Extreme C

Taking you to the limit in Concurrency, OOP, and the most advanced capabilities of C

Kamran Amini

BIRMINGHAM - MUMBAI

Extreme C

Acquisition Editor: Andrew Waldron
Acquisition Editor – Peer Reviews: Suresh Jain
Content Development Editor: Ian Hough
Technical Editor: Gaurav Gavas
Project Editor: Kishor Rit
Proofreader: Safis Editing
Indexer: Rekha Nair
Presentation Designer: Sandip Tadge

First published: October 2019

Production reference: 1301019

Published by Packt Publishing Ltd.
Livery Place
35 Livery Street
Birmingham B3 2PB, UK.

ISBN 978-1-78934-362-5

www.packt.com

Packt>

Contributors

About the author

Kamran Amini is a senior professional specialized in embedded and kernel development. He has worked for numerous well-known Iranian companies as a senior engineer, architect, consultant, and CTO. In 2017, he moved to Europe to work as a senior architect and engineer for highly reputable companies such as Jeppesen, Adecco, TomTom, and ActiveVideo Networks. While residing in Amsterdam, he wrote this book. His main areas of interest are computation theory, distributed systems, machine learning, information theory, and quantum computation. Parallel to his professional career, he is studying astronomy and planetary sciences. His areas of academic interest are related to the early development of the universe, the geometry of black holes, quantum field theory, and string theory.

I want to thank my mother, Ehteram, who devoted her life to raising me and my brother, Ashkan. I'm certain that she is always cheering me on.

And I want to thank my beautiful and beloved wife, Afsaneh, who has supported me at every step, especially while working on this book. Without her patience and encouragement, I'm sure I wouldn't have made it this far.

About the reviewers

Aliakbar Abbasi is a software developer with more than six years of experience using multiple technologies and programming languages. He is an expert in OOP, C/C++, and Python. He likes studying technical books and broadening his knowledge of software development. These days, he lives in Amsterdam with his wife and works for TomTom as a senior software engineer.

Rohit Talwalkar is a vastly experienced software developer expert in the C, C++, and Java languages. He has worked on proprietary **RTOS (Real Time OS)**, Windows and Windows Mobile devices, and the Android platform to develop applications, drivers, and services.

He received his B. Tech from the prestigious Indian Institute of Technology in Mumbai and has a master's degree in computer science and currently works in the mixed reality field as application development lead engineer. He has worked for Motorola and BlackBerry in the past and is currently working at Magic Leap, which makes mixed reality glasses and specializes in spatial computing. In the past, Rohit was involved in reviewing *C++ for the Impatient* by Brian Overland.

I would like to thank Dr. Clovis Tondo, who has taught me C, C++, Java, and many other things in life.

Table of Contents

Preface

In this modern era, we observe mind-blowing technologies on a regular basis and experience luxury and pleasure far beyond what could have been imagined even a few decades ago. We find ourselves on the cusp of autonomous cars becoming a reality on our streets. Advances in physics and other branches of science are changing the way we perceive reality itself. We read news about researchers taking baby steps in quantum computation, rumors about blockchain technology and cryptocurrencies, and plans to colonize other planets. Unbelievably, such a diversity of breakthroughs find their roots in just a few core technologies. This book is about one of those technologies: C.

I started programming with C++ when I was studying in my first year of high school. There, I joined a 2D soccer simulation team for juniors. Soon after C++, I got introduced to Linux and C. I must admit that I didn't know much about the importance of C and Unix in those years, but over time, as I gained more experience in using them through various projects, and as I learned about them through my education, I came to see their critical role and position. The more I knew about C, the bigger my respect for it grew. Finally, I decided to be an expert in this programming language that had so captured my interest. I also decided to be an advocate to spread the knowledge and make people aware of the importance of C. This book is a result of that ambition.

Despite the mistaken belief that C is a dead language, and despite the general ignorance that C receives from tech people, the TIOBE index found at https://www.tiobe.com/tiobe-index demonstrates otherwise. C is, in fact, one of the most popular programming languages of the past 15 years, together with Java, and has gained popularity in recent years.

I come to this book following many years of experience in development and design using C, C++, Golang, Java, and Python on various platforms including various BSD Unix flavors, Linux, and Microsoft Windows. The primary aim of this book is to increase the skill of its audience to the next level; to enable them to take the next step in their use of C, and practically apply it in a way that comes through hard-earned experience. This won't be an easy journey for us and that's why we've called this book *Extreme C*. This journey is the core concern of this book, and we will not be entering into the debate of C versus other programming languages. This book tries to remain practical, but still we have to deal with a significant quantity of hardcore theory that is relevant to practical application. The book is full of examples that aim to prepare you to deal with the things you will encounter within a real system.

It is indeed a great honor to be able to address such a weighty topic. Words won't suffice, so I'll only say that it has been an incredible joy to have the opportunity to write about a topic that is so close to my heart. And I owe this pleasure and astonishment to Andrew Waldron, who let me take on this book as my first experience in book writing.

As part of this, I want to send my special regards and best thanks to Ian Hough, the Development Editor, who was with me chapter by chapter on this journey, to Aliakbar Abbasi for his tireless peer review feedback, and to Kishor Rit, Gaurav Gavas, Veronica Pais, and many more valuable people who have put their best efforts into preparing and publishing this book.

With that said, I invite you to be my companion on this long journey. I hope that the reading of this book will prove to be transformative, helping you to see C in a new light, and to become a better programmer in the process.

Who this book is for

This book is written for an audience that has a minimum level of knowledge regarding C and C++ development. Junior and intermediate C/C++ engineers are the main audience that can get the most from this book and leverage their expertise and knowledge. Hopefully, after reading this book, they can gain a raise in their position and become senior engineers. In addition, after reading this book, their expertise would be a better match for more relevant job opportunities that are challenging and usually well paid. Some topics can still be useful to senior C/C++ engineers, but it is expected that most of the topics are known to them and only some extra details can still be useful.

The other audience that can benefit from reading this book is students and researchers. Students of bachelor's, master's, or PhD degrees studying in any branch of science or engineering such as computer science, software engineering, artificial intelligence, **Internet of Things (IoT)**, astronomy, particle physics, and cosmology, as well as all researchers in these fields, can use the book to increase the level of their knowledge about C/C++, Unix-like operating systems, and the relevant programming skills. This book would be good for engineers and scientists working on complex, multithreaded, or even multi-process systems performing remote device controlling, simulations, big data processing, machine learning, deep learning, and so on.

What this book covers

This book has 7 parts. In each of these 7 parts, we cover some particular aspects of C programming. The first part focuses upon how to build a C project, the second part focuses on memory, the third on object orientation, and the fourth primarily looks at Unix and its relationship to C. The fifth part then discusses concurrency, the sixth covers inter-process communication, and finally the seventh part of the book is about testing and maintenance. Below is a summary of each of the 23 chapters found in this book.

Chapter 1, Essential Features: This chapter is about the essential features found in C that have a profound effect on the way we use C. We will be using these features often throughout the book. The main topics are preprocessing and directives to define macros, variable and function pointers, function call mechanisms, and structures.

Chapter 2, Compilation and Linking: As part of this chapter, we discuss how to build a C project. The compilation pipeline is studied in great detail, both in terms of the pipeline as a whole and in terms of the individual pipeline components.

Chapter 3, Object Files: This chapter looks at the products of a C project after having built it using the compilation pipeline. We introduce object files and their various types. We also take a look inside these object files and see what information can be extracted.

Chapter 4, Process Memory Structure: In this chapter, we explore a process's memory layout. We see what segments can be found in this memory layout and what static and dynamic memory layouts mean.

Chapter 5, Stack and Heap: As part of this chapter, we discuss the Stack and Heap segments specifically. We talk about the Stack and Heap variables and how their lifetime is managed in C. We discuss some best practice regarding Heap variables and the way that they should be managed.

Chapter 6, OOP and Encapsulation: This is the first chapter in a group of four chapters discussing object orientation in C. As part of this chapter, we go through the theory behind object orientation and we give important definitions to the terms often used in the literature.

Chapter 7, Composition and Aggregation: This chapter focuses upon composition and a special form of it: aggregation. We discuss the differences between composition and aggregation and give examples to demonstrate these differences.

Chapter 8, Inheritance and Polymorphism: Inheritance is one of the most important topics in **object-oriented programming (OOP)**. In this chapter, we show how an inheritance relationship can be established between two classes and how it can be done in C. Polymorphism is another big topic that is discussed as part of this chapter.

Chapter 9, Abstraction and OOP in C++: As the final chapter in the third part of the book, we talk about abstraction. We discuss abstract data types and how they can be implemented in C. We discuss the internals of C++ and we demonstrate how object-oriented concepts are implemented in C++.

Chapter 10, Unix – History and Architecture: You cannot talk about C and forget about Unix. In this chapter, we describe why they are strongly bound to each other, and how Unix and C have helped one another to survive thus far. The architecture of Unix is also studied, and we see how a program uses the functionalities exposed by the operating system.

Chapter 11, System Calls and Kernel: In this chapter, we focus on the kernel ring in the Unix architecture. We discuss system calls in greater detail and we add a new system call to Linux. We also talk about various types of kernels, and we write a new simple kernel module for Linux to demonstrate how kernel modules work.

Chapter 12, The Most Recent C: As part of this chapter, we take a look at the most recent version of C standard, C18. We see how it is different from the previous version, C11. We also demonstrate some of the newly added features in comparison to C99.

Chapter 13, Concurrency: This is the first chapter of the fifth part of the book, and it is regarding concurrency. This chapter mainly talks about concurrent environments and their various properties such as interleavings. We explain why these systems are non-determinant and how this property can lead to concurrency issues such as race conditions.

Chapter 14, Synchronization: In this chapter, we continue our discussion regarding concurrent environments, and we discuss the various types of issues that we can expect to observe in a concurrent system. Race conditions, data races, and deadlocks are among the issues that we discuss. We also talk about the techniques that we can utilize to overcome these issues. Semaphores, mutexes, and condition variables are discussed in this chapter.

Chapter 15, Thread Execution: As part of this chapter, we demonstrate how a number of threads can be executed and how they can be managed. We also give real C examples about the concurrency issues discussed in the previous chapter.

Chapter 16, Thread Synchronization: In this chapter, we look at the techniques that we can use to synchronize a number of threads. Semaphores, mutexes, and condition variables are among the notable topics that are discussed and demonstrated in this chapter.

Chapter 17, Process Execution: This chapter talks about the ways that we can create or spawn a new process. We also discuss push-based and pull-based techniques for sharing state among a number of processes. We also demonstrate the concurrency issues discussed in *Chapter 14, Synchronization* using real C examples.

Chapter 18, Process Synchronization: This chapter mainly deals with available mechanisms to synchronize a number of processes residing on the same machine. Process-shared semaphores, process-shared mutexes, and process-shared condition variables are among the techniques discussed in this chapter.

Chapter 19, Single-Host IPC and Sockets: In this chapter, we mainly discuss push-based **interprocess communication (IPC)** techniques. Our focus is on the techniques available to processes residing on the same machine. We also introduce socket programming, and the required background to establish channels between processes residing on different nodes in a network.

Chapter 20, Socket Programming: As part of this chapter, we discuss socket programming through code examples. We drive our discussion by bringing up an example that is going to support various types of sockets. Unix domain sockets, TCP, and UDP sockets operating on either a stream or a datagram channel are discussed.

Chapter 21, Integration with Other Languages: In this chapter, we demonstrate how a C library, built as a shared object file, can be loaded and used in programs written with C++, Java, Python, and Golang.

Chapter 22, Unit Testing and Debugging: This chapter is dedicated to testing and debugging. For the testing half, we explain various levels of testing, but we focus on unit testing in C. We also introduce CMocka and Google Test as two available libraries to write test suites in C. For the debugging half, we go through various available tools that can be used for debugging different types of bugs.

Chapter 23, Build Systems: In the final chapter of the book, we discuss build systems and build script generators. Make, Ninja, and Bazel are the build systems that we explain as part of this chapter. CMake is also the sole build script generator that we discuss in this chapter.

To get the most out of this book

As we have explained before, this book requires you to have a minimum level of knowledge and skill regarding computer programming. The minimum requirements are listed below:

- General knowledge of computer architecture: You should know about memory, CPU, peripheral devices and their characteristics, and how a program interacts with these elements in a computer system.

- General knowledge of programming: You should know what an algorithm is, how its execution can be traced, what source code is, what binary numbers are, and how their related arithmetic works.

- Familiarity with using the *Terminal* and the basic *shell commands* in a Unix-like operating system such as Linux or macOS.

- Intermediate knowledge about programming topics such as conditional statements, different kinds of loops, structures or classes in at least one programming language, pointers in C or C++, functions, and so on.

- Basic knowledge about OOP: This is not mandatory because we will explain OOP in detail, but it can help you to have a better understanding while reading the chapters in third part of the book, *Object Orientation*.

 In addition, it is strongly recommended to download the code repository and follow the commands given in the shell boxes. Please use a platform with Linux or macOS installed. Other POSIX-compliant operating systems can still be used.

Download the example code files

You can download the example code files for this book from your account at www. packt.com/. If you purchased this book elsewhere, you can visit www.packtpub. com/support and register to have the files emailed directly to you.

You can download the code files by following these steps:

1. Log in or register at http://www.packt.com.
2. Select the **Support** tab.
3. Click on **Code Downloads**.
4. Enter the name of the book in the **Search** box and follow the on-screen instructions.

Once the file is downloaded, please make sure that you unzip or extract the folder using the latest version of:

- WinRAR / 7-Zip for Windows
- Zipeg / iZip / UnRarX for Mac
- 7-Zip / PeaZip for Linux

The code bundle for the book is also hosted on GitHub at https://github.com/PacktPublishing/Extreme-C. In case there's an update to the code, it will be updated on the existing GitHub repository.

We also have other code bundles from our rich catalog of books and videos available at https://github.com/PacktPublishing/. Check them out!

Conventions used

In this book, we have used code boxes and shell boxes. Code boxes contain a piece of either C code or pseudo-code. If the content of a code box is brought from a code file, the name of the code file is shown beneath the box. Below, you can see an example of a code box:

```
#include <stdio.h>
#include <unistd.h>

int main(int argc, char** argv) {
  printf("This is the parent process with process ID: %d\n",
         getpid());
  printf("Before calling fork() ...\n");
  pid_t ret = fork();
  if (ret) {
    printf("The child process is spawned with PID: %d\n", ret);
  } else {
    printf("This is the child process with PID: %d\n", getpid());
  }
  printf("Type CTRL+C to exit ...\n");
  while (1);
  return 0;
}
```

Code Box 17-1 [ExtremeC_examples_chapter17_1.c]: Creating a child process using fork API

As you can see, the above code can be found in the ExtremeC_examples_chapter17_1.c file, as part of the code bundle of the book, in the directory of *Chapter 17, Process Execution*. You can get the code bundle from GitHub at https://github.com/PacktPublishing/Extreme-C.

If a code box doesn't have an associated filename, then it contains pseudo-code or C code that cannot be found in the code bundle. An example is given below:

```
Task P {
    1. num = 5
    2. num++
    3. num = num - 2
    4. x = 10
    5. num = num + x
}
```

Code Box 13-1: A simple task with 5 instructions

There can sometimes be some lines shown in bold font within code boxes. These lines are usually the lines of code that are discussed before or after the code box. They are in bold font in order to help you find them more easily.

Shell boxes are used to show the output of the Terminal while running a number of shell commands. The commands are usually in bold font and the output is in the normal font. An example is shown below:

```
$ ls /dev/shm
shm0
$ gcc ExtremeC_examples_chapter17_5.c -lrt -o ex17_5.out
$ ./ex17_5.out
Shared memory is opened with fd: 3
The contents of the shared memory object: ABC

$ ls /dev/shm
$
```

Shell Box 17-6: Reading from the shared memory object created in example 17.4 and finally removing it

The commands start either with $ or #. The commands starting with $ should be run with a normal user, and the commands starting with # should be run with a super user.

The working directory of a shell box is usually the chapter directory found in the code bundle. In cases when a particular directory should be chosen as the working directory, we give you the necessary information regarding that.

Bold: Indicates a new term, an important word. Words that you see on the screen, for example, in menus or dialog boxes, also appear in the text like this. For example: "Select **System info** from the **Administration** panel."

Warnings or important notes appear like this.

 Tips and tricks appear like this.

Get in touch

Feedback from our readers is always welcome.

General feedback: If you have questions about any aspect of this book, mention the book title in the subject of your message and email us at customercare@ packtpub.com.

Errata: Although we have taken every care to ensure the accuracy of our content, mistakes do happen. If you have found a mistake in this book we would be grateful if you would report this to us.

Please visit, www.packtpub.com/support/errata, selecting your book, clicking on the Errata Submission Form link, and entering the details.

Piracy: If you come across any illegal copies of our works in any form on the Internet, we would be grateful if you would provide us with the location address or website name. Please contact us at copyright@packt.com with a link to the material.

If you are interested in becoming an author: If there is a topic that you have expertise in and you are interested in either writing or contributing to a book, please visit authors.packtpub.com.

Reviews

Please leave a review. Once you have read and used this book, why not leave a review on the site that you purchased it from? Potential readers can then see and use your unbiased opinion to make purchase decisions, we at Packt can understand what you think about our products, and our authors can see your feedback on their book. Thank you!

For more information about Packt, please visit packt.com.

Chapter 01

Essential Features

Extreme C is a book that will provide you with both the fundamental and the advanced knowledge you need in order to develop and maintain real C applications. Generally, only knowing the syntax of a programming language is not enough to write successful programs with it – and this is of greater importance in C compared to most other languages. So, we're going to cover all of the concepts you need to write great software in C, from simple single process programs to more complex multiple process systems.

This first chapter is primarily concerned with particular features of C that you'll find extremely useful while you're writing C programs. These features are involved in situations you will encounter regularly while writing in C. Although there are a number of great books and tutorials on C programming that explain everything in detail and cover almost all aspects of C syntax, it would be useful to consider some key features here before we go deeper with C.

These features include preprocessor directives, variable pointers, function pointers, and structures. They are common, of course, in today's more modern programming languages, and it's easy to find their counterparts in Java, C#, Python, and so on. For example, *references* in Java can be considered as similar elements to variable pointers in C. These features and their related concepts are so fundamental, that without them, no piece of software could continue to work, even if it could get executed! Even a simple "hello world" program cannot work without loading a number of shared libraries that require the usage of *function pointers*!

So, whenever you see something like traffic lights, your car's central computer, the microwave oven in your kitchen, the operating system of your smartphone, or probably any other device that you generally don't think about, they all have pieces of software written in C.

Our lives today have been greatly impacted by the invention of the C programming language, and our world would be very different without C.

This chapter focuses on the essential features and machinery required to write expert C code and contains a handpicked collection of features for us to study in depth. We'll explore the following topics:

- **Preprocessor directives, macros, and conditional compilation**: Preprocessing is one of those C features that you can't easily find in other programming languages. Preprocessing brings a lot of advantages, and we'll dive into some of its interesting applications, including *macros* and *conditional directives*.

- **Variable pointers**: This section deep-dives into *variable pointers* and their uses. We'll also find some helpful insights by looking at some of the flaws that could be introduced by misusing variable pointers.

- **Functions**: This section of the chapter is a deep dive into everything we know about functions, beyond just their syntax. In fact, the syntax is the easy part! In this section, we will look at functions as the building blocks for writing *procedural* code. This section also talks about the *function call mechanism* and how a function receives its arguments from the caller function.

- **Function pointers**: Undoubtedly, *function pointers* are one of the most important features of C. A function pointer is a pointer that points to an existing function instead of a variable. The ability to store a pointer to an existing logic is profoundly important in algorithm design, and that's why we have a dedicated section on this topic. Function pointers appear in a vast range of applications ranging from loading dynamic libraries to *polymorphism*, and we'll be seeing plenty more of function pointers across the next couple of chapters.

- **Structures**: C structures might have a simple syntax and convey a simple idea, but they are the main building blocks for writing *well-organized* and more *object-oriented* code. Their importance, together with function pointers, simply cannot be overstated! In the last section of this chapter, we'll revisit all the things that you need to know about structures in C and the tricks around them.

The essential features of C, and their surrounding concepts, play a key role in the Unix ecosystem, and they have led to C being an important and influential technology despite its old age and harsh syntax. We will talk more about the mutual influence of C and Unix upon one another in the upcoming chapters. For now, let's begin this first chapter by talking about preprocessor directives.

Before reading this chapter, bear in mind that you should be already familiar with C. Most of the examples are trivial in this chapter, but it is highly recommended that you know C syntax before moving on to other chapters. For your convenience, below is a list of topics that you should be familiar with before moving on with this book:

General knowledge of computer architecture — you should know about memory, CPU, peripheral devices and their characteristics, and how a program interacts with these elements in a computer system.

General knowledge of programming — you should know what an algorithm is, how its execution can be traced, what a source code is, what binary numbers are, and how their related arithmetic work.

Familiarity with using the Terminal and the basic shell commands in a Unix-like operating system such as Linux or macOS.

Intermediate knowledge about programming topics such as conditional statements, different kinds of loops, structures or classes in at least one programming language, pointers in C or C++, functions, and so on.

Basic knowledge about object-oriented programming — this is not mandatory because we will explain object-oriented programming in detail, but such knowledge will help you to have a better understanding while reading the chapters in the third part of the book; *Object Orientation*.

Preprocessor directives

Preprocessing is a powerful feature in C. We'll cover it fully in *Chapter 2, Compilation and Linking*, but right now let's define preprocessing as something that allows you to engineer and modify your source code before submitting it to the compiler. This means that the C compilation pipeline has at least one step more in comparison to other languages. In other programming languages, the source code is directly sent to the compiler, but in C and C++, it should be preprocessed first.

This extra step has made C (and C++) a unique programming language in the sense that a C programmer can effectively change their source code before submitting it to the compiler. This feature is not present in most higher-level programming languages.

The purpose of preprocessing is to remove the preprocessing directives and substitute them with equivalent generated C code and prepare a final source that is ready to be submitted to the compiler.

The behavior of the C preprocessor can be controlled and influenced using a set of *directives*. C directives are lines of code starting with a # character in both header and source files. These lines are only meaningful to the C preprocessor and never to the C compiler. There are various directives in C, but some of them are very important especially the directives used for macro definition and the directives used for conditional compilation.

In the following section, we'll explain macros and give various examples demonstrating their various uses. We also analyze them further to find their advantages and disadvantages.

Macros

There are many rumors regarding C macros. One says that they make your source code too complicated and less readable. Another says that you face issues while debugging applications if you have used macros in your code. You might have heard some of these statements yourself. But to what extent are they valid? Are macros evils that should be avoided? Or do they have some benefits that can be brought to your project?

The reality is that you'll find macros in any well-known C project. As proof, download a well-known C project such as Apache HTTP Server and do a grep for #define. You will see a list of files where macros are defined. For you as a C developer, there is no way to escape macros. Even if you don't use them yourself, you will likely see them in other people's code. Therefore, you need to learn what they are and how to deal with them.

 The grep command refers to a standard shell utility program in Unix-like operating systems that searches for a pattern in a stream of characters. It can be used to search for a text or a pattern in the content of all files found in a given path.

Macros have a number of applications and you can see some of them as follows:

- Defining a constant
- Using as a function instead of writing a C function
- Loop unrolling
- Header guards
- Code generation
- Conditional compilation

While there are many more possible applications of macros, we'll focus on the above in the following sections.

Defining a macro

Macros are defined using the #define directive. Each macro has a name and a possible list of parameters. It also has a *value* that gets substituted by its *name* in the preprocessing phase through a step called *macro expansion*. A macro can also be *undefined* with the #undef directive. Let's start with a simple example, *example 1.1*:

```
#define ABC 5

int main(int argc, char** argv) {
    int x = 2;
    int y = ABC;

    int z = x + y;
    return 0;
}
```

Code Box 1-1 [ExtremeC_examples_chapter1_1.c]: Defining a macro

In the preceding code box, ABC is not a variable that holds an integer value nor an integer constant. In fact, it's a macro called ABC and its corresponding value is 5. After the macro expansion phase, the resulting code that can be submitted to the C compiler looks similar to the one we see as follows:

```
int main(int argc, char** argv) {
    int x = 2;
    int y = 5;
    int z = x + y;
```

```
    return 0;
}
```

Code Box 1-2: The generated code for the example 1.1 after macro expansion phase

The code in *Code Box 1-2* has a valid C syntax, and now the compiler can proceed and compile it. In the preceding example, the preprocessor did the macro expansion, and as a part of it, the preprocessor simply replaced the macro's name with its value. The preprocessor has also removed the comments on the beginning lines.

Let's now have a look at another example, *example 1.2*:

```
#define ADD(a, b) a + b

int main(int argc, char** argv) {
    int x = 2;
    int y = 3;
    int z = ADD(x, y);
    return 0;
}
```

Code Box 1-3 [ExtremeC_examples_chapter1_2.c]: Defining a function-like macro

In the preceding code box, similar to *example 1.1*, ADD is not a function. It is just a *function-like macro* that accepts arguments. After preprocessing, the resulting code will be like this:

```
int main(int argc, char** argv) {
    int x = 2;
    int y = 3
    int z = x + y;
    return 0;
}
```

Code Box 1-4: Example 1.2 after preprocessing and macro expansion

As you can see in the preceding code box, the expansion that has taken place is as follows. The argument x used as parameter a is replaced with all instances of a in the macro's value. This is the same for the parameter b, and its corresponding argument y. Then, the final substitution occurs, and we get x + y instead of ADD(a, b) in the preprocessed code.

Since function-like macros can accept input arguments, they can mimic C functions. In other words, instead of putting a frequently used logic into a C function, you can name that logic as a function-like macro and use that macro instead.

This way, the macro occurrences will be replaced by the frequently used logic, as part of the preprocessing phase, and there is no need to introduce a new C function. We will discuss this more and compare the two approaches.

Macros only exist before the compilation phase. This means that the compiler, theoretically, doesn't know anything about the macros. This is a very important point to remember if you are going to use macros instead of functions. The compiler knows everything about a function because it is part of the C grammar and it is parsed and being kept in the *parse tree*. But a macro is just a C preprocessor directive only known to the preprocessor itself.

Macros allow you to *generate* code before the compilation. In other programming languages such as Java, you need to use a *code generator* to fulfill this purpose. We will give examples regarding this application of macros.

Modern C compilers are aware of C preprocessor directives. Despite the common belief that they don't know anything about the preprocessing phase, they actually do. The modern C compilers know about the source before entering the preprocessing phase. Look at the following code:

```
#include <stdio.h>

#define CODE \
printf("%d\n", i);

int main(int argc, char** argv) {
  CODE
  return 0;
}
```

Code Box 1-5 [example.c]: Macro definition which yields an undeclared identifier error

If you compile the above code using `clang` in macOS, the following would be the output:

```
$ clang example.c
code.c:7:3: error: use of undeclared identifier 'i'
```

```
CODE
^
code.c:4:16: note: expanded from macro 'CODE'
printf("%d\n", i);
                  ^
1 error generated.
$
```

Shell Box 1-1: The output of the compilation refers to the macro definition

As you see, the compiler has generated an error message that points exactly to the line in which the macro is defined.

As a side note, in most modern compilers, you can view the preprocessing result just before the compilation. For example, when using gcc or clang, you can use the -E option to dump the code after preprocessing. The following shell box demonstrates how to use the -E option. Note that the output is not fully shown:

```
$ clang -E example.c
# 1 "sample.c"# 1 "<built-in>" 1
# 1 "<built-in>" 3
# 361 "<built-in>" 3
...
# 412 "/Library/Developer/CommandLineTools/SDKs/MacOSX10.14.sdk/
usr/include/stdio.h" 2 3 4
# 2 "sample.c" 2
...
int main(int argc, char** argv) {
 printf("%d\n", i);
 return 0;
}
$
```

Shell Box 1-2: The code of example.c after preprocessing phase

Now we come to an important definition. A *translation unit* (or a *compilation unit*) is the preprocessed C code that is ready to be passed to the compiler.

In a translation unit, all directives are substituted with inclusions or macro expansions and a flat long piece of C code has been produced.

Now that you know more about macros, let's work on some more difficult examples. They will show you the power and danger of macros. In my opinion, extreme development deals with dangerous and delicate stuff in a skilled way, and this is exactly what C is about.

The next example is an interesting one. Just pay attention to how the macros are used in sequence to generate a loop:

```
#include <stdio.h>

#define PRINT(a) printf("%d\n", a);
#define LOOP(v, s, e) for (int v = s; v <= e; v++) {
#define ENDLOOP }

int main(int argc, char** argv) {
  LOOP(counter, 1, 10)
    PRINT(counter)
  ENDLOOP
  return 0;
}
```

Code Box 1-6 [ExtremeC_examples_chapter1_3.c]: Using macros to generate a loop

As you see in the preceding code box, the code inside the `main` function is not a valid C code in any way! But after preprocessing, we get a correct C source code that compiles without any problem. Following is the preprocessed result:

```
...
... content of stdio.h ...
...
int main(int argc, char** argv) {
  for (int counter = 1; counter <= 10; counter++) {
    printf("%d\n", counter);
  }
  return 0;
}
```

Code Box 1-7: Example 1.3 after preprocessing phase

In *Code Box 1-6*, in the `main` function, we just used a different and not C-looking set of instructions to write our algorithm. Then after preprocessing, in *Code Box 1-7*, we got a fully functional and correct C program. This is an important application of macros; to define a new **domain specific language** (DSL) and write code using it.

DSLs are very useful in different parts of a project; for example, they are used heavily in testing frameworks such as Google Test framework (gtest) where a DSL is used to write assertions, expectations, and test scenarios.

We should note that we don't have any C directives in the final preprocessed code. This means that the `#include` directive in *Code Box 1-6* has been replaced by the contents of the file it was referring to. That is why you see the content of the `stdio.h` header file (which we replaced with ellipses) in *Code Box 1-7* before the `main` function.

Let's now look at the next example, *example 1.4*, which introduces two new operators regarding macro parameters; the # and ## operators:

```
#include <stdio.h>
#include <string.h>

#define CMD(NAME) \
  char NAME ## _cmd[256]  = ""; \
  strcpy(NAME ## _cmd, #NAME);

int main(int argc, char** argv) {

  CMD(copy)
  CMD(paste)
  CMD(cut)

  char cmd[256];
  scanf("%s", cmd);

  if (strcmp(cmd, copy_cmd) == 0) {
    // ...
  }
  if (strcmp(cmd, paste_cmd) == 0) {
    // ...
  }
  if (strcmp(cmd, cut_cmd) == 0) {
    // ...
  }

  return 0;
}
```

Code Box 1-8 [ExtremeC_examples_chapter1_4.c]: Using # and ## operators in a macro

While expanding the macro, the # operator turns the parameter into its string form surrounded by a pair of quotation marks. For example, in the preceding code, the # operator used before the NAME parameter turns it into `"copy"` in the preprocessed code.

The ## operator has a different meaning. It just concatenates the parameters to other elements in the macro definition and usually forms variable names. Following is the final preprocessed source for *example 1.4*:

```
...
... content of stdio.h ...
...
... content of string.h ...
...
int main(int argc, char** argv) {

  char copy_cmd[256] = ""; strcpy(copy_cmd, "copy");
  char paste_cmd[256] = ""; strcpy(paste_cmd, "paste");
  char cut_cmd[256] = ""; strcpy(cut_cmd, "cut");

  char cmd[256];
  scanf("%s", cmd);

  if (strcmp(cmd, copy_cmd) == 0) {

  }
  if (strcmp(cmd, paste_cmd) == 0) {

  }
  if (strcmp(cmd, cut_cmd) == 0) {
  }

  return 0;
}
```

Code Box 1-9: Example 1.4 after preprocessing phase

Comparing the source before and after preprocessing helps you to realize how # and ## operators are applied to the macro arguments. Note that, in the final preprocessed code, all lines expanded from the same macro definition are on the same line.

It is a good practice to break long macros into multiple lines but do not forget to use \ (one backslash) to let the preprocessor know that the rest of the definition comes on the next line. Note that \ doesn't get substituted with a *newline* character. Instead, it is an indicator that the following line is the continuation of the same macro definition.

Now let's talk about a different type of macros. The next section is going to talk about *variadic macros* which can accept a variable number of arguments.

Variadic macros

The next example, *example 1.5*, is dedicated to variadic macros, which can accept a variable number of input arguments. Sometimes the same variadic macro accepts 2 arguments, sometimes 4 arguments, and sometimes 7. Variadic macros are very handy when you are not sure about the number of arguments in different usages of the same macro. A simple example is given as follows:

```c
#include <stdio.h>
#include <stdlib.h>
#include <string.h>

#define VERSION "2.3.4"

#define LOG_ERROR(format, ...) \
  fprintf(stderr, format, __VA_ARGS__)

int main(int argc, char** argv) {

  if (argc < 3) {
    LOG_ERROR("Invalid number of arguments for version %s\n.",
VERSION);
    exit(1);
  }

  if (strcmp(argv[1], "-n") != 0) {
    LOG_ERROR("%s is a wrong param at index %d for version %s.",
argv[1], 1, VERSION);
    exit(1);
  }

  // ...

  return 0;
}
```

Code Box 1-10 [ExtremeC_examples_chapter1_5.c]: Definition and usage of a variadic macro

In the preceding code box, you see a new identifier: __VA_ARGS__. It is an indicator that tells the preprocessor to replace it with all the remaining input arguments that are not assigned to any parameter yet.

In the preceding example, in the second usage of LOG_ERROR, according to the macro definition, the arguments argv[1], 1, and VERSION are those input arguments that are *not* assigned to any parameter. So, they are going to be used in place of __VA_ARGS__ while expanding the macro.

As a side note, the function fprintf writes to a *file descriptor*. In *example 1.5*, the file descriptor is stderr, which is the *error stream* of the process. Also, note the ending semicolon after each LOG_ERROR usage. It is mandatory because the macro doesn't supply them as part of its definition and the programmer *must* add that semicolon to make the final preprocessed code syntactically correct.

The following code is the final output after passing through the C preprocessor:

```
...
... content of stdio.h ...
...
... content of stdlib.h ...
...
... content of string.h ...
...
int main(int argc, char** argv) {

  if (argc < 3) {
    fprintf(stderr, "Invalid number of arguments for version
%s\n.", "2.3.4");
    exit(1);
  }

  if (strcmp(argv[1], "-n") != 0) {
    fprintf(stderr, "%s is a wrong param at index %d for version
%s.", argv[1], 1, "2.3.4");
    exit(1);
  }

  // ...

  return 0;
}
```

Code Box 1-11: Example 1.5 after preprocessing phase

The next example, *example 1.6*, is a progressive usage of variadic macros that tries to mimic a loop. There is a well-known example about this. Before having foreach in C++, the *boost* framework was (and still is) offering the foreach behavior using a number of macros.

In the following link, you can see how the BOOST_FOREACH macro is defined as the last thing in the header file: https://www.boost.org/doc/libs/1_35_0/boost/foreach.hpp. It is used to iterate over a boost collection, and it is actually a function-like macro.

Our following example, *example 1.6*, is about a simple loop which is not comparable to boost's foreach at all, but yet, it is giving you an idea on how to use variadic macros for repeating a number of instructions:

```c
#include <stdio.h>

#define LOOP_3(X, ...) \
  printf("%s\n", #X);

#define LOOP_2(X, ...) \
  printf("%s\n", #X); \
  LOOP_3(__VA_ARGS__)

#define LOOP_1(X, ...) \
  printf("%s\n", #X); \
  LOOP_2(__VA_ARGS__)

#define LOOP(...) \
  LOOP_1(__VA_ARGS__)

int main(int argc, char** argv) {

  LOOP(copy paste cut)
  LOOP(copy, paste, cut)
  LOOP(copy, paste, cut, select)

  return 0;
}
```

Code Box 1-12 [ExtremeC_examples_chapter1_6.c]: Using variadic macros to mimic a loop

Before starting to explain the example, let's look at the final code after preprocessing. Then, the explanation of what happened will be easier:

```c
...
... content of stdio.h ...
...
int main(int argc, char** argv) {

  printf("%s\n", "copy paste cut"); printf("%s\n", "");
printf("%s\n", "");
```

```
   printf("%s\n", "copy"); printf("%s\n", "paste"); printf("%s\n",
"cut");
   printf("%s\n", "copy"); printf("%s\n", "paste"); printf("%s\n",
"cut");

   return 0;
}
```

Code Box 1-13: Example 1.6 after preprocessing phase

If you look at the preprocessed code carefully, you will see that the LOOP macro has been expanded to multiple printf instructions instead of looping instructions such as for or while. It is obvious why this is the case, and it's because of the fact that the preprocessor doesn't write smart C code for us. It is there to replace macros with the instructions given by us.

The only way to create a loop with a macro is just to put the iteration instructions one after another, and as some separate instructions. This means that a simple macro loop with 1000 iterations will be substituted with 1000 instructions in C and we won't have any actual C loop in the final code.

The preceding technique will lead to a large binary size which can be thought of as a disadvantage. But putting instructions one after another instead of putting them into a loop, which is known as *loop unrolling*, has its own applications, which require an acceptable level of performance in constrained and high-performance environments. According to what we explained so far, it seems that loop unrolling using macros is a trade-off between binary size and performance. We talk more about this in the upcoming section.

There is one more note about the preceding example. As you see, different usages of the LOOP macro in the main function have produced different results. In the first usage, we pass copy paste cut without any commas between the words. The preprocessor accepts it as a single input, so the simulated loop has only one iteration.

In the second usage, the input copy, paste, cut is passed with words separated by commas. Now, the preprocessor treats them as three different arguments; hence, the simulated loop has three iterations. This is clear from the following *Shell Box 1-3*.

In the third usage, we pass four values, copy, paste, cut, select, but only three of them are processed. As you see, the preprocessed code is exactly the same as the second usage. That's because of the fact that our looping macros are only capable of handling lists of up to three elements. Extra elements after the third are ignored.

Note that this doesn't produce compilation errors because nothing wrong has been generated as the final C code, but our macros are limited in the number of elements they can process:

```
$ gcc ExtremeC_examples_chapter1_6.c
$ ./a.out
copy paste cut


copy
paste
cut
$
```

Shell Box 1-3: Compilation and output of example 1.6

Advantages and disadvantages of macros

Let's start the discussion by talking a bit about software design. Defining macros and putting them together is an art, and at times an addictive one! You start building the expected preprocessed code in your mind even before having any macros defined and based on that you define your macros. Since it is an easy way to replicate the code and play with it, it can be overused. Overusing the macros may not be a big issue for you, but it might be for your teammates. But why is that?

Macros have an important characteristic. If you write something in macros, they will be replaced by other lines of code before the compilation phase, and finally, you'll have a flat long piece of code without any modularity at compile time. Of course, you have the modularity in your mind and probably in your macros, but it is not present in your final binaries. This is exactly where using macros can start to cause design issues.

Software design tries to package similar algorithms and concepts in several manageable and reusable *modules*, but macros try to make everything linear and flat. So, when you are using macros as some logical building blocks within your software design, the information regarding them can be lost after the preprocessing phase, as part of the final translation units. That's why the architects and designers use a rule of thumb about macros:

> *If a macro can be written as a C function, then you should write a C function instead!*

From the debugging perspective, again, it is said that macros are evil. A developer uses compilation errors to find the places where there exist *syntax errors* as part of their daily development tasks. They also use *logs* and possibly *compilation warnings* to detect a bug and fix it. The compilation errors and warnings both are beneficial to the bug analysis routine, and both of them are generated by the compilers.

Regarding the macros, and especially with old C compilers, the compiler didn't know anything about the macros and it was treating the compiling source (the translation unit) as a long, linear, flat piece of code. So, for a developer looking at the actual C code with macros and for the C compiler looking at the preprocessed code without macros, there were two different worlds. So, the developer could not understand easily what the compiler reported.

Hopefully, with the help of our modern C compilers, this issue is not that severe anymore. Nowadays, the famous C compilers such as gcc and clang know more about the preprocessing phase, and they try to keep, use, and report according to the source code that the developer sees. Otherwise, the problem with macros could be repeated with #include directives, simply because the main content of a translation unit is only known when all inclusions have happened. As a conclusion, we can say that the problem with debugging is less severe than the problem we explained in the previous paragraph about the software design.

If you remember, we brought up a discussion during the explanation of *example 1.6*. It was about a trade-off between the binary size and the performance of a program. A more general form of this trade-off is between having a single big binary and having multiple small binaries. Both of them are providing the same functionality, but the former can have a better performance.

The number of binaries used in a project, especially when the project is big, is more or less proportional to the degree of *modularization* and the design effort spent on it. As an example, a project having 60 libraries (shared or static) and one executable seems to be developed according to a software plan which is splitting dependencies into multiple libraries and using them in a single main executable.

In other words, when a project is being developed according to the software design principals and best practices, the number of binaries and their sizes are engineered in a careful way and usually will be comprised of multiple lightweight binaries with applicable minimum sizes, instead of having a single huge binary.

Software design tries to have each software component in a suitable position in a giant hierarchy instead of putting them in a linear order. And this is intrinsically against the performance even though its effect on the performance is tiny in most cases.

So, we can conclude that the discussion regarding *example 1.6* was about the trade-off between design and performance. When you need performance, sometimes you need to sacrifice the design and put things in a linear construction. For example, you could avoid loops and use *loop unrolling* instead.

From a different perspective, performance starts with choosing proper algorithms for the problems defined in the design phase. The next step is usually called *optimization* or *performance tuning*. In this phase, gaining performance is equivalent to letting the CPU just compute in a linear and sequential manner and not to force it to jump between different parts of the code. This can be done either by modifying the already used algorithms or by replacing them with some performant and usually more complex algorithms. This stage can come into conflict with the design philosophy. As we said before, design tries to put things in a hierarchy and make them non-linear, but the CPU expects things to be linear, already fetched and ready to be processed. So, this trade-off should be taken care of and balanced for each problem separately.

Let's explain the loop unrolling a bit more. This technique is mostly used in embedded development and especially in environments that suffer from limited processing power. The technique is to remove loops and make them linear to increase the performance and avoid the looping overhead while running iterations.

This is exactly what we did in *example 1.6*; we mimicked a loop with macros, which led to a linear set of instructions. In this sense, we can say that the macros can be used for performance tuning in embedded development and the environments in which a slight change in the way that the instructions are executed will cause a significant performance boost. More than that, macros can bring readability to the code and we can factor out repeated instructions.

Regarding the quote mentioned earlier that says that macros should be replaced by equivalent C functions, we know that the quote is there for the sake of design and it can be ignored in some contexts. In a context where improved performance is a key requirement, having a linear set of instructions that lead to better performance may be a necessity.

Code generation is another common application of macros. They can be used for introducing DSLs into a project. *Microsoft MFC, Qt, Linux Kernel*, and *wxWidgets* are a few projects out of thousands that are using macros to define their own DSLs. Most of them are C++ projects, but they are using this C feature to facilitate their APIs.

As a conclusion, C macros can have advantages if the impacts of their preprocessed form are investigated and known. If you're working on a project within a team, always share your decisions regarding the usage of the macros in the team and keep yourself aligned with the decisions made within the team.

Conditional compilation

Conditional compilation is another unique feature of C. It allows you to have different preprocessed source code based on different conditions. Despite the meaning it implies, the compiler is not doing anything conditionally, but the preprocessed code that is passed to the compiler can be different based on some specified conditions. These conditions are evaluated by the preprocessor while preparing the preprocessed code. There are different directives contributing to the conditional compilation. You can see a list of them as follows:

- `#ifdef`
- `#ifndef`
- `#else`
- `#elif`
- `#endif`

The following example, *example 1.7*, demonstrates a very basic usage of these directives:

```
#define CONDITION

int main(int argc, char** argv) {
#ifdef CONDITION
  int i = 0;
  i++;
#endif
  int j= 0;
  return 0;
}
```

Code Box 1-14 [ExtremeC_examples_chapter1_7.c]: An example of conditional compilation

While preprocessing the preceding code, the preprocessor sees the CONDITION macro's definition and marks it as defined. Note that no value is proposed for the CONDITION macro and this is totally valid. Then, the preprocessor goes down further until it reaches the `#ifdef` statement. Since the CONDITION macro is already defined, all lines between `#ifdef` and `#endif` will be copied to the final source code.

You can see the preprocessed code in the following code box:

```
int main(int argc, char** argv) {
```

```
    int i = 0;
    i++;

    int j= 0;
    return 0;
}
```

Code Box 1-15: Example 1.7 after preprocessing phase

If the macro was not defined, we wouldn't see any replacement for the `#if`-`#endif` directives. Therefore, the preprocessed code could be something like the following:

```
int main(int argc, char** argv) {



    int j= 0;
    return 0;
}
```

Code Box 1-16: Example 1.7 after preprocessing phase assuming that CONDITION macro is not defined

Note the empty lines, in both code boxes *1-15* and *1-16*, which have been remained from the preprocessing phase, after replacing the `#ifdef`-`#endif` section with its evaluated value.

Macros can be defined using `-D` options passed to the compilation command. Regarding the preceding example, we can define the CONDITION macro as follows:

```
$ gcc -DCONDITION -E main.c
```

This is a great feature because it allows you to have macros defined out of source files. This is especially helpful when having a single source code but compiling it for different architectures, for example, Linux or macOS, which have different default macro definitions and libraries.

One of the very common usages of #ifndef is to serve as a *header guard* statement. This statement protects a header file from being included twice in the preprocessing phase, and we can say that almost all C and C++ header files in nearly every project have this statement as their first instruction.

The following code, *example 1.8*, is an example on how to use a header guard statement. Suppose that this is the content of a header file and by chance, it could be included twice in a compilation unit. Note that *example 1.8* is just one header file and it is not supposed to be compiled:

```
#ifndef EXAMPLE_1_8_H
#define EXAMPLE_1_8_H

void say_hello();
int read_age();

#endif
```

Code Box 1-17 [ExtremeC_examples_chapter1_8.h]: An example of a header guard

As you see, all variable and function declarations are put inside the #ifndef and #endif pair and they are protected against multiple inclusions by a macro. In the following paragraph, we explain how.

As the first inclusion happens, the EXAMPLE_1_8_H macro is not yet defined, so the preprocessor continues by entering the #ifndef-#endif block. The next statement defines the EXAMPLE_1_8_H macro, and the preprocessor copies everything to the preprocessed code until it reaches the #endif directive. As the second inclusion happens, the EXAMPLE_1_8_H macro is already defined, so the preprocessor skips all of the content inside the #ifndef-#endif section and moves to the next statement after #endif, if there is any.

It is a common practice that the whole content of a header file is put between the #ifndef-#endif pair, and nothing but comments are left outside.

As a final note in this section, instead of having a pair of #ifndef-#endif directives, one could use #pragma once in order to protect the header file from the *double inclusion* issue. The difference between conditional directives and the #pragma once directive is that the latter is not a C standard, despite the fact that it is supported by almost all C preprocessors. However, it is better to not to use it if *portability* of your code is a requirement.

The following code box contains a demonstration on how to use `#pragma once` in *example 1.8*, instead of `#ifndef`-`#endif` directives:

```
#pragma once

void say_hello();
int read_age();
```

Code Box 1-18: Using #pragma once directive as part of example 1.8

Now, we close the topic of preprocessor directives while we have demonstrated some of their interesting characteristics and various applications. The next section is about variable pointers, which are another important feature of C.

Variable pointers

The concept of a variable pointer, or for short pointer, is one of the most fundamental concepts in C. You can hardly find any direct sign of them in most high-level programming languages. In fact, they have been replaced by some twin concepts, for example, *references* in Java. It is worth mentioning that pointers are unique in the sense that the addresses they point to can be used directly by hardware, but this is not the case for the higher-level twin concepts like references.

Having a deep understanding about pointers and the way they work is crucial to become a skilled C programmer. They are one of the most fundamental concepts in memory management, and despite their simple syntax, they have the potential to lead to a disaster when used in a wrong way. We will cover memory management-related topics in *Chapter 4*, *Process Memory Structure*, and *Chapter 5*, *Stack and Heap*, but here in this chapter, we want to recap everything about pointers. If you feel confident about the basic terminology and the concepts surrounding the pointers, you can skip this section.

Syntax

The idea behind any kind of pointer is very simple; it is just a simple variable that keeps a *memory address*. The first thing you may recall about them is the asterisk character, `*`, which is used for declaring a pointer in C. You can see it in *example 1.9*. The following code box demonstrates how to declare and use a variable pointer:

```
int main(int argc, char** argv) {
  int var = 100;
```

```
    int* ptr = 0;
    ptr = &var;
    *ptr = 200;
    return 0;
}
```

Code Box 1-19 [ExtremeC_examples_chapter1_9.c]: Example on how to declare and use a pointer in C

The preceding example has everything you need to know about the pointer's syntax. The first line declares the var variable on top of the *Stack segment*. We will discuss the Stack segment in *Chapter 4, Process Memory Structure*. The second line declares the pointer ptr with an initial value of zero. A pointer which has the zero value is called a *null pointer*. As long as the ptr pointer retains its zero value, it is considered to be a null pointer. It is very important to *nullify* a pointer if you are *not* going to store a valid address upon declaration.

As you see in *Code Box 1-19*, no header file is included. Pointers are part of the C language, and you don't need to have anything included to be able to use them. Indeed, we can have C programs, which do not include any header file at all.

All of the following declarations are valid in C:

```
int* ptr = 0;

int * ptr = 0;

int *ptr = 0;
```

The third line in the main function introduces the & operator, which is called the *referencing operator*. It returns the address of the variable next to it. We need this operator to obtain the address of a variable. Otherwise, we cannot initialize pointers with valid addresses.

On the same line, the returned address is stored into the ptr pointer. Now, the ptr pointer is not a null pointer anymore. On the fourth line, we see another operator prior to the pointer, which is called the *dereferencing operator* and denoted by *. This operator allows you to have indirect access to the memory cell that the ptr pointer is pointing to. In other words, it allows you to read and modify the var variable through the pointer that is pointing to it. The fourth line is equivalent to the var = 200; statement.

A null pointer is not pointing to a valid memory address. Therefore, dereferencing a null pointer *must* be avoided because it is considered as an *undefined behavior*, which usually leads to a crash.

As a final note regarding the preceding example, we usually have the default macro NULL defined with value 0, and it can be used to nullify pointers upon declaration. It is a good practice to use this macro instead of 0 directly because it makes it easier to distinguish between the variables and the pointers:

```
char* ptr = NULL;
```

Code Box 1-20: Using the NULL macro to nullify a pointer

The pointers in C++ are exactly the same as in C. They need to be nullified by storing 0 or NULL in them, but C++11 has a new keyword for initializing the pointers. It is not a macro like NULL nor an integer like 0. The keyword is nullptr and can be used to nullify the pointers or check whether they are null. The following example demonstrates how it is used in C++11:

```
char* ptr = nullptr;
```

Code Box 1-21: Using nullptr to nullify a pointer in C++11

It is crucial to remember that pointers *must* be initialized upon declaration. If you don't want to store any valid memory address while declaring them, don't leave them uninitialized. *Make it null by assigning* 0 *or* NULL! Do this otherwise you may face a fatal bug!

In most modern compilers, an uninitialized pointer is always nullified. This means that the initial value is 0 for all uninitialized pointers. But this shouldn't be considered as an excuse to declare pointers without initializing them properly. Keep in mind that you are writing code for different architectures, old and new, and this may cause problems on legacy systems. In addition, you will get a list of errors and warnings for these kinds of uninitialized pointers in most *memory profilers*. Memory profilers will be explained thoroughly as part of *Chapter 4, Process Memory Structure*, and *Chapter 5, Stack and Heap*.

Arithmetic on variable pointers

The simplest picture of memory is a very long one-dimensional array of bytes. With this picture in mind, if you're standing on one byte, you can only go back and forth in the array; there's no other possible movement. So, this would be the same for the pointers addressing different bytes in the memory. Incrementing the pointer makes the pointer go forward and decrementing it makes the pointer go backward. No other arithmetic operation is possible for the pointers.

Like we said previously, the arithmetic operations on a pointer are analogous to the movements in an array of bytes. We can use this figure to introduce a new concept: the *arithmetic step size*. We need to have this new concept because when you increment a pointer by 1, it might go forward more than 1 byte in the memory. Each pointer has an arithmetic step size, which means the number of bytes that the pointer will move if it is incremented or decremented by 1. This arithmetic step size is determined by the C *data type* of the pointer.

In every platform, we have one single unit of memory and all pointers store the addresses inside that memory. So, all pointers should have equal sizes in terms of bytes. But this doesn't mean that all of them have equal arithmetic step sizes. As we mentioned earlier, the arithmetic step size of a pointer is determined by its C data type.

For example, an `int` pointer has the same size as a `char` pointer, but they have different arithmetic step sizes. `int*` usually has a 4-byte arithmetic step size and `char*` has a 1-byte arithmetic step size. Therefore, incrementing an integer pointer makes it move forward by 4 bytes in the memory (adds 4 bytes to the current address), and incrementing a character pointer makes it move forward by only 1 byte in the memory. The following example, *example 1.10*, demonstrates the arithmetic step sizes of two pointers with two different data types:

```
#include <stdio.h>

int main(int argc, char** argv) {
  int var = 1;

  int* int_ptr = NULL; // nullify the pointer
  int_ptr = &var;

  char* char_ptr = NULL;
  char_ptr = (char*)&var;

  printf("Before arithmetic: int_ptr: %u, char_ptr: %u\n",
         (unsigned int)int_ptr, (unsigned int)char_ptr);

  int_ptr++;     // Arithmetic step is usually 4 bytes
  char_ptr++;    // Arithmetic step in 1 byte

  printf("After arithmetic: int_ptr: %u, char_ptr: %u\n",
         (unsigned int)int_ptr, (unsigned int)char_ptr);

  return 0;
}
```

Code Box 1-22 [ExtremeC_examples_chapter1_10.c]: Arithmetic step sizes of two pointers

The following shell box shows the output of *example 1.10*. Note that the printed addresses can be different for two successive runs on the same machine, and even from a platform to another, therefore you probably observe different addresses in your output:

```
$ gcc ExtremeC_examples_chapter1_10.c
$ ./a.out
Before arithmetic: int_ptr: 3932338348, char_ptr: 3932338348
After arithmetic:  int_ptr: 3932338352, char_ptr: 3932338349
$
```

Shell Box 1-4: Output of example 1.10 after first run

It is clear from the comparison of the addresses before and after the arithmetic operations that the step size for the integer pointer is 4 bytes, and it is 1 byte for the character pointer. If you run the example again, the pointers probably refer to some other addresses, but their arithmetic step sizes remain the same:

```
$ ./a.out
Before arithmetic: int_ptr: 4009638060, char_ptr: 4009638060
After arithmetic:  int_ptr: 4009638064, char_ptr: 4009638061
$
```

Shell Box 1-5: Output of example 1.10 after second run

Now that you know about the arithmetic step sizes, we can talk about a classic example of using pointer arithmetic to *iterate* over a region of memory. The examples 1.11 and 1.12 are about to print all the elements of an integer array. The trivial approach without using the pointers is brought in *example 1.11*, and the solution based on pointer arithmetic is given as part of *example 1.12*.

The following code box shows the code for *example 1.11*:

```
#include <stdio.h>

#define SIZE 5

int main(int argc, char** argv) {
  int arr[SIZE];
  arr[0] = 9;
  arr[1] = 22;
  arr[2] = 30;
  arr[3] = 23;
```

```
  arr[4] = 18;

  for (int i = 0; i < SIZE; i++) {
    printf("%d\n", arr[i]);
  }

  return 0;
}
```

Code Box 1-23 [ExtremeC_examples_chapter1_11.c]: Iterating over an array without using pointer arithmetic

The code in *Code Box 1-23* should be familiar to you. It just uses a *loop counter* to refer to a specific index of the array and read its content. But if you want to use pointers instead of accessing the elements via the *indexer* syntax (an integer between [and]), it should be done differently. The following code box demonstrates how to use pointers to iterate over the array boundary:

```
#include <stdio.h>

#define SIZE 5

int main(int argc, char** argv) {
  int arr[SIZE];
  arr[0] = 9;
  arr[1] = 22;
  arr[2] = 30;
  arr[3] = 23;
  arr[4] = 18;

  int* ptr = &arr[0];

  for (;;) {
    printf("%d\n", *ptr);
    if (ptr == &arr[SIZE - 1]) {
      break;
    }
    ptr++;
  }

  return 0;
}
```

Code Box 1-24 [ExtremeC_examples_chapter1_12.c]: Iterating over an array using pointer arithmetic

The second approach, demonstrated in *Code Box 1-24*, uses an infinite loop, which breaks when the address of the ptr pointer is the same as the last element of the array.

We know that arrays are adjacent variables inside the memory, so incrementing and decrementing a pointer which is pointing to an element effectively makes it move back and forth inside the array and eventually point to a different element.

As is clear from the preceding code, the `ptr` pointer has the data type `int*`. That's because of the fact that it must be able to point to any individual element of the array which is an integer of type `int`. Note that all the elements of an array are from the same type hence they have equal sizes. Therefore, incrementing the `ptr` pointer makes it point to the next element inside the array. As you see, before the `for` loop, `ptr` points to the first element of the array, and by further increments, it moves forward along the array's memory region. This is a very classic usage of pointer arithmetic.

Note that in C, an array is actually a pointer that points to its first element. So, in the example, the actual data type of `arr` is `int*`. Therefore, we could have written the line as follows:

```
int* ptr = arr;
```

Instead of the line:

```
int* ptr = &arr[0];
```

Generic pointers

A pointer of type `void*` is said to be a generic pointer. It can point to any address like all other pointers, but we don't know its actual data type hence we don't know its arithmetic step size. Generic pointers are usually used to hold the content of other pointers, but they forget the actual data types of those pointers. Therefore, a generic pointer cannot be dereferenced, and one cannot do arithmetic on it because its underlying data type is unknown. The following example, *example 1.13*, shows us that dereferencing a generic pointer is not possible:

```
#include <stdio.h>

int main(int argc, char** argv) {
  int var = 9;
  int* ptr = &var;
  void* gptr = ptr;
  printf("%d\n", *gptr);
```

```
  return 0;
}
```

Code Box 1-25 [ExtremeC_examples_chapter1_13.c]: Dereferencing a generic pointer generates
a compilation error!

If you compile the preceding code using `gcc` in Linux, you will get the following error:

```
$ gcc ExtremeC_examples_chapter1_13.c
In function 'main':
warning: dereferencing 'void *' pointer
  printf("%d\n", *gptr);
                 ^~~~~
error: invalid use of void expression
  printf("%d\n", *gptr);
$
```

Shell Box 1-6: Compiling example 1.13 in Linux

And if you compile it using `clang` in macOS, the error message is different, but it refers to the same issue:

```
$ clang ExtremeC_examples_chapter1_13.c
error: argument type 'void' is incomplete
  printf("%d\n", *gptr);
                  ^
1 error generated.
$
```

Shell Box 1-7: Compiling example 1.13 in macOS

As you see, both compilers don't accept dereferencing a generic pointer. In fact, it is meaningless to dereference a generic pointer! So, what are they good for? In fact, generic pointers are very handy to define *generic functions* that can accept a wide range of different pointers as their input arguments. The following example, *example 1.14*, tries to uncover the details regarding generic functions:

```
#include <stdio.h>

void print_bytes(void* data, size_t length) {
  char delim = ' ';
  unsigned char* ptr = data;
```

```
    for (size_t i = 0; i < length; i++) {
      printf("%c 0x%x", delim, *ptr);
      delim = ',';
      ptr++;
    }
    printf("\n");
}

int main(int argc, char** argv) {
  int a = 9;
  double b = 18.9;

  print_bytes(&a, sizeof(int));
  print_bytes(&b, sizeof(double));

  return 0;
}
```

Code Box 1-26 [ExtremeC_examples_chapter1_14.c]: An example of a generic function

In the preceding code box, the print_bytes function receives an address as a void* pointer and an integer indicating the length. Using these arguments, the function prints all the bytes starting from the given address up to the given length. As you see, the function accepts a generic pointer, which allows the user to pass whatever pointer they want. Keep in mind that assignment to a *void pointer* (generic pointer) does *not* need an explicit cast. That is why we have passed the addresses of a and b without explicit casts.

Inside the print_bytes function, we have to use an unsigned char pointer in order to move inside the memory. Otherwise, we cannot do any arithmetic on the void pointer parameter, data, directly. As you may know, the step size of a char* or unsigned char* is one byte. So, it is the best pointer type for iterating over a range of memory addresses one byte at a time and processing all of those bytes one by one.

As a final note about this example, size_t is a standard and unsigned data type usually used for storing sizes in C.

size_t is defined in section 6.5.3.4 of the ISO/ICE 9899:TC3 standard. This ISO standard is the famous C99 specification revised in 2007. This standard has been the basis for all C implementations up until today. The link to ISO/ICE 9899:TC3 (2007) is http://www.open-std.org/jtc1/sc22/wg14/www/docs/n1256.pdf

Size of a pointer

If you search for the *size of a pointer in* C on Google, you may realize that you cannot find a definitive answer to that. There are many answers out there, and it is true that you cannot define a fixed size for a pointer in different architectures. The size of a pointer depends on the architecture rather than being a specific C concept. C doesn't worry too much about such hardware-related details, and it tries to provide a generic way of working with pointers and other programming concepts. That is why we know C as a standard. Only pointers and the arithmetic on them are important to C.

 Architecture refers to the hardware used in a computer system. You will find more details in the upcoming chapter, *Compilation and Linking.*

You can always use the `sizeof` function to obtain the size of a pointer. It is enough to see the result of `sizeof(char*)` on your target architecture. As a rule of thumb, pointers are 4 bytes in 32-bit architectures and 8 bytes in 64-bit architectures, but you may find different sizes in other architectures. Keep in mind that the code you write *should not* be dependent on a specific value for the size of a pointer, and it should not make any assumptions about it. Otherwise, you will be in trouble while porting your code to other architectures.

Dangling pointers

There are many known issues caused by misusing pointers. The issue of dangling pointers is a very famous one. A pointer usually points to an address to which there is a variable allocated. Reading or modifying an address where there is no variable registered is a big mistake and can result in a crash or a *segmentation fault* situation. Segmentation fault is a scary error that every C/C++ developer should have seen it at least once while working on code. This situation usually happens when you are misusing pointers. You are accessing places in memory that you are not allowed to. You had a variable there before, but it is deallocated by now.

Let's try to produce this situation as part of the following example, *example 1.15*:

```
#include <stdio.h>

int* create_an_integer(int default_value) {
  int var = default_value;
  return &var;
}
```

```
int main() {
    int* ptr = NULL;
    ptr = create_an_integer(10);
    printf("%d\n", *ptr);
    return 0;
}
```

Code Box 1-27 [ExtremeC_examples_chapter1_15.c]: Producing a segmentation fault situation

In the preceding example, the `create_an_integer` function is used to create an integer. It declares an integer with a default value and returns its address to the caller. In the `main` function, the address of the created integer, `var`, is received and it gets stored in the `ptr` pointer. Then, the `ptr` pointer is dereferenced, and the value stored in the `var` variable gets printed.

But things are not that easy. When you want to compile this code using the `gcc` compiler on a Linux machine, it generates a warning as follows, but still successfully finishes the compilation, and you get the final executable:

```
$ gcc ExtremeC_examples_chapter1_15.c
In function 'f':
warning: function returns address of local variable [-Wreturn-
local-addr]
    return &var;
           ^~~
$
```

Shell Box 1-8: Compiling example 1.15 in Linux

This is indeed an important warning message which can be easily missed and forgotten by the programmer. We'll talk more about this later as part of *Chapter 5, Stack and Heap*. Let's see what happens if we proceed and execute the resulting executable.

When you run *example 1.15*, you get a segmentation fault error, and the program crashes immediately:

```
$ ./a.out
Segmentation fault (core dumped)
$
```

Shell Box 1-9: Segmentation fault when running example 1.15

So, what went wrong? The `ptr` pointer is dangling and points to an already deallocated portion of memory that was known to be the memory place of the variable, `var`.

The `var` variable is a local variable to the `create_an_integer` function, and it will be deallocated after leaving the function, but its address can be returned from the function. So, after copying the returned address into `ptr` as part of the `main` function, `ptr` becomes a dangling pointer pointing to an invalid address in memory. Now, dereferencing the pointer causes a serious problem and the program crashes.

If you look back at the warning generated by the compiler, it is clearly stating the problem.

It says that you are *returning the address of a local variable*, which will be deallocated after returning from the function. Smart compiler! If you take these warnings seriously, you won't face these scary bugs.

But what is the proper way to rewrite the example? Yes, using the *Heap memory*. We will cover heap memory fully in *Chapter 4*, *Process Memory Structure*, and *Chapter 5*, *Stack and Heap*, but, for now, we will rewrite the example using *Heap allocation*, and you will see how you can benefit from using *Heap* instead of the *Stack*.

Example 1.16 below shows how to use Heap memory for allocating variables, and enabling the passing addresses between functions without facing any issues:

```c
#include <stdio.h>
#include <stdlib.h>

int* create_an_integer(int default_value) {
    int* var_ptr = (int*)malloc(sizeof(int));
    *var_ptr = default_value;
    return var_ptr;
}

int main() {
    int* ptr = NULL;
    ptr = create_an_integer(10);
    printf("%d\n", *ptr);
    free(ptr);
    return 0;
}
```

Code Box 1-28 [ExtremeC_examples_chapter1_16.c]: Rewriting example 1.15 using Heap memory

As you see in the preceding code box, we have included a new header file, stdlib.h, and we are using two new functions, malloc and free. The simple explanation is like this: the created integer variable inside the create_an_integer function is not a local variable anymore. Instead, it is a variable allocated from the Heap memory and its lifetime is not limited to the function declaring it. Therefore, it can be accessed in the caller (outer) function. The pointers pointing to this variable are not dangling anymore, and they can be dereferenced as long as the variable exists and is not freed. Eventually, the variable becomes deallocated by calling the free function as an end to its lifetime. Note that deallocating a Heap variable is mandatory when it is not needed anymore.

In this section, we went through all the essential discussions regarding variable pointers. In the upcoming section, we'll be talking about functions and their anatomy in C.

Some details about functions

C is a *procedural* programming language. In C, functions act as procedures, and they are building blocks of a C program. So, it is important to know what they are, how they behave, and what is happening when you enter or leave a function. In general, functions (or procedures) are analogous to ordinary variables that store algorithms instead of values. By putting variables and functions together into a new type, we can store relevant values and algorithms under the same concept. This is what we do in *object-oriented programming*, and it will be covered in the third part of the book, *Object Orientation*. In this section, we want to explore functions and discuss their properties in C.

Anatomy of a function

In this section, we want to recap everything about a C function in a single place. If you feel this is familiar to you, you can simply skip this section.

A function is a box of logic that has a name, a list of input parameters, and a list of output results. In C and many other programming languages that are influenced by C, functions return only one value. In object-oriented languages such as C++ and Java, functions (which are usually called *methods*) can also throw an *exception*, which is not the case for C. Functions are invoked by a function call, which is simply using the name of the function to execute its logic. A correct function call should pass all required arguments to the function and wait for its execution. Note that functions are always *blocking* in C. This means that the caller has to wait for the called function to finish and only then can it collect the returned result.

Opposite to a blocking function, we can have a *non-blocking* function. When calling a non-blocking function, the caller doesn't wait for the function to finish and it can continue its execution. In this scheme, there is usually a *callback* mechanism which is triggered when the called (or callee) function is finished. A non-blocking function can also be referred to as an *asynchronous function* or simply an *async function*. Since we don't have async functions in C, we need to implement them using multithreading solutions. We will explain these concepts in more detail in the fifth part of the book, *Concurrency*.

It is interesting to add that nowadays, there is a growing interest in using non-blocking functions over blocking functions. It is usually referred to as *event-oriented programming*. Non-blocking functions are centric in this programming approach, and most of the written functions are non-blocking.

In event-oriented programming, actual function calls happen inside an *event loop*, and proper callbacks are triggered upon the occurrence of an event. Frameworks such as `libuv` and `libev` promote this way of coding, and they allow you to design your software around one or several event loops.

Importance in design

Functions are fundamental building blocks of procedural programming. Since their official support in programming languages, they have had a huge impact on the way we write code. Using functions, we can store logic in semi-variable entities and summon them whenever and wherever they are needed. Using them, we can write a specific logic only once and use it multiple times in various places.

In addition, functions allow us to hide a piece of logic from other existing logic. In other words, they introduce a level of abstraction between various logical components. To give an example, suppose that you have a function, `avg`, which calculates the average of an input array. And you have another function, `main`, which calls the function, `avg`. We say that the logic inside the `avg` function is hidden from the logic inside the `main` function.

Therefore, if you want to change the logic inside `avg`, you don't need to change the logic inside the `main` function. That's because the `main` function only depends on the name and the availability of the `avg` function. This is a great achievement, at least for those years when we had to use punched cards to write and execute programs!

We are still using this feature in designing libraries written in C or even higher-level programming languages such as C++ and Java.

Stack management

If you look at the memory layout of a process running in a Unix-like operating system, you notice that all of the processes share a similar layout. We will discuss this layout in more detail in *Chapter 4*, *Process Memory Structure*, but for now, we want to introduce one of its *segments*; the Stack segment. The Stack segment is the default memory location where all local variables, arrays, and structures are allocated from. So, when you declare a local variable in a function, it is being allocated from the Stack segment. This allocation always happens on top of the Stack segment.

Notice the term *stack* in the name of the segment. It means that this segment behaves like a stack. The variables and arrays are always allocated on top of it, and those at the top are the first variables to get removed. Remember this analogy with the stack concept. We will return to this in the next paragraph.

The Stack segment is also used for function calls. When you call a function, a *stack frame* containing the return address and all of the passing arguments is put on top of the Stack segment, and only then is the function logic executed. When returning from the function, the stack frame is popped out, and the instruction addressed by the return address gets executed, which should usually continue the caller function.

All local variables declared in the function body are put on top of the Stack segment. So, when leaving the function, all Stack variables become freed. That is why we call them *local variables* and that is why a function cannot access the variables in another function. This mechanism also explains why local variables are not defined before entering a function and after leaving it.

Understanding the Stack segment and the way it works is crucial to writing correct and meaningful code. It also prevents common memory bugs from occurring. It is also a reminder that you cannot create any variable on the Stack with any size you like. The Stack is a limited portion of memory, and you could fill it up and potentially receive a *stack overflow* error. This usually happens when we have too many function calls consuming up all the Stack segment by their stack frames. This is very common when dealing with recursive functions, when a function calls itself without any break condition or limit.

Pass-by-value versus pass-by-reference

In most computer programming books, there is a section dedicated to pass-by-value and pass-by-reference regarding the arguments passed to a function. Fortunately, or unfortunately, we have only pass-by-value in C.

There is no reference in C, so there is no pass-by-reference either. Everything is copied into the function's local variables, and you cannot read or modify them after leaving a function.

Despite the many examples that seem to demonstrate pass-by-reference function calls, I should say that passing by reference is an illusion in C. In the rest of this section, we want to uncover this illusion and convince you that those examples are also pass-by-value. The following example will demonstrate this:

```
#include <stdio.h>

void func(int a) {
  a = 5;
}

int main(int argc, char** argv) {
  int x = 3;
  printf("Before function call: %d\n", x);
  func(x);
  printf("After function call: %d\n", x);
  return 0;
}
```

Code Box 1-29 [ExtremeC_examples_chapter1_17.c]: An example of a pass-by-value function call

It is easy to predict the output. Nothing changes about the x variable because it is passed by value. The following shell box shows the output of *example 1.17* and confirms our prediction:

```
$ gcc ExtremeC_examples_chapter1_17.c
$ ./a.out
Before function call: 3
After function call: 3
$
```

Shell Box 1-10: Output of example 1.17

The following example, *example 1.18*, demonstrates that passing by reference doesn't exist in C:

```
#include <stdio.h>

void func(int* a) {
  int b = 9;
```

```
    *a = 5;
    a = &b;
}

int main(int argc, char** argv) {
    int x = 3;
    int* xptr = &x;
    printf("Value before call: %d\n", x);
    printf("Pointer before function call: %p\n", (void*)xptr);
    func(xptr);
    printf("Value after call: %d\n", x);
    printf("Pointer after function call: %p\n", (void*)xptr);
    return 0;
}
```

Code Box 1-30 [ExtremeC_examples_chapter1_18.c]: An example of pass-by-pointer function call which differs from pass-by-reference

And this is the output:

```
$ gcc ExtremeC_examples_chapter1_18.c
$ ./a.out
The value before the call: 3
Pointer before function call: 0x7ffee99a88ec
The value after the call: 5
Pointer after function call: 0x7ffee99a88ec
$
```

Shell Box 1-11: Output of example 1.18

As you see, the value of the pointer is not changed after the function call. This means that the pointer is passed as a pass-by-value argument. Dereferencing the pointer inside the func function has allowed accessing the variable where the pointer is pointing to. But you see that changing the value of the pointer parameter inside the function doesn't change its counterpart argument in the caller function. During a function call in C, all arguments are passed by value and dereferencing the pointers allows the modification of the caller function's variables.

It is worth adding that the above example demonstrates a pass-by-pointer example in which we pass pointers to variables instead of passing them directly. It is usually recommended to use pointers as arguments instead of passing big objects to a function but why? It is easy to guess. Copying 8 bytes of a pointer argument is much more efficient than copying hundreds of bytes of a big object.

Surprisingly, passing the pointer is not efficient in the above example! That's because of the fact that the `int` type is 4 bytes and copying it is more efficient than copying 8 bytes of its pointer. But this is not the case regarding structures and arrays. Since copying structures and arrays is done byte-wise, and all of the bytes in them should be copied one by one, it is usually better to pass pointers instead.

Now that we've covered some details regarding the functions in C, let's talk about function pointers.

Function pointers

Having function pointers is another super feature of the C programming language. The two previous sections were about variable pointers and functions, and this section is going to combine them and talk about a more interesting topic: pointers to functions.

They have many applications, but splitting a large binary into smaller binaries and loading them again in another small executable is one of the most important applications. This has led to *modularization* and software design. Function pointers are building blocks for the implementation of polymorphism in C++ and allow us to extend our existing logic. In this section, we are going to cover them and prepare you for more advanced topics we'll cover over the coming chapters.

Like a variable pointer addressing a variable, a function pointer addresses a function and allows you to call that function indirectly. The following example, *example 1.19*, can be a good starter for this topic:

```c
#include <stdio.h>

int sum(int a, int b) {
  return a + b;
}

int subtract(int a, int b) {
  return a - b;
}

int main() {
  int (*func_ptr)(int, int);
  func_ptr = NULL;

  func_ptr = &sum;
  int result = func_ptr(5, 4);
```

```
    printf("Sum: %d\n", result);

    func_ptr = &subtract;
    result = func_ptr(5, 4);
    printf("Subtract: %d\n", result);

    return 0;
}
```

Code Box 1-31 [ExtremeC_examples_chapter1_19.c]: Using a single function pointer to call different functions

In the preceding code box, `func_ptr` is a function pointer. It can only point to a specific class of functions that match its signature. The signature limits the pointer to only point to functions that accept two integer arguments and return an integer result.

As you see, we have defined two functions called `sum` and `subtract` matching the `func_ptr` pointer's signature. The preceding example uses the `func_ptr` function pointer to point to the `sum` and `subtract` functions separately, then call them with the same arguments and compare the results. This is the output of the example:

```
$ gcc ExtremeC_examples_chapter1_19.c
$ ./a.out
Sum: 9
Subtract: 1
$
```

Shell Box 1-12: Output of example 1.19

As you see in *example 1.19*, we can call different functions for the same list of arguments using a single function pointer, and this is an important feature. If you are familiar with object-oriented programming, the first thing that comes to mind is *polymorphism* and *virtual functions*. In fact, this is the only way to support polymorphism in C and mimic the C++ virtual functions. We will cover OOP as part of the third part of the book, *Object Orientation*.

Like variable pointers, it is important to initialize function pointers properly. For those function pointers which are not going to be initialized immediately upon declaration, it is mandatory to make them null. The nullification of function pointers is demonstrated in the preceding example, and it is pretty similar to variable pointers.

It is usually advised to define a new *type alias* for function pointers. The following example, *example 1.20*, demonstrates the way it should be done:

```
#include <stdio.h>

typedef int bool_t;
typedef bool_t (*less_than_func_t)(int, int);

bool_t less_than(int a, int b) {
  return a < b ? 1 : 0;
}

bool_t less_than_modular(int a, int b) {
  return (a % 5) < (b % 5) ? 1 : 0;
}

int main(int argc, char** argv) {
  less_than_func_t func_ptr = NULL;

  func_ptr = &less_than;
  bool_t result = func_ptr(3, 7);
  printf("%d\n", result);

  func_ptr = &less_than_modular;
  result = func_ptr(3, 7);
  printf("%d\n", result);

  return 0;
}
```

Code Box 1-32 [ExtremeC_examples_chapter1_20.c]: Using a single function pointer to call different functions

The `typedef` keyword allows you to define an alias for an already defined type. There are two new type aliases in the preceding example: `bool_t`, which is an alias for the `int` type, and the `less_than_func_t` type, which is an alias type for the function pointer type, `bool_t (*)(int, int)`. These aliases add readability to the code and let you choose a shorter name for a long and complex type. In C, the name of a new type usually ends with `_t` by convention, and you can find this convention in many other standard type aliases such as `size_t` and `time_t`.

Structures

From the design perspective, structures are one of the most fundamental concepts in C. Nowadays, they are not unique to C, and you can find their twin concepts nearly in every modern programming language.

But we should discuss them in the history of computation when there were no other programming languages offering such a concept. Among many efforts to move away from machine-level programming languages, introducing structures was a great step toward having *encapsulation* in a programming language. For thousands of years, the way we think hasn't changed a lot, and encapsulation has been a centric means for our logical reasoning.

But it was just after C that we finally had some tool, in this case, a programming language, which was able to understand the way we think and could store and process the building blocks of our reasoning. Finally, we got a language that resembles our thoughts and ideas, and all of this happened when we got structures. C structures weren't perfect in comparison to the encapsulation mechanisms found in modern languages, but they were enough for us to build a platform upon which to create our finest tools.

Why structures?

You know that every programming language has some **Primitive Data Types (PDTs)**. Using these PDTs, you can design your data structures and write your algorithms around them. These PDTs are part of the programming language, and they cannot be changed or removed. As an example, you cannot have C without the primitive types, `int` and `double`.

Structures come into play when you need to have your own defined data types, and the data types in the language are not enough. **User-Defined Types (UDTs)** are those types which are created by the user and they are not part of the language.

Note that UDTs are different from the types you could define using `typedef`. The keyword `typedef` doesn't really create a new type, but rather it defines an alias or synonym for an already defined type. But structures allow you to introduce totally new UDTs into your program.

Structures have twin concepts in other programming languages, for example, classes in C++ and Java or packages in Perl. They are considered to be the *type-makers* in these languages.

Why user-defined types?

So, why do we need to create new types in a program? The answer to this question reveals the principles behind software design and the methods we use for our daily software development. We create new types because we do it every day using our brains in a routine analysis.

We don't look at our surroundings as integers, doubles, or characters. We have learned to group related attributes under the same object. We will discuss more the way we analyze our surroundings in *Chapter 6, OOP and Encapsulation*. But as an answer to our starting question, we need new types because we use them to analyze our problems at a higher level of logic, close enough to our human logic.

Here, you need to become familiar with the term *business logic*. Business logic is a set of all entities and regulations found in a business. For example, in the business logic of a banking system, you face concepts such as client, account, balance, money, cash, payment, and many more, which are there to make operations such as money withdrawal possible and meaningful.

Suppose that you had to explain some banking logic in pure integers, floats, or characters. It is almost impossible. If it is possible for programmers, it is almost meaningless to *business analysts*. In a real software development environment that has a well-defined business logic, programmers and business analysts cooperate closely. Therefore, they need to have a shared set of terminology, glossary, types, operations, regulations, logic, and so on.

Today, a programming language that does not support new types in its *type system* can be considered as a dead language. Maybe that's why most people see C as a dead programming language, mainly because they cannot easily define their new types in C, and they prefer to move to a higher-level language such as C++ or Java. Yes, it's not that easy to create a nice type system in C, but everything you need is present there.

Even today, there can be many reasons behind choosing C as the project's main language and accepting the efforts of creating and maintaining a nice type system in a C project and even today many companies do that.

Despite the fact that we need new types in our daily software analysis, CPUs do not understand these new types. CPUs try to stick to the PDTs and fast calculations because they are designed to do that. So, if you have a program written in your high-level language, it should be translated to CPU level instructions, and this may cost you more time and resources.

In this sense, fortunately, C is not very far away from the CPU-level logic, and it has a type system which can be easily translated. You may have heard that C is a low-level or hardware-level programming language. This is one of the reasons why some companies and organizations try to write and maintain their core frameworks in C, even today.

What do structures do?

Structures encapsulate related values under a single unified type. As an early example, we can group red, green, and blue variables under a new single data type called color_t. The new type, color_t, can represent an RGB color in various programs like an image editing application. We can define the corresponding C structure as follows:

```
struct color_t {
  int red;
  int green;
  int blue;
};
```

Code Box 1-33: A structure in C representing an RGB color

As we said before, structures do encapsulation. Encapsulation is one of the most fundamental concepts in software design. It is about grouping and encapsulating related fields under a new type. Then, we can use this new type to define the required variables. We will describe encapsulation thoroughly in *Chapter 6, OOP and Encapsulation*, while talking about object-oriented design.

 Note that we use an _t suffix for naming new data types.

Memory layout

It is usually important to C programmers to know exactly the memory layout of a structure variable. Having a bad layout in memory could cause performance degradations in certain architectures. Don't forget that we code to produce the instructions for the CPU. The values are stored in the memory, and the CPU should be able to read and write them fast enough. Knowing the memory layout helps a developer to understand the way the CPU works and to adjust their code to gain a better result.

The following example, *example 1.21*, defines a new structure type, sample_t, and declares one structure variable, var. Then, it populates its fields with some values and prints the size and the actual bytes of the variable in the memory. This way, we can observe the memory layout of the variable:

```
#include <stdio.h>
```

```
struct sample_t {
  char first;
  char second;
  char third;
  short fourth;
};

void print_size(struct sample_t* var) {
  printf("Size: %lu bytes\n", sizeof(*var));
}

void print_bytes(struct sample_t* var) {
  unsigned char* ptr = (unsigned char*)var;
  for (int i = 0; i < sizeof(*var); i++, ptr++) {
    printf("%d ", (unsigned int)*ptr);
  }
  printf("\n");
}

int main(int argc, char** argv) {
  struct sample_t var;
  var.first = 'A';
  var.second = 'B';
  var.third = 'C';
  var.fourth = 765;
  print_size(&var);
  print_bytes(&var);
  return 0;
}
```

Code Box 1-34 [ExtremeC_examples_chapter1_21.c]: Printing the number of the bytes allocated for a structure variable

The thirst to know the exact memory layout of everything is a bit C/C++ specific, and vanishes as the programming languages become high level. For example, in Java and Python, the programmers tend to know less about the very low-level memory management details, and on the other hand, these languages don't provide many details about the memory.

As you see in *Code Box 1-34*, in C, you have to use the struct keyword before declaring a structure variable. Therefore, in the preceding example we have struct sample_t var, which shows how you should use the keyword before the structure type in the declaration clause. It is trivial to mention that you need to use a . (dot) to access the fields of a structure variable. If it is a structure pointer, you need to use -> (arrow) to access its fields.

In order to prevent typing a lot of `struct`s throughout the code, while defining a new structure type and while declaring a new structure variable, we could use `typedef` to define a new alias type for the structure. Following is an example:

```
typedef struct {
  char first;
  char second;
  char third;
  short fourth;
} sample_t;
```

Now, you can declare the variable without using the keyword `struct`:

```
sample_t var;
```

The following is the output of the preceding example after being compiled and executed on a macOS machine. Note that the numbers generated may vary depending upon the host system:

```
$ clang ExtremeC_examples_chapter1_21.c
$ ./a.out
Size: 6 bytes
65 66 67 0 253 2
$
```

Shell Box 1-13: Output of example 1.21

As you see in the preceding shell box, `sizeof(sample_t)` has returned 6 bytes. The memory layout of a structure variable is very similar to an array. In an array, all elements are adjacent to each other in the memory, and this is the same for a structure variable and its field. The difference is that, in an array, all elements have the same type and therefore the same size, but this is not the case regarding a structure variable. Each field can have a different type, and hence, it can have a different size. Unlike an array, the memory size of which is easily calculated, the size of a structure variable in the memory depends on a few factors and cannot be easily determined.

At first, it seems to be easy to guess the size of a structure variable. For the structure in the preceding example, it has four fields, three `char` fields, and one `short` field. With a simple calculation, if we suppose that `sizeof(char)` is 1 byte and `sizeof(short)` is 2 bytes, each variable of the type `sample_t` should have 5 bytes in its memory layout. But when we look at the output, we see that `sizeof(sample_t)` is 6 bytes. 1 byte more! Why do we have this extra byte?

Again, while looking at the bytes in the memory layout of the structure variable, var, we can see that it is a bit different from our expectation which is 65 66 67 253 2.

For making this clearer and explaining why the size of the structure variable is not 5 bytes, we need to introduce the *memory alignment* concept. The CPU always does all the computations. Besides that, it needs to load values from memory before being able to compute anything and needs to store the results back again in the memory after a computation. Computation is super-fast inside the CPU, but the memory access is very slow in comparison. It is important to know how the CPU interacts with the memory because then we can use the knowledge to boost a program or debug an issue.

The CPU usually reads a specific number of bytes in each memory access. This number of bytes is usually called a *word*. So, the memory is split into words and a word is an atomic unit used by the CPU to read from and write to the memory. The actual number of bytes in a word is an architecture-dependent factor. For example, in most 64-bit machines, the word size is 32 bits or 4 bytes. Regarding the memory alignment, we say that a variable is aligned in the memory if its starting byte is at the beginning of a word. This way, the CPU can load its value in an optimized number of memory accesses.

Regarding the previous example, *example 1.21*, the first 3 fields, first, second, and third, are 1 byte each, and they reside in the first word of the structure's layout, and they all can be read by just one memory access. About the fourth field, fourth occupies 2 bytes. If we forget about the memory alignment, its first byte will be the last byte of the first word, which makes it unaligned.

If this was the case, the CPU would be required to make two memory accesses together with shifting some bits in order to retrieve the value of the field. That is why we see an extra zero after byte 67. The zero byte has been added in order to complete the current word and let the fourth field start in the next word. Here, we say that the first word is padded by one zero byte. The compiler uses the *padding* technique to align values in the memory. Padding is the extra bytes added to match the alignment.

It is possible to turn off the alignment. In C terminology, we use a more specific term for aligned structures. We say that the structure is not packed. *Packed structures* are not aligned and using them may lead to binary incompatibilities and performance degradation. You can easily define a structure that is packed. We will do it in the next example, *example 1.22*, which is pretty similar to the previous example, *example 1.21*. The sample_t structure is packed in this example. The following code box shows *example 1.22*. Note that the similar code are replaced by ellipses:

```
#include <stdio.h>

struct __attribute__((__packed__)) sample_t {
  char first;
  char second;
  char third;
  short fourth;
} ;

void print_size(struct sample_t* var) {
  // ...
}

void print_bytes(struct sample_t* var) {
  // ...
}

int main(int argc, char** argv) {
  // ...
}
```

Code Box 1-35 [ExtremeC_examples_chapter1_22.c]: Declaring a packed structure

In the following shell box, the preceding code is compiled using `clang` and run on macOS:

```
$ clang ExtremeC_examples_chapter1_22.c
$ ./a.out
Size: 5 bytes
65 66 67 253 2
$
```

Shell Box 1-14: Output of example 1.22

As you see in *Shell Box 1-14*, the printed size is exactly what we were expecting as part of *example 1.21*. The final layout is also matched with our expectation. Packed structures are usually used in memory-constrained environments, but they can have a huge negative impact on the performance on most architectures. Only new CPUs can handle reading an unaligned value from multiple words without enforcing extra cost. Note that memory alignment is enabled by default.

Nested structures

As we have explained in the previous sections, in general, we have two kinds of data types in C. There are the types that are primitive to the language and there are types which are defined by the programmers using the `struct` keyword. The former types are PDTs, and the latter are UDTs.

So far, our structure examples have been about UDTs (structures) made up of only PDTs. But in this section, we are going to give an example of UDTs (structures) that are made from other UDTs (structures). These are called *complex data types*, which are the result of nesting a few structures.

Let's begin with the example, *example 1.23*:

```c
typedef struct {
  int x;
  int y;
} point_t;

typedef struct {
  point_t center;
  int radius;
} circle_t;

typedef struct {
  point_t start;
  point_t end;
} line_t;
```

Code Box 1-36 [ExtremeC_examples_chapter1_23.c]: Declaring some nested structures

In the preceding code box, we have three structures; `point_t`, `circle_t`, and `line_t`. The `point_t` structure is a simple UDT because it is made up of only PDTs, but other structures contain a variable of the `point_t` type, which makes them complex UDTs.

The size of a complex structure is calculated exactly the same as a simple structure, by summing up the sizes of all its fields. We should be still careful about the alignment, of course, because it can affect the size of a complex structure. So, `sizeof(point_t)` would be 8 bytes if `sizeof(int)` is 4 bytes. Then, `sizeof(circle_t)` is 12 bytes and `sizeof(line_t)` is 16 bytes.

It is common to call structure variables objects. They are exactly analogous to objects in object-oriented programming, and we will see that they can encapsulate both values and functions. So, it is not wrong at all to call them C objects.

Structure pointers

Like pointers to PDTs, we can have pointers to UDTs as well. They work exactly the same as PDT pointers. They point to an address in memory, and you can do arithmetic on them just like with the PDT pointers. UDT pointers also have arithmetic step sizes equivalent to the size of the UDT. If you don't know anything about the pointers or the allowed arithmetic operations on them, please go to the *Pointers* section and give it a read.

It is important to know that a structure variable points to the address of the first field of the structure variable. In the previous example, *example 1.23*, a pointer of type point_t would point to the address of its first field, x. This is also true for the type, circle_t. A pointer of type circle_t would point to its first field, center, and since it is actually a point_t object, it would point to the address of the first field, x, in the point_t type. Therefore, we can have 3 different pointers addressing the same cell in the memory. The following code will demonstrate this:

```
#include <stdio.h>

typedef struct {
  int x;
  int y;
} point_t;

typedef struct {
  point_t center;
  int radius;
} circle_t;

int main(int argc, char** argv) {
  circle_t c;

  circle_t* p1 = &c;
  point_t*  p2 = (point_t*)&c;
  int*      p3 = (int*)&c;

  printf("p1: %p\n", (void*)p1);
```

```
    printf("p2: %p\n", (void*)p2);
    printf("p3: %p\n", (void*)p3);

    return 0;
}
```

Code Box 1-37 [ExtremeC_examples_chapter1_24.c]: Having three different pointers from three different types addressing the same byte in memory

And this is the output:

```
$ clang ExtremeC_examples_chapter1_24.c
$ ./a.out
p1: 0x7ffee846c8e0
p2: 0x7ffee846c8e0
p3: 0x7ffee846c8e0
$
```

Shell Box 1-15: Output of example 1.24

As you see, all of the pointers are addressing the same byte, but their types are different. This is usually used to extend structures coming from other libraries by adding more fields. This is also the way we implement *inheritance* in C. We will discuss this in *Chapter 8, Inheritance and Polymorphism*.

This was the last section in this chapter. In the upcoming chapter, we will dive into the C compilation pipeline and how to properly compile and link a C project.

Summary

In this chapter, we revisited some of the important features of the C programming language. We tried to go further and show the design aspects of these features and the concepts behind them. Of course, the proper use of a feature requires a deeper insight into the different aspects of that feature. As part of this chapter, we discussed the following:

- We talked about the C preprocessing phase and how various directives can influence the preprocessor to act differently or generate a specific C code for us.

- Macros and the macro expansion mechanism allow us to generate C code before passing the translation unit to the compilation phase.

- Conditional directives allow us to alter the preprocessed code based on certain conditions and allow us to have different code for different situations.

- We also looked at variable pointers, and how they are employed in C.

- We introduced generic pointers and how we can have a function that accepts any kind of pointer.

- We discussed some issues such as segmentation faults and dangling pointers to show a few disastrous situations that can arise from misusing pointers.

- Functions were discussed next, and we reviewed their syntax.

- We explored functions' design aspects and how they contribute to a nicely shaped procedural C program.

- We also explained the function call mechanism and how arguments are passed to a function using stack frames.

- Function pointers were explored in this chapter. The powerful syntax of function pointers allows us to store logics in variable-like entities and use them later. They are, in fact, the fundamental mechanism that every single program uses today to be loaded and operate.

- Structures together with function pointers gave rise to encapsulation in C. We speak more about this in the third part of the book, *Object Orientation*.

- We tried to explain the design aspects of structures and their effect on the way we design programs in C.

- We also discussed the memory layout of structure variables and how they are placed inside memory to maximize CPU utilization.

- Nested structures were also discussed. We also took a look inside the complex structure variables and discussed how their memory layout should look.

- As the final section in this chapter, we talked about structure pointers.

The next chapter will be our first step in building a C project. The C compilation pipeline and linking mechanism will be discussed as part of the next chapter. Reading it thoroughly will be essential to continue with the book and proceed to further chapters.

Chapter 02

From Source to Binary

In programming, everything starts with source code. In reality, *source code*, which sometimes goes by the other name of the *code base*, usually consists of a number of text files. Within that, each of those text files contains textual instructions written in a programming language.

We know that a CPU cannot execute textual instructions. The reality is that these instructions should first be compiled (or translated) to machine-level instructions in order to be executed by a CPU, which eventually will result in a running program.

In this chapter, we go through the steps needed to get a final product out of C source code. This chapter goes into the subject in great depth, and as such we've split it into five distinct sections:

1. **The standard C compilation pipeline**: In the first section, we are going to cover standard C compilation, the various steps in the pipeline, and how they contribute to producing the final product from C source code.

2. **Preprocessor**: In this section, we are going to talk about the preprocessor component, which drives the preprocessing step, in greater depth.

3. **Compiler**: In this section, we are going to have a deeper look at compilers. We will explain how compilers, driving the compilation step, produce *intermediate representations* from source code and then translate them into assembly language.

4. **Assemblers**: After compilers, we also talk about *assemblers*, which play a significant role in translating the assembly instructions, received from compiler, into machine-level instructions. The assembler component drives the assembly step.

5. **Linker**: In the last section, we will discuss the *linker* component, driving the linking step, in greater depth. The linker is a build component that finally creates the actual products of a C project. There are build errors that are specific to this component, and sufficient knowledge of the linker will help us to prevent and resolve them. We also discuss the various final products of a C project, and we will give some hints about disassembling an object file and reading its content. More than that, we discuss briefly what C++ *name mangling* is and how it prevents certain defects in the linking step when building C++ code.

Our discussions in this chapter are mostly themed around Unix-like systems, but we discuss some differences in other operating systems, such as Microsoft Windows.

In the first section, we need to explain the C compilation pipeline. It is vital to know how the pipeline produces the executable and library files from the source code. While there are multiple concepts and steps involved, understanding them thoroughly is vital for us if we are to be prepared for the content in both this and future chapters. Note that the various products of a C project are discussed thoroughly in the next chapter, *Object Files*.

Compilation pipeline

Compiling some C files usually takes a few seconds, but during this brief period of time, the source code enters a pipeline that has four distinct components, with each of them doing a certain task. These components are as follows:

- Preprocessor
- Compiler
- Assembler
- Linker

Each component in this pipeline accepts a certain input from the previous component and produces a certain output for the next component in the pipeline. This process continues through the pipeline until a *product* is generated by the last component.

Source code can be turned into a product if, and only if, it passes through all the required components with success. This means that even a small failure in one of the components can lead to a *compilation* or *linkage* failure, resulting in you receiving relevant error messages.

For certain intermediate products such as *relocatable object files*, it is enough that a single source file goes through the first three components with success. The last component, the *linker*, is usually used to create bigger products, such as an *executable object file*, by merging some of the already prepared relocatable object files. So, building a collection of C source files can create one or sometimes multiple object files, including relocatable, executable, and *shared object files*.

There are currently a variety of C compilers available. While some of them are free and open source, others are proprietary and commercial. Likewise, some compilers will only work on a specific platform while others are cross-platform, although, the important note is that almost every platform has at least one compatible C compiler.

 Note:
For a complete list of available C compilers, please have a look at the following Wikipedia page: `https://en.wikipedia.org/wiki/List_of_compilers#C_compilers`.

Before talking about the default platform and the C compiler that we use throughout this chapter, let's talk a bit more about the term *platform*, and what we mean by it.

A platform is a combination of an operating system running on specific hardware (or architecture), and its CPU's *instruction set* is the most important part of it. The operating system is the software component of a platform, and the architecture defines the hardware part. As an example, we can have Ubuntu running on an ARM-powered board, or we could have Microsoft Windows running on an AMD 64-bit CPU.

Cross-platform software can be run on different platforms. However, it is vital to know that *cross-platform* is different from being *portable*. Cross-platform software usually has different binaries (final object files) and installers for each platform, while portable software uses the same produced binaries and installers on all platforms.

Some C compilers, for example, `gcc` and `clang`, are cross-platform – they can generate code for different platforms – and Java bytecode is portable.

Regarding C and C++, if we say that C/C++ code is portable, we mean that we can compile it for different platforms without any change or with little modification to the source code. This doesn't mean that the final object files are portable, however.

If you have looked at the Wikipedia article we noted before, you can see that there are numerous C compilers. Fortunately for us, all of them follow the same standard compilation pipeline that we are going to introduce in this chapter.

Among these many compilers, we need to choose one of them to work with during this chapter. Throughout this chapter, we will be using gcc 7.3.0 as our default compiler. We are choosing gcc because it is available on most operating systems, in addition to the fact that there are many online resources to be found for it.

We also need to choose our default platform. In this chapter, we have chosen Ubuntu 18.04 as our default operating system running on an AMD 64-bit CPU as our default architecture.

Note:
From time to time this chapter might refer to a different compiler, a different operating system, or a different architecture to compare various platforms and compilers. If we do so, the specification of the new platform or the new compiler will be given beforehand.

In the following sections, we are going to describe the steps in the compilation pipeline. First, we are going to build a simple example to see how the sources inside a C project are compiled and linked. Throughout this example, we will become familiar with new terms and concepts regarding the compilation process. Only after that do we address each component individually in a separate section. There, we go deep in to each component to explain more internal concepts and processes.

Building a C project

In this section, we are going to demonstrate how a C project is built. The project that we are going to work on consists of more than one source file, which is a common characteristic of almost all C projects. However, before we move to the example and start building it, we need to ensure that we understand the structure of a typical C project.

Header files versus source files

Every C project has source code, or code base, together with other documents related to the project description and existing standards. In a C code base, we usually have two kinds of files that contain C code:

- **Header files**, which usually have a .h extension in their names.
- **Source files**, which have a .c extension.

Note:
For convenience, in this chapter, we may use the terms *header* instead of *header file* and *source* instead of *source file*.

A header file usually contains enumerations, macros, and typedefs, as well as the *declarations* of functions, global variables, and structures. In C, some programming elements such as functions, variables, and structures can have their declaration separated from their *definition* placed in different files.

C++ follows the same pattern, but in other programming languages, such as Java, the elements are defined where they are declared. While this is a great feature of both C and C++, as it gives them the power to decouple the declarations from definitions, it also makes the source code more complex.

As a rule of thumb, the declarations are stored in header files, and the corresponding definitions go to source files. This is even more critical with regard to function declarations and function definitions.

It is strongly recommended that you only keep function declarations in header files and move function definitions to the corresponding source files. While this is not necessary, it is an important design practice to keep those function definitions out of the header files.

While the structures could also have separate declarations and definitions, there are special cases in which we move declarations and definitions to different files. We will see an example of this in *Chapter 8, Inheritance and Polymorphism*, where we will be discussing the *inheritance* relationship between classes.

Note:
Header files can include other header files, but never a source file. Source files can only include header files. It is bad practice to let a source file include another source file. If you do, then this usually means that you have a serious design problem in your project.

To elaborate more on this, we are going to look at an example. The following code is the declaration of the average function. A function declaration consists of a *return type* and a *function signature*. A function signature is simply the name of the function together with the list of its input parameters:

```
double average(int*, int);
```

Code Box 2-1: The declaration of the average function

The declaration introduces a function signature whose name is `average` and it receives a pointer to an array of integers together with a second integer argument, which indicates the number of elements in the array. The declaration also states that the function returns a double value. Note that the return type is a part of the declaration but is not often considered a part of the function signature.

As you can see in *Code Box 2-1*, a function declaration ends with a semicolon ";" and it does not have a *body* embraced by curly brackets. We should also take note that the parameters in the function declaration do not have associated names, and this is valid in C, but only in declarations and not in definitions. With that being said, it is recommended that you name the parameters even in declarations.

The function declaration is about how to use the function and the definition defines how that function is implemented. The user doesn't need to know about the parameter names to use the function, and because of that it's possible to hide them in the function declaration.

In the following code, you can find the definition of the `average` function that we declared before. A function definition contains the actual C code representing the function's logic. This always has a body of code embraced by a pair of curly brackets:

```
double average(int* array, int length) {
  if (length <= 0) {
    return 0;
  }
  double sum = 0.0;
  for (int i = 0; i < length; i++) {
    sum += array[i];
  }
  return sum / length;
}
```

Code Box 2-2: The definition of the average function

Like we said before, and to put more emphasis on this, function declarations go to headers, and definitions (or the bodies) go into source files. There are rare cases in which we have enough reason to violate this. In addition, sources need to include header files in order to see and use the declarations, which is how C and C++ work.

If you do not fully understand this now, do not worry as this will become more obvious as we move forward.

Note:
Having more than one definition for any declaration in a *translation unit* will lead to a *compile error*. This is true for all functions, structures, and global variables. Therefore, providing two definitions for a single function declaration is not permitted.

We are going to continue this discussion by introducing our first C example for this chapter. This example is supposed to demonstrate the correct way of compiling a C/C++ project consisting of more than one source file.

Example source files

In *example 2.1*, we have three files, with one being a header file, and the other two being source files, and all are in the same directory. The example wants to calculate the average of an array with five elements.

The header file is used as a bridge between two separate source files and makes it possible to write our code in two separate files but build them together. Without the header file, it's not possible to break our code in two source files, without breaking the rule mentioned above (sources must not include sources). Here, the header file contains everything required by one of the sources to use the functionality of the other one.

The header file contains only one function declaration, `avg`, needed for the program to work. One of the source files contains the definition of the declared function. The other source file contains the `main` function, which is the entry point of the program. Without the `main` function, it is impossible to have an executable binary to run the program with. The `main` function is recognized by the compiler as the starting point of the program.

We are now going to move on and see what the contents of these files are. Here is the header file, which contains an enumeration and a declaration for the `avg` function:

```
#ifndef EXTREMEC_EXAMPLES_CHAPTER_2_1_H
#define EXTREMEC_EXAMPLES_CHAPTER_2_1_Htypedef enum {
  NONE,
  NORMAL,
```

```
    SQUARED
} average_type_t;

// Function declaration
double avg(int*, int, average_type_t);

#endif
```

Code Box 2-3 [ExtremeC_examples_chapter2_1.h]: The header file as part of example 2.1

As you can see, this file contains an enumeration, a set of named integer constants. In C, enumerations cannot have separate declarations and definitions, and they should be declared and defined just once in the same place.

In addition to the enumeration, the *forward declaration* of the avg function can be seen in the code box. The act of declaring a function before giving its definition is called forward declaration. The header file is also protected by the *header guard* statements. They will prevent the header file from being included twice or more while being compiled.

The following code shows us the source file that actually contains the definition of the avg function:

```
#include "ExtremeC_examples_chapter2_1.h"

double avg(int* array, int length, average_type_t type) {
  if (length <= 0 || type == NONE) {
    return 0;
  }
  double sum = 0.0;
  for (int i = 0; i < length; i++) {
    if (type == NORMAL) {
      sum += array[i];
    } else if (type == SQUARED) {
      sum += array[i] * array[i];
    }
  }
  return sum / length;
}
```

Code Box 2-4 [ExtremeC_examples_chapter2_1.c]: The source file containing the definition of avg function

With the preceding code, you should notice that the filename ends with a .c extension. The source file has included the example's header file. This has been done because it needs the declarations of the average_type_t enumeration and the avg function before using them. Using a new type, in this case, the average_type_t enumeration, without declaring it before its usage leads to a compilation error.

Look at the following code box showing the second source file that contains the `main` function:

```c
#include <stdio.h>

#include "ExtremeC_examples_chapter2_1.h"

int main(int argc, char** argv) {
  // Array declaration
  int array[5];

  // Filling the array
  array[0] = 10;
  array[1] = 3;
  array[2] = 5;
  array[3] = -8;
  array[4] = 9;

  // Calculating the averages using the 'avg' function
  double average = avg(array, 5, NORMAL);
  printf("The average: %f\n", average);

  average = avg(array, 5, SQUARED);
  printf("The squared average: %f\n", average);

  return 0;
}
```

Code Box 2-5 [ExtremeC_examples_chapter2_1_main.c]: The main function of example 2.1

In every C project, the `main` function is the entry point of the program. In the preceding code box, the `main` function declares and populates an array of integers and calculates two different averages for it. Note how the `main` function calls the avg function in the preceding code.

Building the example

After introducing the files of *example 2.1* in the previous section, we need to build them and create a final executable binary file that can be run as a program. Building a C/C++ project means that we will compile all the sources within its code base to first produce some *relocatable object files* (known as *intermediate object files* too), and finally combine those relocatable object files to produce the final products, such as *static libraries* or *executable binaries*.

Building a project in other programming languages is also very similar to doing it in either C or C++, but the intermediate and final products have different names and likely different file formats. For example, in Java, the intermediate products are class files containing *Java bytecode*, and the final products are JAR or WAR files.

Note:
To compile the example sources, we will not use an **Integrated Development Environment (IDE)**. Instead, we are going to use the compiler directly without help from any other software. Our approach to building the example is exactly the same as the one that is employed by IDEs and performed in the background while compiling a number of source files.

Before we go any further, there are two important rules that we should remember.

Rule 1: We only compile source files

The first rule is that we only compile source files due to the fact that it is meaningless to compile a header file. Header files should not contain any actual C code other than some declarations. Therefore, for *example 2.1*, we only need to compile two source files: `ExtremeC_examples_chapter2_1.c` and `ExtremeC_examples_chapter2_1_main.c`.

Rule 2: We compile each source file separately

The second rule is that we compile each source file separately. Regarding *example 2.1*, it means that we have to run the compiler twice, each time passing one of the source files.

Note:
It is still possible to pass two source files at once and ask the compiler to compile them in just one command, but we don't recommend it and we don't do that in this book.

Therefore, for a project made up of 100 source files, we need to compile every source file separately, and it means that we have to run the compiler 100 times! Yes, that seems to be a lot, but this is the way that you should compile a C or C++ project. Believe me, you will encounter projects in which several thousand files should be compiled before having a single executable binary!

Note:
If a header file contains a piece of C code that needs to be compiled, we do not compile that header file. Instead, we include it in a source file, and then, we compile the source file. This way, the header's C code will be compiled as part of the source file.

When we compile a source file, no other source files are going to be compiled as part of the same compilation because none of them are included by the compiling source file. Remember, including source files is not allowed if we respect the best practices in C/C++.

Now let's focus on the steps that should be taken in order to build a C project. The first step is preprocessing, and we are going to talk about that in the following section.

Step 1 – Preprocessing

The first step in the C compilation pipeline is *preprocessing*. A source file has a number of header files included. However, before the compilation begins, the contents of these files are gathered by the preprocessor as a single body of C code. In other words, after the preprocessing step, we get a single piece of code created by copying content of the header files into the source file content.

Also, other *preprocessor directives* must be resolved in this step. This preprocessed piece of code is called a *translation unit*. A translation unit is a single logical unit of C code generated by the preprocessor, and it is ready to be compiled. A translation unit is sometimes called a *compilation unit* as well.

Note:
In a translation unit, no preprocessing directives can be found. As a reminder, all preprocessing directives in C (and C++) start with #, for example, #include and #define.

It is possible to ask compilers to dump the translation unit without compiling it further. In the case of gcc, it is enough to pass the -E option (this is case-sensitive). In some rare cases, especially when doing cross-platform development, examining the translation units could be useful when fixing weird issues.

In the following code, you can see the translation unit for ExtremeC_examples_chapter2_1.c, which has been generated by gcc on our default platform:

```
$ gcc -E ExtremeC_examples_chapter2_1.c
# 1 "ExtremeC_examples_chapter2_1.c"
# 1 "<built-in>"
# 1 "<command-line>"
# 31 "<command-line>"
```

```
# 1 "/usr/include/stdc-predef.h" 1 3 4
# 32 "<command-line>" 2
# 1 "ExtremeC_examples_chapter2_1.c"

# 1 "ExtremeC_examples_chapter2_1.h" 1

typedef enum {
  NONE,
  NORMAL,
  SQUARED
} average_type_t;



double avg(int*, int, average_type_t);
# 5 "ExtremeC_examples_chapter2_1.c" 2

double avg(int* array, int length, average_type_t type) {
  if (length <= 0 || type == NONE) {
    return 0;
  }
  double sum = 0;
  for (int i = 0; i < length; i++) {
    if (type == NORMAL) {
      sum += array[i];
    } else if (type == SQUARED) {
      sum += array[i] * array[i];
    }
  }
  return sum / length;
}
$
```

Shell Box 2-1: The produced translation unit while compiling ExtremeC_examples_chapter2_1.c

As you can see, all the declarations are copied from the header file into the translation unit. The comments have also been removed from the translation unit.

The translation unit for ExtremeC_examples_chapter2_1_main.c is very large because it includes the stdio.h header file.

All declarations from this header file, and further inner header files included by it, will be copied into the translation unit recursively. Just to show how big the translation unit of `ExtremeC_examples_chapter2_1_main.c` can be, on our default platform it has 836 lines of C code!

Note:
The `-E` option works also for the `clang` compiler.

This completes the first step. The input to the preprocessing step is a source file, and the output is the corresponding translation unit.

Step 2 – Compilation

Once you have the translation unit, you can go for the second step, which is *compilation*. The input to the compilation step is the translation unit, retrieved from the previous step, and the output is the corresponding *assembly code*. This assembly code is still human-readable, but it is machine-dependent and close to the hardware and still needs further processing in order to become machine-level instructions.

You can always ask `gcc` to stop after performing the second step and dump the resulting assembly code by passing the `-S` option (capital S). The output is a file with the same name as the given source file but with a `.s` extension.

In the following shell box, you can see the assembly of the `ExtremeC_examples_chapter2_1_main.c` source file. However, when reading the code, you should see that some parts of the output are removed:

```
$ gcc -S ExtremeC_examples_chapter2_1.c
$ cat ExtremeC_examples_chapter2_1.s
    .file   "ExtremeC_examples_chapter2_1.c"
    .text
    .globl  avg
    .type   avg, @function
avg:
.LFB0:
    .cfi_startproc
    pushq   %rbp
    .cfi_def_cfa_offset 16
```

```
        .cfi_offset 6, -16
        movq    %rsp, %rbp
        .cfi_def_cfa_register 6
        movq    %rdi, -24(%rbp)
        movl    %esi, -28(%rbp)
        movl    %edx, -32(%rbp)
        cmpl    $0, -28(%rbp)
        jle .L2
        cmpl    $0, -32(%rbp)
        jne .L3
.L2:
        pxor    %xmm0, %xmm0
        jmp .L4
.L3:
        ...
.L8:
        ...
.L6:
        ...
.L7:
        ...
.L5:
        ...
.L4:
        ...
.LFE0:
        .size   avg, .-avg
        .ident  "GCC: (Ubuntu 7.3.0-16ubuntu3) 7.3.0"
        .section    .note.GNU-stack,"",@progbits
$
```

Shell Box 2-2: The produced assembly code while compiling ExtremeC_examples_chapter2_1.c

As part of the compilation step, the compiler parses the translation unit and turns it into assembly code that is specific to the *target architecture*. By the target architecture, we mean the hardware or CPU that the program is being compiled for and is eventually to be run on. The target architecture is sometimes referred to as the *host architecture*.

Shell Box 2-2 shows the assembly code generated for the AMD 64-bit architecture and produced by gcc running on an AMD 64-bit machine. The following shell box contains the assembly code generated for an ARM 32-bit architecture and produced by gcc running on an Intel x86-64 architecture. Both assembly outputs are generated for the same C code:

```
$ cat ExtremeC_examples_chapter2_1.s
    .arch armv5t
    .fpu softvfp
    .eabi_attribute 20, 1
    .eabi_attribute 21, 1
    .eabi_attribute 23, 3
    .eabi_attribute 24, 1
    .eabi_attribute 25, 1
    .eabi_attribute 26, 2
    .eabi_attribute 30, 6
    .eabi_attribute 34, 0
    .eabi_attribute 18, 4
    .file "ExtremeC_examples_chapter2_1.s"
    .global     __aeabi_i2d
    .global     __aeabi_dadd
    .global     __aeabi_ddiv
    .text
    .align      2
    .global     avg
    .syntax unified
    .arm
    .type   avg, %function
avg:
    @ args = 0, pretend = 0, frame = 32
    @ frame_needed = 1, uses_anonymous_args = 0
    push    {r4, fp, lr}
    add     fp, sp, #8
    sub     sp, sp, #36
    str     r0, [fp, #-32]
    str     r1, [fp, #-36]
    str     r2, [fp, #-40]
    ldr     r3, [fp, #-36]
```

```
        cmp     r3, #0
        ble     .L2
        ldr     r3, [fp, #-40]
        cmp     r3, #0
        bne     .L3
.L2:

        ...
.L3:

        ...
.L8:

        ...
.L6:

        ...
.L7:

        ...
.L5:

        ...
.L4:
        mov     r0, r3
        mov     r1, r4
        sub     sp, fp, #8
        @ sp needed
        pop     {r4, fp, pc}
        .size avg, .-avg
        .ident       "GCC: (Ubuntu/Linaro 5.4.0-6ubuntu1~16.04.9) 5.4.0
20160609"
        .section     .note.GNU-stack,"",%progbits
$
```

Shell Box 2-3: The assembly code produced while compiling ExtremeC_examples_chapter2_1.c
for an ARM 32-bit architecture

As you can see in shell boxes 2-2 and 2-3, the generated assembly code is different for the two architectures. This is despite the fact that they are generated for the same C code. For the latter assembly code, we have used the arm-linux-gnueabi-gcc compiler on an Intel x64-86 hardware set running Ubuntu 16.04.

Note:
The target (or host) architecture is the architecture that the source is both being compiled for and will be run on. The *build architecture* is the architecture that we are using to compile the source. They can be different. For example, you can compile a C source for AMD 64-bit hardware on an ARM 32-bit machine.

Producing assembly code from C code is the most important step in the compilation pipeline.

This is because when you have the assembly code, you are very close to the language that a CPU can execute. Because of this important role, the compiler is one of the most important and most studied subjects in computer science.

Step 3 – Assembly

The next step after compilation is *assembly*. The objective here is to generate the actual machine-level instructions (or *machine code*) based on the assembly code generated by the compiler in the previous step. Each architecture has its own *assembler*, which can translate its own assembly code to its own machine code.

A file containing the machine-level instructions that we are going to assemble in this section is called an *object file*. We know that a C project can have several products that are all object files, but in this section, we are mainly interested in relocatable object files. This file is, without a doubt, the most important temporary product that we can obtain during the build process.

Note:
Relocatable object files can be referred to as intermediate object files.

To pull both of the previous steps together, the purpose of this assembly step is to generate a relocatable object file out of the assembly code produced by the compiler. Every other product that we create will be based on the relocatable object files generated by the assembler in this step.

We will talk about these other products in the future sections of this chapter.

Note:
Binary file and *object file* are synonyms that refer to a file containing machine-level instructions. Note however that the term "binary files" in other contexts can have different meanings, for example binary files vs. text files.

In most Unix-like operating systems, we have an assembler tool called `as`, which can be used to produce a relocatable object file from an assembly file.

However, these object files are not executable, and they only contain the machine-level instructions generated for a translation unit. Since each translation unit is made up of various functions and global variables, a relocatable object file simply contains machine-level instructions for the corresponding functions and the pre-allocated entries for the global variables.

In the following shell box, you can see how `as` is used to produce the relocatable object file for `ExtremeC_examples_chapter2_1_main.s`:

```
$ as ExtremeC_examples_chapter2_1.s -o ExtremeC_examples_
chapter2_1.o
$
```

Shell Box 2-4: Producing an object file from the assembly of one of the sources in example 2.1

Looking back at the command in the preceding shell box, we can see that the `-o` option is used to specify the name of the output object file. Relocatable object files usually have a `.o` (or a `.obj` in Microsoft Windows) extension in their names, which is why we have passed a filename with `.o` at the end.

The content of an object file, either `.o` or `.obj`, is not textual, so you would not be able to read it as a human. Therefore, it is common to say that an object file has *binary content*.

Despite the fact that the assembler can be used directly, like what we did in *Shell Box 2-4*, this is not recommended. Instead, good practice would be to use the compiler itself to call `as` indirectly in order to generate the relocatable object file.

Note:
We may use the terms *object file* and *relocatable object file* interchangeably. But not all object files are relocatable object files, and, in some contexts, it may refer to other types of object files such as shared object files.

If you pass the -c option to almost all known C compilers, it will directly generate the corresponding object file for the input source file. In other words, the -c option is equivalent to performing the first three steps all together.

Looking at the following example, you can see that we have used the -c option to compile ExtremeC_examples_chapter2_1.c and generate its corresponding object file:

```
$ gcc -c ExtremeC_examples_chapter2_1.c
$
```

Shell Box 2-5: Compiling one of the sources in example 2.1 and producing its corresponding relocatable object file

All of the steps we have just done – preprocessing, compilation, and assembling – are done as part of the preceding single command. What this means for us is that after running the preceding command, a relocatable object file will be generated. This relocatable object file will have the same name as the input source file; however, it will differ by having a .o extension.

IMPORTANT:
Note that, often, the term *compilation* is used to refer to the first three steps in the compilation pipeline all together, and not just the second step. It is also possible that we use the term "compilation" but actually mean "building;" encompassing all four steps. For instance, we say *C compilation pipeline*, but we actually mean *C build pipeline*.

The assembly is the last step in compiling a single source file. In other words, when we have the corresponding relocatable object file for a source file, we are done with its compilation. At this stage we can put aside the relocatable object file and continue compiling other source files.

In *example 2.1*, we have two source files that need to be compiled. By executing the following commands, it compiles both source files and as a result, produces their corresponding object files:

```
$ gcc -c ExtremeC_examples_chapter2_1.c -o impl.o
$ gcc -c ExtremeC_examples_chapter2_1_main.c -o main.o
$
```

Shell Box 2-6: Producing the relocatable object files for the sources in example 2.1

You can see in the preceding commands that we have changed the names of the object files by specifying our desired names using the -o option. As a result, after compiling both of them, we get the impl.o and main.o relocatable object files.

At this point, we need to remind ourselves that relocatable object files are not executable. If a project is going to have an executable file as its final product, we need to use all, or at the very least, some, of the already produced relocatable object files to build the target executable file through the linking step.

Step 4 – Linking

We know that *example 2.1* needs to be built to an executable file because we have a main function in it. However, at this point, we only have two relocatable object files. Therefore, the next step is to combine these relocatable object files in order to create another object file that is executable. The *linking* step does exactly that.

However, before we go through the linking step, we need to talk about how we add support for a new architecture, or hardware, to an existing Unix-like system.

Supporting new architectures

We know that every architecture has a series of manufactured processors and that every processor can execute a specific instruction set.

The instruction set has been designed by vendor companies such as Intel and ARM for their processors. In addition, these companies also design a specific assembly language for their architecture.

A program can be built for a new architecture if two prerequisites are satisfied:

1. The assembly language is known.
2. The required assembler tool (or program) developed by the vendor company must be at hand. This allows us to translate the assembly code into the equivalent machine-level instructions.

Once these prerequisites are in place, it would be possible to generate machine-level instructions from C source code. Only then, we are able to store the generated machine-level instructions within the object files using an *object file format*. As an example, this could be in the form of either *ELF* or *Mach-O*.

When the assembly language, assembler tool, and object file format are clear, they can be used to develop some further tools that are necessary for us developers when doing C programming. However, you hardly notice their existence since you are often dealing with a C compiler, and it is using these tools on your behalf.

The two immediate tools that are required for a new architecture are as follows:

- C compiler
- Linker

These tools are like the first fundamental building blocks for supporting a new architecture in an operating system. The hardware together with these tools in an operating system give rise to a new platform.

Regarding Unix-like systems, it is important to remember that Unix has a modular design. If you are able to build a few fundamental modules like the assembler, compiler, and linker, you will be able to build other modules on top of them and before long, the whole system is working on a new architecture.

Step details

With all that's been said before, we know that platforms using Unix-like operating systems must have the previously discussed mandatory tools, such as an assembler and a linker, in order to work. Remember, the assembler and the linker can be run separately from the compiler.

In Unix-like systems, `ld` is the default linker. The following command, which you can see in the following shell box, shows us how to use `ld` directly when we want to create an executable from the relocatable object files we produced in the previous sections for *example 2.1*. However, as you will see, it is not that easy to use the linker directly:

```
$ ld impl.o main.o
ld: warning: cannot find entry symbol _start; defaulting to
00000000004000e8
main.o: In function 'main':
ExtremeC_examples_chapter3_1_main.c:(.text+0x7a): undefined
reference to 'printf'
ExtremeC_examples_chapter3_1_main.c:(.text+0xb7): undefined
reference to 'printf'
ExtremeC_examples_chapter3_1_main.c:(.text+0xd0): undefined
reference to '__stack_chk_fail'
$
```

Shell Box 2-7: Trying to link the object files using the ld utility directly

As you see, the command has failed, and it has generated some error messages. If you pay attention to the error messages, they say that in three places in the Text segment `ld` has encountered three function calls (or *references*) that are *undefined*.

Two of these function calls are calls to the `printf` function, which we did in the `main` function. However, the other one, `__stack_chk_fail`, has not been called by us. It is coming from somewhere else, but where? It has been called from the supplementary code that has been put into the relocatable object files by the compiler, and this function is specific to Linux, and you may not find it in the same object files generated on other platforms. However, whatever it is and whatever it does, the linker is looking for its definition and it seems that it cannot find the definition in the provided object files.

Like we said before, the default linker, `ld`, has generated these errors because it has not been able to find the definitions of these functions. Logically, this makes sense, and is true, because we have not defined `printf` and `__stack_chk_fail` ourselves in *example 2.1*.

This means that we should have given `ld` some other object files, though not necessarily relocatable object files, that contain the definitions of the `printf` and `__stack_chk_fail` functions.

Reading what we have just said should explain why it can be very hard to use `ld` directly. Namely, there are more object files and options that need to be specified in order to make `ld` work and generate a working executable.

Fortunately, in Unix-like systems, the most well-known C compilers use `ld` by passing proper options and specifying extra required object files. Hence, we do not need to use `ld` directly.

Therefore, let's look at a much simpler way of producing the final executable file. The following shell box shows us how we can use `gcc` to link the object files from *example 2.1*:

```
$ gcc impl.o main.o
$ ./a.out
The average: 3.800000
The squared average: 55.800000
$
```

Shell Box 2-8: Using gcc to link the object files

As a result of running these commands, we can breathe because we have finally managed to build *example 2.1* and run its final executable!

Note:
Building a project is equivalent to compiling the sources firstly and then linking them together, and possibly other libraries, to create the final products.

It is important to take a minute to pause and reflect on what we have just done. Over the last few sections we have successfully built *example 2.1* by compiling its sources into relocatable object files, and finally linking the generated object files to create the final executable binary.

While this process will be the same for any C/C++ code base, the difference will be in the number of times you need to compile sources, which itself depends on the number of source files in your project.

While the compilation pipeline has some steps, in each step, there is a specific component involved. The focus of the remaining sections of this chapter will be delving into the critical information surrounding each component in the pipeline.

To start this, we are going to focus on the preprocessor component.

Preprocessor

At the very start of this book in *Chapter 1, Essential Features*, we introduced, albeit briefly, the concepts of *C preprocessor*. Specifically, we talked there about macros, conditional compilation, and header guards.

You will remember that at the beginning of the book, we discussed C preprocessing as an essential feature of the C language. Preprocessing is unique due to the fact that it cannot be easily found in other programming languages. In the simplest terms, preprocessing allows you to modify your source code before sending it for compilation. At the same time, it allows you to divide your source code, especially the declarations, into header files so that you can later include them into multiple source files and reuse those declarations.

It is vital to remember that if you have a syntax error in your source code, the preprocessor will not find the error as it does not know anything about the C syntax. Instead, it will just perform some easy tasks, which typically revolve around text substitutions. As an example, imagine that you have a text file named `sample.c` with the following content:

```
#include <stdio.h>
#define file 1000

Hello, this is just a simple text file but ending with .c
extension!
This is not a C file for sure!
But we can preprocess it!
```

Code Box 2-6: C code containing some text!

Having the preceding code, let us preprocess the file using `gcc`. Note that some parts of the following shell box have been removed. This is because including `stdio.h` makes the translation unit very big:

```
$ gcc -E sample.c
# 1 "sample.c"
# 1 "<built-in>" 1
# 1 "<built-in>" 3
# 341 "<built-in>" 3
# 1 "<command line>" 1
# 1 "<built-in>" 2
# 1 "sample.c" 2
# 1 "/usr/include/stdio.h" 1 3 4
# 64 "/usr/include/stdio.h" 3 4
# 1 "/usr/include/_stdio.h" 1 3 4
# 68 "/usr/include/_stdio.h" 3 4
# 1 "/usr/include/sys/cdefs.h" 1 3 4
# 587 "/usr/include/sys/cdefs.h" 3 4
# 1 "/usr/include/sys/_symbol_aliasing.h" 1 3 4
# 588 "/usr/include/sys/cdefs.h" 2 3 4
# 653 "/usr/include/sys/cdefs.h" 3 4
...
...
extern int __vsnprintf_chk (char * restrict, size_t, int, size_t,
        const char * restrict, va_list);
# 412 "/usr/include/stdio.h" 2 3 4
# 2 "sample.c" 2



Hello, this is just a simple text 1000 but ending with .c
extension!
This is not a C 1000 for sure!
But we can preprocess it!
$
```

Shell Box 2-9: The preprocessed sample C code seen in Code Box 2-6

As you see in the preceding shell box, the content of `stdio.h` is copied before the text.

If you pay more attention, you will see that another interesting substitution has also happened. The occurrences of the `file` have been replaced by `1000` in the text.

This example shows us exactly how the preprocessor works. The preprocessor only does simple tasks, such as inclusion, by copying contents from a file or expanding the macros by text substitution. It does not know anything about C though; it needs a parser to parse the input file before performing any further tasks. This means that a C preprocessor uses a parser, which looks for directives in the input code.

Note:
Generally, a parser is a program that processes the input data and extracts some certain parts of it for further analysis and processing. Parsers need to know the structure of the input data in order to break it down into some smaller and useful pieces of data.

The preprocessor's parser is different from the parser used by a C compiler because it uses grammar that is almost independent of C grammar. This enables us to use it in circumstances other than preprocessing a C file.

Note:
By exploiting the functionalities of a C preprocessor, you could use file inclusion and macro expansion for other purposes other than building a C program. They could be used to process other text files as well.

The GNU C Preprocessor Internals – `http://www.chiark.greenend.org.uk/doc/cpp-4.3-doc/cppinternals.html` – is a great source for learning more about the `gcc` preprocessor. This document is an official source that describes how the GNU C preprocessor works. The GNU C preprocessor is used by the `gcc` compiler to preprocess the source files.

In the preceding link, you can find how the preprocessor parses the directives and how it creates the *parse tree*. The document also provides an explanation of the different macro expansion algorithms. While it is outside of the scope of this chapter, if you wanted to implement your own preprocessor for a specific in-house programming language, or just for processing some text files, then the above link provides some great context.

In most Unix-like operating systems, there is a tool called **cpp**, which stands for **C Pre-Processor** – and not C Plus Plus! cpp is part of the C development bundle that is shipped with each flavor of Unix. It can be used to preprocess a C file. In the background, the tool is used by a C compiler, like gcc, to preprocess a C file. If you have a source file, you can use it, in a similar way to what we have done next, to preprocess a source file:

```
$ cpp ExtremeC_examples_chapter2_1.c
# 1 "ExtremeC_examples_chapter2_1.c"
# 1 "<built-in>" 1
# 1 "<built-in>" 3
# 340 "<built-in>" 3
# 1 "<command line>" 1
# 1 "<built-in>" 2
. . .
. . .
# 5 "ExtremeC_examples_chapter2_1.c" 2

double avg(int* array, int length, average_type_t type) {
  if (length <= 0 || type == NONE) {
    return 0;
  }
  double sum = 0;
  for (int i = 0; i < length; i++) {
    if (type == NORMAL) {
      sum += array[i];
    } else if (type == SQUARED) {
      sum += array[i] * array[i];
    }
  }
  return sum / length;
}
$
```

Shell Box 2-10: Using the cpp utility to preprocess source code

As a final note in this section, if you pass a file with the extension .i to a C compiler, then it will bypass the preprocessor step. It does this because a file with a .i extension is supposed to have already been preprocessed. Therefore, it should be sent directly to the compilation step.

If you insist on running the C preprocessor for a file with a `.i` extension, then you will get the following warning message. Note that the following shell box is produced with the `clang` compiler:

```
$ clang -E ExtremeC_examples_chapter2_1.c  > ex2_1.i
$ clang -E ex2_1.i
clang: warning: ex2_1.i: previously preprocessed input
[-Wunused-command-line-argument]
$
```

Shell Box 2-11: Passing an already preprocessed file, with extension .i, to the clang compiler

As you can see, `clang` warns us that the file has been already preprocessed.

In the next section of this chapter, we are going to specifically talk about the compiler component in the C compilation pipeline.

Compiler

As we discussed in the previous sections, the compiler accepts the translation unit prepared by the preprocessor and generates the corresponding assembly instructions. When multiple C sources are compiled into their equivalent assembly code, the existing tools in the platform, such as the assembler and the linker, manage the rest by making relocatable object files out of the generated assembly code and finally linking them together (and possibly with other object files) to form a library or an executable file.

As an example, we spoke about `as` and `ld` as two examples among the many available tools in Unix for C development. These tools are mainly used to create platform-compatible object files. These tools exist necessarily outside of `gcc` or any other compiler. By existing outside of any compiler, we actually mean that they are not developed as a part of `gcc` (we have chosen `gcc` as an example) and they should be available on any platform even without having `gcc` installed. `gcc` only uses them in its compilation pipeline, and they are not embedded into `gcc`.

That is because the platform itself is the most knowledgeable entity that knows about the instruction set accepted by its processor and the operating system-specific formats and restrictions. The compiler is not usually aware of these constraints unless it wants to do some *optimization* on the translation unit. Therefore, we can conclude that the most important task that `gcc` does is to translate the translation unit into assembly instructions. This is what we actually call compilation.

One of the challenges in C compilation is to generate correct assembly instructions that can be accepted by the target architecture. It is possible to use gcc to compile the same C code for various architectures such as ARM, Intel x86, AMD, and many more. As we discussed before, each architecture has an instruction set that is accepted by its processor, and gcc (or any C compiler) is the sole responsible entity that should generate correct assembly code for a specific architecture.

The way that gcc (or any other C compiler) overcomes this difficulty is to split the mission into two steps, first parsing the translation unit into an relocatable and C-independent data structure called an **Abstract Syntax Tree (AST)**, and then using the created AST to generate the equivalent assembly instructions for the target architecture. The first part is architecture-independent and can be done regardless of the target instruction set. But the second step is architecture-dependent, and the compiler should be aware of the target instruction set. The subcomponent that performs the first step is called a *compiler frontend*, and the subcomponent that performs the later step is called a *compiler backend*.

In the following sections, we are going to discuss these steps in more depth. First, let's talk about the AST.

Abstract syntax tree

As we have explained in the previous section, a C compiler frontend should parse the translation unit and create an intermediate data structure. The compiler creates this intermediate data structure by parsing the C source code according to the C *grammar* and saving the result in a tree-like data structure that is *not* architecture-dependent. The final data structure is commonly referred to as an AST.

ASTs can be generated for any programming language, not only C, so the AST structure must be abstract enough to be independent of C syntax.

This is enough to change the compiler frontend to support other languages. This is exactly why you can find **GNU Compiler Collection (GCC)**, which gcc is a part of as the C compiler, or **Low-Level Virtual Machine (LLVM)**, which clang is a part of as the C compiler, as a collection of compilers for many languages beyond just C and C++ such as Java, Fortran, and so on.

Once the AST is produced, the compiler backend can start to optimize the AST and generate assembly code based on the optimized AST for a target architecture. To get a better understanding of ASTs, we are going to take a look at a real AST. In this example, we have the following C source code:

```
int main() {
```

```
int var1 = 1;
double var2 = 2.5;
int var3 = var1 + var2;
return 0;
}
```

Code Box 2-7 [ExtremeC_examples_chapter2_2.c]: Simple C code whose AST is going to be generated

The next step is to use `clang` to dump the AST within the preceding code. In the following figure, *Figure 2-1*, you can see the AST:

Figure 2-1: The AST generated and dumped for example 2.2

So far, we have used `clang` in various places as a C compiler, but let's introduce it properly. `clang` is a C compiler frontend developed by the LLVM Developer Group for the `llvm` compiler backend. The *LLVM Compiler Infrastructure Project* uses an *intermediate representation* – or *LLVM IR* – as its abstract data structure used between its frontend and its backend. LLVM is famous for its ability to dump its IR data structure for research purposes. The preceding tree-like output is the IR generated from the source code of *example 2.2*.

What we have done here is introduce you to the basics of AST. We are not going through the details of the preceding AST output because each compiler has its own AST implementation. We would require several chapters to cover all of the details on this, and that is beyond the scope of this book.

However, if you pay attention to the above figure, you can find a line that starts with -FunctionDecl. This represents the main function. Before that, you can find meta information regarding the translation unit passed to the compiler.

If you continue after FunctionDecl, you will find tree entries – or *nodes* – for declaration statements, binary operator statements, the return statement, and even implicit cast statements. There are lots of interesting things residing in an AST, with countless things to learn!

Another benefit of having an AST for source code is that you can rearrange the order of instructions, prune some unused branches, and replace branches so that you have better performance but preserve the purpose of the program. As we pointed out before, it is called optimization and it is usually done to a certain configurable extent by any C compiler.

The next component that we are going to discuss in more detail is the assembler.

Assembler

As we explained before, a platform has to have an assembler in order to produce object files that contain correct machine-level instructions. In a Unix-like operating system, the assembler can be invoked by using the as utility program. In the rest of this section, we are going to discuss what can be put in an object file by the assembler.

If you install two different Unix-like operating systems on the same architecture, the installed assemblers might not be the same, which is very important. What this means is that, despite the fact that the machine-level instructions are the same, because of being on the same hardware, the produced object files can be different!

If you compile a program and produce the corresponding object file on Linux for an AMD64 architecture, it could be different from if you had tried to compile the same program in a different operating system such as FreeBSD or macOS, and on the same hardware. This implies that while the object files cannot be the same, they do contain the same machine-level instructions. This proves that object files can have different formats in various operating systems.

In other words, each operating system defines its own specific binary format or *object file format* when it comes to storing machine-level instructions within object files. Therefore, there are two factors that specify the contents of an object file: the architecture (or hardware) and the operating system. Typically, we will use the term platform for such a combination.

To round off this section, we usually say that object files, hence the assembler generating them, are platform-specific. In Linux, we use the **Executable and Linking Format** (**ELF**). As the name implies, all executable files, object files, and shared libraries should use this format. In other words, in Linux, the assembler produces ELF object files. In the upcoming chapter, *Object Files*, we will discuss object files and their formats in greater detail.

In the following section, we will take a deeper look at the *linker* component. We will demonstrate and explain how the component actually produces the final products in a C project.

Linker

The first big step in building a C project is compiling all the source files to their corresponding relocatable object files. This step is a necessary step in preparing the final products, but alone, it is not enough, and one more step is still needed. Before going through the details of this step, we need to have a quick look at the possible *products* (sometimes referred to as *artifacts*) in a C project.

A C/C++ project can lead to the following products:

- A number of executable files that usually have the .out extension in most Unix-like operating systems. These files usually have the .exe extension in Microsoft Windows.

- A number of static libraries that usually have the .a extension in most Unix-like operating systems. These files have the .lib extension in Microsoft Windows.

- A number of dynamic libraries or shared object files that usually have the .so extension in most Unix-like operating systems. These files have the .dylib extension in macOS, and .dll in Microsoft Windows.

Relocatable object files are not considered as one of these products; hence, you cannot find them in the preceding list. Relocatable object files are temporary products simply because they only take part in the linking step to produce the preceding products, and after that, we don't need them anymore. The linker component has the sole responsibility of producing the preceding products from the given relocatable object files.

One final and important note about the used terminology: all these three products are called *object files*. Therefore, it is best to use the term **relocatable** before the term object file when referring to an object file produced by the assembler as an intermediate product.

We'll now briefly describe each of the final products. The upcoming chapter is totally dedicated to the object files and it will discuss these final products in greater detail.

An executable object file can be run as a *process*. This file usually contains a substantial portion of the features provided by a project. It must have an entry point where the machine-level instructions are executed. While the `main` function is the entry point of a C program, the entry point of an executable object file is platform-dependent, and it is not the `main` function. The `main` function will eventually be called after some preparations made by a group of platform-specific instructions, which have been added by the linker as the result of the linking step.

A static library is nothing more than an archive file that contains several relocatable object files. Therefore, a static library file is not produced by the linker directly. Instead, it is produced by the default archive program of the system, which on a Unix-like system is the `ar` program.

Static libraries are usually linked to other executable files, and they then become part of those executable files. They are the simplest and easiest way to encapsulate a piece of logic so that you can use it at a later point. There is an enormous number of static libraries that exist within an operating system, with each of them containing a specific piece of logic that can be used to access a certain functionality within that operating system.

Shared object files, which have a more complicated structure rather than simply being an archive, are created directly by the linker. They are also used differently; namely, before they are used, they need to be loaded into a running process at runtime.

This is in opposition to static libraries that are used at *link time* to become part of the final executable file. In addition, a single shared object file can be loaded and used by multiple different processes at the same time. As part of the next chapter, we demonstrate how shared object files can be loaded and used by a C program at *runtime*.

In the upcoming section, we explain what happens in the linking step and what elements are involved and used by the linker to produce the final products, especially executable files.

How does the linker work?

In this section, we are going to explain how the linker component works and what we exactly mean by linking. Suppose that you are building a C project that contains five source files, with the final product being an executable. As part of the build process, you have compiled all the source files, and now you have five relocatable object files. What you now need is a linker to complete the last step and produce the final executable file.

Based on what we have said so far, to put it simply, a linker combines all of the relocatable object files, in addition to specified static libraries, in order to create the final executable object file. However, you would be wrong if you thought that this step was straightforward.

There are a few concerns, which come from the contents of the object files, that need to be considered when we are combining the object files in order to produce a working executable object file. In order to see how the linker works, we need to know how it uses the relocatable object files, and for this purpose, we need to find out what is inside an object file.

The simple answer is that an object file contains the equivalent machine-level instructions for a translation unit. However, these instructions are not put into the file in random order. Instead, they are grouped under sections called *symbols*.

In fact, there are many things in an object file, but symbols are one component that explains how the linker works and how it ties some object files together to produce a larger one. In order to explain symbols, let's talk about them in the context of an example: *example 2.3*. Using this example, we want to demonstrate how some functions are compiled and placed in the corresponding relocatable object file. Take a look at the following code, which contains two functions:

```c
int average(int a, int b) {
  return (a + b) / 2;
}

int sum(int* numbers, int count) {
  int sum = 0;
  for (int i = 0; i < count; i++) {
    sum += numbers[i];
  }
  return sum;
}
```

Code Box 2-8 [ExtremeC_examples_chapter2_3.c]: A code with two function definitions

Firstly, we need to compile the preceding code in order to produce the corresponding object file. The following command produces the object file, `target.o`. We are compiling the code on our default platform:

```
$ gcc -c ExtremeC_examples_chapter2_3.c -o target.o
$
```

Shell Box 2-12: Compiling the source file in example 2.3

Next, we use the nm utility to look into the `target.o` object file. The nm utility allows us to see the symbols that can be found inside an object file:

```
$ nm target.o
0000000000000000 T average
000000000000001d T sum
$
```

Shell Box 2-13: Using the nm utility to see the defined symbols in a relocatable object file

The preceding shell box shows the symbols defined in the object file. As you can see, their names are exactly the same as the function defined in *Code Box 2-8*.

If you use the readelf utility, like we have done in the following shell box, you can see the *symbol table* existing in the object file. A symbol table contains all the symbols defined in an object file and it can give you more information about the symbols:

```
$ readelf -s target.o

Symbol table '.symtab' contains 10 entries:
   Num:    Value          Size Type    Bind   Vis      Ndx Name
     0: 0000000000000000     0 NOTYPE  LOCAL  DEFAULT  UND
     1: 0000000000000000     0 FILE    LOCAL  DEFAULT  ABS
ExtremeC_examples_chapter
     2: 0000000000000000     0 SECTION LOCAL  DEFAULT    1
     3: 0000000000000000     0 SECTION LOCAL  DEFAULT    2
     4: 0000000000000000     0 SECTION LOCAL  DEFAULT    3
     5: 0000000000000000     0 SECTION LOCAL  DEFAULT    5
     6: 0000000000000000     0 SECTION LOCAL  DEFAULT    6
     7: 0000000000000000     0 SECTION LOCAL  DEFAULT    4
     8: 0000000000000000    29 FUNC    GLOBAL DEFAULT    1 average
     9: 000000000000001d    69 FUNC    GLOBAL DEFAULT    1 sum
$
```

Shell Box 2-14: Using the readelf utility to see the symbol table of a relocatable object file

As you can see in the output of readelf, there are two function symbols in the symbol table. There are also other symbols in the table that refer to different sections within the object file. We will discuss some of these symbols in this chapter and the next chapter.

If you want to see the disassembly of the machine-level instructions, under each function symbol, then you can use the `objdump` tool:

```
$ objdump -d target.o

target.o:      file format elf64-x86-64


Disassembly of section .text:

0000000000000000 <average>:
   0:   55                      push   %rbp
   1:   48 89 e5                mov    %rsp,%rbp
   4:   89 7d fc                mov    %edi,-0x4(%rbp)
   7:   89 75 f8                mov    %esi,-0x8(%rbp)
   a:   8b 55 fc                mov    -0x4(%rbp),%edx
   d:   8b 45 f8                mov    -0x8(%rbp),%eax
  10:   01 d0                   add    %edx,%eax
  12:   89 c2                   mov    %eax,%edx
  14:   c1 ea 1f                shr    $0x1f,%edx
  17:   01 d0                   add    %edx,%eax
  19:   d1 f8                   sar    %eax
  1b:   5d                      pop    %rbp
  1c:   c3                      retq

000000000000001d <sum>:
  1d:   55                      push   %rbp
  1e:   48 89 e5                mov    %rsp,%rbp
  21:   48 89 7d e8             mov    %rdi,-0x18(%rbp)
  25:   89 75 e4                mov    %esi,-0x1c(%rbp)
  28:   c7 45 f8 00 00 00 00    movl   $0x0,-0x8(%rbp)
  2f:   c7 45 fc 00 00 00 00    movl   $0x0,-0x4(%rbp)
  36:   eb 1d                   jmp    55 <sum+0x38>
  38:   8b 45 fc                mov    -0x4(%rbp),%eax
  3b:   48 98                   cltq
  3d:   48 8d 14 85 00 00 00    lea    0x0(,%rax,4),%rdx
  44:   00
  45:   48 8b 45 e8             mov    -0x18(%rbp),%rax
```

```
49:     48 01 d0              add     %rdx,%rax
4c:     8b 00                 mov     (%rax),%eax
4e:     01 45 f8              add     %eax,-0x8(%rbp)
51:     83 45 fc 01           addl    $0x1,-0x4(%rbp)
55:     8b 45 fc              mov     -0x4(%rbp),%eax
58:     3b 45 e4              cmp     -0x1c(%rbp),%eax
5b:     7c db                 jl      38 <sum+0x1b>
5d:     8b 45 f8              mov     -0x8(%rbp),%eax
60:     5d                    pop     %rbp
61:     c3                    retq
$
```

Shell Box 2-15: Using the objdump utility to see the instructions of the symbols defined
in a relocatable object file

Based on what we see, each function symbol corresponds to a function that has been defined in the source code. When you need to link several relocatable object files, in order to produce an executable object file, this shows that each of the relocatable object files contains only a portion of the whole required function symbols needed to build a complete executable program.

Now, going back to the topic of this section, the linker gathers all the symbols from the various relocatable object files before putting them together in a bigger object file to form a complete executable binary. In order to demonstrate this in a real scenario, we need a different example that has some functions distributed in a number of source files. This way, we can show how the linker looks up the symbols in the given relocatable object files, in order to produce an executable file.

Example 2.4 consists of four C files – three source files and one header file. In the header file, we have declared two functions, with each one defined in its own source file. The third source file contains the `main` function.

The functions in *example 2.4* are amazingly simple, and after compilation, each function will contain a few machine-level instructions within their corresponding object files. In addition, *example 2.4* will not include any of the standard C header files. We have chosen this in order to have a small translation unit for each source file.

The following code box shows the header file:

```
#ifndef EXTREMEC_EXAMPLES_CHAPTER_2_4_DECLS_H
```

```
#define EXTREMEC_EXAMPLES_CHAPTER_2_4_DECLS_H

int add(int, int);
int multiply(int, int);

#endif
```

Code Box 2-9 [ExtremeC_examples_chapter2_4_decls.h]: The declaration of the functions in example 2.4

Looking at that code, you can see that we used the header guard statements to prevent *double inclusion*. More than that, two functions with similar *signatures* are declared. Each of them receives two integers as input and will return another integer as a result.

As we said before, each of these functions are implemented in separate source files. The first source file looks as follows:

```
int add(int a, int b) {
  return a + b;
}
```

Code Box 2-10 [ExtremeC_examples_chapter2_4_add.c]: The definition of the add function

We can clearly see that the source file has not included any other header files. However, it does define a function that follows the exact same signature that we have declared in the header file.

As we can see next, the second source file is similar to the first one. This one contains the definition of the multiply function:

```
int multiply(int a, int b) {
  return a * b;
}
```

Code Box 2-11 [ExtremeC_examples_chapter2_4_multiply.c]: The definition of the multiply function

We can now move onto the third source file, which contains the main function:

```
#include "ExtremeC_examples_chapter2_4_decls.h"

int main(int argc, char** argv) {
  int x = add(4, 5);
  int y = multiply(9, x);
  return 0;
```

```
}
```

Code Box 2-12 [ExtremeC_examples_chapter2_4_main.c]: The main function of example 2.4

The third source file has to include the header file in order to obtain the declarations of both functions. Otherwise, the source file will not be able to use the add and multiply functions, simply because they are not declared, and this may result in a compilation failure.

In addition, the main function does not know anything about the definitions of either add or multiply. Therefore, we need to ask an important question: how does the main function find these definitions when it does not even know about the other source files? Note that the file shown in *Code Box 2-12* has only included one header file, and therefore it has no relationship with the other two source files.

The above question can be resolved by bringing the linker into consideration. The linker will gather the required definitions from various object files and put them together, and this way, the code written in the main function can finally use the code written in another function.

Note:
To compile a source file that uses a function, the declaration is enough. However, to actually run your program, the definition should be provided to the linker in order to be put into the final executable file.

Now, it's time to compile *example 2.4* and demonstrate what we've said so far. Using the following commands, we create corresponding relocatable object files. You need to remember that we only compile source files:

```
$ gcc -c ExtremeC_examples_chapter2_4_add.c -o add.o
$ gcc -c ExtremeC_examples_chapter2_4_multiply.c -o multiply.o
$ gcc -c ExtremeC_examples_chapter2_4_main.c -o main.o
$
```

Shell Box 2-16: Compiling all sources in example 2.4 to their corresponding relocatable object files

For the next step, we are going to look at the symbol table contained in each relocatable object file:

```
$ nm add.o
```

```
0000000000000000 T add
$
```

Shell Box 2-17: Listing the symbols defined in add.o

As you see, the `add` symbol has been defined. The next object file:

```
$ nm multiply.o
0000000000000000 T multiply
$
```

Shell Box 2-18: Listing the symbols defined in multiply.o

The same happens to the `multiply` symbol within `multiply.o`. And the final object file:

```
$ nm main.o
                 U add
                 U _GLOBAL_OFFSET_TABLE_
0000000000000000 T main
                 U multiply
$
```

Shell Box 2-19: Listing the symbols defined in main.o

Despite the fact that the third source file, *Code Box 2-12*, has only the `main` function, we see two symbols for `add` and `multiply` in its corresponding object file. However, they are different from the `main` symbol, which has an address inside the object file. They are marked as `U`, or *unresolved*. This means that while the compiler has seen these symbols in the translation unit, it has not been able to find their actual definitions. And this is exactly what we expected and explained before.

The source file containing the `main` function, *Code Box 2-12*, should not know anything about the definitions of other functions if they are not defined in the same translation unit, but the fact that the `main` definition is dependent on the declarations of `add` and `multiply` should be somehow pointed out in the corresponding relocatable object file.

To summarize where we are now, we have three intermediate object files, with one of them having two unresolved symbols. This has now made the job of the linker clear; we need to give the linker the necessary symbols that can be found in other object files. After having found all of the required symbols, the linker can continue to combine them in order to create a final executable binary that works.

If the linker is not able to find the definition of an unresolved symbol, it will fail, and inform us by printing a *linkage error*.

For the next step, we want to link the preceding object files together. The following command will do that:

```
$ gcc add.o multiply.o main.o
$
```

Shell Box 2-20: Linking all object files together

We should note here that running `gcc` with a list of object files, without passing any option, will result in the linking step trying to create an executable object file out of the input object files. Actually, it calls the linker in the background with the given object files, together with some other static libraries and object files, that are required on the platform.

To examine what happens if the linker fails to find proper definitions, we are going to provide the linker with only two intermediate object files, `main.o` and `add.o`:

```
$ gcc add.o main.o
main.o: In function 'main':
ExtremeC_examples_chapter2_4_main.c:(.text+0x2c): undefined
reference to 'multiply'
collect2: error: ld returned 1 exit status
$
```

Shell Box 2-21: Linking only two of the object files: add.o and main.o

As you can see, the linker has failed because it could not find the `multiply` symbol in the provided object files.

Moving on, let's provide the other two object files, `main.o` and `multiply.o`:

```
$ gcc main.o multiply.o
main.o: In function 'main':
ExtremeC_examples_chapter2_4_main.c:(.text+0x1a): undefined
reference to 'add'
collect2: error: ld returned 1 exit status
$
```

Shell Box 2-22: Linking only two of the object files, multiply.o and main.o

As expected, the same thing occurred. This happened since the `add` symbol could not be found in the provided object files.

Finally, let's provide the only remaining combination of two object files, `add.o` and `multiply.o`. Before we run it, we should expect it to work since neither object file has unresolved symbols in their symbol tables. Let's see what happens:

```
$ gcc add.o multiply.o
/usr/lib/gcc/x86_64-linux-gnu/7/../../../x86_64-linux-gnu/Scrt1.o:
In function '_start':
(.text+0x20): undefined reference to 'main'
collect2: error: ld returned 1 exit status
$
```

Shell Box 2-23: Linking only two of the object files, add.o and multiply.o

As you see, the linker has failed again! Looking at the output, we can see the reason was that none of the object files contain the `main` symbol that is necessary to create an executable. The linker needs an entry point for the program, which is the `main` function according to the C standard.

At this point – and I cannot emphasize this enough – pay attention to the place where a reference to the `main` symbol has been made. It has been made in the `_start` function in a file located at `/usr/lib/gcc/x86_64-Linux-gnu/7/../../../x86_64-Linux-gnu/Scrt1.o`.

The `Scrt1.o` file seems to be a relocatable object file that has not been created by us. `Scrt1.o` is actually a file that is part of a group of default C object files. These default object files have been compiled for Linux as a part of the `gcc` bundle and are linked to any program in order to make it runnable.

As you have just seen, there are a lot of different things that are happening around your source code that can cause conflicts. Not only that, but there are a number of other object files that need to be linked to your program in order to make it executable.

Linker can be fooled!

To make our current discussion even more interesting, there are rare scenarios when the linking step will perform as we planned, but the final binary step does not work as expected. In this section, we are going to look at an example of this occurring.

Example 2.5 is based on an incorrect definition having been gathered by the linker and put into the final executable object file.

This example has two source files, one of which contains the definition of a function with the same name, but a different signature from the declaration used by the `main` function. The following code boxes are the contents of these two source files. Here's the first source file:

```
int add(int a, int b, int c, int d) {
  return a + b + c + d;
}
```

Code Box 2-13 [ExtremeC_examples_chapter2_5_add.c]: Definition of the add function in example 2.5

And, following is the second source file:

```
#include <stdio.h>

int add(int, int);

int main(int argc, char** argv) {
  int x = add(5, 6);
  printf("Result: %d\n", x);
  return 0;
}
```

Code Box 2-14 [ExtremeC_examples_chapter2_5_main.c]: The main function in example 2.5

As you can see, the `main` function is using another version of the `add` function with a different signature, accepting two integers, but the `add` function defined in the first source file, *Code Box 2-13*, is accepting four integers.

These functions are usually said to be the *overloads* of each other. For sure, there should be something wrong if we compile and link these source files. It's interesting to see if we can build the example successfully.

The next step is to compile and link the relocatable object files, which we can do by running the following code:

```
$ gcc -c ExtremeC_examples_chapter2_5_add.c -o add.o
$ gcc -c ExtremeC_examples_chapter2_5_main.c -o main.o
$ gcc add.o main.o -o ex2_5.out
$
```

Shell Box 2-24: Building example 2.5

As you can see in the shell output, the linking step went well, and the final executable has been produced! This clearly shows that the symbols can fool the linker. Now let's look at the output after running the executable:

```
$ ./ex2_5.out
Result: -1885535197
$ ./ex2_5.out
Result: 1679625283
$
```

Shell Box 2-25: Running example 2.5 twice and the strange results!

As you can see, the output is wrong; it even changes in different runs! This example shows that bad things can happen when the linker picks up the wrong version of a symbol. Regarding the function symbols, they are just names and they don't carry any information regarding the signature of the corresponding function. Function arguments are nothing more than a C concept; in fact, they do not truly exist in either assembly code or machine-level instructions.

In order to investigate more, we are going to look at the *disassembly* of the add functions in a different example. In *example 2.6*, we have two add functions with the same signatures that we had in *example 2.5*.

To study this, we are going to work from the idea that we have the following source files in *example 2.6*:

```
int add(int a, int b, int c, int d) {
    return a + b + c + d;
}
```

Code Box 2-15 [ExtremeC_examples_chapter2_6_add_1.c]: The first definition of add in example 2.6

The following code is the other source file:

```
int add(int a, int b) {
    return a + b;
}
```

Code Box 2-16 [ExtremeC_examples_chapter2_6_add_2.c]: The second definition of add in example 2.6

The first step, just like before, is to compile both source files:

```
$ gcc -c ExtremeC_examples_chapter2_6_add_1.c -o add_1.o
$ gcc -c ExtremeC_examples_chapter2_6_add_2.c -o add_2.o
$
```

Shell Box 2-26: Compiling the source files in example 2.6 to their corresponding object files

We then need to have a look at the disassembly of the add symbol in different object files. Therefore, we start with the add_1.o object file:

```
$ objdump -d add_1.o

add_1.o:       file format elf64-x86-64


Disassembly of section .text:

0000000000000000 <add>:
   0:   55                      push   %rbp
   1:   48 89 e5                mov    %rsp,%rbp
   4:   89 7d fc                mov    %edi,-0x4(%rbp)
   7:   89 75 f8                mov    %esi,-0x8(%rbp)
   a:   89 55 f4                mov    %edx,-0xc(%rbp)
   d:   89 4d f0                mov    %ecx,-0x10(%rbp)
  10:   8b 55 fc                mov    -0x4(%rbp),%edx
  13:   8b 45 f8                mov    -0x8(%rbp),%eax
  16:   01 c2                   add    %eax,%edx
  18:   8b 45 f4                mov    -0xc(%rbp),%eax
  1b:   01 c2                   add    %eax,%edx
  1d:   8b 45 f0                mov    -0x10(%rbp),%eax
  20:   01 d0                   add    %edx,%eax
  22:   5d                      pop    %rbp
  23:   c3
$
```

Shell Box 2-27: Using objdump to look at the disassembly of the add symbol in add_1.o

The following shell box shows us the disassembly of the add symbol found in the other object file, add_2.o:

```
$ objdump -d add_2.o

add_2.o:        file format elf64-x86-64


Disassembly of section .text:

0000000000000000 <add>:
   0:    55                          push    %rbp
   1:    48 89 e5                    mov     %rsp,%rbp
   4:    89 7d fc                    mov     %edi,-0x4(%rbp)
   7:    89 75 f8                    mov     %esi,-0x8(%rbp)
   a:    8b 55 fc                    mov     -0x4(%rbp),%edx
   d:    8b 45 f8                    mov     -0x8(%rbp),%eax
  10:    01 d0                       add     %edx,%eax
  12:    5d                          pop     %rbp
  13:    c3                          retq
$
```

Shell Box 2-28: Using objdump to look at the disassembly of the add symbol in add_2.o

When a function call takes place, a new *stack frame* is created on top of the stack. This stack frame contains both the arguments passed to the function and the return address. You will read more about the function call mechanism in *Chapter 4, Process Memory Structure*, and *Chapter 5, Stack and Heap*.

In shell boxes *2-27* and *2-28*, you can clearly see how the arguments are collected from the stack frame. In the disassembly of add_1.o, *Shell Box 2-27*, you can see the following lines:

```
   4:    89 7d fc                    mov     %edi,-0x4(%rbp)
   7:    89 75 f8                    mov     %esi,-0x8(%rbp)
   a:    89 55 f4                    mov     %edx,-0xc(%rbp)
   d:    89 4d f0                    mov     %ecx,-0x10(%rbp)
```

Code Box 2-17: The assembly instructions to copy the arguments from the stack frame
to the registers for the first add function

These instructions copy four values from the memory addresses, which have been pointed by the %rbp register, and put them into the local registers.

Note:
Registers are locations within a CPU that can be accessed quickly. Therefore, it would be highly efficient for the CPU to bring the values from main memory into its registers first, and then perform calculations on them. The register %rbp is the one that points to the current stack frame, containing the arguments passed to a function.

If you look at the disassembly of the second object file, while it is very similar, it differs by not having the copy operation four times:

```
4:   89 7d fc                    mov     %edi,-0x4(%rbp)
7:   89 75 f8                    mov     %esi,-0x8(%rbp)
```

Code Box 2-18: The assembly instructions to copy the arguments from the stack frame to the registers for the second add function

These instructions copy two values simply because the function only expects two arguments. This is why we saw those strange values in the output of *example 2.5*. The main function only puts two values into the stack frame while calling the add function, but the add definition was actually expecting four arguments. So, it is likely that the wrong definition continues to go beyond the stack frame to read the missing arguments, which results in the wrong values for the sum operation.

We could prevent this by changing the function symbol names based on the input types. This is usually referred to as *name mangling* and is mostly used in C++ because of its *function overloading* feature. We discuss this briefly in the last section of the chapter.

C++ name mangling

To highlight how name mangling works in C++, we are going to compile *example 2.6* using a C++ compiler. Therefore, we will use the GNU C++ compiler g++ for this purpose.

Once we have done that, we can use readelf to dump the symbol tables for each generated object file. By doing this, we can see how C++ has changed the name of the function symbols based on the types of input parameters.

As we have noted before, the compilation pipelines of C and C++ are very similar. Therefore, we can expect to have relocatable object files as a result of C++ compilation. Let's look at both of the object files produced as part of compiling *example 2.6*:

```
$ g++ -c ExtremeC_examples_chapter2_6_add_1.o
$ g++ -c ExtremeC_examples_chapter2_6_add_2.o
$ readelf -s ExtremeC_examples_chapter2_6_add_1.o

Symbol table '.symtab' contains 9 entries:
   Num:    Value            Size Type    Bind   Vis     Ndx Name
     0: 0000000000000000       0 NOTYPE  LOCAL  DEFAULT UND
     1: 0000000000000000       0 FILE    LOCAL  DEFAULT ABS ExtremeC_
examples_chapter
     2: 0000000000000000       0 SECTION LOCAL  DEFAULT   1
     3: 0000000000000000       0 SECTION LOCAL  DEFAULT   2
     4: 0000000000000000       0 SECTION LOCAL  DEFAULT   3
     5: 0000000000000000       0 SECTION LOCAL  DEFAULT   5
     6: 0000000000000000       0 SECTION LOCAL  DEFAULT   6
     7: 0000000000000000       0 SECTION LOCAL  DEFAULT   4
     8: 0000000000000000      36 FUNC    GLOBAL DEFAULT   1 _Z3addiiii
$ readelf -s ExtremeC_examples_chapter2_6_add_2.o

Symbol table '.symtab' contains 9 entries:
   Num:    Value            Size Type    Bind   Vis     Ndx Name
     0: 0000000000000000       0 NOTYPE  LOCAL  DEFAULT UND
     1: 0000000000000000       0 FILE    LOCAL  DEFAULT ABS ExtremeC_
examples_chapter
     2: 0000000000000000       0 SECTION LOCAL  DEFAULT   1
     3: 0000000000000000       0 SECTION LOCAL  DEFAULT   2
     4: 0000000000000000       0 SECTION LOCAL  DEFAULT   3
     5: 0000000000000000       0 SECTION LOCAL  DEFAULT   5
     6: 0000000000000000       0 SECTION LOCAL  DEFAULT   6
     7: 0000000000000000       0 SECTION LOCAL  DEFAULT   4
     8: 0000000000000000      20 FUNC    GLOBAL DEFAULT   1 _Z3addii
$
```

Shell Box 2-29: Using readelf the see the symbol tables of the object files produced by a C++ compiler

As you can see in the output, we have two different symbol names for different overloads of the add function. The overload that accepts four integers has the symbol name _Z3addiiii, and the other overload, which accepts two integers, has the symbol name _Z3addii.

Every i in the symbol name refers to one of the integer input parameters.

From that, you can see the symbol names are different, and if you try to use the wrong one, you will get a linking error as a result of the linker not being able to find the definition of a wrong symbol. Name mangling is the technique that enables C++ to support function overloading and it helps to prevent the problems we encountered in the previous section.

Summary

In this chapter, we covered the fundamental steps and components required to build a C project. Without knowing how to build a project, it is pointless to just write code. In this chapter:

- We went through the C compilation pipeline and its various steps. We discussed each step and described the inputs and the outputs.

- We defined the term *platform* and how different assemblers can lead to different machine-level instructions for the same C program.

- We continued to discuss each step and the component driving that step in a greater detail.

- As part of the compiler component, we explained what the compiler frontends and backends are, and how GCC and LLVM use this separation to support many languages.

- As part of our discussion regarding the assembler component, we saw that object files are platform-dependent, and they should have an exact file format.

- As part of the linker component, we discussed what a linker does and how it uses symbols to find the missing definitions in order to put them together and form the final product. We also explained various possible products of a C project. We explained why relocatable (or intermediate) object files should not be considered as products.

- We demonstrated how the linker can be fooled when a symbol is provided with a wrong definition. We showed this in *example 2.5*.

- We explained the C++ name mangling feature and how problems like what we saw in *example 2.5* can be prevented because of that.

We will continue our discussion regarding object files and their internal structure in the next chapter, *Object Files*.

Chapter 03

Object Files

This chapter details the various products that a C/C++ project can have. Possible products include relocatable object files, executable object files, static libraries, and shared object files. However, relocatable object files are considered to be temporary products and they act as ingredients for making other types of products that are final.

It seems that today in C, it's crucial to have further discussion about the various types of object files and their internal structures. The majority of C books only talk about the C syntax and the language itself; but, in real-world you need more in-depth knowledge to be a successful C programmer.

When you are creating software, it is not just about the development and the programming language. In fact, it is about the whole process: writing the code, compilation, optimization, producing correct products, and further subsequent steps, in order to run and maintain those products on the target platforms.

You should be knowledgeable about these intermediate steps, to the extent that you are able to solve any issues you might encounter. This is even more serious regarding embedded development, as the hardware architectures and the instruction sets can be challenging and atypical.

This chapter is divided into the following sections:

1. **Application binary interface**: Here, we are first going to talk about the **Application Binary Interface (ABI)** and its importance.
2. **Object file formats**: In this section, we talk about various object file formats that exist today or they have become obsolete over the years. We also introduce ELF as the most used object file format in Unix-like systems.
3. **Relocatable object files**: Here we discuss relocatable object files and the very first products of a C project. We take a look inside ELF relocatable object files to see what we can find there.

4. **Executable object files**: As part of this section, we talk about the executable object files. We also explain how they are created from a number of relocatable object files. We discuss the differences between ELF relocatable and executable object files in terms of their internal structure.

5. **Static library**: In this section, we talk about static libraries and how we can create them. We also demonstrate how to write a program and use already built static libraries.

6. **Dynamic library**: Here we talk about shared object files. We demonstrate how to create them out of a number of relocatable object files and how to use them in a program. We also briefly talk about the internal structure of an ELF shared object file.

Our discussions in this chapter will be mostly themed around Unix-like systems, but we will discuss some differences in other operating systems like Microsoft Windows.

Note:
Before moving on to read this chapter, you need to be familiar with the basic ideas and steps required for building a C project. You need to know what a translation unit is and how linking is different from compilation. Please read the previous chapter before moving on with this one.

Let's begin the chapter by talking about ABI.

Application binary interface (ABI)

As you may already know, every library or framework, regardless of the technologies or the programming language used, exposes a set of certain functionalities, which is known as its **Application Programming Interface** (**API**). If a library is supposed to be used by another code, then the consumer code should use the provided API. To be clear, nothing other than the API should be used in order to use a library because it is the public interface of the library and everything else is seen as a black box, hence cannot be used.

Now suppose after some time, the library's API undergoes some modifications. In order for the consumer code to continue using the newer versions of the library, the code must adapt itself to the new API; otherwise, it won't be able to use it anymore. The consumer code could stick to a certain version of the library (maybe an old one) and ignore the newer versions, but let's assume that there is a desire to upgrade to the latest version of the library.

To put it simply, an API is like a convention (or standard) accepted between two software components to serve or use each other. An ABI is pretty similar to API, but at a different level. While the API guarantees the compatibility of two software components to continue their functional cooperation, the ABI guarantees that two programs are compatible at the level of their machine-level instructions, together with their corresponding object files.

For instance, a program cannot use a dynamic or static library that has a different ABI. Perhaps worse than that, an executable file (which is, in fact, an object file) cannot be run on a system supporting a different ABI than the one that the executable file was built for. A number of vital and obvious system functionalities, such as *dynamic linking*, *loading an executable*, and *function calling convention*, should be done precisely according to an agreed upon ABI.

An ABI will typically cover the following things:

- The instruction set of the target architecture, which includes the processor instructions, memory layout, endianness, registers, and so on.

- Existing data types, their sizes, and the alignment policy.

- The function calling convention describes how functions should be called. For example, subjects like the structure of the *stack frame* and the pushing order of the arguments are part of it.

- Defining how *system calls* should be called in a Unix-like system.

- Used *object file format*, which we will explain in the following section, for having *relocatable, executable*, and *shared object files*.

- Regarding object files produced by a C++ compiler, the *name mangling*, *virtual table* layout, is part of the ABI.

The *System V ABI* is the most widely used ABI standard among Unix-like operating systems like Linux and the BSD systems. **Executable and Linking Format (ELF)** is the standard object file format used in the System V ABI.

 Note:
The following link is the System V ABI for AMD 64-bit architecture: `https://www.uclibc.org/docs/psABI-x86_64.pdf`. You can go through the list of contents and see the areas it covers.

In the following section, we will discuss the object file formats, particularly ELF.

Object file formats

As we explained in the previous chapter, *Chapter 2, Compilation and Linking*, on a platform, object files have their own specific format for storing machine-level instructions. Note that this is about the structure of object files and this is different from the fact that each architecture has its own instruction set. As we know from the previous discussion, these two variations are different parts of the ABI in a platform; the object file format and the architecture's instruction set.

In this section, we are going to have a brief look into some widely known object file formats. To start with, let's look at some object file formats used in various operating systems:

- **ELF** used by Linux and many other Unix-like operating systems
- **Mach-O** used in OS X (macOS and iOS) systems
- **PE** used in Microsoft Windows

To give some history and context about the current and past object file formats, we can say that all object file formats that exist today are successors to the old a.out object file format. It was designed for early versions of Unix.

The term **a.out** stands for **assembler output**. Despite the fact that the file format is obsolete today, the name is still used as the default filename for the executable files produced by most linkers. You should remember seeing a.out in a number of examples in the first chapter of the book.

However, the a.out format was soon replaced by **COFF** or the **Common Object File Format**. COFF is the basis for ELF – the object format that we use in most Unix-like systems. Apple also replaced a.out with Mach-O as part of OS/X. Windows uses the **PE** or **Portable Execution** file format for its object files, which is based on COFF.

Note:
A deeper history of object file formats can be found here: https://en.wikipedia.org/wiki/COFF#History. Knowing about the history of a specific topic will help you to get a better understanding of its evolution path and current and past characteristics.

As you can see, all of today's major object file formats are based on the historic object file format a.out, and then COFF, and in many ways share the same ancestry.

ELF is the standard object file format used in Linux and most Unix-like operating systems. In fact, ELF is the object file format used as part of the System V ABI, heavily employed in most Unix systems. Today, it is the most widely accepted object file format used by operating systems.

ELF is the standard binary file format for operating systems including, but not limited to:

- Linux
- FreeBSD
- NetBSD
- Solaris

This means that as long as the architecture beneath them remains the same, an ELF object file created for one of these operating systems can be run and used in others. ELF, like all other *file formats*, has a structure that we will describe briefly in the upcoming sections.

Note:
More information about ELF and its details can be found here: `https://www.uclibc.org/docs/psABI-x86_64.pdf`. Note that this link refers to the System V ABI for AMD 64-bits (`amd64`) architecture.

You can also read the HTML version of the System V ABI here: `http://www.sco.com/developers/gabi/2003-12-17/ch4.intro.html`.

In the upcoming sections, we are going to talk about the temporary and final products of a C project. We start with relocatable object files.

Relocatable object files

In this section, we are going to talk about relocatable object files. As we explained in the previous chapter, these object files are the output of the assembly step in the C compilation pipeline. These files are considered to be temporary products of a C project, and they are the main ingredients to produce further and final products. For this reason, it would be useful to have a deeper look at them and see what we can find in a relocatable object file.

In a relocatable object file, we can find the following items regarding the compiled translation unit:

- The machine-level instructions produced for the functions found in the translation unit (code).

- The values of the initialized global variables declared in the translation unit (data).

- The *symbol table* containing all the defined and reference symbols found in the translation unit.

These are the key items that can be found in any relocatable object file. Of course, the way that they are put together depends on the object file format, but using proper tools, you should be able to extract these items from a relocatable object file. We are going to do this for an ELF relocatable object file shortly.

But before delving into the example, let's talk about the reason why relocatable object files are named like this. In other words, what does the *relocatable* mean after all? The reason comes from the process that a linker performs in order to put some relocatable object files together and form a bigger object file – an executable object file or a shared object file.

We discuss what can be found in an executable file in the next section, but for now, we should know that the items we find in an executable object file are the sum of all the items found in all the constituent relocatable object files. Let's just talk about machine-level instructions.

The machine-level instructions found in one relocatable object file should be put next to the machine-level instructions coming from another relocatable object file. This means that the instructions should be easily *movable* or *relocatable*. For this to happen, the instructions have no addresses in a relocatable object file, and they obtain their addresses only after the linking step. This is the main reason why we call these object files relocatable. To elaborate more on this, we need to show it in a real example.

Example 3.1 is about two source files, one containing the definitions of two functions, max and max_3, and the other source file containing the main function using the declared functions max and max_3. Next, you can see the content of the first source file:

```
int max(int a, int b) {
  return a > b ? a : b;
}

int max_3(int a, int b, int c) {
  int temp = max(a, b);
  return c > temp ? c : temp;
}
```

Code Box 3-1 [ExtremeC_examples_chapter3_1_funcs.c]: A source file containing two function definitions

And the second source file looks like the following code box:

```
int max(int, int);
int max_3(int, int, int);

int a = 5;
int b = 10;

int main(int argc, char** argv) {
  int m1 = max(a, b);
  int m2 = max_3(5, 8, -1);
  return 0;
}
```

Code Box 3-2 [ExtremeC_examples_chapter3_1.c]: The main function using the already declared functions. Definitions are put in a separate source file.

Let's produce the relocatable object files for the preceding source files. This way, we can investigate the content and that which we explained before. Note that, since we are compiling these sources on a Linux machine, we expect to see ELF object files as the result:

```
$ gcc -c ExtremeC_examples_chapter3_1_funcs.c  -o funcs.o
$ gcc -c ExtremeC_examples_chapter3_1.c -o main.o
$
```

Shell Box 3-1: Compiling source files to their corresponding relocatable object files

Both `funcs.o` and `main.o` are relocatable ELF object files. In an ELF object file, the items described to be in a relocatable object file are put into a number of sections. In order to see the present sections in the preceding relocatable object files, we can use the `readelf` utility as follows:

```
$ readelf -hSl funcs.o
[7/7]
ELF Header:
  Magic:   7f 45 4c 46 02 01 01 00 00 00 00 00 00 00 00 00
  Class:                             ELF64
  Data:                              2's complement, little endian
  Version:                           1 (current)
  OS/ABI:                            UNIX - System V
  ABI Version:                       0
  Type:                              REL (Relocatable file)
```

```
Machine:                              Advanced Micro Devices X86-64
...
Number of section headers:        12
Section header string table index: 11


Section Headers:
  [Nr] Name                Type            Address        Offset
       Size                EntSize         Flags  Link  Info  Align
  [ 0]                     NULL            0000000000000000
00000000
       0000000000000000    0000000000000000        0     0     0
  [ 1] .text               PROGBITS        0000000000000000
00000040
       0000000000000045    0000000000000000  AX    0     0     1
...

  [ 3] .data               PROGBITS        0000000000000000
00000085
       0000000000000000    0000000000000000  WA    0     0     1
  [ 4] .bss                NOBITS          0000000000000000
00000085
       0000000000000000    0000000000000000  WA    0     0     1
...

  [ 9] .symtab             SYMTAB          0000000000000000
00000110
       00000000000000f0    0000000000000018       10     8     8
  [10] .strtab             STRTAB          0000000000000000
00000200
       0000000000000030    0000000000000000        0     0     1
  [11] .shstrtab           STRTAB          0000000000000000
00000278
       0000000000000059    0000000000000000        0     0     1
...
$
```

Shell Box 3-2: The ELF content of the funcs.o object file

As you can see in the preceding shell box, the relocatable object file has 11 sections. The sections in bold font are the sections that we have introduced as items existing in an object file. The .text section contains all the machine-level instructions for the translation unit. The .data and .bss sections contain the values for initialized global variables, and the number of bytes required for uninitialized global variables respectively. The .symtab section contains the symbol table.

Note that, the sections existing in both preceding object files are the same, but their content is different. Therefore, we don't show the sections for the other relocatable object file.

As we mentioned before, one of the sections in an ELF object file contains the symbol table. In the previous chapter, we had a thorough discussion about the symbol table and its entries. We described how it is being used by the linker to produce executable and shared object files. Here, we want to draw your attention to something about the symbol table that we didn't discuss in the previous chapter. This would be in accordance with our explanation on why relocatable object files are named in this manner.

Let's dump the symbol table for `funcs.o`. In the previous chapter, we used `objdump` but now, we are going to use `readelf` to do so:

```
$ readelf -s funcs.o

Symbol table '.symtab' contains 10 entries:
   Num:    Value          Size Type    Bind    Vis      Ndx Name
     0: 0000000000000000     0 NOTYPE  LOCAL   DEFAULT  UND
...
     6: 0000000000000000     0 SECTION LOCAL   DEFAULT    7
     7: 0000000000000000     0 SECTION LOCAL   DEFAULT    5
     8: 0000000000000000    22 FUNC    GLOBAL  DEFAULT    1 max
     9: 0000000000000016    47 FUNC    GLOBAL  DEFAULT    1 max_3
$
```

Shell Box 3-3: The symbol table of the funcs.o object file

As you can see in the `Value` column, the address assigned to `max` is `0` and the address assigned to `max_3` is `22` (hexadecimal `16`). This means that the instructions related to these symbols are adjacent and their addresses start from 0. These symbols, and their corresponding machine-level instructions, are ready to be relocated to other places in the final executable. Let's look at the symbol table of `main.o`:

```
$ readelf -s main.o

Symbol table '.symtab' contains 14 entries:
   Num:    Value          Size Type    Bind    Vis      Ndx Name
     0: 0000000000000000     0 NOTYPE  LOCAL   DEFAULT  UND
...
```

```
   8: 0000000000000000        4 OBJECT   GLOBAL DEFAULT      3 a
   9: 0000000000000004        4 OBJECT   GLOBAL DEFAULT      3 b
  10: 0000000000000000       69 FUNC     GLOBAL DEFAULT      1 main
  11: 0000000000000000        0 NOTYPE   GLOBAL DEFAULT    UND _
GLOBAL_OFFSET_TABLE_
  12: 0000000000000000        0 NOTYPE   GLOBAL DEFAULT    UND max
  13: 0000000000000000        0 NOTYPE   GLOBAL DEFAULT    UND max_3
$
```

Shell Box 3-4: The symbol table of the main.o object file

As you can see, the symbols associated with global variables a and b, as well as the symbol for the main function are put at addresses that don't seem be the final addresses that they should be placed at. This is a sign of being a relocatable object file. As we have said before, the symbols in a relocatable object files don't have any final and absolute addresses and their addresses will be determined as part of the linking step.

In the following section, we continue to produce an executable file from the preceding relocatable object files. You will see that the symbol table is different.

Executable Object Files

Now, it's time to talk about executable object files. You should know by now that executable object file is one of the final products of a C project. Like relocatable object files, they have the same items in them; the machine-level instructions, the values for initialized global variables, and the symbol table; however, the arrangement can be different. We can show this regarding the ELF executable object files since it would be easy to generate them and study their internal structure.

In order to produce an executable ELF object file, we continue with *example 3.1*. In the previous section, we generated relocatable object files for the two sources existing in the example, and in this section, we are going to link them to form an executable file.

The following commands do that for you, as explained in the previous chapter:

```
$ gcc funcs.o main.o -o ex3_1.out
$
```

Shell Box 3-5: Linking previously built relocatable object files in example 3.1

In the previous section, we spoke about sections being present in an ELF object file. We should say that more sections exist in an ELF executable object file, but together with some segments. Every ELF executable object file, and as you will see later in this chapter, every ELF shared object file, has a number of *segments* in addition to sections. Each segment consists of a number of sections (zero or more), and the sections are put into segments based on their content.

For example, all sections containing machine-level instructions go into the same segment. You will see in *Chapter 4, Process Memory Structure,* that these segments nicely map to static *memory segments* found in the memory layout of a running process.

Let's look at the contents of an executable file and meet these segments. Similarly, to relocatable object files, we can use the same command to show the sections, and the segments found in an executable ELF object file.

```
$ readelf -hSl ex3_1.out
ELF Header:
  Magic:   7f 45 4c 46 02 01 01 00 00 00 00 00 00 00 00 00
  Class:                             ELF64
  Data:                              2's complement, little endian
  Version:                           1 (current)
  OS/ABI:                            UNIX - System V
  ABI Version:                       0
  Type:                              DYN (Shared object file)
  Machine:                           Advanced Micro Devices X86-64
  Version:                           0x1
  Entry point address:               0x4f0
  Start of program headers:          64 (bytes into file)
  Start of section headers:          6576 (bytes into file)
  Flags:                             0x0
  Size of this header:               64 (bytes)
  Size of program headers:           56 (bytes)
  Number of program headers:         9
  Size of section headers:           64 (bytes)
  Number of section headers:         28
  Section header string table index: 27

Section Headers:
  [Nr] Name              Type            Address          Offset
       Size              EntSize         Flags  Link  Info  Align
  [ 0]                   NULL            0000000000000000
00000000
```

```
        0000000000000000  0000000000000000           0    0    0
   [ 1] .interp          PROGBITS        0000000000000238
00000238
        000000000000001c  0000000000000000  A        0    0    1
   [ 2] .note.ABI-tag    NOTE            0000000000000254
00000254
        0000000000000020  0000000000000000  A        0    0    4
   [ 3] .note.gnu.build-i NOTE           0000000000000274
00000274
        0000000000000024  0000000000000000  A        0    0    4
...
   [26] .strtab          STRTAB          0000000000000000
00001678
        0000000000000239  0000000000000000           0    0    1
   [27] .shstrtab        STRTAB          0000000000000000
000018b1
        00000000000000f9  0000000000000000           0    0    1
Key to Flags:
  W (write), A (alloc), X (execute), M (merge), S (strings), I
(info),
  L (link order), O (extra OS processing required), G (group), T
(TLS),
  C (compressed), x (unknown), o (OS specific), E (exclude),
  l (large), p (processor specific)


Program Headers:
  Type           Offset            VirtAddr          PhysAddr
                 FileSiz           MemSiz            Flags
Align
  PHDR           0x0000000000000040 0x0000000000000040
0x0000000000000040
                 0x00000000000001f8 0x00000000000001f8  R     0x8
  INTERP         0x0000000000000238 0x0000000000000238
0x0000000000000238
                 0x000000000000001c 0x000000000000001c  R     0x1
      [Requesting program interpreter: /lib64/ld-linux-x86-64.
so.2]
...
  GNU_EH_FRAME   0x0000000000000714 0x0000000000000714
0x0000000000000714
                 0x000000000000004c 0x000000000000004c  R     0x4
```

```
   GNU_STACK        0x0000000000000000 0x0000000000000000
0x0000000000000000
                    0x0000000000000000 0x0000000000000000   RW
0x10
   GNU_RELRO        0x0000000000000df0 0x0000000000200df0
0x0000000000200df0
                    0x0000000000000210 0x0000000000000210   R       0x1

Section to Segment mapping:
  Segment Sections...
   00
   01      .interp
   02      .interp .note.ABI-tag .note.gnu.build-id .gnu.hash
.dynsym .dynstr .gnu.version .gnu.version_r .rela.dyn .init .plt
.plt.got .text .fini .rodata .eh_frame_hdr .eh_frame
   03      .init_array .fini_array .dynamic .got .data .bss
   04      .dynamic
   05      .note.ABI-tag .note.gnu.build-id
   06      .eh_frame_hdr
   07
   08      .init_array .fini_array .dynamic .got
$
```

Shell Box 3-6: The ELF content of ex3_1.out executable object file

There are multiple notes about the above output:

- We can see that the type of object file from the ELF point of view, is a shared object file. In other words, in ELF, an executable object file is a shared object file that has some specific segments like INTERP. This segment (actually the .interp section which is referred to by this segment) is used by the loader program to load and execute the executable object file.

- We have made four segments bold. The first one refers to the INTERP segment which is explained in the previous bullet point. The second one is the TEXT segment. It contains all the sections having machine-level instructions. The third one is the DATA segment that contains all the values that should be used to initialize the global variables and other early structures. The fourth segment refers to the section that *dynamic linking* related information can be found, for instance, the shared object files that need to be loaded as part of the execution.

- As you see, we've got more sections in comparison to a relocatable shared object, probably filled with data required to load and execute the object file.

As we explained in the previous section, the symbols found in the symbol table of a relocatable object file do not have any absolute and determined addresses. That's because the sections containing machine-level instructions are not linked yet.

In a deeper sense, linking a number of relocatable object files is actually to collect all similar sections from the given relocatable object files and put them together to form a bigger section, and finally put the resulting section into the output executable or the shared object file. Therefore, only after this step, the symbols can be finalized and obtain the addresses that are not going to change. In executable object files, the addresses are absolute, while in shared object files, the *relative addresses* are absolute. We will discuss this more in the section dedicated to dynamic libraries.

Let's look at the symbol table found in the executable file ex3_1.out. Note that the symbol table has many entries and that's why the output is not fully shown in the following shell box:

```
$ readelf -s ex3_1.out
Symbol table '.dynsym' contains 6 entries:
   Num:    Value          Size Type    Bind   Vis      Ndx Name
     0: 0000000000000000     0 NOTYPE  LOCAL  DEFAULT  UND
...
     5: 0000000000000000     0 FUNC    WEAK   DEFAULT  UND __cxa_
finalize@GLIBC_2.2.5 (2)


Symbol table '.symtab' contains 66 entries:
   Num:    Value          Size Type    Bind   Vis      Ndx Name
     0: 0000000000000000     0 NOTYPE  LOCAL  DEFAULT  UND
...
    45: 0000000000201000     0 NOTYPE  WEAK   DEFAULT   22 data_
start
    46: 0000000000000610    47 FUNC    GLOBAL DEFAULT   13 max_3
    47: 0000000000201014     4 OBJECT  GLOBAL DEFAULT   22 b
    48: 0000000000201018     0 NOTYPE  GLOBAL DEFAULT   22 _edata
    49: 0000000000000704     0 FUNC    GLOBAL DEFAULT   14 _fini
    50: 00000000000005fa    22 FUNC    GLOBAL DEFAULT   13 max
    51: 0000000000000000     0 FUNC    GLOBAL DEFAULT  UND __libc_
start_main@@GLIBC_
...
```

```
    64: 0000000000000000        0 FUNC     WEAK    DEFAULT   UND __cxa_
finalize@@GLIBC_2.2
    65: 00000000000004b8        0 FUNC     GLOBAL DEFAULT     10 _init
$
```

Shell Box 3-7: The symbol tables found in the ex3_1.out executable object file

As you see in the preceding shell box, we have two different symbol tables in an executable object file. The first one, .dynsym, contains the symbols that should be resolved when loading the executable, but the second symbol table, .symtab, contains all the resolved symbols together with unresolved symbols brought from the dynamic symbol table. In other words, the symbol table contains the unresolved symbols from the dynamic table as well.

As you see, the resolved symbols in the symbol table have absolute corresponding addresses that they have obtained after the linking step. The addresses for max and max_3 symbols are shown in bold font.

In this section, we took a brief look into the executable object file. In the next section, we are going to talk about static libraries.

Static libraries

As we have explained before, a static library is one of the possible products of a C project. In this section, we are going to talk about static libraries and the way they are created and used. We will then continue this discussion by introducing dynamic libraries in the next section.

A static library is simply a Unix archive made from the relocatable object files. Such a library is usually linked together with other object files to form an executable object file.

Note that a static library itself is not considered as an object file, rather it is a container for them. In other words, static libraries are not ELF files in Linux systems, nor are they Mach-O files in macOS systems. They are simply archived files that have been created by the Unix ar utility.

When a linker is about to use a static library in the linking step, it first tries to extract the relocatable object files from it, then it starts to look up and resolve the undefined symbols that may be found in some of them.

Now, it's time to create a static library for a project with multiple source files. The first step is to create some relocatable object files. Once you have compiled all of the source files in a C/C++ project, you can use the Unix archiving tool, ar, to create the static library's archive file.

In Unix systems, static libraries are usually named according to an accepted and widely used convention. The name starts with `lib`, and it ends with the `.a` extension. This can be different for other operating systems; for instance, in Microsoft Windows, static libraries carry the `.lib` extension.

Suppose that, in an imaginary C project, you have the source files `aa.c`, `bb.c`, all the way up to `zz.c`. In order to produce the relocatable object files, you will need to compile the source files in a similar manner to how we use the commands next. Note that the compilation process has been thoroughly explained in the previous chapter:

```
$ gcc -c aa.c -o aa.o
$ gcc -c bb.c -o bb.o
.
.
.
$ gcc -c zz.c -o zz.o
$
```

Shell Box 3-8: Compiling a number of sources to their corresponding relocatable object files

By running the preceding commands, we will get all the required relocatable object files. Note that this can take a considerable amount of time if the project is big and contains thousands of source files. Of course, having a powerful build machine, together with running the compilation jobs in parallel, can reduce the build time significantly.

When it comes to creating a static library file, we simply need to run the following command:

```
$ ar crs libexample.a aa.o bb.o ... zz.o
$
```

Shell Box 3-9: The general recipe for making a static library out of a number of relocatable object files

As a result, `libexample.a` is created, which contains all of the preceding relocatable object files as a single archive. Explaining the `crs` option passed to `ar` would be out of the scope of this chapter, but in the following link, you can read about its meaning: `https://stackoverflow.com/questions/29714300/what-does-the-rcs-option-in-ar-do`.

Note:
The ar command does not necessarily create a *compressed* archive file. It is only used to put files together to form a single file that is an archive of all those files. The tool ar is general purpose, and you can use it to put any kind of files together and create your own archive out of them.

Now that we know how to create a static library, we are going to create a real one as part of *example 3.2*.

First, we are going to presume that *example 3.2* is a C project about geometry. The example consists of three source files and one header file. The purpose of the library is to define a selection of geometry related functions that can be used in other applications.

To do this, we need to create a static library file named libgeometry.a out of the three source files. By having the static library, we can use the header file and the static library file together in order to write another program that will use the geometry functions defined in the library.

The following code boxes are the contents of the source and header files. The first file, ExtremeC_examples_chapter3_2_geometry.h, contains all of the declarations that need to be exported from our geometry library. These declarations will be used by future applications that are going to use the library.

Note:
All the commands provided for creating object files are run and tested on Linux. Some modifications might be necessary if you're going to execute them on a different operating system.

We need to take note that future applications *must* be only dependent on the declarations and not the definitions at all. Therefore, firstly, let's look at the declarations of the geometry library:

```
#ifndef EXTREME_C_EXAMPLES_CHAPTER_3_2_H
#define EXTREME_C_EXAMPLES_CHAPTER_3_2_H

#define PI 3.14159265359
```

```
typedef struct {
  double x;
  double y;
} cartesian_pos_2d_t;

typedef struct {
  double length;
  // in degrees
  double theta;
} polar_pos_2d_t;

typedef struct {
  double x;
  double y;
  double z;
} cartesian_pos_3d_t;

typedef struct {
  double length;
  // in degrees
  double theta;
  // in degrees
  double phi;
} polar_pos_3d_t;

double to_radian(double deg);
double to_degree(double rad);

double cos_deg(double deg);
double acos_deg(double deg);

double sin_deg(double deg);
double asin_deg(double deg);

cartesian_pos_2d_t convert_to_2d_cartesian_pos(
        const polar_pos_2d_t* polar_pos);
polar_pos_2d_t convert_to_2d_polar_pos(
        const cartesian_pos_2d_t* cartesian_pos);

cartesian_pos_3d_t convert_to_3d_cartesian_pos(
        const polar_pos_3d_t* polar_pos);
polar_pos_3d_t convert_to_3d_polar_pos(
        const cartesian_pos_3d_t* cartesian_pos);

#endif
```

Code Box 3-3 [ExtremeC_examples_chapter3_2_geometry.h]: The header file of example 3.2

The second file, which is a source file, contains the definitions of the trigonometry functions, the first six functions declared in the preceding header file:

```c
#include <math.h>

// We need to include the header file since
// we want to use the macro PI
#include "ExtremeC_examples_chapter3_2_geometry.h"

double to_radian(double deg) {
  return (PI * deg) / 180;
}

double to_degree(double rad) {
  return (180 * rad) / PI;
}

double cos_deg(double deg) {
  return cos(to_radian(deg));
}

double acos_deg(double deg) {
  return acos(to_radian(deg));
}

double sin_deg(double deg) {
  return sin(to_radian(deg));
}

double asin_deg(double deg) {
  return asin(to_radian(deg));
}
```

Code Box 3-4 [ExtremeC_examples_chapter3_2_trigon.c]: The source file containing the definitions of the trigonometry functions

Note that it is not necessary for sources to include the header file unless they are going to use a declaration like PI or to_degree, which is declared in the header file.

The third file, which is a source file again, contains the definitions of all 2D Geometry functions:

```c
#include <math.h>
```

```
// We need to include the header file since we want
// to use the types polar_pos_2d_t, cartesian_pos_2d_t,
// etc and the trigonometry functions implemented in
// another source file.
#include "ExtremeC_examples_chapter3_2_geometry.h"

cartesian_pos_2d_t convert_to_2d_cartesian_pos(
        const polar_pos_2d_t* polar_pos) {
  cartesian_pos_2d_t result;
  result.x = polar_pos->length * cos_deg(polar_pos->theta);
  result.y = polar_pos->length * sin_deg(polar_pos->theta);
  return result;
}


polar_pos_2d_t convert_to_2d_polar_pos(
        const cartesian_pos_2d_t* cartesian_pos) {
  polar_pos_2d_t result;
  result.length = sqrt(cartesian_pos->x * cartesian_pos->x +
    cartesian_pos->y * cartesian_pos->y);
  result.theta =
      to_degree(atan(cartesian_pos->y / cartesian_pos->x));
  return result;
}
```

Code Box 3-5 [ExtremeC_examples_chapter3_2_2d.c]: The source file containing the definitions
of the 2D functions

And finally, the fourth file that contains the definitions of 3D Geometry functions:

```
#include <math.h>

// We need to include the header file since we want to
// use the types polar_pos_3d_t, cartesian_pos_3d_t,
// etc and the trigonometry functions implemented in
// another source file.
#include "ExtremeC_examples_chapter3_2_geometry.h"

cartesian_pos_3d_t convert_to_3d_cartesian_pos(
        const polar_pos_3d_t* polar_pos) {
  cartesian_pos_3d_t result;
  result.x = polar_pos->length *
      sin_deg(polar_pos->theta) * cos_deg(polar_pos->phi);
  result.y = polar_pos->length *
      sin_deg(polar_pos->theta) * sin_deg(polar_pos->phi);
  result.z = polar_pos->length * cos_deg(polar_pos->theta);
  return result;
}
```

```
polar_pos_3d_t convert_to_3d_polar_pos(
        const cartesian_pos_3d_t* cartesian_pos) {
  polar_pos_3d_t result;
  result.length = sqrt(cartesian_pos->x * cartesian_pos->x +
    cartesian_pos->y * cartesian_pos->y +
    cartesian_pos->z * cartesian_pos->z);
  result.theta =
      to_degree(acos(cartesian_pos->z / result.length));
  result.phi =
      to_degree(atan(cartesian_pos->y / cartesian_pos->x));
  return result;
}
```

Code Box 3-6 [ExtremeC_examples_chapter3_2_3d.c]: The source file containing
the definitions of the 3D functions

Now we'll create the static library file. To do this, firstly we need to compile the preceding sources to their corresponding relocatable object files. You need to note that we cannot link these object files to create an executable file as there is no main function in any of the preceding source files. Therefore, we can either keep them as relocatable object files or archive them to form a static library. We have another option to create a shared object file out of them, but we'll wait until the next section to look at this.

In this section, we have chosen to archive them in order to create a static library file. The following commands will do the compilation on a Linux system:

```
$ gcc -c ExtremeC_examples_chapter3_2_trigon.c -o trigon.o
$ gcc -c ExtremeC_examples_chapter3_2_2d.c -o 2d.o
$ gcc -c ExtremeC_examples_chapter3_2_3d.c -o 3d.o
$
```

Shell Box 3-10: Compiling source files to their corresponding relocatable object files

When it comes to archiving these object files into a static library file, we need to run the following command:

```
$ ar crs libgeometry.a trigon.o 2d.o 3d.o
$ mkdir -p /opt/geometry
$ mv libgeometry.a /opt/geometry
$
```

Shell Box 3-11: Creating the static library file out of the relocatable object files

As we can see, the file `libgeometry.a` has been created. As you see, we have moved the library file to the `/opt/geometry` directory to be easily locatable by any other program. Again, using the `ar` command, and via passing the `t` option, we can see the content of the archive file:

```
$ ar t /opt/geometry/libgeometry.a
trigon.o
2d.o
3d.o
$
```

Shell Box 3-12: Listing the content of the static library file

As is clear from the preceding shell box, the static library file contains three relocatable object files as we intended. The next step is to use the static library file.

Now that we have created a static library for our geometry example, *example 3.2*, we are going to use it in a new application. When using a C library, we need to have access to the declarations that are exposed by the library together with its static library file. The declarations are considered as the *public interface* of the library, or more commonly, the API of the library.

We need declarations in the compile stage, when the compiler needs to know about the existence of types, function signatures, and so on. Header files serve this purpose. Other details such as type sizes and function addresses are needed at later stages; linking and loading.

As we said before, we usually find a C API (an API exposed by a C library) as a group of header files. Therefore, the header file from *example 3.2*, and the created static library file `libgeometry.a`, are enough for us to write a new program that uses our geometry library.

When it comes to using the static library, we need to write a new source file that includes the library's API and make use of its functions. We write the new code as a new example, *example 3.3*. The following code is the source that we have written for *example 3.3*:

```c
#include <stdio.h>

#include "ExtremeC_examples_chapter3_2_geometry.h"

int main(int argc, char** argv) {
  cartesian_pos_2d_t cartesian_pos;
  cartesian_pos.x = 100;
  cartesian_pos.y = 200;
  polar_pos_2d_t polar_pos =
```

```
        convert_to_2d_polar_pos(&cartesian_pos);
    printf("Polar Position: Length: %f, Theta: %f (deg)\n",
        polar_pos.length, polar_pos.theta);
    return 0;
}
```

Code Box 3-7 [ExtremeC_examples_chapter3_3.c]: The main function testing some of the geometry functions

As you can see, *example 3.3* has included the header file from *example 3.2*. It has done this because it needs the declarations of the functions that it is going to use.

We now need to compile the preceding source file to create its corresponding relocatable object file in a Linux system:

```
$ gcc -c ExtremeC_examples_chapter3_3.c -o main.o
$
```

Shell Box 3-13: Compiling example 3.3

After we have done that, we need to link it with the static library that we created for *example 3.2*. In this case, we assume that the file `libgeometry.a` is located in the `/opt/geometry` directory, as we had in *Shell Box 3-11*. The following command will complete the build by performing the linking step and creating the executable object file, *ex3_3.out*:

```
$ gcc main.o -L/opt/geometry -lgeometry -lm -o ex3_3.out
$
```

Shell Box 3-14: Linking with the static library created as part of example 3.2

To explain the preceding command, we are going to explain each passing option separately:

- `-L/opt/geometry` tells `gcc` to consider the directory `/opt/geometry` as one of the various locations in which static and shared libraries could be found. There are well-known paths like `/usr/lib` or `/usr/local/lib` in which the linker searches for library files by default. If you do not specify the `-L` option, the linker only searches its default paths.

- `-lgeometry` tells `gcc` to look for the file `libgeometry.a` or `libgeometry.so`. A file ending with `.so` is a shared object file, which we explain in the next section. Note the convention used. If you pass the option `-lxyz` for instance, the linker will search for the file `libxyz.a` or `libxyz.so` in the default and specified directories. If the file is not found, the linker stops and generates an error.

- `-lm` tells `gcc` to look for another library named `libm.a` or `libm.so`. This library keeps the definitions of mathematical functions in *glibc*. We need it for the `cos`, `sin`, and `acos` functions. Note that we are building *example 3.3* on a Linux machine, which uses *glibc* as its default C library's implementation. In macOS and possibly some other Unix-like systems, you don't need to specify this option.

- `-o ex3_3.out` tells `gcc` that the output executable file should be named `ex3_3.out`.

After running the preceding command, if everything goes smoothly, you will have an executable binary file that contains all the relocatable object files found in the static library `libgeometry.a` plus `main.o`.

Note that there will not be any dependency on the existence of the static library file after linking, as everything is *embedded* inside the executable file itself. In other words, the final executable file can be run on its own without needing the static library to be present.

However, executable files produced from the linkage of many static libraries usually have huge sizes. The more static libraries and the more relocatable object files inside them, the bigger the size of the final executable. Sometimes it can go up to several hundred megabytes or even a few gigabytes.

It is a trade-off between the size of the binary and the dependencies it might have. You can have a smaller binary, but by using shared libraries. It means that the final binary is not complete and cannot be run if the external shared libraries do not exist or cannot be found. We talk more about this in the upcoming sections.

In this section, we described what static libraries are and how they should be created and used. We also demonstrated how another program can use the exposed API and get linked to an existing static library. In the following section, we are going to talk about dynamic libraries and how to produce a shared object file (dynamic library) from sources in *example 3.2*, instead of using a static library.

Dynamic libraries

Dynamic libraries, or shared libraries, are another way to produce libraries for reuse. As their name implies, unlike the static libraries, dynamic libraries are not part of the final executable itself. Instead, they should be loaded and brought in while loading a process for execution.

Since static libraries are part of the executable, the linker puts everything found in the given relocatable files into the final executable file. In other words, the linker detects the undefined symbols, and required definitions, and tries to find them in the given relocatable object files, then puts them all in the output executable file.

The final product is only produced when every undefined symbol is found. From a unique perspective, we detect all dependencies and resolve them at linking time. Regarding dynamic libraries, it is possible to have undefined symbols that are not resolved at linking time. These symbols are searched for when the executable product is about to be loaded and begin the execution.

In other words, a different kind of linking step is needed when you have undefined dynamic symbols. A *dynamic linker*, or simply the *loader*, usually does the linking while loading an executable file and preparing it to be run as a process.

Since the undefined dynamic symbols are not found in the executable file, they should be found somewhere else. These symbols should be loaded from shared object files. These files are sister files to static library files. While the static library files have a .a extension in their names, the shared object files carry the .so extension in most Unix-like systems. In macOS, they have the .dylib extension.

When loading a process and about to be launched, a shared object file will be loaded and mapped to a memory region accessible by the process. This procedure is done by a dynamic linker (or loader), which loads and executes an executable file.

Like we said in the section dedicated to executable object files, both ELF executable and shared object files have segments in their ELF structure. Each segment has zero or more sections in them. There are two main differences between an ELF executable object file and an ELF shared object file. Firstly, the symbols have relative absolute addresses that allow them to be loaded as part of many processes at the same time.

This means that while the address of each instruction is different in any process, the distance between two instructions remains fixed. In other words, the addresses are fixed relative to an offset. This is because the relocatable object files are *position independent*. We talk more about this in the last section of this chapter.

For instance, if two instructions are located at addresses 100 and 200 in a process, in another process they may be at 140 and 240, and in another one they could be at 323 and 423. The related addresses are absolute, but the actual addresses can change. These two instructions will always be 100 addresses apart from each other.

The second difference is that some segments related to loading an ELF executable object file are not present in shared object files. This effectively means that shared object files cannot be executed.

Before giving more details on how a shared object is accessed from different processes, we need to show an example of how they are created and used. Therefore, we are going to create dynamic libraries for the same geometry library, *example 3.2*, that we worked on in the previous section.

In the previous section we created a static library for the geometry library. In this section, we want to compile the sources again in order to create a shared object file out of them. The following commands show you how to compile the three sources into their corresponding relocatable object files, with just one difference in comparison to what we did for *example 3.2*. In the following commands, note the -fPIC option that is passed to gcc:

```
$ gcc -c ExtremeC_examples_chapter3_2_2d.c -fPIC -o 2d.o
$ gcc -c ExtremeC_examples_chapter3_2_3d.c -fPIC -o 3d.o
$ gcc -c ExtremeC_examples_chapter3_2_trigon.c -fPIC -o trigon.o
$
```

Shell Box 3-15: Compiling the sources of example 3.2 to corresponding position-independent relocatable object files

Looking at the commands, you can see that we have passed an extra option,-fPIC, to gcc while compiling the sources. This option is *mandatory* if you are going to create a shared object file out of some relocatable object files. **PIC** stands for **position independent code**. As we explained before, if a relocatable object file is position independent, it simply means that the instructions within it don't have fixed addresses. Instead, they have relative addresses; hence they can obtain different addresses in different processes. This is a requirement because of the way we use shared object files.

There is no guarantee that the loader program will load a shared object file at the same address in different processes. In fact, the loader creates memory mappings to the shared object files, and the address ranges for those mappings can be different. If the instruction addresses were absolute, we couldn't load the same shared object file in various processes, and in various memory regions, at the same time.

Note:
For more detailed information on how the dynamic loading of programs and shared object files works, you can see the following resources:

- https://software.intel.com/sites/default/files/m/a/1/e/dsohowto.pdf

- https://www.technovelty.org/linux/plt-and-got-the-key-to-code-sharing-and-dynamic-libraries.html

To create shared object files, you need to use the compiler, in this case, gcc, again. Unlike a static library file, which is a simple archive, a shared object file is an object file itself. Therefore, they should be created by the same linker program, for instance ld, that we used to produce the relocatable object files.

We know that, on most Unix-like systems, ld does that. However, it is strongly recommended not to use ld directly for linking object files for the reasons we explained in the previous chapter.

The following command shows how you should create a shared object file out of a number of relocatable object files that have been compiled using the -fPIC option:

```
$ gcc -shared 2d.o 3d.o trigon.o -o libgeometry.so
$ mkdir -p /opt/geometry
$ mv libgeometry.so /opt/geometry
$
```

Shell Box 3-16: Creating a shared object file out of the relocatable object files

As you can see in the first command, we passed the -shared option, to ask gcc to create a shared object file out of the relocatable object files. The result is a shared object file named libgeometry.so. We have moved the shared object file to /opt/geometry to make it easily available to other programs willing to use it. The next step is to compile and link *example 3.3* again.

Previously, we compiled and linked *example 3.3* with the created static library file, libgeometry.a. Here, we are going to do the same, but instead, link it with libgeometry.so, a dynamic library.

While everything seems to be the same, especially the commands, they are in fact different. This time, we are going to link *example 3.3* with libgeometry.so instead of libgeometry.a, and more than that, the dynamic library won't get embedded into the final executable, instead it will load the library upon execution. While practicing this, make sure that you have removed the static library file, libgeometry.a, from /opt/geometry before linking *example 3.3* again:

```
$ rm -fv /opt/geometry/libgeometry.a
$ gcc -c ExtremeC_examples_chapter3_3.c -o main.o
$ gcc main.o -L/opt/geometry-lgeometry -lm -o ex3_3.out
$
```

Shell Box 3-17: Linking example 3.3 against the built shared object file

As we explained before, the option -lgeometry tells the compiler to find and use a library, either static or shared, to link it with the rest of the object files. Since we have removed the static library file, the shared object file is picked up. If both the static library and shared object files exist for a defined library, then gcc prefers to pick the shared object file and link it with the program.

If you now try to run the executable file ex3_3.out, you will most probably face the following error:

```
$ ./ex3_3.out
./ex3_3.out: error while loading shared libraries: libgeometry.so:
cannot open shared object file: No such file or directory
$
```

Shell Box 3-18: Trying to run example 3.3

We haven't seen this error so far, because we were using static linkage and a static library. But now, by introducing dynamic libraries, if we are going to run a program that has *dynamic dependencies*, we should provide the required dynamic libraries to have it run. But what has happened and why we've received the error message?

The ex3_3.out executable file depends on libgeometry.so. That's because some of the definitions it needs can only be found inside that shared object file. We should note that this is not true for the static library libgeometry.a. An executable file linked with a static library can be run on its own as a standalone executable, since it has copied everything from the static library file, and therefore, doesn't rely on its existence anymore.

This is not true for the shared object files. We received the error because the program loader (dynamic linker) could not find libgeometry.so in its default search paths. Therefore, we need to add /opt/geometry to its search paths, so that it finds the libgeometry.so file there. To do this, we will update the environment variable LD_LIBRARY_PATH to point to the current directory.

The loader will check the value of this environment variable, and it will search the specified paths for the required shared libraries. Note that more than one path can be specified in this environment variable (using the separator colon :).

```
$ export LD_LIBRARY_PATH=/opt/geometry
$ ./ex3_3.out
Polar Position: Length: 223.606798, Theta: 63.434949 (deg)
$
```

Shell Box 3-19: Running example 3.3 by specifying LD_LIBRARY_PATH

This time, the program has successfully been run! This means that the program loader has found the shared object file and the dynamic linker has loaded the required symbols from it successfully.

Note that, in the preceding shell box, we used the `export` command to change the `LD_LIBRARY_PATH`. However, it is common to set the environment variable together with the execution command. You can see this in the following shell box. The result would be the same for both usages:

```
$ LD_LIBRARY_PATH=/opt/geometry ./ex3_3.out
Polar Position: Length: 223.606798, Theta: 63.434949 (deg)
$
```

Shell Box 3-20: Running example 3.3 by specifying LD_LIBRARY_PATH as part of the same command

By linking an executable with several shared object files, as we did before, we tell the system that this executable file needs a number of shared libraries to be found and loaded at runtime. Therefore, before running the executable, the loader searches for those shared object files automatically, and the required symbols are mapped to the proper addresses that are accessible by the process. Only then can the processor begin the execution.

Manual loading of shared libraries

Shared object files can also be loaded and used in a different way, in which they are not loaded *automatically* by the loader program (dynamic linker). Instead, the programmer will use a set of functions to load a shared object file *manually* before using some symbols (functions) that can be found inside that shared library. There are applications for this manual loading mechanism, and we'll talk about them once we've discussed the example we'll look at in this section.

Example 3.4 demonstrates how to load a shared object file lazily, or manually, without having it in the linking step. This example borrows the same logic from *example 3.3*, but instead, it loads the shared object file `libgeometry.so` manually inside the program.

Before going through *example 3.4*, we need to produce `libgeometry.so` a bit differently in order to make *example 3.4* work. To do this, we have to use the following command in Linux:

```
$ gcc -shared 2d.o 3d.o trigon.o -lm -o libgeometry.so
$
```

Shell Box 3-21: Linking the geometry shared object file against the standard math library

Looking at the preceding command, you can see a new option, -lm, which tells the linker to link the shared object file against the standard math library, libm.so. That is done because when we load libgeometry.so manually, its dependencies should, somehow, be loaded automatically. If they're not, then we will get errors about the symbols that are required by libgeometry.so itself, such as cos or sqrt. Note that we won't link the final executable file with the math standard library, and it will be resolved automatically by the loader when loading libgeometry.so.

Now that we have a linked shared object file, we can proceed to *example 3.4*:

```
#include <stdio.h>
#include <stdlib.h>
#include <dlfcn.h>

#include "ExtremeC_examples_chapter3_2_geometry.h"

polar_pos_2d_t (*func_ptr)(cartesian_pos_2d_t*);

int main(int argc, char** argv) {

  void* handle = dlopen ("/opt/geometry/libgeometry.so", RTLD_
LAZY);
  if (!handle) {
    fprintf(stderr, "%s\n", dlerror());
    exit(1);
  }

  func_ptr = dlsym(handle, "convert_to_2d_polar_pos");
  if (!func_ptr) {
    fprintf(stderr, "%s\n", dlerror());
    exit(1);
  }

  cartesian_pos_2d_t cartesian_pos;
  cartesian_pos.x = 100;
  cartesian_pos.y = 200;
  polar_pos_2d_t polar_pos = func_ptr(&cartesian_pos);
  printf("Polar Position: Length: %f, Theta: %f (deg)\n",
    polar_pos.length, polar_pos.theta);
  return 0;
}
```

Code Box 3-8 [ExtremeC_examples_chapter3_4.c]: Example 3.4 loading the geometry shared object file manually

Looking at the preceding code, you can see how we have used the functions `dlopen` and `dlsym` to load the shared object file and then find the symbol `convert_to_2d_polar_pos` in it. The function `dlsym` returns a function pointer, which can be used to invoke the target function.

It is worth noting that the preceding code searches for the shared object file in `/opt/geometry`, and if there is no such object file, then an error message is shown. Note that in macOS, the shared object files end in the `.dylib` extension. Therefore, the preceding code should be modified in order to load the file with the correct extension.

The following command compiles the preceding code and runs the executable file:

```
$ gcc ExtremeC_examples_chapter3_4.c -ldl -o ex3_4.out
$ ./ex3_4.out
Polar Position: Length: 223.606798, Theta: 63.434949 (deg)
$
```

Shell Box 3-22: Running example 3.4

As you can see, we did not link the program with the file `libgeometry.so`. We didn't do this because we want to instead load it manually when it is needed. This method is often referred to as the *lazy loading* of shared object files. Yet, despite the name, in certain scenarios, lazy loading the shared object files can be really useful.

One such case is when you have different shared object files for different implementations or versions of the same library. Lazy loading gives you increased freedom to load the desired shared objects according to your own logic and when it is needed, instead of having them automatically loaded at load time, where you have less control over them.

Summary

This chapter mainly talked about various types of object files, as products of a C/C++ project after building. As part of this chapter, we covered the following points:

- We discussed the API and ABI, along with their differences.

- We went through various object file formats and looked at a brief history of them. They all share the same ancestor, but they have changed in their specific paths to become what they are today.

- We talked about relocatable object files and their internal structure regarding ELF relocatable object files.

- We discussed executable object files and the differences between them and relocatable object files. We also took a look at an ELF executable object file.

- We showed static and dynamic symbol tables and how their content can be read using some command-line tools.

- We discussed static linking and dynamic linking and how various symbol tables are looked up in order to produce the final binary or execute a program.

- We discussed static library files and the fact that they are just archive files that contain a number of relocatable object files.

- Shared object files (dynamic libraries) were discussed and we demonstrated how they can be made out of a number of relocatable object files.

- We explained what position-independent code is and why the relocatable object files participating in the creation of a shared library must be position-independent.

In the following chapter, we will go through the memory structure of a process; another key topic in C/C++ programming. The various memory segments will be described as part of the next chapter and we'll see how we can write code that has no memory issues in it.

Chapter 04

Process Memory Structure

In this chapter, we are going to talk about memory and its structure within a process. For a C programmer, memory management is always a crucial topic, and applying its best practices requires a basic knowledge about memory structure. In fact, this is not limited to C. In many programming languages such as C++ or Java, you need to have a fundamental understanding of memory and the way it works; otherwise, you face some serious issues that cannot be easily traced and fixed.

You might know that memory management is fully manual in C, and more than that, the programmer is the sole responsible person who allocates memory regions and deallocates them once they're no longer needed.

Memory management is different in high-level programming languages such as Java or C#, and it is done partly by the programmer and partly by the underlying language platform, such as **Java Virtual Machine (JVM)** in the case of using Java. In these languages, the programmer only issues memory allocations, but they are not responsible for the deallocations. A component called the *garbage collector* does the deallocation and frees up the allocated memory automatically.

Since there is no such garbage collector in C and C++, having some dedicated chapters for covering the concepts and issues regarding memory management is essential. That's why we have dedicated this chapter and the next to memory-related concepts, and these chapters together should give you a basic understanding of how memory works in C/C++.

Throughout this chapter:

- We start by looking at the typical memory structure of a process. This will help us to discover the anatomy of a process and the way it interacts with the memory.

- We discuss static and dynamic memory layouts.

- We introduce the segments found in the aforementioned memory layouts. We see that some of them reside in the executable object file and the rest are created while the process is loading.

- We introduce the probing tools and commands which can help us to detect the segments and see their content, both inside an object file and deep within a running process.

As part of this chapter, we get to know two segments called *Stack* and *Heap*. They are part of the dynamic memory layout of a process and all the allocations and deallocations happen in these segments. In the following chapter, we will discuss Stack and Heap segments in a greater detail because in fact, they are the segments that a programmer interacts with the most.

Let's start this chapter by talking about the *process memory layout*. This will give you an overall idea about how the memory of a running process is segmented, and what each segment is used for.

Process memory layout

Whenever you run an executable file, the operating system creates a new process. A process is a live and running program that is loaded into the memory and has a unique **Process Identifier** (**PID**). The operating system is the sole responsible entity for spawning and loading new processes.

A process remains running until it either exits normally, or the process is given a signal, such as SIGTERM, SIGINT, or SIGKILL, which eventually makes it exit. The SIGTERM and SIGINT signals can be ignored, but SIGKILL will kill the process immediately and forcefully.

Note:

The signals mentioned in the preceding section are explained as follows:

SIGTERM: This is the termination signal. It allows the process to clean up.

SIGINT: This is the interrupt signal usually sent to the foreground process by pressing *Ctrl* + *C*.

SIGKILL: This is the kill signal and it closes the process forcefully without letting it clean up.

When creating a process, one of the first things that operating systems do is allocate a portion of memory dedicated to the process and then apply a predefined memory layout. This predefined memory layout is more or less the same in different operating systems, especially in Unix-like operating systems.

In this chapter, we're going to explore the structure of this memory layout, and a number of important and useful terms are introduced.

The memory layout of an ordinary process is divided into multiple parts. Each part is called a *segment*. Each segment is a region of memory which has a definite task and it is supposed to store a specific type of data. You can see the following list of segments being part of the memory layout of a running process:

- Uninitialized data segment or **Block Started by Symbol** (**BSS**) segment
- Data segment
- Text segment or Code segment
- Stack segment
- Heap segment

In the following sections, we will study each of these segments individually, and we discuss the way they contribute to the execution of a program. In the next chapter, we will focus on Stack and Heap segments and we'll discuss them thoroughly. As part of our quest, let's introduce some tools that help us inspect the memory before going into the specifics of the above segments.

Discovering memory structure

Unix-like operating systems provide a set of tools for inspecting the memory segments of a process. You learn in this section that some of these segments reside within the executable object file, and other segments are created dynamically at runtime, when the process is spawned.

As you should already know from the two previous chapters, an executable object file and a process are not the same thing, therefore it is expected to have different tools for inspecting each of them.

From the previous chapters, we know that an executable object file contains the machine instructions, and it is produced by the compiler. But a process is a running program spawned by executing an executable object file, consuming a region of the main memory, and the CPU is constantly fetching and executing its instructions.

A process is a living entity that is being executed inside the operating system while the executable object file is just a file containing a premade initial layout acting as a basis for spawning future processes. It is true that in the memory layout of a running process, some segments come directly from the base executable object file, and the rest are built dynamically at runtime while the process is being loaded. The former layout is called the **static memory layout**, and the latter is called the **dynamic memory layout**.

Static and dynamic memory layouts both have a predetermined set of segments. The content of the static memory layout is prewritten into the executable object file by the compiler, when compiling the source code. On the other hand, the content of the dynamic memory layout is written by the process instructions allocating memory for variables and arrays, and modifying them according to the program's logic.

With all that said, we can guess the content of the static memory layout either by just looking at the source code or the compiled object file. But this is not that easy regarding the dynamic memory layout as it cannot be determined without running the program. In addition, different runs of the same executable file can lead to different content in the dynamic memory layout. In other words, the dynamic content of a process is unique to that process and it should be investigated while the process is still running.

Let's begin with inspecting the static memory layout of a process.

Probing static memory layout

The tools used for inspecting the static memory layout usually work on the object files. To get some initial insight, we'll start with an example, *example 4.1*, which is a minimal C program that doesn't have any variable or logic as part of it:

```
int main(int argc, char** argv) {
  return 0;
}
```

Code Box 4-1 [ExtremeC_examples_chapter4_1.c]: A minimal C program

First, we need to compile the preceding program. We compile it in Linux using `gcc`:

```
$ gcc ExtremeC_examples_chapter4_1.c -o ex4_1-linux.out
$
```

Shell Box 4-1: Compiling example 4.1 using gcc in Linux

After a successful compilation and having the final executable binary linked, we get an executable object file named `ex4_1-linux.out`. This file contains a predetermined static memory layout that is specific to the Linux operating system, and it will exist in all future processes spawned based on this executable file.

The `size` command is the first tool that we want to introduce. It can be used to print the static memory layout of an executable object file.

You can see the usage of the `size` command in order to see the various segments found as part of the static memory layout as follows:

```
$ size ex4_1-linux.out
   text     data      bss      dec      hex    filename
   1099      544        8     1651      673    ex4_1-linux.out
$
```

Shell Box 4-2: Using the size command to see the static segments of ex4_1-linux.out

As you see, we have Text, Data, and BSS segments as part of the static layout. The shown sizes are in bytes.

Now, let's compile the same code, *example 4.1*, in a different operating system. We have chosen macOS and we are going to use the `clang` compiler:

```
$ clang ExtremeC_examples_chapter4_1.c -o ex4_1-macos.out
$
```

Shell Box 4-3: Compiling example 4.1 using clang in macOS

Since macOS is a POSIX-compliant operating system just like Linux, and the `size` command is specified to be part of the POSIX utility programs, macOS should also have the `size` command. Therefore, we can use the same command to see the static memory segments of `ex4_1-macos.out`:

```
$ size ex4_1-macos.out
__TEXT   __DATA   __OBJC   others        dec           hex
4096     0        0        4294971392    4294975488    100002000
$ size -m ex4_1-macos.out
Segment __PAGEZERO: 4294967296
Segment __TEXT: 4096
    Section __text: 22
    Section __unwind_info: 72
    total 94
Segment __LINKEDIT: 4096
total 4294975488
$
```

Shell Box 4-4: Using the size command to see the static segments of ex4_1-macos.out

In the preceding shell box, we have run the `size` command twice; the second run gives us more details about the found memory segments. You might have noticed that we have Text and Data segments in macOS, just like Linux, but there is no BSS segment. Note that the BSS segment also exists in macOS, but it is not shown in the `size` output. Since the BSS segment contains uninitialized global variables, there is no need to allocate some bytes as part of the object file and it is enough to know how many bytes are required for storing those global variables.

In the preceding shell boxes, there is an interesting point to note. The size of the Text segment is 1,099 bytes in Linux while it is 4 KB in macOS. It can also be seen that the Data segment for a minimal C program has a non-zero size in Linux, but it is empty in macOS. It is apparent that the low-level memory details are different on various platforms.

Despite these little differences between Linux and macOS, we can see that both platforms have the Text, Data, and BSS segments as part of their static layout. From now on, we gradually explain what each of these segments are used for. In the upcoming sections, we'll discuss each segment separately and we give an example slightly different from *example 4.1* for each, in order to see how differently each segment responds to the minor changes in the code.

BSS segment

We start with the BSS segment. **BSS** stands for **Block Started by Symbol**. Historically, the name was used to denote reserved regions for uninitialized words. Basically, that's the purpose that we use the BSS segment for; either uninitialized global variables or global variables set to zero.

Let's expand *example 4.1* by adding a few uninitialized global variables. You see that uninitialized global variables will contribute to the BSS segment. The following code box demonstrates *example 4.2*:

```
int global_var1;
int global_var2;
int global_var3 = 0;

int main(int argc, char** argv) {
  return 0;
}
```

Code Box 4-2 [ExtremeC_examples_chapter4_2.c]: A minimal C program with a few global variables either uninitialized or set to zero

The integers `global_var1`, `global_var2`, and `global_var3` are global variables which are uninitialized. For observing the changes made to the resulting executable object file in Linux, in comparison to *example 4.1*, we again run the `size` command:

```
$ gcc ExtremeC_examples_chapter4_2.c -o ex4_2-linux.out
$ size ex4_2-linux.out
   text    data    bss     dec     hex    filename
   1099     544     16    1659     67b    ex4_2-linux.out
$
```

Shell Box 4-5: Using the size command to see the static segments of ex4_2-linux.out

If you compare the preceding output with a similar output from *example 4.1*, you will notice that the size of the BSS segment has changed. In other words, declaring global variables that are *not* initialized or set to zero will add up to the BSS segment. These special global variables are part of the static layout and they become preallocated when a process is loading, and they never get deallocated until the process is alive. In other words, they have a static lifetime.

Note:

Because of design concerns, we usually prefer to use local variables in our algorithms. Having too many global variables can increase the binary size. In addition, keeping sensitive data in the global scope, it can introduce security concerns. Concurrency issues, especially data races, namespace pollution, unknown ownership, and having too many variables in the global scope, are some of the complications that global variables introduce.

Let's compile *example 4.2* in macOS and have a look at the output of the `size` command:

```
$ clang ExtremeC_examples_chapter4_2.c -o ex4_2-macos.out
$ size ex4_2-macos.out
__TEXT   __DATA   __OBJC   others        dec          hex
4096     4096         0    4294971392    4294979584   100003000
```

```
$ size -m ex4_2-macos.out
Segment __PAGEZERO: 4294967296
Segment __TEXT: 4096
    Section __text: 22
    Section __unwind_info: 72
    total 94
Segment __DATA: 4096
    Section __common: 12
    total 12
Segment __LINKEDIT: 4096
total 4294979584
$
```

Shell Box 4-6: Using the size command to see the static segments of ex4_2-macos.out

And again, it is different from Linux. In Linux, we had preallocated 8 bytes for the BSS segment, when we had no global variables. In *example 4.2*, we added three new uninitialized global variables whose sizes sum up to 12 bytes, and the Linux C compiler expanded the BSS segment by 8 bytes. But in macOS, we still have no BSS segment as part of the size's output, but the compiler has expanded the data segment from 0 bytes to 4KB, which is the default page size in macOS. This means that clang has allocated a new memory page for the data segment inside the layout. Again, this simply shows how much the details of the memory layout can be different in various platforms.

Note:
While allocating the memory, it doesn't matter how many bytes a program needs to allocate. The *allocator* always acquires memory in terms of *memory pages* until the total allocated size covers the program's need. More information about the Linux memory allocator can be found here: https://www.kernel.org/doc/gorman/html/understand/understand009.html.

In *Shell Box 4-6*, we have a section named __common, inside the _DATA segment, which is 12 bytes, and it is in fact referring to the BSS segment that is not shown as BSS in the size's output. It refers to 3 uninitialized global integer variables or 12 bytes (each integer being 4 bytes). It's worth taking note that uninitialized global variables are set to *zero* by default. There is no other value that could be imagined for uninitialized variables.

Let's now talk about the next segment in the static memory layout; the Data segment.

Data segment

In order to show what type of variables are stored in the Data segment, we are going to declare more global variables, but this time we initialize them with non-zero values. The following example, *example 4.3*, expands *example 4.2* and adds two new initialized global variables:

```c
int global_var1;
int global_var2;
int global_var3 = 0;

double global_var4 = 4.5;
char global_var5 = 'A';

int main(int argc, char** argv) {
  return 0;
}
```

Code Box 4-3 [ExtremeC_examples_chapter4_3.c]: A minimal C program with both initialized and uninitialized global variables

The following shell box shows the output of the `size` command, in Linux, and for *example 4.3*:

```
$ gcc ExtremeC_examples_chapter4_3.c -o ex4_3-linux.out
$ size ex4_3-linux.out
   text      data      bss      dec      hex filename
   1099       553       20     1672      688 ex4_3-linux.out
$
```

Shell Box 4-7: Using the size command to see the static segments of ex4_3-linux.out

We know that the Data segment is used to store the initialized global variables set to a non-zero value. If you compare the output of the `size` command for *examples 4.2* and *4.3*, you can easily see that the Data segment is increased by 9 bytes, which is the sum of the sizes of the two newly added global variables (one 8-byte `double` and one 1-byte `char`).

Let's look at the changes in macOS:

```
$ clang ExtremeC_examples_chapter4_3.c -o ex4_3-macos.out
```

```
$ size ex4_3-macos.out
__TEXT __DATA __OBJC  others         dec          hex
4096    4096     0    4294971392   4294979584   100003000
$ size -m ex4_3-macos.out
Segment __PAGEZERO: 4294967296
Segment __TEXT: 4096
    Section __text: 22
    Section __unwind_info: 72
    total 94
Segment __DATA: 4096
    Section __data: 9
    Section __common: 12
    total 21
Segment __LINKEDIT: 4096
total 4294979584
$
```

Shell Box 4-8: Using the size command to see the static segments of ex4_3-macos.out

In the first run, we see no changes since the size of all global variables summed together is still way below 4KB. But in the second run, we see a new section as part of the _DATA segment; the __data section. The memory allocated for this section is 9 bytes, and it is in accordance with the size of the newly introduced initialized global variables. And still, we have 12 bytes for uninitialized global variables as we had in *example 4.2*, and in macOS.

On a further note, the size command only shows the size of the segments, but not their contents. There are other commands, specific to each operating system, that can be used to inspect the content of segments found in an object file. For instance, in Linux, you have readelf and objdump commands in order to see the content of *ELF* files. These tools can also be used to probe the static memory layout inside the object files. As part of two previous chapters we explored some of these commands.

Other than global variables, we can have some static variables declared inside a function. These variables retain their values while calling the same function multiple times. These variables can be stored either in the Data segment or the BSS segment depending on the platform and whether they are initialized or not. The following code box demonstrates how to declare some static variables within a function:

```
void func() {
    static int i;
```

```
static int j = 1;
    ...
}
```

Code Box 4-4: Declaration of two static variables, one initialized and the other one uninitialized

As you see in *Code Box 4-4*, the i and j variables are static. The i variable is uninitialized and the j variable is initialized with value 1. It doesn't matter how many times you enter and leave the func function, these variables keep their most recent values.

To elaborate more on how this is done, at runtime, the func function has access to these variables located in either the Data segment or the BSS segment, which has a static lifetime. That's basically why these variables are called *static*. We know that the j variable is located in the Data segment simply because it has an initial value, and the i variable is supposed to be inside the BSS segment since it is not initialized.

Now, we want to introduce the second command to examine the content of the BSS segment. In Linux, the objdump command can be used to print out the content of memory segments found in an object file. This corresponding command in macOS is gobjdump which should be installed first.

As part of *example 4.4*, we try to examine the resulting executable object file to find the data written to the Data segment as some global variables. The following code box shows the code for *example 4.4*:

```
int     x = 33;          // 0x00000021
int     y = 0x12153467;
char z[6] = "ABCDE";

int main(int argc, char**argv) {
    return 0;
}
```

Code Box 4-5 [ExtremeC_examples_chapter4_4.c]: Some initialized global variables which should be written to the Data segment

The preceding code is easy to follow. It just declares three global variables with some initial values. After compilation, we need to dump the content of the Data segment in order to find the written values.

The following commands will demonstrate how to compile and use objdump to see the content of the Data segment:

```
$ gcc ExtremeC_examples_chapter4_4.c -o ex4_4.out
```

```
$ objdump -s -j .data ex4_4.out

a.out:      file format elf64-x86-64

Contents of section .data:
 601020 00000000 00000000 00000000 00000000   ..............
 601030 21000000 67341512 41424344 4500       !....4..ABCDE.
$
```

Shell Box 4-9: Using the objdump command to see the content of the Data segment

Let's explain how the preceding output, and especially the contents of the section .data, should be read. The first column on the left is the address column. The next four columns are the contents, and each of them is showing 4 bytes of data. So, in each row, we have the contents of 16 bytes. The last column on the right shows the ASCII representation of the same bytes shown in the middle columns. A dot character means that the character cannot be shown using alphanumerical characters. Note that the option -s tells objdump to show the full content of the chosen section and the option -j .data tells it to show the content of the section .data.

The first line is 16 bytes filled by zeros. There is no variable stored here, so nothing special for us. The second line shows the contents of the Data segment starting with the address 0x601030. The first 4 bytes is the value stored in the x variable found in *example 4.4*. The next 4 bytes also contain the value for the y variable. The final 6 bytes are the characters inside the z array. The contents of z can be clearly seen in the last column.

If you pay enough attention to the content shown in *Shell Box 4-9*, you see that despite the fact that we write 33, in decimal base, as 0x00000021, in hexadecimal base it is stored differently in the segment. It is stored as 0x21000000. This is also true for the content of the y variable. We have written it as 0x12153467, but it is stored differently as 0x67341512. It seems that the order of bytes is reversed.

The effect explained is because of the *endianness* concept. Generally, we have two different types of endianness, *big-endian* and *little-endian*. The value 0x12153467 is the big-endian representation for the number 0x12153467, as the biggest byte, 0x12, comes first. But the value 0x67341512 is the little-endian representation for the number 0x12153467, as the smallest byte, 0x67, comes first.

No matter what the endianness is, we always read the correct value in C. Endianness is a property of the CPU and with a different CPU you may get a different byte order in your final object files. This is one of the reasons why you cannot run an executable object file on hardware with different endianness.

It would be interesting to see the same output on a macOS machine. The following shell box demonstrates how to use the `gobjdump` command in order to see the content of the Data segment:

```
$ gcc ExtremeC_examples_chapter4_4.c -o ex4_4.out
$ gobjdump -s -j .data ex4_4.out


a.out:      file format mach-o-x86-64


Contents of section .data:
 100001000 21000000 67341512 41424344 4500        !...g4..ABCDE.
$
```

Shell Box 4-10: Using the gobjdump command in macOS to see the content of the Data segment

It should be read exactly like the Linux output found as part of *Shell Code 4-9*. As you see, in macOS, there are no 16-byte zero headers in the data segment. Endianness of the contents also shows that the binary has been compiled for a little-endian processor.

As a final note in this section, other tools like `readelf` in Linux and `dwarfdump` in macOS can be used in order to inspect the content of object files. The binary content of the object files can also be read using tools such as `hexdump`.

In the following section, we will discuss the Text segment and how it can be inspected using `objdump`.

Text segment

As we know from *Chapter 2, Compilation and Linking*, the linker writes the resulting machine-level instructions into the final executable object file. Since the Text segment, or the Code segment, contains all the machine-level instructions of a program, it should be located in the executable object file, as part of its static memory layout. These instructions are fetched by the processor and get executed at runtime when the process is running.

To dive deeper, let's have a look at the Text segment of a real executable object file. For this purpose, we propose a new example. The following code box shows *example 4.5*, and as you see, it is just an empty `main` function:

```
int main(int argc, char** argv) {
  return 0;
}
```

Code Box 4-6 [ExtremeC_examples_chapter4_5.c]: A minimal C program

We can use the `objdump` command to dump the various parts of the resulting executable object file. Note that the `objdump` command is only available in Linux, while other operating systems have their own set of commands to do the same.

The following shell box demonstrates using the `objdump` command to extract the content of various sections present in the executable object file resulting from *example 4.5*. Note that the output is shortened in order to only show the `main` function's corresponding section and its assembly instructions:

```
$ gcc ExtremeC_examples_chapter4_5.c -o ex4_5.out
$ objdump -S ex4_5.out

ex4_5.out:      file format elf64-x86-64
Disassembly of section .init:

0000000000400390 <_init>:
... truncated.
.

.

Disassembly of section .plt:

00000000004003b0 <__libc_start_main@plt-0x10>:
... truncated

00000000004004d6 <main>:
  4004d6:    55                       push    %rbp
  4004d7:    48 89 e5                 mov     %rsp,%rbp
  4004da:    b8 00 00 00 00           mov     $0x0,%eax
  4004df:    5d                       pop     %rbp
  4004e0:    c3                       retq
  4004e1:    66 2e 0f 1f 84 00 00     nopw    %cs:0x0(%rax,%rax,1)
  4004e8:    00 00 00
  4004eb:    0f 1f 44 00 00           nopl    0x0(%rax,%rax,1)


00000000004004f0 <__libc_csu_init>:
... truncated
.

.

.

0000000000400564 <_fini>:
... truncated
$
```

Shell Box 4-11: Using objdump to show the content of the section corresponding to the main function

As you see in the preceding shell box, there are various sections containing machine-level instructions: the `.text`, `.init`, and `.plt` sections and some others, which all together allow a program to become loaded and running. All of these sections are part of the same Text segment found in the static memory layout, inside the executable object file.

Our C program, written for *example 4.5*, had only one function, the `main` function, but as you see, the final executable object file has a dozen other functions.

The preceding output, seen as part of *Shell Box 4-11*, shows that the `main` function is not the first function to be called in a C program and there are logics before and after `main` that should be executed. As explained in *Chapter 2*, *Compilation and Linking*, in Linux, these functions are usually borrowed from the `glibc` library, and they are put together by the linker to form the final executable object file.

In the following section, we start to probe the dynamic memory layout of a process.

Probing dynamic memory layout

The dynamic memory layout is actually the runtime memory of a process, and it exists as long as the process is running. When you execute an executable object file, a program called *loader* takes care of the execution. It spawns a new process and it creates the initial memory layout which is supposed to be dynamic. To form this layout, the segments found in the static layout will be copied from the executable object file. More than that, two new segments will also be added to it. Only then can the process proceed and become running.

In short, we expect to have five segments in the memory layout of a running process. Three of these segments are directly copied from the static layout found in the executable object file. The two newly added segments are called Stack and Heap segments. These segments are dynamic, and they exist only when the process is running. This means that you cannot find any trace of them as part of the executable object file.

In this section, our ultimate goal is to probe the Stack and Heap segments and introduce tools and places in an operating system which can be used for this purpose. From time to time, we might refer to these segments as the process's dynamic memory layout, without considering the other three segments copied from the object file, but you should always remember that the dynamic memory of a process consists of all five segments together.

The Stack segment is the default memory region where we allocate variables from. It is a limited region in terms of size, and you cannot hold big objects in it. In contrast, the Heap segment is a bigger and adjustable region of memory which can be used to hold big objects and huge arrays. Working with the Heap segment requires its own API which we introduce as part of our discussion.

Remember, dynamic memory layout is different from *Dynamic Memory Allocation*. You should not mix these two concepts, since they are referring to two different things! As we progress, we'll learn more about different types of memory allocations, especially dynamic memory allocation.

The five segments found in the dynamic memory of a process are referring to parts of the main memory that are already *allocated*, *dedicated*, and *private* to a running process. These segments, excluding the Text segment, which is literally static and constant, are dynamic in a sense that their contents are always changing at runtime. That's due to the fact that these segments are constantly being modified by the algorithm that the process is executing.

Inspecting the dynamic memory layout of a process requires its own procedure. This implies that we need to have a running process before being able to probe its dynamic memory layout. This requires us to write examples which remain running for a fairly long time in order to keep their dynamic memory in place. Then, we can use our inspection tools to study their dynamic memory structure.

In the following section, we give an example on how to probe the structure of dynamic memory.

Memory mappings

Let's start with a simple example. *Example 4.6* will be running for an indefinite amount of time. This way, we have a process that never dies, and in the meantime, we can probe its memory structure. And of course, we can *kill* it whenever we are done with the inspection. You can find the example in the following code box:

```
#include <unistd.h> // Needed for sleep function

int main(int argc, char** argv) {
  // Infinite loop
  while (1) {
    sleep(1); // Sleep 1 second
  };
  return 0;
}
```

Code Box 4-6 [ExtremeC_examples_chapter4_6.c]: Example 4.6 used for probing dynamic memory layout

As you see, the code is just an infinite loop, which means that the process will run forever. So, we have enough time to inspect the process's memory. Let's first build it.

Note:
The unistd.h header is available only on Unix-like operating systems; to be more precise, in POSIX-compliant operating systems. This means that on Microsoft Windows, which is not POSIX-compliant, you have to include the windows.h header instead.

The following shell box shows how to compile the example in Linux:

```
$ gcc ExtremeC_examples_chapter4_6.c -o ex4_6.out
$
```

Shell Box 4-12: Compiling example 4.6 in Linux

Then, we run it as follows. In order to use the same prompt for issuing further commands while the process is running, we should start the process in the background:

```
$ ./ ex4_6.out &
[1] 402
$
```

Shell Box 4-13: Running example 4.6 in the background

The process is now running in the background. According to the output, the PID of the recently started process is 402, and we will use this PID to kill it in the future. The PID is different every time you run a program; therefore, you'll probably see a different PID on your computer. Note that whenever you run a process in the background, the shell prompt returns immediately, and you can issue further commands.

Note:
If you have the PID (Process ID) of a process, you can easily end it using the kill command. For example, if the PID is 402, the following command will work in Unix-like operating systems: kill -9 402.

The PID is the identifier we use to inspect the memory of a process. Usually, an operating system provides its own specific mechanism to query various properties of a process based on its PID. But here, we are only interested in the dynamic memory of a process and we'll use the available mechanism in Linux to find more about the dynamic memory structure of the above running process.

On a Linux machine, the information about a process can be found in files under the /proc directory. It uses a special filesystem called *procfs*. This filesystem is not an ordinary filesystem meant for keeping actual files, but it is more of a hierarchical interface to query about various properties of an individual process or the system as a whole.

Note:

procfs is not limited to Linux. It is usually part of Unix-like operating systems, but not all Unix-like operating systems use it. For example, FreeBSD uses this filesystem, but macOS doesn't.

Now, we are going to use procfs to see the memory structure of the running process. The memory of a process consists of a number of *memory mappings*. Each memory mapping represents a dedicated region of memory which is mapped to a specific file or segment as part of the process. Shortly, you'll see that both Stack and Heap segments have their own memory mappings in each process.

One of the things that you can use procfs for is to observe the current memory mappings of the process. Next, we are going to show this.

We know that the process is running with PID 402. Using the ls command, we can see the contents of the /proc/402 directory, shown as follows:

```
$ ls -l /proc/402
total of 0
dr-xr-xr-x  2 root root 0 Jul 15 22:28 attr
-rw-r--r--  1 root root 0 Jul 15 22:28 autogroup
-r--------  1 root root 0 Jul 15 22:28 auxv
-r--r--r--  1 root root 0 Jul 15 22:28 cgroup
--w-------  1 root root 0 Jul 15 22:28 clear_refs
-r--r--r--  1 root root 0 Jul 15 22:28 cmdline
-rw-r--r--  1 root root 0 Jul 15 22:28 comm
-rw-r--r--  1 root root 0 Jul 15 22:28 coredump_filter
-r--r--r--  1 root root 0 Jul 15 22:28 cpuset
lrwxrwxrwx  1 root root 0 Jul 15 22:28 cwd -> /root/codes
-r--------  1 root root 0 Jul 15 22:28 environ
lrwxrwxrwx  1 root root 0 Jul 15 22:28 exe -> /root/codes/a.out
dr-x------  2 root root 0 Jul 15 22:28 fd
dr-x------  2 root root 0 Jul 15 22:28 fdinfo
-rw-r--r--  1 root root 0 Jul 15 22:28 gid_map
```

```
-r--------  1 root root 0 Jul 15 22:28 io
-r--r--r--  1 root root 0 Jul 15 22:28 limits
...
$
```

Shell Box 4-14: Listing the content of /proc/402

As you can see, there are many files and directories under the /proc/402 directory. Each of these files and directories corresponds to a specific property of the process. For querying the memory mappings of the process, we have to see the contents of the file maps under the PID directory. We use the cat command to dump the contents of the /proc/402/maps file. It can be seen as follows:

```
$ cat /proc/402/maps
00400000-00401000 r-xp 00000000 08:01 790655          .../
extreme_c/4.6/ex4_6.out
00600000-00601000 r--p 00000000 08:01 790655          .../
extreme_c/4.6/ex4_6.out
00601000-00602000 rw-p 00001000 08:01 790655          .../
extreme_c/4.6/ex4_6.out
7f4ee16cb000-7f4ee188a000 r-xp 00000000 08:01 787362   /lib/
x86_64-linux-gnu/libc-2.23.so
7f4ee188a000-7f4ee1a8a000 ---p 001bf000 08:01 787362   /lib/
x86_64-linux-gnu/libc-2.23.so
7f4ee1a8a000-7f4ee1a8e000 r--p 001bf000 08:01 787362   /lib/
x86_64-linux-gnu/libc-2.23.so
7f4ee1a8e000-7f4ee1a90000 rw-p 001c3000 08:01 787362   /lib/
x86_64-linux-gnu/libc-2.23.so
7f4ee1a90000-7f4ee1a94000 rw-p 00000000 00:00 0
7f4ee1a94000-7f4ee1aba000 r-xp 00000000 08:01 787342   /lib/
x86_64-linux-gnu/ld-2.23.so
7f4ee1cab000-7f4ee1cae000 rw-p 00000000 00:00 0
7f4ee1cb7000-7f4ee1cb9000 rw-p 00000000 00:00 0
7f4ee1cb9000-7f4ee1cba000 r--p 00025000 08:01 787342   /lib/
x86_64-linux-gnu/ld-2.23.so
7f4ee1cba000-7f4ee1cbb000 rw-p 00026000 08:01 787342   /lib/
x86_64-linux-gnu/ld-2.23.so
7f4ee1cbb000-7f4ee1cbc000 rw-p 00000000 00:00 0
7ffe94296000-7ffe942b7000 rw-p 00000000 00:00 0        [stack]
7ffe943a0000-7ffe943a2000 r--p 00000000 00:00 0        [vvar]
```

```
7ffe943a2000-7ffe943a4000 r-xp 00000000 00:00 0            [vdso]
ffffffffff600000-ffffffffff601000 r-xp 00000000 00:00 0
[vsyscall]
$
```

Shell Box 4-15: Dumping the content of /proc/402/maps

As you see in *Shell Box 4-15*, the result consists of a number of rows. Each row represents a memory mapping that indicates a range of memory addresses (a region) that are allocated and mapped to a specific file or segment in the dynamic memory layout of the process. Each mapping has a number of fields separated by one or more spaces. Next, you can find the descriptions of these fields from left to right:

- **Address range**: These are the start and end addresses of the mapped range. You can find a file path in front of them if the region is mapped to a file. This is a smart way to map the same loaded shared object file in various processes. We have talked about this as part of *Chapter 3, Object Files*.

- **Permissions**: This indicates whether the content can be executed (x), read (r), or modified (w). The region can also be shared (s) by the other processes or be private (p) only to the owning process.

- **Offset**: If the region is mapped to a file, this is the offset from the beginning of the file. It is usually 0 if the region is not mapped to a file.

- **Device**: If the region is mapped to a file, this would be the device number (in the form of m:n), indicating a device that contains the mapped file. For example, this would be the device number of the hard disk that contains a shared object file.

- **The inode**: If the region is mapped to a file, that file should reside on a filesystem. Then, this field would be the inode number of the file in that filesystem. An *inode* is an abstract concept within filesystems such as *ext4* which are mostly used in Unix-like operating systems. Each inode can represent both files and directories. Every inode has a number that is used to access its content.

- **Pathname or description**: If the region is mapped to a file, this would be the path to that file. Otherwise, it would be left empty, or it would describe the purpose of the region. For example, [stack] indicates that the region is actually the Stack segment.

The maps file provides even more useful information regarding the dynamic memory layout of a process. We'll need a new example to properly demonstrate this.

Stack segment

First, let's talk more about the Stack segment. The Stack is a crucial part of the dynamic memory in every process, and it exists in almost all architectures. You have seen it in the memory mappings described as `[stack]`.

Both Stack and Heap segments have dynamic contents which are constantly changing while the process is running. It is not easy to see the dynamic contents of these segments and most of the time you need a debugger such as `gdb` to go through the memory bytes and read them while a process is running.

As pointed out before, the Stack segment is usually limited in size, and it is not a good place to store big objects. If the Stack segment is full, the process cannot make any further function calls since the function call mechanism relies heavily on the functionality of the Stack segment.

If the Stack segment of a process becomes full, the process gets terminated by the operating system. *Stack overflow* is a famous error that happens when the Stack segment becomes full. We discuss the function call mechanism in future paragraphs.

As explained before, the Stack segment is a default memory region that variables are allocated from. Suppose that you've declared a variable inside a function, as follows:

```
void func() {
  // The memory required for the following variable is
  // allocated from the stack segment.
  int a;
  ...
}
```

Code Box 4-7: Declaring a local variable which has its memory allocated from the Stack segment

In the preceding function, while declaring the variable, we have not mentioned anything to let the compiler know which segment the variable should be allocated from. Because of this, the compiler uses the Stack segment by default. The Stack segment is the first place that allocations are made from.

As its name implies, it is a *stack*. If you declare a local variable, it becomes allocated on top of the Stack segment. When you're leaving the scope of the declared local variable, the compiler has to pop the local variables first in order to bring up the local variables declared in the outer scope.

Note:
Stack, in its abstract form, is a **First In, Last Out (FILO)** or **Last In, First Out (LIFO)** data structure. Regardless of the implementation details, each entry is stored (pushed) on top of the stack, and it will be buried by further entries. One entry cannot be popped out without removing the above entries first.

Variables are not the only entities that are stored in the Stack segment. Whenever you make a function call, a new entry called a *stack frame* is placed on top of the Stack segment. Otherwise, you cannot return to the calling function or return the result back to the caller.

Having a healthy stacking mechanism is vital to have a working program. Since the size of the Stack is limited, it is a good practice to declare small variables in it. Also, the Stack shouldn't be filled by too many stack frames as a result of making infinite *recursive* calls or too many function calls.

From a different perspective, the Stack segment is a region used by you, as a programmer, to keep your data and declare the local variables used in your algorithms, and by the operating system, as the program runner, to keep the data needed for its internal mechanisms to execute your program successfully.

In this sense, you should be careful when working with this segment because misusing it or corrupting its data can interrupt the running process or even make it crash. The Heap segment is the memory segment that is only managed by the programmer. We will cover the Heap segment in the next section.

It is not easy to see the contents of the Stack segment from outside if we are only using the tools we've introduced for probing the static memory layout. This part of memory contains private data and can be sensitive. It is also private to the process, and other processes cannot read or modify it.

So, for sailing through the Stack memory, one has to attach something to a process and see the Stack segment through the eyes of that process. This can be done using a *debugger* program. A debugger attaches to a process and allows a programmer to control the target process and investigate its memory content. We will use this technique and examine the Stack memory in the following chapter. For now, we leave the Stack segment to discuss more about the Heap segment. We will get back to the Stack in the next chapter.

Heap segment

The following example, *example 4.7*, shows how memory mappings can be used to find regions allocated for the Heap segment. It is quite similar to *example 4.6*, but it allocates a number of bytes from the Heap segment before entering the infinite loop.

Therefore, just like we did for *example 4.6*, we can go through the memory mappings of the running process and see which mapping refers to the Heap segment.

The following code box contains the code for *example 4.7*:

```
#include <unistd.h> // Needed for sleep function
#include <stdlib.h> // Needed for malloc function
#include <stdio.h> // Needed for printf

int main(int argc, char** argv) {
  void* ptr = malloc(1024); // Allocate 1KB from heap
  printf("Address: %p\n", ptr);
  fflush(stdout); // To force the print
  // Infinite loop
  while (1) {
    sleep(1); // Sleep 1 second
  };
  return 0;
}
```

Code Box 4-8 [ExtremeC_examples_chapter4_7.c]: Example 4.7 used for probing the Heap segment

In the preceding code, we used the `malloc` function. It's the primary way to allocate extra memory from the Heap segment. It accepts the number of bytes that should be allocated, and it returns a generic pointer.

As a reminder, a generic pointer (or a void pointer) contains a memory address but it cannot be *dereferenced* and used directly. It should be cast to a specific pointer type before being used.

In *example 4.7*, we allocate 1024 bytes (or 1KB) before entering the loop. The program also prints the address of the pointer received from `malloc` before starting the loop. Let's compile the example and run it as we did for *example 4.7*:

```
$ g++ ExtremeC_examples_chapter4_7.c -o ex4_7.out
$ ./ex4_7.out &
[1] 3451
Address: 0x19790010
$
```

Shell Box 4-16: Compiling and running example 4.7

Now, the process is running in the background, and it has obtained the PID 3451.

Let's see what memory regions have been mapped for this process by looking at its maps file:

```
$ cat /proc/3451/maps
00400000-00401000 r-xp 00000000 00:2f 176521            .../
extreme_c/4.7/ex4_7.out
00600000-00601000 r--p 00000000 00:2f 176521            .../
extreme_c/4.7/ex4_7.out
00601000-00602000 rw-p 00001000 00:2f 176521            .../
extreme_c/4.7/ex4_7.out
01979000-0199a000 rw-p 00000000 00:00 0                 [heap]
7f7b32f12000-7f7b330d1000 r-xp 00000000 00:2f 30        /lib/
x86_64-linux-gnu/libc-2.23.so
7f7b330d1000-7f7b332d1000 ---p 001bf000 00:2f 30        /lib/
x86_64-linux-gnu/libc-2.23.so
7f7b332d1000-7f7b332d5000 r--p 001bf000 00:2f 30        /lib/
x86_64-linux-gnu/libc-2.23.so
7f7b332d5000-7f7b332d7000 rw-p 001c3000 00:2f 30        /lib/
x86_64-linux-gnu/libc-2.23.so
7f7b332d7000-7f7b332db000 rw-p 00000000 00:00 0
7f7b332db000-7f7b33301000 r-xp 00000000 00:2f 27        /lib/
x86_64-linux-gnu/ld-2.23.so
7f7b334f2000-7f7b334f5000 rw-p 00000000 00:00 0
7f7b334fe000-7f7b33500000 rw-p 00000000 00:00 0
7f7b33500000-7f7b33501000 r--p 00025000 00:2f 27        /lib/
x86_64-linux-gnu/ld-2.23.so
7f7b33501000-7f7b33502000 rw-p 00026000 00:2f 27        /lib/
x86_64-linux-gnu/ld-2.23.so
7f7b33502000-7f7b33503000 rw-p 00000000 00:00 0
7ffdd63c2000-7ffdd63e3000 rw-p 00000000 00:00 0         [stack]
7ffdd63e7000-7ffdd63ea000 r--p 00000000 00:00 0         [vvar]
7ffdd63ea000-7ffdd63ec000 r-xp 00000000 00:00 0         [vdso]
ffffffffff600000-ffffffffff601000 r-xp 00000000 00:00 0
[vsyscall]
$
```

Shell Box 4-17: Dumping the content of /proc/3451/maps

If you look at *Shell Box 4-17* carefully, you will see a new mapping which is highlighted, and it is being described by [heap]. This region has been added because of using the malloc function. If you calculate the size of the region, it is 0x21000 bytes or 132 KB. This means that to allocate only 1 KB in the code, a region of the size 132 KB has been allocated.

This is usually done in order to prevent further memory allocations when using `malloc` again in the future. That's simply because the memory allocation from the Heap segment is not cheap and it has both memory and time overheads.

If you go back to the code shown in *Code Box 4-8*, the address that the `ptr` pointer is pointing to is also interesting. The Heap's memory mapping, shown in *Shell Box 4-17*, is allocated from the address `0x01979000` to `0x0199a000`, and the address stored in `ptr` is `0x19790010`, which is obviously inside the Heap range, located at an offset of `16` bytes.

The Heap segment can grow to sizes far greater than 132 KB, even to tens of gigabytes, and usually it is used for permanent, global, and very big objects such as arrays and bit streams.

As pointed out before, allocation and deallocation within the heap segment require a program to call specific functions provided by the C standard. While you can have local variables on top of the Stack segment, and you can use them directly to interact with the memory, the Heap memory can be accessed only through pointers, and this is one of the reasons why knowing pointers and being able to work with them is crucial to every C programmer. Let's bring up *example 4.8*, which demonstrates how to use pointers to access the Heap space:

```
#include <stdio.h>   // For printf function
#include <stdlib.h>  // For malloc and free function

void fill(char* ptr) {
    ptr[0] = 'H';
    ptr[1] = 'e';
    ptr[2] = 'l';
    ptr[3] = 'l';
    ptr[5] = 0;
}

int main(int argc, char** argv) {
    void* gptr = malloc(10 * sizeof(char));
    char* ptr = (char*)gptr;
    fill(ptr);
    printf("%s!\n", ptr);
    free(ptr);
    return 0;
}
```

Code Box 4-9 [ExtremeC_examples_chapter4_8.c]: Using pointers to interact with the Heap memory

The preceding program allocates 10 bytes from the Heap space using the `malloc` function. The `malloc` function receives the number of bytes that should be allocated and returns a generic pointer addressing the first byte of the allocated memory block.

For using the returned pointer, we have to cast it to a proper pointer type. Since we are going to use the allocated memory to store some characters, we choose to cast it to a `char` pointer. The casting is done before calling the `fill` function.

Note that the local pointer variables, `gptr` and `ptr`, are allocated from the Stack. These pointers need memory to store their values, and this memory comes from the Stack segment. But the address that they are pointing to is inside the Heap segment. This is the theme when working with Heap memories. You have local pointers which are allocated from the Stack segment, but they are actually pointing to a region allocated from the Heap segment. We show more of these in the following chapter.

Note that the `ptr` pointer inside the `fill` function is also allocated from the Stack but it is in a different scope, and it is different from the `ptr` pointer declared in the `main` function.

When it comes to Heap memory, the program, or actually the programmer, is responsible for memory allocation. The program is also responsible for deallocation of the memory when it is not needed. Having a piece of allocated Heap memory that is not *reachable* is considered a *memory leak*. By not being reachable, we mean that there is no pointer that can be used to address that region.

Memory leaks are fatal to programs because having an incremental memory leak will eventually use up the whole allowed memory space, and this can kill the process. That's why the program is calling the `free` function before returning from the `main` function. The call to the `free` function will deallocate the acquired Heap memory block, and the program shouldn't use those Heap addresses anymore.

More on Stack and Heap segments will come in the next chapter.

Summary

Our initial goal in this chapter was to provide an overview of the memory structure of a process in a Unix-like operating system. As we have covered a lot in this chapter, take a minute to read through what we've been through, as you should now feel comfortable in understanding what we have accomplished:

- We described the dynamic memory structure of a running process as well as the static memory structure of an executable object file.

- We observed that the static memory layout is located inside the executable object file and it is broken into pieces which are called segments. We found out that the Text, Data, and BSS segments are part of the static memory layout.

- We saw that the Text segment or Code segment is used to store the machine-level instructions meant to be executed when a new process is spawned out of the current executable object file.

- We saw that the BSS segment is used to store global variables that are either uninitialized or set to zero.

- We explained that the Data segment is used to store initialized global variables.

- We used the `size` and `objdump` commands to probe the internals of object files. We can also use object file dumpers like `readelf` in order to find these segments inside an object file.

- We probed the dynamic memory layout of a process. We saw that all segments are copied from the static memory layout into the dynamic memory of the process. However, there are two new segments in the dynamic memory layout; the Stack segment, and the Heap segment.

- We explained that the Stack segment is the default memory region used for allocations.

- We learned that the local variables are always allocated on top of the Stack region.

- We also observed that the secret behind the function calls lies within the Stack segment and the way it works.

- We saw that we have to use a specific API, or a set of functions, in order to allocate and deallocate Heap memory regions. This API is provided by the C standard library.

- We discussed memory leakage and how it can happen regarding Heap memory regions.

The next chapter is about the Stack and Heap segments specifically. It will use the topics we have covered within this chapter, and it will add more to those foundations. More examples will be given, and new probing tools will be introduced; this will complete our discussion regarding memory management in C.

Chapter 05

Stack and Heap

In the previous chapter, we ran an investigation of the memory layout of a running process. System programming without knowing enough about the memory structure and its various segments is like doing surgery without knowing the anatomy of the human body. The previous chapter just gave us the basic information regarding the different segments in the process memory layout, but this chapter wants us to just focus on the most frequently used segments: Stack and Heap.

As a programmer, you are mostly busy working with Stack and Heap segments. Other segments such as Data or BSS are less in use, or you have less control over them. That's basically because of the fact that the Data and BSS segments are generated by the compiler, and usually, they take up a small percentage of the whole memory of a process during its lifetime. This doesn't mean that they are not important, and, in fact, there are issues that directly relate to these segments. But as you are spending most of your time with Stack and Heap, most memory issues have roots in these segments.

As part of this chapter, you will learn:

- How to probe the Stack segment and the tools you need for this purpose
- How memory management is done automatically for the Stack segment
- The various characteristics of the stack segment
- The guidelines and best practices on how to use the Stack segment
- How to probe the Heap segment
- How to allocate and deallocate a Heap memory block
- The guidelines and best practices regarding the usage of the Heap segment
- Memory-constrained environments and tuning memory in performant environments

Let's begin our quest by discussing the Stack segment in more detail.

Stack

A process can continue working without the Heap segment but not without the Stack segment. This says a lot. The Stack is the main part of the process metabolism, and it cannot continue execution without it. The reason is hiding behind the mechanism driving the function calls. As briefly explained in the previous chapter, calling a function can only be done by using the Stack segment. Without a Stack segment, no function call can be made, and this means no execution at all.

With that said, the Stack segment and its contents are engineered carefully to result in the healthy execution of the process. Therefore, messing with the Stack content can disrupt the execution and halt the process. Allocation from the Stack segment is fast, and it doesn't need any special function call. More than that, the deallocation and all memory management tasks happen automatically. All these facts are all very tempting and encourage you to overuse the Stack.

You should be careful about this. Using the Stack segment brings its own complications. The stack is not very big, therefore you cannot store large objects in it. In addition, incorrect use of the Stack content can halt the execution and result in a crash. The following piece of code demonstrates this:

```
#include <string.h>

int main(int argc, char** argv) {
  char str[10];
  strcpy(str,
"akjsdhkhqiueryo34928739r27yeiwuyfiusdciuti7twe79ye");
  return 0;
}
```

Code Box 5-1: A buffer overflow situation. The strcpy function will overwrite the content of the Stack

When running the preceding code, the program will most likely crash. That's because the strcpy is overwriting the content of the Stack, or as it is commonly termed, *smashing* the stack. As you see in *Code Box 5-1*, the str array has 10 characters, but the strcpy is writing way more than 10 characters to the str array. As you will see shortly, this effectively writes on the previously pushed variables and stack frames, and the program jumps to a wrong instruction after returning from the main function. And this eventually makes it impossible to continue the execution.

I hope that the preceding example has helped you to appreciate the delicacy of the Stack segment. In the first half of this chapter, we are going to have a deeper look into the Stack and examine it closely. We first start by probing into the Stack.

Probing the Stack

Before knowing more about the Stack, we need to be able to read and, probably, modify it. As stated in the previous chapter, the Stack segment is a private memory that only the owner process has the right to read and modify. If we are going to read the Stack or change it, we need to become part of the process owning the Stack.

This is where a new set of tools come in: *debuggers*. A debugger is a program that attaches to another process in order to *debug* it. One of the usual tasks while debugging a process is to observe and manipulate the various memory segments. Only when debugging a process are we able to read and modify the private memory blocks. The other thing that can be done as part of debugging is to control the order of the execution of the program instructions. We give examples on how to do these tasks using a debugger shortly, as part of this section.

Let's start with an example. In *example 5.1*, we show how to compile a program and make it ready for debugging. Then, we demonstrate how to use `gdb`, the GNU debugger, to run the program and read the Stack memory. This example declares a character array allocated on top of the Stack and populates its elements with some characters, as can be seen in the following code box:

```c
#include <stdio.h>

int main(int argc, char** argv) {
  char arr[4];
  arr[0] = 'A';
  arr[1] = 'B';
  arr[2] = 'C';
  arr[3] = 'D';
  return 0;
}
```

Code Box 5-2 [ExtremeC_examples_chapter5_1.c]: Declaration of an array allocated on top of the Stack

The program is simple and easy to follow, but the things that are happening inside the memory are interesting. First of all, the memory required for the `arr` array is allocated from the Stack simply because it is not allocated from the Heap segment and we didn't use the `malloc` function. Remember, the Stack segment is the default place for allocating variables and arrays.

In order to have some memory allocated from the Heap, one should acquire it by calling `malloc` or other similar functions, such as `calloc`. Otherwise, the memory is allocated from the Stack, and more precisely, on top of the Stack.

In order to be able to debug a program, the binary must be built for debugging purposes. This means that we have to tell the compiler that we want a binary that contains *debug symbols*. These symbols will be used to find the code lines that have been executing or those that caused a crash. Let's compile *example 5.1* and create an executable object file that contains debugging symbols.

First, we build the example. We're doing our compilation in a Linux environment:

```
$ gcc -g ExtremeC_examples_chapter5_1.c -o ex5_1_dbg.out
$
```

Shell Box 5-1: Compiling the example 5.1 with debug option -g

The -g option tells the compiler that the final executable object file must contain the debugging information. The size of the binary is also different when you compile the source with and without the debug option. Next, you can see the difference between the sizes of the two executable object files, the first one built without the -g option and the second one with the -g option:

```
$ gcc ExtremeC_examples_chapter2_10.c -o ex5_1.out
$ ls -al ex5_1.out
-rwxrwxr-x 1 kamranamini kamranamini 8640 jul 24 13:55 ex5_1.out
$ gcc -g ExtremeC_examples_chapter2_10.c -o ex5_1_dbg.out
$ ls -al ex5_1.out
-rwxrwxr-x 1 kamranamini kamranamini 9864 jul 24 13:56 ex5_1_dbg.
out
$
```

Shell Box 5-2: The size of the output executable object file with and without the -g option

Now that we have an executable file containing the debug symbols, we can use the debugger to run the program. In this example, we are going to use gdb for debugging *example 5.1*. Next, you can find the command to start the debugger:

```
$ gdb ex5_1_dbg.out
```

Shell Box 5-3: Starting the debugger for the example 5.1

Note:
gdb is usually installed as part of the build-essentials package on Linux systems. In macOS systems, it can be installed using the brew package manager like this: brew install gdb.

After running the debugger, the output will be something similar to the following shell box:

```
$ gdb ex5_1_dbg.out
GNU gdb (Ubuntu 7.11.1-0ubuntu1~16.5) 7.11.1
Copyright (C) 2016 Free Software Foundation, Inc.
License GPLv3+: GNU GPL version 3 or later http://gnu.org/
licenses/gpl.html
...
Reading symbols from ex5_1_dbg.out...done.
(gdb)
```

Shell Box 5-4: The output of the debugger after getting started

As you may have noticed, I've run the preceding command on a Linux machine. gdb has a command-line interface that allows you to issue debugging commands. Enter the r (or run) command in order to execute the executable object file, specified as an input to the debugger. The following shell box shows how the run command executes the program:

```
...
Reading symbols from ex5_1_dbg.out...done.
(gdb) run
Starting program: .../extreme_c/5.1/ex5_1_dbg.out
[Inferior 1 (process 9742) exited normally]
(gdb)
```

Shell Box 5-5: The output of the debugger after issuing the run command

In the preceding shell box, after issuing the run command, gdb has started the process, attached to it, and let the program execute its instructions and exit. It did not interrupt the program because we have not set a *breakpoint*. A breakpoint is an indicator that tells gdb to pause the program execution and wait for further instructions. You can have as many breakpoints as you want.

Next, we set a breakpoint on the main function using the b (or break) command. After setting the breakpoint, gdb pauses the execution when the program enters the main function. You can see how to set a breakpoint on the main function in the following shell box:

```
(gdb) break main
Breakpoint 1 at 0x400555: file ExtremeC_examples_chapter5_1.c,
```

```
line 4.
(gdb)
```

Shell Box 5-6: Setting a breakpoint on the main function in gdb

Now, we run the program again. This creates a new process, and gdb attaches to it. Next, you can find the result:

```
(gdb) r
Starting program: .../extreme_c/5.1/ex5_1_dbg.out

Breakpoint 1, main (argc=1, argv=0x7fffffffcbd8) at ExtremeC_
examples_chapter5_1.c:3
3           int main(int argc, char** argv) {
(gdb)
```

Shell Box 5-7: Running the program again after setting the breakpoint

As you can see, the execution has paused at line 3, which is just the line of the main function. Then, the debugger waits for the next command. Now, we can ask gdb to run the next line of code and pause again. In other words, we run the program step by step and line by line. This way, you have enough time to look around and check the variables and their values inside the memory. In fact, this is the method we are going to use to probe the Stack and the Heap segments.

In the following shell box, you can see how to use the n (or next) command to run the next line of code:

```
(gdb) n
5           arr[0] = 'A';
(gdb) n
6           arr[1] = 'B';
(gdb) next
7           arr[2] = 'C';
(gdb) next
8           arr[3] = 'D';
(gdb) next
9           return 0;
(gdb)
```

Shell Box 5-8: Using the n (or next) command to execute upcoming lines of code

Now, if you enter the `print arr` command in the debugger, it will show the content of the array as a string:

```
(gdb) print arr
$1 = "ABCD"
(gdb)
```

Shell Box 5-9: Printing the content of the arr array using gdb

To get back to the topic, we introduced `gdb` to be able to see inside the Stack memory. Now, we can do it. We have a process that has a Stack segment, and it is paused, and we have a `gdb` command line to explore its memory. Let's begin and print the memory allocated for the `arr` array:

```
(gdb) x/4b arr
0x7fffffffcae0:  0x41     0x42     0x43     0x44
(gdb) x/8b arr
0x7fffffffcae0:  0x41     0x42     0x43     0x44     0xff     0x7f
0x00     0x00
(gdb)
```

Shell Box 5-10: Printing bytes of memory starting from the arr array

The first command, `x/4b`, shows 4 bytes from the location that `arr` is pointing to. Remember that `arr` is a pointer that actually is pointing to the first element of the array, so it can be used to move along the memory.

The second command, `x/8b`, prints 8 bytes after `arr`. According to the code written for *example 5.1*, and found in *Code Box 5-2*, the values A, B, C, and D are stored in the array, `arr`. You should know that ASCII values are stored in the array, not the real characters. The ASCII value for A is 65 decimal or 0x41 hexadecimal. For B, it is 66 or 0x42. As you can see, the values printed in the `gdb` output are the values we just stored in the `arr` array.

What about the other 4 bytes in the second command? They are part of the Stack, and they probably contain data from the recent Stack frame put on top of the Stack while calling the `main` function.

Note that the Stack segment is filled in an opposite fashion in comparison to other segments.

Other memory regions are filled starting from the smaller addresses and they move forward to bigger addresses, but this is not the case with the Stack segment.

The Stack segment is filled from the bigger addresses and moves backward to the smaller addresses. Some of the reasons behind this design lie in the development history of modern computers, and some in the functionality of the Stack segment, which behaves like a stack data structure.

With all that said, if you read the Stack segment from an addresses toward the bigger addresses, just like we did in *Shell Box 5-10*, you are effectively reading the already pushed content as part of the Stack segment, and if you try to change those bytes, you are altering the Stack, and this is not good. We will demonstrate why this is dangerous and how this can be done in future paragraphs.

Why are we able to see more than the size of the arr array? Because gdb goes through the number of bytes in the memory that we have requested. The x command doesn't care about the array's boundary. It just needs a starting address and the number of bytes to print the range.

If you want to change the values inside the Stack, you have to use the set command. This allows you to modify an existing memory cell. In this case, the memory cell refers to an individual byte in the arr array:

```
(gdb) x/4b arr
0x7fffffffcae0: 0x41      0x42      0x43      0x44
(gdb) set arr[1] = 'F'
(gdb) x/4b arr
0x7fffffffcae0: 0x41      0x46      0x43      0x44
(gdb) print arr
$2 = "AFCD"
(gdb)
```

Shell Box 5-11: Changing an individual byte in the array using the set command

As you can see, using the set command, we have set the second element of the arr array to F. If you are going to change an address that is not in the boundaries of your arrays, it is still possible through gdb.

Please observe the following modification carefully. Now, we want to modify a byte located in a far bigger address than arr, and as we explained before, we will be altering the already pushed content of the Stack. Remember, the Stack memory is filled in an opposite manner compared to other segments:

```
(gdb) x/20x arr
0x7fffffffcae0: 0x41      0x42      0x43      0x44      0xff      0x7f
0x00      0x00
```

```
0x7fffffffcae8:  0x00     0x96     0xea     0x5d     0xf0     0x31
0xea     0x73
0x7fffffffcaf0:  0x90     0x05     0x40     0x00
(gdb) set *(0x7fffffffcaed) = 0xff
(gdb) x/20x arr
0x7fffffffcae0:  0x41     0x42     0x43     0x44     0xff     0x7f
0x00     0x00
0x7fffffffcae8:  0x00     0x96     0xea     0x5d     0xf0     0xff
0x00     0x00
0x7fffffffcaf0:  0x00     0x05     0x40     0x00
(gdb)
```

Shell Box 5-12: Changing an individual byte outside of the array's boundary

That is all. We just wrote the value `0xff` in the `0x7fffffffcaed` address, which is out of the boundary of the `arr` array, and probably a byte within the stack frame pushed before entering the `main` function.

What will happen if we continue the execution? If we have modified a critical byte in the Stack, we expect to see a crash or at least have this modification detected by some mechanism and have the execution of the program halted. The command `c` (or `continue`) will continue the execution of the process in `gdb`, as you can see next:

```
(gdb) c
Continuing.
*** stack smashing detected ***: .../extreme_c/5.1/ex5_1_dbg.out
terminated

Program received signal SIGABRT, Aborted.
0x00007ffff7a42428 in __GI_raise (sig=sig@entry=6) at ../sysdeps/
Unix/sysv/linux/raise.c:54
54          ../sysdeps/Unix/sysv/linux/raise.c: No such file or
directory.
(gdb)
```

Shell Box 5-13: Having a critical byte changed in the Stack terminates the process

As you can see in the preceding shell box, we've just smashed the Stack! Modifying the content of the Stack in addresses that are not allocated by you, even by 1 byte, can be very dangerous and it usually leads to a crash or a sudden termination.

As we have said before, most of the vital procedures regarding the execution of a program are done within the Stack memory. So, you should be very careful when writing to Stack variables. You should not write any values outside of the boundaries defined for variables and arrays simply because the addresses grow backward in the Stack memory, which makes it likely to overwrite the already written bytes.

When you're done with debugging, and you're ready to leave the gdb, then you can simply use the command q (or quit). Now, you should be out of the debugger and back in the terminal.

As another note, writing unchecked values into a *buffer* (another name for a byte or character array) allocated on top of the Stack (not from the Heap) is considered a vulnerability. An attacker can carefully design a byte array and feed it to the program in order to take control of it. This is usually called an *exploit* because of a *buffer overflow* attack.

The following program shows this vulnerability:

```
int main(int argc, char** argv) {
  char str[10];
  strcpy(str, argv[1]);
  printf("Hello %s!\n", str);
}
```

Code Box 5-3: A program showing the buffer overflow vulnerability

The preceding code does not check the argv[1] input for its content and its size and copies it directly into the str array, which is allocated on top of the Stack.

If you're lucky, this can lead to a crash, but in some rare but dangerous cases, this can lead to an exploit attack.

Points on using the Stack memory

Now that you have a better understanding of the Stack segment and how it works, we can talk about the best practices and the points you should be careful about. You should be familiar with the *scope* concept. Each Stack variable has its own scope, and the scope determines the lifetime of the variable. This means that a Stack variable starts its lifetime in one scope and dies when that scope is gone. In other words, the scope determines the lifetime of a Stack variable.

We also have automatic memory allocation and deallocation for Stack variables, and it is only applicable to the Stack variables. This feature, automatic memory management, comes from the nature of the Stack segment.

Whenever you declare a Stack variable, it will be allocated on top of the Stack segment. Allocation happens automatically, and this can be marked as the start of its lifetime. After this point, many more variables and other stack frames are put on top of it inside the Stack. As long as the variable exists in the Stack and there are other variables on top of it, it survives and continues living.

Eventually, however, this stuff will get popped out of the Stack because at some point in the future the program has to be finished, and the stack should be empty at that moment. So, there should be a point in the future when this variable is popped out of the stack. So, the deallocation, or getting popped out, happens automatically, and that can be marked as the end of the variable's lifetime. This is basically the reason why we say that we have automatic memory management for the Stack variables that is not controlled by the programmer.

Suppose that you have defined a variable in the `main` function, as we see in the following code box:

```
int main(int argc, char** argv) {
    int a;
    ...
    return 0;
}
```

Code Box 5-4: Declaring a variable on top of the Stack

This variable will stay in the Stack until the `main` function returns. In other words, the variable exists until its scope (the `main` function) is valid. Since the `main` function is the function in which all the program runs, the lifetime of the variable is almost like a global variable that is declared throughout the runtime of the program.

It is like a global variable, but not exactly one, because there will be a time that the variable is popped out from the Stack, whereas a global variable always has its memory even when the main function is finished and the program is being finalized. Note that there are two pieces of code that are run before and after the `main` function, bootstrapping and finalizing the program respectively. As another note, global variables are allocated from a different segment, Data or BSS, that does not behave like the Stack segment.

Let's now look at an example of a very common mistake. It usually happens to an amateur programmer while writing their first C programs. It is about returning an address to a local variable inside a function.

The following code box shows *example 5.2*:

```
int* get_integer() {
    int var = 10;
```

```
    return &var;
}

int main(int argc, char** argv) {
    int* ptr = get_integer();
    *ptr = 5;
    return 0;
}
```

Code Box 5-5 [ExtremeC_examples_chapter5_2.c]: Declaring a variable on top of the Stack

The `get_integer` function returns an address to the local variable, `var`, which has been declared in the scope of the `get_integer` function. The `get_integer` function returns the address of the local variable. Then, the `main` function tries to dereference the received pointer and access the memory region behind. The following is the output of the `gcc` compiler while compiling the preceding code on a Linux system:

```
$ gcc ExtremeC_examples_chapter5_2.c -o ex5_2.out
ExtremeC_examples_chapter5_2.c: In function 'get_integer':
ExtremeC_examples_chapter5_2.c:3:11: warning: function returns
address of local variable [-Wreturn-local-addr]
    return &var;
           ^~~~
$
```

Shell Box 5-14: Compiling the example 5.2 in Linux

As you can see, we have received a warning message. Since returning the address of a local variable is a common mistake, compilers already know about it, and they show a clear warning message like `warning: function returns address of a local variable`.

And this is what happens when we execute the program:

```
$ ./ex5_2.out
Segmentation fault (core dumped)
$
```

Shell Box 5-15: Executing the example 5.2 in Linux

As you can see in *Shell Box 5-15*, a segmentation fault has happened. It can be translated as a crash. It is usually because of invalid access to a region of memory that had been allocated at some point, but now it is deallocated.

Note:

Some warnings should be treated as errors. For example, the preceding warning should be an error because it usually leads to a crash. If you want to make all warning to be treated as errors, it is enough to pass the -Werror option to gcc compiler. If you want to treat only one specific warning as an error, for example, the preceding warning, it is enough to pass the -Werror=return-local-addr option.

If you run the program with gdb, you will see more details regarding the crash. But remember, you need to compile the program with the -g option otherwise gdb won't be that helpful.

It is always mandatory to compile the sources with -g option if you are about to debug the program using gdb or other debugging tools such as valgrind. The following shell box demonstrates how to compile and run *example 5.2* in the debugger:

```
$ gcc -g ExtremeC_examples_chapter5_2.c -o ex5_2_dbg.out
ExtremeC_examples_chapter5_2.c: In function 'get_integer':
ExtremeC_examples_chapter5_2.c:3:11: warning: function returns
address of local variable [-Wreturn-local-addr]
    return &var;
           ^~~~
$ gdb ex5_2_dbg.out
GNU gdb (Ubuntu 8.1-0ubuntu3) 8.1.0.20180409-git
...
Reading symbols from ex5_2_dbg.out...done.
(gdb) run
Starting program: .../extreme_c/5.2/ex5_2_dbg.out

Program received signal SIGSEGV, Segmentation fault.
0x00005555555546c4 in main (argc=1, argv=0x7fffffffdf88) at
ExtremeC_examples_chapter5_2.c:8
8       *ptr = 5;
(gdb) quit
$
```

Shell Box 5-16: Running the example 5.2 in the debugger

As is clear from the `gdb` output, the source of the crash is located at line 8 in the `main` function, exactly where the program tries to write to the returned address by dereferencing the returned pointer. But the `var` variable has been a local variable to the `get_integer` function and it doesn't exist anymore, simply because at line 8 we have already returned from the `get_integer` function and its scope, together with all variables, have vanished. Therefore, the returned pointer is a *dangling pointer*.

It is usually a common practice to pass the pointers addressing the variables in the current scope to other functions but not the other way around, because as long as the current scope is valid, the variables are there. Further function calls only put more stuff on top of the Stack segment, and the current scope won't be finished before them.

Note that the above statement is not a good practice regarding concurrent programs because in the future, if another concurrent task wants to use the received pointer addressing a variable inside the current scope, the current scope might have vanished already.

To end this section and have a conclusion about the Stack segment, the following points can be extracted from what we have explained so far:

- Stack memory has a limited size; therefore, it is not a good place to store big objects.

- The addresses in Stack segment grow backward, therefore reading forward in the Stack memory means reading already pushed bytes.

- Stack has automatic memory management, both for allocation and deallocation.

- Every Stack variable has a scope and it determines its lifetime. You should design your logic based on this lifetime. You have no control over it.

- Pointers should only point to those Stack variables that are still in a scope.

- Memory deallocation of Stack variables is done automatically when the scope is about to finish, and you have no control over it.

- Pointers to variables that exist in the current scope can be passed to other functions as arguments only when we are sure that the current scope will be still in place when the code in the called functions is about to use that pointer. This condition might break in situations when we have concurrent logic.

In the next section, we will talk about the Heap segment and its various features.

Heap

Almost any code, written in any programming language, uses Heap memory in some way. That's because the Heap has some unique advantages that cannot be achieved by using the Stack.

On the other hand, it also has some disadvantages; for example, it is slower to allocate a region of Heap memory in comparison to a similar region in Stack memory.

In this section, we are going to talk more about the Heap itself and the guidelines we should keep in mind when using Heap memory.

Heap memory is important because of its unique properties. Not all of them are advantageous and, in fact, some of them can be considered as risks that should be mitigated. A great tool always has good points and some bad points, and if you are going to use it properly, you are required to know both sides very well.

Here, we are going to list these features and see which ones are beneficial and which are risky:

1. **The Heap doesn't have any memory blocks that are allocated automatically**. Instead, the programmer must use `malloc` or similar functions to obtain Heap memory blocks, one by one. In fact, this could be regarded as a weak point for Stack memory that is resolved by Heap memory. Stack memory can contain stack frames, which are not allocated and pushed by the programmer but as a result of function calls, and in an automatic fashion.

2. **The Heap has a large memory size**. While the size of the Stack is limited and it is not a good choice for keeping big objects, the Heap allows the storing of very big objects even tens of gigabytes in size. As the Heap size grows, the allocator needs to request more heap pages from the operating system, and the Heap memory blocks are spread among these pages. Note that, unlike the Stack segment, the allocating addresses in the Heap memory move forward to bigger addresses.

3. **Memory allocation and deallocation inside Heap memory are managed by the programmer**. This means that the programmer is the sole responsible entity for allocating the memory and then freeing it when it is not needed anymore. In many recent programming languages, freeing allocated Heap blocks is done automatically by a parallel component called *garbage collector*. But in C and C++, we don't have such a concept and freeing the Heap blocks should be done manually. This is indeed a risk, and C/C++ programmers should be very careful while using heap memory. Failing to free the allocated Heap blocks usually leads to *memory leaks*, which can be fatal in most cases.

4. **Variables allocated from the Heap do not have any scope**, unlike variables in the Stack.

5. This is a risk because it makes memory management much harder. You don't know when you need to deallocate the variable, and you have to come up with some new definitions for the *scope* and the *owner* of the memory block in order to do the memory management effectively. Some of these methods are covered in the upcoming sections.

6. **We can only use pointers to address a Heap memory block**. In other words, there is no such concept as a Heap variable. The Heap region is addressed via pointers.

7. **Since the Heap segment is private to its owner process, we need to use a debugger to probe it**. Fortunately, C pointers work with the Heap memory block exactly the same as they work with Stack memory blocks. C does this abstraction very well, and because of this, we can use the same pointers to address both memories. Therefore, we can use the same methods that we used to examine the Stack to probe the Heap memory.

In the next section, we are going to discuss how to allocate and deallocate a heap memory block.

Heap memory allocation and deallocation

As we said in the previous section, Heap memory should be obtained and released manually. This means that the programmer should use a set of functions or API (the C standard library's memory allocation functions) in order to allocate or free a memory block in the Heap.

These functions do exist, and they are defined in the header, `stdlib.h`. The functions used for obtaining a Heap memory block are `malloc`, `calloc`, and `realloc`, and the sole function used for releasing a Heap memory block is `free`. *Example 5.3* demonstrates how to use some of these functions.

 Note:
In some texts, dynamic memory is used to refer to Heap memory. *Dynamic memory allocation* is a synonym for Heap memory allocation.

The following code box shows the source code of *example 5.3*. It allocates two Heap memory blocks, and then it prints its own memory mappings:

```
#include <stdio.h>  // For printf function
#include <stdlib.h> // For C library's heap memory functions
```

```
void print_mem_maps() {
#ifdef __linux__
  FILE* fd = fopen("/proc/self/maps", "r");
  if (!fd) {
    printf("Could not open maps file.\n");
    exit(1);
  }
  char line[1024];
  while (!feof(fd)) {
    fgets(line, 1024, fd);
    printf("> %s", line);
  }
  fclose(fd);
#endif
}

int main(int argc, char** argv) {
  // Allocate 10 bytes without initialization
  char* ptr1 = (char*)malloc(10 * sizeof(char));
  printf("Address of ptr1: %p\n", (void*)&ptr1);
  printf("Memory allocated by malloc at %p: ", (void*)ptr1);
  for (int i = 0; i < 10; i++) {
    printf("0x%02x ", (unsigned char)ptr1[i]);
  }
  printf("\n");

  // Allocation 10 bytes all initialized to zero
  char* ptr2 = (char*)calloc(10, sizeof(char));
  printf("Address of ptr2: %p\n", (void*)&ptr2);
  printf("Memory allocated by calloc at %p: ", (void*)ptr2);
  for (int i = 0; i < 10; i++) {
    printf("0x%02x ", (unsigned char)ptr2[i]);
  }
  printf("\n");

  print_mem_maps();

  free(ptr1);
  free(ptr2);

  return 0;
}
```

Code Box 5-6 [ExtremeC_examples_chapter5_3.c]: Example 5.3 showing the memory mappings after allocating two Heap memory blocks

The preceding code is cross-platform, and you can compile it on most Unix-like operating systems. But the print_mem_maps function only works on Linux since the __linux__ macro is only defined in Linux environments. Therefore, in macOS, you can compile the code, but the print_mem_maps function won't do anything.

The following shell box is the result of running the example in a Linux environment:

```
$ gcc ExtremeC_examples_chapter5_3.c -o ex5_3.out
$ ./ex5_3.out
Address of ptr1: 0x7ffe0ad75c38
Memory allocated by malloc at 0x564c03977260: 0x00 0x00 0x00 0x00
0x00 0x00 0x00 0x00 0x00 0x00
Address of ptr2: 0x7ffe0ad75c40
Memory allocated by calloc at 0x564c03977690: 0x00 0x00 0x00 0x00
0x00 0x00 0x00 0x00 0x00 0x00
> 564c01978000-564c01979000 r-xp 00000000 08:01 5898436
/home/kamranamini/extreme_c/5.3/ex5_3.out
> 564c01b79000-564c01b7a000 r--p 00001000 08:01 5898436
/home/kamranamini/extreme_c/5.3/ex5_3.out
> 564c01b7a000-564c01b7b000 rw-p 00002000 08:01 5898436
/home/kamranamini/extreme_c/5.3/ex5_3.out
> 564c03977000-564c03998000 rw-p 00000000 00:00 0          [heap]
> 7f31978ec000-7f3197ad3000 r-xp 00000000 08:01 5247803    /lib/
x86_64-linux-gnu/libc-2.27.so
...
> 7f3197eef000-7f3197ef1000 rw-p 00000000 00:00 0
> 7f3197f04000-7f3197f05000 r--p 00027000 08:01 5247775    /lib/
x86_64-linux-gnu/ld-2.27.so
> 7f3197f05000-7f3197f06000 rw-p 00028000 08:01 5247775    /lib/
x86_64-linux-gnu/ld-2.27.so
> 7f3197f06000-7f3197f07000 rw-p 00000000 00:00 0
> 7ffe0ad57000-7ffe0ad78000 rw-p 00000000 00:00 0
[stack]
> 7ffe0adc2000-7ffe0adc5000 r--p 00000000 00:00 0          [vvar]
> 7ffe0adc5000-7ffe0adc7000 r-xp 00000000 00:00 0          [vdso]
> ffffffffff600000-ffffffffff601000 r-xp 00000000 00:00 0
[vsyscall]
$
```

Shell Box 5-17: Output of example 5.3 in Linux

The preceding output has a lot to say. The program prints the addresses of the pointers ptr1 and ptr2. If you find the memory mapping of the Stack segment, as part of the printed memory mappings, you see that the Stack region starts from 0x7ffe0ad57000 and ends at 0x7ffe0ad78000. The pointers are within this range.

This means that the pointers are allocated from the Stack, but they are pointing to a memory region outside of the Stack segment, in this case, the Heap segment. It is very common to use a Stack pointer to address a Heap memory block.

Keep in mind that the ptr1 and ptr2 pointers have the same scope and they will be freed when the main function returns, but there is no scope to the Heap memory blocks obtained from the Heap segment. They will remain allocated until the program frees them manually. You can see that before returning from the main function, both memory blocks are freed using the pointers pointing to them and using the free function.

As a further note regarding the above example, we can see that the addresses returned by the malloc and calloc functions are located inside the Heap segment. This can be investigated by comparing the returned addresses and the memory mapping described as [heap]. The region marked as heap starts from 0x564c03977000 and ends at 0x564c03998000. The ptr1 pointer points to the address 0x564c03977260 and the ptr2 pointer points to the address 0x564c03977690, which are both inside the heap region.

Regarding the Heap allocation function, as their names imply, calloc stands for **clear and allocate** and malloc stands for **memory allocate**. So, this means that calloc clears the memory block after allocation, but malloc leaves it uninitialized until the program does it itself if necessary.

Note:
In C++, the new and delete keywords do the same as malloc and free respectively. Additionally, new operator infers the size of the allocated memory block from the operand type and also converts the returned pointer to the operand type automatically.

But if you look at the bytes in the two allocated blocks, both of them have zero bytes. So, it seems that malloc has also initialized the memory block after the allocation. But based on the description of malloc in the C Specification, malloc doesn't initialize the allocated memory block. So, why is that? To move this further, let's run the example in a macOS environment:

```
$ clang ExtremeC_examples_chapter5_3.c -o ex5_3.out
$ ./ ex5_3.out
Address of ptr1: 0x7ffee66b2888
Memory allocated by malloc at 0x7fc628c00370: 0x00 0x00 0x00 0x00
```

```
0x00 0x00 0x00 0x80 0x00 0x00

Address of ptr2: 0x7ffee66b2878

Memory allocated by calloc at 0x7fc628c02740: 0x00 0x00 0x00 0x00
0x00 0x00 0x00 0x00 0x00 0x00

$
```

Shell Box 5-18: Output of example 5.3 on macOS

If you look carefully, you can see that the memory block allocated by `malloc` has some non-zero bytes, but the memory block allocated by `calloc` is all zeros. So, what should we do? Should we assume that the memory block allocated by `malloc` in Linux is always zeros?

If you are going to write a cross-platform program, always be aligned with the C specification. The specification says `malloc` does not initialize the allocated memory block.

Even when you are writing your program only for Linux and not for other operating systems, be aware that future compilers may behave differently. Therefore, according to the C specification, we must always assume that the memory block allocated by the `malloc` is not initialized and it should be initialized manually if necessary.

Note that since `malloc` doesn't initialize the allocated memory, it is usually faster than `calloc`. In some implementations, `malloc` doesn't actually allocate the memory block and defer the allocation until when the memory block is accessed (either read or write). This way, memory allocations happen faster.

If you are going to initialize the memory after `malloc`, you can use the `memset` function. Here is an example:

```c
#include <stdlib.h> // For malloc
#include <string.h> // For memset

int main(int argc, char** argv) {
  char* ptr = (char*)malloc(16 * sizeof(char));
  memset(ptr, 0, 16 * sizeof(char));     // Fill with 0
  memset(ptr, 0xff, 16 * sizeof(char)); // Fill with 0xff
  ...
  free(ptr);
  return 0;
}
```

Code Box 5-7: Using the memset function to initialize a memory block

The `realloc` function is another function that is introduced as part of the Heap allocation functions. It was not used as part of *example 5.3*. It actually reallocates the memory by resizing an already allocated memory block. Here is an example:

```
int main(int argc, char** argv) {
   char* ptr = (char*)malloc(16 * sizeof(char));
   ...
   ptr = (char*)realloc(32 * sizeof(char));
   ...
   free(ptr);

   return 0;
}
```

Code Box 5-8: Using the realloc function to change the size of an already allocated block

The `realloc` function does not change the data in the old block and only expands an already allocated block to a new one. If it cannot expand the currently allocated block because of *fragmentation*, it will find another block that's large enough and copy the data from the old block to the new one. In this case, it will also free the old block. As you can see, reallocation is not a cheap operation in some cases because it involves many steps, hence it should be used with care.

The last note about *example 5.3* is on the `free` function. In fact, it deallocates an already allocated Heap memory block by passing the block's address as a pointer. As it is said before, any allocated Heap block should be freed when it is not needed. Failing to do so leads to *memory leakage*. Using a new example, *example 5.4*, we are going to show you how to detect memory leaks using the `valgrind` tool.

Let's first produce some memory leaks as part of *example 5.4*:

```
#include <stdlib.h> // For heap memory functions

int main(int argc, char** argv) {
   char* ptr = (char*)malloc(16 * sizeof(char));
   return 0;
}
```

Code Box 5-9: Producing a memory leak by not freeing the allocated block when returning from the main function

The preceding program has a memory leak because when the program ends, we have 16 bytes of Heap memory allocated and not freed. This example is very simple, but when the source code grows and more components are involved, it would be too hard or even impossible to detect it by sight.

Memory profilers are useful programs that can detect the memory issues in a running process. The famous `valgrind` tool is one of the most well knowns.

In order to use `valgrind` to analyze *example 5.4*, first we need to build the example with the debug option, `-g`. Then, we should run it using `valgrind`. While running the given executable object file, `valgrind` records all of the memory allocations and deallocations. Finally, when the execution is finished or a crash happens, `valgrind` prints out the summary of allocations and deallocations and the amount of memory that has not been freed. This way, it can let you know how much memory leak has been produced as part of the execution of the given program.

The following shell box demonstrates how to compile and use `valgrind` for *example 5.4*:

```
$ gcc -g ExtremeC_examples_chapter5_4.c -o ex5_4.out
$ valgrind ./ex5_4.out
==12022== Memcheck, a memory error detector
==12022== Copyright (C) 2002-2017, and GNU GPL'd, by Julian Seward
et al.
==12022== Using Valgrind-3.13.0 and LibVEX; rerun with -h for
copyright info
==12022== Command: ./ex5_4.out
==12022==
==12022==
==12022== HEAP SUMMARY:
==12022==     in use at exit: 16 bytes in 1 blocks
==12022==   total heap usage: 1 allocs, 0 frees, 16 bytes
allocated
==12022==
==12022== LEAK SUMMARY:
==12022==    definitely lost: 16 bytes in 1 blocks
==12022==    indirectly lost: 0 bytes in 0 blocks
==12022==      possibly lost: 0 bytes in 0 blocks
==12022==    still reachable: 0 bytes in 0 blocks
==12022==         suppressed: 0 bytes in 0 blocks
==12022== Rerun with --leak-chck=full to see details of leaked
memory
==12022==
==12022== For counts of detected and suppressed errors, rerun
with: -v
```

```
==12022== ERROR SUMMARY: 0 errors from 0 contexts (suppressed: 0
from 0)
$
```

Shell Box 5-19: Output of valgrind showing the 16-byte memory leak as part of the execution of example 5.4

If you look into the HEAP SUMMARY section in *Shell Box 5-19*, you can see that we had 1 allocation and 0 frees, and 16 bytes remained allocated while exiting. If you come down a bit to the LEAK SUMMARY section, it states that 16 bytes are definitely lost, and this means a memory leak!

If you want to know exactly at which line the mentioned leaking memory block has been allocated, you can use valgrind with a special option designed for this. In the following shell box, you will see how to use valgrind to find the lines responsible for the actual allocation:

```
$ gcc -g ExtremeC_examples_chapter5_4.c -o ex5_4.out
$ valgrind --leak-check=full ./ex5_4.out
==12144== Memcheck, a memory error detector
==12144== Copyright (C) 2002-2017, and GNU GPL'd, by Julian Seward
et al.
==12144== Using Valgrind-3.13.0 and LibVEX; rerun with -h for
copyright info
==12144== Command: ./ex5_4.out
==12144==
==12144==
==12144== HEAP SUMMARY:
==12144==     in use at exit: 16 bytes in 1 blocks
==12144==   total heap usage: 1 allocs, 0 frees, 16 bytes
allocated
==12144==
==12144== 16 bytes in 1 blocks are definitely lost in loss record
1 of 1
==12144==     at 0x4C2FB0F: malloc (in /usr/lib/valgrind/vgpreload_
memcheck-amd64-linux.so)
==12144==     by 0x108662: main (ExtremeC_examples_chapter5_4.c:4)
==12144==
==12144== LEAK SUMMARY:
==12144==    definitely lost: 16 bytes in 1 blocks
==12144==    indirectly lost: 0 bytes in 0 blocks
```

```
==12144==        possibly lost: 0 bytes in 0 blocks
==12144==      still reachable: 0 bytes in 0 blocks
==12144==           suppressed: 0 bytes in 0 blocks
==12144==
==12144== For counts of detected and suppressed errors, rerun with
: -v
==12144== ERROR SUMMARY: 1 errors from 1 contexts (suppressed: 0
from 0)
$
```

Shell Box 5-20: Output of valgrind showing the line that is responsible for the actual allocation

As you can see, we have passed the --leak-check=full option to valgrind, and now it shows the line of code that is responsible for the leaking Heap memory. It clearly shows that line 4 in *Code Box 5-9*, which is a malloc call, is where the leaking Heap block has been allocated. This can help you to trace it further and find the right place that the mentioned leaking block should be freed.

OK, let's change the preceding example so that it frees the allocated memory. We just need to add the free(ptr) instruction before the return statement, as we can see here:

```c
#include <stdlib.h> // For heap memory functions

int main(int argc, char** argv) {
  char* ptr = (char*)malloc(16 * sizeof(char));
  free(ptr);
  return 0;
}
```

Code Box 5-10: Freeing up the allocated memory block as part of example 5.4

Now with this change, the only allocated Heap block is freed. Let's build and run valgrind again:

```
$ gcc -g ExtremeC_examples_chapter5_4.c -o ex5_4.out
$ valgrind --leak-check=full ./ex5_4.out
==12175== Memcheck, a memory error detector
==12175== Copyright (C) 2002-2017, and GNU GPL'd, by Julian Seward
et al.
==12175== Using Valgrind-3.13.0 and LibVEX; rerun with -h for
copyright info
==12175== Command: ./ex5_4.out
```

```
==12175==
==12175==
==12175== HEAP SUMMARY:
==12175==     in use at exit: 0 bytes in 0 blocks
==12175==   total heap usage: 1 allocs, 1 frees, 16 bytes
allocated
==12175==
==12175== All heap blocks were freed -- no leaks are possible
==12175==
==12175== For counts of detected and suppressed errors, rerun with
-v
==12175== ERROR SUMMARY: 0 errors from 0 contexts (suppressed: 0
from 0)
$
```

Shell Box 5-20: Output of valgrind after freeing the allocated memory block

As you can see, `valgrind` says that `All Heap blocks were freed`, and this effectively means that we have no further memory leakage in our program. Running programs with `valgrind` can slow them down noticeably by a factor of 10 to 50, but it can help you to spot the memory issues very easily. It's a good practice to let your written programs run inside a memory profiler and catch memory leaks as soon as possible.

Memory leaks can be considered both as *technical debts*, if you have a bad design that causes the leaks, or as *risks*, where it's known that we have a leak, but we don't know what will happen if the leak continues to grow. But in my opinion, they should be treated as *bugs*; otherwise, it will take a while for you to look back at them. Usually, in teams, memory leaks are treated as bugs that should be fixed as soon as possible.

There are other memory profilers other than `valgrind`. **LLVM Address Sanitizer (or ASAN)** and **MemProf** are also other well-known memory profilers. Memory profilers can profile memory usage and allocations using various methods. Next, we discuss some of them:

- Some profilers can behave like a sandbox, running the target program inside and monitoring all their memory activities. We've used this method to run *example 5.4* inside a `valgrind` sandbox. This method does not require you to recompile your code.

- Another method is to use the libraries provided by some memory profilers, which wrap memory-related system calls. This way, the final binary will contain all of the logic required for the profiling task.

valgrind and ASAN can be linked to the final executable object file as a memory profiler library. This method requires the recompilation of your target source code and even making some modifications to your source code as well.

- Programs can also *preload* different libraries instead of the default C standard libraries, which contain memory *function interpositions* of the C library's standard memory allocation functions. This way, you are not required to compile your target source code. You just need to specify the libraries of such profilers in the LD_PRELOAD environment variable to be preloaded instead of the default libc libraries. MemProf uses this method.

Note:
A *function interposition* is a wrapper function defined in a dynamic library loaded before the target dynamic library, which propagates calls to the target function. Dynamic libraries can be preloaded using the LD_PRELOAD environment variable.

Heap memory principles

As pointed out before, Heap memory is different from Stack memory in several ways. Therefore, heap memory has its own guidelines regarding memory management. In this section, we are going to focus on these differences and come up with some dos and don'ts that we should consider when working with the Heap space.

Every memory block (or a variable) in the Stack has a scope. So, it is an easy task to define the lifetime of a memory block based on its scope. Whenever we are out of scope, all of the variables in that scope are gone. But this is different and much more complex with Heap memory.

A Heap memory block doesn't have any scope, so its lifetime is unclear and should be redefined. This is the reason behind having manual deallocation or *generational garbage collection* in modern languages such as Java. The Heap lifetime cannot be determined by the program itself or the C libraries used, and the programmer is the sole person who defines the lifetime of a Heap memory block.

When the discussion comes to the programmer's decision, especially in this case, it is complicated and hard to propose a universal silver bullet solution. Every opinion is debatable and can lead to a trade-off.

One of the best proposed strategies to overcome the complexity of the Heap lifetime, which of course is not a complete solution, is to define an *owner* for a memory block instead of having a scope that encompasses the memory block.

The owner is the sole entity responsible for managing the lifetime of a Heap memory block and is the one who allocates the block in the first place and frees it when the block is not needed anymore.

There are many classic examples of how to use this strategy. Most of the well-known C libraries use this strategy to handle their Heap memory allocations. *Example 5.5* is a very simple implementation of this method that is used to manage the lifetime of a queue object written in C. The following code box tries to demonstrate the *ownership* strategy:

```c
#include <stdio.h> // For printf function
#include <stdlib.h> // For heap memory functions

#define QUEUE_MAX_SIZE 100

typedef struct {
  int front;
  int rear;
  double* arr;
} queue_t;

void init(queue_t* q) {
  q->front = q->rear = 0;
  // The heap memory block allocated here is owned
  // by the queue object.
  q->arr = (double*)malloc(QUEUE_MAX_SIZE * sizeof(double));
}

void destroy(queue_t* q) {
  free(q->arr);
}

int size(queue_t* q) {
  return q->rear - q->front;
}

void enqueue(queue_t* q, double item) {
  q->arr[q->rear] = item;
  q->rear++;
}

double dequeue(queue_t* q) {
  double item = q->arr[q->front];
  q->front++;
  return item;
}

int main(int argc, char** argv) {
```

```
// The heap memory block allocated here is owned
// by the function main
queue_t* q = (queue_t*)malloc(sizeof(queue_t));

// Allocate needed memory for the queue object
init(q);

enqueue(q, 6.5);
enqueue(q, 1.3);
enqueue(q, 2.4);

printf("%f\n", dequeue(q));
printf("%f\n", dequeue(q));
printf("%f\n", dequeue(q));

// Release resources acquired by the queue object
destroy(q);

// Free the memory allocated for the queue object
// acquired by the function main
free(q);
return 0;
}
```

Code Box 5-11 [ExtremeC_examples_chapter5_5.c]: The example 5.5 demonstrating the ownership strategy for Heap lifetime management

The preceding example contains two different ownerships each of which owning a specific object. The first ownership is about the Heap memory block addressed by the `arr` pointer in the `queue_t` structure that is owned by the queue object. As long as the queue object exists, this memory block must remain in place and allocated.

The second ownership is regarding the Heap memory block acquired by the `main` function as a placeholder for the queue object, `q`, that is owned by the `main` function itself. It is very important to distinguish between the Heap memory blocks owned by the queue object and the Heap memory blocks owned by the `main` function because releasing one of them doesn't release another.

To demonstrate how a memory leak can happen in the preceding code, suppose that you forget to call the `destroy` function on the queue object. It will definitely lead to a memory leak because the Heap memory block acquired inside the `init` function would be still allocated and not freed.

Note that if an entity (an object, function, and so on) owns a Heap memory block, it should be expressed in the comments. Nothing should free a Heap memory block if it does not own the block.

Note that multiple deallocations of the same Heap memory block will lead to a *double free* situation. A double-free situation is a memory corruption issue and like any other memory corruption issue, it should be dealt with and resolved soon after detection. Otherwise, it can have serious consequences like sudden crashes.

Other than the ownership strategy, one could use a garbage collector. The garbage collector is an automatic mechanism that is embedded in a program and tries to collect memory blocks that have no pointer addressing them. One of the old well-known garbage collectors for C is the *Boehm-Demers-Weiser Conservative Garbage Collector*, which provides a set of memory allocation functions that should be called instead of `malloc` and other standard C memory allocation functions.

 Further Reading:
More information about the Boehm-Demers-Weiser garbage collector can be found here: `http://www.hboehm.info/gc/`.

Another technique to manage the lifetime of a Heap block is using a RAII object. **RAII** stands for **Resource Acquisition Is Initialization**. It means that we can bind the lifetime of a resource, possibly a Heap allocated memory block, to the lifetime of an object. In other words, we use an object that upon its construction initializes the resource, and upon its destruction frees the resource. Unfortunately, this technique cannot be used in C because we are not notified about the destruction of an object. But in C++, using destructors, this technique can be used effectively. In RAII objects, resource initialization happens in the constructor and the code required to de-initialize the resource is put into the destructor. Note that in C++, the destructor is invoked automatically when an object is going out of scope or being deleted.

As a conclusion, the following guidelines are important when working with Heap memory:

- Heap memory allocation is not free, and it has its own costs. Not all memory allocation functions have the same cost and, usually, `malloc` is the cheapest one.

- All memory blocks allocated from the Heap space must be freed either immediately when they are not needed anymore or just before ending the program.

- Since Heap memory blocks have no scope, the program must be able to manage the memory in order to avoid any possible leakage.

- Sticking to a chosen memory management strategy for each Heap memory block seems to be necessary.

- The chosen strategy and its assumptions should be documented throughout the code wherever the block is accessed so that future programmers will know about it.

- In certain programming languages like C++, we can use RAII objects to manage a resource, possibly a Heap memory block.

So far, we have considered that we have enough memory to store big objects and run any kind of program. But in the following section, we are going to put some constraints on the available memory and discuss the environments where the memory is low, or it is costly (in terms of money, time, performance, and so on) to add further memory storage. In such cases, we need to use the available memory in the most efficient way.

Memory management in constrained environments

There are environments in which memory is a precious resource, and it is often limited. There are also other environments in which performance is a key factor and programs should be fast, no matter how much memory we have. Regarding memory management, each of these environments requires a specific technique to overcome the memory shortage and performance degradation. First, we need to know what a constrained environment is.

A constrained environment does not necessarily have a low memory capacity. There are usually some *constraints* that limit the memory usage for a program. These constraints can be your customer's hard limits regarding memory usage, or it could be because of a hardware that provides the low memory capacity, or it can be because of an operating system that does not support a bigger memory (for example, MS-DOS).

Even if there are no constraints or hardware limitations, we as programmers try our best to use the least possible amount of memory and use it in an optimal way. Memory consumption is one of the key *non-functional requirements* in a project and should be monitored and tuned carefully.

In this section, we'll first introduce the techniques used in low memory environments for overcoming the shortage issue, and then we will talk about the memory techniques usually used in performant environments in order to boost the performance of the running programs.

Memory-constrained environments

In these environments, limited memory is always a constraint, and algorithms should be designed in a way in order to cope with memory shortages. Embedded systems with a memory size of tens to hundreds of megabytes are usually in this category. There are a few tips about memory management in such environments, but none of them work as well as having a nicely tuned algorithm. In this case, algorithms with a low memory complexity are usually used. These algorithms usually have a higher *time complexity*, which should be traded off with their low memory usage.

To elaborate more on this, every algorithm has specific *time* and *memory* complexities. Time complexity describes the relationship between the input size and the time that the algorithm takes to complete. Similarly, memory complexity describes the relationship between the input size and the memory that the algorithm consumes to complete its task. These complexities are usually denoted as *Big-O functions*, which we don't want to deal with in this section. Our discussion is qualitative, so we don't need any math to talk about memory-constrained environments.

An algorithm should ideally have a low time complexity and also a low memory complexity. In other words, having a fast algorithm consuming a low amount of memory is highly desirable, but it is unusual to have this "best of both worlds" situation. It is also unexpected to have an algorithm with high memory consumption while not performing well

Most of the time, we have a trade-off between memory and speed, which represents time. As an example, a sorting algorithm that is faster than another algorithm usually consumes more memory than the other, despite the fact that both of them do the same job.

It is a good but conservative practice, especially when writing a program, to assume that we are writing code for a memory-constrained system, even if we know that we will have more than enough memory in the final production environment. We make this assumption because we want to mitigate the risk of having too much memory consumption.

Note that the driving force behind this assumption should be controlled and adjusted based on a fairly accurate guess about the average memory availability, in terms of size, as part of the final setup. Algorithms designed for memory-constrained environments are intrinsically slower, and you should be careful about this trap.

In the upcoming sections, we will cover some techniques that can help us to collect some wasted memory or to use less memory in memory-constrained environments.

Packed structures

One of the easiest ways to use less memory is to use packed structures. Packed structures discard the memory alignment and they have a more compact memory layout for storing their fields.

Using packed structures is actually a trade-off. You consume less memory because you discard memory alignments and eventually end up with more memory read time while loading a structure variable. This will result in a slower program.

This method is simple but not recommended for all programs. For more information regarding this method, you can read the *Structures* section found in *Chapter 1, Essential Features*.

Compression

This is an effective technique, especially for programs working with a lot of textual data that should be kept inside the memory. Textual data has a high *compression ratio* in comparison to binary data. This technique allows a program to store the compressed form instead of the actual text data with a huge memory return.

However, saving memory is not free; since compression algorithms are *CPU-bound* and computation-intensive, the program would have worse performance in the end. This method is ideal for programs that keep textual data that is not required often; otherwise, a lot of compression/decompression operations are needed, and the program would be almost unusable eventually.

External data storage

Using external data storage in the forms of a network service, a cloud infrastructure, or simply a hard drive is a very common and useful technique for resolving low memory issues. Since it is usually considered that a program might be run in a limited or low memory environment, there are a lot of examples that use this method to be able to consume less memory even in environments in which enough memory is available.

This technique usually assumes that memory is not the main storage, but it acts as *cache* memory. Another assumption is that we cannot keep the whole data in the memory and at any moment, only a portion of data or a *page* of data can be loaded into the memory.

These algorithms are not directly addressing the low memory problem, but they are trying to solve another issue: slow external data storage. External data storage is always too slow in comparison to the main memory. So, the algorithms should balance the reads from the external data store and their internal memory. All database services, such as PostgreSQL and Oracle, use this technique.

In most projects, it is not very wise to design and write these algorithms from scratch because these algorithms are not that trivial and simple to write. The teams behind famous libraries such as SQLite have been fixing bugs for years.

If you need to access an external data storage such as a file, a database, or a host on the network while having a low memory footprint, there are always options out there for you.

Performant environments

As we have explained in the previous sections about the time and memory complexities of an algorithm, it is usually expected to consume more memory when you want to have a faster algorithm. In this section, we therefore expect to consume more memory for the sake of increased performance.

An intuitive example of this statement can be using a cache in order to increase the performance. Caching data means consuming more memory, but we could expect to get better performance if the cache is used properly.

But adding extra memory is not always the best way to increase performance. There are other methods that are directly or indirectly related to memory and can have a substantial impact on the performance of an algorithm. Before jumping to these methods, let's talk about caching first.

Caching

Caching is a general term for all similar techniques utilized in many parts of a computer system when two data storages with different read/write speeds are involved. For example, the CPU has a number of internal registers that perform quickly in terms of reading and writing operations. In addition, the CPU has to fetch data from the main memory, which is many times slower than its registers. A caching mechanism is needed here; otherwise, the lower speed of the main memory becomes dominant, and it hides the high computational speed of the CPU.

Working with database files is another example. Database files are usually stored on an external hard disk, which is far slower than the main memory, by orders of magnitude. Definitely, a caching mechanism is required here; otherwise, the slowest speed becomes dominant, and it determines the speed of the whole system.

Caching and the details around it deserve to have a whole dedicated chapter since there are abstract models and specific terminology that should be explained.

Using these models, one can predict how well a cache would behave and how much *performance gain* could be expected after introducing the cache. Here, we try to explain caching in a simple and intuitive manner.

Suppose that you have slow storage that can contain many items. You also have another fast storage, but it can contain a limited number of items. This is an obvious tradeoff. We can call the faster but smaller storage a *cache*. It would be reasonable if you bring items from the slow storage into the fast one and process them on the fast storage, simply because it is faster.

From time to time, you have to go to slow storage in order to bring over more items. It is obvious that you won't bring only one item over from the slow storage, as this would be very inefficient. Rather, you will bring a *bucket* of items into the faster storage. Usually, it is said that the items are cached into the faster storage.

Suppose that you are processing an item that requires you to load some other item from the slow storage. The first thing that comes to mind is to search for the required item inside the recently brought bucket, which is in the cache storage at the moment.

If you could find the item in the cache, there is no need to retrieve it from the slow storage, and this is called a *hit*. If the item is missing from the cache storage, you have to go to the slow storage and read another bucket of items into the cache memory. This is called a *miss*. It is clear that the more hits you observe, the more performance you get.

The preceding description can be applied to the CPU cache and the main memory. The CPU cache stores recent instructions and data read from the main memory, and the main memory is slow compared to the CPU cache memory.

In the following section, we discuss cache-friendly code, and we observe why cache-friendly code can be executed faster by the CPU.

Cache-friendly code

When the CPU is executing an instruction, it has to fetch all required data first. The data is located in the main memory at a specific address that is determined by the instruction.

The data has to be transferred to the CPU registers before any computation. But the CPU usually brings more blocks than are expected to be fetched and puts them inside its cache.

Next time, if a value is needed in the *proximity* of the previous address, it should exist in the cache, and the CPU can use the cache instead of the main memory, which is far faster than reading it from the main memory. As we explained in the previous section, this is a *cache hit*. If the address is not found in the CPU cache, it is a *cache miss*, and the CPU has to access the main memory to read the target address and bring required data which is quite slow. In general, higher hit rates result in faster executions.

But why does the CPU fetch the neighboring addresses (the proximity) around an address? It is because of the *principle of locality*. In computer systems, it is usually observed that the data located in the same neighborhood is more frequently accessed. So, the CPU behaves according to this principle and brings more data from a local reference. If an algorithm can exploit this behavior, it can be executed faster by the CPU. This is why we refer to such algorithm as a *cache-friendly* algorithm.

Example 5.6 demonstrates the difference between the performances of cache-friendly code and non-cache-friendly code:

```c
#include <stdio.h>  // For printf function
#include <stdlib.h> // For heap memory functions
#include <string.h> // For strcmp function

void fill(int* matrix, int rows, int columns) {
  int counter = 1;
  for (int i = 0; i < rows; i++) {
    for (int j = 0; j < columns; j++) {
      *(matrix + i * columns + j) = counter;
    }
    counter++;
  }
}

void print_matrix(int* matrix, int rows, int columns) {
  int counter = 1;
  printf("Matrix:\n");
  for (int i = 0; i < rows; i++) {
    for (int j = 0; j < columns; j++) {
      printf("%d ", *(matrix + i * columns + j));
    }
    printf("\n");
  }
}

void print_flat(int* matrix, int rows, int columns) {
  printf("Flat matrix: ");
  for (int i = 0; i < (rows * columns); i++) {
    printf("%d ", *(matrix + i));
  }
  printf("\n");
}

int friendly_sum(int* matrix, int rows, int columns) {
  int sum = 0;
  for (int i = 0; i < rows; i++) {
    for (int j = 0; j < columns; j++) {
      sum += *(matrix + i * columns + j);
    }
  }
  return sum;
```

```
}

int not_friendly_sum(int* matrix, int rows, int columns) {
  int sum = 0;
  for (int j = 0; j < columns; j++) {
    for (int i = 0; i < rows; i++) {
      sum += *(matrix + i * columns + j);
    }
  }
  return sum;
}

int main(int argc, char** argv) {

  if (argc < 4) {
    printf("Usage: %s [print|friendly-sum|not-friendly-sum] ");
    printf("[number-of-rows] [number-of-columns]\n", argv[0]);
    exit(1);
  }
  char* operation = argv[1];
  int rows = atol(argv[2]);
  int columns = atol(argv[3]);

  int* matrix = (int*)malloc(rows * columns * sizeof(int));
  fill(matrix, rows, columns);

  if (strcmp(operation, "print") == 0) {
    print_matrix(matrix, rows, columns);
    print_flat(matrix, rows, columns);
  }
  else if (strcmp(operation, "friendly-sum") == 0) {
    int sum = friendly_sum(matrix, rows, columns);
    printf("Friendly sum: %d\n", sum);
  }
  else if (strcmp(operation, "not-friendly-sum") == 0) {
    int sum = not_friendly_sum(matrix, rows, columns);
    printf("Not friendly sum: %d\n", sum);
  }
  else {
    printf("FATAL: Not supported operation!\n");
    exit(1);
  }

  free(matrix);
  return 0;
}
```

Code Box 5-12 [ExtremeC_examples_chapter5_6.c]: Example 5.6 demonstrates the performance of cache-friendly code and non-cache-friendly code

The preceding program computes and prints the sum of all elements in a matrix, but it also does more than that.

The user can pass options to this program, which alters its behavior. Suppose that we want to print a 2 by 3 matrix that is initialized by an algorithm written in the fill function. The user has to pass the print option with the desired number of rows and columns. Next, you can see how these options are passed to the final executable binary:

```
$ gcc ExtremeC_examples_chapter5_6.c -o ex5_6.out
$ ./ex5_6.out print 2 3
Matrix:
1 1 1
2 2 2
Flat matrix: 1 1 1 2 2 2
$
```

Shell Box 5-21: Output of example 5.6 showing a 2 by 3 matrix

The output consists of two different prints for the matrix. The first is the 2D representation of the matrix and the second is the *flat* representation of the same matrix. As you can see, the matrix is stored as a *row-major order* in memory. This means that we store it row by row. So, if something from a row is fetched by the CPU, it is probable that all of the elements in that row are fetched too. Hence, it would be better to do our summation in row-major order and not *column-major* order.

If you look at the code again, you can see that the summation done in the friendly_sum function is row-major, and the summation performed in the not_friendly_sum function is column-major. Next, we can compare the time it takes to perform the summation of a matrix with 20,000 rows and 20,000 columns. As you can see, the difference is very clear:

```
$ time ./ex5_6.out friendly-sum 20000 20000
Friendly sum: 1585447424

real    0m5.192s
user    0m3.142s
sys     0m1.765s

$ time ./ex5_6.out not-friendly-sum 20000 20000
Not friendly sum: 1585447424
```

```
real    0m15.372s
user    0m14.031s
sys     0m0.791s
$
```

Shell Box 5-22: Demonstration of the time difference between the column-major and row-major matrix summation algorithms

The difference between the measured times is about 10 seconds! The program is compiled on a macOS machine using the `clang` compiler. The difference means that the same logic, using the same amount of memory, can take much longer – just by selecting a different order of accessing the matrix elements! This example clearly shows the effect of cache-friendly code.

 Note:
The `time` utility is available in all Unix-like operating systems. It can be used to measure the time a program takes to finish.

Before continuing to the next technique, we should talk a bit more about the allocation and deallocation cost.

Allocation and deallocation cost

Here, we want to specifically talk about the cost of Heap memory allocation and deallocation. This might be a bit of a surprise if you realize that Heap memory allocation and deallocation operations are time-and memory-consuming and are usually expensive, especially when you need to allocate and deallocate Heap memory blocks many times per second.

Unlike Stack allocation, which is relatively fast and the allocation itself requires no further memory, Heap allocation requires finding a free block of memory with enough size, and this can be costly.

There are many algorithms designed for memory allocation and deallocation, and there is always a tradeoff between the allocation and deallocation operations. If you want to allocate quickly, you have to consume more memory as part of the allocation algorithm and vice versa if you want to consume less memory you can choose to spend more time with a slower allocation.

There are memory allocators for C other than those provided by the default C standard library through the `malloc` and `free` functions. Some of these memory allocator libraries are `ptmalloc`, `tcmalloc`, `Haord`, and `dlmalloc`.

Going through all allocators here is beyond the scope of this chapter, but it would be good practice for you to go through them and give them a try for yourself.

What is the solution to this silent problem? It is simple: allocate and deallocate less frequently. This may seem impossible in some programs that are required to have a high rate of Heap allocations. These programs usually allocate a big block of the Heap memory and try to manage it themselves. It is like having another layer of allocation and deallocation logic (maybe simpler than implementations of `malloc` and `free`) on top of a big block of the Heap memory.

There is also another method, which is using *memory pools*. We'll briefly explain this technique before we come to the end of this chapter.

Memory pools

As we described in the previous section, memory allocation and deallocation are costly. Using a pool of preallocated fixed-size Heap memory blocks is an effective way to reduce the number of allocations and gain some performance. Each block in the pool usually has an identifier, which can be acquired through an API designed for pool management. Also, the block can be released later when it is not needed. Since the amount of allocated memory remains almost fixed, it is an excellent choice for algorithms willing to have deterministic behavior in memory-constrained environments.

Describing memory pools in further detail is beyond the scope of this book; many useful resources on this topic exist online if you wish to read more about it.

Summary

As part of this chapter, we mainly covered the Stack and Heap segments and the way they should be used. After that, we briefly discussed memory-constrained environments and we saw how techniques like caching and memory pools can increase the performance.

In this chapter:

- We discussed the tools and techniques used for probing both Stack and Heap segments.
- We introduced debuggers and we used `gdb` as our main debugger to troubleshoot memory-related issues.
- We discussed memory profilers and we used `valgrind` to find memory issues such as leakages or dangling pointers happening at runtime.

- We compared the lifetime of a Stack variable and a Heap block and we explained how we should judge the lifetime of such memory blocks.

- We saw that memory management is automatic regarding Stack variables, but it is fully manual with Heap blocks.

- We went through the common mistakes that happen when dealing with Stack variables.

- We discussed the constrained environments and we saw how memory tuning can be done in these environments.

- We discussed the performant environments and what techniques can be used to gain some performance.

The next four chapters together cover object orientation in C. This might at first glance seem to be unrelated to C, but in fact, this is the correct way to write object-oriented code in C. As part of these chapters, you will be introduced to the proper way of designing and solving a problem in an object-oriented fashion, and you will get guidance through writing readable and correct C code.

The next chapter covers encapsulation and the basics of object-oriented programming by providing the required theoretical discussion and examples to explore the topics discussed.

Chapter 06

OOP and Encapsulation

There are many great books and articles on the subject of object-oriented programming or OOP. But I don't think that many of them address the same topic using a non-OOP language such as C! How is that even possible? Are we even able to write object-oriented programs with a programming language that has no support for it? To be precise, is it possible to write an object-oriented program using C?

The short answer to the above question is yes, but before explaining how, we need to explain why. We need to break the question down and see what OOP really means. Why is it possible to write an object-oriented program using a language that has no claim for object-orientation support? This seems like a paradox, but it's not, and our effort in this chapter is to explain why that's possible and how it should be done.

Another question that may puzzle you is that what's the point of having such discussions and knowing about OOP when you are going to use C as your primary programming language? Almost all existing mature C code bases such as open source kernels, implementation of services like HTTPD, Postfix, nfsd, ftpd, and many other C libraries such as OpenSSL and OpenCV, are all written in an object-oriented fashion. This doesn't mean that C is object-oriented; instead, the approach these projects have taken to organize their internal structure comes from an object-oriented mindset.

I highly recommend reading this chapter together with the next three chapters and getting to know more about OOP because firstly, it will enable you to think and design like the engineers who have designed the libraries mentioned before, and secondly, it would be highly beneficial when reading the sources of such libraries.

C does not support object-oriented concepts such as classes, inheritance, and virtual functions in its syntax. However, it does support object-oriented concepts – in an indirect way. In fact, nearly all the computer languages through history have supported OOP intrinsically – way before the days of Smalltalk, C++, and Java. That's because there must be a way in every general-purpose programming language to extend its data types and it is the first step towards OOP.

C cannot and *should not* support object-oriented features in its syntax; not because of its age, but because of very good reasons that we're going to talk about in this chapter. Simply put, you can still write an object-oriented program using C, but it takes a bit of extra effort to get around the complexity.

There are a few books and articles regarding OOP in C, and they usually try to create a *type system* for writing classes, implementing inheritance, polymorphism, and more, using C. These books look at adding OOP support as a set of functions, macros, and a preprocessor, all of which can be used together to write object-oriented programs with C. This won't be the approach we take in this chapter. We are not going to create a new C++ out of C; instead, we want to speculate how C has the potential to be used for OOP.

It is usually said that OOP is another programming paradigm together with procedural and functional paradigms. But OOP is more than that. OOP is more like a way of thinking about and analyzing a problem. It is an attitude towards the universe and the hierarchy of objects within it. It is part of our ancient, intrinsic, and inherited method for comprehending and analyzing the physical and abstract entities around us. It is so fundamental to our understanding of nature.

We've always thought about every problem from an object-oriented point of view. OOP is just about applying the same point of view that humans have always adopted, but this time using a programming language to solve a computational problem. All this explains why OOP is the most common programming paradigm used for writing software.

This chapter, together with the following three chapters, are going to show that any concept within OOP can be implemented in C – even though it might be complex to do. We know we can have OOP with C because some people have already done it, especially when they created C++ on top of C, and since they have built many complex and successful programs in C in an object-oriented fashion.

What these chapters are *not* going to suggest is a certain library or set of macros that you should use for declaring a class or establishing an inheritance relation or working with other OOP concepts. In addition, we won't impose any methodology or discipline such as specific naming conventions. We will simply use raw C to implement OOP concepts.

The reason why we're dedicating **four whole chapters** to OOP with C is because of the heavy theory behind object orientation and the various examples that are necessary to be explored in order to demonstrate all of it. Most of the essential theory behind OOP is going to be explained in this chapter, while the more practical topics will be dealt with in the following chapters. With all that said, we need to discuss the theory because the OOP concepts are usually new to most skilled C programmers, even those with many years of experience.

The upcoming four chapters together cover almost anything that you might come across in OOP. In this chapter, we are going to discuss the following:

- First of all, we'll give definitions for the most fundamental terms used in OOP literature. We'll define classes, objects, attributes, behaviors, methods, domains, and more. These terms will be used heavily throughout these four chapters. They are also vital to your understanding of other OOP-related resources because they are a staple part of the accepted language of OOP.

- The first part of this chapter is not wholly about terminology; we'll also heavily discuss the roots of object orientation and the philosophy behind it, exploring the nature of object-oriented thinking.

- The second section of this chapter is dedicated to C and why it is not, and cannot, be object-oriented. This is an important question that should be asked and properly answered. This topic will be further discussed in *Chapter 10, Unix – History and Architecture*, where we will be exploring Unix and its close relationship to C.

- The third section of this chapter talks about *encapsulation*, which is one of the most fundamental concepts of OOP. Put simply, it's what allows you to create objects and use them. The fact that you can put variables and methods inside an object comes directly from encapsulation. This is discussed thoroughly in the third section, and several examples are given.

- The chapter then moves on to *information-hiding*, which is something of a side effect (though a very important one) of having encapsulation. Without information-hiding, we wouldn't be able to isolate and decouple software modules, and we'd effectively be unable to provide implementation-independent APIs to clients. This is the last thing we discuss as part of this chapter.

As mentioned, the whole topic will cover four chapters, with the following chapters picking up from the *composition* relationship. From there, the upcoming chapters will cover *aggregation, inheritance, polymorphism, abstraction*.

In this chapter, though, we'll start with the theory behind OOP and look at how we can extract an object model from our thought process regarding a software component.

Object-oriented thinking

As we said in the chapter introduction, object-oriented thinking is the way in which we break down and analyze what surrounds us. When you're looking at a vase on a table, you're able to understand that the vase and the table are separate objects without any heavy analysis.

Unconsciously, you are aware that there is a border between them that separates them. You know that you could change the color of the vase, and the color of the table would remain unchanged.

These observations show us that we view our environment from an object-oriented perspective. In other words, we are just creating a reflection of the surrounding object-oriented reality in our minds. We also see this a lot in computer games, 3D modeling software, and engineering software, all of which can entail many objects interacting with each other.

OOP is about bringing object-oriented thinking to software design and development. Object-oriented thinking is our default way of processing our surroundings, and that's why OOP has become the most commonly used paradigm for writing software.

Of course, there are problems that would be hard to solve if you go with the object-oriented approach, and they would have been analyzed and resolved easier if you chose another paradigm, but these problems can be considered relatively rare.

In the following sections, we are going to find out more about the translation of object-oriented thinking into writing object-oriented code.

Mental concepts

You'd be hard-pressed to find a program that completely lacks at least some traces of object-oriented thinking, even if it had been written using C or some other non-OOP language. If a human writes a program, it will be naturally object-oriented. This will be evident even just in the variable names. Look at the following example. It declares the variables required to keep the information of 10 students:

```
char*    student_first_names[10];
char*    student_surnames[10];
  int    student_ages[10];
double   student_marks[10];
```

Code Box 6-1: Four arrays related by having the student_ prefix, according to a naming convention, supposed to keep the information of 10 students

The declarations found in *Code Box 6-1* show how we use variable names to group some variables under the same concept, which in this case is the *student*. We have to do this; else we would get confused by ad hoc names that don't make any sense to our object-oriented minds. Suppose that we had something such as this instead:

```
   char*   aaa[10];
   char*   bbb[10];
     int   ccc[10];
  double   ddd[10];
```

Code Box 6-2: Four arrays with ad hoc names supposed to keep the information of 10 students!

Using such variable names as seen in *Code Box 6-2*, however much experience in programming you have, you must admit that you'd have a lot of trouble dealing with this when writing an algorithm. Variable naming is – and has always been – important, because the names remind us of the concepts in our mind and the relationships between data and those concepts. By using this kind of ad hoc naming, we lose those concepts and their relationships in the code. This may not pose an issue for the computer, but it complicates the analysis and troubleshooting for us programmers and increases the likelihood of us making mistakes.

Let's clarify more about what we mean by a concept in our current context. A concept is a mental or abstract image that exists in the mind as a thought or an idea. A *concept* could be formed by the perception of a real-world entity or could simply be entirely imaginary and abstract. When you look at a tree or when you think about a car, their corresponding images come to mind as two different concepts.

Note that sometimes we use the term concept in a different context, such as in "object-oriented concepts," which obviously doesn't use the word concept in the same way as the definition we just gave. The word concept, used in relation to technology-related topics, simply refers to the principles to understand regarding a topic. For now, we'll use this technology-related definition.

Concepts are important to object-oriented thinking because if you cannot form and maintain an understanding of objects in your mind, you cannot extract details about what they represent and relate to, and you cannot understand their interrelations.

So, object-oriented thinking is about thinking in terms of concepts and their relationships. It follows, then, that if you want to write a proper object-oriented program, you need to have a proper understanding of all the relevant objects, their corresponding concepts, and also their relationships, in your mind.

An object-oriented map formed in your mind, which consists of many concepts and their mutual interrelations, cannot be easily communicated to others, for instance when approaching a task as a team. More than that, such mental concepts are volatile and elusive, and they can get forgotten very easily. This also puts an extra emphasis on the fact that you will need models and other tools for representation, in order to translate your mind map into communicable ideas.

Mind maps and object models

In this section, we look at an example to understand further what we've been discussing so far. Suppose that we have a written description of a scene. The purpose of describing something is to communicate the related specific concepts to the audience. Think of it this way: the one who is describing has a map in their mind that lays out various concepts and how they all link together; their aim is to communicate that mind map to the audience. You might say that this is more or less the goal of all artistic expression; it is actually what's happening when you look at a painting, listen to a piece of music, or read a novel.

Now we are going to look at a written description. It describes a classroom. Relax your mind and try to imagine what you are reading about. Everything you see in your mind is a concept communicated by the following description:

Our classroom is an old room with two big windows. When you enter the room, you can see the windows on the opposite wall. There are a number of brown wooden chairs in the middle of the room. There are five students sitting on the chairs, and two of them are boys. There is a green, wooden blackboard on the wall to your right, and the teacher is talking to the students. He is an old man wearing a blue shirt.

Now, let's see what concepts have formed in our minds. Before we do that though, bear in mind that your imagination can run away without you noticing. So, let's do our best to limit ourselves to the boundaries of the description. For example, I could imagine more and say that the girls are blonde. But that is not mentioned in the description, so we won't take that into account. In the next paragraph, I explain what has been shaped in my mind, and before continuing, you should also try to do that for yourself.

In my mind, there are five concepts (or mental images, or objects), one for each student in the class. There are also another five concepts for the chairs. There is another concept for the wood and another one for the glass. And I know that every chair is made from wood. This is a relationship, between the concept of wood and the concepts of the chairs. In addition, I know that every student is sitting on a chair. As such, there are five relationships – between chairs and students. We could continue to identify more concepts and relate them. In no time, we'd have a huge and complex graph describing the relationships of hundreds of concepts.

Now, pause for a moment and see how differently you were extracting the concepts and their relationships. That's a lesson that everyone can do this in a different way. This procedure also happens when you want to solve a particular problem. You need to create a mind map before attacking the problem. This is the phase that we call the *understanding phase*.

You solve a problem using an approach that is based on the concepts of the problem and the relationships you find between them. You explain your solution in terms of those concepts, and if someone wants to understand your solution, they should understand the concepts and their relationships first.

You'd be surprised if I told you this is what exactly happens when you try to solve a problem using a computer, but that is exactly the case. You break the problem into objects (same as the concepts in a mental context) and the relationships between them, and then you try to write a program, based on those objects, that eventually resolves the problem.

The program that you write simulates the concepts and their relations as you have them in your mind. The computer runs the solution, and you can verify whether it works. You are still the person who solves the problem, but now a computer is your colleague, since it can execute your solution, which is now described as a series of machine-level instructions translated from your mind map, much faster and more accurately.

An object-oriented program simulates concepts in terms of objects, and while we create a mind map for a problem in our minds, the program creates an object model in its memory. In other words, the terms *concept*, *mind*, and *mind map* are equivalent to *object*, *memory*, and *object model* respectively, if we are going to compare a human with an object-oriented program. This is the most important correlation we offer in this section, which relates the way we think to an object-oriented program.

But why are we using computers to simulate our mind maps? Because computers are good when it comes to speed and precision. This is a very classic answer to such questions, but it is still a relevant answer to our question. Creating and maintaining a big mind map and the corresponding object model is a complex task and is one that computers can do very well. As another advantage, the object model created by a program can be stored on a disk and used later.

A mind map can be forgotten or altered by emotions, but computers are emotionless, and object models are far more robust than human thoughts. That's why we should write object-oriented programs: to be able to transfer the concepts of our minds to effective programs and software.

 Note:
So far, nothing has been invented that can download and store a mind map from someone's mind – but perhaps in the future!

Objects are not in code

If you look at the memory of a running object-oriented program, you'll find it full of objects, all of which are interrelated. That's the same for humans. If you consider a human as a machine, you could say that they are always up and running until they die. Now, that's an important analogy. Objects can only exist in a running program, just as concepts can only exist in a living mind. That means you have objects only when you have a running program.

This may look like a paradox because when you are writing a program (an object-oriented one), the program doesn't yet exist and so cannot be running! So, how can we write object-oriented code when there is no running program and no objects?

Note:
When you are writing object-oriented code, no object exists. The objects are created once you build the code into an executable program and run it.

OOP is not actually about creating objects. It is about creating a set of instructions that will lead to a fully dynamic object model when the program is run. So, the object-oriented code should be able to create, modify, relate, and even delete objects, once compiled and run.

As such, writing object-oriented code is a tricky task. You need to imagine the objects and their relations before they exist. This is exactly the reason why OOP can be complex and why we need a programming language that supports object-orientation. The art of imagining something which is not yet created and describing or engineering its various details is usually called *design*. That's why this process is usually called **object-oriented design** (OOD) in object-oriented programming.

In object-oriented code, we only plan to create objects. OOP leads to a set of instructions for when and how an object should be created. Of course, it is not only about creation. All the operations regarding an object can be detailed using a programming language. An OOP language is a language that has a set of instructions (and grammar rules) that allow you to write and plan different object-related operations.

So far, we've seen that there is a clear correspondence between concepts in the human mind and objects in a program's memory. So, there should be a correspondence between the operations that can be performed on concepts and objects.

Every object has a dedicated life cycle. This is also true for concepts in the mind. At some point, an idea comes to mind and creates a mental image as a concept, and at some other point, it fades away. The same is true for objects. An object is constructed at one point and is destructed at another time.

As a final note, some mental concepts are very firm and constant (as opposed to volatile and transient concepts which come and go). It seems that these concepts are independent of any mind and have been in existence even when there were no minds to comprehend them. They are mostly mathematical concepts. The number 2 is an example. We have only one number 2 in the whole universe! That's amazing. It means that you and I have the very same concept in our minds of the number 2; if we tried to change it, it would no longer be the number 2. This is exactly where we leave the object-oriented realm, and we step into another realm, full of immutable objects, that is described under the title of the *functional programming* paradigm.

Object attributes

Each concept in any mind has some attributes associated with it. If you remember, in our classroom description, we had a chair, named *chair1*, that was brown. In other words, every chair object has an attribute called color and it was brown for the *chair1* object. We know that there were four other chairs in the classroom, and they had their color attributes which could have different values. In our description, all of them were brown, but it could be that in another description, one or two of them were yellow.

An object can have more than one attribute or a set of attributes. We call the values assigned to these attributes, collectively, the *state* of an object. The state can be thought of simply as a list of values, each one belonging to a certain attribute, attached to an object. An object can be modified during its lifetime. Such an object is said to be *mutable*. This simply means that the state can be changed during its lifetime. Objects can also be *stateless*, which means that they don't carry any state (or any attributes).

An object can be *immutable* as well, exactly like the concept (or object) corresponding to the number 2, which cannot be altered — being immutable means that the state is determined upon construction and cannot be modified after that.

Note:
A stateless object can be thought of as an immutable object because its state cannot be changed throughout its lifetime. In fact, it has no state to be changed.

As a final note, immutable objects are especially important. The fact that their state cannot be altered is an advantage, especially when they are shared in a multithreaded environment.

Domain

Every program written to solve a particular problem, even an exceedingly small one, has a well-defined domain. Domain is another big term that is used widely in the literature of software engineering. The domain defines the boundaries in which software exhibits its functionality. It also defines the requirements that software should address.

A domain uses a specific and predetermined terminology (glossary) to deliver its mission and have engineers stay within its boundaries. Everyone participating in a software project should be aware of the domain in which their project is defined.

As an example, banking software is usually built for a very well-defined domain. It has a set of well-known terms as its glossary which includes account, credit, balance, transfer, loan, interest, and so on.

The definition of a domain is made clear by the terms found in its glossary; you wouldn't find the terms patient, medicine, and dosage in the banking domain, for instance.

If a programming language doesn't provide facilities for working with the concepts specific to a given domain (such as the concepts of patients and medicines in the healthcare domain), it would be difficult to write the software for that domain using that programming language – not impossible, but certainly complex. Moreover, the bigger the software is, the harder it becomes to develop and maintain.

Relations among objects

Objects can be inter-related; they can refer to each other to denote relationships. For example, as part of our classroom description, the object *student4* (the fourth student) might be related to the object *chair3* (the third chair) in regard to a relationship named *sitting on*. In other words, *student4* sits on *chair3*. This way, all objects within a system refer to each other and form a network of objects called an object model. As we've said before, an object model is the correspondent of the mind map that we form in our minds.

When two objects are related, a change in the state of one might affect the state of the other. Let's explain this by giving an example. Suppose that we have two unrelated objects, p1 and p2, representing pixels.

Object p1 has a set of attributes as follows: {x: 53, y: 345, red: 120, green: 45, blue: 178}. Object p2 has the attributes {x: 53, y: 346, red: 79, green: 162, blue: 23}.

Note:
The notation we used is almost but not quite the same as **JavaScript Object Notation** or **JSON**. In this notation, the attributes of an individual object are embraced within two curly braces, and the attributes are separated by commas. Each attribute has a corresponding value separated from the attribute by a colon.

Now, in order to make them related, they need to have an extra attribute to denote the relationship between themselves. The state of object p1 would change to {x: 53, y: 345, red: 120, green: 45, blue: 178, adjacent_down_pixel: p2}, and that of p2 would change to {x: 53, y: 346, red: 79, green: 162, blue: 23, adjacent_up_pixel: p1}.

The adjacent_down_pixel and adjacent_up_pixel attributes denote the fact that these pixel objects are adjacent; their y attributes differ only by 1 unit. Using such extra attributes, the objects realize that they are in a relationship with other objects. For instance, p1 knows that its adjacent_down_pixel is p2, and p2 knows that its adjacent_up_pixel is p1.

So, as we can see, if a relationship is formed between two objects, the states of those objects (or the lists of the values corresponding to their attributes) are changed. So, the relationship among objects is created by adding new attributes to them and because of that, the relationship becomes part of the objects' states. This, of course, has ramifications for the mutability or immutability of these objects.

Note that the subset of the attributes which define the state and immutability of an object can be changed from a domain to another, and it doesn't necessarily encompass all the attributes. In one domain, we might use only non-referring attributes (x, y, red, green, and blue, in the preceding example) as the state and in another domain, we might combine them all together with referring attributes (adjacent_up_pixel and adjacent_down_pixel in the preceding example).

Object-oriented operations

An OOP language allows us to plan the object construction, object destruction, and altering the states of an object in a soon-to-be-running program. So, let's start by looking at the object construction.

Note:
The term *construction* has been chosen carefully. We could use creation or building, but these terms are not accepted as part of the standard terminology in OOP literature. Creation refers to the memory allocation for an object, while construction means the initialization of its attributes.

There are two ways to plan the construction of an object:

- The first approach involves either constructing an empty object – one *without* any attributes in its state – or, more commonly, an object with a set of minimum attributes.

- More attributes will be determined and added as the code is being run. Using this method, the same object can have different attributes in two different executions of the same program, in accordance with the changes found in the surrounding environment.

- Each object is treated as a separate entity, and any two objects, even if they seem to belong to the same group (or class), by having a list of common attributes, may get different attributes in their states as the program continues.

- As an example, the already mentioned pixel objects p1 and p2 are both pixels (or they both belong to the same class named pixel) because they have the same attributes – x, y, red, green, and blue. After forming a relationship, they would have different states because they then have new and different attributes: p1 has the adjacent_down_pixel attribute, and p2 has the adjacent_up_pixel attribute.

- This approach is used in programming languages such as JavaScript, Ruby, Python, Perl, and PHP. Most of them are *interpreted programming languages*, and the attributes are kept as a *map* (or a *hash*) in their internal data structures that can be easily changed at runtime. This technique is usually called **prototype-based OOP**.

- The second approach involves constructing an object whose attributes are predetermined and won't change in the middle of execution. No more attributes are allowed to be added to such an object at runtime, and the object will retain its structure. Only the values of the attributes are allowed to change, and that's possible only when the object is mutable.

- To apply this approach, a programmer should create a predesigned *object template* or *class* that keeps track of all the attributes that need to be present in the object at runtime. Then, this template should be compiled and fed into the object-oriented language at runtime.

- In many programming languages, this object template is called a class. Programming languages such as Java, C++, and Python use this term to denote their object templates. This technique is usually known as **class-based OOP**. Note that Python supports both prototype-based and class-based OOP.

Note:
A class only determines the list of attributes present in an object but not the actual values assigned to them at runtime.

Note that an object and an *instance* are the same thing, and they can be used interchangeably. However, in some texts, there might be some slight differences between them. There is also another term, *reference*, which is worth mentioning and explaining. The term object or instance is used to refer to the actual place allocated in the memory for the values of that object, while a reference is like a pointer that refers to that object. So, we can have many references referring to the same object. Generally speaking, an object usually has no name, but a reference does have a name.

Note:
In C, we have pointers as the corresponding syntax for references. We also have both Stack objects and Heap objects. A Heap object does not have a name and we use pointers to refer to it. In contrast, a Stack object is actually a variable and hence has a name.

While it is possible to use both approaches, C and especially C++ are officially designed in a way to support the class-based approach. Therefore, when a programmer wants to create an object in C or C++, they need to have a class first. We will talk more about the class and its role in OOP in future sections.

The following discussion might seem a bit unrelated, but, in fact, it isn't. There are two schools of thought regarding how humans grow through life, and they match quite accurately the object construction approaches that we've talked about. One of these philosophies says that the human is empty at birth and has no essence (or state).

By living and experiencing different good and bad events in life, their essence starts to grow and evolves into something that has an independent and mature character. *Existentialism* is a philosophical tradition that promotes this idea.

Its famous precept is "Existence precedes essence". This simply means that the human first comes to existence and then gains their essence through life experience. This idea is awfully close to our prototype-based approach to object construction, in which the object is constructed empty and then evolves at runtime.

The other philosophy is older and is promoted mostly by religions. In this, the human is created based on an image (or an essence), and this image has been determined before the human comes to exist. This is most similar to the way in which we plan to construct an object based on a template or class. As the object creators, we prepare a class, and then a program starts to create objects according to that class.

Note:
There has been a great correspondence between the approaches that people in novels or stories, including both literature and history sources, take to overcome a certain difficulty and the algorithms we have designed in computer science to solve similar problems. I deeply believe that the way humans live and the reality they experience are in great harmony with what we understand about algorithms and data structures as part of computer science. The preceding discussion was a great example of such harmony between OOP and Philosophy.

Like object construction, object destruction happens at runtime; we have only the power to plan it in code. All resources allocated by an object throughout its lifetime should be released when it is destroyed. When an object is being destructed, all other related objects should be changed so that they no longer refer to the destroyed object. An object shouldn't have an attribute that refers to a non-existent object, otherwise we lose the *referential integrity* in our object model. It can lead to runtime errors such as memory corruption or segmentation fault, as well as logical errors such as miscalculations.

Modifying an object (or altering the state of an object) can happen in two different ways. It could simply be either a change in the value of an existing attribute or it could be the addition or removal of an attribute to/from the set of attributes in that object. The latter can only happen if we have chosen the prototype-based approach to object construction. Remember that altering the state of an object that is immutable is forbidden and usually, it is not permitted by an object-oriented language.

Objects have behaviors

Every object, together with its attributes, has a certain list of functionalities that it can perform. For instance, a car object is able to speed up, slow down, turn, and so on. In OOP, these functionalities are always in accordance with the domain requirements. For example, in a banking object model, a client can order a new account but cannot eat. Of course, the client is a person and can eat, but as long as eating functionality is not related to the banking domain, we don't consider it as a necessary functionality for a client object.

Every functionality is able to change the state of an object by altering the values of its attributes. As a simple example, a car object can accelerate. Acceleration is a functionality of the car object, and by accelerating, the speed of the car, which is one of its attributes, changes.

In summary, an object is simply a group of attributes and functionalities. In the later sections, we'll talk more about how to put these things together in an object.

So far, we have explained the fundamental terminology needed to study and understand OOP. The next step is to explain the fundamental concept of encapsulation. But, as a break, let's read about why C cannot be an OOP language.

C is not object-oriented, but why?

C is not object-oriented, but not because of its age. If age was a reason, we could have found a way to make it object-oriented by now. But, as you will see in *Chapter 12, The Most Recent C*, the latest standard of the C programming language, C18, doesn't try to make C an object-oriented language.

On the other hand, we have C++, which is the result of all efforts to have an OOP language based on C. If the fate of C was for it to be replaced by an object-oriented language, then there wouldn't be any demand for C today, mainly because of C++ – but the current demand for C engineers shows that this is not the case.

A human thinks in an object-oriented way, but a CPU executes machine-level instructions which are procedural. A CPU just executes a set of instructions one by one, and from time to time, it has to jump, fetch, and execute other instructions from a different address in memory; quite similar to function calls in a program written using a procedural programming language like C.

C cannot be object-oriented because it is located on the barrier between object orientation and procedural programming. Object orientation is the human understanding of a problem and procedural execution is what a CPU can do. Therefore, we need something to be in this position and make this barrier. Otherwise high-level programs, which are usually written in an object-oriented way, cannot be translated directly into procedural instructions to be fed into the CPU.

If you look at high-level programming languages like Java, JavaScript, Python, Ruby, and so on, they have a component or layer within their architecture which bridges between their environment and the actual C library found inside the operating system (the Standard C Library in Unix-like systems and Win32 API in Windows systems). For instance, **Java Virtual Machine** (**JVM**) does that in a Java platform. While not all these environments are necessarily object-oriented (for example JavaScript or Python can be both procedural and object-oriented), they need this layer to translate their high-level logic to low-level procedural instructions.

Encapsulation

In the previous sections, we saw that each object has a set of attributes and a set of functionalities attached to it. Here, we are going to talk about putting those attributes and functionalities into an entity called an object. We do this through a process called *encapsulation*.

Encapsulation simply means putting related things together into a *capsule* that represents an object. It happens first in your mind, and then it should be transferred to the code. The moment that you feel an object needs to have some attributes and functionalities, you are doing encapsulation in your mind; that encapsulation then needs to be transferred to the code level.

It is crucial to be able to encapsulate things in a programming language, otherwise keeping related variables together becomes an untenable struggle (we mentioned using naming conventions to accomplish this).

An object is made from a set of attributes and a set of functionalities. Both of these should be encapsulated into the object capsule. Let's first talk about *attribute encapsulation*.

Attribute encapsulation

As we saw before, we can always use variable names to do encapsulation and tie different variables together and group them under the same object. Following is an example:

```
int pixel_p1_x      = 56;
int pixel_p1_y      = 34;
int pixel_p1_red    = 123;
int pixel_p1_green  = 37;
int pixel_p1_blue   = 127;

int pixel_p2_x      = 212;
int pixel_p2_y      = 994;
int pixel_p2_red    = 127;
int pixel_p2_green  = 127;
int pixel_p2_blue   = 0;
```

Code Box 6-3: Some variables representing two pixels grouped by their names

This example clearly shows how variable names are used to group variables under p1 and p2, which somehow are *implicit* objects. By implicit, we mean that the programmer is the only one who is aware of the existence of such objects; the programming language doesn't know anything about them.

The programming language only sees 10 variables that seem to be independent of each other. This would be a very low level of encapsulation, to such an extent that it would not be officially considered as encapsulation. Encapsulation by variable names exists in all programming languages (because you can name variables), even in an assembly language.

What we need are approaches offering *explicit* encapsulation. By explicit, we mean that both the programmer and the programming language are aware of the encapsulation and the capsules (or objects) that exist. Programming languages that do not offer explicit *attribute encapsulation* are very hard to use.

Fortunately, C does offer explicit encapsulation, and that's one of the reasons behind why we are able to write so many intrinsically object-oriented programs with it more or less easily. On the other hand, as we see shortly in the next section, C doesn't offer explicit behavior encapsulation, and we have to come up with an implicit discipline to support this.

Note that having an explicit feature such as encapsulation in a programming language is always desired. Here, we only spoke about encapsulation, but this can be extended to many other object-oriented features, such as inheritance and polymorphism. Such explicit features allow a programming language to catch relevant errors at compile time instead of runtime.

Resolving errors at runtime is a nightmare, and so we should always try to catch errors at compile time. This is the main advantage of having an object-oriented language, which is completely aware of the object-oriented way of our thinking. An object-oriented language can find and report errors and violations in our design at compile time and keep us from having to resolve many severe bugs at runtime. Indeed, this is the reason why we are seeing more complex programming languages every day – to make everything explicit to the language.

Unfortunately, not all object-oriented features are explicit in C. That's basically why it is hard to write an object-oriented program with C. But there are more explicit features in C++ and, indeed, that's why it is called an object-oriented programming language.

In C, structures offer encapsulation. Let's change the code inside *Code Box 6-3*, and rewrite it using structures:

```
typedef struct {
    int x, y;
    int red, green, blue;
} pixel_t;
```

```
pixel_t p1, p2;

p1.x = 56;
p1.y = 34;
p1.red = 123;
p1.green = 37;
p1.blue = 127;

p2.x = 212;
p2.y = 994;
p2.red = 127;
p2.green = 127;
p2.blue = 0;
```

Code Box 6-4: The pixel_t structure and declaring two pixel_t variables

There are some important things to note regarding *Code Box 6-4*:

- The attribute encapsulation happens when we put the x, y, red, green, and blue attributes into a new type, pixel_t.

- Encapsulation always creates a new type; attribute encapsulation does this particularly in C. This is very important to note. In fact, this is the way that we make encapsulation explicit. Please note the _t suffix at the end of the pixel_t. It is very common in C to add the _t suffix to the end of the name of new types, but it is not mandatory. We use this convention throughout this book.

- p1 and p2 will be our explicit objects when this code is executed. Both of them are of the pixel_t type, and they have only the attributes dictated by the structure. In C, and especially C++, types dictate the attributes to their objects.

- The new type, pixel_t, is only the attributes of a class (or the object template). The word "class," remember, refers to a template of objects containing both attributes and functionalities. Since a C structure only keeps attributes, it cannot be a counterpart for a class. Unfortunately, we have no counterpart concept for a class in C; attributes and functionalities exist separately, and we implicitly relate them to each other in the code. Every class is implicit to C and it refers to a single structure together with a list of C functions. You'll see more of this in the upcoming examples, as part of this chapter and the future chapters.

- As you see, we are constructing objects based on a template (here, the structure of pixel_t), and the template has the predetermined attributes that an object should have at birth. Like we said before, the structure only stores attributes and not the functionalities.

- Object construction is very similar to the declaration of a new variable. The type comes first, then the variable name (here the object name) after that. While declaring an object, two things happen almost at the same time: first the memory is allocated for the object (creation), and then, the attributes are initialized (construction) using the default values. In the preceding example, since all attributes are integers, the default integer value in C is going to be used which is 0.

- In C and many other programming languages, we use a dot (.) to access an attribute inside an object, or an arrow (->) while accessing the attributes of a structure indirectly through its address stored in a pointer. The statement p1.x (or p1->x if p1 is a pointer) should be read as *the x attribute in the p1 object*.

As you know by now, attributes are certainly not the only things that can be encapsulated into objects. Now it is time to see how functionalities are encapsulated.

Behavior encapsulation

An object is simply a capsule of attributes and methods. The method is another standard term that we usually use to denote a piece of logic or functionality being kept in an object. It can be considered as a C function that has a name, a list of arguments, and a return type. Attributes convey *values* and methods convey *behaviors*. Therefore, an object has a list of values and can perform certain behaviors in a system.

In class-based object-oriented languages such as C++, it is very easy to group a number of attributes and methods together in a class. In prototype-based languages such as JavaScript, we usually start with an empty object (*ex nihilo*, or "from nothing") or clone from an existing object. To have behaviors in the object, we need to add methods. Look at the following example, which helps you gain an insight into how prototype-based programming languages work. It is written in JavaScript:

```javascript
// Construct an empty object
var clientObj = {};

// Set the attributes
clientObj.name = "John";
clientObj.surname = "Doe";

// Add a method for ordering a bank account
clientObj.orderBankAccount = function () {
    ...
```

```
}

...

// Call the method
clientObj.orderBankAccount();
```

Code Box 6-5: Constructing a client object in JavaScript

As you see in this example, on the 2nd line, we create an empty object. In the following two lines, we add two new attributes, name and surname, to our object. And on the following line, we add a new method, orderBankAccount, which points to a function definition. This line is an assignment actually. On the right-hand side is an *anonymous function*, which does not have a name and is assigned to the orderBankAccount attribute of the object, on the left-hand side. In other words, we store a function into the orderBankAccount attribute. On the last line, the object's method orderBankAccount is called. This example is a great demonstration of prototype-based programming languages, which only rely on having an empty object at first and nothing more.

The preceding example would be different in a class-based programming language. In these languages, we start by writing a class because without having a class, we can't have any object. The following code box contains the previous example but written in C++:

```
class Client {
public:
  void orderBankAccount() {
    ...
  }
  std::string name;
  std::string surname:
};
...
Client clientObj;
clientObj.name = "John";
clientObj.surname = "Doe";
...
clientObj.orderBankAccount ();
```

Code Box 6-6: Constructing the client object in C++

As you see, we started by declaring a new class, Client. On the 1st line, we declared a class, which immediately became a new C++ type. It resembles a capsule and is surrounded by braces. After declaring the class, we constructed the object clientObj from the Client type.

On the following lines, we set the attributes, and finally, we called the
`orderBankAccount` method on the `clientObj` object.

 Note:
In C++, methods are usually called *member functions* and
attributes are called *data members*.

If you look at the techniques employed by open source and well-known C
projects in order to encapsulate some items, you notice that there is a common
theme among them. In the rest of this section, we are going to propose a behavior
encapsulation technique which is based on the similar techniques observed in
such projects.

Since we'll be referring back to this technique often, I'm going to give it a name.
We call this technique **implicit encapsulation**. It's implicit because it doesn't offer
an explicit behavior encapsulation that C knows about. Based on what we've got
so far in the ANSI C standard, it is not possible to let C know about classes. So,
all techniques that try to address object orientation in C have to be implicit.

The implicit encapsulation technique suggests the following:

- Using C structures to keep the attributes of an object (explicit attribute
  encapsulation). These structures are called **attribute structures**.

- For behavior encapsulation, C functions are used. These functions are
  called **behavior functions**. As you might know, we cannot have functions
  in structures in C. So, these functions have to exist outside the attribute
  structure (implicit behavior encapsulation).

- Behavior functions must accept a structure pointer as one of their
  arguments (usually the first argument or the last one). This pointer
  points to the attribute structure of the object. That's because the behavior
  functions might need to read or modify the object's attributes, which is
  very common.

- Behavior functions should have proper names to indicate that they are
  related to the same class of objects. That's why sticking to a consistent
  naming convention is very important when using this technique. This
  is one of the two naming conventions that we try to stick to in these
  chapters in order to have a clear encapsulation. The other one is using
  `_t` suffix in the names of the attribute structures. However, of course, we
  don't force them and you can use your own custom naming conventions.

- The declaration statements corresponding to the behavior functions are
  usually put in the same header file that is used for keeping the declaration
  of the attribute structure. This header is called the **declaration header**.

- The definitions of the behavior functions are usually put in one or various separate source files which include the declaration header.

Note that with implicit encapsulation, classes do exist, but they are implicit and known only to the programmer. The following example, *example 6.1*, shows how to use this technique in a real C program. It is about a car object that accelerates until it runs out of fuel and stops.

The following header file, as part of *example 6.1*, contains the declaration of the new type, car_t, which is the attribute structure of the Car class. The header also contains the declarations required for the behavior functions of the Car class. We use the phrase "the Car class" to refer to the implicit class that is missing from the C code and it encompasses collectively the attribute structure and the behavior functions:

```
#ifndef EXTREME_C_EXAMPLES_CHAPTER_6_1_H
#define EXTREME_C_EXAMPLES_CHAPTER_6_1_H

// This structure keeps all the attributes
// related to a car object
typedef struct {
  char name[32];
  double speed;
  double fuel;
} car_t;

// These function declarations are
// the behaviors of a car object
void car_construct(car_t*, const char*);
void car_destruct(car_t*);
void car_accelerate(car_t*);
void car_brake(car_t*);
void car_refuel(car_t*, double);

#endif
```

Code Box 6-7 [ExtremeC_examples_chapter6_1.h]: The declarations of the attribute structure and the behavior functions of the Car class

As you see, the attribute structure car_t has three fields – name, speed, and fuel – which are the attributes of the car object. Note that car_t is now a new type in C, and we can now declare variables of this type. The behavior functions are also usually declared in the same header file, as you can see in the preceding code box. They start with the car_ prefix to put emphasis on the fact that all of them belong to the same class.

Something very important regarding the implicit encapsulation technique: each object has its own unique attribute structure variable, but all objects share the same behavior functions. In other words, we have to create a dedicated variable from the attribute structure type for each object, but we only write behavior functions once and we call them for different objects.

Note that the `car_t` attribute structure is not a class itself. It only contains the attributes of the `Car` class. The declarations all together make the implicit `Car` class. You'll see more examples of this as we go on.

There are many famous open source projects that use the preceding technique to write semi-object-oriented code. One example is `libcurl`. If you have a look at its source code, you will see a lot of structures and functions starting with `curl_`. You can find the list of such functions here: `https://curl.haxx.se/libcurl/c/allfuncs.html`.

The following source file contains the definitions of the behavior functions as part of example 6.1:

```c
#include <string.h>

#include "ExtremeC_examples_chapter6_1.h"

// Definitions of the above functions
void car_construct(car_t* car, const char* name) {
  strcpy(car->name, name);
  car->speed = 0.0;
  car->fuel = 0.0;
}

void car_destruct(car_t* car) {
  // Nothing to do here!
}

void car_accelerate(car_t* car) {
  car->speed += 0.05;
  car->fuel -= 1.0;
  if (car->fuel < 0.0) {
    car->fuel = 0.0;
  }
}

void car_brake(car_t* car) {
  car->speed -= 0.07;
  if (car->speed < 0.0) {
    car->speed = 0.0;
  }
```

```
    car->fuel -= 2.0;
    if (car->fuel < 0.0) {
      car->fuel = 0.0;
    }
  }

  void car_refuel(car_t* car, double amount) {
    car->fuel = amount;
  }
```

Code Box 6-8 [ExtremeC_examples_chapter6_1.c]: The definitions of the behavior functions
as part of the Car class

The Car's behavior functions are defined in *Code Box 6-8*. As you can see, all the functions accept a car_t pointer as their first argument. This allows the function to read and modify the attributes of an object. If a function is not receiving a pointer to an attribute structure, then it can be considered as an ordinary C function that does not represent an object's behavior.

Note that the declarations of behavior functions are usually found next to the declarations of their corresponding attribute structure. That's because the programmer is the sole person in charge of maintaining the correspondence of the attribute structure and the behavior functions, and the maintenance should be easy enough. That's why keeping these two sets close together, usually in the same header file, helps in maintaining the overall structure of the class, and eases the pain for future efforts.

In the following code box, you'll find the source file that contains the main function and performs the main logic. All the behavior functions will be used here:

```
#include <stdio.h>

#include "ExtremeC_examples_chapter6_1.h"

// Main function
int main(int argc, char** argv) {

  // Create the object variable
  car_t car;

  // Construct the object
  car_construct(&car, "Renault");

  // Main algorithm
```

```
  car_refuel(&car, 100.0);
  printf("Car is refueled, the correct fuel level is %f\n",
    car.fuel);
  while (car.fuel > 0) {
    printf("Car fuel level: %f\n", car.fuel);
    if (car.speed < 80) {
      car_accelerate(&car);
      printf("Car has been accelerated to the speed: %f\n",
car.speed);
    } else {
      car_brake(&car);
      printf("Car has been slowed down to the speed: %f\n",
car.speed);
    }
  }

  printf("Car ran out of the fuel! Slowing down ...\n");
  while (car.speed > 0) {
    car_brake(&car);
    printf("Car has been slowed down to the speed: %f\n",
      car.speed);
  }

  // Destruct the object
  car_destruct(&car);

  return 0;
}
```

Code Box 6-9 [ExtremeC_examples_chapter6_1_main.c]: The main function of example 6.1

As the first instruction in the `main` function, we've declared the `car` variable from the `car_t` type. The variable `car` is our first `car` object. On this line, we have allocated the memory for the object's attributes. On the following line, we constructed the object. Now on this line, we have initialized the attributes. You can initialize an object only when there is memory allocated for its attributes. In the code, the constructor accepts a second argument as the car's name. You may have noticed that we are passing the address of the `car` object to all `car_*` behavior functions.

Following that in the `while` loop, the `main` function reads the `fuel` attribute and checks whether its value is greater than zero. The fact that the `main` function, which is not a behavior function, is able to access (read and write) the `car`'s attributes is an important thing. The `fuel` and `speed` attributes, for instance, are examples of *public* attributes, which functions (external code) other than the behavior functions can access. We will come back to this point in the next section.

Before leaving the `main` function and ending the program, we've destructed the `car` object. This simply means that resources allocated by the object have been released at this phase. Regarding the `car` object in this example, there is nothing to be done for its destruction, but it is not always the case and destruction might have steps to be followed. We will see more of this in the upcoming examples. The destruction phase is mandatory and prevents memory leaks in the case of Heap allocations.

It would be good to see how we could write the preceding example in C++. This would help you to get an insight into how an OOP language understands classes and objects and how it reduces the overhead of writing proper object-oriented code.

The following code box, as part of *example 6.2*, shows the header file containing the `Car` class in C++:

```
#ifndef EXTREME_C_EXAMPLES_CHAPTER_6_2_H
#define EXTREME_C_EXAMPLES_CHAPTER_6_2_H

class Car {
public:
  // Constructor
  Car(const char*);
  // Destructor
  ~Car();

  void Accelerate();
  void Brake();
  void Refuel(double);

  // Data Members (Attributes in C)
  char name[32];
  double speed;
  double fuel;
};

#endif
```

Code Box 6-10 [ExtremeC_examples_chapter6_2.h]: The declaration of the Car class in C++

The main feature of the preceding code is the fact that C++ knows about classes. Therefore, the preceding code demonstrates an explicit encapsulation; both attribute and behavior encapsulations. More than that, C++ supports more object-oriented concepts such as constructors and destructors.

In the C++ code, all the declarations, both attributes and behaviors, are encapsulated in the class definition. This is the explicit encapsulation. Look at the two first functions that we have declared as the constructor and the destructor of the class. C doesn't know about the constructors and destructors; but C++ has a specific notation for them. For instance, the destructor starts with ~ and it has the same name as the class does.

In addition, as you can see, the behavior functions are missing the first pointer argument. That's because they all have access to the attributes inside the class. The next code box shows the content of the source file that contains the definition of the declared behavior functions:

```
#include <string.h>

#include "ExtremeC_examples_chapter6_2.h"

Car::Car(const char* name) {
  strcpy(this->name, name);
  this->speed = 0.0;
  this->fuel = 0.0;
}

Car::~Car() {
  // Nothing to do
}

void Car::Accelerate() {
  this->speed += 0.05;
  this->fuel -= 1.0;
  if (this->fuel < 0.0) {
    this->fuel = 0.0;
  }
}

void Car::Brake() {
  this->speed -= 0.07;
  if (this->speed < 0.0) {
    this->speed = 0.0;
  }
  this->fuel -= 2.0;
  if (this->fuel < 0.0) {
    this->fuel = 0.0;
  }
}

void Car::Refuel(double amount) {
  this->fuel = amount;
}
```

Code Box 6-11 [ExtremeC_examples_chapter6_2.cpp]: The definition of the Car class in C++

If you look carefully, you'll see that the car pointer in the C code has been replaced by a this pointer, which is a keyword in C++. The keyword this simply means the current object. I'm not going to explain it any further here, but it is a smart workaround to eliminate the pointer argument in C and make behavior functions simpler.

And finally, the following code box contains the `main` function that uses the preceding class:

```cpp
// File name: ExtremeC_examples_chapter6_2_main.cpp
// Description: Main function

#include <iostream>

#include "ExtremeC_examples_chapter6_2.h"

// Main function
int main(int argc, char** argv) {

  // Create the object variable and call the constructor
  Car car("Renault");

  // Main algorithm
  car.Refuel(100.0);
  std::cout << "Car is refueled, the correct fuel level is "
    << car.fuel << std::endl;
  while (car.fuel > 0) {
    std::cout << "Car fuel level: " << car.fuel << std::endl;
    if (car.speed < 80) {
      car.Accelerate();
      std::cout << "Car has been accelerated to the speed: "
        << car.speed << std::endl;
    } else {
      car.Brake();
      std::cout << "Car has been slowed down to the speed: "
        << car.speed << std::endl;
    }
  }

  std::cout << "Car ran out of the fuel! Slowing down ..."
    << std::endl;
  while (car.speed > 0) {
    car.Brake();
    std::cout << "Car has been slowed down to the speed: "
      << car.speed << std::endl;
  }
  std::cout << "Car is stopped!" << std::endl;

  // When leaving the function, the object 'car' gets
  // destructed automatically.
  return 0;
}
```

Code Box 6-12 [ExtremeC_examples_chapter6_2_main.cpp]: The main function of example 6.2

The `main` function written for C++ is very similar to the one we wrote for C, except that it allocates the memory for a class variable instead of a structure variable.

In C, we can't put attributes and behavior functions in a bundle that is known to C. Instead, we have to use files to group them. But in C++, we have a syntax for this bundle, which is the *class definition*. It allows us to put data members (or attributes) and member functions (or behavior functions) in the same place.

Since C++ knows about the encapsulation, it is redundant to pass the pointer argument to the behavior functions, and as you can see, in C++, we don't have any first pointer arguments in member function declarations like those we see in the C version of the `Car` class.

So, what happened? We wrote an object-oriented program in both C, which is a procedural programming language, and in C++, which is an object-oriented one. The biggest change was using `car.Accelerate()` instead of `car_accelerate(&car)`, or using `car.Refuel(1000.0)` instead of `car_refuel(&car, 1000.0)`.

In other words, if we are doing a call such as `func(obj, a, b, c, ...)` in a procedural programming language, we can do it as `obj.func(a, b, c, ...)` in an object-oriented language. They are equivalent but coming from different programming paradigms. Like we said before, there are numerous examples of C projects that use this technique.

Note:
In *Chapter 9, Abstraction and OOP in C++*, you will see that C++ uses exactly the same preceding technique in order to translate high-level C++ function calls to low-level C function calls.

As a final note, there is an important difference between C and C++ regarding object destruction. In C++, the destructor function is invoked automatically whenever an object is allocated on top of the Stack and it is going out of scope, like any other Stack variable. This is a great achievement in C++ memory management, because in C, you may easily forget to call the destructor function and eventually experience a memory leak.

Now it is time to talk about other aspects of encapsulation. In the next section, we will talk about a consequence of encapsulation: information-hiding.

Information hiding

So far, we've explained how encapsulation bundles attributes (which represent values) and functionalities (which represent behaviors) together to form objects. But it doesn't end there.

Encapsulation has another important purpose or consequence, which is *information-hiding*. Information-hiding is the act of protecting (or hiding) some attributes and behaviors that should not be visible to the outer world. By the outer world, we mean all parts of the code that do not belong to the behaviors of an object. By this definition, no other code, or simply no other C function, can access a private attribute or a private behavior of an object if that attribute or behavior is not part of the public interface of the class.

Note that the behaviors of two objects from the same type, such as car1 and car2 from the Car class, can access the attributes of any object from the same type. That's because of the fact that we write behavior functions once for all objects in a class.

In *example 6.1*, we saw that the main function was easily accessing the speed and fuel attributes in the car_t attribute structure. This means that all attributes in the car_t type were public. Having a public attribute or behavior can be a bad thing because it might have some long-lasting and dangerous.

As a consequence, the implementation details could leak out. Suppose that you are going to use a car object. Usually, it is only important to you that it has a behavior that accelerates the car; and you are not curious about how it is done. There may be even more internal attributes in the object that contribute to the acceleration process, but there is no valid reason that they should be visible to the consumer logic.

For instance, the amount of the electrical current being delivered to the engine starter could be an attribute, but it should be just private to the object itself. This also holds for certain behaviors that are internal to the object. For example, injecting the fuel into the combustion chamber is an internal behavior that should not be visible and accessible to you, otherwise, you could interfere with that and interrupt the normal process of the engine.

From another point of view, the implementation details (how the car works) vary from one car manufacturer to another but being able to accelerate a car is a behavior that is provided by all car manufacturers. We usually say that being able to accelerate a car is part of the *public API* or the *public interface* of the Car class.

Generally, the code using an object becomes dependent on the public attributes and behaviors of that object. This is a serious concern. Leaking out an internal attribute by declaring it public at first and then making it private can effectively break the build of the dependent code. It is expected that other parts of the code that are using that attribute as a public thing won't get compiled after the change.

This would mean you've broken the backward compatibility. That's why we choose a conservative approach and make every single attribute private by default until we find sound reasoning for making it public.

To put it simply, exposing private code from a class effectively means that rather than being dependent on a light public interface, we have been dependent on a thick implementation. These consequences are serious and have the potential to cause a lot of rework in a project. So, it is important to keep attributes and behaviors as private as they can be.

The following code box, as part of *example 6.3*, will demonstrate how we can have private attributes and behaviors in C. The example is about a List class that is supposed to store some integer values:

```
#ifndef EXTREME_C_EXAMPLES_CHAPTER_6_3_H
#define EXTREME_C_EXAMPLES_CHAPTER_6_3_H

#include <unistd.h>

// The attribute structure with no disclosed attribute
struct list_t;

// Allocation function
struct list_t* list_malloc();

// Constructor and destructor functions
void list_init(struct list_t*);
void list_destroy(struct list_t*);

// Public behavior functions
int list_add(struct list_t*, int);
int list_get(struct list_t*, int, int*);
void list_clear(struct list_t*);
size_t list_size(struct list_t*);
void list_print(struct list_t*);

#endif
```

Code Box 6-13 [ExtremeC_examples_chapter6_3.h]: The public interface of the List class

What you see in the preceding code box is the way that we make the attributes private. If another source file, such as the one that contains the main function, includes the preceding header, it'll have no access to the attributes inside the list_t type. The reason is simple. The list_t is just a declaration without a definition, and with just a structure declaration, you cannot access the fields of the structure. You cannot even declare a variable out of it. This way, we guarantee the information-hiding. This is actually a great achievement.

Once again, before creating and publishing a header file, it is mandatory to double-check whether we need to expose something as public or not. By exposing a public behavior or a public attribute, you'll create dependencies whose breaking would cost you time, development effort, and eventually money.

The following code box demonstrates the actual definition of the list_t attribute structure. Note that it is defined inside a source file and not a header file:

```
#include <stdio.h>
#include <stdlib.h>

#define MAX_SIZE 10

// Define the alias type bool_t
typedef int bool_t;

// Define the type list_t
typedef struct {
  size_t size;
  int* items;
} list_t;

// A private behavior which checks if the list is full
bool_t __list_is_full(list_t* list) {
  return (list->size == MAX_SIZE);
}

// Another private behavior which checks the index
bool_t __check_index(list_t* list, const int index) {
  return (index >= 0 && index <= list->size);
}

// Allocates memory for a list object
list_t* list_malloc() {
  return (list_t*)malloc(sizeof(list_t));
}

// Constructor of a list object
void list_init(list_t* list) {
  list->size = 0;
  // Allocates from the heap memory
  list->items = (int*)malloc(MAX_SIZE * sizeof(int));
}

// Destructor of a list object
void list_destroy(list_t* list) {
  // Deallocates the allocated memory
  free(list->items);
```

```
}

int list_add(list_t* list, const int item) {
  // The usage of the private behavior
  if (__list_is_full(list)) {
    return -1;
  }
  list->items[list->size++] = item;
  return 0;
}

int list_get(list_t* list, const int index, int* result) {
  if (__check_index(list, index)) {
    *result = list->items[index];
    return 0;
  }
  return -1;
}

void list_clear(list_t* list) {
  list->size = 0;
}

size_t list_size(list_t* list) {
  return list->size;
}

void list_print(list_t* list) {
  printf("[");
  for (size_t i = 0; i < list->size; i++) {
    printf("%d ", list->items[i]);
  }
  printf("]\n");
}
```

Code Box 6-14 [ExtremeC_examples_chapter6_3.c]: The definition of the List class

All the definitions that you see in the preceding code box are private. The external logic that is going to use a list_t object does not know anything about the preceding implementations, and the header file is the only piece of code that the external code will be dependent on.

Note that the preceding file has not even included the header file! As long as the definitions and function signatures match the declarations in the header file, that's all that's needed. However, it is recommended to do so because it guarantees the compatibility between the declarations and their corresponding definitions. As you've seen in *Chapter 2, Compilation and Linking*, the source files are compiled separately and finally linked together.

In fact, the linker brings private definitions to the public declarations and makes a working program out of them.

Note:
We can use a different notation for private behavior functions. We use the prefix __ in their names. As an example, the __ check_index function is a private function. Note that a private function does not have any corresponding declaration in the header file.

The following code box contains *example 6.3*'s main function that creates two list objects, populates the first one, and uses the second list to store the reverse of the first list. Finally, it prints them out:

```c
#include <stdlib.h>

#include "ExtremeC_examples_chapter6_3.h"

int reverse(struct list_t* source, struct list_t* dest) {
  list_clear(dest);
  for (size_t i = list_size(source) - 1; i >= 0; i--) {
    int item;
    if (list_get(source, i, &item)) {
      return -1;
    }
    list_add(dest, item);
  }
  return 0;
}

int main(int argc, char** argv) {
  struct list_t* list1 = list_malloc();
  struct list_t* list2 = list_malloc();

  // Construction
  list_init(list1);
  list_init(list2);

  list_add(list1, 4);
  list_add(list1, 6);
  list_add(list1, 1);
  list_add(list1, 5);

  list_add(list2, 9);

  reverse(list1, list2);
```

```
    list_print(list1);
    list_print(list2);

    // Destruction
    list_destroy(list1);
    list_destroy(list2);

    free(list1);
    free(list2);
    return 0;
}
```

Code Box 6-15 [ExtremeC_examples_chapter6_3_main.c]: The main function of example 6.3

As you can see in the preceding code box, we wrote the main and reverse functions only based on the things declared in the header file. In other words, these functions are using only the public API (or public interface) of the List class; the declarations of the attribute structure list_t and its behavior functions. This example is a nice demonstration of how to break the dependencies and hide the implementation details from other parts of the code.

Note:

Using the public API, you can write a program that compiles, but it cannot turn into a real working program unless you provide the corresponding object files of the private part and link them together.

There are some points related to the preceding code that we explore in more detail here. We needed to have a list_malloc function in order to allocate memory for a list_t object. Then, we can use the function free to release the allocated memory when we're done with the object.

You cannot use malloc directly in the preceding example. That's because if you are going to use malloc inside the main function, you have to pass sizeof(list_t) as the required number of bytes that should be allocated. However, you cannot use sizeof for an incomplete type.

The list_t type included from the header file is an *incomplete type* because it is just a declaration that doesn't give any information regarding its internal fields, and we don't know its size while compiling it. The real size will be determined only at link time when we know the implementation details. As a solution, we had to have the list_malloc function defined and have malloc used in a place where sizeof(list_t) is determined.

In order to build *example 6.3*, we need to compile the sources first. The following commands produce the necessary object files before the linking phase:

```
$ gcc -c ExtremeC_examples_chapter6_3.c -o private.o
$ gcc -c ExtremeC_examples_chapter6_3_main.c -o main.o
```

Shell Box 6-1: Compiling example 6.3

As you see, we have compiled the private part into `private.o` and the main part into `main.o`. Remember that we don't compile header files. The public declarations in the header are included as part of the `main.o` object file.

Now we need to link the preceding object files together, otherwise `main.o` alone cannot turn into an executable program. If you try to create an executable file using only `main.o`, you will see the following errors:

```
$ gcc main.o -o ex6_3.out
main.o: In function 'reverse':
ExtremeC_examples_chapter6_3_main.c:(.text+0x27): undefined
reference to 'list_clear'
...
main.o: In function 'main':
ExtremeC_examples_chapter6_3_main.c:(.text+0xa5): undefined
reference to 'list_malloc'
...
collect2: error: ld returned 1 exit status
$
```

Shell Box 6-2: Trying to link example 6.3 by just providing main.o

You see that the linker cannot find the definitions of the functions declared in the header file. The proper way to link the example is as follows:

```
$ gcc main.o private.o -o ex6_3.out
$ ./ex6_3.out
[4 6 1 5 ]
[5 1 6 4 ]
$
```

Shell Box 6-3: Linking and running example 6.3

What happens if you change the implementation behind the `List` class?

Say, instead of using an array, you use a linked list. It seems that we don't need to generate the `main.o` again, because it is nicely independent of the implementation details of the list it uses. So, we need only to compile and generate a new object file for the new implementation; for example, `private2.o`. Then, we just need to relink the object files and get the new executable:

```
$ gcc main.o private2.o -o ex6_3.out
$ ./ex6_3.out
[4 6 1 5 ]
[5 1 6 4 ]
$
```

Shell Box 6-4: Linking and running example 6.3 with a different implementation of the List class

As you see, from the user's point of view, nothing has changed, but the underlying implementation has been replaced. That is a great achievement and this approach is being used heavily in C projects.

What if we wanted to not repeat the linking phase in case of a new list implementation? In that case, we could use a shared library (or `.so` file) to contain the private object file. Then, we could load it dynamically at runtime, removing the need to relink the executable again. We have discussed shared libraries as part of *Chapter 3, Object Files*.

Here, we bring the current chapter to an end and we will continue our discussion in the following chapter. The next two chapters will be about the possible relationships which can exist between two classes.

Summary

In this chapter, the following topics have been discussed:

- We gave a thorough explanation of object-orientation philosophy and how you can extract an object model from your mind map.
- We also introduced the concept of the domain and how it should be used to filter the mind map to just keep relevant concepts and ideas.
- We also introduced the attributes and behaviors of a single object and how they should be extracted from either the mind map or the requirements given in the description of a domain.

- We explained why C cannot be an OOP language and explored its role in the translation of OOP programs into low-level assembly instructions that eventually will be run on a CPU.

- Encapsulation, as the first principle in OOP, was discussed. We use encapsulation to create capsules (or objects) that contain a set of attributes (placeholders for values) and a set of behaviors (placeholders for logic).

- Information-hiding was also discussed, including how it can lead to interfaces (or APIs) that can be used without having to become dependent on the underlying implementation.

- While discussing information-hiding, we demonstrated how to make attributes or methods private in C code.

The next chapter will be the opening to the discussion regarding possible relations between classes. We start *Chapter 7, Composition, and Aggregation,* with talking about composition relationship and then, we continue with inheritance and polymorphism as part of *Chapter 8, Inheritance and Polymorphism.*

Chapter 07
Composition and Aggregation

In the previous chapter, we talked about encapsulation and information hiding. In this chapter, we continue with object orientation in C and we'll discuss the various relationships that can exist between two classes. Eventually, this will allow us to expand our object model and express the relations between objects as part of the upcoming chapters.

As part of this chapter, we discuss:

- Types of relations that can exist between two objects and their corresponding classes: We will talk about *to-have* and *to-be* relationships, but our focus will be on to-have relations in this chapter.

- *Composition* as our first to-have relation: An example will be given to demonstrate a real composition relationship between two classes. Using the given example, we explore the memory structure which we usually have in case of composition.

- *Aggregation* as the second to-have relation: It is similar to composition since both of them address a to-have relationship. But they are different. We will give a separate complete example to cover an aggregation case. The difference among aggregation and composition will shine over the memory layout associated with these relationships.

This is the second of the four chapters covering OOP in C. The to-be relationship, which is also called *inheritance*, will be covered in the next chapter.

Relations between classes

An object model is a set of related objects. The number of relations can be many, but there are a few relationship types that can exist between two objects. Generally, there are two categories of relationships found between objects (or their corresponding classes): to-have relationships and to-be relationships.

We'll explore to-have relationships in depth in this chapter, and we'll cover to-be relationships in the next chapter. In addition, we will also see how the relationships between various objects can lead to relationships between their corresponding classes. Before dealing with that, we need to be able to distinguish between a class and an object.

Object versus class

If you remember from the previous chapter, we have two approaches for constructing objects. One approach is *prototype-based* and the other is *class-based*.

In the prototype-based approach, we construct an object either empty (without any attribute or behavior), or we clone it from an existing object. In this context, *instance* and *object* mean the same thing. So, the prototype-based approach can be read as the object-based approach; an approach that begins from empty objects instead of classes.

In the class-based approach, we cannot construct an object without having a blueprint that is often called a *class*. So, we should start from a class. And then, we can instantiate an object from it. In the previous chapter, we explained the implicit encapsulation technique that defines a class as a set of declarations put in a header file. We also gave some examples showing how this works in C.

Now, as part of this section, we want to talk more about the differences between a class and an object. While the differences seem to be trivial, we want to dive deeper and study them carefully. We begin by giving an example.

Suppose that we define a class, `Person`. It has the following attributes: `name`, `surname`, and `age`. We won't talk about the behaviors because the differences usually come from the attributes, and not the behaviors.

In C, we can write the `Person` class with public attributes as follows:

```
typedef struct {
  char name[32];
  char surname[32];
  unsigned int age;
} person_t;
```

Code Box 7-1: The Person attribute structure in C

And in C++:

```
class Person {
```

```
public:
  std::string name;
  std::string family;
  uint32_t age;
};
```

Code Box 7-2: The Person class's class in C++

The preceding code boxes are identical. In fact, the current discussion can be applied to both C and C++, and even other OOP languages such as Java. A class (or an object template) is a blueprint that only determines the attributes required to be present in every object, and *not* the values that these attributes might have in one specific object. In fact, each object has its own specific set of values for the same attributes that exist in other objects instantiated from the same class.

When an object is created based on a class, its memory is allocated first. This allocated memory will be a placeholder for the attribute values. After that, we need to initialize the attribute values with some values. This is an important step, otherwise, the object might have an invalid state after being created. As you've already seen, this step is called *construction*.

There is usually a dedicated function that performs the construction step, which is called the *constructor*. The functions list_init and car_construct in the examples, found in the previous chapter, were constructor functions. It is quite possible that as part of constructing an object, we need to allocate even more memory for resources such as other objects, buffers, arrays, streams, and so on required by that object. The resources owned by the object must have been released before having the owner object freed.

We also have another function, similar to the constructor, which is responsible for freeing any allocated resources. It is called the *destructor*. Similarly, the functions list_destroy and car_destruct in the examples found in the previous chapter were destructors. After destructing an object, its allocated memory is freed, but before that, all the owned resources and their corresponding memories must be freed.

Before moving on, let's sum up what we've explained so far:

- A class is a blueprint that is used as a map for creating objects.
- Many objects can be made from the same class.
- A class determines which attributes should be present in every future object created based on that class. It doesn't say anything about the possible values they can have.

- A class itself does not consume any memory (except in some programming languages other than C and C++) and only exists at the source level and at compile time. But objects exist at runtime and consume memory.

- When creating an object, memory allocation happens first. In addition, memory deallocation is the last operation for an object.

- When creating an object, it should be constructed right after memory allocation. It should be also destructed right before deallocation.

- An object might be owning some resources such as streams, buffers, arrays, and so on, that must be released before having the object destroyed.

Now that you know the differences between a class and an object, we can move on and explain the different relationships that can exist between two objects and their corresponding classes. We'll start with composition.

Composition

As the term "composition" implies, when an object contains or possesses another object – in other words, it is composed of another object – we say that there is a composition relationship between them.

As an example, a car has an engine; a car is an object that contains an engine object. Therefore, the car and engine objects have a composition relationship. There is an important condition that a composition relationship must have: *the lifetime of the contained object is bound to the lifetime of the container object.*

As long as the container object exists, the contained object must exist. But when the container object is about to get destroyed, the contained object must have been destructed first. This condition implies that the contained object is often internal and private to the container.

Some parts of the contained object may be still accessible through the public interface (or behavior functions) of the container class, but the lifetime of the contained object must be managed internally by the container object. If a piece of code can destruct the contained object without destructing the container object, it is a breach of the composition relationship and the relationship is no longer a composition.

The following example, *example 7.1*, demonstrates the composition relationship between a car object and an engine object.

It is composed of five files: two header files, which declare the public interfaces of the Car and Engine classes; two source files, which contain the implementation of the Car and Engine classes; and finally, a source file, which contains the main function and executes a simple scenario using a car and its engine object.

Note that, in some domains, we can have engine objects outside of the car objects; for example, in mechanical engineering CAD software. So, the type of relationships between the various objects is determined by the problem domain. For the sake of our example, imagine a domain in which engine objects could not exist outside of car objects.

The following code box shows the header file for the Car class:

```
#ifndef EXTREME_C_EXAMPLES_CHAPTER_7_1_CAR_H
#define EXTREME_C_EXAMPLES_CHAPTER_7_1_CAR_H

struct car_t;

// Memory allocator
struct car_t* car_new();

// Constructor
void car_ctor(struct car_t*);

// Destructor
void car_dtor(struct car_t*);

// Behavior functions
void car_start(struct car_t*);
void car_stop(struct car_t*);
double car_get_engine_temperature(struct car_t*);

#endif
```

Code Box 7-3 [ExtremeC_examples_chapter7_1_car.h]: The public interface of the Car class

As you see, the preceding declarations have been made in a similar way to what we did for the List class in the last example of the previous chapter, *example 6.3*. One of the differences is that we have chosen a new suffix for the constructor function; car_new instead of car_construct. The other difference is that we have only declared the attribute structure car_t. We have not defined its fields, and this is called a *forward declaration*. The definition for the structure car_t will be in the source file which comes in the code box 7-5. Note that in the preceding header file, the type car_t is considered an incomplete type which is not defined yet.

The following code box contains the header file for the `Engine` class:

```
#ifndef EXTREME_C_EXAMPLES_CHAPTER_7_1_ENGINE_H
#define EXTREME_C_EXAMPLES_CHAPTER_7_1_ENGINE_H

struct engine_t;

// Memory allocator
struct engine_t* engine_new();

// Constructor
void engine_ctor(struct engine_t*);

// Destructor
void engine_dtor(struct engine_t*);

// Behavior functions
void engine_turn_on(struct engine_t*);
void engine_turn_off(struct engine_t*);
double engine_get_temperature(struct engine_t*);

#endif
```

Code Box 7-4 [ExtremeC_examples_chapter7_1_engine.h]: The public interface of the Engine class

The following code boxes contains the implementations done for the `Car` and `Engine` classes. We begin with the `Car` class:

```
#include <stdlib.h>

// Car is only able to work with the public interface of Engine
#include "ExtremeC_examples_chapter7_1_engine.h"

typedef struct {
  // Composition happens because of this attribute
  struct engine_t* engine;
} car_t;

car_t* car_new() {
  return (car_t*)malloc(sizeof(car_t));
}

void car_ctor(car_t* car) {
  // Allocate memory for the engine object
  car->engine = engine_new();

  // Construct the engine object
```

```
    engine_ctor(car->engine);
}

void car_dtor(car_t* car) {
  // Destruct the engine object
  engine_dtor(car->engine);

  // Free the memory allocated for the engine object
  free(car->engine);
}

void car_start(car_t* car) {
  engine_turn_on(car->engine);
}

void car_stop(car_t* car) {
  engine_turn_off(car->engine);
}

double car_get_engine_temperature(car_t* car) {
  return engine_get_temperature(car->engine);
}
```

Code Box 7-5 [ExtremeC_examples_chapter7_1_car.c]: The definition of the Car class

The preceding code box shows how the car has contained the engine. As you see, we have a new attribute as part of the car_t attribute structure, and it is of the struct engine_t* type. Composition happens because of this attribute.

Though the type struct engine_t* is still incomplete inside this source file, it can point to an object from a complete engine_t type at runtime. This attribute will point to an object that is going to be constructed as part of the Car class's constructor, and it will be freed inside the destructor. At both places, the car object exists, and this means that the engine's lifetime is included in the car's lifetime.

The engine pointer is private, and no pointer is leaking from the implementation. That's an important note. When you are implementing a composition relationship, no pointer should be leaked out otherwise it causes external code to be able to change the state of the contained object. Just like encapsulation, no pointer should be leaked out when it gives direct access to the private parts of an object. Private parts should always be accessed indirectly via behavior functions.

The car_get_engine_temperature function in the code box gives access to the temperature attribute of the engine. However, there is an important note regarding this function. It uses the public interface of the engine. If you pay attention, you'll see that the *car's private implementation* is consuming the *engine's public interface*.

This means that the car itself doesn't know anything about the implementation details of the engine. This is the way that it should be.

Two objects that are not of the same type, in most cases, must not know about each other's implementation details. This is what information hiding dictates. Remember that the car's behaviors are considered external to the engine.

This way, we can replace the implementation of the engine with an alternative one, and it should work, as long as the new implementation provides definitions for the same public functions declared in the engine's header file.

Now, let's look at the implementation of the `Engine` class:

```c
#include <stdlib.h>

typedef enum {
  ON,
  OFF
} state_t;

typedef struct {
  state_t state;
  double temperature;
} engine_t;

// Memory allocator
engine_t* engine_new() {
  return (engine_t*)malloc(sizeof(engine_t));
}

// Constructor
void engine_ctor(engine_t* engine) {
  engine->state = OFF;
  engine->temperature = 15;
}

// Destructor
void engine_dtor(engine_t* engine) {
  // Nothing to do
}

// Behavior functions
void engine_turn_on(engine_t* engine) {
  if (engine->state == ON) {
    return;
  }
  engine->state = ON;
  engine->temperature = 75;
```

```
}

void engine_turn_off(engine_t* engine) {
  if (engine->state == OFF) {
    return;
  }
  engine->state = OFF;
  engine->temperature = 15;
}

double engine_get_temperature(engine_t* engine) {
  return engine->temperature;
}
```

Code Box 7-6 [ExtremeC_examples_chapter7_1_engine.c]: The definition of the Engine class

The preceding code is just using the implicit encapsulation approach for its private implementation, and it is very similar to previous examples. But there is one thing to note about this. As you see, the `engine` object doesn't know that an external object is going to contain it in a composition relationship. This is like the real world. When a company is building engines, it is not clear which engine will go into which car. Of course, we could have kept a pointer to the container `car` object, but in this example, we didn't need to.

The following code box demonstrates the scenario in which we create a `car` object and invoke some of its public API to extract information about the car's engine:

```
#include <stdio.h>
#include <stdlib.h>

#include "ExtremeC_examples_chapter7_1_car.h"

int main(int argc, char** argv) {

  // Allocate memory for the car object
  struct car_t *car = car_new();

  // Construct the car object
  car_ctor(car);

  printf("Engine temperature before starting the car: %f\n",
          car_get_engine_temperature(car));
  car_start(car);
  printf("Engine temperature after starting the car: %f\n",
          car_get_engine_temperature(car));
  car_stop(car);
```

```
        printf("Engine temperature after stopping the car: %f\n",
                car_get_engine_temperature(car));

        // Destruct the car object
        car_dtor(car);

        // Free the memory allocated for the car object
        free(car);

        return 0;
}
```

Code Box 7-7 [ExtremeC_examples_chapter7_1_main.c]: The main function of example 7.1

To build the preceding example, firstly we need to compile the previous three source files. Then, we need to link them together to generate the final executable object file. Note that the main source file (the source file that contains the main function) only depends on the car's public interface. So, when linking, it only needs the private implementation of the car object. However, the private implementation of the car object relies on the public interface of the engine interface; then, while linking, we need to provide the private implementation of the engine object. Therefore, we need to link all three object files in order to have the final executable.

The following commands show how to build the example and run the final executable:

```
$ gcc -c ExtremeC_examples_chapter7_1_engine.c -o engine.o
$ gcc -c ExtremeC_examples_chapter7_1_car.c -o car.o
$ gcc -c ExtremeC_examples_chapter7_1_main.c -o main.o
$ gcc engine.o car.o main.o -o ex7_1.out
$ ./ex7_1.out
Engine temperature before starting the car: 15.000000
Engine temperature after starting the car: 75.000000
Engine temperature after stopping the car: 15.000000
$
```

Shell Box 7-1: The compilation, linking, and execution of example 7.1

In this section, we explained one type of relationship that can exist between two objects. In the next section, we'll talk about the next relationship. It shares a similar concept to the composition relationship, but there are some significant differences.

Aggregation

Aggregation also involves a container object that contains another object. The main difference is that in aggregation, the lifetime of the contained object is independent of the lifetime of the container object.

In aggregation, the contained object could be constructed even before the container object is constructed. This is opposite to composition, in which the contained object should have a lifetime shorter than or equal to the container object.

The following example, *example 7.2*, demonstrates an aggregation relationship. It describes a very simple game scenario in which a player picks up a gun, fires multiple times, and drops the gun.

The player object would be a container object for a while, and the gun object would be a contained object as long as the player object holds it. The lifetime of the gun object is independent of the lifetime of the player object.

The following code box shows the header file of the Gun class:

```
#ifndef EXTREME_C_EXAMPLES_CHAPTER_7_2_GUN_H
#define EXTREME_C_EXAMPLES_CHAPTER_7_2_GUN_H

typedef int bool_t;

// Type forward declarations
struct gun_t;

// Memory allocator
struct gun_t* gun_new();

// Constructor
void gun_ctor(struct gun_t*, int);

// Destructor
void gun_dtor(struct gun_t*);

// Behavior functions
bool_t gun_has_bullets(struct gun_t*);
void gun_trigger(struct gun_t*);
void gun_refill(struct gun_t*);

#endif
```

Code Box 7-8 [ExtremeC_examples_chapter7_2_gun.h]: The public interface of the Gun class

As you see, we have only declared the gun_t attribute structure as we have not defined its fields. As we have explained before, this is called a forward declaration and it results in an incomplete type which cannot be instantiated.

The following code box shows the header file of the Player class:

```
#ifndef EXTREME_C_EXAMPLES_CHAPTER_7_2_PLAYER_H
#define EXTREME_C_EXAMPLES_CHAPTER_7_2_PLAYER_H

// Type forward declarations
struct player_t;
struct gun_t;

// Memory allocator
struct player_t* player_new();

// Constructor
void player_ctor(struct player_t*, const char*);

// Destructor
void player_dtor(struct player_t*);

// Behavior functions
void player_pickup_gun(struct player_t*, struct gun_t*);
void player_shoot(struct player_t*);
void player_drop_gun(struct player_t*);

#endif
```

Code Box 7-9 [ExtremeC_examples_chapter7_2_player.h]: The public interface of the Player class

The preceding code box defines the public interface of all player objects. In other words, it defines the public interface of the Player class.

Again, we have to forward the declaration of the gun_t and player_t structures. We need to have the gun_t type declared since some behavior functions of the Player class have arguments of this type.

The implementation of the Player class is as follows:

```
#include <stdlib.h>
#include <string.h>
#include <stdio.h>

#include "ExtremeC_examples_chapter7_2_gun.h"

// Attribute structure
```

```
typedef struct {
  char* name;
  struct gun_t* gun;
} player_t;

// Memory allocator
player_t* player_new() {
  return (player_t*)malloc(sizeof(player_t));
}

// Constructor
void player_ctor(player_t* player, const char* name) {
  player->name =
      (char*)malloc((strlen(name) + 1) * sizeof(char));
  strcpy(player->name, name);
  // This is important. We need to nullify aggregation pointers
  // if they are not meant to be set in constructor.
  player->gun = NULL;
}

// Destructor
void player_dtor(player_t* player) {
  free(player->name);
}

// Behavior functions
void player_pickup_gun(player_t* player, struct gun_t* gun) {
  // After the following line the aggregation relation begins.
  player->gun = gun;
}

void player_shoot(player_t* player) {
  // We need to check if the player has picked up the gun
  // otherwise, shooting is meaningless
  if (player->gun) {
    gun_trigger(player->gun);
  } else {
    printf("Player wants to shoot but he doesn't have a gun!");
    exit(1);
  }
}

void player_drop_gun(player_t* player) {
  // After the following line the aggregation relation
  // ends between two objects. Note that the object gun
  // should not be freed since this object is not its
  // owner like composition.
  player->gun = NULL;
}
```

Code Box 7-10 [ExtremeC_examples_chapter7_2_player.c]: The definition of the Player class

Inside the `player_t` structure, we declare the pointer attribute `gun` that is going to point to a `gun` object soon. We need to nullify this in the constructor because unlike composition, this attribute is not meant to be set as part of the constructor.

If an aggregation pointer is required to be set upon construction, the address of the target object should be passed as an argument to the constructor. Then, this situation is called a *mandatory aggregation*.

If the aggregation pointer can be left as null in the constructor, then it is an *optional aggregation*, as in the preceding code. It is important to nullify the optional aggregation pointers in the constructor.

In the function `player_pickup_gun`, the aggregation relationship begins, and it ends in the function `player_drop_gun` when the player drops the gun.

Note that we need to nullify the pointer `gun` after dropping the aggregation relationship. Unlike in composition, the container object is not the *owner* of the contained object. So, it has no control over its lifetime. Therefore, we should not free the gun object in any place inside the player's implementation code.

In optional aggregation relations, we may not have set the contained object at some point in the program. Therefore, we should be careful while using the aggregation pointer since any access to a pointer that is not set, or a pointer that is `null`, can lead to a segmentation fault. That's basically why in the function `player_shoot`, we check the `gun` pointer is valid. If the aggregation pointer is null, it means that the code using the player object is misusing it. If that's the case, we abort the execution by returning 1 as the *exit* code of the process.

The following code is the implementation of the `Gun` class:

```
#include <stdlib.h>

typedef int bool_t;

// Attribute structure
typedef struct {
  int bullets;
} gun_t;

// Memory allocator
gun_t* gun_new() {
  return (gun_t*)malloc(sizeof(gun_t));
}
```

```
// Constructor
void gun_ctor(gun_t* gun, int initial_bullets) {
  gun->bullets = 0;
  if (initial_bullets > 0) {
    gun->bullets = initial_bullets;
  }
}

// Destructor
void gun_dtor(gun_t* gun) {
  // Nothing to do
}

// Behavior functions
bool_t gun_has_bullets(gun_t* gun) {
  return (gun->bullets > 0);
}

void gun_trigger(gun_t* gun) {
  gun->bullets--;
}

void gun_refill(gun_t* gun) {
  gun->bullets = 7;
}
```

Code Box 7-11 [ExtremeC_examples_chapter7_2_gun.c]: The definition of the Gun class

The preceding code is straightforward, and it is written in a way that a gun object doesn't know that it will be contained in any object.

Finally, the following code box demonstrates a short scenario that creates a player object and a gun object. Then, the player picks up the gun and fires with it until no ammo is left. After that, the player refills the gun and does the same. Finally, they drop the gun:

```
#include <stdio.h>
#include <stdlib.h>

#include "ExtremeC_examples_chapter7_2_player.h"
#include "ExtremeC_examples_chapter7_2_gun.h"

int main(int argc, char** argv) {
```

```
// Create and constructor the gun object
struct gun_t* gun = gun_new();
gun_ctor(gun, 3);

// Create and construct the player object
struct player_t* player = player_new();
player_ctor(player, "Billy");

// Begin the aggregation relation.
player_pickup_gun(player, gun);

// Shoot until no bullet is left.
while (gun_has_bullets(gun)) {
  player_shoot(player);
}

// Refill the gun
gun_refill(gun);

// Shoot until no bullet is left.
while (gun_has_bullets(gun)) {
  player_shoot(player);
}

// End the aggregation relation.
player_drop_gun(player);

// Destruct and free the player object
player_dtor(player);
free(player);

// Destruct and free the gun object
gun_dtor(gun);
free(gun);

return 0;
}
```

Code Box 7-12 [ExtremeC_examples_chapter7_2_main.c]: The main function of example 7.2

As you see here, the gun and player objects are independent of each other. The responsible logic for creating and destroying these objects is the main function. At some point in the execution, they form an aggregation relationship and perform their roles, then at another point, they become separated. The important thing in aggregation is that the container object shouldn't alter the lifetime of the contained object, and as long as this rule is followed, no memory issues should arise.

The following shell box shows how to build the example and run the resulting executable file. As you see, the `main` function in *Code Box 7-12* doesn't produce any output:

```
$ gcc -c ExtremeC_examples_chapter7_2_gun.c -o gun.o
$ gcc -c ExtremeC_examples_chapter7_2_player.c -o player.o
$ gcc -c ExtremeC_examples_chapter7_2_main.c -o main.o
$ gcc gun.o player.o main.o -o ex7_2.out
$ ./ex7_2.out
$
```

Shell Box 7-2: The compilation, linking, and execution of example 7.2

In an object model created for a real project, the amount of aggregation relationships is usually greater than the number of composition relationships. Also, aggregation relationships are more visible externally because, in order to make an aggregation relationship, some dedicated behavior functions are required, at least in the public interface of the container object, to set and reset the contained object.

As you see in the preceding example, the `gun` and `player` objects are separated from the start. They become related for a short period of time, and then they become separated again. This means that the aggregation relationship is temporary, unlike the composition relationship, which is permanent. This shows that composition is a stronger form of *possession* (to-have) relationship between objects, while aggregation exhibits a weaker relationship.

Now, a question comes to mind. If an aggregation relationship is temporary between two objects, is it temporary between their corresponding classes? The answer is no. The aggregation relationship is permanent between the types. If there is a small chance that in the future, two objects from two different types become related based on an aggregation relationship, their types should be in the aggregation relationship permanently. This holds for composition as well.

Even a low chance of there being an aggregation relationship should cause us to declare some pointers in the attribute structure of the container object, and this means that the attribute structure is changed permanently. Of course, this is only true for class-based programming languages.

Composition and aggregation both describe the possession of some objects. In other words, these relationships describe a "to-have" or "has-a" situation; a player **has** a gun, or a car **has** an engine. Every time you feel that an object possesses another one, it means there should either be a composition relationship or an aggregation relationship between them (and their corresponding classes).

In the next chapter, we'll continue our discussion regarding relationship types by looking at the *inheritance* or *extension* relationship.

Summary

In this chapter, the following topics have been discussed:

- The possible relationship types between classes and objects.
- The differences and similarities between a class, an object, an instance, and a reference.
- Composition, which entails that a contained object is totally dependent on its container object.
- Aggregation, in which the contained object can live freely without any dependency on its container object.
- The fact that aggregation can be temporary between objects, but it is defined permanently between their types (or classes).

In the next chapter, we continue to explore OOP, primarily addressing the two further pillars upon which it is based: inheritance and polymorphism.

Chapter 08

Inheritance
and Polymorphism

This chapter is a continuation of the previous two chapters, where we introduced how you can do OOP in C and reached the concepts of composition and aggregation. This chapter mainly continues the discussion regarding relationships between objects and their corresponding classes and covers inheritance and polymorphism. As part of this chapter, we conclude this topic and we continue with *Abstraction* in the following chapter.

This chapter is heavily dependent on the theory explained in the previous two chapters, where we were discussing the possible relationships between classes. We explained *composition* and *aggregation* relationships, and now we are going to talk about the *extension* or *inheritance* relationship in this chapter, along with a few other topics.

The following are the topics that will be explained throughout this chapter:

- As explained earlier, the inheritance relationship is the first topic that we discuss. The methods for implementing the inheritance relationship in C will be covered, and we will conduct a comparison between them.

- The next big topic is *polymorphism*. Polymorphism allows us to have different versions of the same behavior in the child classes, in the case of having an inheritance relationship between those classes. We will discuss the methods for having a polymorphic function in C; this will be the first step in our understanding of how C++ offers polymorphism.

Let's start our discussion with the inheritance relationship.

Inheritance

We closed the previous chapter by talking about *to-have* relationships, which eventually led us to composition and aggregation relationships. In this section, we are going to talk about *to-be* or *is-a* relationships. The inheritance relationship is a to-be relationship.

An inheritance relationship can also be called an *extension relationship* because it only adds extra attributes and behaviors to an existing object or class. In the following sections, we'll explain what inheritance means and how it can be implemented in C.

There are situations when an object needs to have the same attributes that exist in another object. In other words, the new object is an extension to the other object.

For example, a student has all the attributes of a person, but may also have extra attributes. See *Code Box 8-1*:

```
typedef struct {
  char first_name[32];
  char last_name[32];
  unsigned int birth_year;
} person_t;

typedef struct {
  char first_name[32];
  char last_name[32];
  unsigned int birth_year;
  char student_number[16]; // Extra attribute
  unsigned int passed_credits; // Extra attribute
} student_t;
```

Code Box 8-1: The attribute structures of the Person class and the Student class

This example clearly shows how `student_t` extends the attributes of `person_t` with new attributes, `student_number` and `passed_credits`, which are student-specific attributes.

As we have pointed out before, inheritance (or extension) is a to-be relationship, unlike composition and aggregation, which are to-have relationships. Therefore, for the preceding example, we can say that "a student is a person," which seems to be correct in the domain of educational software. Whenever a to-be relationship exists in a domain, it is probably an inheritance relationship. In the preceding example, `person_t` is usually called the *supertype*, or the *base* type, or simply the *parent* type, and `student_t` is usually called the *child* type or the *inherited subtype*.

The nature of inheritance

If you were to dig deeper and see what an inheritance relationship really is, you would find out that it is really a composition relationship in its nature. For example, we can say that a student has a person's nature inside of them. In other words, we can suppose that there is a private person object inside the `Student` class's attribute structure. That is, an inheritance relationship can be equivalent to a one-to-one composition relationship.

So, the structures in *Code Box 8-1* can be written as:

```
typedef struct {
  char first_name[32];
  char last_name[32];
  unsigned int birth_year;
} person_t;

typedef struct {
  person_t person;
  char student_number[16]; // Extra attribute
  unsigned int passed_credits; // Extra attribute
} student_t;
```

Code Box 8-2: The attribute structures of the Person and Student classes but nested this time

This syntax is totally valid in C, and in fact nesting structures by using structure variables (not pointers) is a powerful setup. It allows you to have a structure variable inside your new structure that is really an extension to the former.

With the preceding setup, necessarily having a field of type `person_t` as the first field, a `student_t` pointer can be easily cast to a `person_t` pointer, and both of them can point to the same address in memory.

This is called *upcasting*. In other words, casting a pointer of the type of the child's attribute structure to the type of the parent's attribute structure is upcasting. Note that with structure variables, you cannot have this feature.

Example 8.1 demonstrates this as follows:

```
#include <stdio.h>

typedef struct {
  char first_name[32];
  char last_name[32];
  unsigned int birth_year;
} person_t;
```

```
typedef struct {
  person_t person;
  char student_number[16]; // Extra attribute
  unsigned int passed_credits; // Extra attribute
} student_t;

int main(int argc, char** argv) {
  student_t s;
  student_t* s_ptr = &s;
  person_t* p_ptr = (person_t*)&s;
  printf("Student pointer points to %p\n", (void*)s_ptr);
  printf("Person pointer points to %p\n", (void*)p_ptr);
  return 0;
}
```

Code Box 8-3 [ExtremeC_examples_chapter8_1.c]: Example 8.1, showing upcasting between Student and Person object pointers

As you can see, we expect that the s_ptr and p_ptr pointers are pointing to the same address in memory. The following is the output after building and running *example 8.1*:

```
$ gcc ExtremeC_examples_chapter8_1.c -o ex8_1.out
$ ./ex8_1.out
Student pointer points to 0x7ffeecd41810
Person pointer points to 0x7ffeecd41810
$
```

Shell Box 8-1: The output of example 8.1

And yes, they are pointing to the same address. Note that the shown addresses can be different in each run, but the point is that the pointers are referring to the same address. This means that a structure variable of the type student_t is really inheriting the person_t structure in its memory layout. This implies that we can use the function behaviors of the Person class with a pointer that is pointing to a student object. In other words, the Person class's behavior functions can be reused for the student objects, which is a great achievement.

Note that the following is wrong, and the code won't compile:

```
struct person_t;

typedef struct {
```

```
    struct person_t person; // Generates an error!
    char student_number[16]; // Extra attribute
    unsigned int passed_credits; // Extra attribute
} student_t;
```

Code Box 8-4: Establishing an inheritance relationship which doesn't compile!

The line declaring the `person` field generates an error because you cannot create a variable from an *incomplete type*. You should remember that the forward declaration of a structure (similar to the first line in *Code Box 8-4*) results in the declaration of an incomplete type. You can have only pointers of incomplete types, *not* variables. As you've seen before, you cannot even allocate Heap memory for an incomplete type.

So, what does this mean? It means that if you're going to use nested structure variables in order to implement inheritance, the `student_t` structure should see the actual definition of `person_t`, which, based on what we learned about encapsulation, should be private and not visible to any other class.

Therefore, you have two approaches for implementing the inheritance relationship:

- Make it so that the child class has access to the private implementation (actual definition) of the base class.

- Make it so that the child class only has access to the public interface of the base class.

The first approach for having inheritance in C

We'll demonstrate the first approach in the following example, *example 8.2*, and the second approach in *example 8.3*, which will come up in the next section. Both of them represent the same classes, `Student` and `Person`, with some behavior functions, having some objects playing in a simple scenario in the `main` function.

We'll start with *example 8.2*, in which the `Student` class needs to have access to the actual private definition of the `Person` class's attribute structure. The following code boxes present the headers and the sources for the `Student` and `Person` classes together with the `main` function. Let's start with the header file declaring the `Person` class:

```
#ifndef EXTREME_C_EXAMPLES_CHAPTER_8_2_PERSON_H
#define EXTREME_C_EXAMPLES_CHAPTER_8_2_PERSON_H
```

```
// Forward declaration
struct person_t;

// Memory allocator
struct person_t* person_new();

// Constructor
void person_ctor(struct person_t*,
                 const char*  /* first name */,
                 const char*  /* last name */,
                 unsigned int /* birth year */);

// Destructor
void person_dtor(struct person_t*);

// Behavior functions
void person_get_first_name(struct person_t*, char*);
void person_get_last_name(struct person_t*, char*);
unsigned int person_get_birth_year(struct person_t*);

#endif
```

Code Box 8-5 [ExtremeC_examples_chapter8_2_person.h]: Example 8.2, the public interface of the Person class

Look at the constructor function in *Code Box 8-5*. It accepts all the values required for creating a `person` object: `first_name`, `second_name`, and `birth_year`. As you see, the attribute structure `person_t` is incomplete, hence the `Student` class cannot use the preceding header file for establishing an inheritance relationship, similar to what we demonstrated in the previous section.

On the other hand, the preceding header file must not contain the actual definition of the attribute structure `person_t`, since the preceding header file is going to be used by other parts of the code which should not know anything about the `Person` internals. So, what should we do? We want a certain part of the logic to know about a structure definition that other parts of the code must not know about. That's where *private header files* jump in.

A private header file is an ordinary header file that is supposed to be included and used by a certain part of code or a certain class that actually needs it. Regarding *example 8.2*, the actual definition of `person_t` should be part of a private header. In the following code box, you will see an example of a private header file:

```
#ifndef EXTREME_C_EXAMPLES_CHAPTER_8_2_PERSON_P_H
#define EXTREME_C_EXAMPLES_CHAPTER_8_2_PERSON_P_H
```

```
// Private definition
typedef struct {
  char first_name[32];
  char last_name[32];
  unsigned int birth_year;
} person_t;

#endif
```

Code Box 8-6 [ExtremeC_examples_chapter8_2_person_p.h]: The private header file which contains the actual
definition of person_t

As you see, it only contains the definition of the person_t structure and nothing
more than that. This is the part of the Person class which should stay private,
but it needs to become public to the Student class. We are going to need this
definition for defining the student_t attribute structure. The next code box
demonstrates the private implementation of the Person class:

```
#include <stdlib.h>
#include <string.h>

// person_t is defined in the following header file.
#include "ExtremeC_examples_chapter8_2_person_p.h"

// Memory allocator
person_t* person_new() {
  return (person_t*)malloc(sizeof(person_t));
}

// Constructor
void person_ctor(person_t* person,
                 const char* first_name,
                 const char* last_name,
                 unsigned int birth_year) {
  strcpy(person->first_name, first_name);
  strcpy(person->last_name, last_name);
  person->birth_year = birth_year;
}

// Destructor
void person_dtor(person_t* person) {
  // Nothing to do
}

// Behavior functions
void person_get_first_name(person_t* person, char* buffer) {
```

```
  strcpy(buffer, person->first_name);
}

void person_get_last_name(person_t* person, char* buffer) {
  strcpy(buffer, person->last_name);
}

unsigned int person_get_birth_year(person_t* person) {
  return person->birth_year;
}
```

Code Box 8-7 [ExtremeC_examples_chapter8_2_person.c]: The definition of the Person class

There is nothing special about the definition of the `Person` class and it is like all previous examples. The following code box shows the public interface of the `Student` class:

```
#ifndef EXTREME_C_EXAMPLES_CHAPTER_8_2_STUDENT_H
#define EXTREME_C_EXAMPLES_CHAPTER_8_2_STUDENT_H

//Forward declaration
struct student_t;

// Memory allocator
struct student_t* student_new();

// Constructor
void student_ctor(struct student_t*,
                  const char*  /* first name */,
                  const char*  /* last name */,
                  unsigned int /* birth year */,
                  const char*  /* student number */,
                  unsigned int /* passed credits */);

// Destructor
void student_dtor(struct student_t*);

// Behavior functions
void student_get_student_number(struct student_t*, char*);
unsigned int student_get_passed_credits(struct student_t*);

#endif
```

Code Box 8-8 [ExtremeC_examples_chapter8_2_student.h]: The public interface of the Student class

As you can see, the constructor of the class accepts similar arguments to the `Person` class's constructor. That's because a `student` object actually contains a `person` object and it needs those values for populating its composed `person` object.

This implies that the student constructor needs to set the attributes for the person part of the student.

Note that we have only two additional behavior functions as part of the Student class, and that's because we can use the Person class's behavior functions for student objects as well.

The next code box contains the private implementation of the Student class:

```c
#include <stdlib.h>
#include <string.h>

#include "ExtremeC_examples_chapter8_2_person.h"

// person_t is defined in the following header
// file and we need it here.
#include "ExtremeC_examples_chapter8_2_person_p.h"

//Forward declaration
typedef struct {
    // Here, we inherit all attributes from the person class and
    // also we can use all of its behavior functions because of
    // this nesting.
    person_t person;
    char* student_number;
    unsigned int passed_credits;
} student_t;

// Memory allocator
student_t* student_new() {
    return (student_t*)malloc(sizeof(student_t));
}

// Constructor
void student_ctor(student_t* student,
                  const char* first_name,
                  const char* last_name,
                  unsigned int birth_year,
                  const char* student_number,
                  unsigned int passed_credits) {
    // Call the constructor of the parent class
    person_ctor((struct person_t*)student,
            first_name, last_name, birth_year);
    student->student_number = (char*)malloc(16 * sizeof(char));
    strcpy(student->student_number, student_number);
    student->passed_credits = passed_credits;
}
```

```
// Destructor
void student_dtor(student_t* student) {
  // We need to destruct the child object first.
  free(student->student_number);
  // Then, we need to call the destructor function
  // of the parent class
  person_dtor((struct person_t*)student);
}

// Behavior functions
void student_get_student_number(student_t* student,
                                char* buffer) {
  strcpy(buffer, student->student_number);
}

unsigned int student_get_passed_credits(student_t* student) {
  return student->passed_credits;
}
```

Code Box 8-9 [ExtremeC_examples_chapter8_2_student.c]: The private definition of the Student class

The preceding code box contains the most important code regarding the inheritance relationship. Firstly, we needed to include the private header of the Person class because as part of defining student_t, we want to have the first field from the person_t type. And, since that field is an actual variable and not a pointer, it requires that we have person_t already defined. Note that this variable must be the *first field* in the structure. Otherwise, we lose the possibility of using the Person class's behavior functions.

Again, in the preceding code box, as part of the Student class's constructor, we call the parent's constructor to initialize the attributes of the parent (composed) object. Look at how we cast the student_t pointer to a person_t pointer when passing it to the person_ctor function. This is possible just because the person field is the first member of student_t.

Similarly, as part of the Student class's destructor, we called the parent's destructor. This destruction should happen first at the child level and then the parent level, in the opposite order of construction. The next code box contains *example 8.2*'s main scenario, which is going to use the Student class and create an object of type Student:

```
#include <stdio.h>
#include <stdlib.h>
```

```
#include "ExtremeC_examples_chapter8_2_person.h"
#include "ExtremeC_examples_chapter8_2_student.h"

int main(int argc, char** argv) {
  // Create and construct the student object
  struct student_t* student = student_new();
  student_ctor(student, "John", "Doe",
        1987, "TA5667", 134);

  // Now, we use person's behavior functions to
  // read person's attributes from the student object
  char buffer[32];

  // Upcasting to a pointer of parent type
  struct person_t* person_ptr = (struct person_t*)student;

  person_get_first_name(person_ptr, buffer);
  printf("First name: %s\n", buffer);

  person_get_last_name(person_ptr, buffer);
  printf("Last name: %s\n", buffer);

  printf("Birth year: %d\n", person_get_birth_year(person_ptr));

  // Now, we read the attributes specific to the student object.
  student_get_student_number(student, buffer);
  printf("Student number: %s\n", buffer);

  printf("Passed credits: %d\n",
        student_get_passed_credits(student));

  // Destruct and free the student object
  student_dtor(student);
  free(student);

  return 0;
}
```

Code Box 8-10 [ExtremeC_examples_chapter8_2_main.c]: The main scenario of example 8.2

As you see in the main scenario, we have included the public interfaces of both the `Person` and `Student` classes (not the private header file), but we have only created one `student` object. As you can see, the `student` object has inherited all attributes from its internal `person` object, and they can be read via the `Person` class's behavior functions.

The following shell box shows how to compile and run *example 8.2*:

```
$ gcc -c ExtremeC_examples_chapter8_2_person.c -o person.o
$ gcc -c ExtremeC_examples_chapter8_2_student.c -o student.o
$ gcc -c ExtremeC_examples_chapter8_2_main.c -o main.o
$ gcc person.o student.o main.o -o ex8_2.out
$ ./ex8_2.out
First name: John
Last name: Doe
Birth year: 1987
Student number: TA5667
Passed credits: 134
$
```

Shell Box 8-2: Building and running example 8.2

The following example, *example 8.3*, will address the second approach to implementing inheritance relationships in C. The output should be very similar to *example 8.2*.

The second approach to inheritance in C

Using the first approach, we kept a structure variable as the first field in the child's attribute structure. Now, using the second approach, we'll keep a pointer to the parent's structure variable. This way, the child class can be independent of the implementation of the parent class, which is a good thing, considering information-hiding concerns.

We gain some advantages, and we lose some by choosing the second approach. After demonstrating *example 8.3* we will conduct a comparison between the two approaches, and you will see the advantages and disadvantages of using each of these techniques.

Example 8.3, below, is remarkably similar to *example 8.2*, especially in terms of the output and the final results. However, the main difference is that as part of this example, the Student class only relies on the public interface of the Person class, and not its private definition. This is great because it decouples the classes and allows us to easily change the implementation of the parent class without altering the implementation of the child class.

In the preceding example, the `Student` class didn't strictly violate information-hiding principles, but it could have done that because it had access to the actual definition of `person_t` and its fields. As a result, it could read or modify the fields without using `Person`'s behavior functions.

As noted, *example 8.3* is remarkably similar to *example 8.2*, but it has some fundamental differences. The `Person` class has the same public interface as part of the new example. But this is not true regarding the `Student` class and its public interface has to be changed. The following code box shows the `Student` class's new public interface:

```
#ifndef EXTREME_C_EXAMPLES_CHAPTER_8_3_STUDENT_H
#define EXTREME_C_EXAMPLES_CHAPTER_8_3_STUDENT_H

//Forward declaration
struct student_t;

// Memory allocator
struct student_t* student_new();

// Constructor
void student_ctor(struct student_t*,
                  const char*  /* first name */,
                  const char*  /* last name */,
                  unsigned int /* birth year */,
                  const char*  /* student number */,
                  unsigned int /* passed credits */);

// Destructor
void student_dtor(struct student_t*);

// Behavior functions
void student_get_first_name(struct student_t*, char*);
void student_get_last_name(struct student_t*, char*);
unsigned int student_get_birth_year(struct student_t*);
void student_get_student_number(struct student_t*, char*);
unsigned int student_get_passed_credits(struct student_t*);

#endif
```

Code Box 8-11 [ExtremeC_examples_chapter8_3_student.h]: The new public interface of the Student class

For reasons you will realize shortly, the `Student` class has to repeat all the behavior functions declared as part of the `Person` class. That's because of the fact that we can no longer cast a `student_t` pointer to a `person_t` pointer. In other words, upcasting doesn't work anymore regarding `Student` and `Person` pointers.

While the public interface of the Person class is not changed from *example 8.2*, its implementation has changed. The following code box demonstrates the implementation of the Person class as part of *example 8.3*:

```
#include <stdlib.h>
#include <string.h>

// Private definition
typedef struct {
  char first_name[32];
  char last_name[32];
  unsigned int birth_year;
} person_t;

// Memory allocator
person_t* person_new() {
  return (person_t*)malloc(sizeof(person_t));
}

// Constructor
void person_ctor(person_t* person,
                 const char* first_name,
                 const char* last_name,
                 unsigned int birth_year) {
  strcpy(person->first_name, first_name);
  strcpy(person->last_name, last_name);
  person->birth_year = birth_year;
}

// Destructor
void person_dtor(person_t* person) {
  // Nothing to do
}

// Behavior functions
void person_get_first_name(person_t* person, char* buffer) {
  strcpy(buffer, person->first_name);
}

void person_get_last_name(person_t* person, char* buffer) {
  strcpy(buffer, person->last_name);
}

unsigned int person_get_birth_year(person_t* person) {
  return person->birth_year;
}
```

Code Box 8-12 [ExtremeC_examples_chapter8_3_person.c]: The new implementation of the Person class

As you see, the private definition of person_t is placed inside the source file and we are not using a private header anymore. This means that we are not going to share the definition with other classes such as the Student class at all. We want to conduct a complete encapsulation of the Person class and hide all its implementation details.

The following is the private implementation of the Student class:

```c
#include <stdlib.h>
#include <string.h>

// Public interface of the person class
#include "ExtremeC_examples_chapter8_3_person.h"

//Forward declaration
typedef struct {
  char* student_number;
  unsigned int passed_credits;
  // We have to have a pointer here since the type
  // person_t is incomplete.
  struct person_t* person;
} student_t;

// Memory allocator
student_t* student_new() {
  return (student_t*)malloc(sizeof(student_t));
}

// Constructor
void student_ctor(student_t* student,
                  const char* first_name,
                  const char* last_name,
                  unsigned int birth_year,
                  const char* student_number,
                  unsigned int passed_credits) {
  // Allocate memory for the parent object
  student->person = person_new();
  person_ctor(student->person, first_name,
          last_name, birth_year);
  student->student_number = (char*)malloc(16 * sizeof(char));
  strcpy(student->student_number, student_number);
  student->passed_credits = passed_credits;
}

// Destructor
void student_dtor(student_t* student) {
  // We need to destruct the child object first.
  free(student->student_number);
```

```
    // Then, we need to call the destructor function
    // of the parent class
    person_dtor(student->person);
    // And we need to free the parent object's allocated memory
    free(student->person);
}


// Behavior functions
void student_get_first_name(student_t* student, char* buffer) {
    // We have to use person's behavior function
    person_get_first_name(student->person, buffer);
}

void student_get_last_name(student_t* student, char* buffer) {
    // We have to use person's behavior function
    person_get_last_name(student->person, buffer);
}

unsigned int student_get_birth_year(student_t* student) {
    // We have to use person's behavior function
    return person_get_birth_year(student->person);
}

void student_get_student_number(student_t* student,
                                char* buffer) {
    strcpy(buffer, student->student_number);
}

unsigned int student_get_passed_credits(student_t* student) {
    return student->passed_credits;
}
```

Code Box 8-13 [ExtremeC_examples_chapter8_3_student.c]: The new implementation of the Student class

As demonstrated in the preceding code box, we've used the Person class's public interface by including its header file. In addition, as part of the definition of student_t, we've added a pointer field, which points to the parent Person object. This should remind you of the implementation of a composition relationship done as part of the previous chapter.

Note that there is no need for this pointer field to be the first item in the attribute structure. This is in contrast to what we saw in the first approach. The pointers of the types student_t and person_t are no longer interchangeable, and they are pointing to different addresses in the memory that are not necessarily adjacent. This is again in contrast to what we did in the previous approach.

Note that, as part of the Student class's constructor, we instantiate the parent object. Then, we construct it by calling the Person class's constructor and passing the required parameters. That's the same for destructors as well and we destruct the parent object lastly in the Student class's destructor.

Since we cannot use the behaviors of the Person class to read the inherited attributes, the Student class is required to offer its set of behavior functions to expose those inherited and private attributes.

In other words, the Student class has to provide some wrapper functions to expose the private attributes of its inner parent person object. Note that the Student object itself doesn't know anything about the private attributes of the Person object, and this is in contrast with what we saw in the first approach.

The main scenario is also very similar to how it was as part of *example 8.2*. The following code box demonstrates that:

```
#include <stdio.h>
#include <stdlib.h>

#include "ExtremeC_examples_chapter8_3_student.h"

int main(int argc, char** argv) {
  // Create and construct the student object
  struct student_t* student = student_new();
  student_ctor(student, "John", "Doe",
        1987, "TA5667", 134);

  // We have to use student's behavior functions because the
  // student pointer is not a person pointer and we cannot
  // access to private parent pointer in the student object.
  char buffer[32];
  student_get_first_name(student, buffer);
  printf("First name: %s\n", buffer);

  student_get_last_name(student, buffer);
  printf("Last name: %s\n", buffer);

  printf("Birth year: %d\n", student_get_birth_year(student));

  student_get_student_number(student, buffer);
  printf("Student number: %s\n", buffer);

  printf("Passed credits: %d\n",
        student_get_passed_credits(student));
```

```
    // Destruct and free the student object
    student_dtor(student);
    free(student);

    return 0;
}
```

Code Box 8-14 [ExtremeC_examples_chapter8_3_main.c]: The main scenario of example 8.3

In comparison to the main function in *example 8.2*, we have not included the public interface of the `Person` class. We have also needed to use the `Student` class's behavior functions because the `student_t` and `person_t` pointers are not interchangeable anymore.

The following shell box demonstrates how to compile and run *example 8.3*. As you might have guessed, the outputs are identical:

```
$ gcc -c ExtremeC_examples_chapter8_3_person.c -o person.o
$ gcc -c ExtremeC_examples_chapter8_3_student.c -o student.o
$ gcc -c ExtremeC_examples_chapter8_3_main.c -o main.o
$ gcc person.o student.o main.o -o ex8_3.out
$ ./ex8_3.out
First name: John
Last name: Doe
Birth year: 1987
Student number: TA5667
Passed credits: 134
$
```

Shell Box 8-3: Building and running example 8.3

In the following section, we're going to compare the aforementioned approaches to implement an inheritance relationship in C.

Comparison of two approaches

Now that you've seen two different approaches that we can take to implement inheritance in C, we can compare them. The following bullet points outline the similarities and differences between the two approaches:

- Both approaches intrinsically show composition relationships.

- The first approach keeps a structure variable in the child's attribute structure and relies on having access to the private implementation of the parent class. However, the second approach keeps a structure pointer from the incomplete type of the parent's attribute structure, and hence, it doesn't rely on the private implementation of the parent class.

- In the first approach, the parent and child types are strongly dependent. In the second approach, the classes are independent of each other, and everything inside the parent implementation is hidden from the child.

- In the first approach, you can have only one parent. In other words, it is a way to implement *single inheritance* in C. However, in the second approach, you can have as many parents as you like, thereby demonstrating the concept of *multiple inheritance*.

- In the first approach, the parent's structure variable must be the first field in the attribute structure of the child class, but in the second approach, the pointers to parent objects can be put anywhere in the structure.

- In the first approach, there were no two separate parent and child objects. The parent object was included in the child object, and a pointer to the child object was actually a pointer to the parent object.

- In the first approach, we could use the behavior functions of the parent class, but in the second approach, we needed to forward the parent's behavior functions through new behavior functions in the child class.

So far, we have only talked about inheritance itself and we haven't gone through its usages. One of the most important usages of inheritance is to have *polymorphism* in your object model. In the following section, we're going to talk about polymorphism and how it can be implemented in C.

Polymorphism

Polymorphism is not really a relationship between two classes. It is mostly a technique for keeping the same code while having different behaviors. It allows us to extend code or add functionalities without having to recompile the whole code base.

In this section, we try to cover what polymorphism is and how we can have it in C. This also gives us a better view of how modern programming languages such as C++ implement polymorphism. We'll start by defining polymorphism.

What is polymorphism?

Polymorphism simply means to have different behaviors by just using the same public interface (or set of behavior functions).

Suppose that we have two classes, Cat and Duck, and they each have a behavior function, sound, which makes them print their specific sound. Explaining polymorphism is not an easy task to do and we'll try to take a top-down approach in explaining it. First, we'll try to give you an idea of how polymorphic code looks and how it behaves, and then we'll dive into implementing it in C. Once you get the idea, it will be easier to move into the implementation. In the following code boxes, we first create some objects, and then we see how we would expect a polymorphic function to behave if polymorphism was in place. First, let's create three objects. We have already assumed that both the Cat and Duck classes are children of the Animal class:

```
struct animal_t* animal = animal_malloc();
animal_ctor(animal);

struct cat_t* cat = cat_malloc();
cat_ctor(cat);

struct duck_t* duck = duck_malloc();
duck_ctor(duck);
```

Code Box 8-15: Creating three objects of types Animal, Cat, and Duck

Without polymorphism, we would have called the sound behavior function for each object as follows:

```
// This is not a polymorphism
animal_sound(animal);
cat_sound(cat);
duck_sound(duck);
```

Code Box 8-16: Calling the sound behavior function on the created objects

And the output would be as follows:

```
Animal: Beeeep
Cat: Meow
Duck: Quack
```

Shell Box 8-4: The output of the function calls

The preceding code box is not demonstrating polymorphism because it uses different functions, `cat_sound` and `duck_sound`, to call specific behaviors from the `Cat` and `Duck` objects. However, the following code box shows how we expect a polymorphic function to behave. The following code box contains a perfect example of polymorphism:

```
// This is a polymorphism
animal_sound(animal);
animal_sound((struct animal_t*)cat);
animal_sound((struct animal_t*)duck);
```

Code Box 8-17: Calling the same sound behavior function on all three objects

Despite calling the same function three times, we expect to see different behaviors. It seems that passing different object pointers changes the actual behavior behind `animal_sound`. The following shell box would be the output of *Code Box 8-17* if `animal_sound` was polymorphic:

```
Animal: Beeeep
Cat: Meow
Duck: Quake
```

Shell Box 8-5: The output of the function calls

As you see in *Code Box 8-17*, we have used the same function, `animal_sound`, but with different pointers, and as a result, different functions have been invoked behind the scenes.

CAUTION:
Please don't move forward if you're having trouble understanding the preceding code; if you are, please recap the previous section.

The preceding polymorphic code implies that there should be an inheritance relationship between the `Cat` and `Duck` classes with a third class, `Animal`, because we want to be able to cast the `duck_t` and `cat_t` pointers to an `animal_t` pointer. This also implies something else: we have to use the first approach of implementing inheritance in C in order to benefit from the polymorphism mechanism we introduced before.

You may recall that in the first approach to implementing inheritance, the child class had access to the private implementation of the parent class, and here a structure variable from the `animal_t` type should have been put as the first field in the definitions of the `duck_t` and `cat_t` attribute structures. The following code shows the relationship between these three classes:

```
typedef struct {
  ...
} animal_t;

typedef struct {
  animal_t animal;
  ...
} cat_t;

typedef struct {
  animal_t animal;
  ...
} duck_t;
```

Code Box 8-18: The definitions of the attribute structures of classes Animal, Cat, and Duck

With this setup, we can cast the `duck_t` and `cat_t` pointers to the `animal_t` pointers, and then we can use the same behavior functions for both child classes.

So far, we have shown how a polymorphic function is expected to behave and how an inheritance relationship should be defined between the classes. What we haven't shown is how this polymorphic behavior is fulfilled. In other words, we haven't talked about the actual mechanism behind the polymorphism.

Suppose that the behavior function `animal_sound` is defined as it can be seen in code box 8-19. No matter the pointer you send inside as the argument, we will have always one behavior and the function calls won't be polymorphic without the underlying mechanism. The mechanism will be explained as part of *example 8.4* which you will see shortly:

```
void animal_sound(animal_t* ptr) {
  printf("Animal: Beeeep");
}

// This could be a polymorphism, but it is NOT!
animal_sound(animal);
animal_sound((struct animal_t*)cat);
animal_sound((struct animal_t*)duck);
```

Code Box 8-19: The function animal_sound is not polymorphic yet!

As you see next, calling the behavior function `animal_sound` with various pointers won't change the logic of the behavior function; in other words, it is not polymorphic. We will make this function polymorphic as part of the next example, *example 8.4*:

```
Animal: Beeeep
Animal: Beeeep
Animal: Beeeep
```

Shell Box 8-6: The output of the functional calls in Code Box 8-19

So, what is the underlying mechanism that enables polymorphic behavior functions? We answer that question in the upcoming sections, but before that we need to know why we want to have polymorphism in the first place.

Why do we need polymorphism?

Before talking further about the way in which we're going to implement polymorphism in C, we should spend some time talking about the reasons behind the need for polymorphism. The main reason why polymorphism is needed is that we want to keep a piece of code "as is," even when using it with various subtypes of a base type. You are going to see some demonstration of this shortly in the examples.

We don't want to modify the current logic very often when we add new subtypes to the system, or when the behavior of one subtype is being changed. It's just not realistic to have zero changes when a new feature is added – there will always be some changes – but using polymorphism, we can significantly reduce the number of changes that are needed.

Another motivation for having polymorphism is due to the concept of *abstraction*. When we have abstract types (or classes), they usually have some vague or unimplemented behavior functions that need to be *overridden* in child classes and polymorphism is the key way to do this.

Since we want to use abstract types to write our logic, we need a way to call the proper implementation when dealing with pointers of very abstract types. This is another place where polymorphism comes in. No matter what the language is, we need a way to have polymorphic behaviors, otherwise the cost of maintaining a big project can grow quickly, for instance when we are going to add a new subtype to our code.

Now that we've established the importance of polymorphism, it's time to explain how we can have it in C.

How to have polymorphic behavior in C

If we want to have polymorphism in C, we need to use the first approach we explored to implementing inheritance in C. To achieve polymorphic behavior, we can utilize *function pointers*. However, this time, these function pointers need to be kept as some fields in the attribute structure. Let's implement the animal sound example to illustrate this.

We have three classes, Animal, Cat, and Duck, and Cat and Duck are subtypes of Animal. Each class has one header and one source. The Animal class has an extra private header file that contains the actual definition of its attribute structure. This private header is required since we are taking the first approach to implement inheritance. The private header is going to be used by the Cat and Duck classes.

The following code box shows the public interface of the Animal class:

```
#ifndef EXTREME_C_EXAMPLES_CHAPTER_8_4_ANIMAL_H
#define EXTREME_C_EXAMPLES_CHAPTER_8_4_ANIMAL_H

// Forward declaration
struct animal_t;

// Memory allocator
struct animal_t* animal_new();

// Constructor
void animal_ctor(struct animal_t*);

// Destructor
void animal_dtor(struct animal_t*);

// Behavior functions
void animal_get_name(struct animal_t*, char*);
void animal_sound(struct animal_t*);

#endif
```

Code Box 8-20 [ExtremeC_examples_chapter8_4_animal.h]: The public interface of the Animal class

The `Animal` class has two behavior functions. The `animal_sound` function is supposed to be polymorphic and can be overridden by the child classes, while the other behavior function, `animal_get_name`, is not polymorphic, and children cannot override it.

The following is the private definition of the `animal_t` attribute structure:

```c
#ifndef EXTREME_C_EXAMPLES_CHAPTER_8_4_ANIMAL_P_H
#define EXTREME_C_EXAMPLES_CHAPTER_8_4_ANIMAL_P_H

// The function pointer type needed to point to
// different morphs of animal_sound
typedef void (*sound_func_t)(void*);

// Forward declaration
typedef struct {
  char* name;
  // This member is a pointer to the function which
  // performs the actual sound behavior
  sound_func_t sound_func;
} animal_t;

#endif
```

Code Box 8-21 [ExtremeC_examples_chapter8_4_animal_p.h]: The private header of the Animal class

In polymorphism, every child class can provide its own version of the `animal_sound` function. In other words, every child class can override the function inherited from its parent class. Therefore, we need to have a different function for each child class that wants to override it. This means, if the child class has overridden the `animal_sound`, its own overridden function should be called.

That's why we are using function pointers here. Each instance of `animal_t` will have a function pointer dedicated to the behavior `animal_sound`, and that pointer is pointing to the actual definition of the polymorphic function inside the class.

For each polymorphic behavior function, we have a dedicated function pointer. Here, you will see how we use this function pointer to do the correct function call in each subclass. In other words, we show how the polymorphism actually works.

The following code box shows the definition of the `Animal` class:

```c
#include <stdlib.h>
#include <string.h>
#include <stdio.h>
```

```
#include "ExtremeC_examples_chapter8_4_animal_p.h"

// Default definition of the animal_sound at the parent level
void __animal_sound(void* this_ptr) {
  animal_t* animal = (animal_t*)this_ptr;
  printf("%s: Beeeep\n", animal->name);
}

// Memory allocator
animal_t* animal_new() {
  return (animal_t*)malloc(sizeof(animal_t));
}

// Constructor
void animal_ctor(animal_t* animal) {
  animal->name = (char*)malloc(10 * sizeof(char));
  strcpy(animal->name, "Animal");
  // Set the function pointer to point to the default definition
  animal->sound_func = __animal_sound;
}

// Destructor
void animal_dtor(animal_t* animal) {
  free(animal->name);
}

// Behavior functions
void animal_get_name(animal_t* animal, char* buffer) {
  strcpy(buffer, animal->name);
}

void animal_sound(animal_t* animal) {
  // Call the function which is pointed by the function pointer.
  animal->sound_func(animal);
}
```

Code Box 8-22 [ExtremeC_examples_chapter8_4_animal.c]: The definition of the Animal class

The actual polymorphic behavior is happening in *Code Box 8-22*, inside the function `animal_sound`. The private function `__animal_sound` is supposed to be the default behavior of the `animal_sound` function when the subclasses decide not to override it. You will see in the next chapter that polymorphic behavior functions have a default definition which will get inherited and used if the subclass doesn't provide the overridden version.

Moving on, inside the constructor `animal_ctor`, we store the address of __ animal_sound into the `sound_func` field of the `animal` object. Remember that `sound_func` is a function pointer. In this setup, every child object inherits this function pointer, which points to the default definition __animal_sound.

And the final step, inside the behavior function animal_sound, we just call the function that is being pointed to by the `sound_func` field. Again, `sound_func` is the function pointer field pointing to the actual definition of the sound behavior which in the preceding case is __animal_sound. Note that the `animal_sound` function behaves more like a relay to the actual behavior function.

Using this setup, if the `sound_func` field was pointing to another function, then that function would have been called if animal_sound was invoked. That's the trick we are going to use in the `Cat` and `Duck` classes to override the default definition of the sound behavior.

Now, it's time to show the `Cat` and `Duck` classes. The following code boxes will show the `Cat` class's public interface and private implementation. First, we show the `Cat` class's public interface:

```
#ifndef EXTREME_C_EXAMPLES_CHAPTER_8_4_CAT_H
#define EXTREME_C_EXAMPLES_CHAPTER_8_4_CAT_H

// Forward declaration
struct cat_t;

// Memory allocator
struct cat_t* cat_new();

// Constructor
void cat_ctor(struct cat_t*);

// Destructor
void cat_dtor(struct cat_t*);

// All behavior functions are inherited from the animal class.

#endif
```

Code Box 8-23 [ExtremeC_examples_chapter8_4_cat.h]: The public interface of the Cat class

As you will see shortly, it will inherit the `sound` behavior from its parent class, the `Animal` class.

The following code box shows the definition of the Cat class:

```
#include <stdio.h>
#include <stdlib.h>
#include <string.h>

#include "ExtremeC_examples_chapter8_4_animal.h"
#include "ExtremeC_examples_chapter8_4_animal_p.h"

typedef struct {
  animal_t animal;
} cat_t;

// Define a new behavior for the cat's sound
void __cat_sound(void* ptr) {
  animal_t* animal = (animal_t*)ptr;
  printf("%s: Meow\n", animal->name);
}

// Memory allocator
cat_t* cat_new() {
  return (cat_t*)malloc(sizeof(cat_t));
}

// Constructor
void cat_ctor(cat_t* cat) {
  animal_ctor((struct animal_t*)cat);
  strcpy(cat->animal.name, "Cat");
  // Point to the new behavior function. Overriding
  // is actually happening here.
  cat->animal.sound_func = __cat_sound;
}

// Destructor
void cat_dtor(cat_t* cat) {
  animal_dtor((struct animal_t*)cat);
}
```

Code Box 8-24 [ExtremeC_examples_chapter8_4_cat.c]: The private implementation of the Cat class

As you see in the previous code box, we have defined a new function for the cat's sound, __cat_sound. Then inside the constructor, we make the sound_func pointer point to this function.

Now, overriding is happening, and from now on, all cat objects will actually call __cat_sound instead of __animal_sound. The same technique is used for the Duck class.

The following code box shows the public interface of the Duck class:

```
#ifndef EXTREME_C_EXAMPLES_CHAPTER_8_4_DUCK_H
#define EXTREME_C_EXAMPLES_CHAPTER_8_4_DUCK_H

// Forward declaration
struct duck_t;

// Memory allocator
struct duck_t* duck_new();

// Constructor
void duck_ctor(struct duck_t*);

// Destructor
void duck_dtor(struct duck_t*);

// All behavior functions are inherited from the animal class.

#endif
```

Code Box 8-25 [ExtremeC_examples_chapter8_4_duck.h]: The public interface of the Duck class

As you see, that's quite similar to the Cat class. Let's bring up the private definition of the Duck class:

```
#include <stdio.h>
#include <stdlib.h>
#include <string.h>

#include "ExtremeC_examples_chapter8_4_animal.h"
#include "ExtremeC_examples_chapter8_4_animal_p.h"

typedef struct {
  animal_t animal;
} duck_t;

// Define a new behavior for the duck's sound
void __duck_sound(void* ptr) {
  animal_t* animal = (animal_t*)ptr;
  printf("%s: Quacks\n", animal->name);
}

// Memory allocator
duck_t* duck_new() {
  return (duck_t*)malloc(sizeof(duck_t));
}
```

```
// Constructor
void duck_ctor(duck_t* duck) {
  animal_ctor((struct animal_t*)duck);
  strcpy(duck->animal.name, "Duck");
  // Point to the new behavior function. Overriding
  // is actually happening here.
  duck->animal.sound_func = __duck_sound;
}

// Destructor
void duck_dtor(duck_t* duck) {
  animal_dtor((struct animal_t*)duck);
}
```

Code Box 8-26 [ExtremeC_examples_chapter8_4_duck.c]: The private implementation of the Duck class

As you can see, the technique has been used to override the default definition of the sound behavior. A new private behavior function, __duck_sound, has been defined that does the duck-specific sound, and the sound_func pointer is updated to point to this function. This is basically the way that polymorphism is introduced to C++. We will talk more about this in the next chapter.

Finally, the following code box demonstrates the main scenario of *example 8.4*:

```
#include <stdio.h>
#include <stdlib.h>
#include <string.h>

// Only public interfaces
#include "ExtremeC_examples_chapter8_4_animal.h"
#include "ExtremeC_examples_chapter8_4_cat.h"
#include "ExtremeC_examples_chapter8_4_duck.h"

int main(int argc, char** argv) {
  struct animal_t* animal = animal_new();
  struct cat_t* cat = cat_new();
  struct duck_t* duck = duck_new();

  animal_ctor(animal);
  cat_ctor(cat);
  duck_ctor(duck);

  animal_sound(animal);
  animal_sound((struct animal_t*)cat);
  animal_sound((struct animal_t*)duck);
```

```
    animal_dtor(animal);
    cat_dtor(cat);
    duck_dtor(duck);

    free(duck);
    free(cat);
    free(animal);
    return 0;
}
```

Code Box 8-27 [ExtremeC_examples_chapter8_4_main.c]: The main scenario of example 8.4

As you see in the preceding code box, we are only using the public interfaces of the `Animal`, `Cat`, and `Duck` classes. So, the `main` function doesn't know anything about the internal implementation of the classes. Calling the `animal_sound` function with passing different pointers demonstrates how a polymorphic behavior should work. Let's look at the output of the example.

The following shell box shows how to compile and run *example 8.4*:

```
$ gcc -c ExtremeC_examples_chapter8_4_animal.c -o animal.o
$ gcc -c ExtremeC_examples_chapter8_4_cat.c -o cat.o
$ gcc -c ExtremeC_examples_chapter8_4_duck.c -o duck.o
$ gcc -c ExtremeC_examples_chapter8_4_main.c -o main.o
$ gcc animal.o cat.o duck.o main.o -o ex8_4.out
$ ./ex8_4.out
Animal: Beeeep
Cat: Meow
Duck: Quake
$
```

Shell Box 8-7: The compilation, execution, and output of example 8.4

As you can see in *example 8.4*, in class-based programming languages the behavior functions which we want to be polymorphic need special care and should be treated differently. Otherwise, a simple behavior function without the underlying mechanism that we discussed as part of *example 8.4* cannot be polymorphic. That's why we have a special name for these behavior functions, and why we use specific keywords to denote a function to be polymorphic in a language such as C++. These functions are called *virtual* functions. Virtual functions are behavior functions that can be overridden by child classes. Virtual functions need to be tracked by the compiler, and proper pointers should be placed in the corresponding objects to point to the actual definitions when overridden. These pointers are used at runtime to execute the right version of the function.

In the next chapter, we'll see how C++ handles object-oriented relationships between classes. Also, we will find out how C++ implements polymorphism. We will also discuss *Abstraction* which is a direct result of polymorphism.

Summary

In this chapter, we continued our exploration of topics in OOP, picking up from where we left off in the previous chapter. The following topics were discussed in this chapter:

- We explained how inheritance works and looked at the two approaches that we can use to implement inheritance in C.

- The first approach allows direct access to all the private attributes of the parent class, but the second approach has a more conservative approach, hiding the private attributes of the parent class.

- We compared these approaches, and we saw that each of them can be suitable in some use cases.

- Polymorphism was the next topic that we explored. To put it simply, it allows us to have different versions of the same behavior and invoke the correct behavior using the public API of an abstract supertype.

- We saw how to write polymorphic code in C and saw how function pointers contribute to choosing the correct version of a particular behavior at runtime.

The next chapter will be our final chapter about object orientation. As part of it, we'll explore how C++ handles encapsulation, inheritance, and polymorphism. More than that, we will discuss the topic of abstraction and how it leads to a bizarre type of class which is called an *abstract class*. We cannot create objects from these classes!

Chapter 09

Abstraction and OOP in C++

This is the final chapter on OOP in C. In this chapter, we are going to cover the remaining topics and introduce you to a new programming paradigm. In addition, we explore C++ and look at how it implements object-oriented concepts behind the scenes.

As part of this chapter, we will cover the following topics:

- Firstly, we discuss the *Abstraction*. This continues our discussion regarding inheritance and polymorphism and will be the last topic that we cover as part of OOP in C. We show how abstraction helps us in designing object models that have the maximum extendibility and the minimum dependencies between its various components.

- We talk about how object-oriented concepts have been implemented in a famous C++ compiler, g++ in this case. As part of this, we see that how close the approaches that we have discussed so far are in accordance with the approaches that g++ has taken to provide the same concepts.

Let's start the chapter by talking about abstraction.

Abstraction

Abstraction can have a very general meaning in various fields of science and engineering. But in programming, and especially in OOP, abstraction essentially deals with *abstract data types*. In class-based object orientation, abstract data types are the same as *abstract classes*. Abstract classes are special classes that we cannot create an object from; they are not ready or complete enough to be used for object creation. So, why do we need to have such classes or data types? This is because when we work with abstract and general data types, we avoid creating strong dependencies between various parts of code.

As an example, we can have the following relationships between the *Human* and *Apple* classes:

An object of the Human class eats an object of the Apple class.

An object of the Human class eats an object of the Orange class.

If the classes that an object from the *Human* class can eat were expanded to more than just *Apple* and *Orange*, we would need to add more relations to the *Human* class. Instead, though, we could create an abstract class called *Fruit* that is the parent of both *Apple* and *Orange* classes, and we could set the relation to be between *Human* and *Fruit* only. Therefore, we can turn our preceding two statements into one:

An object of the Human class eats an object from a subtype of the Fruit class.

The *Fruit* class is abstract because it lacks information about shape, taste, smell, color, and many more attributes of a specific fruit. Only when we have an apple or an orange do we know the exact values of the different attributes. The *Apple* and *Orange* classes are said to be *concrete types*.

We can even add more abstraction. The *Human* class can eat *Salad* or *Chocolate* as well. So, we can say:

An object of the Human type eats an object from a subtype of the Eatable class.

As you can see, the abstraction level of *Eatable* is even higher than that of *Fruit*. Abstraction is a great technique for designing an object model that has minimal dependency on concrete types and allows the maximum future extension to the object model when more concrete types are introduced to the system.

Regarding the preceding example, we could also add further abstraction by using the fact that *Human* is an *Eater*. Then, we could make our statement even more abstract:

An object from a subtype of the Eater class eats an object from a subtype of the Eatable class.

We can continue to abstract everything in an object model and find abstract data types that are more abstract than the level we need to solve our problem. This is usually called *over-abstraction*. It happens when you try to create abstract data types that have no real application, either for your current or your future needs. This should be avoided at all costs because abstraction can cause problems, despite all the benefits it provides.

A general guide regarding the amount of abstraction that we need can be found as part of the *abstraction principle*. I got the following quote from its Wikipedia page, `https://en.wikipedia.org/wiki/Abstraction_principle_(computer_ programming)`. It simply states:

Each significant piece of functionality in a program should be implemented in just one place in the source code. Where similar functions are carried out by distinct pieces of code, it is generally beneficial to combine them into one by abstracting out the varying parts.

While at first glance you may not see any sign of object orientation or inheritance in this statement, by giving some further thought to it you will notice that what we did with inheritance was based on this principle. Therefore, as a general rule, whenever you don't expect to have variations in a specific logic, there is no need to introduce abstraction at that point.

In a programming language, inheritance and polymorphism are two capabilities that are required in order to create abstraction. An abstract class such as *Eatable* is a supertype in relation to its concrete classes, such as *Apple*, and this is accomplished by inheritance.

Polymorphism also plays an important role. There are behaviors in an abstract type that *cannot* have default implementation at that abstraction level. For example, *taste* as an attribute implemented using a behavior function such as `eatable_get_taste` as part of the *Eatable* class cannot have an exact value when we are talking about an *Eatable* object. In other words, we cannot create an object directly from the *Eatable* class if we don't know how to define the `eatable_get_taste` behavior function.

The preceding function can only be defined when the child class is concrete enough. For example, we know that *Apple* objects should return *sweet* for their taste (we've assumed here that all apples are sweet). This is where polymorphism helps. It allows a child class to override its parent's behaviors and return the proper taste, for example.

If you remember from the previous chapter, the behavior functions that can be overridden by child classes are called *virtual functions*. Note that it is possible that a virtual function doesn't have any definition at all. Of course, this makes the owner class abstract.

By adding more and more abstraction, at a certain level, we reach classes that have no attributes and contain only virtual functions with no default definitions. These classes are called *interfaces*. In other words, they expose functionalities but they don't offer any implementation at all, and they are usually used to create dependencies between various components in a software project. As an example, in our preceding examples, the *Eater* and *Eatable* classes are interfaces. Note that, just like abstract classes, you must not create an object from an interface. The following code shows why this cannot be done in a C code.

The following code box is the equivalent code written for the preceding interface *Eatable* in C using the techniques we introduced in the previous chapter to implement inheritance and polymorphism:

```
typedef enum {SWEET, SOUR} taste_t;

// Function pointer type
typedef taste_t (*get_taste_func_t)(void*);

typedef struct {
  // Pointer to the definition of the virtual function
  get_taste_func_t get_taste_func;
} eatable_t;

eatable_t* eatable_new() { ... }

void eatable_ctor(eatable_t* eatable) {
  // We don't have any default definition for the virtual function
  eatable->get_taste_func = NULL;
}


// Virtual behavior function
taste_t eatable_get_taste(eatable_t* eatable) {
  return eatable->get_taste_func(eatable);
}
```

Code Box 9-1: The Eatable interface in C

As you can see, in the constructor function we have set the `get_taste_func` pointer to NULL. So, calling the `eatable_get_taste` virtual function can lead to a segmentation fault. From the coding perspective, that's basically why that we must not create an object from the *Eatable* interface other than the reasons we know from the definition of the interface and the design point of view.

The following code box demonstrates how creating an object from the *Eatable* interface, which is totally possible and allowed from a C point of view, can lead to a crash and must not be done:

```
eatable_t *eatable = eatable_new();
eatable_ctor(eatable);
taste_t taste = eatable_get_taste(eatable); // Segmentation fault!
free(eatable);
```

Code Box 9-2: Segmentation fault when creating an object from the Eatable interface and calling a pure virtual function from it

To prevent ourselves from creating an object from an abstract type, we can remove the *allocator function* from the class's public interface. If you remember the approaches that we took in the previous chapter to implement inheritance in C, by removing the allocator function, only child classes are able to create objects from the parent's attribute structure.

External codes are then no longer able to do so. For instance, in the preceding example, we do not want any external code to be able to create any object from the structure `eatable_t`. In order to do that, we need to have the attribute structure forward declared and make it an incomplete type. Then, we need to remove the public memory allocator `eatable_new` from the class.

To summarize what we need to do to have an abstract class in C, you need to nullify the virtual function pointers that are not meant to have a default definition at that abstraction level. At an extremely high level of abstraction, we have an interface whose all function pointers are null. To prevent any external code from creating objects from abstract types, we should remove the allocator function from the public interface.

In the following section, we are going to compare similar object-oriented features in C and C++. This gives us an idea how C++ has been developed from pure C.

Object-oriented constructs in C++

In this section, we are going to compare what we did in C and the underlying mechanisms employed in a famous C++ compiler, `g++` in this case, for supporting encapsulation, inheritance, polymorphism, and abstraction.

We want to show that there is a close accordance between the methods by which object-oriented concepts are implemented in C and C++. Note that, from now on, whenever we refer to C++, we are actually referring to the implementation of `g++` as one of the C++ compilers, and not the C++ standard. Of course, the underlying implementations can be different for various compilers, but we don't expect to see a lot of differences. We will also be using `g++` in a 64-bit Linux setup.

We are going to use the previously discussed techniques to write an object-oriented code in C, and then we write the same program in C++, before jumping to the final conclusion.

Encapsulation

It is difficult to go deep into a C++ compiler and see how it uses the techniques that we've been exploring so far to produce the final executable, but there is one clever trick that we can use to actually see this. The way to do this is to compare the assembly instructions generated for two similar C and C++ programs.

This is exactly what we are going to do to demonstrate that the C++ compiler ends up generating the same assembly instructions as a C program that uses the OOP techniques that we've been discussing in the previous chapters.

Example 9.1 is about two C and C++ programs addressing the same simple object-oriented logic. There is a `Rectangle` class in this example, which has a behavior function for calculating its area. We want to see and compare the generated assembly codes for the same behavior function in both programs. The following code box demonstrates the C version:

```
#include <stdio.h>

typedef struct {
  int width;
  int length;
} rect_t;

int rect_area(rect_t* rect) {
  return rect->width * rect->length;
}

int main(int argc, char** argv) {
  rect_t r;
  r.width = 10;
  r.length = 25;
  int area = rect_area(&r);
  printf("Area: %d\n", area);
  return 0;
}
```

Code Box 9-3 [ExtremeC_examples_chapter9_1.c]: Encapsulation example in C

And the following code box shows the C++ version of the preceding program:

```
#include <iostream>

class Rect {
public:
  int Area() {
    return width * length;
  }
  int width;
  int length;
};

int main(int argc, char** argv) {
  Rect r;
  r.width = 10;
  r.length = 25;
  int area = r.Area();
  std::cout << "Area: " << area << std::endl;
  return 0;
```

```
}
```

Code Box 9-4 [ExtremeC_examples_chapter9_1.cpp]: Encapsulation example in C++

So, let's generate the assembly codes for the preceding C and C++ programs:

```
$ gcc -S ExtremeC_examples_chapter9_1.c -o ex9_1_c.s
$ g++ -S ExtremeC_examples_chapter9_1.cpp -o ex9_1_cpp.s
$
```

Shell Box 9-1: Generating the assembly outputs for the C and C++ codes

Now, let's dump the ex9_1_c.s and ex9_1_cpp.s files and look for the definition of the behavior functions. In ex9_1_c.s, we should look for the rect_area symbol, and in ex9_1_cpp.s, we should look for the _ZN4Rect4AreaEv symbol. Note that C++ mangles the symbol names, and that's why you need to search for this strange symbol. Name mangling in C++ has been discussed in *Chapter 2, Compilation and Linking*.

For the C program, the following is the generated assembly for the rect_area function:

```
$ cat ex9_1_c.s
...
rect_area:
.LFB0:
    .cfi_startproc
    pushq   %rbp
    .cfi_def_cfa_offset 16
    .cfi_offset 6, -16
    movq    %rsp, %rbp
    .cfi_def_cfa_register 6
    movq    %rdi, -8(%rbp)
    movq    -8(%rbp), %rax
    movl    (%rax), %edx
    movq    -8(%rbp), %rax
    movl    4(%rax), %eax
    imull   %edx, %eax
    popq    %rbp
    .cfi_def_cfa 7, 8
    Ret
```

```
    .cfi_endproc
...
$
```

Shell Box 9-2: The generated assembly code of the rect_area function

The following is the generated assembly instructions for the Rect::Area function:

```
$ cat ex9_1_cpp.s
...
_ZN4Rect4AreaEv:
.LFB1493:
    .cfi_startproc
    pushq   %rbp
    .cfi_def_cfa_offset 16
    .cfi_offset 6, -16
    movq    %rsp, %rbp
    .cfi_def_cfa_register 6
    movq    %rdi, -8(%rbp)
    movq    -8(%rbp), %rax
    movl    (%rax), %edx
    movq    -8(%rbp), %rax
    movl    4(%rax), %eax
    imull   %edx, %eax
    popq    %rbp
    .cfi_def_cfa 7, 8
    Ret
    .cfi_endproc
...
$
```

Shell Box 9-3: The generated assembly code of the Rect::Area function

Unbelievably, they are exactly the same! I'm not sure how the C++ code turns into the preceding assembly code, but I'm sure that the assembly code generated for the preceding C function is almost, to high degree of accuracy, equivalent to the assembly code generated for the C++ function.

We can conclude from this that the C++ compiler has used a similar approach to that which we used in C, introduced as *implicit encapsulation* as part of *Chapter 6, OOP and Encapsulation*, to implement the encapsulation. Like what we did with implicit encapsulation, you can see in *Code Box 9-3* that a pointer to the attribute structure is passed to the rect_area function as the first argument.

As part of the boldened assembly instructions in both shell boxes, the width and length variables are being read by adding to the memory address passed as the first argument. The first pointer argument can be found in the %rdi register according to *System V ABI*. So, we can infer that C++ has changed the Area function to accept a pointer argument as its first argument, which points to the object itself.

As a final word on encapsulation, we saw how C and C++ are closely related regarding encapsulation, at least in this simple example. Let's see if the same is true regarding inheritance as well.

Inheritance

Investigating inheritance is easier than encapsulation. In C++, the pointers from a child class can be assigned to the pointers from the parent class. Also, the child class should have access to the private definition of the parent class.

Both of these behaviors imply that C++ is using our first approach to implementing inheritance, which was discussed in the previous chapter, *Chapter 8, Inheritance and Polymorphism*, along with the second approach. Please refer back to the previous chapter if you need to remind yourself of the two approaches.

However, C++ inheritance seems more complex because C++ supports multiple inheritances that we can't support in our first approach. In this section, we will check the memory layouts of two objects instantiated from two similar classes in C and C++, as demonstrated in *example 9.2*.

Example 9.2 is about a simple class inheriting from another simple class, both of which have no behavior functions. The C version is as follows:

```
#include <string.h>

typedef struct {
  char c;
  char d;
} a_t;
```

```
typedef struct {
  a_t parent;
  char str[5];
} b_t;

int main(int argc, char** argv) {
  b_t b;
  b.parent.c = 'A';
  b.parent.d = 'B';
  strcpy(b.str, "1234");
  // We need to set a break point at this line to see the memory
layout.
  return 0;
}
```

Code Box 9-5 [ExtremeC_examples_chapter9_2.c]: Inheritance example in C

And the C++ version comes within the following code box:

```
#include <string.h>

class A {
public:
  char c;
  char d;
};

class B : public A {
public:
  char str[5];
};

int main(int argc, char** argv) {
  B b;
  b.c = 'A';
  b.d = 'B';
  strcpy(b.str, "1234");
  // We need to set a break point at this line to see the memory
layout.
  return 0;
}
```

Code Box 9-6 [ExtremeC_examples_chapter9_2.cpp]: Inheritance example in C++

Firstly, we need to compile the C program and use gdb to set a breakpoint on the last line of the main function. When the execution pauses, we can examine the memory layout as well as the existing values:

```
$ gcc -g ExtremeC_examples_chapter9_2.c -o ex9_2_c.out
$ gdb ./ex9_2_c.out
...
(gdb) b ExtremeC_examples_chapter9_2.c:19
Breakpoint 1 at 0x69e: file ExtremeC_examples_chapter9_2.c, line
19.
(gdb) r
Starting program: .../ex9_2_c.out

Breakpoint 1, main (argc=1, argv=0x7fffffffe358) at ExtremeC_
examples_chapter9_2.c:20
20      return 0;
(gdb) x/7c &b
0x7fffffffe261: 65 'A'  66 'B'  49 '1'  50 '2'  51 '3'  52 '4'  0
'\000'
(gdb) c
[Inferior 1 (process 3759) exited normally]
(gdb) q
$
```

Shell Box 9-4: Running the C version of example 9.2 in gdb

As you can see, we have printed seven characters, starting from the address of b object, which are as follows: 'A', 'B', '1', '2', '3', '4', '\0'. Let's do the same for the C++ code:

```
$ g++ -g ExtremeC_examples_chapter9_2.cpp -o ex9_2_cpp.out
$ gdb ./ex9_2_cpp.out
...
(gdb) b ExtremeC_examples_chapter9_2.cpp:20
Breakpoint 1 at 0x69b: file ExtremeC_examples_chapter9_2.cpp, line
20.
(gdb) r
Starting program: .../ex9_2_cpp.out

Breakpoint 1, main (argc=1, argv=0x7fffffffe358) at ExtremeC_
examples_chapter9_2.cpp:21
21      return 0;
(gdb) x/7c &b
```

```
0x7ffffffe251: 65 'A'  66 'B'  49 '1'  50 '2'  51 '3'  52 '4'  0
'\000'
```

(qdb) c

[Inferior 1 (process 3804) exited normally]

(qdb) q

$

Shell Box 9-5: Running the C++ version of example 9.2 in gdb

As you can see in the preceding two shell boxes, the memory layout and the values stored in the attributes are the same. You shouldn't get confused by having the behavior functions and attributes together in a class in C++; they are going to be treated separately from the class. In C++, the attributes, no matter where you put them in a class, are always collected within the same memory block regarding a specific object, and functions will always be independent of the attributes, just as we saw when looking at *implicit encapsulation* as part of *Chapter 6, OOP and Encapsulation*.

The previous example demonstrates *single inheritance*. So, what about *multiple inheritance*? In the previous chapter, we explained why our first approach to implementing inheritance in C could not support multiple inheritance. We again demonstrate the reason in the following code box:

```
typedef struct { ... } a_t;
typedef struct { ... } b_t;

typedef struct {
  a_t a;
  b_t b;
  ...
} c_t;

c_t c_obj;
a_t* a_ptr = (a_ptr*)&c_obj;
b_t* b_ptr = (b_ptr*)&c_obj;
c_t* c_ptr = &c_obj;
```

Code Box 9-7: Demonstration of why multiple inheritance cannot work with our proposed first approach for implementing inheritance in C

In the preceding code box, the c_t class desires to inherit both a_t and b_t classes. After declaring the classes, we create the c_obj object. In the following lines of preceding code, we create different pointers.

An important note here is that *all of these pointers must be pointing to the same address*. The a_ptr and c_ptr pointers can be used safely with any behavior function from the a_t and c_t classes, but the b_ptr pointer is dangerous to use because it is pointing to the a field in the c_t class, which is an a_t object. Trying to access the fields inside b_t through b_ptr results in an undefined behavior.

The following code is the correct version of the preceding code, where all pointers can be used safely:

```
c_t c_obj;
a_t* a_ptr = (a_ptr*)&c_obj;
b_t* b_ptr = (b_ptr*)(&c_obj + sizeof(a_t));
c_t* c_ptr = &c_obj;
```

Code Box 9-8: Demonstration of how casts should be updated to point to the correct fields

As you can see on the third line in *Code Box 9-8*, we have added the size of an a_t object to the address of c_obj; this eventually results in a pointer pointing to the b field in c_t. Note that casting in C does not do any magic; it is there to convert types and it doesn't modify the transferring value, the memory address in the preceding case. Eventually, after the assignment, the address from the right-hand side would be copied to the left-hand side.

For now, let's see the same example in C++ with a look at *example 9.3*. Suppose that we have a D class that inherits from three different classes, A, B, and C. The following is the code written for *example 9.3*:

```
#include <string.h>

class A {
public:
    char a;
    char b[4];
};

class B {
public:
    char c;
    char d;
};

class C {
public:
    char e;
    char f;
};
```

```
class D : public A, public B, public C {
public:
  char str[5];
};

int main(int argc, char** argv) {
  D d;
  d.a = 'A';
  strcpy(d.b, "BBB");
  d.c = 'C';
  d.d = 'D';
  d.e = 'E';
  d.f = 'F';
  strcpy(d.str, "1234");
  A* ap = &d;
  B* bp = &d;
  C* cp = &d;
  D* dp = &d;
  // We need to set a break point at this line.
  return 0;
}
```

Code Box 9-9 [ExtremeC_examples_chapter9_3.cpp]: Multiple inheritance in C++

Let's compile the example and run it with gdb:

```
$ g++ -g ExtremeC_examples_chapter9_3.cpp -o ex9_3.out
$ gdb ./ex9_3.out
...
(gdb) b ExtremeC_examples_chapter9_3.cpp:40
Breakpoint 1 at 0x100000f78: file ExtremeC_examples_chapter9_3.
cpp, line 40.
(gdb) r
Starting program: .../ex9_3.out

Breakpoint 1, main (argc=1, argv=0x7ffffffe358) at ExtremeC_
examples_chapter9_3.cpp:41
41      return 0;
(gdb) x/14c &d
0x7ffffffe25a: 65 'A'   66 'B'   66 'B'   66 'B'   0 '\000'     67 'C'
68 'D'   69 'E'
0x7ffffffe262: 70 'F'   49 '1'   50 '2'   51 '3'   52 '4'   0 '\000'
(gdb)
```

```
$
```

Shell Box 9-6: Compiling and running example 9.3 in gdb

As you can see, the attributes are placed adjacent to each other. This shows that multiple objects of the parent classes are being kept inside the same memory layout of the d object. What about the ap, bp, cp, and dp pointers? As you can see, in C++, we can cast implicitly when assigning a child pointer to a parent pointer (upcasting).

Let's examine the values of these pointers in the current execution:

```
(gdb) print ap
$1 = (A *) 0x7ffffffe25a
(gdb) print bp
$2 = (B *) 0x7ffffffe25f
(gdb) print cp
$3 = (C *) 0x7ffffffe261
(gdb) print dp
$4 = (D *) 0x7ffffffe25a
(gdb)
```

Shell Box 9-7: Printing the addresses stored in the pointers as part of example 9.3

The preceding shell box shows that the starting address of the d object, shown as $4, is the same as the address being pointed to by ap, shown as $1. So, this clearly shows that C++ puts an object of the type *A* as the first field in the corresponding attribute structure of the *D* class. Based on the addresses in the pointers and the result we got from the x command, an object of the *B* type and then an object of the *C* type, are put into the same memory layout belonging to object d.

In addition, the preceding addresses show that the cast in C++ is not a passive operation, and it can perform some pointer arithmetic on the transferring address while converting the types. For example, in *Code Box 9-9*, while assigning the bp pointer in the main function, five bytes or sizeof(A), are added to the address of d. This is done in order to overcome the problem we found in implementing multiple inheritance in C. Now, these pointers can easily be used in all behavior functions without needing to do the arithmetic yourself. As an important note, C casts and C++ casts are different, and you may see different behavior if you assume that C++ casts are as passive as C casts.

Now it's time to look at the similarities between C and C++ in the case of polymorphism.

Polymorphism

Comparing the underlying techniques for having polymorphism in C and C++ is not an easy task. In the previous chapter, we came up with a simple method for having a polymorphic behavior function in C, but C++ uses a much more sophisticated mechanism to bring about polymorphism, though the basic underlying idea is still the same. If we want to generalize our approach for implementing polymorphism in C, we can do it as the pseudo-code that can be seen in the following code box:

```
// Typedefing function pointer types
typedef void* (*func_1_t)(void*, ...);
typedef void* (*func_2_t)(void*, ...);
...
typedef void* (*func_n_t)(void*, ...);

// Attribute structure of the parent class
typedef struct {
  // Attributes
  ...
  // Pointers to functions
  func_1_t func_1;
  func_2_t func_2;
  ...
  func_n_t func_t;
} parent_t;

// Default private definitions for the
// virtual behavior functions
void* __default_func_1(void* parent, ...) {  // Default definition
}
void* __default_func_2(void* parent, ...) {  // Default definition
}
...
void* __default_func_n(void* parent, ...) {  // Default definition
}
// Constructor
void parent_ctor(parent_t *parent) {
  // Initializing attributes
  ...
  // Setting default definitions for virtual
  // behavior functions
  parent->func_1 = __default_func_1;
  parent->func_2 = __default_func_2;
  ...
  parent->func_n = __default_func_n;
}
```

```
// Public and non-virtual behavior functions
void* parent_non_virt_func_1(parent_t* parent, ...) { // Code }
void* parent_non_virt_func_2(parent_t* parent, ...) { // Code }
...
void* parent_non_virt_func_m(parent_t* parent, ...) { // Code }

// Actual public virtual behavior functions
void* parent_func_1(parent_t* parent, ...) {
  return parent->func_1(parent, ...);
}
void* parent_func_2(parent_t* parent, ...) {
  return parent->func_2(parent, ...);
}
...
void* parent_func_n(parent_t* parent, ...) {
  return parent->func_n(parent, ...);
}
```

Code Box 9-10: Pseudo-code demonstrating how virtual functions can be declared and defined in a C code

As you can see in the preceding pseudo-code, the parent class has to maintain a list of function pointers in its attribute structure. These function pointers (in the parent class) either point to the default definitions for the virtual functions, or they are null. The pseudo-class defined as part of *Code Box 9-10* has m non-virtual behavior functions and n virtual behavior functions.

Note:
Not all behavior functions are polymorphic. Polymorphic behavior functions are called virtual behavior functions or simply virtual functions. In some languages, such as Java, they are called *virtual methods*.

Non-virtual functions are not polymorphic, and you never get various behaviors by calling them. In other words, a call to a non-virtual function is a simple function call and it just performs the logic inside the definition and doesn't relay the call to another function. However, virtual functions need to redirect the call to a proper function, set by either the parent or the child constructor. If a child class wants to override some of the inherited virtual functions, it should update the virtual function pointers.

Note:
The void* type for the output variables can be replaced by any other pointer type. I used a generic pointer to show that anything can be returned from the functions in the pseudo-code.

The following pseudo-code shows how a child class overrides a few of the virtual functions found in *Code Box 9-10*:

```
Include everything related to parent class ...

typedef struct {
  parent_t parent;
  // Child attributes
  ...
} child_t;

void* __child_func_4(void* parent, ...) { // Overriding definition
}
void* __child_func_7(void* parent, ...) { // Overriding definition
}

void child_ctor(child_t* child) {
  parent_ctor((parent_t*)child);
  // Initialize child attributes
  ...
  // Update pointers to functions
  child->parent.func_4 = __child_func_4;
  child->parent.func_7 = __child_func_7;
}

// Child's behavior functions
...
```

Code Box 9-11: Pseudo-code in C demonstrating how a child class can override some
virtual functions inherited from the parent class

As you can see in *Code Box 9-11*, the child class needs only to update a few pointers in the parent's attribute structure. C++ takes a similar approach. When you declare a behavior function as virtual (using the `virtual` keyword), C++ creates an array of function pointers, pretty similar to the way we did in *Code Box 9-10*.

As you can see, we added one function pointer attribute for each virtual function, but C++ has a smarter way of keeping these pointers. It just uses an array called a *virtual table* or *vtable*. The virtual table is created when an object is about to be created. It is first populated while calling the constructor of the base class, and then as part of the constructor of the child class, just as we've shown in *Code Boxes 9-10* and *9-11*.

Since the virtual table is only populated in the constructors, calling a polymorphic method in a constructor, either in the parent or in the child class, should be avoided, as its pointer may have not been updated yet and it might be pointing to an incorrect definition.

As our last discussion regarding the underlying mechanisms used for having various object-oriented concepts in C and C++, we are going to talk about abstraction.

Abstract classes

Abstraction in C++ is possible using *pure virtual* functions. In C++ if you define a member function as a virtual function and set it to zero, you have declared a pure virtual function. Look at the following example:

```
enum class Taste { Sweet, Sour };

// This is an interface
class Eatable {
public:
  virtual Taste GetTaste() = 0;
};
```

Code Box 9-12: The Eatable interface in C++

Inside the class `Eatable`, we have a `GetTaste` virtual function that is set to zero. `GetTaste` is a pure virtual function and makes the whole class abstract. You can no longer create objects from the *Eatable* type, and C++ doesn't allow this. In addition, *Eatable* is an interface, because all of its member functions are purely virtual. This function can be overridden in a child class.

The following shows a class that is overriding the `GetTaste` function:

```
enum class Taste { Sweet, Sour };

// This is an interface
class Eatable {
public:
  virtual Taste GetTaste() = 0;
};

class Apple : public Eatable {
public:
  Taste GetTaste() override {
    return Taste::Sweet;
  }
};
```

Code Box 9-13: Two child classes implementing the Eatable interface

Pure virtual functions are remarkably similar to virtual functions. The addresses to the actual definitions are being kept in the virtual table in the same way as virtual functions, but with one difference. The initial values for the pointers of pure virtual functions are null, unlike the pointers of normal virtual functions, which need to point to a default definition while the construction is in progress.

Unlike a C compiler, which doesn't know anything about abstract types, a C++ compiler is aware of abstract types and generates a compilation error if you try to create an object from an abstract type.

In this section, we took various object-oriented concepts and compared them in C, using the techniques introduced in the past three chapters, and in C++, using the g++ compiler. We showed that, in most cases, the approaches we employed are in accordance with the techniques that a compiler like g++ uses.

Summary

In this chapter, we concluded our exploration of topics in OOP, picking up from abstraction and moving on by showing the similarities between C and C++ regarding object-oriented concepts.

The following topics were discussed as part of this chapter:

- Abstract classes and interfaces were initially discussed. Using them, we can have an interface or a partially abstract class, which could be used to create concrete child classes with polymorphic and different behaviors.

- We then compared the output of the techniques we used in C to bring in some OOP features, with the output of what g++ produces. This was to demonstrate how similar the results are. We concluded that the techniques that we employed can be very similar in their outcomes.

- We discussed virtual tables in greater depth.

- We showed how pure virtual functions (which is a C++ concept but does have a C counterpart) can be used to declare virtual behaviors that have no default definition.

The next chapter is about Unix and its correspondence to C. It will review the history of Unix and the invention of C. It will also explain the layered architecture of a Unix system.

Chapter 10

Unix – History and Architecture

You might have asked yourself why there should be a chapter about Unix in the middle of a book about expert-level C. If you have not, I invite you to ask yourself, how can these two topics, C and Unix, be related in such a way that there's a need for two dedicated chapters (this and the next chapter) in the middle of a book that should talk about C?

The answer is simple: if you think they are unrelated, then you are making a big mistake. The relationship between the two is simple; Unix is the first operating system that is implemented with a fairly high-level programming language, C, which is designed for this purpose, and C got its fame and power from Unix. Of course, our statement about C being a high-level programming language is not true anymore, and C is no longer considered to be so high-level.

Back in the 1970s and 1980s, if the Unix engineers at Bell Labs had decided to use another programming language, instead of C, to develop a new version of Unix, then we would be talking about that language today, and this book wouldn't be *Extreme C* anymore. Let's pause for a minute to read this quote from Dennis M. Ritchie, one of the pioneers of C, about the effect of Unix on the success of C:

> *"Doubtless, the success of Unix itself was the most important factor;*
> *it made the language available to hundreds of thousands of people.*
> *Conversely, of course, Unix's use of C and its consequent portability*
> *to a wide variety of machines was important in the system's success."*
>
> *- Dennis M. Ritchie – The Development of the C Language*

Available at `https://www.bell-labs.com/usr/dmr/www/chist.html`.

As part of this chapter, we cover the following topics:

- We briefly talk about the history of Unix and how the invention of C happened.

- We explain how C has been developed based on B and BCPL.

- We discuss the Unix onion architecture and how it was designed based on the Unix philosophy.

- We describe the user application layer together with shell ring and how the programs consume the API exposed by the shell ring. The SUS and POSIX standards are explained as part of this section.

- We discuss the kernel layer and what features and functionalities should be present in a Unix kernel.

- We talk about the Unix devices and how they can be used in a Unix system.

Let's start the chapter by talking about the Unix history.

Unix history

In this section, we are going to give a bit of history about Unix. This is not a history book, so we're going to keep it short and straight to the point, but the goal here is to gain some hints of history in order to develop a basis for having Unix side by side with C forever in your minds.

Multics OS and Unix

Even before having Unix, we had the Multics OS. It was a joint project launched in 1964 as a cooperative project led by MIT, General Electric, and Bell Labs. Multics OS was a huge success because it could introduce the world to a real working and secure operating system. Multics was installed everywhere from universities to government sites. Fast-forward to 2019, and every operating system today is borrowing some ideas from Multics indirectly through Unix.

In 1969, because of the various reasons that we will talk about shortly, some people at Bell Labs, especially the pioneers of Unix, such as Ken Thompson and Dennis Ritchie, gave up on Multics and, subsequently, Bell Labs quit the Multics project. But this was not the end for Bell Labs; they had designed their simpler and more efficient operating system, which was called Unix.

You can read more about Multics and its history here: `https://multicians. org/history.html`, where you can get a breakdown of the history of Multics.

The following link: `https://www.quora.com/Why-did-Unix-succeed-and-not-Multics`, is also a good one that explains why Unix continued to live while Multics became discontinued.

It is worthwhile to compare the Multics and Unix operating systems. In the following list, you will see similarities and differences found while comparing Multics and Unix:

- **Both follow the onion architecture as their internal structure**. We mean that they both have more or less the same rings in their onion architecture, especially kernel and shell rings. Therefore, programmers could write their own programs on top of the shell ring. Also, Unix and Multics expose a list of utility programs such as `ls` and `pwd`. In the following sections, we will explain the various rings found in the Unix architecture.

- **Multics needed expensive resources and machines to be able to work**. It was not possible to install it on ordinary commodity machines, and that was one of the main drawbacks that let Unix thrive and finally made Multics obsolete after about 30 years.

- **Multics was complex by design**. This was the reason behind the frustration of Bell Labs employees and, as we said earlier, the reason why they left the project. But Unix tried to remain simple. In the first version, it was not even multitasking or multi-user!

You can read more about Unix and Multics online, and follow the events that happened in that era. Both were successful projects, but Unix has been able to thrive and survive to this day.

It is worth sharing that Bell Labs has been working on a new distributed operating system called *Plan 9*, which is based on the Unix project. You can read more about it at Wikipedia: `https://en.wikipedia.org/wiki/Plan_9_from_Bell_Labs`.

Figure 10-1: Plan 9 from Bell Labs (from Wikipedia)

I suppose that it is enough for us to know that Unix was a simplification of the ideas and innovations that Multics presented; it was not something new, and so, I can quit talking about Unix and Multics history at this point.

So far, there are no traces of C in the history because it has not been invented yet. The first versions of Unix were purely written using assembly language. Only in 1973 was Unix version 4 written using C.

Now, we are getting close to discussing C itself, but before that, we must talk about BCPL and B because they have been the gateway to C.

BCPL and B

BCPL was created by Martin Richards as a programming language invented for the purpose of writing compilers. The people from Bell Labs were introduced to the language when they were working as part of the Multics project. After quitting the Multics project, Bell Labs first started to write Unix using assembly programming language. That's because, back then, it was an anti-pattern to develop an operating system using a programming language other than assembly!

For instance, it was strange that the people at the Multics project were using PL/1 to develop Multics but, by doing that, they showed that operating systems could be successfully written using a higher-level programming language other than assembly. So, because of that, Multics became the main inspiration for using another language for developing Unix.

The attempt to write operating system modules using a programming language other than assembly remained with Ken Thompson and Dennis Ritchie at Bell Labs. They tried to use BCPL, but it turned out that they needed to apply some modifications to the language to be able to use it in minicomputers such as the DEC PDP-7. These changes led to the B programming language.

We are going to avoid going too deep into the properties of the B language here, but you can read more about it and the way it was developed in the following links:

- The B Programming Language, at `https://en.wikipedia.org/wiki/B_ (programming_language)`
- *The Development of the C Language*, at `https://www.bell-labs.com/usr/ dmr/www/chist.html`

Dennis Ritchie authored the latter article himself, and it is a good way to explain the development of the C programming language while still sharing valuable information about B and its characteristics.

B also had its shortcomings in terms of being a system programming language. B was typeless, which meant that it was only possible to work with a *word* (not a byte) in each operation. This made it hard to use the language on machines with a different word length.

This is why, over time, further modifications were made to the language until it led to developing the **NB (New B)** language, and later it derived the structures from the B language. These structures were typeless in B, but they became typed in C. Finally, in 1973, the fourth version of Unix could be developed using C, in which there were still many assembly codes.

In the next section, we talk about the differences between B and C, and why C is a top-notch modern system programming language for writing an operating system.

The way to C

I do not think we can find anyone better than Dennis Ritchie himself to explain why C was invented after the difficulties met with B. In this section, we're going to list the causes that made Dennis Ritchie, Ken Thompson, and others create a new programming language instead of using B for writing Unix.

Following is the list of flaws found in B, which led to the creation of C:

- **B could only work with words in memory**: Every single operation should have been performed in terms of words. Back then, having a programming language that was able to work with bytes was a dream. This was because of the available hardware at the time, which was addressing the memory in a word-based scheme.

- **B was typeless**: The more accurate statement we could say is that B was a single-type language. All variables were from the same type: word. So, if you had a string with 20 characters (21 plus the null character at the end), you had to divide it up by words and store it in more than one variable. For example, if a word was 4 bytes, you would have 6 variables to store 21 characters of the string.

- **Being typeless meant that multiple byte-oriented algorithms, such as string manipulation algorithms, were not efficiently written with B**: This was because B was using the memory words not bytes, and they could not be used efficiently to manage multi-byte data types such as integers and strings.

- **B was not supporting floating-point operations**: At the time, these were becoming increasingly available on the new hardware, but there was no support for that in the B language.

- Through the availability of machines such as PDP-1, which were able to address memory on a byte basis, B showed that it could be inefficient in addressing bytes of memory: This became even clearer with B pointers, which could only address the words in the memory, and not the bytes. In other words, for a program wanting to access a specific byte or a byte range in the memory, more computations had to be done to calculate the corresponding word indexes.

The difficulties with B, particularly its slow development and execution on machines that were available at the time, forced Dennis Ritchie to produce a new language. This new language was called NB, or New B at first, but it eventually turned out to be C.

This newly developed language, C, tried to cover the difficulties and flaws of B and became a *de facto* programming language for system development, instead of the assembly language. In less than 10 years, newer versions of Unix were completely written in C, and all newer operating systems that were based on Unix got tied with C and its crucial presence in the system.

As you can see, C was not born as an ordinary programming language, but instead, it was designed by having a complete set of requirements in mind and, nowadays, it has no competitor. You may consider languages such as Java, Python, and Ruby to be higher-level languages, but they cannot be considered as direct competitors as they are different and serve different purposes. For instance, you cannot write a device driver or a kernel module with Java or Python, and they themselves have been built on top of a layer written in C.

Unlike many programming languages, C is standardized by ISO, and if it is required to have a certain feature in the future, then the standard can be modified to support the new feature.

In the next section, we'll discuss Unix architecture. This is a fundamental concept in understanding how a program evolves within the Unix environment.

Unix architecture

In this section, we are going to explore the philosophy that the Unix creators had in mind and what they were expecting it to be when they created the architecture.

As we've explained in the previous section, the people involved in Unix from Bell Labs were working for the Multics project. Multics was a big project, the proposed architecture was complex, and it was tuned to be used on expensive hardware. But we should remember that despite all the difficulties, Multics had big goals. The ideas behind the Multics project revolutionized the way we were thinking about the operating systems.

Despite the challenges and difficulties discussed previously the ideas presented in the project were successful because Multics managed to live for around 40 years, until the year 2000. Not only that, but the project created a huge revenue stream for its owner company.

People such as Ken Thompson and his colleagues brought ideas into Unix even though Unix was, initially, supposed to be simple. Both Multics and Unix tried to bring in similar architecture, but they had two vastly different fates. Multics, since the turn of the century, has started to be forgotten, while Unix, and the operating system families based on it such as BSD, have been growing since then.

We're going to move on to talk about the Unix philosophy. It is simply a set of high-level requirements that the design of Unix is based on. After that, we're going to talk about the Unix multi-ring, onion-like architecture and the role of each ring in the overall behavior of the system.

Philosophy

The philosophy of Unix has been explained several times by its founders. As such, a thorough breakdown of the entire topic is beyond the scope of this book. What we will do is summarize all of the main viewpoints.

Before we do that, I've listed below some great external literature that could help you on the subject of Unix philosophy:

- Wikipedia, *Unix philosophy*: `https://en.wikipedia.org/wiki/Unix_philosophy`

- *The Unix Philosophy: A Brief Introduction*: `http://www.linfo.org/unix_philosophy.html`

- Eric Steven Raymond, *The Art of Unix Programming*: `https://homepage.cs.uri.edu/~thenry/resources/unix_art/ch01s06.html`

Equally, in the following link, you'll see a quite angry opposite view to the Unix philosophy. I've included this because it's always great to know both sides since, intrinsically, nothing is perfect:

- *The Collapse of UNIX Philosophy*: `https://kukuruku.co/post/the-collapse-of-the-unix-philosophy/`

To summarize these viewpoints, I've grouped the key Unix philosophies as follows:

- **Unix is mainly designed and developed to be used by programmers and not ordinary end users**: Therefore, many considerations addressing user interface and user experience requirements are not part of the Unix architecture.

- **A Unix system is made up of many small and simple programs**: Each of them is designed to perform a small and simple task. There are lots of examples of these small and simple programs, such as `ls`, `mkdir`, `ifconfig`, `grep`, and `sed`.

- **A complex task can be performed by executing a sequence of these small and simple programs in a chain**: It means that essentially more than one program is involved in a big and complex task and that, together, each of the programs could be executed multiple times in order to accomplish the task. A good example of this is to use shell scripts instead of writing a program from scratch. Note that shell scripts are often portable between Unix systems, and Unix encourages programmers to break down their big and complex programs into small and simple programs.

- **Each small and simple program should be able to pass its output as the input of another program, and this chain should continue**: This way, we can use small programs in a chain that has the potential to perform complex tasks. In this chain, each program can be considered as a transformer that receives the output of the previous program, transforms it based on its logic, and passes it to the next program in the chain. A particularly good example of this is *piping* between Unix commands, which is denoted by a vertical bar, such as `ls -l | grep a.out`.

- **Unix is very text-oriented**: All configurations are text files, and it has a textual command line. Shell scripts are also text files that use simple grammar to write an algorithm that executes other Unix shell programs.

- **Unix suggests choosing simplicity over perfection**: For example, if a simple solution is working in most cases, don't design a complicated solution that only works marginally better.

- **Programs written for a certain Unix-compliant operating system should be easily usable in other Unix systems**: This is mainly satisfied by having a single code base that can be built and executed on various Unix-compliant systems.

The points we've just listed have been extracted and interpreted by different people, but in general, they've been agreed upon as the main principles driving Unix philosophy and, as a result, have shaped the design of Unix.

If you have had experience with a Unix-like operating system, for example, Linux, then you'll be able to align your experience with the preceding statements. As we explained in the previous section regarding the history of Unix, it was supposed to be a simpler version of Multics, with the experiences the Unix founders had with Multics leading them to the preceding philosophies.

But back to the topic of C. You may be asking how C has been contributing to the preceding philosophy? Well, almost all of the essential things reflected in the preceding statements are written in C. In other words, the abovementioned small and simple programs that propel much of Unix are all written in C.

It's often better to show rather than simply tell. So, let's look at an example. The C source code for the ls program in NetBSD can be found here: `http://cvsweb.netbsd.org/bsdweb.cgi/~checkout~/src/bin/ls/ls.c?rev=1.67`. As you should know, the ls program lists the contents of a directory and does nothing more than that, and this simple logic has been written in C as you can see in the link. But this is not the only contribution of C in Unix. We will explain more about this in future sections while talking about the C Standard Library.

Unix onion

Now, it is time to explore the Unix architecture. An *onion model*, as we briefly mentioned before, can describe the Unix overall architecture. It is onion-like because it consists of a few *rings*, each of which acts as a wrapper for internal rings.

Figure 10-2 demonstrates the proposed famous onion model for the Unix architecture:

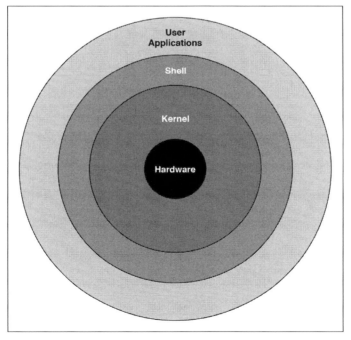

Figure 10-2: The onion model of Unix architecture

The model looks quite simple at first glance. However, to understand it fully requires you to write a few programs in Unix. Only after that can you understand what each ring is really doing. We're going to try and explain the model as simply as possible in order to develop an initial foundation before moving forward with writing real examples.

Let's explain the onion model from the innermost ring.

At the core of the preceding model is **Hardware**. As we know, the main task of an operating system is to allow the user to interact with and use the hardware. That's why hardware is at the core of the model in *Figure 10-2*. This simply shows us that one of the main goals of Unix is to make hardware available to the programs willing to have access to it. Everything that we've read about the Unix philosophy in the previous section focuses upon delivering these services in the best possible manner.

The ring around the hardware is the **Kernel**. The kernel is the most important part of an operating system. This is because it is the closest layer to the hardware, and it acts as a wrapper to expose the functionalities of the attached hardware directly. Because of this direct access, the kernel has the highest privilege to use the whole available resources in a system. This unlimited access to everything is the best justification for having other rings in the architecture that don't have that unlimited access. In fact, this was behind the separation between the *kernel space* and the *user space*. We discuss this in further detail in this chapter and the following one.

Note that writing the kernel takes most of the effort needed when writing a new Unix-like operating system, and, as you can see, its ring is drawn thicker than the other rings. There are many different units inside a Unix kernel, and each of them are playing a vital role in the Unix ecosystem. Later on in this chapter, we will explain more about the internal structure of a Unix kernel.

The next ring is called **Shell**. It is simply a shell around the kernel that allows user applications to interact with the kernel and use its many services. Take note that the shell ring alone brings mainly most of the requirements addressed by the Unix philosophy that we explained in the previous section. We will elaborate more on this in the upcoming paragraphs.

The shell ring consists of many small programs, which, together, form a set of tools that allows a user or an application to use the kernel services. It also contains a set of libraries, all written in C, which will allow a programmer to write a new application for Unix.

Based on the libraries found in **Simple Unix Specification (SUS)**, the shell ring must expose a standard and a precisely defined interface for programmers. Such standardizations will make Unix programs portable, or at least compilable, on various Unix implementations. We will reveal some shocking secrets about this ring in the following sections!

Finally, the outermost ring, **User Applications**, consists of all of the actual applications written to be used on Unix systems, such as database services, web services, mail services, web browsers, worksheet programs, and word editor programs.

These applications should use the APIs and tools provided by the shell ring instead of accessing the kernel directly (via *system calls*, which we will discuss shortly) to accomplish their tasks. This is done because of the portability principle in the Unix philosophy. Note that in our current context, by the term *user*, we usually mean the user applications, and not necessarily the people working with these applications.

Being restricted to use just the shell ring also helps these applications to be compliable on various Unix-like operating systems that are not true Unix-compliant operating systems. The best example is the various Linux distributions, which are just Unix-like. We like to have big pieces of software available on both Unix-compliant and Unix-like operating systems with a single code base. As we progress, you find out more about the differences between Unix-like and Unix-compliant systems.

One general theme in the Unix onion is the fact that the inner rings should provide some interface for the outer rings in order to let them use their services. In fact, these interfaces between the rings are more important than the rings themselves. For example, we are more interested in knowing how to use the existing kernel services rather than just digging down the kernel, which is different from one Unix implementation to another.

The same could be said of the shell ring and the interface it exposes to the user applications. In fact, these interfaces are our main subject focus across these two chapters while looking at Unix. In the following sections, we're going to talk about each ring individually and discuss its exposed interface in some detail.

Shell interface to user applications

A *human user* either uses a Terminal or a specific GUI program such as a web browser to use the functionalities available on a Unix system. Both are referred to as user applications, or just simply applications or programs, that allow the hardware to be used through the shell ring. Memory, CPU, network adapter, and hard drives are typical examples of hardware that are usually used by most Unix programs through the API provided by the shell ring. The API provided is one of the topics that we are going to talk about.

From a developer's perspective, there is not much difference between an application and a program. But from a human user's perspective, an application is a program that has a means such as a **Graphical User interface (GUI)** or **Command-Line Interface (CLI)** to interact with the user, but a program is a piece of software running on a machine that has no UI, such as a running service. This book does not distinguish between programs and applications, and we use the terms interchangeably.

There is a wide range of programs that have been developed for Unix in C. Database services, web servers, mail servers, games, office applications, and many others are among various types of programs that exist in a Unix environment. There is one common feature among these applications, and that is that their code is portable on most Unix and Unix-like operating systems with some slight changes. But how is that possible? How can you write a program in C that can be built on various versions of Unix and through various types of hardware?

The answer is simple: all Unix systems expose the same **Application Programming Interface (API)** from their shell ring. A piece of C source code that is only using the exposed standard interface can be built and run across all Unix systems.

But what exactly do we mean by exposing an API? An API, as we have explained before, is a bunch of header files that contain a set of declarations. In Unix, these headers, and the declared functions in them, are the same throughout all Unix systems, but the implementation of those functions, in other words the static and dynamic libraries written for each UNIX-compliant system, can be unique and different from others.

Note that we are looking at Unix as a standard and not an operating system. There are systems that are built fully compatible with the Unix standard, and we call them *Unix-compliant systems*, such as BSD Unix, while there are systems that partly comply with the Unix standard, and which are called *Unix-like systems*, such as Linux.

The same API is being exposed from the shell ring in more or less all Unix systems. As an example, the `printf` function must always be declared in the `stdio.h` header file, as specified by the Unix standard. Whenever you want to print something to the standard output in a Unix-compliant system, you should use `printf` or `fprintf` from the `stdio.h` header file.

In fact, `stdio.h` is not part of C even though all C books explain this header and the declared functions in it. It's part of the C standard library specified in the SUS standard. A C program written for Unix is not aware of the actual implementation of a specific function, such as `printf` or `fopen`. In other words, the shell ring is seen as a black box by the programs in the outer ring.

The various APIs exposed by the shell ring are collected under the SUS standard. This standard is maintained by **The Open Group** consortium and has had multiple iterations since the creation of Unix. The most recent version is SUS version 4, which goes back to 2008. However, the most recent version has itself some revisions in 2013, 2016, and finally in 2018.

The following link will take you to the document explaining the exposed interfaces in SUS version 4: `http://www.unix.org/version4/GS5_APIs.pdf`. As you can see in the link, there are different kinds of APIs that are exposed by the shell ring. Some of these are mandatory, and some others are optional. The following is the list of APIs found in SUS v4:

- **System interfaces**: This is a list of all functions that should be usable by any C program. SUS v4 has 1,191 functions that need to be implemented by a Unix system. The table also describes the fact that a specific function either is mandatory or optional for a specific version of C. Take note that the version we are interested in is C99.

- **Header interfaces**: This is a list of header files that can be available in an SUS v4-compatible Unix system. In this version of SUS, there are 82 header files that can be accessible to all C programs. If you go through the list, you will find many famous header files, such as `stdio.h`, `stdlib.h`, `math.h`, and `string.h`. Based on the Unix version and the C version used, some of them are mandatory, while others are optional. The optional headers could be missing in a Unix system, but mandatory header files certainly exist somewhere in the filesystem.

- **Utility interfaces**: This is a list of utility programs, or command-line programs, that should be available in a SUS v4-compatible Unix system. If you go through the tables, you will see lots of commands that are familiar to you, for example, `mkdir`, `ls`, `cp`, `df`, `bc`, and many more, which make up to 160 utility programs. Note that these are usually programs that must have already been written by a specific Unix vendor before shipping as part of its installation bundle.

  These utility programs are mostly used in Terminals or in shell scripts and are not often called by another C program. These utility programs usually use the same system interfaces that are exposed to an ordinary C program written in the user application ring.

  As an example, the following is a link to the `mkdir` utility program's source code written for macOS High Sierra 10.13.6, which is a Berkeley Software Distribution (BSD) - based Unix system. The source code is published on the Apple Open Source website, macOS High Sierra (10.13.6), and is available at `https://opensource.apple.com/source/file_cmds/file_cmds-272/mkdir/mkdir.c`.

If you open the link and go through the source, you see that it is using `mkdir` and `umask` functions declared as part of the system interfaces.

- **Scripting interface**: This interface is a language that is used to write *shell scripts*. It is mainly used for writing automated tasks that are using utility programs. This interface is usually denoted as a *shell scripting language* or a *shell command language*.

- **XCURSES interfaces**: XCURSES is a set of interfaces that allow a C program to interact with the user in a minimalistic text-based GUI.

  In the following screenshot, you can see an example of the GUI that has been written using `ncurses` that is an implementation for XCURSES.

  In SUS v4, there are 379 functions located in 3 headers, together with 4 utility programs, which make up the XCURSES interface.

  Many programs today are still using XCURSES to interact with the user through a better interface. It's worth noting that, by using XCURSES-based interfaces, you don't need to have a graphics engine. Likewise, it is usable over remote connections such as **Secure Shell** (**SSH**) as well.

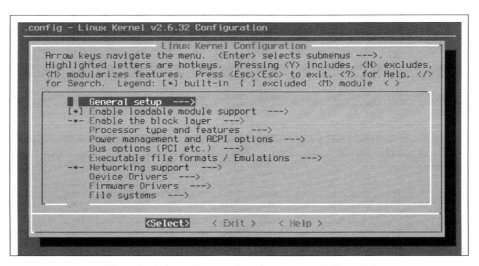

Figure 10-3: A config menu based on ncurses (Wikipedia)

As you can see, SUS doesn't talk about the filesystem hierarchy and the place where header files should be found. It only states which headers should be available and present in the system. A widely used convention for the path of standard header files says that these headers should be found in either `/usr/include` or `/usr/local/include`, but it is still up to the operating system and the user to make the final decision. These are the default paths for the header files. However, systems can be configured to use other paths instead of default ones.

If we put system interfaces and header interfaces together with the implementation of the exposed functions, which are different in each Unix flavor (or implementation), then we get the **C Standard Library** or **libc**. In other words, libc is a set of functions placed in specific header files, all according to SUS, together with the static and shared libraries containing the implementation of the exposed functions.

The definition of libc is entangled tightly with standardizations of Unix systems. Every C program being developed in a Unix system uses libc for communicating further down to the kernel and the hardware levels.

It's important to remember that not all operating systems are Unix fully compatible systems. Microsoft Windows and operating systems using the Linux kernel, for example, Android, are examples of that. These operating systems are not Unix-compliant systems, but they can be Unix-like systems. We have used the terms Unix-compliant and Unix-like across earlier chapters without explaining their true meanings, but now we are going to define them carefully.

A Unix-compliant system is fully compliant to SUS standards, but this isn't true of a Unix-like system that is only partially compliant with the standard. What this means is that the Unix-like systems are only conforming to a specific subset of SUS standards and not all of them. This means, theoretically, that the programs developed for a Unix-compliant system are supposed to be portable to other Unix-compatible systems, but may not be ported to a Unix-like operating system. This is especially the case regarding the programs being ported from Linux to, or to Linux from, other Unix-compliant systems.

Having lots of Unix-like operating systems developed, especially after the birth of Linux, became the basis for giving this subset of SUS standards a specific name. They called it the **Portable Operating System Interface (POSIX)**. We can say that POSIX is a subset of SUS standards that Unix-like systems chose to comply with.

In the following link, you can find all of the different interfaces that should be exposed in a POSIX system: `http://pubs.opengroup.org/onlinepubs/9699919799/`.

As you can see in the link, there are similar interfaces in POSIX, just like there are in SUS. The standards are remarkably similar, but POSIX has enabled Unix standards to be applicable to a broader range of operating systems.

Unix-like operating systems, such as most Linux distributions, are POSIX-compliant from the beginning. That's why if you've worked with Ubuntu, you can work with FreeBSD Unix in the same manner.

However, that's not true for some operating systems such as Microsoft Windows. Microsoft Windows cannot be considered as POSIX-compliant, but further tools can be installed to make it a POSIX operating system, for example, *Cygwin*, a POSIX-compatible environment that runs natively on the Windows operating system.

This again shows that POSIX compatibility is about having a standard shell ring and not the kernel.

On a slight tangent, it was quite the story when Microsoft Windows became POSIX-compliant in the 1990s. However, over time, that support became deprecated.

Both SUS and POSIX standards dictate the interfaces. They both state what should be available, but they don't talk about how it should become available. Each Unix system has its own implementation of POSIX or SUS implementation. These implementations are then put in libc libraries that are part of the shell ring. In other words, in a Unix system, the shell ring contains a libc implementation that is exposed in a standard way. Subsequently, the shell ring will pass the request further down to the kernel ring to be processed.

Kernel interface to shell ring

In the previous section, we explained that the shell ring in a Unix system exposes the interfaces defined in the SUS or POSIX standard. There are mainly two ways to invoke a certain logic in the shell ring, either through the libc or using shell utility programs. A user application should either get linked with libc libraries to execute shell routines, or it should execute an existing utility program that's available in the system.

Note that the existing utility programs are themselves using the libc libraries. Therefore, we can generalize and state that all shell routines can be found in libc libraries. This gives even more importance to standard C libraries. If you want to create a new Unix system from scratch, you must write your own libc after having the kernel up and ready.

If you have followed the flow of this book and have read the previous chapters, you'll see that pieces of the puzzle are coming together. We needed to have a compilation pipeline and a linking mechanism to be able to design an operating system that exposes an interface and has been implemented using a set of library files. At this point, you are able to see that every feature of C is acting in favor of having Unix. The more you understand about the relationship between C and Unix, the more you find them tied together.

Now that the relationship between user applications and the shell ring is clear, we need to see how the shell ring (or libc) communicates with the kernel ring. Before we go any further, note that, in this section, we are not going to explain what a kernel is. Instead, we are going to look at it as a black box exposing certain functionalities.

The main mechanism that libc (or the functions in shell ring) uses to consume a kernel functionality is through using *system calls*. To explain this mechanism, we need to have an example to follow down the rings of the onion model in order to find the place where system calls are used to do certain things.

We also need to choose a real libc implementation, so we can track down the sources and find the system calls. We choose FreeBSD for further investigations. FreeBSD is a Unix-like operating system branched from the BSD Unix.

Note:
The Git repository of FreeBSD can be found here: `https://github.com/freebsd/freebsd`. This repository contains the sources for FreeBSD's kernel and shell rings. The sources for FreeBSD libc can be found in the `lib/libc` directory.

Let's start with the following example. *Example 10.1* is a simple program that just waits for one second. Likewise, the program is considered to be in the application ring, which means it is a user application, even though it is remarkably simple.

So, let's first look at the source code of *example 10.1*:

```
#include <unistd.h>

int main(int argc, char** argv) {
  sleep(1);
  return 0;
}
```

Code Box 10-1 [ExtremeC_examples_chapter10_1.c]: Example 10.1 calling the sleep function included from the shell ring

As you can see, the code includes the `unistd.h` header file and calls the `sleep` function, both of which are part of the SUS exposed interfaces. But then what happens next, especially in the `sleep` function? As a C programmer, you may have never asked yourself this question before, but knowing it can enhance your understanding of a Unix system.

We have always used functions such as `sleep`, `printf`, and `malloc`, without knowing how they work internally, but now we want to take a leap of faith and discover the mechanism that libc uses to communicate with the kernel.

We know that system calls, or *syscalls* for short, are being triggered by the codes written in a libc implementation. In fact, this is the way that kernel routines are triggered. In SUS, and subsequently in POSIX-compatible systems, there is a program that is used to trace system calls when a program is running.

We are almost certain that a program that doesn't call system calls literally cannot do anything. So, as a result, we know that every program that we write has to use system calls through calling the libc functions.

Let's compile the preceding example and find out the system calls that it triggers. We can start this process by running:

```
$ cc ExtremeC_examples_chapter10_1.c -lc -o ex10_1.out
$ truss ./ex10_1.out
...
$
```

Shell Box 10-1: Building and running example 10.1 using truss to trace the system calls that it invokes

As you can see in *Shell Box 10-1*, we have used a utility program called truss. The following text is an excerpt from the FreeBSD's manual page for truss:

> *"The truss utility traces the system calls called by the specified process or program. The output is to the specified output file or standard error by default. It does this by stopping and restarting the process being monitored via ptrace(2)."*

As the description implies, truss is a program for seeing all system calls that a program has invoked during the execution. Utilities similar to truss are available in most Unix-like systems. For instance, strace can be used in Linux systems.

The following shell box shows the output of truss being used to monitor the system calls invoked by the preceding example:

```
$ truss ./ex10_1.out
mmap(0x0,32768,PROT_READ|PROT_WRITE,MAP_PRIVATE|MAP_ANON,-1,0x0) =
34366160896 (0x800620000)
issetugid()                                            = 0 (0x0)
lstat("/etc",{ mode=drwxr-xr-x ,inode=3129984,size=2560,blksi
ze=32768 }) = 0 (0x0)
lstat("/etc/libmap.conf",{ mode=-rw-r--r-- ,in
ode=3129991,size=109,blksize=32768 }) = 0 (0x0)
openat(AT_FDCWD,"/etc/libmap.conf",O_RDONLY|O_CLOEXEC,00) = 3
(0x3)
fstat(3,{ mode=-rw-r--r-- ,inode=3129991,size=109,blksize=32768 })
= 0 (0x0)
...
```

```
openat(AT_FDCWD,"/var/run/ld-elf.
so.hints",O_RDONLY|O_CLOEXEC,00) = 3 (0x3)
read(3,"Ehnt\^A\0\0\0\M^@\0\0\0Q\0\0\0\0"...,128) = 128 (0x80)
fstat(3,{ mode=-r--r--r-- ,inode=7705382,size=209,blksize=32768 })
= 0 (0x0)
lseek(3,0x80,SEEK_SET)                          = 128 (0x80)
read(3,"/lib:/usr/lib:/usr/lib/compat:/u"...,81) = 81 (0x51)
close(3)                                        = 0 (0x0)
access("/lib/libc.so.7",F_OK)                   = 0 (0x0)
```

openat(AT_FDCWD,"/lib/libc.so.7",O_RDONLY|O_CLOEXEC|O_VERIFY,00) = 3 (0x3)

```
...
sigprocmask(SIG_BLOCK,{ SIGHUP|SIGINT|SIGQUIT|SIGKILL|SIGPIPE|SIGA
LRM|SIGTERM|SIGURG|SIGSTOP|SIGTSTP|SIGCONT|SIGCHLD|SIGTTIN|SIGTTOU
|SIGIO|SIGXCPU|SIGXFSZ|SIGVTALRM|SIGPROF|SIGWINCH|SIGINFO|SIGUSR1|
SIGUSR2 },{ }) = 0 (0x0)
sigprocmask(SIG_SETMASK,{ },0x0)                = 0 (0x0)
sigprocmask(SIG_BLOCK,{ SIGHUP|SIGINT|SIGQUIT|SIGKILL|SIGPIPE|SIGA
LRM|SIGTERM|SIGURG|SIGSTOP|SIGTSTP|SIGCONT|SIGCHLD|SIGTTIN|SIGTTOU
|SIGIO|SIGXCPU|SIGXFSZ|SIGVTALRM|SIGPROF|SIGWINCH|SIGINFO|SIGUSR1|
SIGUSR2 },{ }) = 0 (0x0)
sigprocmask(SIG_SETMASK,{ },0x0)                = 0 (0x0)
```

nanosleep({ 1.000000000 })   = 0 (0x0)

```
sigprocmask(SIG_BLOCK,{ SIGHUP|SIGINT|SIGQUIT|SIGKILL|SIGPIPE|SIGA
LRM|SIGTERM|SIGURG|SIGSTOP|SIGTSTP|SIGCONT|SIGCHLD|SIGTTIN|SIGTTOU
|SIGIO|SIGXCPU|SIGXFSZ|SIGVTALRM|SIGPROF|SIGWINCH|SIGINFO|SIGUSR1|
SIGUSR2 },{ }) = 0 (0x0)
...
sigprocmask(SIG_SETMASK,{ },0x0)                = 0 (0x0)
exit(0x0)
process exit, rval = 0
$
```

Shell Box 10-2: Output of truss showing the system calls invoked by example 10.1

As you can see in the preceding output, there are many system calls initiated by our simple example, with some of them being about loading shared object libraries, especially when initializing the process. The first system call shown in bold opens the libc.so.7 shared object library file. This shared object library contains the actual implementation of FreeBSD's libc.

In the same shell box, you can see that the program is calling the nanosleep system call. The value passed to this system call is **1000000000** nanoseconds, which is equivalent to 1 second.

System calls are like function calls. Note that each system call has a dedicated and predetermined constant number, and subsequently, together with that, it has a specific name, and a list of arguments. Each system call also performs a specific task. In this case, nanosleep makes the calling thread sleep for the specified number of nanoseconds.

More information regarding the system calls can be found in the FreeBSD *system calls manual*. The following shell box shows the page dedicated to the nanosleep system call in the manual:

```
$ man nanosleep
NANOSLEEP(2)                    FreeBSD System Calls Manual
NANOSLEEP(2)


NAME
     nanosleep - high resolution sleep

LIBRARY
     Standard C Library (libc, -lc)

SYNOPSIS
     #include <time.h>

     Int
     clock_nanosleep(clockid_t clock_id, int flags,
         const struct timespec *rqtp, struct timespec *rmtp);

     int
     nanosleep(const struct timespec *rqtp, struct timespec
*rmtp);

DESCRIPTION
     If the TIMER_ABSTIME flag is not set in the flags argument,
then
     clock_nanosleep() suspends execution of the calling thread
until either
     the time interval specified by the rqtp argument has elapsed,
or a signal
     is delivered to the calling process and its action is to
invoke a signal-
     catching function or to terminate the process.  The clock
```

```
used to measure
     the time is specified by the clock_id argument
...
...
$
```

Shell Box 10-3: The manual page dedicated to the nanosleep system call

The preceding manual page describes the following:

- `nanosleep` is a system call.

- The system call is accessible through calling the `nanosleep` and `clock_nanosleep` functions from the shell ring defined in `time.h`. Note that we used the `sleep` function from `unitsd.h`. We could also use the preceding two functions from `time.h`. It's also worth noting that both header files and all of the preceding functions, together with the functions actually used, are part of SUS and POSIX.

- If you want to be able to call these functions, you need to link your executable against libc by passing the `-lc` option to your linker. This might be specific to FreeBSD only.

- This manual page doesn't talk about the system call itself, but it talks about the standard C API, which is exposed from the shell ring. These manuals are written for application developers and, as such, they won't discuss the systems calls and kernel internals often. Instead, they focus on the APIs exposed from the shell ring.

Now, let's find the place in libc where the system call is actually invoked. We will be using FreeBSD sources on GitHub. The commit hash we are using is `bf78455d496` from the **master** branch. In order to clone and use the proper commit from the repository, run the following commands:

```
$ git clone https://github.com/freebsd/freebsd
...
$ cd freebsd
$ git reset --hard bf78455d496
...
$
```

Shell Box 10-4: Cloning the FreeBSD project and going to a specific commit

It is also possible to navigate the FreeBSD project on the GitHub website itself using the following link: `https://github.com/freebsd/freebsd/tree/bf78455d496`. No matter what method you use to navigate the project, you should be able to find the following line of codes.

If you go into the `lib/libc` directory and do a `grep` for `sys_nanosleep`, you will find the following file entries:

```
$ cd lib/libc
$ grep sys_nanosleep . -R
./include/libc_private.h:int          __sys_nanosleep(const struct
timespec *, struct timespec *);
./sys/Symbol.map:          __sys_nanosleep;
./sys/nanosleep.c:__weak_reference(__sys_nanosleep, __nanosleep);
./sys/interposing_table.c:     SLOT(nanosleep, __sys_nanosleep),
$
```

Shell Box 10-5: Finding the entries related to the nanosleep system call in FreeBSD libc files

As you can see in the `lib/libc/sys/interposing_table.c` file, the `nanosleep` function is mapped to the `__sys_nanosleep` function. Therefore, any function call targeted at `nanosleep` will cause `__sys_nanosleep` to be invoked.

The functions starting with `__sys` are actual system call functions in FreeBSD convention. Note that this is part of the libc implementation, and the used naming convention and other implementation-related configurations are highly specific to FreeBSD.

Having said all of that there's also another interesting point in the preceding shell box. The `lib/libc/include/libc_private.h` file contains the private and internal function declarations required for the wrapper functions around the system calls.

So far, we have seen how shell rings route the function calls made to libc to the inner rings by using system calls. But why do we need system calls in the first place? Why is it called a system call and not a function call? When looking at an ordinary function in a user application or libc, how is it different from a system call in the kernel ring? In *Chapter 11*, *System Calls and Kernels*, we will discuss this further by giving a more concrete definition of a system call.

The next section is about the kernel ring and its internal units, which are common in kernels used by most Unix-compliant and Unix-like systems.

Kernel

The main purpose of the kernel ring is to manage the hardware attached to a system and expose its functionalities as system calls. The following diagram shows how a specific hardware functionality is exposed through different rings before a user application can finally use it:

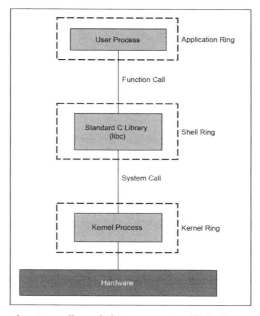

Figure 10-4: Function calls and system calls made between various Unix rings in order to expose a hardware functionality

The preceding diagram shows a summary of what we have explained so far. In this section, we are going to focus on the kernel itself and see what the kernel is. A kernel is a process that, like any other processes that we know, executes a sequence of instructions. But a **kernel process** is fundamentally different from an ordinary process, which we know as a **user process**.

The following list compares a kernel process and a user process. Note that our comparison is biased to a monolithic kernel such as Linux. We will explain the different types of kernels in the next chapter.

- A kernel process is the first thing that is loaded and executed, but user processes need to have the kernel process loaded and running before being spawned.

- We only have one kernel process, but we can have many user processes working at the same time.

- The kernel process is created by copying a kernel image into the main memory by the boot loader, but a user process is created using the `exec` or `fork` system calls. These system calls exist in most Unix systems.

- The kernel process handles and executes system calls, but a user process invokes the system call and waits for its execution handled by the kernel process. This means that, when a user process demands the execution of a system call, the flow of execution is transferred to the kernel process and it is the kernel itself that executes the system call's logic on behalf of the user process. We will clarify this in the second part of our look into Unix, *Chapter 11, System Calls and Kernel.*

- The kernel process sees the physical memory and all of the attached hardware in a *privileged* mode, but a user process sees the virtual memory, which is mapped to a portion of physical memory, where the user process doesn't know anything about the physical memory layout. Likewise, the user process has controlled and supervised access to resources and hardware. We can say that the user process is being executed in a sandbox simulated by the operating system. This also implies that a user process cannot see the memory of another user process.

As it is understood from the preceding comparison, we have two different execution modes in an operating system's runtime. One of them is dedicated to the kernel process, and the other is dedicated to the user processes.

The former execution mode is called *kernel land* or *kernel space*, and the latter is called *user land* or *user space*. Calling system calls by user processes is a way to bring these two lands together. Basically, we invented the system calls because we needed to isolate the kernel space and the user space from each other. Kernel space has the most privileged access to the system resources, and the user space has the least privileged and supervised access.

The internal structure of a typical Unix kernel can be discerned by the tasks a kernel performs. In fact, managing the hardware is not the only task that a kernel performs. The following is the list of a Unix kernel's responsibilities. Note that we have included the hardware management tasks as well in the following list:

- **Process management**: User processes are created by the kernel via a system call. Allocating memory for a new process and loading its instructions are some of the operations, among all of the operations, that should be performed before running a process.

- **Inter-Process Communication (IPC)**: User processes on the same machine can use different methods for exchanging data among them. Some of these methods are shared memories, pipes, and Unix domain sockets. These methods should be facilitated by the kernel, and some of them need the kernel to control the exchange of data. We will explain these methods in *Chapter 19, Single Host IPC and Sockets*, while talking about IPC techniques.

- **Scheduling**: Unix has always been known as a multi-tasking operating system. The kernel manages access to CPU cores and tries to balance access to them. Scheduling is a name given to the task that shares the CPU time among many processes based on their priority and importance. We will explain more about multi-tasking, multithreading, and multi-processing in the following chapters.

- **Memory management**: Without doubt, this is one of the key tasks of a kernel. The kernel is the only process that sees the whole physical memory and has superuser access to it. So, the task of breaking it into allocatable pages, assigning new pages to the processes in case of Heap allocation, freeing the memory, and many more memory-related tasks besides, should be performed and managed by the kernel.

- **System startup**: Once the kernel image is loaded into the main memory and the kernel process is started, it should initialize the user space. This is usually done by creating the first user process with the **Process Identifier (PID)** 1. In some Unix systems such as Linux, this process is called *init*. After having this process started, further services and daemons will be started by it.

- **Device management**: Apart from the CPU and memory, the kernel should be able to manage hardware through an abstraction made over all of them. A *device* is a real or virtual hardware attached to a Unix system. A typical Unix system uses the /dev path to store mapped device files. All attached hard drives, network adapters, USB devices, etc. are mapped to files found in the /dev path. These device files can be used by user processes to communicate with these devices.

The following diagram shows the most common internal structure of a Unix kernel based on the preceding list:

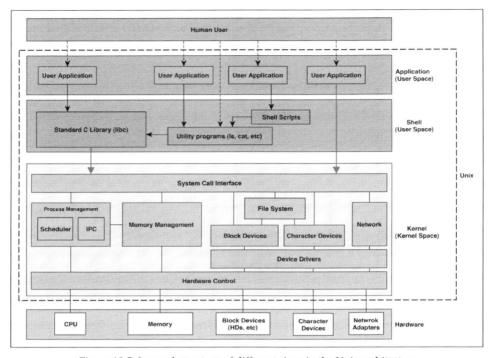

Figure 10-5: Internal structure of different rings in the Unix architecture

The preceding figure is a detailed illustration of Unix rings. It clearly shows that, in the shell ring, we have three parts that are exposed to the user applications. It also shows a detailed inner structure of the kernel ring.

At the top in the kernel ring, we have the system call interface. As is clear in the figure, all of the preceding units that are in the user space must communicate with the bottom units only through the system call interface. This interface is like a gate or a barrier between user and kernel spaces.

There are various units in the kernel such as the **Memory Management unit** (**MMU**) that manages the available physical memory. The **Process Management unit** creates processes in the user space and allocates resources for them. It also makes IPC available to processes. The diagram also shows the **Character** and **Block devices** that are mediated by the **Device Drivers** to expose the various I/O functionalities. We explain character and block devices in the following section. The **File System** unit is an essential part of the kernel, which is an abstraction over the block and character devices and lets the processes and the kernel itself use the same shared file hierarchy.

In the next section, we are going to talk about hardware.

Hardware

The final purpose of every operating system is to allow the user and the applications to be able to use and interact with hardware. Unix also aims to provide access to the attached hardware in an abstract and transparent way, using the same set of utility programs and commands in all existing and future platforms.

By having this transparency and abstraction, Unix abstracts all of the different hardware to be a number of devices attached to a system. So, the term *device* is centric in Unix, and every connected piece of hardware is considered to be a device connected to the Unix system.

The hardware attached to a computer can be categorized into two different categories: *mandatory* and *peripheral*. The CPU and main memory are mandatory devices attached to a Unix system. All other hardware such as the hard drive, network adapter, mouse, monitor, graphics card, and Wi-Fi adapter, are peripheral devices.

A Unix machine cannot work without mandatory hardware, but you can have a Unix machine that doesn't have a hard drive or a network adapter. Note that having a filesystem, which is essential for a Unix kernel to operate, doesn't necessarily require a hard disk!

A Unix kernel completely hides the CPU and physical memory. They are managed directly by the kernel, and no access is allowed to be made from the user space. The **Memory Management** and **Scheduler** units in a Unix kernel are responsible for managing the physical memory and the CPU, respectively.

This is not the case with other peripheral devices connected to a Unix system. They are exposed through a mechanism called *device files*. You can see these files in a Unix system as part of the /dev path.

The following is the list of files that can be found on an ordinary Linux machine:

```
$ ls -l /dev
total 0
crw-r--r--  1 root    root     10, 235 Oct 14 16:55 autofs
drwxr-xr-x  2 root    root         280 Oct 14 16:55 block
drwxr-xr-x  2 root    root          80 Oct 14 16:55 bsg
crw-rw----  1 root    disk     10, 234 Oct 14 16:55 btrfs-control
drwxr-xr-x  3 root    root          60 Oct 14 17:02 bus
```

```
lrwxrwxrwx 1 root    root           3 Oct 14 16:55 cdrom -> sr0
drwxr-xr-x 2 root    root        3500 Oct 14 16:55 char
crw------- 1 root    root      5,   1 Oct 14 16:55 console
lrwxrwxrwx 1 root    root          11 Oct 14 16:55 core -> /proc/
kcore
crw------- 1 root    root     10,  59 Oct 14 16:55 cpu_dma_latency
crw------- 1 root    root     10, 203 Oct 14 16:55 cuse
drwxr-xr-x 6 root    root         120 Oct 14 16:55 disk
drwxr-xr-x 3 root    root          80 Oct 14 16:55 dri
lrwxrwxrwx 1 root    root           3 Oct 14 16:55 dvd -> sr0
crw------- 1 root    root     10,  61 Oct 14 16:55 ecryptfs
crw-rw---- 1 root    video    29,   0 Oct 14 16:55 fb0
lrwxrwxrwx 1 root    root          13 Oct 14 16:55 fd -> /proc/
self/fd
crw-rw-rw- 1 root    root      1,   7 Oct 14 16:55 full
crw-rw-rw- 1 root    root     10, 229 Oct 14 16:55 fuse
crw------- 1 root    root    245,   0 Oct 14 16:55 hidraw0
crw------- 1 root    root     10, 228 Oct 14 16:55 hpet
drwxr-xr-x 2 root    root           0 Oct 14 16:55 hugepages
crw------- 1 root    root     10, 183 Oct 14 16:55 hwrng
crw------- 1 root    root     89,   0 Oct 14 16:55 i2c-0
...
crw-rw-r-- 1 root    root     10,  62 Oct 14 16:55 rfkill
lrwxrwxrwx 1 root    root           4 Oct 14 16:55 rtc -> rtc0
crw------- 1 root    root    249,   0 Oct 14 16:55 rtc0
brw-rw---- 1 root    disk      8,   0 Oct 14 16:55 sda
brw-rw---- 1 root    disk      8,   1 Oct 14 16:55 sda1
brw-rw---- 1 root    disk      8,   2 Oct 14 16:55 sda2
crw-rw----+ 1 root   cdrom    21,   0 Oct 14 16:55 sg0
crw-rw---- 1 root    disk     21,   1 Oct 14 16:55 sg1
drwxrwxrwt 2 root    root          40 Oct 14 16:55 shm
crw------- 1 root    root     10, 231 Oct 14 16:55 snapshot
drwxr-xr-x 3 root    root         180 Oct 14 16:55 snd
brw-rw----+ 1 root   cdrom    11,   0 Oct 14 16:55 sr0
lrwxrwxrwx 1 root    root          15 Oct 14 16:55 stderr -> /
proc/self/fd/2
lrwxrwxrwx 1 root    root          15 Oct 14 16:55 stdin -> /proc/
self/fd/0
```

```
lrwxrwxrwx  1 root    root        15 Oct 14 16:55 stdout -> /
proc/self/fd/1
crw-rw-rw-  1 root    tty      5,  0 Oct 14 16:55 tty
crw--w----  1 root    tty      4,  0 Oct 14 16:55 tty0
...
$
```

Shell Box 10-6: Listing the content of /dev on a Linux machine

As you can see, it is quite a list of devices attached to the machine. But of course, not all of them are physical. The abstraction over the hardware devices in Unix has given it the ability to have *virtual devices*.

For example, you can have a virtual network adapter that has no physical counterpart, but is able to perform additional operations on the network data. This is one of the ways that VPNs are being used in Unix-based environments. The physical network adapter brings the real network functionality, and the virtual network adapter gives the ability to transmit the data through a secure tunnel.

As is clear from the preceding output, each device has its own file in the /dev directory. The lines starting with c and b are device files representing character devices and block devices, respectively. Character devices are supposed to deliver and consume data byte by byte. Examples of such devices are serial ports, and parallel ports. Block devices are supposed to deliver and consume chunks of data that have more than one byte. Hard disks, network adapters, cameras, and so on are examples of block devices. In the preceding shell box, the lines starting with '1' are symbolic links to other devices, and the lines starting with d represent directories that may contain other device files.

User processes use these device files in order to access the corresponding hardware. These files can be written or can be read in order to send or receive data to and from the device.

In this book, we won't go deeper than this, but if you are curious to know more about devices and device drivers, you should read more around this subject. In the next chapter, *Chapter 11, System Calls and Kernels*, we continue our talk about system calls in greater detail, and we will add a new system call to an existing Unix kernel.

Summary

In this chapter, we started to discuss Unix and how it is interrelated with C. Even in non-Unix operating systems, you see some traces of a similar design to Unix systems.

As part of this chapter, we went through the history of the early 1970s and explained how Unix appeared from Multics and how C was derived from the B programming language. After that, we talked about the Unix architecture, an onion-like architecture that consists of four layers: user applications, the shell, the kernel, and hardware.

We briefly went over the various layers in the Unix onion model and provided detailed explanations of the shell layer. We introduced the C standard library and how it is used through POSIX and SUS standards to give programmers the ability to write programs that can be built on various Unix systems.

In the second part of our look into Unix, *Chapter 11, System Calls and Kernels*, we will continue our discussion about Unix and its architecture, and we will provide explanations of the kernel and the system call interface surrounding it in greater depth.

Chapter 11

System Calls and Kernels

In the previous chapter, we discussed the history of Unix and its onion-like architecture. We also introduced and talked about the POSIX and SUS standards governing the shell ring in Unix, before explaining how the C standard library is there to provide common functionalities exposed by a Unix-compliant system.

In this chapter, we are going to continue our discussion of the *system call interface* and the Unix *kernel*. This will give us a complete insight into how a Unix system works.

After reading this chapter, you will be able to analyze the system calls a program invokes, you will be able to explain how the process lives and evolves inside the Unix environment, and you will also be able to use system calls directly or through libc. We'll also talk about Unix kernel development and show you how you can add a new system call to the Linux kernel and how it can be invoked from the shell ring.

In the last part of this chapter, we will talk about *monolithic* kernels and *microkernels* and how they differ. We will introduce the Linux kernel as a monolithic kernel, and we will write a *kernel module* for it that can be loaded and unloaded dynamically.

Let's start this chapter by talking about system calls.

System calls

In the previous chapter, we briefly explained what a system call is. In this section, we want to take a deeper look and explain the mechanism that is used behind system calls to transfer the execution from a user process to the kernel process.

However, before we do that, we need to explain a bit more about both the kernel space and the user space, because this will be beneficial in our understanding of how the system calls work behind the scenes. We will also write a simple system call to gain some ideas about kernel development.

What we're about to do is crucial if you want to be able to write a new system call when you're going to add a new functionality into the kernel that wasn't there before. It also gives you a better understanding of the kernel space and how it differs from the user space because, in reality, they are very different.

System calls under the microscope

As we discussed in the previous chapter, a separation happens when moving from the shell ring into the kernel ring. You find that whatever resides in the first two rings, the user application and the shell, belongs to the user space. Likewise, what ever appears in the kernel ring or the hardware ring belongs to the kernel space.

There is one rule about this separation, and that is nothing in the two most inner rings – kernel and hardware – can be accessed directly by the user space. In other words, no processes in the user space can access the hardware, internal kernel data structures, and algorithms directly. Instead, they should be accessed via system calls.

That said you may think that it seems a little contradictory to whatever you know and have experienced about Unix-like operating systems, such as Linux. If you don't see the issue, let me explain it to you. It seems to be a contradiction because, for instance, when a program reads some bytes from a network socket, it is not the program that actually reads those bytes from the network adapter. It is the kernel that reads the bytes and copies them to the user space, and then the program can pick them up and use them.

We can clarify this by going through all the steps taken from the user space to the kernel space and vice versa in an example. When you want to read a file from a hard disk drive, you write a program in the user application ring. Your program uses a libc I/O function called fread (or another similar function) and will eventually be running as a process in the user space. When the program makes a call to the fread function, the implementation behind libc gets triggered.

So far, everything is still in the user process. Then, the fread implementation eventually invokes a system call, while fread is receiving an already opened *file descriptor* as the first argument, the address of a buffer allocated in the process's memory, which is in the user space, as the second argument, and the length of the buffer as the third argument.

When the system call is triggered by the libc implementation, the kernel gets control of execution on behalf of the user process. It receives the arguments from the user space and keeps them in the kernel space. Then, it is the kernel that reads from the file by accessing the filesystem unit inside the kernel (as can be seen in *Figure 10-5* in the previous chapter).

When the `read` operation is complete in the kernel ring, the read data will be copied to the buffer in the user space, as specified by the second augment when calling the `fread` function, and the system call leaves and returns the control of execution to the user process. Meanwhile, the user process usually waits while the system call is busy with the operation. In this case, the system call is blocking.

There are some important things to note about this scenario:

- We only have one kernel that performs all the logic behind system calls.

- If the system call is *blocking*, when that system call is in progress, the caller user process has to wait while the system call is busy and has not finished. Conversely, if the system call is *non-blocking*, the system call returns very quickly, but the user process has to make extra system calls to check if the results are available.

- Arguments together with input and output data will be copied from/to user space. Since the actual values are copied, system calls are supposed to be designed in such a way that they accept tiny variables and pointers as input arguments.

- The kernel has full privileged access to all resources of a system. Therefore, there should be a mechanism to check if the user process is able to make such a system call. In this scenario, if the user is not the owner of the file, `fread` should fail with an error about the lack of required permissions.

- A similar separation exists between the memory dedicated to the user space and the kernel space. User processes can only access the user space memory. Multiple transfers might be required in order to fulfil a certain system call.

Before we move onto the next section, I want to ask you a question. How does a system call transfer the control of execution to the kernel? Take a minute to think about that, because in the next section we're going to work on the answer to it.

Bypassing standard C – calling a system call directly

Before answering the raised question, let's go through an example that bypasses the standard C library and calls a system call directly. In other words, the program calls a system call without going through the shell ring. As we have noted before, this is considered an anti-pattern, but when certain system calls are not exposed through libc, a user application can call the system calls directly.

In every Unix system, there is a specific method for invoking system calls directly. For example, in Linux, there is a function called syscall located in the <sys/syscall.h> header file that can be used for this purpose.

The following code box, *example 11.1*, is a different Hello World example that does not use libc to print to the standard output. In other words, the example does not use the printf function that can be found as part of shell ring and the POSIX standard. Instead, it invokes a specific system call directly, hence the code is only compilable on Linux machines, not other Unix systems. In other words, the code is not portable between various Unix flavors:

```c
// We need to have this to be able to use non-POSIX stuff
#define _GNU_SOURCE

#include <unistd.h>

// This is not part of POSIX!
#include <sys/syscall.h>

int main(int argc, char** argv) {
  char message[20] = "Hello World!\n";
  // Invokes the 'write' system call that writes
  // some bytes into the standard output.
  syscall(__NR_write, 1, message, 13);
  return 0;
}
```

Code Box 11-1 [ExtremeC_examples_chapter11_1.c]: A different Hello World example that invokes the write system call directly

As the first statement in the preceding code box, we have to define _GNU_SOURCE to indicate that we are going to use parts of the **GNU C Library** (**glibc**) that are not part of POSIX, or SUS standards. This breaks the portability of the program, and because of that, you may not be able to compile your code on another Unix machine. In the second include statement, we include one of the glibc-specific header files that doesn't exist in other POSIX systems using implementations other than glibc as their main libc backbone.

In the main function, we make a system call by calling the syscall function. First of all, we have to specify the system call by passing a number. This is an integer that refers to a specific system call. Every system call has its own unique specific *system call number* in Linux.

In the example code, the __R_write constant has been passed instead of the system call number, and we don't know its exact numerical value. After looking it up in the unistd.h header file, apparently 64 is the number of the write system call.

After passing the system call number, we should pass the arguments that are required for the system call.

Note that, despite the fact that the preceding code is very simple, and it just contains a simple function call, you should know that `syscall` is not an ordinary function. It is an assembly procedure that fills some proper CPU registers and actually transfers the control of execution from the user space to the kernel space. We will talk about this shortly.

For `write`, we need to pass three arguments: the file descriptor, which here is 1 to refer to the standard output; the second is the *pointer to a buffer* allocated in the user space; and finally, the *length of bytes* that should be copied from the buffer.

The following is the output of *example 11.1*, compiled and run in Ubuntu 18.04.1 using `gcc`:

```
$ gcc ExtremeC_examples_chapter11_1.c -o ex11_1.out
$ ./ex11_1.out
Hello World!
$
```

Shell Box 11-1: The output of example 11.1

Now it's time to use `strace`, introduced in the previous chapter, to see the actual system calls that *example 11.1* has invoked. The output of `strace`, shown as follows, demonstrates that the program has invoked the desired system call:

```
$ strace ./ex11_1.out
execve("./ex11_1.out", ["./ex11_1.out"], 0x7ffcb94306b0 /* 22 vars
*/) = 0
brk(NULL)                               = 0x55ebc30fb000
access("/etc/ld.so.nohwcap", F_OK)      = -1 ENOENT (No such file
or directory)
access("/etc/ld.so.preload", R_OK)      = -1 ENOENT (No such file
or directory)
openat(AT_FDCWD, "/etc/ld.so.cache", O_RDONLY|O_CLOEXEC) = 3
...

...
arch_prctl(ARCH_SET_FS, 0x7f24aa5624c0) = 0
mprotect(0x7f24aa339000, 16384, PROT_READ) = 0
mprotect(0x55ebc1e04000, 4096, PROT_READ) = 0
mprotect(0x7f24aa56a000, 4096, PROT_READ) = 0
```

```
munmap(0x7f24aa563000, 26144)            = 0
write(1, "Hello World!\n", 13Hello World!
)                = 13
exit_group(0)                            = ?
+++ exited with 0 +++
$
```

Shell Box 11-2: The output of strace while running example 11.1

As you can see as a bold in *Shell Box 11-2*, the system call has been recorded by `strace`. Look at the return value, which is 13. It means that the system call has successfully written 13 bytes into the given file, the standard output in this case.

Note:
A user application should never try to use system calls directly. There are usually steps that should be taken before and after calling the system call. Libc implementations do these steps. When you're not going to use libc, you have to do these steps yourself, and you must know that these steps vary from one Unix system to another.

Inside the syscall function

However, what happens inside the `syscall` function? Note that the current discussion is only applicable to glibc and not to the rest of the libc implementations. Firstly, we need to find `syscall` in glibc. Here is the link to the `syscall` definition: https://github.com/lattera/glibc/blob/master/sysdeps/unix/sysv/linux/x86_64/syscall.S.

If you open the preceding link in a browser, you will see that this function is written in assembly language.

Note:
Assembly language can be used together with C statements in a C source file. In fact, this is one of the great features of C that makes it suitable for writing an operating system. For the `syscall` function, we have a declaration written in C, but the definition is in assembly.

Here is the source code you find as part of `syscall.S`:

```
/* Copyright (C) 2001-2018 Free Software Foundation, Inc.
   This file is part of the GNU C Library.
...
   <http://www.gnu.org/licenses/>.  */

#include <sysdep.h>

/* Please consult the file sysdeps/unix/sysv/linux/x86-64/sysdep.h
for
   more information about the value -4095 used below.  */

/* Usage: long syscall (syscall_number, arg1, arg2, arg3, arg4,
arg5, arg6)
   We need to do some arg shifting, the syscall_number will be in
   rax.  */


   .text
ENTRY (syscall)
    movq %rdi, %rax              /* Syscall number -> rax.  */
    movq %rsi, %rdi             /* shift arg1 - arg5.  */
    movq %rdx, %rsi
    movq %rcx, %rdx
    movq %r8, %r10
    movq %r9, %r8
    movq 8(%rsp),%r9            /* arg6 is on the stack.  */
    syscall                     /* Do the system call.  */
    cmpq $-4095, %rax           /* Check %rax for error.  */
    jae SYSCALL_ERROR_LABEL     /* Jump to error handler if error.
*/
    ret                         /* Return to caller.  */

PSEUDO_END (syscall)
```

Code Box 11-2: The definition of the syscall function in glibc

These instructions are short and simple despite the fact that making a system call in this way seems to be more complex. The usage comment explains that a system call in glibc can be provided up to six arguments in each invocation.

What this means is that if the underlying kernel supports system calls with more than six arguments, glibc cannot provide certain kernel functionalities, and it should be changed to support them. Fortunately, six arguments have been fine in most cases, and for system calls that need more than six arguments, we can pass pointers to structure variables allocated in the user space memory.

In the preceding code box, after the `movq` instructions, the assembly code calls the `syscall` subroutine. It simply generates an *interrupt*, which allows a specific part of the kernel, which is waiting for such interrupts, to wake up and handle the interrupt.

As you can see on the first line of the `syscall` procedure, the system call number is moved to the `%rax` register. On the following lines, we are copying other arguments into the different registers. When the system call interrupt is fired, the kernel's interrupt handler unit picks up the call and gathers the system call number and the arguments. Then it searches its *system call table* to find the appropriate function that should be invoked on the kernel side.

An interesting point is that, by the time the interrupt handler is being executed in the CPU, the user code that has initiated the system call has left the CPU, and the kernel is doing the job. This is the main mechanism behind system calls. When you initiate a system call, the CPU changes its mode, and the kernel instructions are fetched into the CPU and the user space application is no longer being executed. That's basically why we say that the kernel performs the logic behind the system call on behalf of the user application.

In the next section, we're going to give an example of this by writing a system call that prints a hello message. It can be considered a progressive version of *example 11.1* that accepts an input string and returns a greeting string.

Add a system call to Linux

In this section, we are going to add a new system call to the system call table of an existing Unix-like kernel. This may be the first time that most of you reading this book have written C code that is supposed to be run within the kernel space. All of the past examples that we wrote in previous chapters, and almost all of the codes that we will write in future chapters, run in the user space.

In fact, most of the programs we write are meant to be running in the user space. In fact, this is what we call *C programming* or *C development*. However, if we are going to write a C program that is supposed to run in the kernel space, we use a different name; we call it *kernel development*.

We are going through the next example, *example 11.2*, but before that we need to explore the kernel environment to see how it is different from the user space.

Kernel development

This section will be beneficial to those of you who are seeking to be a kernel developer or a security researcher in the field of operating systems. In the first part, before jumping to the system call itself, we want to explain the differences between the kernel development and the ordinary C development.

The development of kernels is different from the development of ordinary C programs in a number of ways. Before looking at the differences, one thing we should note is that C development usually takes place in the user space.

In the following list, we have provided six of the key differences between the development efforts happening in the kernel and the user space:

- There is only one kernel process that runs everything. This simply means that if your code causes a crash in the kernel, you probably need to reboot the machine and let the kernel become initialized again. So, with the kernel process, the development cost is very high, and you cannot try various solutions without rebooting the machine, which you can do very easily for user space programs while working on them. Upon a crash in the kernel, a *kernel crash dump* is generated, which can be used to diagnose the cause.

- In the kernel ring, there is no C standard library like glibc! In other words, this is a realm in which SUS and POSIX standards are no longer valid. So, you cannot include any libc header files, such as `stdio.h` or `string.h`. In this case, you have a dedicated set of functions that should be used for various operations. These functions are usually located in *kernel headers* and can be different from one Unix flavor to another because there is no standardization in this field.

  As an example, if you are doing kernel development in Linux, you may use `printk` to write a message into the kernel's *message buffer*. However, in FreeBSD, you need to use the `printf` family of functions, which are different from the libc `printf` functions. You will find these `printf` functions in the `<sys/system.h>` header file in a FreeBSD system. The equivalent function while doing XNU kernel development is `os_log`. Note that XNU is the kernel of macOS.

- You can read or modify files in the kernel, but not using libc functions. Each Unix kernel has its own method of accessing files inside the kernel ring. This is the same for all functionalities exposed through libc.

- You have full access to the physical memory and many other services in the kernel ring. So, writing secure and reliable code is very important.

- There is no system call mechanism in the kernel. System calls are the main user space mechanism to enable user processes to communicate with the kernel ring. So, once you're in the kernel, there is no need for it.

- The kernel process is created by copying the kernel image into the physical memory, performed by the *boot loader*. You cannot add a new system call without having to create the kernel image from scratch and reload it again by rebooting the system. In kernels that support *kernel modules*, you can easily add or remove a module when the kernel is up and running, but you cannot do the same with system calls.

As you can see with the points we've just listed, kernel development takes place in a different flow compared to the ordinary C development. Testing written logic is not an easy task, and buggy code can cause a system crash.

In the next section, we will do our first kernel development by adding a new system call. We're doing this not because it's common to add a system call when you want to introduce a new functionality into the kernel, but we're going to give it a try in order to get familiar with kernel development.

Writing a Hello World system call for Linux

In this section, we're going to write a new system call for Linux. There are many great sources on the internet that explain how to add a system call to an existing Linux kernel, but the following forum post, *Adding a Hello World System Call to Linux Kernel* – available at `https://medium.com/anubhav-shrimal/adding-a-hello-world-system-call-to-linux-kernel-dad32875872` – was used as the basis to build my own system call in Linux.

Example 11.2 is an advanced version of *example 11.1* that uses a different and custom system call, which we are going to write in this section. The new system call receives four arguments. The first two are for the input name and the second two are for the greeting string output. Our system call accepts a name using its first two arguments, one char pointer addressing an already allocated buffer in the user space and one integer as the buffer's length, and returns the greeting string using its second two arguments, a pointer that is different from the input buffer and is again allocated in the user space and another integer as its length.

WARNING:
Please don't perform this experiment in a Linux installation that is supposed to be used for work or home usage purposes. Run the following commands on an experimental machine, which is strongly recommended to be a virtual machine. You can easily create virtual machines by using emulator applications such as VirtualBox or VMware.

The following instructions have the potential to corrupt your system and make you lose part, if not all, of your data if they are used inappropriately or in the wrong order. Always consider some backup solutions to make a copy of your data if you're going to run the following commands on a none-experimental machine.

First of all, we need to download the latest source code of the Linux kernel. We will use the Linux GitHub repository to clone its source code and then we will pick a specific release. Version 5.3 was released on 15 September 2019, and so we're going to use this version for this example.

Note:
Linux is a kernel. It means that it can only be installed in the kernel ring in a Unix-like operating system, but a *Linux distribution* is a different thing. A Linux distribution has a specific version of the Linux kernel in its kernel ring and a specific version of GNU libc and Bash (or GNU shell) in its shell ring.

Each Linux distribution is usually shipped with a complete list of user applications in its external rings. So, we can say a Linux distribution is a complete operating system. Note that, *Linux distribution*, *Linux distro*, and *Linux flavor* all refer to the same thing.

In this example, I'm using the Ubuntu 18.04.1 Linux distribution on a 64-bit machine.

Before we start, it's vital to make sure that the prerequisite packages are installed by running the following commands:

```
$ sudo apt-get update
$ sudo apt-get install -y build-essential autoconf libncurses5-dev
libssl-dev bison flex libelf-dev git
. . .
. . .
$
```

Shell Box 11-3: Installing the prerequisite packages required for example 11.2

Some notes about the preceding instructions: apt is the main package manager in Debian-based Linux distributions, while sudo is a utility program that we use to run a command in *superuser* mode. It is available on almost every Unix-like operating system.

The next step is to clone the Linux GitHub repository. We also need to check out the release 5.3 after cloning the repository. The version can be checked out by using the release tag name, as you can see in the following commands:

```
$ git clone https://github.com/torvalds/linux
$ cd linux
$ git checkout v5.3
$
```

Shell Box 11-4: Cloning the Linux kernel and checking out version 5.3

Now, if you look at the files in the root directory, you will see lots of files and directories that combined build up the Linux kernel code base:

```
$ ls
total 760K
drwxrwxr-x  33 kamran kamran 4.0K Jan 28  2018 arch
drwxrwxr-x   3 kamran kamran 4.0K Oct 16 22:11 block
drwxrwxr-x   2 kamran kamran 4.0K Oct 16 22:11 certs
...
drwxrwxr-x 125 kamran kamran  12K Oct 16 22:11 Documentation
drwxrwxr-x 132 kamran kamran 4.0K Oct 16 22:11 drivers
-rw-rw-r--   1 kamran kamran 3.4K Oct 16 22:11 dropped.txt
drwxrwxr-x   2 kamran kamran 4.0K Jan 28  2018 firmare
drwxrwxr-x  75 kamraln kamran 4.0K Oct 16 22:11 fs
drwxrwxr-x  27 kamran kamran 4.0K Jan 28  2018 include
...
-rw-rw-r--   1 kamran kamran  287 Jan 28  2018 Kconfig
drwxrwxr-x  17 kamran kamran 4.0K Oct 16 22:11 kernel
drwxrwxr-x  13 kamran kamran  12K Oct 16 22:11 lib
-rw-rw-r--   1 kamran kamran 429K Oct 16 22:11 MAINTAINERS
-rw-rw-r--   1 kamran kamran  61K Oct 16 22:11 Makefile
drwxrwxr-x   3 kamran kamran 4.0K Oct 16 22:11 mm
drwxrwxr-x  69 kamran kamran 4.0K Jan 28  2018 net
-rw-rw-r--   1 kamran kamran  722 Jan 28  2018 README
drwxrwxr-x  28 kamran kamran 4.0K Jan 28  2018 samples
drwxrwxr-x  14 kamran kamran 4.0K Oct 16 22:11 scripts
...
drwxrwxr-x   4 kamran kamran 4.0K Jan 28  2018 virt
drwxrwxr-x   5 kamran kamran 4.0K Oct 16 22:11 zfs
$
```

Shell Box 11-5: The content of the Linux kernel code base

As you can see, there are directories that might seem familiar: fs, mm, net, arch, and so on. I should point out that we are not going to give more details on each of these directories as it can vary massively from a kernel to another, but one common feature is that all kernels follow almost the same internal structure.

Now that we have the kernel source, we should begin to add our new Hello World system call. However, before we do that, we need to choose a unique numerical identifier for our system call; in this case, I give it the name hello_world, and I choose 999 as its number.

Firstly, we need to add the system call function declaration to the end of the include/linux/syscalls.h header file. After this modification, the file should look like this:

```
/*
 * syscalls.h - Linux syscall interfaces (non-arch-specific)
 *
 * Copyright (c) 2004 Randy Dunlap
 * Copyright (c) 2004 Open Source Development Labs
 *
 * This file is released under the GPLv2.
 * See the file COPYING for more details.
 */

#ifndef _LINUX_SYSCALLS_H
#define _LINUX_SYSCALLS_H

struct epoll_event;
struct iattr;
struct inode;

...

asmlinkage long sys_statx(int dfd, const char __user *path,
unsigned flags,
                        unsigned mask, struct statx __user
*buffer);

asmlinkage long sys_hello_world(const char __user *str,
                        const size_t str_len,
                        char __user *buf,
                        size_t buf_len);
#endif
```

Code Box 11-3 [include/linux/syscalls.h]: Declaration of the new Hello World system call

The description at the top says that this is a header file that contains the Linux syscall interfaces, which are not *architecture specific*. This means that on all architectures, Linux exposes the same set of system calls.

At the end of the file, we have declared our system call function, which accepts four arguments. As we have explained before, the first two arguments are the input string and its length, and the second two arguments are the output string and its length.

Note that input arguments are `const`, but the output arguments are not. Additionally, the `__user` identifier means that the pointers are pointing to memory addresses within the user space. As you can see, every system call has an integer value being returned as part of its function signature, which will actually be its execution result. The range of returned values and their meanings is different from one system call to another. In the case of our system call, `0` means success and any other number is a failure.

We now need to define our system call. To do this, we must first create a folder named `hello_world` in the root directory, which we accomplish using the following commands:

```
$ mkdir hello_world
$ cd hello_world
$
```

Shell Box 11-6: Creating the hello_world directory

Next, we create a file named `sys_hello_world.c` inside the `hello_world` directory. The contents of this file should be as follows:

```c
#include <linux/kernel.h>    // For printk
#include <linux/string.h>    // For strcpy, strcat, strlen
#include <linux/slab.h>      // For kmalloc, kfree
#include <linux/uaccess.h>   // For copy_from_user, copy_to_user
#include <linux/syscalls.h>  // For SYSCALL_DEFINE4

// Definition of the system call
SYSCALL_DEFINE4(hello_world,
        const char __user *, str,      // Input name
        const unsigned int, str_len,   // Length of input name
        char __user *, buf,            // Output buffer
        unsigned int, buf_len) {       // Length of output buffer
  // The kernel stack variable supposed to keep the content
  // of the input buffer
  char name[64];
  // The kernel stack variable supposed to keep the final
  // output message.
  char message[96];
```

```
printk("System call fired!\n");
if (str_len >= 64) {
  printk("Too long input string.\n");
  return -1;
}

// Copy data from user space into kernel space
if (copy_from_user(name, str, str_len)) {
  printk("Copy from user space failed.\n");
  return -2;
}

// Build up the final message
strcpy(message, "Hello ");
strcat(message, name);
strcat(message, "!");

// Check if the final message can be fit into the output binary
if (strlen(message) >= (buf_len - 1)) {
  printk("Too small output buffer.\n");
  return -3;
}

// Copy back the message from the kernel space to the user space
if (copy_to_user(buf, message, strlen(message) + 1)) {
  printk("Copy to user space failed.\n");
  return -4;
}

// Print the sent message into the kernel log
printk("Message: %s\n", message);
return 0;
}
```

Code Box 11-4: The definition of the Hello World system call

In the *Code Box 11-4*, we have used the SYSCALL_DEFINE4 macro to define our function definition, with the DEFINE4 suffix simply meaning that it accepts four arguments.

At the beginning of the function body, we have declared two-character arrays on the top of the kernel Stack. Much like ordinary processes, the kernel process has an address space that contains a Stack. After we've achieved that, we copy the data from the user space into the kernel space. Following that, we create the greeting message by concatenating some strings. This string is still in the kernel memory. Finally, we copy back the message to the user space and make it available for the caller process.

In the case of errors, appropriate error numbers are returned in order to let the caller process know about the result of the system call.

The next step to make our system call work is to update one more table. There is only one system call table for both x86 and x64 architectures, and the newly added system calls should be added to this table to become exposed.

Only after this step the system calls are available in x86 and x64 machines. To add the system call to the table, we need to add `hello_word` and its function name, `sys_hello_world`.

To do this, open the `arch/x86/entry/syscalls/syscall_64.tbl` file and add the following line to the end of the file:

```
999        64       hello_world              __x64_sys_hello_world
```

Code Box 11-5: Adding the newly added Hello World system call to the system call table

After the modification, the file should look like this:

```
$ cat arch/x86/entry/syscalls/syscall_64.tbl
...
...
546        x32      preadv2                  __x32_compat_sys_
preadv64v2
547        x32      pwritev2                 __x32_compat_sys_
pwritev64v2
999        64       hello_world              __x64_sys_hello_world
$
```

Shell Box 11-7: Hello World system call added to the system call table

Note the `__x64_` prefix in the name of the system call. This is an indication that the system call is only exposed in x64 systems.

The Linux kernel uses the Make build system to compile all the source files and build the final kernel image. Moving on, you must make a file named `Makefile` in the `hello_world` directory. Its content, which is a single line of text, should be the following:

```
obj-y := sys_hello_world.o
```

Code Box 11-6: Makefile of the Hello World system call

Then, you need to add `hello_world` directory to the main `Makefile` in the root directory. Change to the kernel's root directory, open the `Makefile` file, and find the following line:

```
core-y   += kernel/certs/mm/fs/ipc/security/crypto/block/
```

Code Box 11-7: The target line that should be modified in the root Makefile

Add `hello_world/` to this list. All of these directories are simply the directories that should be built as part of the kernel.

We need to add the directory of the Hello World system call in order to include it in the build process and have it included in the final kernel image. The line should look like the following code after the modification:

```
core-y   += kernel/certs/mm/fs/hello_world/ipc/security/crypto/block/
```

Code Box 11-8: The target line after modification

The next step is to build the kernel.

Building the kernel

To build the kernel, we must first go back to the kernel's root directory because before we start to build the kernel, you need to provide a configuration. A configuration has a list of features and units that should be built as part of the build process.

The following command tries to make the target configuration based on the current Linux kernel's configuration. It uses the existing values in your kernel and asks you about confirmation if a newer configuration value exists in the kernel we are trying to build. If it does, you can simply accept all newer versions by just pressing the *Enter* key:

```
$ make localmodconfig
...
...
#
# configuration written to .config
#
$
```

Shell Box 11-8: Creating a kernel configuration based on the current running kernel

Now you can start the build process. Since the Linux kernel contains a lot of source files, the build can take hours to complete. Therefore, we need to run the compilations in parallel.

If you're using a virtual machine, please configure your machine to have more than one core in order to have an effective boost in the build process:

```
$ make -j4
SYSHDR   arch/x86/include/generated/asm/unistd_32_ia32.h
SYSTBL   arch/x86/include/generated/asm/syscalls_32.h
HOSTCC   scripts/basic/bin2c
SYSHDR   arch/x86/include/generated/asm/unistd_64_x32.h
...
...
UPD      include/generated/compile.h
CC       init/main.o
CC       hello_world/sys_hello_world.o
CC       arch/x86/crypto/crc32c-intel_glue.o
...
...
LD [M]   net/netfilter/x_tables.ko
LD [M]   net/netfilter/xt_tcpudp.ko
LD [M]   net/sched/sch_fq_codel.ko
LD [M]   sound/ac97_bus.ko
LD [M]   sound/core/snd-pcm.ko
LD [M]   sound/core/snd.ko
LD [M]   sound/core/snd-timer.ko
LD [M]   sound/pci/ac97/snd-ac97-codec.ko
LD [M]   sound/pci/snd-intel8x0.ko
LD [M]   sound/soundcore.ko
$
```

Shell Box 11-9: Output of the kernel build. Please note the line indicating the compilation of the Hello World system call

Note:
Make sure that you have installed the prerequisite packages introduced in the very first part of this section; otherwise, you will get compilation errors.

As you can see, the build process has started with four jobs trying to compile C files in parallel. You need to wait for it to complete. When it's finished, you can easily install the new kernel and reboot the machine:

```
$ sudo make modules_install install
INSTALL arch/x86/crypto/aes-x86_64.ko
INSTALL arch/x86/crypto/aesni-intel.ko
INSTALL arch/x86/crypto/crc32-pclmul.ko
INSTALL arch/x86/crypto/crct10dif-pclmul.ko
...
...
run-parts: executing /et/knel/postinst.d/initam-tools 5.3.0+ /
boot/vmlinuz-5.3.0+
update-iniras: Generating /boot/initrd.img-5.3.0+
run-parts: executing /etc/keneostinst.d/unattende-urades 5.3.0+ /
boot/vmlinuz-5.3.0+
...
...
Found initrd image: /boot/initrd.img-4.15.0-36-generic
Found linux image: /boot/vmlinuz-4.15.0-29-generic
Found initrd image: /boot/initrd.img-4.15.0-29-generic
done.
$
```

Shell Box 11-10: Creating and installing the new kernel image

As you can see, a new kernel image for the version 5.3.0 has been created and installed. Now we 're ready to reboot the system. Don't forget to check the current kernel's version before rebooting if you don't know it. In my case, my version is 4.15.0-36-generic. I've used the following commands to find it out:

```
$ uname -r
4.15.0-36-generic
$
```

Shell Box 11-11: Checking the version of the currently installed kernel

Now, reboot the system using the following command:

```
$ sudo reboot
```

Shell Box 11-12: Rebooting the system

While the system is booting up, the new kernel image will be picked up and used. Note that boot loaders won't pick up the older kernels; therefore, if you've had a kernel with version above 5.3, you are going to need to load the built kernel image manually. This link can help you with that: `https://askubuntu.com/questions/82140/how-can-i-boot-with-an-older-kernel-version`.

When the operating system boot is complete, you should have the new kernel running. Check the version. It must look like this:

```
$ uname -r
5.3.0+
$
```

Shell Box 11-13: Checking the kernel version after the reboot.

If everything has gone well, the new kernel should be in place. Now we can continue to write a C program that invokes our newly added Hello World system call. It will be very similar to *example 11.1*, that called the `write` system call. You can find *example 11.2* next:

```c
// We need to have this to be able to use non-POSIX stuff
#define _GNU_SOURCE

#include <stdio.h>
#include <unistd.h>

// This is not part of POSIX!
#include <sys/syscall.h>

int main(int argc, char** argv) {
  char str[20] = "Kam";
  char message[64] = "";

  // Call the hello world system call
  int ret_val = syscall(999, str, 4, message, 64);
  if (ret_val < 0) {
    printf("[ERR] Ret val: %d\n", ret_val);
    return 1;
  }
  printf("Message: %s\n", message);
  return 0;
}
```

Code Box 11-9 [ExtremeC_examples_chapter11_2.c]: Example 11.2 invoking the newly added Hello World system call

As you can see, we have invoked the system call with the number 999. We pass Kam as the input, and we expect to receive Hello Kam! as the greeting message. The program waits for the result and prints the message buffer that is filled by the system call in the kernel space.

In the following code, we build and run the example:

```
$ gcc ExtremeC_examples_chapter11_2.c -o ex11_2.out
$ ./ex11_2.out
Message: Hello Kam!
$
```

Shell Box 11-14: Compiling and running example 11.2

After running the example, and if you look at the kernel logs using the dmesg command, you will see the generated logs using printk:

```
$ dmesg
...
...
[  112.273783] System call fired!
[  112.273786] Message: Hello Kam!
$
```

Shell Box 11-15: Using dmesg to see the logs generated by the Hello World system call

If you run *example 11.2* with strace, you can see that it actually calls system call 999. You can see it in the line starting with syscall_0x3e7(...). Note that 0x3e7 is the hexadecimal value for 999:

```
$ strace ./ex11_2.out
...
...
mprotect(0x557266020000, 4096, PROT_READ) = 0
mprotect(0x7f8dd6d2d000, 4096, PROT_READ) = 0
munmap(0x7f8dd6d26000, 27048)           = 0
syscall_0x3e7(0x7fffe7d2af30, 0x4, 0x7fffe7d2af50, 0x40,
0x7f8dd6b01d80, 0x7fffe7d2b088) = 0
fstat(1, {st_mode=S_IFCHR|0620, st_rdev=makedev(136, 0), ...}) = 0
brk(NULL)                               = 0x5572674f2000
```

```
brk(0x557267513000)
...
...
exit_group(0)                                    = ?
+++ exited with 0 +++
$
```

Shell Box 11-16: Monitoring the system calls made by example 11.2

In *Shell Box 11-16,* you can see that `syscall_0x3e7` has been called and `0` has been returned. If you change the code in *example 11.2* to pass a name with more than 64 bytes, you will receive an error. Let's change the example and run it again:

```
int main(int argc, char** argv) {
   char name[84] = "A very very long message! It is really hard to
produce a big string!";
   char message[64] = "";
   ...
   return 0;
}
```

Code Box 11-10: Passing a long message (more than 64 bytes) to our Hello World system call

Let's compile and run it again:

```
$ gcc ExtremeC_examples_chapter11_2.c -o ex11_2.out
$ ./ex11_2.out
[ERR] Ret val: -1
$
```

Shell Box 11-17: Compiling and running example 11.2 after the modification

As you see, the system call returns `-1` based on the logic we have written for it. Running with `strace` also shows that system call has returned `-1`:

```
$ strace ./ex11_2.out
...
...
munmap(0x7f1a900a5000, 27048)                    = 0
```

```
syscall_0x3e7(0x7ffdf74e10f0, 0x54, 0x7ffdf74e1110, 0x40,
0x7f1a8fe80d80, 0x7ffdf74e1248) = -1 (errno 1)
fstat(1, {st_mode=S_IFCHR|0620, st_rdev=makedev(136, 0), ...}) = 0
brk(NULL)                                    = 0x5646802e2000
...

...
exit_group(1)                                = ?
+++ exited with 1 +++
$
```

Shell Box 11-18: Monitoring the system calls made by example 11.2 after the modification

In the next section, we talk about the approaches we can take in designing kernels. As part of our discussion, we introduce the kernel modules and explore how they are used in kernel development.

Unix kernels

In this section, we are going to talk about the architectures that Unix kernels have been developed with throughout the last 30 years. Before talking about the different types of kernels, and there are not very many, we should know that there is no standardization about the way a kernel should be designed.

The best practices that we have obtained are based on our experiences over the years, and they have led us to a high-level picture of the internal units in a Unix kernel, which results in illustrations such as *Figure 10-5* in the previous chapter. Therefore, each kernel is somewhat different in comparison to another. The main thing that all of them have in common is that they should expose their functionalities through a system call interface. However, every kernel has its own way of handling system calls.

This variety and the debates around it have made it one of the hottest computer architecture-related topics of the 1990s, with large groups of people taking part in these debates – the *Tanenbaum-Torvalds* debate being considered the most famous one.

We are not going to go into the details of these debates, but we want to talk a bit about the two major dominant architectures for designing a Unix kernel: *monolithic* and *microkernel*. There are still other architectures, such as *hybrid kernels*, *nanokernels*, and *exokernels*, all of which have their own specific usages.

We, however, are going to focus on monolithic kernels and microkernels by creating a comparison so that we can learn about their characteristics.

Monolithic kernels versus microkernels

In the previous chapter where we looked at Unix architecture, we described the kernel as a single process containing many units, but in reality, we were actually talking about a monolithic kernel.

A monolithic kernel is made up of one kernel process with one address space that contains multiple smaller units within the same process. Microkernels take the opposite approach. A microkernel is a minimal kernel process that tries to push out services such as filesystem, device drivers, and process management to the user space in order to make the kernel process smaller and thinner.

Both of these architectures have advantages and disadvantages, and as a result, they've been the topic of one of the most famous debates in the history of operating systems. It goes back to 1992, just after the release of the first version of Linux. A debate was started on *Usenet* by a post written by **Andrew S. Tanenbaum**. The debate is known as the Tanenbaum-Torvalds debate. You can read more at https://en.wikipedia.org/wiki/Tanenbaum-Torvalds_debate.

That post was the starting point for a flame war between the Linux creator **Linus Torvalds** and Tanenbaum and a bunch of other enthusiasts, who later became the first Linux developers. They were debating the nature of monolithic kernels and microkernels. Many different aspects of kernel design and the influence of hardware architecture on kernel design were discussed as part of this flame war.

Further discussion of the debates and topics described would be lengthy and complex and therefore beyond the scope of this book, but we want to compare these two approaches and let you get familiar with the advantages and disadvantages of each approach.

The following is a list of differences between monolithic kernels and microkernels:

- A monolithic kernel is made up of a single process containing all the services provided by the kernel. Most early Unix kernels were developed like this, and it is considered to be an old approach. Microkernels are different because they have separate processes for every service the kernel offers.

- A monolithic kernel process resides in the kernel space, whereas the *server processes* in a microkernel are usually in the user space. Server processes are those processes that provide the kernel's functionalities, such as memory management, filesystem, and so on. Microkernels are different in that they let server processes be in the user space. This means some operating systems are more microkernel-like than the others.

- Monolithic kernels are usually faster. That's because all kernel services are performed inside the kernel process, but microkernels need to do some *message passing* between the user space and the kernel space, hence more system calls and context switches.

- In a monolithic kernel, all device drivers are loaded into the kernel. Therefore, device drivers written by third-party vendors will be run as a part of the kernel. Any flaw in any device driver or any other unit inside the kernel may lead to a kernel crash. This is not the case with microkernels because all of the device drivers and many other units are run in the user space, which we could hypothesize as the reason why monolithic kernels are not used in mission-critical projects.

- In monolithic kernels, injecting a small piece of malicious code is enough to compromise the whole kernel, and subsequently the whole system. However, this can't happen easily in a microkernel because many server processes are in the user space, and only a minimal set of critical functionalities are concentrated in the kernel space.

- In a monolithic kernel, even a simple change to the kernel source needs the whole kernel to be compiled again, and a new kernel image should be generated. Loading the new image also requires the machine to be rebooted. But changes in a microkernel can lead to a compilation of only a specific server process, and probably loading the new functionality without rebooting the system. In monolithic kernels, a similar functionality can be obtained to some extent using kernel modules.

MINIX is one of the best-known examples of microkernels. It was written by Andrew S. Tanenbaum and was initiated as an educational operating system. Linus Torvalds used MINIX as his development environment to write his own kernel, called Linux, in 1991 for the 80386 microprocessor.

As Linux has been the biggest and most successful defender of monolithic kernels for nearly 30 years, we're going to talk more about Linux in the next section.

Linux

You've already been introduced to the Linux kernel in the previous section of this chapter, when we were developing a new system call for it. In this section, we want to focus a bit more on the fact that Linux is monolithic and that every kernel functionality is inside the kernel.

However, there should be a way to add a new functionality to the kernel without needing it to be recompiled. New functionalities cannot be added to the kernel as new system calls simply because, as you saw, by adding a new system call, many fundamental files need to be changed, and this means we need to recompile the kernel in order to have the new functionalities.

The new approach is different. In this technique, kernel modules are written and plugged into the kernel dynamically, which we will discuss in the first section, before moving on to writing a kernel module for Linux.

Kernel modules

Monolithic kernels are usually equipped with another facility that enables kernel developers to hot-plug new functionalities into an up-and-running kernel. These pluggable units are called kernel modules. These are not the same as server processes in microkernels.

Unlike server processes in a microkernel, which are in fact separate processes using IPC techniques to communicate with each other, kernel modules are *kernel object files* that are already compiled and can be loaded dynamically into the kernel process. These kernel object files can either become statically built as part of the kernel image or become loaded dynamically when the kernel is up and running.

Note that the kernel object files are twin concepts to the ordinary object files produced in C development.

It's worth noting again that if the kernel module does something bad inside the kernel, a *kernel crash* can happen.

The way you communicate with kernel modules is different from system calls, and they cannot be used by calling a function or using a given API. Generally, there are three ways to communicate with a kernel module in Linux and some similar operating systems:

- **Device files in the /dev directory**: Kernel modules are mainly developed to be used by device drivers, and that's why devices are the most common way to communicate with kernel modules. As we explained in the previous chapter, devices are accessible as device files located in the /dev directory. You can read from and write to these files and, using them, you can send and receive data to/from the modules.

- **Entries in procfs**: Entries in the /proc directory can be used to read meta-information about a specific kernel module. These files can also be used to pass meta-information or control commands to a kernel module. We shortly demonstrate the usage of procfs in the next example, *example 11.3*, as part of the following section.

- **Entries in sysfs**: This is another filesystem in Linux that allows scripts and users to control user processes and other kernel-related units, such as kernel modules. It can be considered as a new version of procfs.

In fact, the best way to see a kernel module is to write one, which is what we are going to do in the next section, where we write a Hello World kernel module for Linux. Note that kernel modules are not limited to Linux; monolithic kernels such as FreeBSD also benefit from the kernel module mechanism.

Adding a kernel module to Linux

In this section, we are going to write a new kernel module for Linux. This is the Hello World kernel module, which creates an entry in procfs. Then, using this entry, we read the greeting string.

In this section, you will become familiar with writing a kernel module, compiling it, loading it into the kernel, unloading it from the kernel, and reading data from a procfs entry. The main purpose of this example is to get your hands dirty with writing a kernel module and, as a result more development can be done by yourself.

Note:
Kernel modules are compiled into kernel object files that can be loaded directly into the kernel at run-time. There is no need to reboot the system after loading the kernel module object file as long as it doesn't do something bad in the kernel that leads to a kernel crash. That's also true for unloading the kernel module.

The first step is to create a directory that is supposed to contain all files related to the kernel module. We name it `ex11_3` since this is the third example in this chapter:

```
$ mkdir ex11_3
$ cd ex11_3
$
```

Shell Box 11-19: Making the root directory for example 11.3

Then, create a file named `hwkm.c`, which is just an acronym made up of the first letters of "Hello World Kernel Module," with the following content:

```c
#include <linux/module.h>
#include <linux/kernel.h>
#include <linux/init.h>
#include <linux/proc_fs.h>

// The structure pointing to the proc file
struct proc_dir_entry *proc_file;

// The read callback function
ssize_t proc_file_read(struct file *file, char __user *ubuf,
size_t count, loff_t *ppos) {
  int copied = 0;
  if (*ppos > 0) {
    return 0;
```

```
  }
  copied = sprintf(ubuf, "Hello World From Kernel Module!\n");
  *ppos = copied;
  return copied;
}

static const struct file_operations proc_file_fops = {
 .owner = THIS_MODULE,
 .read  = proc_file_read
};

// The module initialization callback
static int __init hwkm_init(void) {
  proc_file = proc_create("hwkm", 0, NULL, &proc_file_fops);
  if (!proc_file) {
    return -ENOMEM;
  }
  printk("Hello World module is loaded.\n");
  return 0;
}

// The module exit callback
static void __exit hkwm_exit(void) {
  proc_remove(proc_file);
  printk("Goodbye World!\n");
}

// Defining module callbacks
module_init(hwkm_init);
module_exit(hkwm_exit);
```

Code Box 11-11 [ex11_3/hwkm.c]: The Hello World kernel module

Using the two last statements in *Code Box 11-11*, we have registered the module's initialization and exit callbacks. These functions are called when the module is being loaded and unloaded respectively. The initialization callback is the first code to be executed.

As you can see inside the hwkm_init function, it creates a file named hwkm inside the /proc directory. There is also an exit callback. Inside the hwkm_exit function, it removes the hwkm file from the /proc path. The /proc/hwkm file is the contact point for the user space to be able to communicate with the kernel module.

The proc_file_read function is the read callback function. This function is called when the user space tries to read the /proc/hwkm file. As you will soon see, we use the cat utility program to read the file. It simply copies the Hello World From Kernel Module! string to the user space.

Note that at this stage, the code written inside a kernel module has total access to almost anything inside the kernel, and it can leak out any kind of information to the user space. This is a major security issue, and further reading about the best practices for writing a secure kernel module should be undertaken.

To compile the preceding code, we need to use an appropriate compiler, including possibly linking it with the appropriate libraries. In order to make life easier, we create a file named Makefile that will trigger the necessary build tools in order to build the kernel module.

The following code box shows the content of the Makefile:

```
obj-m += hwkm.o

all:
    make -C /lib/modules/$(shell uname -r)/build M=$(PWD) modules

clean:
    make -C /lib/modules/$(shell uname -r)/build M=$(PWD) clean
```

Code Box 11-12: Makefile of the Hello World kernel module

Then, we can run the make command. The following shell box demonstrates this:

```
$ make
make -C /lib/modules/54.318.0+/build M=/home/kamran/extreme_c/
ch11/codes/ex11_3 modules
make[1]: Entering directory '/home/kamran/linux'
  CC [M]  /home/kamran/extreme_c/ch11/codes/ex11_3/hwkm.o
  Building modules, stage 2.
  MODPOST 1 modules
WARNING: modpost: missing MODULE_LICENSE() in /home/kamran/
extreme_c/ch11/codes/ex11_3/hwkm.o
see include/linux/module.h for more information
  CC      /home/kamran/extreme_c/ch11/codes/ex11_3/hwkm.mod.o
  LD [M]  /home/kamran/extreme_c/ch11/codes/ex11_3/hwkm.ko
make[1]: Leaving directory '/home/kamran/linux'
$
```

Shell Box 11-20: Building the Hello World kernel module

As you can see, the compiler compiles the code and produces an object file. Then, it continues by linking the object file with other libraries to create a .ko file. Now, if you look at the generated files, you find a file named hwkm.ko.

Notice the .ko extension, which simply means that the output file is a kernel object file. It is something like a shared library that can be dynamically loaded into the kernel and become running.

Please note that in *Shell Box 11-20*, the build process has produced a warning message. It says that the module has no license associated with it. It is a highly recommended practice to generate licensed modules when developing or deploying kernel modules in test and production environments.

The following shell box shows the list of files that can be found after building the kernel module:

```
$ ls -l
total 556
-rw-rw-r-- 1 kamran kamran    154 Oct 19 00:36 Makefile
-rw-rw-r-- 1 kamran kamran      0 Oct 19 08:15 Module.symvers
-rw-rw-r-- 1 kamran kamran   1104 Oct 19 08:05 hwkm.c
-rw-rw-r-- 1 kamran kamran 272280 Oct 19 08:15 hwkm.ko
-rw-rw-r-- 1 kamran kamran    596 Oct 19 08:15 hwkm.mod.c
-rw-rw-r-- 1 kamran kamran 104488 Oct 19 08:15 hwkm.mod.o
-rw-rw-r-- 1 kamran kamran 169272 Oct 19 08:15 hwkm.o
-rw-rw-r-- 1 kamran kamran     54 Oct 19 08:15 modules.order
$
```

Shell Box 11-21: List of existing files after building the Hello World kernel module

Note:
We have used module build tools from Linux kernel version 5.3.0 You might get a compilation error if you compile this example using a kernel version below 3.10.

To load the hwkm kernel module, we use the insmod command in Linux, which simply loads and installs the kernel module, as we have done in the following shell box:

```
$ sudo insmod hwkm.ko
$
```

Shell Box 11-22: Loading and installing the Hello World kernel module

Now, if you look at the kernel logs, you will see the lines that are produced by the initializer function. Just use the dmesg command to see the latest kernel logs, which is what we have done next:

```
$ dmesg
...
...
[ 7411.519575] Hello World module is loaded.
$
```

Shell Box 11-23: Checking the kernel log messages after installing the kernel module

Now, the module has been loaded, and the `/proc/hwkm` file should have been created. We can read it now by using the `cat` command:

```
$ cat /proc/hwkm
Hello World From Kernel Module!
$ cat /proc/hwkm
Hello World From Kernel Module!
$
```

Shell Box 11-24: Reading the/proc/hwkm file using cat

As you can see in the preceding shell box, we have read the file twice, and both times, it returns the same `Hello World From Kernel Module!` string. Note that the string is copied into the user space by the kernel module, and the `cat` program has just printed it to the standard output.

When it comes to unloading the module, we can use the `rmmod` command in Linux, as we have done next:

```
$ sudo rmmod hwkm
$
```

Shell Box 11-25: Unloading the Hello World kernel module

Now that the module has been unloaded, look at the kernel logs again to see the goodbye message:

```
$ dmesg
...
...
[ 7411.519575] Hello World module is loaded.
```

```
[ 7648.950639] Goodbye World!
$
```

Shell Box 11-26: Checking the kernel log messages after unloading the kernel module

As you saw in the preceding example, kernel modules are very handy when it comes to writing kernel codes.

To finish off this chapter, I believe it would be helpful to give you a list of the features that we have seen so far regarding kernel modules:

- Kernel modules can be loaded and unloaded without needing to reboot the machine.

- When loaded, they become part of the kernel and can access any unit or structure within the kernel. This can be thought of as a vulnerability, but a Linux kernel can be protected against installing unwanted modules.

- In the case of kernel modules, you only need to compile their source code. But for system calls, you have to compile the whole kernel, which can easily take an hour of your time.

Finally, kernel modules can be handy when you are going to develop a code that needs to be run within the kernel behind a system call. The logic that is going to be exposed using a system call can be loaded into the kernel using a kernel module first, and after being developed and tested properly, it can go behind a real system call.

Developing system calls from scratch can be a tedious job because you have to reboot your machine countless times. Having the logic firstly written and tested as part of a kernel module can ease the pain of kernel development. Note that if your code is trying to cause a kernel crash, it doesn't matter if it is in a kernel module or behind a system call; it causes a kernel crash and you must reboot your machine.

In this section, we talked about various types of kernels. We also showed how a kernel module can be used within a monolithic kernel to have transient kernel logic by loading and unloading it dynamically.

Summary

We've now completed our two-chapter discussion about Unix. In this chapter, we learned about the following:

- What a system call is and how it exposes a certain functionality
- What happens behind the invocation of a system call
- How a certain system call can be invoked from C code directly
- How to add a new system call to an existing Unix-like kernel (Linux) and how to recompile the kernel
- What a monolithic kernel is and how it differs from a microkernel
- How kernel modules work within a monolithic kernel and how to write a new kernel module for Linux

In the following chapter, we're going to talk about the C standards and the most recent version of C, C18. You will become familiar with the new features introduced as part of it.

Chapter 12

The Most Recent C

Change cannot be prevented, and C is no exception. The C programming language is standardized by an ISO standard, and it is constantly under revision by a group of people who are trying to make it better and bring new features to it. This doesn't mean that the language will necessarily get easier, however; we might see novel and complex features emerge in the language as new content is added.

In this chapter, we are going to have a brief look at C11's features. You might know that C11 has replaced the old C99 standard, and it has been superseded by the C18 standard. In other words, C18 is the latest version of the C standard, and just before that we had C11.

It's interesting to know that C18 doesn't offer any new features; it just contains fixes for the issues found in C11. Therefore, talking about C11 is basically the same as talking about C18, and it will lead us to the most recent C standard. As you can see, we are observing constant improvement in the C language... contrary to the belief that it is a long-dead language!

This chapter will give a brief overview of the following topics:

- How to detect the C version and how to write a piece of C code which is compatible with various C versions
- New features for writing optimized and secure code, such as *no-return* functions and *bounds-checking* functions
- New data types and memory alignment techniques
- Type-generic functions
- Unicode support in C11, which was missing from the language in the older standards
- Anonymous structures and unions
- Standard support for multithreading and synchronization techniques in C11

Let's begin the chapter by talking about C11 and its new features.

C11

Gathering a new standard for a technology that has been in use for more than 30 years is not an easy task. Millions (if not billions!) of lines of C code exist, and if you are about to introduce new features, this must be done while keeping previous code or features intact. New features shouldn't create new problems for the existing programs, and they should be bug-free. While this view seems to be idealistic, it is something that we should be committed to.

The following PDF document resides on the *Open Standards* website and contains the worries and thoughts that people in the C community had in mind before starting to shape C11: `http://www.open-std.org/JTC1/SC22/wg14/www/docs/n1250.pdf`. It would be useful to give it a read because it will introduce you to the experience of authoring a new standard for a programming language that several thousand pieces of software have been built upon.

Finally, with these things in mind, we consider the release of C11. When C11 came out, it was not in its ideal form and was in fact suffering from some serious defects. You can see the list of these defects here: `http://www.open-std.org/jtc1/sc22/wg14/www/docs/n2244.htm`.

Seven years after the launch of C11, C18 was introduced, which came about to fix the defects found in C11. Note that C18 is also *informally* referred to as C17, and both C17 and C18 refer to the same C standard. If you open the previous link you will see the defects and their current statuses. If the status of a defect is "C17," it means that the defect is solved as part of C18. This shows how hard and delicate process it is to assemble a standard that has as many users as C does.

In the following sections, we'll talk about the new features of C11. Before going through them however, we need a way to be sure that we are really writing C11 code, and that we are using a compatible compiler. The following section will address this requirement.

Finding a supported version of C standard

At the time of writing, it has been almost 8 years since C11 came out. Therefore, it would be expected that many compilers should support the standard, and this is indeed the case. Open source compilers such as `gcc` and `clang` both support C11 perfectly, and they can switch back to C99 or even older versions of C if needed. In this section, we show how to use specific macros to detect the C version and, depending on the version, how to use the supported features.

The first thing that is necessary when using a compiler that supports different versions of the C standard is being able to identify which version of the C standard is currently in use. Every C standard defines a special macro that can be used to find out what version is being used. So far, we have used gcc in Linux and clang in macOS systems. As of version 4.7, gcc offers C11 as one of its supported standards.

Let's look at the following example and see how already-defined macros can be used to detect the current version of the C standard at runtime:

```
#include <stdio.h>

int main(int argc, char** argv) {
#if __STDC_VERSION__ >= 201710L
  printf("Hello World from C18!\n");
#elif __STDC_VERSION__ >= 201112L
  printf("Hello World from C11!\n");
#elif __STDC_VERSION__ >= 199901L
  printf("Hello World from C99!\n");
#else
  printf("Hello World from C89/C90!\n");
#endif
  return 0;
}
```

Code Box 12-1 [ExtremeC_examples_chapter12_1.c]: Detecting the version of the C standard

As you can see, the preceding code can distinguish between various versions of the C standard. In order to see how various C versions can lead to various printings, we have to compile the preceding source code multiple times with various versions of C standard that are supported by the compiler.

To ask the compiler to use a specific version of the C standard, we have to pass the -std=CXX option to the C compiler. Look at the following commands and the produced output:

```
$ gcc ExtremeC_examples_chapter12_1.c -o ex12_1.out
$ ./ex12_1.out
Hello World from C11!
$ gcc ExtremeC_examples_chapter12_1.c -o ex12_1.out -std=c11
$ ./ex12_1.out
Hello World from C11!
$ gcc ExtremeC_examples_chapter12_1.c -o ex12_1.out -std=c99
```

```
$ ./ex12_1.out
Hello World from C99!
$ gcc ExtremeC_examples_chapter12_1.c -o ex12_1.out -std=c90
$ ./ex12_1.out
Hello World from C89/C90!
$ gcc ExtremeC_examples_chapter12_1.c -o ex12_1.out -std=c89
$ ./ex12_1.out
Hello World from C89/C90!
$
```

Shell Box 12-1: Compiling example 12.1 with various versions of C standard

As you can see, the default C standard version in newer compilers is C11. With older versions, you have to specify the version using the -std option, if you want to enable C11. Note the comments made at the beginning of the file. I have used /* ... */ comments (multiline comments) instead of // comments (one-line comments). That's because one-line comments were not supported in standards before C99. Therefore, we had to use multiline comments in order to have the preceding code compiled with all C versions.

Removal of the gets function

In C11, the famous gets function is removed. The gets function was subject to *buffer overflow* attacks, and in older versions it was decided to make the function *deprecated*. Later, as part of the C11 standard, it was removed. Therefore, older source code that uses the gets function won't be compiled using a C11 compiler.

The fgets function can be used instead of gets. The following is an excerpt from the gets manual page (man page) in macOS:

SECURITY CONSIDERATIONS

The gets() function cannot be used securely. Because of its lack of bounds checking, and the inability for the calling program to reliably determine the length of the next incoming line, the use of this function enables malicious users to arbitrarily change a running program's functionality through a buffer overflow attack. It is strongly suggested that the fgets() function be used in all cases. (See the FSA.)

Changes to fopen function

The `fopen` function is usually used for opening a file and returning a file descriptor to that file. The concept of a file is very general in Unix, and by using the term *file*, we don't necessarily mean a file located on the filesystem. The `fopen` function has the following signatures:

```
FILE* fopen(const char *pathname, const char *mode);
FILE* fdopen(int fd, const char *mode);
FILE* freopen(const char *pathname, const char *mode, FILE
*stream);
```

Code Box 12-2: Various signatures of the family of fopen functions

As you can see, all of the preceding signatures accept a `mode` input. This input parameter is a string that determines how the file should be opened. The following description in *Shell Box 12-2* is obtained from the FreeBSD manual for the `fopen` function and explains how `mode` should be used:

```
$ man 3 fopen
...
The argument mode points to a string beginning with one of the
following letters:

      "r"       Open for reading.  The stream is positioned at the
beginning
                of the file.  Fail if the file does not exist.


      "w"       Open for writing.  The stream is positioned at the
beginning
                of the file.  Create the file if it does not exist.


      "a"       Open for writing.  The stream is positioned at the
end of
                the file. Subsequent writes to the file will always
end up
                at the then current end of file, irrespective of
                any intervening fseek(3) or similar. Create the file
                if it does not exist.


      An optional "+" following "r", "w", or "a" opens the file
```

```
      for both reading and writing.  An optional "x" following "w"
or
      "w+" causes the fopen() call to fail if the file already
exists.
      An optional "e" following the above causes the fopen() call
to set
      the FD_CLOEXEC flag on the underlying file descriptor.


      The mode string can also include the letter "b" after either
      the "+" or the first letter.

...
$
```

Shell Box 12-2: An excerpt from the fopen's manual page in FreeBSD

The mode x, explained in the preceding extract from the fopen manual page, has been introduced as part of C11. To open a file in order to write to it, the mode w or w+ should be supplied to fopen. The problem is that, if the file already exists, the w or w+ mode will truncate (empty) the file.

Therefore, if the programmer wants to append to a file and keep its current content, they have to use a different mode, a. Hence, they have to check for the file's existence, using a filesystem API such as stat, before calling fopen, and then choose the proper mode based on the result. Now however, with the new mode x, the programmer first tries with the mode wx or w+x, and if the file already exists the fopen will fail. Then the programmer can continue with the a mode.

Thus, less boilerplate code needs to be written to open a file without using the filesystem API to check for the file's existence. From now on, fopen is enough to open a file in every desired mode.

Another change in C11 was the introduction of the fopen_s API. This function serves as a secure fopen. According to the documentation for fopen_s found at https://en.cppreference.com/w/c/io/fopen, performs extra checking on the provided buffers and their boundaries in order to detect any flaw in them.

Bounds-checking functions

One of the serious problems with C programs operating on strings and byte arrays is the ability to go easily beyond the boundary defined for a buffer or a byte array.

As a reminder, a buffer is a region of memory that is used as the place holder for a byte array or a string variable. Going beyond the boundary of a buffer causes a *buffer overflow* and based on that a malicious entity can organize an attack (usually called a *buffer overflow attack*). This type of attack either results in a **denial of service (DOS)** or in *exploitation* of the victim C program.

Most such attacks usually start in a function operating on character or byte arrays. String manipulation functions found in string.h, such as strcpy and strcat, are among the *vulnerable* functions that lack a boundary checking mechanism to prevent buffer overflow attacks.

However, as part of C11, a new set of functions has been introduced. *Bounds-checking* functions borrow the same name from the string manipulation functions but with an _s at the end. The suffix _s distinguishes them as a *secure* or *safe* flavor of those functions that conduct more runtime checks in order to shut down the vulnerabilities. Functions such as strcpy_s and strcat_s have been introduced as part of bounds-checking functions in C11.

These functions accept some extra arguments for the input buffers that restrict them from performing dangerous operations. As an example, the strcpy_s function has the following signature:

```
errno_t strcpy_s(char *restrict dest, rsize_t destsz, const char
*restrict src);
```

Code Box 12-3: Signature of the strcpy_s function

As you can see, the second argument is the length of the dest buffer. Using that, the function performs some runtime checks, such as ensuring that the src string is shorter than or at the same size of the dest buffer in order to prevent writing to unallocated memory.

No-return functions

A function call can end either by using the return keyword or by reaching the end of the function's block. There are also situations in which a function call never ends, and this is usually done intentionally. Look at the following code example contained in *Code Box 12-4*:

```
void main_loop() {
  while (1) {
    ...
  }
}
```

```
int main(int argc, char** argv) {
  ...
  main_loop();
  return 0;
}
```

Code Box 12-4: Example of a function that never returns

As you can see, the function `main_loop` performs the main task of the program, and if we return from the function, the program could be considered as finished. In these exceptional cases, the compiler can perform some more optimizations, but somehow, it needs to know that the function `main_loop` never returns.

In C11, you have the ability to mark a function as a *no-return* function. The `_Noreturn` keyword from the `stdnoreturn.h` header file can be used to specify that a function never exits. So, the code in *Code Box 12-4* can be changed for C11 to look like this:

```
_Noreturn void main_loop() {
  while (true) {
    ...
  }
}
```

Code Box 12-5: Using the _Noreturn keyword to mark main_loop as a never-ending function

There are other functions, such as `exit`, `quick_exit` (added recently as part of C11 for quick termination of the program), and `abort`, that are considered to be no-return functions. In addition, knowing about no-return functions allows the compiler to recognize function calls that unintentionally won't return and produce proper warnings because they could be a sign of a logical bug. Note that if a function marked as `_Noreturn` returns, then this would be an *undefined behavior* and it is highly discouraged.

Type generic macros

In C11, a new keyword has been introduced: `_Generic`. It can be used to write macros that are type-aware at compile time. In other words, you can write macros that can change their value based on the type of their arguments. This is usually called *generic selection*. Look at the following code example in *Code Box 12-6*:

```
#include <stdio.h>
```

```
#define abs(x) _Generic((x), \
                        int: absi, \
                        double: absd)(x)
int absi(int a) {
  return a > 0 ? a : -a;
}

double absd(double a) {
  return a > 0 ? a : -a;
}

int main(int argc, char** argv) {
  printf("abs(-2): %d\n", abs(-2));
  printf("abs(2.5): %f\n", abs(2.5));;
  return 0;
}
```

Code Box 12-6: Example of a generic macro

As you can see in the macro definition, we have used different expressions based on the type of the argument x. We use `absi` if it is an integer value, and `absd` if it is a double value. This feature is not new to C11, and you can find it in older C compilers, but it wasn't part of the C standard. As of C11, it is now standard, and you can use this syntax to write type-aware macros.

Unicode

One of the greatest features that has been added to the C11 standard is support for Unicode through UTF-8, UTF-16, and UTF-32 encodings. C was missing this feature for a long time, and C programmers had to use third-party libraries such as **IBM International Components for Unicode (ICU)** to fulfill their needs.

Before C11, we only had `char` and `unsigned char` types, which were 8-bit variables used to store ASCII and Extended ASCII characters. By creating arrays of these ASCII characters, we could create ASCII strings.

Note:
ASCII standard has 128 characters which can be stored in 7 bits. Extended ASCII is an extension to ASCII which adds another 128 characters to make them together 256 characters. Then, an 8-bit or one-byte variable is enough to store all of them. In the upcoming text, we will only use the term ASCII, and by that we refer to both ASCII standard and Extended ASCII.

Note that support for ASCII characters and strings is fundamental, and it will never be removed from C. Thus, we can be confident that we will always have ASCII support in C. From C11, they have added support for new characters, and therefore new strings that use a different number of bytes, not just one byte, for each character.

To explain this further, in ASCII, we have one byte for each character. Therefore, the bytes and characters can be used interchangeably, but this is *not* true in general. Different encodings define new ways to store a wider range of characters in multiple bytes.

In ASCII, altogether we have 256 characters. Therefore, a single one-byte (8-bit) character is enough to store all of them. If we are going to have more than 256 characters, however, we must use more than one byte to store their numerical values after 255. Characters that need more than one byte to store their values are usually called *wide characters*. By this definition, ASCII characters are not considered as wide characters.

The Unicode standard introduced various methods of using more than one byte to encode all characters in ASCII, Extended ASCII, and wide characters. These methods are called *encodings*. Through Unicode, there are three well-known encodings: UTF-8, UTF-16, and UTF-32. UTF-8 uses the first byte for storing the first half of the ASCII characters, and the next bytes, usually up to 4 bytes, for the other half of ASCII characters together with all other wide characters. Hence, UTF-8 is considered as a variable-sized encoding. It uses certain bits in the first byte of the character to denote the number of actual bytes that should be read to retrieve the character fully. UTF-8 is considered a superset of ASCII because for ASCII characters (not Extended ASCII characters) the representation is the same.

Like UTF-8, UTF-16 uses one or two *words* (each word has 16 bits within) for storing all characters; hence it is also a variable-sized encoding. UTF-32 uses exactly 4 bytes for storing the values of all characters; therefore, it is a fixed-sized encoding. UTF-8, and after that, UTF-16, are suitable for the applications in which a smaller number of bytes should be used for more frequent characters.

UTF-32 uses a fixed number of bytes even for ASCII characters. So, it consumes more memory space to store strings using this encoding compared to others; but it requires less computation power when using UTF-32 characters. UTF-8 and UTF-16 can be considered as compressed encodings, but they need more computation to return the actual value of a character.

Note:
More information about UTF-8, UTF-16, and UTF-32 strings and how to decode them can be found on Wikipedia or other sources like:

https://unicodebook.readthedocs.io/unicode_encodings.html

https://javarevisited.blogspot.com/2015/02/difference-between-utf-8-utf-16-and-utf.html

In C11 we have support for all the above Unicode encodings. Look at the following example, *example 12.3*. It defines various ASCII, UTF-8, UTF-16, and UTF-32 strings, and counts the number of actual bytes used to store them and the number of characters observed within them. We present the code in multiple steps in order to give additional comments on the code. The following code box demonstrates the inclusions and declarations required:

```
#include <stdlib.h>
#include <stdio.h>
#include <string.h>

#ifdef __APPLE__

#include <stdint.h>

typedef uint16_t char16_t;
typedef uint32_t char32_t;

#else
#include <uchar.h> // Needed for char16_t and char32_t
#endif
```

Code Box 12-7 [ExtremeC_examples_chapter12_3.c]: Inclusions and declarations required for example 12.3 to get built

The preceding lines are the `include` statements for *example 12.3*. As you can see, in macOS we do not have the `uchar.h` header and we have to define new types for the `char16_t` and `char32_t` types. The whole functionality of Unicode strings is supported, however. On Linux, we don't have any issues with Unicode support in C11.

The next part of the code demonstrates the functions used for counting the number of bytes and characters in various kinds of Unicode strings. Note that no utility function is offered by C11 to operate on Unicode strings, therefore we have to write a new `strlen` for them. In fact, our versions of `strlen` functions do more just than returning the number of characters; they return the number of consumed bytes as well. The implementation details won't be described, but it is strongly recommended to give them a read:

```
typedef struct {
  long num_chars;
  long num_bytes;
} unicode_len_t;

unicode_len_t strlen_ascii(char* str) {
  unicode_len_t res;
  res.num_chars = 0;
  res.num_bytes = 0;
  if (!str) {
    return res;
  }
  res.num_chars = strlen(str) + 1;
  res.num_bytes = strlen(str) + 1;
  return res;
}

unicode_len_t strlen_u8(char* str) {
  unicode_len_t res;
  res.num_chars = 0;
  res.num_bytes = 0;
  if (!str) {
    return res;
  }
  // Last null character
  res.num_chars = 1;
  res.num_bytes = 1;
  while (*str) {
    if ((*str | 0x7f) == 0x7f) { // 0x7f = 0b01111111
      res.num_chars++;
      res.num_bytes++;
      str++;
    } else if ((*str & 0xc0) == 0xc0) { // 0xc0 = 0b11000000
      res.num_chars++;
      res.num_bytes += 2;
      str += 2;
    } else if ((*str & 0xe0) == 0xe0) { // 0xe0 = 0b11100000
      res.num_chars++;
      res.num_bytes += 3;
```

```
            str += 3;
        } else if ((*str & 0xf0) == 0xf0) { // 0xf0 = 0b11110000
            res.num_chars++;
            res.num_bytes += 4;
            str += 4;
        } else {
            fprintf(stderr, "UTF-8 string is not valid!\n");
            exit(1);
        }
    }
    return res;
}

unicode_len_t strlen_u16(char16_t* str) {
    unicode_len_t res;
    res.num_chars = 0;
    res.num_bytes = 0;
    if (!str) {
        return res;
    }
    // Last null character
    res.num_chars = 1;
    res.num_bytes = 2;
    while (*str) {
        if (*str < 0xdc00 || *str > 0xdfff) {
            res.num_chars++;
            res.num_bytes += 2;
            str++;
        } else {
            res.num_chars++;
            res.num_bytes += 4;
            str += 2;
        }
    }
    return res;
}
unicode_len_t strlen_u32(char32_t* str) {
    unicode_len_t res;
    res.num_chars = 0;
    res.num_bytes = 0;
    if (!str) {
        return res;
    }
    // Last null character
    res.num_chars = 1;
    res.num_bytes = 4;
    while (*str) {
        res.num_chars++;
```

```
      res.num_bytes += 4;
      str++;
  }
  return res;
}
```

Code Box 12-8 [ExtremeC_examples_chapter12_3.c]: The definitions of the functions used in example 12.3

The last part is the `main` function. It declares some different strings in English, Persian, and some alien language to evaluate the preceding functions:

```
int main(int argc, char** argv) {

  char ascii_string[32] = "Hello World!";

  char utf8_string[32] = u8"Hello World!";
  char utf8_string_2[32] = u8"درود دنیا!";

  char16_t utf16_string[32] = u"Hello World!";
  char16_t utf16_string_2[32] = u"درود دنیا!";
  char16_t utf16_string_3[32] = u"इह!";

  char32_t utf32_string[32] = U"Hello World!";
  char32_t utf32_string_2[32] = U"درود دنیا!";
  char32_t utf32_string_3[32] = U"इह!";

  unicode_len_t len = strlen_ascii(ascii_string);
  printf("Length of ASCII string:\t\t\t %ld chars, %ld bytes\n\n",
      len.num_chars, len.num_bytes);

  len = strlen_u8(utf8_string);
  printf("Length of UTF-8 English string:\t\t %ld chars, %ld
bytes\n",
      len.num_chars, len.num_bytes);
  len = strlen_u16(utf16_string);
  printf("Length of UTF-16 english string:\t %ld chars, %ld
bytes\n",
      len.num_chars, len.num_bytes);
  len = strlen_u32(utf32_string);
  printf("Length of UTF-32 english string:\t %ld chars, %ld bytes\
n\n",
      len.num_chars, len.num_bytes);

  len = strlen_u8(utf8_string_2);
  printf("Length of UTF-8 Persian string:\t\t %ld chars, %ld
bytes\n",
```

```
        len.num_chars, len.num_bytes);
    len = strlen_u16(utf16_string_2);
    printf("Length of UTF-16 persian string:\t %ld chars, %ld
bytes\n",
        len.num_chars, len.num_bytes);
    len = strlen_u32(utf32_string_2);
    printf("Length of UTF-32 persian string:\t %ld chars, %ld bytes\
n\n",
        len.num_chars, len.num_bytes);

    len = strlen_u16(utf16_string_3);
    printf("Length of UTF-16 alien string:\t\t %ld chars, %ld
bytes\n",
        len.num_chars, len.num_bytes);
    len = strlen_u32(utf32_string_3);
    printf("Length of UTF-32 alien string:\t\t %ld chars, %ld
bytes\n",
        len.num_chars, len.num_bytes);

    return 0;
}
```

Code Box 12-9 [ExtremeC_examples_chapter12_3.c]: The main function of example 12.3

Now, we must compile the preceding example. Note that the example can only be compiled using a C11 compiler. You can try using older compilers and take a look at the resulting errors. The following commands compile and run the preceding program:

```
$ gcc ExtremeC_examples_chapter12_3.c -std=c11 -o ex12_3.out
$ ./ex12_3.out
Length of ASCII string:              13 chars, 13 bytes

Length of UTF-8 english string:      13 chars, 13 bytes
Length of UTF-16 english string:     13 chars, 26 bytes
Length of UTF-32 english string:     13 chars, 52 bytes

Length of UTF-8 persian string:      11 chars, 19 bytes
Length of UTF-16 persian string:     11 chars, 22 bytes
Length of UTF-32 persian string:     11 chars, 44 bytes

Length of UTF-16 alien string:       5 chars, 14 bytes
```

```
Length of UTF-32 alien string:      5 chars, 20 bytes
$
```

Shell Box 12-3: Compiling and running example 12.3

As you can see, the same string with the same number of characters uses a different number of bytes to encode and store the same value. UTF-8 uses the least number of bytes, especially when a large number of characters in a text are ASCII characters, simply because most of the characters will use only one byte.

As we go through the characters that are more distinct from the Latin characters, such as characters in Asian languages, UTF-16 has a better balance between the number of characters and the number of used bytes, because most of the characters will use up to two bytes.

UTF-32 is rarely used, but it can be used in systems where having a fixed-length *code print* for characters is useful; for example, if the system suffers from low computational power or is benefiting from some parallel processing pipelines. Therefore, UTF-32 characters can be used as keys in mappings from the characters to any kind of data. In other words, they can be used to build up some indexes to look up data very quickly.

Anonymous structures and anonymous unions

Anonymous structures and anonymous unions are type definitions without names, and they are usually used in other types as a nested type. It is easier to explain them with an example. Here, you can see a type that has both an anonymous structure and an anonymous union in one place, displayed in *Code Box 12-10*:

```
typedef struct {
  union {
    struct {
      int x;
      int y;
    };
    int data[2];
  };
} point_t;
```

Code Box 12-10: Example of an anonymous structure together with an anonymous union

The preceding type uses the same memory for the anonymous structure and the byte array field `data`. The following code box shows how it can be used in a real example:

```c
#include <stdio.h>

typedef struct {
  union {
    struct {
      int x;
      int y;
    };
    int data[2];
  };
} point_t;

int main(int argc, char** argv) {
  point_t p;
  p.x = 10;
  p.data[1] = -5;
  printf("Point (%d, %d) using an anonymous structure inside an
anonymous union.\n", p.x, p.y);
  printf("Point (%d, %d) using byte array inside an anonymous
union.\n",
      p.data[0], p.data[1]);
  return 0;
}
```

Code box 12-11 [ExtremeC_examples_chapter12_4.c]: The main function using an anonymous structure together with an anonymous union

In this example we are creating an anonymous union that has an anonymous structure within. Therefore, the same memory region is used to store an instance of the anonymous structure and the two-element integer array. Next, you can see the output of the preceding program:

```
$ gcc ExtremeC_examples_chapter12_4.c -std=c11 -o ex12_4.out
$ ./ex12_4.out
Point (10, -5) using anonymous structure.
Point (10, -5) using anonymous byte array.
$
```

Shell Box 12-4: Compiling and running example 12.4

As you can see, any changes to the two-element integer array can be seen in the structure variable, and vice versa.

Multithreading

Multithreading support has been available in C for a long time via POSIX threading functions, or the `pthreads` library. We have covered multithreading thoroughly in *Chapter 15*, *Thread Execution*, and *Chapter 16*, *Thread Synchronization*.

The POSIX threading library, as the name implies, is only available in POSIX-compliant systems such as Linux and other Unix-like systems. Therefore, if you are on a non-POSIX compliant operating system such as Microsoft Windows, you have to use the library provided by the operating system. As part of C11, a standard threading library is provided that can be used on all systems that are using standard C, regardless of whether it's POSIX-compliant or not. This is the biggest change we see in the C11 standard.

Unfortunately, C11 threading is not implemented for Linux and macOS. Therefore, we cannot provide working examples at the time of writing.

A bit about C18

As we've mentioned in the earlier sections, the C18 standard contains all the fixes that were made in C11, and no new feature has been introduced as part of it. As said before, the following link takes you to a page on which you can see the issues created and being tracked for C11 and the discussions around them: http://www.open-std.org/jtc1/sc22/wg14/www/docs/n2244.htm.

Summary

In this chapter, we went through C11, C18, and the most recent C standards, and we explored C11's various new features. Unicode support, anonymous structures and unions, and the new standard threading library (despite the fact that it is not available in recent compilers and platforms to date) are among the most important features that have been introduced in modern C. We will look forward to seeing new versions of the C standard in the future.

In the next chapter, we begin to talk about concurrency and the theory behind concurrent systems. This will begin a long journey through six chapters in which we'll cover multithreading and multi-processing in order to fulfil our purpose to be able to write concurrent systems.

Chapter 13

Concurrency

Over the course of the next two chapters we are going to talk about *concurrency* and the theoretical background that is required for developing concurrent programs, not only in C, but necessarily in other languages as well. As such, these two chapters won't contain any C code and instead use pseudo-code to represent concurrent systems and their intrinsic properties.

The topic of concurrency, due to its length, has been split into two chapters. In this chapter we will be looking at the basic concepts regarding concurrency itself, before moving to *Chapter 14, Synchronization*, where we will discuss concurrency-related issues and the *synchronization* mechanisms used in concurrent programs to resolve said issues. The collective end goal of these two chapters is to provide you with enough theoretical knowledge to proceed with the multithreading and multi-processing topics discussed in upcoming chapters.

The background knowledge we build in this chapter will also be useful when working with the *POSIX threading library*, which we use throughout this book.

In this first chapter on concurrency, we will be working on understanding:

- How parallel systems differ from concurrent systems
- When we need concurrency
- What a *task scheduler* is, and what the widely used scheduling algorithms are
- How a concurrent program is run and what the interleavings are
- What a shared state is and how various tasks can access it

Let's start our look into concurrency by giving an introduction to the concept, and understanding broadly what it means for us.

Introducing concurrency

Concurrency simply means having multiple pieces of logic within a program being executed simultaneously. Modern software systems are often concurrent, as programs need to run various pieces of logic at the same time. As such, concurrency is something that every program today is using to a certain extent.

We can say that concurrency is a powerful tool that lets you write programs that can manage different tasks at the same time, and the support for it usually lies in the kernel, which is at the heart of the operating system.

There are numerous examples in which an ordinary program manages multiple jobs simultaneously. For example, you can surf the web while downloading files. In this case, tasks are being executed in the context of the browser process concurrently. Another notable example is in a *video streaming* scenario, such as when you are watching a video on YouTube. The video player might be in the middle of downloading future chunks of the video while you are still watching previously downloaded chunks.

Even simple word-processing software has several concurrent tasks running in the background. As I write this chapter on Microsoft Word, a spell checker and a formatter are running in the background. If you were to be reading this on the Kindle application on an iPad, what programs do you think might be running concurrently as part of the Kindle program?

Having multiple programs being run at the same time sounds amazing, but as with most technology, concurrency brings along with it several headaches in addition to its benefits. Indeed, concurrency brings some of the most painful headaches in the history of computer science! These "headaches," which we will address later on, can remain hidden for a long time, even for months after a release, and they are usually hard to find, reproduce, and resolve.

We started this section describing concurrency as having tasks being executed at the same time, or concurrently. This description implies that the tasks are being run in parallel, but that's not strictly true. Such a description is too simple, as well as inaccurate, because *being concurrent is different from being parallel*, and we have not yet explained the differences between the two. Two concurrent programs are different from two parallel programs, and one of our goals in this chapter is to shine a light on these differences and give some definitions used by the official literature in this field.

In the following sections, we are going to explain some basic concurrency-related concepts such as *tasks*, *scheduling*, *interleavings*, *state*, and *shared state*, which are some of the terms you will come across frequently in this book. It's worth pointing out that most of these concepts are abstract and can be applied to any concurrent system, not just in C.

To understand the difference between parallel and concurrent, we are going to briefly touch upon parallel systems.

Note that in this chapter we stick to simple definitions. Our sole purpose is to give you a basic idea of how concurrent systems work, as going beyond this would be outside of the scope of this book on C.

Parallelism

Parallelism simply means having two tasks run at the same time, or *in parallel*. The phrase "in parallel" is the key element that differentiates parallelism from concurrency. Why is this? Because parallel implies that two things are happening simultaneously. This is not the case in a concurrent system; in concurrent systems, you need to pause one task in order to let another continue execution. Note that this definition can be too simple and incomplete regarding the modern concurrent systems, but it is sufficient for us to give you a basic idea.

We meet parallelism regularly in our daily lives. When you and your friend are doing two separate tasks simultaneously, those tasks are being done in parallel. To have a number of tasks in parallel, we need separate and isolated *processing units*, each of which is assigned to a certain task. For instance, in a computer system, each *CPU core* is a processor unit that can handle one task at a time.

For a minute, look at yourself as the sole reader of this book. You cannot read two books in parallel; you would have to pause in reading one of them in order to read the other. Yet, if you added your friend into the mix, then it's possible for two books to be read in parallel.

What would happen if you had a third book that needed to be read? Since neither of you can read two books in parallel, then one of you would need to pause in reading your book to continue with the third one. This simply means that either you or your friend need to divide your time properly in order to read all three books.

In a computer system, there must be at least two separate and independent processing units in order to have two parallel tasks being executed on that system. Modern CPUs have a number of *cores* inside, and those cores are the actual processing units. For example, a 4-core CPU has 4 processing units, and therefore can support 4 parallel tasks being run simultaneously. For simplicity, in this chapter we will suppose that our imaginary CPU has only one core inside and therefore cannot perform parallel tasks. There will be some discussion regarding multi-core CPUs later, within relevant sections.

Suppose that you get two laptops with our imaginary CPU inside, with one playing a piece of music, and the other one finding the solution to a differential equation. Both of them are functioning in parallel, but if you want them to do both on the same laptop using only one CPU, and with one core, then it *cannot* be parallel and it is in fact concurrent.

Parallelism is about tasks that can be parallelized. This means that the actual algorithm can be divided and run on multiple processor units. But most of the algorithms we write, as of today, are *sequential* and not parallel in nature. Even in multithreading, each thread has a number of sequential instructions that cannot be broken into some parallel *execution flows*.

In other words, a sequential algorithm cannot be easily broken into some parallel flows of execution automatically by the operating system, and this should be done by a programmer. Therefore, with having a multi-core CPU, you still need to assign each of the execution flows to a certain CPU core, and in that core, if you have more than one flow assigned, you cannot have both of them running in parallel, and you immediately observe a concurrent behavior.

In short, of course having two flows, each assigned to a different core, can end up in two parallel flows but assigning them to just one core, would result in two concurrent flows. In multi-core CPUs we effectively observe a mixed behavior, both parallelism between the cores, and concurrency on the same core.

Despite its simple meaning and numerous everyday examples, parallelism is a complex and tough topic in computer architecture. In fact, it is a separate academic subject from concurrency, with its own theories, books, and literature. Being able to have an operating system that can break a sequential algorithm into some parallel execution flows is an open field of research and the current operating systems cannot do that.

As stated, the purpose of this chapter is not to go into any depth in parallelism, but only to provide an initial definition for the concept. Since further depth of discussion about parallelism is beyond the scope of this book, let's begin with the concept of concurrency.

Firstly, we'll talk about concurrent systems and what it really means in comparison to parallelism.

Concurrency

You may have heard about *multitasking* – well, concurrency has the same idea. If your system is managing multiple tasks at the same time, you need to understand that it does not necessarily mean that the tasks are being run in parallel. Instead, there can be a *task scheduler* in the middle; this simply switches very quickly between the different tasks and performs a tiny bit of each of them in a fairly small amount of time.

This certainly happens when you have just one processor unit. For the rest of our discussion in this section, we assume that we are operating on just one processor unit.

If a task scheduler is sufficiently *fast* and *fair*, you won't notice the *switching* between the tasks, and they'll appear to be running in parallel from your perspective. That's the magic of concurrency, and the very reason why it is being used in most of the widely known operating systems, including Linux, macOS, and Microsoft Windows.

Concurrency could be seen as a simulation of performing tasks in parallel, using a single processor unit. In fact, the whole idea can be referred to as a form of artificial parallelism. For old systems that only had a single CPU, with only one core, it was a huge advance when people were able to use that single core in a multitasking fashion.

As a side note, *Multics* was one of the first operating systems designed to multitask and manage simultaneous processes. You'll remember that in *Chapter 10, Unix – History and Architecture*, Unix was built based on the ideas gained from the Multics project.

As we've explained previously, almost all operating systems can perform concurrent tasks through multitasking, especially POSIX-compliant operating systems, since the ability is clearly exposed in the POSIX standard.

Task scheduler unit

As we've said before, all multitasking operating systems are required to have a *task scheduler* unit, or simply a *scheduler unit*, in their kernel. In this section, we're going to see how this unit works and how it contributes to the seamless execution of some concurrent tasks.

Some facts regarding the task scheduler unit are listed as follows:

- The scheduler has a *queue* for tasks waiting to be executed. *Tasks* or *jobs* are simply the pieces of work that should be performed in separate flows of execution.

- This queue is usually *prioritized*, with the high-priority tasks being chosen to start first.

- The processor unit is managed and shared among all the tasks by the task scheduler. When the processor unit is free (no task is using it), the task scheduler must select another task from its queue before letting it use the processor unit. When the task is finished, it releases the processor unit and make it available again, then the task scheduler selects another task. This goes on in a continuous loop. This is called *task scheduling*, and it is the sole responsibility of the task scheduler to do this.

- There are many *scheduling algorithms* that the task scheduler can operate, but all of them should address specific requirements. For example, all of them should be *fair*, and no task should be *starved* in the queue as a result of not being chosen for a prolonged period of time.

- Based on a chosen *scheduling strategy*, the scheduler should either dedicate a specific *time slice* or *time quantum* to the task in order to use the processor unit, or alternatively, the scheduler must wait for the task to release the processor unit.

- If the scheduling strategy is *preemptive*, the scheduler should be able to forcefully take back the CPU core from the running task in order to give it to the next task. This is called *preemptive scheduling*. There is also another scheme in which the task releases the CPU voluntarily, which is called *cooperative scheduling*.

- Preemptive scheduling algorithms try to share *time slices* evenly and fairly between different tasks. Prioritized tasks may get chosen more frequently, or they may even get longer time slices depending upon the implementation of the scheduler.

A task is a general abstract concept, used to refer to any piece of work that should be done in a concurrent system, not necessarily a computer system. We'll look at what exactly these non-computer systems are shortly. Likewise, CPUs are not the only type of resource that can be shared between tasks. Humans have been scheduling and prioritizing tasks for as long as we have existed, when we are faced with tasks that we cannot complete simultaneously. In the next few paragraphs, we will consider such a situation as a good example for understanding scheduling.

Let's suppose that we are at the beginning of the twentieth century and there is only one telephone booth in the street, and 10 people are waiting to use the telephone. In this case, these 10 people should follow a scheduling algorithm in order to share the booth fairly between themselves.

First of all, they need to stand in a queue. This is the most basic decision that enters the civilized mind in such a situation – to stand in the queue and wait for your turn. However, this alone is not enough; we also need some regulations to support this method. The first person, who is currently using the phone, can't talk as much as they might like to when there are nine other people waiting for the booth. The first person must leave the booth after a certain amount of time in order to allow the next person in the queue their turn.

In the rare case that they have not finished their conversation yet, the first person should stop using the phone after a certain amount of time, leave the booth, and go back to the end of the queue. They must then wait for their next turn so that they can continue their talk. This way, each of the 10 people will need to continue entering the booth, until they have completed their conversation.

This is just an example. We encounter examples of sharing resources between a number of consumers every day, and humans have invented many ways to share these resources fairly between themselves – to the extent that human nature allows! In the next section, we return to considering scheduling within the context of a computer system.

Processes and threads

Throughout this book, we are mainly interested in task scheduling within computer systems. In an operating system, tasks are either *processes* or *threads*. We'll explain them and their differences in the upcoming chapters, but for now, you should know that most operating systems treat both in basically the same way: as some tasks that need to be executed concurrently.

An operating system needs to use a task scheduler to share the CPU cores among the many tasks, be they processes or threads, that are willing to use the CPU for their execution. When a new process or a new thread is created, it enters the scheduler queue as a new task, and it waits to obtain a CPU core before it starts running.

In cases in which a *time-sharing* or *preemptive scheduler* is in place, if the task cannot finish its logic in a certain amount of time, then the CPU core will be taken back forcefully by the task scheduler and the task enters the queue again, just like in the telephone booth scenario.

In this case, the task should wait in the queue until it obtains the CPU core once more, and then it can continue running. If it cannot finish its logic in the second round, the same process continues until it is able to finish.

Every time a preemptive scheduler stops a process in the middle of running and puts another process into the running state, it is said that a *context switch* has occurred. The faster the context switches are, the more a user will feel as if the tasks are being run in parallel. Interestingly, most operating systems today use a preemptive scheduler, something that will be our main focus for the rest of this chapter.

 Note:
From now on, all schedulers are assumed to be preemptive. I will specify in instances where this is not the case.

When a task is running, it may experience hundreds or even thousands of context switches before being finished. However, context switches have a very bizarre and unique characteristic – they are not *predictable*. In other words, we are not able to predict when, or even at which instruction, a context switch is going to happen. Even in two remarkably close successive runs of a program on the same platform, the context switches will happen differently.

The importance of this, and the impact it has, cannot be overstated; context switches cannot be predicted! Shortly, through the given examples, you'll observe the consequences of this for yourself.

Context switches are highly unpredictable, to such an extent that the best way to deal with this uncertainty is to assume that the probability of having a context switch on a specific instruction is the same for all instructions. In other words, you should expect that all instructions are subject to experiencing a context switch in any given run. What this means, simply, is that you may have gaps between the execution of any two adjacent instructions.

With that being said, let's now move on and take a look at the only certainties that do exist in a concurrent environment.

Happens-before constraint

We established in the previous section that context switches are not predictable; there is uncertainty about the time at which they are likely to occur in our programs. Despite that, there is certainty about the instructions that are being executed concurrently.

Let's continue with a simple example. To start with, we're going to work on the basis that we've got a task like the one you see next in *Code Box 13-1*, which has five instructions. Note that these instructions are abstract, and they don't represent any real instructions like C or machine instructions:

```
Task P {
    1. num = 5
    2. num++
    3. num = num - 2
    4. x = 10
    5. num = num + x
}
```

Code Box 13-1: A simple task with 5 instructions

As you can see, the instructions are ordered, which means that they *must* be executed in that specified order in order to satisfy the purpose of the task. We are certain about this. In technical terms, we say that we have a *happens-before constraint* between every two adjacent instructions. The instruction num++ must happen before num = num - 2 and this constraint must be kept satisfied no matter how the context switches are happening.

Note that we still have uncertainty about when the context switches are going to happen; it's key to remember that they can happen anywhere between the instructions.

Here, we are going to present two possible executions of the preceding task, with different context switches:

```
Run 1:
    1. num = 5
    2. num++
>>>>> Context Switch <<<<<
    3. num = num - 2
    4. x = 10
>>>>> Context Switch <<<<<
    5. num = num + x
```

Code Box 13-2: One possible run of the above task together with the context switches

And for the second run, it is executed as the following:

```
Run 2:
    num = 5
    >> Context Switch <<
    num++
    num = num - 2
    >> Context Switch <<
    x = 10
    >> Context Switch <<
    num = num + x
```

Code Box 13-3: Another possible run together with the context switches

As you can see in *Code Box 13-2*, the number of context switches and the places they occur can both change in each run. Yet, as we said before, there are certain happens-before constraints that should be followed.

This is the reason we can have an overall deterministic behavior for a specific task. No matter how context switches happen in different runs, the *overall state* of a task remains the same. By the overall state of a task, we mean the set of variables and their corresponding values after the execution of the last instruction in the task. For example, for the preceding task, we always have the final state, including the num variables with a value of 14, and the variable x with a value of 10, regardless of the context switches.

By knowing that the overall state of a single task does not change in different runs, we might be tempted to conclude that due to having to follow the order of execution and the happens-before constraints, concurrency cannot affect the overall state of a task. Yet, we should be careful about this conclusion.

Let's assume that we have a system of concurrent tasks, all having read/write permissions over a *shared resource*, say a variable. If all the tasks only read the shared variable and none of them are going to write to it (change its value), we can say that no matter how context switches are happening, and no matter how many times you run the tasks, we always get the same results. Note that this is also true about a system of concurrent tasks that have no shared variable at all.

Yet, if just one of the tasks is going to write to the shared variable, then the context switches imposed by the task scheduler unit will affect the overall state of all tasks. This means that it can be different from one run to another! Consequently, a proper control mechanism should be employed to avoid any unwanted results. This is all due to the fact that context switches cannot be predicted, and the tasks' *intermediate states* can vary from one run to another. An intermediate state, as opposed to overall state, is a set of variables together with their values at a certain instruction. Every task has only one overall state that is determined when it is finished, but it has numerous intermediate states that correspond to the variables and their values after executing a certain instruction.

In summary, when you have a concurrent system containing several tasks with a shared resource that can be written to by any of those tasks, then different runs of the system will yield different results. Hence, proper *synchronization* methods should be used in order to cancel the effect of context switches and obtain the same deterministic results in various runs.

We now have some of the basic concepts of concurrency, which is the dominant topic of this chapter. The concepts explained in this section are fundamental to our understanding of many topics, and you will hear them again and again in future sections and chapters of this book.

You'll remember that we also said concurrency could be problematic and in turn, it can make things more complicated for us. So, you may be asking, when do we need it? In the next section of this chapter, we'll answer that question.

When to use concurrency

Based on our explanations given so far, it seems that having only one task is less problematic than having multiple tasks do the same thing concurrently. This is quite right; if you can write a program that runs acceptably without introducing concurrency, it is highly recommended that you do so. There are some general patterns we can use to know when we have to use concurrency.

In this section, we are going to walk through what these general patterns are, and how they lead us to split a program into concurrent flows.

A program, regardless of the programming language used, is simply a set of instructions that should be executed in sequence. In other words, a given instruction won't be executed until the preceding instruction has been executed. We call this concept a *sequential execution*. It doesn't matter how long the current instruction takes to finish; the next instruction must wait until the current one has been completed. It is usually said that the current instruction is *blocking* the next instruction; this is sometimes described as the current instruction being a *blocking instruction*.

In every program, all of the instructions are blocking, and the execution flow is sequential in each flow of execution. We can only say a program is running quickly if each instruction blocks the following instruction for a relatively short time in terms of a few milliseconds. Yet, what happens if a blocking instruction takes too much time (for example 2 seconds or 2000 milliseconds), or the time that it takes cannot be determined? These are two patterns that tell us we need to have a concurrent program.

To elaborate further, every blocking instruction consumes an amount of time when trying to get completed. For us, the best scenario is that a given instruction takes a relatively short time to complete and after that, the next instruction can be executed immediately. However, we are not always so fortunate.

There are certain scenarios where we cannot determine the time that a blocking instruction takes to complete. This usually happens when a blocking instruction is waiting either for a certain event to occur, or for some data to become available.

Let's continue with an example. Suppose that we have a server program that is serving a number of client programs. There is an instruction in the server program that waits for a client program to get connected. From the server program's point of view, no one can say for sure when a new client is about to connect. Therefore, the next instruction cannot be executed on the server side because we don't know when we will be done with the current one. It depends entirely on the time at which a new client tries to connect.

A simpler example is when you read a string from the user. From the program's point of view, no one can say for sure when the user will enter their input; hence, future instructions cannot be executed. This is the *first pattern* that leads to a concurrent system of tasks.

The first pattern for concurrency then, is when you have an instruction that can block the flow of execution for an indefinite amount of time. At this point you should split the existing flow into two separate flows or tasks. You would do this if you need to have the later instructions being executed, and you cannot wait for the current instruction to complete first. More importantly for this scenario, we assume that the later instructions are not dependent on the result of the current instructions being completed.

By splitting our preceding flow into two concurrent tasks, while one of the tasks is waiting for the blocking instruction to complete, the other task can continue and execute those instructions that were blocked in the preceding non-concurrent setup.

The following example that we're going to focus on in this section shows how the first pattern can result in a system of concurrent tasks. We will be using pseudo-code to represent the instructions in each task.

Note:
No prior knowledge of computer networks is needed to understand the upcoming example.

The example we're going to focus on is about a server program that has three objectives:

- It calculates the sum of two numbers read from a client and returns the result back to the client.

- It writes the number of served clients to a file regularly, regardless of whether any client is being served or not.

- It must also be able to serve multiple clients at once.

Before talking about the final concurrent system that satisfies preceding objectives, let's first suppose that in this example we are going to use only one task (or flow) and then we are going to show that a single task cannot accomplish the preceding objectives. You can see the pseudo-code for the server program, in a single-task setup, in *Code Box 13-4*:

```
Calculator Server {
    Task T1 {
        1. N = 0
        2. Prepare Server
        3. Do Forever {
        4.      Wait for a client C
        5.      N = N + 1
        6.      Read the first number from C and store it in X
        7.      Read the second number from C and store it in Y
        8.      Z = X + Y
        9.      Write Z to C
       10.      Close the connection to C
       11.      Write N to file
            }
        }
    }
```

Code Box 13-4: A server program operating using a single task

As you can see, our single flow waits for a client on the network to get connected. It then reads two numbers from the client, then calculates their sum and returns it to the client. Finally, it closes the client connection and writes the number of served clients to a file before continuing to wait for the next client to join in. Shortly, we'll show that the preceding code cannot satisfy our aforementioned objectives.

This pseudo-code contains only one task, T1. It has 12 lines of instructions, and as we've said before, they are executed sequentially, and all the instructions are blocking. So, what exactly is this code showing us? Let's walk through it:

- The first instruction, N = 0, is simple and finishes very quickly.

- The second instruction, Prepare Server, is expected to finish in a reasonable time so that it won't block the execution of the server program.

- The third instruction is just starting the main loop and it should finish quickly as we proceed to go inside the loop.

- The fourth command, Wait for a client C, is a blocking instruction with an unknown completion time. Therefore, commands 5, 6, and the rest won't be executed. Hence, it seems that they must wait for a new client to join in, and only after that, these instructions can be executed.

As we said before, having instructions 5 to 10 wait for a new client is must. In other words, those instructions are dependent on the output of instruction 4 and they cannot be executed without having a client accepted. However, instruction 11, Write N to file, needs to be executed regardless of having a client or not. This is dictated by the second objective that we've defined for this example. By the preceding configuration, we write N to file only if we have a client, despite this being against our initial requirement, that is, we write N to file *regardless* of whether we have a client or not.

The preceding code has another problem in its flow of instructions; both instructions 6 and 7 can potentially block the flow of execution. These instructions wait for the client to enter two numbers, and since this is up to the client we cannot predict exactly when these instructions are going to finish. This prevents the program from continuing its execution.

More than that, these instructions potentially block the program from accepting new clients. This is because the flow of executions won't reach the command 4 again, if commands 6 and 7 are going to take a long time to complete. Therefore, the server program cannot serve multiple clients at once, which is again not in accordance with our defined objectives.

To resolve the aforementioned issues, we need to break our single task into three concurrent tasks that together will satisfy our requirements for the server program.

In the following pseudo-code in *Code Box 13-5*, you will find three flows of execution, T1, T2, and T3, that satisfy our defined objectives based on a concurrent solution:

```
Calculator Server {
    Shared Variable: N

    Task T1 {
        1. N = 0
        2. Prepare Server
        3. Spawn task T2
        4. Do Forever {
        5.      Write N to file
        6.      Wait for 30 seconds
           }
    }
    Task T2 {
        1. Do Forever {
        2.      Wait for a client C
        3.      N = N + 1
        4.      Spawn task T3 for C
           }
    }

    Task T3 {
        1. Read first number from C and store it in X
        2. Read first number from C and store it in Y
        3. Z = X + Y
        4. Write Z to C
        5. Close the connection to C
    }
}
```

Code Box 13-5: A server program operating using three concurrent tasks

The program starts by executing task T1. T1 is said to be the main task of the program because it is the first task that is going to be executed. Take note that each program has at least one task and that all other tasks are initiated by this task, either directly or indirectly.

In the preceding code box, we have two other tasks that are spawned by the main task, T1. There is also a shared variable, N, which stores the number of served clients and can be accessed (read or written) by all the tasks.

The program starts with the first instruction in task T1; through this, it initializes the variable N to zero. Then the second instruction prepares the server. As part of this instruction, some preliminary steps should be taken in order for the server program to be able to accept the incoming connections. Note that so far there hasn't been any other concurrent task running next to task T1.

The third instruction in task T1 creates a new *instance* of task T2. The creation of a new task is usually fast and takes no time. Therefore, task T1 enters the infinite loop immediately after the creation of task T2, where it continues to write the value of the shared variable N to a file every 30 seconds. This was our first objective defined for the server program that has now been satisfied. Based on that, without having any interruption or blockage from other instructions, task T1 writes the value of N to a file regularly, until the program finishes.

Let's talk about the spawned task. The sole responsibility of task T2 is to accept the incoming clients as soon as they send the connection request. It's also worth remembering that all the instructions in task T2 are run inside an infinite loop. The second command in task T2 waits for a new client. Here, it blocks other instructions in task T2 from executing, but this is only applied to the instructions in task T2. Note that if we had spawned two instances of task T2 instead of one, having instructions blocked in one of them would not block the instructions in the other instance.

Other concurrent tasks, in this case only T1, continue to execute their instructions without any blockage. This is what concurrency enables; while some tasks are blocked for a certain event, other tasks can continue their work without any interruption. As we said before, this has an important design principle at its core: *Whenever you have a blocking operation where either its finishing time is unknown, or it takes a long time to complete, then you should break the task into two concurrent tasks.*

Now, suppose that a new client joins. We've already seen in *Code Box 13-4*, in the non-concurrent version of the server program, that the read operations could block the acceptance of new clients. Based on the design principle that we pointed out just now, since the read instructions are blocking, we need to break the logic into two concurrent tasks, which is why we have introduced task T3.

Whenever a new client joins, task T2 spawns a new instance of task T3 in order to communicate with the newly joined client. This was done by instruction 4 in task T2, which, to remind you, was the following command:

```
4.      Spawn task T3 for C
```

Code Box 13-6: Instruction 4 in task T2

It's important to note that before spawning a new task, task T2 increments the value of the shared variable N as an indication of having a new client served. Again, a spawn instruction is fairly quick and doesn't block the acceptance of new clients.

In task T2, when instruction 4 is finished, the loop continues, and it goes back to instruction 2, which waits for another client to join. Note that based on the pseudo-code that we have, while we have only one instance of task T1 and one instance of task T2, we can have multiple instances of T3 for every client.

The sole responsibility of task T3 is to communicate to the client and read the input numbers. It then continues by calculating the sum and sending it back to the client. As pointed out before, the blocking instructions inside task T3 cannot block the execution of other tasks, and its blocking behavior is limited to the same instance of T3. Even the blocking instructions in a specific instance of T3 cannot block the instructions in another instance of T3. This way, the server program can satisfy all of our desired objectives in a concurrent way.

So, the next question might be, when do the tasks finish? We know that generally, when all the instructions within a task are executed, the task is finished. That being said, when we have an infinite loop wrapping all instructions inside a task, the task won't finish, and its lifetime is dependent on its *parent task* that has spawned it. We will discuss this specifically regarding processes and threads in future chapters. For the sake of our example, in our preceding concurrent program the parent task of all instances of T3 is the only instance of task T2. As you can see, a specific instance of task T3 finishes either when it closes the connection to the client after passing two blocking read instructions or when the only instance of task T2 is finished.

In a rare but possible scenario, if all read operations take too much time to complete (and this can be either intentional or accidental), and the number of incoming clients increases rapidly, then there should be a moment where we have too many instances of task T3 running and all of them are waiting for their clients to provide their input numbers. This situation would result in consuming a considerable amount of resources. Then, after some time, by having more and more incoming connections, either the server program would be terminated by the operating system, or it simply cannot serve any more clients.

Whatever happens in the preceding case, the server program ceases to serve the clients. When this occurs, it's called a **denial of service (DoS)**. Systems with concurrent tasks should be designed in such a way to overcome these extreme situations that stop them from serving clients in a reasonable fashion.

Note:
When under a DoS attack, congestion of resources on a server machine occurs in order to bring it down and make it non-responsive. DoS attacks belong to a group of network attacks that try to block a certain service in order to make it unavailable to its clients. They cover a wide range of attacks, including *exploits*, with the intention of stopping a service. This can even include the *flooding* of a network in order to bring down the network infrastructure.

In the preceding example of the server program, we described a situation in which we had a blocking instruction whose completion time could not be determined, and this was the first pattern for the use of concurrency. There is another pattern that is similar to this, but slightly different.

If an instruction or a group of instructions take too much time to complete, then we can put them in a separate task and run the new task concurrent to the main task. This is different from the first pattern because, while we do have an estimate of the completion time, albeit not a very accurate one, we do know that it won't be soon.

The last thing to note about the preceding example, regarding the shared variable, N, is that one of the tasks, specifically the instance of task T2, could change its value. Based on our previous discussions in this chapter, this system of concurrent tasks is therefore prone to concurrency problems because of it having a shared variable that can be modified by one of the tasks.

It's important to note that the solution we proposed for the server program is far from perfect. In the next chapter, you'll be introduced to concurrency issues, and through it you will see that the preceding example suffers from a serious *data race* issue over the shared variable, N. As a result, proper control mechanisms should be employed to resolve the issues created by concurrency.

In the following and final section in this chapter, we are going to talk about the *states* that are shared between some concurrent tasks. We will also introduce the concept of *interleaving* and its important consequences for a concurrent system with a modifiable shared state.

Shared states

In the previous section, we talked about the patterns suggesting that we require a concurrent system of tasks. Before that, we also briefly explained how the uncertainty in the pattern of context switches during the execution of a number of concurrent tasks, together with having a modifiable shared state, can lead to non-determinism occurring in the overall states of all tasks. This section provides an example to demonstrate how this non-determinism can be problematic in a simple program.

In this section, we are going to continue our discussion and bring in *shared states* to see how they contribute to the non-determinism we talked about. As a programmer, the term *state* should remind you of a set of variables and their corresponding values at a specific time. Therefore, when we are talking about the *overall state* of a task, as we defined it in the first section, we are referring to the set of all existing non-shared variables, together with their corresponding values, at the exact moment when the last instruction of the task has been executed.

Similarly, an *intermediate state* of a task is the set of all existing non-shared variables, together with their values when the task has executed a certain instruction. Therefore, a task has a different intermediate state for each of its instructions, and the number of intermediate states is equal to the number of instructions. According to our definitions, the last intermediate state is the same as the overall state of the task.

A shared state is also a set of variables together with their corresponding values at a specific time which can be read or modified by a system of concurrent tasks. A shared state is not owned by a task (it is not local to a task), and it can be read or modified by any of the tasks running in the system, and of course at any time.

Generally, we are not interested in shared states that are read-only. They are usually safe to be read by many concurrent tasks, and they don't yield any problem. However, a shared state that is modifiable usually yields some serious problems if it is not protected carefully. Therefore, all the shared states covered by this section are considered to be modifiable by at least by one of the tasks.

Ask yourself this question: what can go wrong if a shared state is modified by one of the concurrent tasks in a system? To answer this, we start by giving an example of a system of two concurrent tasks accessing a single shared variable, which, in this case, is a simple integer variable.

Let's suppose that we have the following system as displayed in *Code Box 13-7*:

```
Concurrent System {

    Shared State {
        X : Integer = 0
    }

    Task P {
        A : Integer
            1. A = X
            2. A = A + 1
            3. X = A
            4. print X
    }

    Task Q {
        B : Integer
            1. B = X
            2. B = B + 2
            3. X = B
            4. print X
    }
}
```

Code Box 13-7: A system of two concurrent tasks with a modifiable shared state

Suppose that in the preceding system, tasks P and Q are not concurrently run. Therefore, they become executed sequentially. Suppose that the instructions in P are executed first, before Q. If that was the case, then the overall state of the whole system, regardless of the overall state of any individual task, would be the shared variable, X, with a value of 3.

If you run the system in reverse order, first the instructions in Q and then the instructions in P, you will get the same overall state. However, this is not usually the case and running two different tasks in a reversed order probably leads to a different overall state.

As you can see, running these tasks sequentially produces a deterministic result without worrying about context switches.

Now, suppose that they are run concurrently on the same CPU core. There are many possible scenarios for putting the instructions of P and Q into execution by considering various context switches occurring at various instructions.

The following is a possible scenario:

```
        Task P        |    Task Scheduler    |    Task Q
----------------------------------------------------------------
                      |    Context Switch    |
                      |                      |  B = X
                      |                      |  B = B + 2
                      |    Context Switch    |
     A = X            |                      |
                      |    Context Switch    |
                      |                      |  X = B
                      |    Context Switch    |
     A = A + 1        |                      |
     X = A            |                      |
                      |    Context Switch    |
                      |                      |  print X
                      |    Context Switch    |
     print X          |                      |
                      |    Context Switch    |
```

Code Box 13-8: A possible interleaving of tasks P and Q when run concurrently

This scenario is only one of many possible scenarios with context switches happening at certain places. Each scenario is called an *interleaving*. So, for a system of concurrent tasks, there are a number of possible interleavings based on the various places that context switches can happen, and in each run only one of these many interleavings will happen. This, as a result, makes them unpredictable.

For the preceding interleaving, as you can see in the first and last column, the order of instructions and happens-before constraints are preserved, but there could be *gaps* between the executions. These gaps are not predictable, and as we trace the execution, the preceding interleaving leads to a surprising result. Process P prints the value 1 and process Q prints the value 2, yet it was expected that both of them would print 3 as their final result.

Note that in the preceding example, the constraint for accepting the final result has been defined like this – the program should print two 3s in the output. This constraint could be something else, and independent of the visible output of the program. More than that, there exist other critical constraints that should remain *invariant* when facing unpredictable context switches. These could include not having any *data race* or *race condition*, having no memory leak at all, or even not to crash. All of these constraints are far more important than the visible output of the program. In many real applications, a program doesn't even have an output at all.

The following in *Code Box 13-9* is another interleaving with a different result:

```
     Task P      |    Task Scheduler    |    Task Q
- - - - - - - - - - - - - - - - - - - - - - - - - - - -
                 |   Context Switch     |
                 |                      |    B = X
                 |                      |    B = B + 2
                 |                      |    X = B
                 |   Context Switch     |
    A = X        |                      |
    A = A + 1    |                      |
                 |   Context Switch     |
                 |                      |    print X
                 |   Context Switch     |
    X = A        |                      |
    print X      |                      |
                 |   Context Switch     |
```

Code Box 13-9: Another possible interleaving of tasks P and Q when run concurrently

In this interleaving, task P prints 3, but task Q prints 2. This occurs due to the fact that task P hasn't been lucky enough to update the value of the shared variable X before the third context switch. Therefore, task Q just printed the value of X, which was 2 at that moment. This condition is called a *data race* over the variable X, and we explain this further in the upcoming chapter.

In a real C program, we usually write X++ or X = X + 1 instead of firstly copying X into A and then incrementing A, and finally putting it back into X. You will see an example of this in *Chapter 15, Thread Execution*.

This clearly shows that a simple x++ statement in C consists of three smaller instructions that won't be executed in a single time slice. In other words, it is not an *atomic instruction*, but it has been made up of three smaller atomic instructions. An atomic instruction cannot be broken down into smaller operations and it cannot be interrupted by context switches. We will see more of this in later chapters regarding multithreading.

There is another thing to consider regarding the preceding example. In the preceding example, the tasks P and Q were not the only running tasks in the system; there were also other tasks being executed concurrently to our tasks P and Q, but we didn't consider them in our analysis, and we only discussed those two tasks. Why is that?

The answer to this question relies on the fact that the different interleavings between any of these two tasks and the other tasks in the system could not change the intermediate states of the task P or Q. In other words, the other tasks have no shared state with P and Q, and as we have explained before, when there are no shared resources between some tasks, interleavings won't matter, as we can see in this case. Therefore, we could assume that there are no other tasks besides P and Q in our hypothetical system.

The only effect that the other tasks have upon P and Q is that, if there are too many of them, they can make P and Q's execution slower. That's simply a result of having long gaps between two successive instructions in P or Q. In other words, the CPU core needs to be shared among more tasks. Therefore, tasks P and Q would need to wait in the queue more often than normally, delaying their execution.

Using this example, you saw how even a single shared state between only two concurrent tasks could lead to a lack of determinism in the overall result. We have shown the problems associated with a lack of determinism; we don't want to have a program that yields to a different result in each run. The tasks in our example were relatively simple, containing four trivial instructions, but real concurrent applications that are present in the production environment are much more complex than this.

More than that, we have various kinds of shared resources that don't necessarily reside in the memory, such as files or services that are available on the network.

Likewise, the number of tasks trying to access a shared resource can be high, and therefore we need to study concurrency issues in a deeper sense and find mechanisms to bring back determinism. In the next chapter, we'll continue our discussions by talking about concurrency issues and the solutions to fix them.

Before finishing this chapter, let's briefly talk about the task scheduler and how it works. If we only have one CPU core, then, at any given moment, we can only have one task using that CPU core.

We also know that the task scheduler itself is a piece of program that needs a slice of the CPU core to be executed. So, how does it manage different tasks in order to use the CPU core when another task is using it? Let's suppose that the task scheduler itself is using the CPU core. Firstly, it selects a task from its queue before it sets a timer for a *timer interrupt* to happen, and it then leaves the CPU core and gives its resources over to the selected task.

Now that we have assumed that the task scheduler will give each task a certain amount of time, there is a time that the interrupt will act, and the CPU core stops the execution of the current task and immediately loads the task scheduler back into the CPU. Now, the scheduler stores the latest status of the previous task and loads the next one from the queue. All of this goes on until the kernel is up and running. Regarding a machine having a CPU with multiple cores, this can change, and the kernel can use various cores while scheduling the tasks for other cores.

In this section, we briefly went over the concept of shared states and the way they participate in concurrent systems. The discussions will be continued in the next chapter by talking about concurrency issues and synchronization techniques.

Summary

In this chapter, we went through the basics of concurrency, and the essential concepts and terminology that you need to know in order to understand the upcoming topics of multithreading and multi-processing.

Specifically, we discussed the following:

- The definitions of concurrency and parallelism – the fact that each parallel task needs to have its own processor unit, while concurrent tasks can share a single processor.

- Concurrent tasks use a single processor unit while a task scheduler manages the processor time and shares it between different tasks. This will lead to a number context switches and different interleavings for each task.

- An introduction to blocking instructions. We also explained the patterns that suggest when we require concurrency, and the way we could break a single task into two or three concurrent tasks.

- We described what a shared state is. We also showed how a shared state could lead to serious concurrency issues like data races when multiple tasks try to read and write the same shared state.

In the following chapter, we complete our discussion on the topic of concurrency, and we explain the several types of issues that you will experience in a concurrent environment. Talking about the solutions to concurrency-related issues will also be a part of our discussions in the following chapter.

Chapter 14

Synchronization

In the previous chapter, we went through the basic concepts and the widely used terminology of concurrency. In this chapter, we are going to focus on issues that might appear as a result of using concurrency in a program. Like the previous chapter, we won't deal with any C source code; instead, we'll place our focus solely on the concepts and the theoretical background around concurrency issues and resolving them.

As part of this chapter, we're going to learn about:

- **Concurrency-related issues, namely, race conditions, and data races**: We will discuss the effect of having a shared state among multiple tasks and how simultaneous access to the shared variable can lead to issues.

- **Concurrency control techniques used to synchronize access to a shared state**: We will be mainly talking about these techniques from a theoretical point of view, and we will be explaining the approaches we could take to overcome concurrency-related issues.

- **Concurrency in POSIX**: As part of this topic, we discuss how POSIX can standardize the way we should develop concurrent programs. We briefly explain and compare multithreaded and multi-process programs.

In the first section, we will further discuss how the non-deterministic nature of concurrent environments can lead to concurrency issues, as we mentioned in the previous chapter. We will also talk about how we can categorize such issues.

Concurrency issues

Throughout the previous chapter, we have seen that a modifiable shared state can cause issues when some concurrent tasks are able to change the shared state's value. Exploring this further we might ask, what kind of issues may occur? What is the main reason behind them? We will answer these questions within this section.

First of all, we need to distinguish the different types of concurrency issues that might occur. Some concurrency issues only exist when no concurrency control mechanism is in place, and some are introduced by using a concurrency control technique.

Regarding the issues in the first group, they happen when you can see that different interleavings result in different *overall states*. Upon identifying one of these issues, the next step of course will be to begin thinking about a suitable fix to resolve said issue.

Regarding the second group, they only arise following a fix being put in place. This means that when you fix a concurrency issue, you may introduce a new issue that has a totally different nature and a different root cause; this is what makes concurrent programs problematic to deal with.

As an example, suppose that you have a number of tasks that all have read/write access to the same shared data source. After running the tasks multiple times, you find out that your algorithms, written for different tasks, do not function as they are supposed to. This is leading to accidental crashes or logical errors that occur randomly. Since the occurrences of crashes and wrong results are random and not predictable in your case, you could reasonably presume that it might be concurrency issues.

You begin to analyze the algorithms over and over again, and finally you find the problem; there is a *data race* over the shared data source. Now you need to come up with a fix that tries to control the access to the shared data source. You implement a solution and run the system again, and surprisingly you find out that sometimes some of the tasks never get the chance to access the data source. We technically say that these tasks are *starved*. A new issue, with a completely different nature from the first issue, has been introduced by your changes!

Therefore, we now have two different groups of concurrency issues, these being:

- The issues that exist in a concurrent system while having no control (synchronization) mechanism in place. We call them *intrinsic concurrency issues*.

- The issues that happen after the attempted resolution of an issue in the first group. We call them *post-synchronization issues*.

The reason behind calling the first group *intrinsic* is due to the fact that these issues are present intrinsically in all concurrent systems. You cannot avoid them, and you have to deal with them via the use of control mechanisms. In a way, they can be considered as a property of the concurrent systems rather than being issues. Despite that, we treat them as issues because their non-deterministic nature interferes with our ability to develop the deterministic programs that we require.

The issues in the second group only happen when you use control mechanisms in the wrong way. Note that control mechanisms are not problematic at all and indeed are necessary to bring back the determinism to our programs. If they are used in the wrong fashion, however, they can lead to secondary concurrency problems. These secondary problems, or post-concurrency issues, can be considered as new bugs being introduced by a programmer, rather than being an intrinsic property of a concurrent system.

In the following sections, we are going to introduce the issues in both groups. First, we start with intrinsic issues and we discuss the main reason behind having these intrinsic problematic properties in concurrent environments.

Intrinsic concurrency issues

Every concurrent system with more than one task can have a number of possible interleavings, which can be thought of as an intrinsic property of the system. From what we've learned so far, we know that this property has a non-deterministic nature, which causes the instructions of different tasks to be executed in a chaotic order in each run, while still following the *happens-before constraints*. Note that this is something that has already been explained in the previous chapter.

Interleavings are not problematic by themselves and, as we've explained before, they're an intrinsic property of a concurrent system. But in some cases, this property dissatisfies some constraints that are meant to be conserved. This is exactly when interleavings yield issues.

We know that it's possible to have many interleavings while a number of tasks are being executed concurrently. Yet issues only arise when a constraint of the system, which should have been invariant, happens to be changed by the interleavings from one run to another. Therefore, our goal is to employ some control mechanisms, which sometimes are referred to as *synchronization mechanisms*, in order to keep that constraint unchanged and invariant.

This constraint is usually expressed through a list of conditions and criteria, which from now on we will refer to as *invariant constraints*. These constraints can be about almost anything in a concurrent system.

The invariant constraints can be something very simple, like the example we gave in previous chapters, in which the program should have printed two 3s in its output. They can also be very complex, like conserving the *data integrity* of all the external data sources in a huge concurrent software program.

Note:
It's very hard to produce every possible interleaving. In some cases, a specific interleaving is only possible with a very low probability. It might happen one time in a million, if at all.

This is another dangerous aspect of concurrent development. While some interleavings might only occur once in a million, when they do go wrong, they go wrong badly. They can cause, for example, a plane crash or a serious device malfunction during a brain surgery!

Every concurrent system has some least well-defined invariant constraints. As we progress through the chapter, we give examples and for every example, we shall discuss its invariant constraints. This is because we need these constraints to be able to design a specific concurrent system that will satisfy them and keep them invariant.

The interleavings happening in a concurrent system should satisfy the already defined invariant constraints. If they do not, something is wrong with the system. This is where invariant constraints become a very important factor. Whenever there are interleavings that dissatisfy the invariant constraints of a system, we say that we have a *race condition* in the system.

A race condition is an issue that is caused by the intrinsic property of concurrent systems, or in other words, the interleavings. Whenever we get a race condition, the invariant constraints of the system are in danger of being missed.

The consequences of failing to satisfy the invariant constraints can be observed as either logical errors or sudden crashes. There are numerous examples in which the values stored in the shared variables are not reflecting the true state. This is mainly because of having different interleavings that corrupt the *data integrity* of the shared variable.

We will explain data integrity-related issues later on in this chapter but, for now, let's look at the following example. Like we said before, we have to define the invariant constraints of an example before being able to jump to it. *Example 14.1* shown in *Code Box 14-1* has only one invariant constraint, and it is to have the final correct value in the shared Counter variable, which should be 3. There are three concurrent tasks in this example. Every task is supposed to increment the Counter by one, and this is the logic that we have aimed for in the following code box:

```
Concurrent System {

    Shared State {
        Counter : Integer = 0
    }

    Task T1 {
        A : Integer
            1.1. A = Counter
            1.2. A = A + 1
            1.2. Counter = A
    }

    Task T2 {
        B : Integer
            2.1. B = Counter
```

```
        2.2. B = B + 1
        2.2. Counter = B
    }

    Task T3 {
       A : Integer
        3.1. A = Counter
        3.2. A = A + 1
        3.2. Counter = A
    }
}
```

Code Box 14-1: A system of three concurrent tasks operating a single shared variable

In the preceding code box, you see a concurrent system written in pseudo-code. As you can see, there are three tasks in the concurrent system. There is also a section for shared states. In the preceding system, `Counter` is the only shared variable that is accessible by all three tasks.

Every task can have a number of local variables. These local variables are private to the task and other tasks cannot see them. That's why we can have two local variables with the same A, but every one of them is different and local to its owner task.

Note that tasks cannot operate directly on the shared variables, and they can only read their values or change their values. That's basically why you need to have some local variables. As you can see, the tasks can only increment a local variable and not the shared variable directly. This is in close harmony with what we see in multithreading and multi-processing systems, and that's why we've chosen the preceding configuration to represent a concurrent system.

The example shown in *Code Box 14-1* shows us how the race condition can result in a logical error. It is easy to find an interleaving that results in having the value 2 in the shared `Counter` variable. Just look at the interleaving in *Code Box 14-2*:

```
   Task Scheduler |    Task T1    |    Task T2    |  Task T3
-------------------------------------------------------------------
   Context Switch |               |               |
                  | A = Counter   |               |
                  | A = A + 1     |               |
                  | Counter = A   |               |
   Context Switch |               |               |
                  |               | B = Counter   |
                  |               | B = B + 1     |
   Context Switch |               |               |
                  |               |               | A = Counter
   Context Switch |               |               |
```

```
                    |                |   Counter = B  |
 Context Switch     |                |                |
                    |                |                |   A = A + 1
                    |                |                |   Counter = A
```

Code Box 14-2: An interleaving violating the invariant constraint defined for Code Box 14.1

Here, it is easy to trace the interleaving. Instructions 2.3 and 3.3 (as seen in *Code Box 14-1*) both store the value 2 inside the shared Counter variable. The preceding situation is called a *data race*, something that we explain in more detail later in this section.

The next example, shown in *Code Box 14-3*, demonstrates how a race condition can result in a crash.

Note:

In the following section we will be using a C pseudo-codes example. This is because we have not yet introduced the POSIX API, which is necessary for writing C codes that create and manage threads or processes.

The following code is an example that can result in a segmentation fault if it is written with C:

```
Concurrent System {

    Shared State {
        char *ptr = NULL; // A shared char pointer which is
                          // supposed to point to a memory
                          // address in the Heap space. It
                          // becomes null by default.
    }

    Task P {
        1.1. ptr = (char*)malloc(10 * sizeof(char));
        1.2. strcpy(ptr, "Hello!");
        1.3. printf("%s\n", ptr);
    }

    Task Q {
        2.1. free(ptr);
        2.2. ptr = NULL;
    }
}
```

Code Box 14-3: An interleaving violating the invariant constraint of the example seen in Code Box 14-1

One of the obvious invariant constraints that we are concerned about as part of this example is to not let a task crash, something that is *implicitly* included in our invariant constraints. If a task cannot survive to complete its job, then having an invariant constraint is contradictory in the first place.

There are some interleavings that cause the preceding tasks to crash. Next, we explain two of them:

- Firstly, suppose that instruction 2.1 is executed first. Since ptr is null, then task Q will crash, while task P continues. As a result, and in the multithreading use case where both tasks (threads) belong to the same process, the whole program containing two tasks will crash. The main reason behind the crash is deleting a null pointer.

- The other interleaving is when instruction 2.2 is executed before 1.2 but after 1.1. In this case, task P will crash, while task Q finishes without a problem. The main reason behind the crash is dereferencing a null pointer.

Therefore, as you see in the previous examples, having a race condition in a concurrent system can lead to different situations, like logical errors or sudden crashes. Two occurrences that obviously need to be resolved properly.

It's worth taking a moment to make sure that we understand that not all race conditions in a concurrent system can be easily identified. Some of the race conditions remain hidden until they show themselves much later. This is why I opened this chapter by saying that concurrent programs are problematic to deal with.

With that said, sometimes we'll use *race detectors* to find the existing race conditions in branches of code that would be executed less often. They can be used in fact to identify the interleavings leading to a race condition.

Note:
The race condition can be detected by a group of programs called *race detectors*. They are grouped based on being static or dynamic.

Static race detectors will go through the source code and try to produce all the interleavings based on the observed instructions, while *dynamic race detectors* run the program first and then wait for a code execution that is suspected to be a race condition. Both are used in combination to mitigate the risk of having race conditions.

Now, it is time for a question. Is there a single primary reason behind all race conditions? We need to answer this question in order to come up with a solution that removes the race conditions. We know that whenever an interleaving dissatisfies the invariant constraint, a race condition happens. Therefore, to answer the question, we need to conduct a deeper analysis of the possible invariant constraints and see how they can be missed.

From what we've observed across various concurrent systems, in order to keep an invariant constraint satisfied there are always a number of instructions found in different tasks that should be executed in a strict order across all interleavings.

Hence, those interleavings that follow this order don't violate the invariant constraint. We are satisfied with regard to these interleavings, and we observe the desired output. The interleavings that don't keep to the strict order will dissatisfy the invariant constraint and thus can be considered as problematic interleavings.

For these interleavings, we need to employ mechanisms to restore the order and make sure that the invariant constraints are always satisfied. *Example 14.2* can be seen in *Code Box 14-4*. The constraint that should remain invariant is to **have 1 printed in the output**. While this constraint is a bit immature, and you won't see it in real concurrent applications, it serves to help us understand the concepts we are discussing:

```
Concurrent System {

  Shared State {
    X : Integer = 0
  }

  Task P {
      1.1. X = 1
  }

  Task Q {
      2.1. print X
  }
}
```

Code Box 14-4: A very simple concurrent system suffering from a race condition

The preceding example can have two different outputs based on the interleavings it has. If we want to have 1 printed in the output, which is enforced by the invariant constraint, then we need to define a strict order for the instructions in the two different tasks.

For this purpose, the print instructions, 2.1, must be executed only after instruction 1.1. Since there is another interleaving that easily violates such order, hence the invariant constraint, then we have a race condition. We need a strict order between these instructions. However, putting them in the desired order is not an easy job. We will be discussing the ways to restore this order later on in this chapter.

Let's look at *example 14.3*, below. In the following code, we have a system of three tasks. We should note that there is no shared state in this system. Yet, with that being said, we have a race condition. Let's define the invariant constraint of the following system to be **printing always 1 first, 2 second, and 3 last**:

```
Concurrent System {

    Shared State {
    }

    Task P {
        1.1. print 3
    }

    Task Q {
        2.1. print 1
    }

    Task R {
        3.1. print 2
    }
}
```

Code Box 14-5: Another very simple concurrent system suffering from race condition
but without having any shared state

Even in this very simple system, you cannot guarantee which task is going to begin first, and because of that, we have a race condition. Therefore, to satisfy the invariant constraint, we need to execute the instructions in the following order: 2.1, 3.1, 1.1. This order must be kept in all possible interleavings.

The preceding example reveals an important feature of race conditions, that is: To have a race condition in a concurrent system, we don't need to have a shared state. Instead, to avoid having a race condition, we need to keep some of the instructions in a strict order all the time. We should take note that race conditions only happen because a small set of instructions, usually known as a *critical section*, that are executed out of order, while other instructions can be executed in any order.

Having both a writable shared state and a specific invariant constraint in regard to the shared state can impose a strict order between the *read* and *write* instructions targeting that shared state. One of the most important constraints about a writable shared state is the data integrity. It simply means that all tasks should always be able to read the latest and the freshest value of the shared state, in addition to being aware of any update made to the shared state before continuing with their own instructions that modify the shared state.

Example 14.4, shown in *Code Box 14-6*, explains the data integrity constraint and, more importantly, how it can be missed easily:

```
Concurrent System {

  Shared State {
    X : Integer = 2
  }

  Task P {
    A : Integer
      1.1. A = X
      1.2. A = A + 1
      1.3. X = A
  }

  Task Q {
    B : Integer
      2.1. B = X
      2.2. B = B + 3
      2.3. X = B
  }
}
```

Code Box 14-6: A concurrent system suffering from a data race over shared variable X

Consider the following interleaving. Firstly, instruction 1.1 is executed. Therefore, the value of X is copied to the local variable A. However, task P is not so lucky, so a context switch happens, and the CPU is granted to task Q. Instruction 2.1 is then executed, and then the value of X is copied to the local variable B. Therefore, both variables A and B have the same value, 2.

Now, task Q is lucky and can continue its execution. Instruction 2.2 is then executed, and B becomes 5. Task Q continues and writes the value 5 to the shared state X. So, X becomes 5.

Now, the next context switch happens, and the CPU is given back to task P. It continues with instruction 1.2. This is where the integrity constraint is missed.

The shared state X has been updated by task Q, but task P is using the old value 2 for the rest of its calculations. Eventually, it resets the value of X to 3, something that can hardly be a result that the programmer wishes for. To keep the constraint of the data integrity satisfied, we have to make sure that instruction 1.1 is executed only after instruction 2.3, or that instruction 2.1 is executed only after instruction 1.3, otherwise the data integrity is potentially compromised.

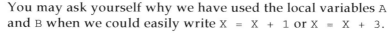

Note:
You may ask yourself why we have used the local variables A and B when we could easily write X = X + 1 or X = X + 3.

As we explained in the previous chapter, the instruction X = X + 1, which in C is written as X++, is not an *atomic* instruction. It simply means that it cannot be done in just one instruction and it needs more than one. This is because we never have direct access to a variable in memory when doing an operation on it.

We always use a temporary variable, or a CPU register, to keep the latest value and perform the operation on the temporary variable or register and then transfer the result back to memory. Therefore, no matter how you write it, there is always a temporary variable locally associated to the task.

You will see that the situation is even worse in systems with more than one CPU core. We have also CPU caches that cache the variables and don't transfer the result back to the variable in the main memory immediately.

Let's talk about another definition. Whenever some interleavings invalidate the constraint of the data integrity related to a shared state, it is said that we have a data race over that shared state.

Data races are very similar to race conditions, but to have a data race we need to have a shared state among different tasks and that shared state must be modifiable (writable) by at least one of the tasks. In other words, the shared state should not be read-only for all tasks, and there should be at least one task which may write to the shared state based on its logic.

As we said before, for a read-only shared state, we *can't* have a data race. This is due to the fact that one cannot ruin the data integrity of a read-only shared state since the value of the shared state cannot be modified.

Example 14.5, shown in *Code Box 14-7*, shows how we can have a race condition, while at the same time no data race is possible over a read-only shared state:

```
Concurrent System {

  Shared State {
    X : Integer (read-only) = 5
  }

  Task P {
    A : Integer
      1.1. A = X
      1.2. A = A + 1
      1.2. print A
  }

  Task Q {
      2.1. print X
  }

  Task R {
    B : Integer
      3.1. B = X + 1
      3.2. B = B + 1
      3.3. print B
  }
}
```

Code Box 14-7: A concurrent system with a read-only shared state

Suppose that the invariant constraint of the preceding example is to **keep the data integrity of X and first print 5, then 6, and finally 7.** Certainly, we have a race condition because a strict order is required among different `print` instructions.

However, since the shared variable is read-only, there is no data race. Note that instructions `1.2` and `3.2` only modify their local variables, and thus they cannot be considered as modifications to the shared state.

As the final note in this section: Don't expect race conditions to be resolved easily! You will certainly need to employ some synchronization mechanisms in order to create the required order between certain instructions from different tasks. This will force all possible interleavings follow the given order. In fact, you will see in the next section that we have to introduce some new interleavings that obey the desired order.

We will talk about these mechanisms later in this chapter; before that, we need to explain the concurrency-related issues occurring after using some synchronization methods. The next section is all about *post-synchronization* issues and how they are different from intrinsic issues.

Post-synchronization issues

Next, we're going to talk about three of the key issues that are expected to occur as a result of misusing the control mechanisms. You could experience one or even all of these issues together because they have different root causes:

- **New intrinsic issues**: Applying control mechanisms may result in having different race conditions or data races. Control mechanisms are to enforce a strict order between instructions, and this may cause newer intrinsic issues to occur. The fact that control mechanisms introduce new interleavings is the basis of experiencing new concurrency-related behaviors and issues. As a consequence of having new race conditions and new data races, new logical errors and crashes can occur. You'll have to go through the employed synchronization techniques and tune them based on your program's logic in order to fix these new issues.

- **Starvation**: When a task in a concurrent system doesn't have access to a shared resource for a long period of time, mainly because of employing a specific control mechanism, it is said that the task has become starved. A starved task cannot access the shared resource, and thus it cannot execute its purpose effectively. If other tasks rely on the cooperation of a starved task, they themselves may also get starved.

- **Deadlock**: When all the tasks in a concurrent system are waiting for each other and none of them is advancing, we say that a deadlock is reached. It happens mainly due to a control mechanism being applied in the wrong way, which in turn makes tasks enter an infinite loop waiting for the other task to release a shared resource or unlock a lock object, and so on. This is usually called a *circular wait*. While the tasks are waiting, none of them will be able to continue their execution, and as a result, the system will go into a coma-like situation. Some illustration describing a deadlock situation can be found on the Wikipedia page found at: `https://en.wikipedia.org/wiki/Deadlock`.

  In a deadlock situation, all the tasks are stuck and waiting for each other. But there are often situations in which only a portion of tasks, only one or two of them, are stuck and the rest can continue. We call them *semi-deadlock* situations. We are going to see more of these semi-deadlock situations in the upcoming sections.

- **Priority inversion**: There are situations in which, after employing a synchronization technique, a task with a higher priority to use a shared resource is blocked behind a low priority task and this way, their priorities are reversed. This is another type of secondary issues that can happen because of a wrongly implemented synchronization technique.

Starvation doesn't exist by default in a concurrent system; when no synchronization technique is imposed upon the operating system's task scheduler, the system is fair and doesn't allow any task to become starved. Only having some control mechanisms employed by the programmer can lead to starvation. Likewise, the occurrence of a deadlock also doesn't exist within a concurrent system until the programmer gets involved. The main reason for most deadlock situations is when locks are employed in such a way that all tasks in a concurrent system are waiting for each other to release the lock. Generally, deadlocks are a more common issue than starvation within a concurrent system.

Now, we should move on and talk about the control mechanisms. In the next section, we will be talking about various synchronization techniques that can be used to overcome race conditions.

Synchronization techniques

In this section, we're going to talk about the synchronization techniques, or concurrency control techniques, or concurrent control mechanisms, that are used to overcome intrinsic concurrency-related issues. Looking back at what we've explained so far, control mechanisms try to overcome the problems that a portion of interleavings may cause in a system.

Each concurrent system has its own invariant constraints, and not all interleavings are going to keep all of them satisfied. For those interleavings that dissatisfy the system's invariant constraints, we need to invent a method to impose a specific order between instructions. In other words, we should *create* new interleavings that satisfy the invariant constraint and replace the bad interleavings with them. After using a certain synchronization technique, we will have a totally new concurrent system with some new interleavings, and our hope is that the new system is going to keep the invariant constraints satisfied and not to produce any post-synchronization issues.

Note that in order to employ a synchronization technique, we will need to both write new code and change the existing code. When you change the existing code, you are effectively changing the order of instructions, and hence the interleavings. Changing the code simply creates a new concurrent system with new interleavings.

How does having new interleavings solve our concurrent issues? By introducing newly added engineered interleavings we impose some extra happens-before constraints between different instructions from different tasks, which keeps the invariant constraints satisfied.

Note that happens-before constraints always exist between two adjacent instructions in a single task, but we don't have them between two instructions from two different tasks in a concurrent system and by using synchronization techniques, we define some new happens-before constraints that govern the order of execution between two different tasks.

Having a totally new concurrent system means having new, different, issues. The first-hand concurrent system was a natural system in which the task scheduler was the only entity driving the context switches. But in the later system, we are facing an artificial and engineered concurrent system where the task scheduler is not the only effective element. The concurrency control mechanisms employed to conserve the system's invariant constraints are other important factors. Therefore, newer issues called *post-synchronization issues*, which were discussed in the previous section, will show up.

Employing a proper control technique to synchronize a number of tasks and make them obey a specific order is dependent on the first-hand concurrent environment. As an example, the control mechanisms used in a multi-processing program can be different from the methods that are used in a multithreading program.

Because of this, we cannot discuss the control mechanisms here in great detail without using real C code. We will therefore discuss them in an abstract way that is true for all concurrent systems, regardless of their implementation methods. The following techniques and concepts are therefore valid in all concurrent systems, but their implementations are greatly dependent upon the true nature of the surrounding environment and the system itself.

Busy-waits and spin locks

As a generic solution, in order to force an instruction from a task to be executed after another instruction from another task, the former task should wait for the later task to execute its instruction first. In the meantime, the former task may gain the CPU because of a context switch, but it shouldn't continue execution, and it should still wait. In other words, the former task should pause and wait until the later task has executed its instruction.

When the latter task is able to complete the execution of its instruction, then there are two options available. Either the former task itself checks again and sees that the latter task has done its job or there should be a way for the latter task to notify the former task and let it know that it can now continue to execute its instruction.

The scenario described is similar to a situation in which two people try to do something in a defined order. One of them must wait for the other to complete their job, and only then the other person can continue to do their own job. We can say that almost all control mechanisms use an approach analogous to this, but the implementations of this are diverse, and they are mostly dependent on the available mechanisms in a specific environment. We'll explain one of these environments, a POSIX-compliant system, and the available mechanisms in it, as part of the last section in this chapter.

Let's explain the preceding control technique, which is central to all other techniques, using an example. *Example 14.6*, shown in *Code Box 14-8*, is a system of two concurrent tasks, and we want to define the invariant constraint as **having first A, and then B printed in the output**. Without any control mechanism in place, it looks like the following code box:

```
Concurrent System {

  Task P {
    1.1. print 'A'
  }

  Task Q {
    2.1. print 'B'
  }
}
```

Code Box 14-8: A concurrent system representing example 14.6 before introducing an control mechanism

It is clear that we have a race condition based on the defined invariant constraint. The interleaving {2.1, 1.1} prints B and then A, which is against the invariant constraint. Therefore, we need to use a control mechanism to keep a specific order between the preceding instructions.

We want to have 2.1 executed only when instruction 1.1 has been executed. The following pseudo-code shown in *Code Box 14-9* demonstrates how we design and employ the previously-explained approach in order to bring back the order between the instructions:

```
Concurrent System {

  Shared State {
    Done : Boolean = False
  }

  Task P {
    1.1. print 'A'
```

```
      1.2. Done = True
    }

  Task Q {
    2.1. While Not Done Do Nothing
    2.2. print 'B'
    }
}
```

Code Box 14-9: A solution for example 14.6 using busy-waiting

As you can see, we had to add more instructions to synchronize the tasks. Therefore, it seems we have added a bunch of new interleavings. To be more precise, we are facing a completely new concurrent system in comparison to the previous one. This new system has its own set of interleavings that are in no way comparable to interleavings in the old system.

One thing is common among all these new interleavings, and that is the fact that instruction 1.1 always happens before instruction 2.2; this is what we wanted to achieve by adding the control mechanism. No matter which interleaving is chosen or how the context switches occur, we have enforced a happens-before constraint between instructions 1.1 and 2.2.

How is this possible? In the preceding system, we introduced a new shared state, Done, which is a Boolean variable initially set to False. Whenever task P prints A, it sets Done to True. Then, task Q, which was waiting for Done to become True, exits the while loop at line 2.1 and prints B. In other words, task Q waits in a while loop until the shared state Done becomes True and it is an indication that the task P has completed its print command. Everything seems to be fine with the proposed solution, and in fact, it just works fine.

Try to imagine the following interleaving. When task P loses the CPU core and task Q gains the CPU core, if Done is not true, then task Q remains in the loop until it loses the CPU core again. This means, while the task Q has the CPU core, the required condition is not met yet, it doesn't leave the loop, and it tries to use its *time slice* to do almost nothing other than *polling* and checking whether the condition has been met. It does it until the CPU core is taken back. In other words, the task Q waits and *wastes* its time until the CPU core is granted back to task P and task P can now print A.

In technical language, we say that the task Q is in a *busy-wait* until a specific condition is met. It monitors (or polls) a condition continuously in a busy-wait until it becomes true and then it exits the busy-wait. Whatever you call it, the task Q is wasting the CPU's precious time despite the fact that the preceding solution solves our problem perfectly.

Note:
Busy-waiting is not an efficient approach to wait for an event to happen, but it is a simple one. Since inside a busy-wait nothing special can be done by a task, it wastes its given time slice completely. Busy-waits are avoided in long waits. That wasted time of CPU could be granted to some other task in order to complete a portion of its job. However, in some circumstances in which the waiting times are expected to be short, busy-waits are used.

In real C programs, and also in other programming languages, *locks* are usually used to enforce some strict order. A lock is simply an object, or a variable, that we use to wait for a condition to be met or an event to happen. Note that in the previous example, Done is not a lock but a flag.

To comprehend the term *lock*, we can think of it as if we were trying to acquire a lock before executing instruction 2.2. Only once the lock is acquired can you continue and exit the loop. Inside the loop, we are waiting for the lock to become available. We can have various types of locks, which we explain in future sections.

In the next section, we're going to do the waiting scenario discussed previously, but this time using a more efficient approach that doesn't waste the CPU core's time. It has many names, but we can call it *wait/notify* or the *sleep/notify* mechanism.

Sleep/notify mechanism

Rather than using a busy-wait loop as discussed in the previous section, a different scenario can also be imagined. Task Q could go to sleep instead of busy-waiting on the Done flag and the task P could notify it about the change in the flag when it made the flag True.

In other words, task Q goes to sleep as soon as it finds the flag is not True and lets the task P acquire the CPU core faster and execute its logic. In return, the task P will awaken the task Q after modifying the flag to True. In fact, this approach is the *de facto* implementation in most operating systems to avoid busy-waits and bring control mechanisms into the play more efficiently.

The following pseudo-code demonstrates how to use this approach to rewrite the solution to the example given in the previous section:

```
Concurrent System {

  Task P {
      1.1. print 'A'
      1.2. Notify Task Q
  }

  Task Q {
      2.1. Go To Sleep Mode
      2.2. print 'B'
  }
}
```

Code Box 14-10: A solution for example 14.6 using sleep/notify

We'll need to review some new concepts before being able to explain the preceding pseudo-code. The first is how a task can *sleep*. As long as a task is asleep, it won't get any CPU share. When a task puts itself into the sleeping mode, the task scheduler will become aware of this. After this, the task scheduler won't give any time slice to the asleep task.

What is the benefit of tasks going to sleep? The tasks that go to sleep won't waste the CPU's time by going into a busy-wait. Instead of starting a busy-wait to poll a condition, the tasks go to sleep and get notified when the condition has been met. This will significantly increase the *CPU utilization* factor, and the tasks that really need the CPU share will obtain it.

When a task goes into the sleeping mode, there should be a mechanism to wake it up. This mechanism is normally done by *notifying* or *signaling* the asleep task. A task can be notified to leave the sleeping mode, and as soon as it becomes awake and notified, the task scheduler puts it back in the queue and gives it the CPU again. Then the task will continue execution just after the line that has put it into sleeping mode.

In the code we wrote, the task Q enters the sleeping mode as soon as it starts to execute. When it goes into sleeping mode, it won't have any CPU share until it becomes notified and awakened by task P. Task P notifies task Q only when it has printed A. Then, task Q becomes awake and it obtains the CPU, and it continues and prints B.

With this method there's no busy-wait, and there is no wasting of the CPU's time. Note when going to the sleeping mode and notifying an asleep task, both have specific system calls and are supported in most operating systems, especially the POSIX-compliant ones.

At first glance, it seems that the preceding solution has solved our problem, and in an efficient manner – indeed, it does! Yet, there is an interleaving that yields a post-synchronization issue. It happens when you have the following order of execution in the preceding system:

```
1.1 print 'A'
1.2. Notify Task Q
2.1. Go To Sleep Mode
2.2. print 'B'
```

Code Box 14-11: An interleaving that puts the concurrent system presented in Code Box 14-10 into a semi-deadlock situation

In the preceding interleaving, the task P has printed A, and then it has notified task Q, which is not asleep yet because it hasn't yet obtained the CPU. When the task Q gains the CPU, it goes into sleeping mode immediately. However, there are no other tasks running to notify it. Therefore, task Q won't obtain the CPU anymore simply because the task scheduler doesn't give the CPU core to an asleep task. This is the first example of employing a synchronization technique and observing its consequence as a post-synchronization issue.

For solving this issue, we need to use a Boolean flag again. Now, task Q should check the flag before going to sleep. Here is our final solution:

```
Concurrent System {

  Shared State {
    Done : Boolean = False
  }

  Task P {
      1.1. print 'A'
      1.2. Done = True
      1.3. Notify Task Q
  }

  Task Q {
      2.1. While Not Done {
      2.2.     Go To Sleep Mode If Done is False (Atomic)
      2.3. }
      2.4. print 'B'
  }
}
```

Code Box 14-12: An improved solution for example 14.6 based on the sleep/notify approach

As you see in the preceding pseudo-code, task Q sleeps if the flag Done has not been set to True. Instruction 2.2 is put inside a loop that simply checks the flag and goes to sleep only if Done is False. One important note about instruction 2.2 is that it must be an atomic instruction, otherwise the solution is not complete, and it would suffer from the same problem.

Note:
For those of you who have some experience with concurrent systems, having this instruction declared as atomic might seem a bit surprising. The main reason behind this is the fact that regarding the preceding example, a true tangible synchronization only happens when we define a clear critical section and protect it using a mutex. As we go forward, this becomes more evident and after going through more conceptual topics, we can finally provide a tangible and real solution.

The loop is required because an asleep task could be notified by anything in the system, not only the task P. In real systems, operating systems and other tasks can notify a task but here, we are only interested in notifications received from task P.

Therefore, when the task is notified and awakened, it should check the flag again and go back to sleep if the flag has not yet been set. As we explained before, this solution seems to be working based on the explanations that we've given so far, but it's not a complete solution, as it can also cause a semi-deadlock situation on a machine with multiple CPU cores. We explain this further in the section, *Multiple processor units*.

Note:
Solutions based on the wait/notify mechanism are usually developed using condition variables. Condition variables also have counterparts in POSIX API, and we will cover them conceptually in a dedicated section, which comes shortly.

All synchronization mechanisms have some sort of waiting involved. This is the only way you can keep some tasks synchronized. At some point, some of them should wait, and some others should continue. This is the point that we need to introduce *semaphores*; these are the standard tools for making a piece of logic wait or continue in a concurrent environment. We focus on this in the next section.

Semaphores and mutexes

It was in the 1960s when Edsger Dijkstra, a very well-known Dutch computer scientist and mathematician, together with his team designed a new operating system called *THE Multiprogramming System* or *THE OS* for the Electrologica X8 computer, which had its own unique architecture at the time.

It was less than 10 years before the invention of Unix, and later C, by Bell Labs. They were using assembly for wiring THE OS. THE OS was a multitasking operating system, and it had a multi-level architecture. The highest level was the user, and the lowest level was the task scheduler. In Unix terminology, the lowest level was equivalent to having *task scheduler* and *process management unit* together in the kernel ring. One of the ideas that Dijkstra and his team invented to overcome certain concurrency-related difficulties, and for sharing different resources among different tasks, was the concept of *semaphores*.

Semaphores are simply variables, or objects, which are used to synchronize access to a shared resource. We are going to explain them thoroughly in this section and introduce a specific type of semaphores, mutexes that are used widely in concurrent programs and exist in almost any programming language today.

When a task is going to access a shared resource, which can be a simple variable or a shared file, the task should check a predefined semaphore first and ask for permission to continue and access the shared resource. We can use an analogous example to explain a semaphore and its role.

Imagine a doctor, and some patients wishing to be visited by the doctor. Suppose that there is no mechanism for having a prescheduled appointment, and the patients can go to the doctor whenever they want. Our doctor has a secretary who manages the patients, keeps them in a queue, and grants them permission to go into the doctor's room.

We assume that the doctor can see multiple patients (up to a certain number) at a time, which is a bit unusual based on our daily experiences, but you can assume that our doctor is extraordinary and can see multiple patients at once; perhaps multiple patients are happy to sit together within one consultation. In certain real use cases, semaphores protect resources that can be used by many consumers. So, please bear with the preceding assumption for now.

Whenever a new patient arrives at the doctor's office, they should go to the secretary first in order to be registered. The secretary has a list that is simply written on a piece of paper, where they'll write the name of the new patient. Now, the patient should wait for the secretary to summon them and grant them access to the doctor's room. On the other hand, whenever a patient leaves the doctor's room, this information goes to the secretary, who will remove the patient's name from the list.

At each moment, the secretary's list reflects the patients inside the doctor's room and being visited plus those patients who are waiting to be visited. When a new patient leaves the doctor's room, a new patient who is waiting on the list can enter the doctor's room. This process continues until all the patients have seen the doctor.

Now, let's map it to a concurrent computer system to see how semaphores do the same thing as the secretary in our analogy.

In the example, the doctor is a shared resource. They can be accessed by a number of patients, which are analogous to the tasks wishing to access the shared resource. The secretary is a semaphore. Like the secretary who has a list, each semaphore has a queue of pending tasks that are waiting to obtain access to the shared resource. The doctor's room can be considered as a *critical section*.

A critical section is simply a set of instructions that are protected by a semaphore. Tasks cannot enter it without waiting behind a semaphore. On the other hand, it is the semaphore's job to protect the critical section. Whenever a task tries to enter a critical section, it should let a specific semaphore know about it.

Likewise, when a task is done and wants to exit the critical section, it should let the same semaphore know about it. As you can see, there is a very good correspondence between our doctor example and the semaphores. Let's continue with a more programmatic example and try to find the semaphores and other elements in it.

Note:
Critical sections should satisfy certain conditions. These conditions will be explained as we progress through the chapter.

The following example, *example 14.7*, shown in *Code Box 14-13*, is again about two tasks trying to increment a shared counter. We have already discussed this example in previous sections in multiple places, but this time, we are going to give a solution based on semaphores:

```
Concurrent System {

  Shared State {
    S : Semaphore which allows only 1 task at a time
    Counter: Integer = 0
  }

  Task P {
    A : Local Integer
      1.1. EnterCriticalSection(S)
      1.2. A = Counter
      1.3. A = A + 1
```

```
        1.4. Counter = A
        1.5. LeaveCriticalSection(S)
    }

    Task Q {
      B : Local Integer
        2.1. EnterCriticalSection(S)
        2.2. B = Counter
        2.3. B = B + 2
        2.4. Counter = B
        2.5. LeaveCriticalSection(S)
    }
}
```

Code Box 14-13: Using semaphores to synchronize two tasks

In the preceding system, we have two different shared states: a shared semaphore S that is supposed to protect the access to another shared variable Counter. S only allows one task at a time to enter a critical section being protected by it. The critical sections are the instructions encompassed by EnterCriticalSection(S) and LeaveCriticalSection(S) instructions, and as you can see, each task has a different critical section protected by S.

To enter a critical section, a task should execute the instruction EnterCriticalSection(S). If another task is already in its own critical section, the instruction EnterCriticalSection(S) becomes blocking and doesn't finish, and so the current task should wait until the semaphore allows it to pass and enter its critical section.

The EnterCriticalSection(S) instruction can have various implementations depending on the scenario. It can be simply a busy-wait, or it can just make the waiting task go to the sleeping mode. The latter approach is more common, and the tasks waiting for their critical sections usually go to sleep.

In the preceding example, the semaphore S was used in a way that only one task could enter its critical section. But semaphores are more generic, and they can allow more than one task (up to a certain number defined when creating the semaphore) to enter their critical sections. A semaphore that only allows one task to enter the critical section at a time is usually called a *binary semaphore* or a *mutex*. Mutexes are far more common than semaphores, and you will always see them in concurrent codes. The POSIX API exposes both semaphores and mutexes, and you can use them depending on the situation.

The term **mutex** stands for **mutual exclusion**. Suppose that we have two tasks and each of them have a critical section accessing the same shared resource. In order to have a solution based on mutual exclusion that is race condition free, the following conditions should be met regarding the tasks:

- Only one of them can enter the critical section at any time, and the other task should wait until the former task leaves the critical section.

- The solution should be deadlock free. A task waiting behind a critical section should be able to enter it eventually. In some cases, an upper limit for the waiting time (the *contention time*) is assumed.

- The task in the critical section cannot be pulled out by *preemption* in order to let the other task enter the critical section. In other words, the solution should be *preemption free* and *collaborative*.

Mutexes exist to allow such solutions based on mutual exclusion to be developed. Note that the critical sections should also follow similar conditions. They should allow only one task inside, and they should be deadlock free. Note that the semaphores also satisfy the last two conditions, but they can allow more than one task to enter their critical sections at a time.

We can say that mutual exclusion is the most important concept in concurrency and is a dominant factor in various control mechanisms that we have at hand. In other words, in every synchronization technique that you might know, you will see a footprint of mutual exclusion through using semaphores and mutexes (but mostly mutexes).

Semaphores and mutexes are said to be *lockable* objects. In a different but more formal terminology, the act of waiting for a semaphore and entering the critical section is the same as *locking* the semaphore. Likewise, the act of leaving a critical section and updating the semaphore is the same as to *unlocking* the semaphore.

Therefore, locking and unlocking the semaphores can be considered as two algorithms used to wait and acquire the access to the critical section and to release the critical section respectively. As an example, *spin locking* is acquiring access to a critical section by busy-waiting on a semaphore, and certainly, we can have other types of locking and unlocking algorithms as well. We will explain these various locking algorithms while we are developing concurrent programs using POSIX API in *Chapter 16, Thread Synchronization*.

If we are going to write the preceding solution based on locking and unlocking terminology, it would be like the following:

```
Concurrent System {

  Shared State {
    S : Semaphore which allows only 1 task at a time
    Counter: Integer = 0
  }
```

```
Task P {
   A : Local Integer
      1.1. Lock(S)
      1.2. A = Counter
      1.3. A = A + 1
      1.4. Counter = A
      1.5. Unlock(S)
}

Task Q {
   B : Local Integer
      2.1. Lock(S)
      2.2. B = Counter
      2.3. B = B + 2
      2.4. Counter = B
      2.5. Unlock(S)
   }
}
```

Code Box 14-14: Using lock and unlock operations to work with semaphores

From now on, we will be using the locking and unlocking terminology in our pseudo-code snippets, and this terminology has been used throughout the POSIX API as well.

We are going to finish this section by giving the final definition. When a number of tasks are willing to enter a critical section, they are trying to lock a semaphore, but only a certain number of them (depending on the semaphore) can acquire the lock and enter the critical section. The other tasks will be waiting to acquire the lock. The act of waiting to acquire a lock over a semaphore is called *contention*. More tasks yield more contention, and the contention time is a measure of how much the execution of tasks is slowed down.

Obviously, it takes some time for the tasks in contention to acquire the lock, and as more tasks we get, the more they should wait to enter their critical sections. The amount of time that a task waits in the contention state is usually called the *contention time*. The contention time can be a non-functional requirement for a concurrent system that should be monitored carefully to prevent any performance degradation.

We could conclude that mutexes are our primary tool to synchronize some concurrent tasks. We also have mutexes in POSIX threading API and almost every programming language that supports concurrency. Apart from mutexes, *condition variables* also play an important role when we need to wait for an indefinite amount of time in order to satisfy a certain condition.

We are going to discuss the condition variables, but before that, we need to talk about memory barriers and concurrent environments with multiple processor units, either multiple CPUs or a CPU with multiple cores. Therefore, the next section is dedicated to this topic.

Multiple processor units

When you have only one processor unit in your computer system, a CPU with only one core, the tasks trying to access a specific address in the main memory always read the latest and freshest value even if that address is cached in the CPU core. It's a common practice to cache the value of certain memory addresses inside the CPU core as part of its *local cache* and even keep the changes made to those addresses inside the cache as well. This will increase the performance by reducing the number of reading and writing operations on the main memory. On certain events, the CPU core will propagate the changes in its local cache back to the main memory in order to keep its cache and the main memory synchronized.

These local caches still exist when you have more than one processor unit. By multiple processor units, we mean either one CPU with more than one core or multiple CPUs with any number of cores. Note that every CPU core has its own local cache.

Therefore, when two different tasks are executed on two different CPU cores, working on the same address in the main memory, each CPU core has cached the value of the same memory address in its own local cache. This means if one of them tries to write to the shared memory address, the changes are only applied to its local cache, and not to the main memory and the other CPU core's local cache.

Doing this leads to many different problems because when the task running in the other CPU core tries to read the latest value from the shared memory address, it cannot see the latest changes since it would read from its local cache, which doesn't have the latest changes.

This problem, which comes from having a different local cache for each CPU core, is solved by introducing a *memory coherence protocol* among CPU cores. Therefore, by following a coherence protocol, all tasks running on different CPU cores will see the same value in their local caches when the value is changed in one of the CPU cores. In other words, we say that the memory address is visible to all other processors. Following a memory coherence protocol brings *memory visibility* to all tasks running on different processor units. Cache coherence and memory visibility are two important factors that should be considered in concurrent systems being run on more than one processor unit.

Let's go back to our first sleep-notify-based solution for *example 14.6* that was explained in the previous two sections. The invariant constraint for *example 14.6* was to **have first A and then B in the output**.

The following pseudo-code was our final solution, and we used the sleep/notify mechanism to enforce the desired ordering between `print` instructions. We said that the solution is not bug-free and can yield post-synchronization issues. In the following paragraph, we will explain how the problem shows up:

```
Concurrent System {

  Shared State {
    Done : Boolean = False
  }

  Task P {
      1.1. print 'A'
      1.2. Done = True
      1.3. Notify Task Q
  }

  Task Q {
      2.1. While Not Done {
      2.2.      Go To Sleep Mode If Done is False (Atomic)
      2.3. }
      2.4. print 'B'
  }
}
```

Code Box 14-15: The solution proposed for example 14.6 based on the sleep/notify technique

Suppose that the tasks P and Q are running on different CPU cores. In this case, each CPU core has an entry for the shared variable Done in its local cache. Note that, again, we have declared instruction 2.2 to be atomic, and note that this is an essential assumption until we come up with a proper mutex-based solution to resolve this. Suppose an interleaving in which the task P executes instruction 1.2 and notifies task Q, which could be sleeping. Therefore, task P updates the value of Done in its local cache, but it doesn't mean that it writes it back to the main memory or it updates the other CPU core's local cache.

With that being said, there's no guarantee that we will see a change in the main memory and the task Q's local cache. Therefore, there is a chance that when the task Q obtains CPU and reads its local cache, it sees that Done has the value False and goes into the sleeping mode while task P is finished and has sent its notification signal a while ago, and no more notifying signals will be emitted by the task P. Eventually, the task Q goes to sleep forever and a semi-deadlock situation happens.

To resolve this issue, one needs to use memory barriers or memory fences. They are instructions that act like a barrier and upon executing (passing) them, all values updated in just one local cache are propagated into the main memory and other local caches. They become visible to all tasks executing in other CPU cores. In other words, memory barriers synchronize all CPU cores' local caches and the main memory.

Finally, we can propose our complete solution as follows. Note that, again, we have declared instruction 2.3 to be atomic, and note that this is an essential assumption until we come up with a proper mutex-based solution to resolve this:

```
Concurrent System {

  Shared State {
      Done : Boolean = False
  }

  Task P {
      1.1. print 'A'
      1.2. Done = True
      1.3. Memory Barrier
      1.4. Notify Task Q
  }

  Task Q {
      2.1. Do {
      2.2.      Memory Barrier
      2.3.      Go To Sleep Mode If Done is False (Atomic)
      2.4. } While Not Done
      2.5. print 'B'
  }
}
```

Code Box 14-16: Improving the solution proposed for example 14.6 using memory barriers

By employing memory barriers in the preceding pseudo-code, we are certain that any updates to the shared variable Done can be seen by task Q. It would be a good idea for you to go through different possible interleavings and see for yourself how the memory barrier helps to make the shared variable Done visible to task Q and prevent any unwanted semi-deadlock situation.

Note that creating a task, locking a semaphore, and unlocking a semaphore are three operations that act as memory barriers and synchronize all the CPU cores' local caches and main memory, and propagate the recent changes made to the shared states.

The following pseudo-code is the same as the preceding solution but using mutexes this time. As part of the following solution, we are going to use a mutex and finally resolve the issue that made us declare the instruction Go To Sleep Mode If Done is False as atomic. Though take note that mutexes are semaphores, which allows only one task to be in the critical section at each time and, like semaphores, locking and unlocking mutexes can act as a memory barrier:

```
Concurrent System {
```

```
Shared State {
    Done : Boolean = False
    M : Mutex
}

Task P {
    1.1. print 'A'
    1.2. Lock(M)
    1.3. Done = True
    1.4. Unlock(M)
    1.5. Notify Task Q
}

Task Q {
    2.1. Lock(M)
    2.2. While Not Done {
    2.3.      Go To Sleep Mode And Unlock(M)  (Atomic)
    2.4.      Lock(M)
    2.5. }
    2.6. Unlock(M)
    2.7. print 'B'
}
}
```

Code Box 14-17: Improving the solution proposed for example 14.6 using a mutex

The instructions Lock(M) and Unlock(M) act as memory barriers so guarantees memory visibility in all tasks. As a reminder, the instructions between Lock(M) and Unlock(M) are considered as critical sections in each task.

Note that when a task locks a mutex (or semaphore), there are three occasions in which the mutex gets unlocked automatically:

- The task uses the Unlock command to unlock a mutex.
- When a task is finished, all the locked mutexes become unlocked.
- When a task goes into sleeping mode, the locked mutexes become unlocked.

Note:
The third bullet point in the preceding list is not generally true. If a task wants to sleep for a certain amount of time inside a critical section being protected by a mutex, it is certainly possible to sleep without needing to unlock the mutex. That's why we have declared instruction 2.3 as atomic and we have added Unlock(M) to it. For a complete appreciation of such scenarios, we need to touch on *condition variables*, which come shortly in the upcoming sections.

Therefore, when instruction 2.3 is executed as an atomic instruction, the already locked mutex M becomes unlocked. When the task is notified again, it will reobtain the lock using instruction 2.4, and then it can proceed into its critical section again.

As a final note in this section, when a task has locked a mutex, it cannot lock it again, and attempting to lock it further usually leads to a deadlock situation. Only a *recursive mutex* can be locked many times by a single task. Note that while a recursive mutex is locked (no matter how many times), all other tasks will be blocked upon trying to lock it. Lock and unlock operations always come in pairs, therefore if a task has locked a recursive mutex twice, it should unlock it twice as well.

So far, we have discussed and used the sleep/notify technique in a number of examples. You will get a full appreciation of sleep/notify technique only when you become introduced to a new concept: condition variables. Condition variables together with mutexes have built a basis for implementing control techniques, which effectively synchronize many tasks on a single shared resource. But before that, let's talk about another possible solution to *example 14.6*.

Spin locks

Before starting to talk about the condition variables and the true way that the sleep/notify technique should get implemented, let's go back a little bit and use busy-waiting together with mutexes to write a new solution for *example 14.6*. As a reminder, the example was about **having first A and then B printed in the standard output**.

The following is the proposed solution that uses a mutex equipped with the spin locking algorithm. The mutex acts as a memory barrier, so we won't have any memory visibility issues, and it effectively synchronizes the tasks P and Q over the Done shared flag:

```
Concurrent System {

    Shared State {
        Done : Boolean = False
        M : Mutex
    }

    Task P {
        1.1. print 'A'
        1.2. SpinLock(M)
        1.2. Done = True
        1.3. SpinUnlock(M)
    }

    Task Q {
```

```
2.1  SpinLock(M)
2.2. While Not Done {
2.3.    SpinUnlock(M)
2.4.    SpinLock(M)
2.5. }
2.6. SpinUnlock(M)
2.4. print 'B'
    }
}
```

Code Box 14-18: The solution for example 14.6 using a mutex and spin locking algorithms

The preceding pseudo-code is the first solution that can be written as a valid C code using the POSIX threading API. None of the previously given pseudo-codes could be written as real programs because either they were too abstract to be implemented or they were problematic in certain scenarios, like being run in a system with multiple processor units. But the preceding pseudo-code can be translated into any programming language that supports concurrency.

In the preceding code, we are using *spinlocks*, which are simply busy-waiting algorithms. Whenever you lock a spinlock mutex, it goes into a busy-wait loop until the mutex becomes available and then it continues.

I think everything in the preceding pseudo-code is easy to follow, except instructions 2.3 and 2.4, which are strange successive lock and unlock instructions inside a loop! Actually, this is the most beautiful part of the code. A series of locking and unlocking the spinlock mutex M is in progress while the task Q obtains the CPU core.

What if we didn't have instructions 2.3 and 2.4? Then the lock at instruction 2.1 would have kept the mutex locked until instruction 2.6, which means that task P never could find a chance to get the access to the shared flag Done. Those locking and unlocking instructions allow the task P to find a chance and update the flag Done via instruction 1.2. Otherwise, the mutex will be held by the task Q all the time and the task P can never proceed to instruction 1.2. In other words, the system goes into a semi-deadlock situation. The pseudo-code demonstrates a beautiful harmony of locking/unlocking operations, which nicely solves our problem using spinlocks.

Note that in high-performance systems in which putting a task into sleeping mode is very expensive in comparison to the rate of events happening in the system, spin locks are very common. When using spin locks, the tasks should be written in a way that they can unlock a mutex as soon as possible. For this to happen, the critical sections should be small enough. As you can see in our code, we have a critical section with only one Boolean check (the loop condition).

In the next section, we explore condition variables and their properties.

Condition variables

The solutions we have provided in the previous sections to satisfy *example 14.6* cannot be implemented using a programming language because we don't know how to put a task into sleep mode and how to notify another task programmatically. In this section, we are going to introduce condition variables, a new concept that can help us to make a task wait and get notified accordingly.

Condition variables are simple variables (or objects) that can be used to put a task into sleeping mode or notify other sleeping tasks and wake them up. Note that sleeping mode discussed here is different from sleeping for a number of seconds or milliseconds to make a delay and it particularly means that the task doesn't want to receive any more CPU share. Like mutexes that are used to protect a critical section, condition variables are used to enable *signaling* between different tasks.

Again, like mutexes that have associated *lock* and *unlock* operations, the condition variables have *sleep* and *notify* operations. However, every programming language has its own terminology here, and in some of them you may find *wait* and *signal* instead of sleep and notify, but the logic behind them remains the same.

A condition variable must be used together with a mutex. Having a solution that uses a condition variable without a mutex simply lacks the *mutual exclusion* property. Remember that a condition variable must be shared between multiple tasks to be helpful and, as a shared resource, we need synchronized access to it. This is often achieved with a mutex that guards the critical sections. The following pseudo-code shows how we can use condition variables and mutexes to wait for a certain condition, or an event in general, and specifically to wait for the shared flag Done to become True in *example 14.6*:

```
Concurrent System {

  Shared State {
      Done : Boolean = False
      CV   : Condition Variable
      M    : Mutex
  }

  Task P {
        1.1. print 'A'
        1.2. Lock(M)
        1.3. Done = True
        1.4. Notify(CV)
        1.5. Unlock(M)
  }

  Task Q {
        2.1. Lock(M)
```

```
          2.2. While Not Done {
          2.3.     Sleep(M, CV)
          2.4. }
          2.5. Unlock(M)
          2.6. print 'B'
     }
}
```

Code Box 14-19: The solution for example 14.6 using a condition variable

The preceding solution is the most genuine way to use condition variables to implement strict ordering between two instructions in a concurrent system. Instructions 1.4 and 2.3 are using the condition variable CV. As you can see, the operation Sleep needs to know about both the mutex M and the condition variable CV because it needs to unlock M when the task Q is going to sleep and reacquiring the lock over M when it has become notified.

Note that when the task Q is notified, it continues its logic that is inside the Sleep operation, and locking M again is part of that. Instruction 1.4 also only works when you have acquired the lock over M, otherwise race conditions happen. It would be a good and beneficial challenge to go through possible interleavings and see how the preceding mutex and condition variable are going to enforce the desired order between instructions 1.1 and 2.6 all the time.

As a final definition in this section, a mutex object together with a condition variable is usually referred to as a *monitor* object. We also have a concurrency-related design pattern called *monitor object*, which is about employing the preceding technique to reorder instructions in some concurrent tasks.

In the previous sections, we showed how semaphores, mutexes, and condition variables together with locking, unlocking, sleep, and notify algorithms can be used to implement control mechanisms that are used to enforce a strict order between some instructions in various concurrent tasks and to protect critical sections. These concepts will be used in the upcoming chapters in order to write multithreaded and multi-process programs in C. The next section will talk about the concurrency support in the POSIX standard that has been implemented and provided by many Unix-like operating systems.

Concurrency in POSIX

As we explained in the previous sections, concurrency or multitasking is a functionality provided by the kernel of an operating system. Not all kernels have been concurrent since their birth, but most of them support concurrency today. It is nice to know that the first version of Unix was not concurrent, but it gained this feature very soon after its birth.

If you remember *Chapter 10, Unix – History and Architecture*, we explained how single Unix specification and POSIX tried to standardize the API exposed by the shell ring in a Unix-like operating system. Concurrency has been part of these standards for a long time, and so far, it has allowed many developers to write concurrent programs for POSIX-compliant operating systems. The concurrency support in POSIX has been widely used and implemented in a vast range of operating systems, such as Linux and macOS.

Concurrency in a POSIX-compliant operating system is generally provided in two ways. You can either have a concurrent program executing as some different processes, which is called *multi-processing*, or you can have your concurrent program running as some different threads as part of the same process, which is called *multithreading*. In this section, we are going to talk about these two methods and compare them from a programmer's point of view. But before that, we need to know more about the internals of a kernel supporting concurrency. The next section briefly explains what you will find in such a kernel.

Kernels supporting concurrency

Almost all kernels being developed and maintained today are multitasking. As we already know, every kernel has a *task scheduler unit* that shares CPU cores among many running processes and threads that were generally referred to as tasks in this and the previous chapter.

Before being able to move on, we need to describe processes and threads and their differences with respect to concurrency. Whenever you run a program, a new process is created, and the program's logic is run inside that process. Processes are isolated from each other, and one process cannot have access to another process's internals, like its memory.

Threads are very similar to processes, but they are local to a certain process. They are used to bring concurrency into a single process through having multiple threads of execution that together execute multiple series of instructions in a concurrent way. A single thread cannot be shared between two processes, and it is local and bound to its owner process. All threads in a process are able to access their owner process's memory as a shared resource, while every thread has its own Stack region that of course is accessible by other threads in the same process. In addition, both processes and threads can use CPU share, and the task scheduler in most kernels uses the same *scheduling* algorithm for sharing the CPU cores among them.

Note that when we're talking at the kernel level, we prefer to use the term *task* instead of the terms *thread* or *process*. From the kernel's point of view, there is a queue of tasks waiting to have a CPU core to execute their instructions, and it is the duty of the task scheduler unit to provide this facility to all of them in a fair fashion.

Note:
In Unix-like kernels, we usually use the term *task* for both processes and threads. In fact, the terms thread or process are *userspace* terms, and they cannot be used in kernel terminology. Therefore, Unix-like kernels have task scheduler units that try to fairly manage access to CPU cores among various tasks.

In different kernels, the task schedulers use different strategies and algorithms to do the scheduling. But most of them can be grouped into two giant categories of scheduling algorithms:

- Cooperative scheduling
- Preemptive scheduling

Cooperative scheduling is about granting the CPU core to a task and waiting for the task's cooperation to release the CPU core. This approach is not *preemptive* in the sense that in most normal cases, there is no force employed to take back the CPU core from the task. There should be a high priority *preemptive signal* to make the scheduler to take back the CPU core by preemption. Otherwise, the scheduler and all tasks in the system should wait until the active task releases the CPU core at will. Modern kernels are not usually designed this way, but you can still find kernels employing cooperative scheduling for very specific applications, like *real-time processing*. Early versions of macOS and Windows used cooperative scheduling, but nowadays they use a preemptive scheduling approach.

In contrast to cooperative scheduling, we have preemptive scheduling. In preemptive scheduling, a task is allowed to use a CPU core until it is taken back by the scheduler. In a specific type of preemptive scheduling, a task is allowed to use the given CPU core for a certain amount of time. This type of preemptive scheduling is called *time-sharing*, and it is the most employed scheduling strategy in current kernels. The time interval that has been given to a task to use the CPU has various names, and it can be called a *time slice*, a *time slot*, or a *quantum* in various academic sources.

There are also various types of time-sharing scheduling based on the algorithm used. *Round-robin* is the most widely used time-sharing algorithm and has been employed by various kernels, with some modifications of course. The round-robin algorithm allows fair and *starvation-free* access to a shared resource, which is a CPU core in this case.

Despite the fact that the round-robin algorithm is simple and not prioritized, it can be modified to allow multiple priority levels for tasks. Having different priority levels is usually a requirement for modern kernels because there are certain types of tasks that are initiated by the kernel itself or other important units inside the kernel, and these tasks should be served before any other ordinary task.

As we said before, there are two ways of bringing concurrency into a piece of software. The first approach is multi-processing, which uses *user processes* to do parallel tasks in a multitasking environment. The second approach is multithreading, which uses *user threads* to break tasks into parallel flows of execution inside a single process. It is also very common to use a combination of both techniques in a big software project. Despite the fact that both techniques bring concurrency to software, they have fundamental differences in respect to their different natures.

In the following two sections, we will talk about multi-processing and multithreading in greater detail. In the next two chapters, we will cover multithreaded development in C, and in the two chapters after that, we will discuss multi-processing.

Multi-processing

Multi-processing simply means using processes to do concurrent tasks. A very good example is the **Common Gateway Interface** (**CGI**) standard in web servers. The web servers employing this technique launch a new *interpreter process* for each HTTP request. This way, they can serve multiple requests simultaneously.

On such web servers, for a high throughput of requests, you might see that many interpreter processes are spawned and running at the same time, each of which is handling a different HTTP request. Since they are different processes, they are isolated and cannot see the memory regions of each other. Fortunately, in the CGI use case, the interpreter processes don't need to communicate with each other or share data. But this is not always the case.

There are many examples in which a number of processes are doing some concurrent tasks, and they need to share crucial pieces of information in order to let the software continue functioning. As an example, we can refer to the Hadoop infrastructure. There are many nodes in a Hadoop cluster, and each node has a number of processes keeping the cluster running.

These processes need to constantly share pieces of information in order to keep the cluster up and running. There are many more examples of such distributed systems with multiple nodes, like Gluster, Kafka, and cryptocurrency networks. All of them need a great deal of intercommunication and message-passing between processes located on different nodes in order to remain up and running.

As long as the processes or threads are functioning without having a shared state in the middle, there is not much difference between multi-processing and multithreading. You probably can use processes instead of threads and vice versa. But with introducing a shared state between them, we see a huge difference between using processes or threads, or even a combination of both. One difference is in the available synchronization techniques. While the APIs exposed to use these mechanisms are more or less the same, the complexity of working in multi-process environments is much higher and the underlying implementations are different. Another difference between multi-processing and multithreading is the techniques we use for having shared states. While threads are able to use all the techniques available to processes, they have the luxury that they can use the same memory region to share a state. As you see in the upcoming chapters, this makes a big difference.

To elaborate more, a process has a private memory, and other processes cannot read or modify it, so it's not that easy to use the process's memory for sharing something with other processes. But this is much simpler with threads. All threads within the same process have access to the same process's memory; hence they can use it for storing a shared state.

Next, you can find the techniques that can be used by processes to access a shared state among themselves. More information regarding these techniques will be given in upcoming chapters:

- **File system**: This can be considered as the simplest way to share data between a number of processes. This approach is very old and is supported by almost all operating systems. An example is configuration files that are read by many processes in a software project. If the file is going to be written by one of the processes, synchronization techniques should be employed in order to prevent data races and other concurrency-related issues.

- **Memory-mapped file**: In all POSIX-compliant operating systems and Microsoft Windows, we can have memory regions that are mapped to files on disk. These memory regions can be shared among a number of processes to be read and modified.

    This technique is very similar to the file system approach, but it has fewer headaches caused by streaming data to and from a file descriptor using the File API. Proper synchronization mechanisms should be employed if the content of the mapped region can be modified by any of the processes that have access to it.

- **Network**: For processes located on different computers, the only way to communicate is by using the network infrastructure and the socket programming API. The socket programming API is a great part of the SUS and POSIX standards, and it exists in almost every operating system.

The details regarding this technique are huge, and many books exist just to cover this technique. Various protocols, various architectures, different methods for handling data flow, and many more details all exist as subparts of this technique. We try to cover part of it in *Chapter 20, Socket Programming*, but it may need a completely separate book to go through the different aspects of IPC via networks.

- **Signals**: Processes being run within the same operating system can send signals to each other. While this is more used for passing command signals, it can be also used for sharing a small state (payload). The value for the shared state can be carried on the signal and intercepted by the target process.

- **Shared memory**: In POSIX-compliant operating systems and Microsoft Windows, we can have a region of memory shared among a number of processes. Therefore, they can use this shared region to store variables and share some values. Shared memory is not protected against data races, so the processes willing to use it as a placeholder for their modifiable shared states need to employ a proper synchronization mechanism in order to avoid any concurrency problems. A shared memory region can be used by many processes at the same time.

- **Pipes**: In POSIX-compliant operating systems and Microsoft Windows, pipes are one-way communication channels. They can be used in order to transfer a shared state between two processes. One of the processes writes to the pipe, and the other one reads from it.

  A pipe can be either named or anonymous, each of which has its own specific use cases. We will give more details and examples in *Chapter 19, Single-Host IPC and Sockets*, when talking about various available IPC techniques on a single machine.

- **Unix domain sockets**: In POSIX-compliant operating systems, and recently Windows 10, we have communication endpoints known as *Unix sockets*. Processes located on the same machine and running within the same operating system can use *Unix domain sockets* to pass information over a full-duplex channel. Unix domain sockets are very similar to network sockets, but all the data is transferred through the kernel, hence it provides a very fast way of transferring data. Multiple processes can use the same Unix domain socket in order to communicate and share data. Unix domain sockets can also be used for special use cases, like transferring a file descriptor between processes on the same machine. The good thing about Unix domain sockets is that we need to use the same socket programming API as if they were network sockets.

- **Message queue**: This exists in almost every operating system. A message queue is maintained in the kernel that can be used by various processes to send and receive a number of messages. The processes are not required to know about each other, and it is enough for them to only have access to the message queue.

  This technique is only used to make processes on the same machine able to communicate with each other.

- **Environment variables**: Unix-like operating systems and Microsoft Windows offer a set of variables that are kept in the operating system itself.

  These variables are called environment variables, and they can be accessible to processes within the system.

As an example, this method is heavily used in CGI implementations introduced in the first paragraph of this section, especially when the main webserver process wants to pass HTTP request data to the spawned interpreter process.

Regarding the control techniques to make a number of threads/processes synchronized, you will see that the techniques used in multi-processing and multithreading environments share a very similar API provided by the POSIX standard. But probably the underlying implementation of a mutex or a condition variable is different in multithreading and multiprocessing usages. We will give examples of this in the upcoming chapters.

Multithreading

Multithreading is about employing *user threads* to perform parallel tasks in a concurrent environment. It's very rare to find a non-trivial program that has only a single thread; almost every program you'll encounter is multithreaded. Threads can only exist inside processes; we cannot have any thread without an owner process. Each process has at least one thread, which is usually called the *main thread*. A program that is using a single thread to perform all its tasks is called a *single-threaded* program. All threads within a process have access to the same memory regions, and this means that we won't have to come up with a complex scenario to share a piece of data, like we do in multi-processing.

Since threads are very similar to processes, they can use all the techniques that processes use to share or transfer a state. Therefore, all the techniques explained in the previous section can be employed by threads to access a shared state or transfer data among themselves. But threads have another advantage over processes in this sense, and that's having access to the same memory regions. Hence, one of the common methods of sharing a piece of data among a number of threads is to use the memory by declaring some variables.

Since each thread has its own Stack memory, it can be used as a placeholder for keeping shared states. A thread can give an address pointing to somewhere inside its Stack to another thread, and it can be easily accessed by the other thread because all of these memory addresses belong to the process's Stack segment. The threads can also easily access the same Heap space owned by the process and use it as a place holder to store their shared states. We will give several examples of using the Stack and Heap regions as some placeholders for shared states in the next chapter.

The synchronization techniques are also very similar to the techniques used by the processes. Even the POSIX API remains the same between processes and threads. It's likely due to the fact that a POSIX-compliant operating system treats processes and threads in almost the same way. In the next chapter, we will explain how to use the POSIX API to declare semaphores, mutexes, and condition variables and more in a multithreaded program.

As a final note on Windows, regarding the POSIX Threading API (pthreads), Microsoft Windows doesn't support it. Therefore, Windows has its own API, which creates and manages threads. This API is part of the Win32 native library, which we won't go through in this book, but you can certainly find many resources on the web that cover it.

Summary

In this chapter, we discussed the issues we might expect to encounter while developing a concurrent program, and the solutions we should employ to resolve them. The following are the main points that we covered in this chapter.

- We covered concurrency issues. Intrinsic issues exist in all concurrent systems when different interleavings dissatisfy the invariant constraints of a system.

- We discussed post-synchronization issues that only occur after employing a synchronization technique in a poor and wrong way.

- We explored the control mechanisms employed to keep the invariant constraints satisfied.

- Semaphores are key tools in implementing control mechanisms. Mutexes are a special category of semaphores that allow only one task at a time to enter a critical section based on mutual exclusion conditions.

- Monitor objects that encapsulate a mutex and a condition variable can be used in situations when a task is waiting for a condition to be met.

- We finally took the first step towards concurrency development by introducing multi-processing and multithreading in the POSIX standard.

The next chapter is the first of a pair of chapters (*Chapter 15, Thread Execution,* and *Chapter 16, Thread Synchronization*) that discuss multithreaded development in POSIX-compliant operating systems. *Chapter 15, Thread Execution* mainly talks about threads and how they are executed. *Chapter 16, Thread Synchronization* goes through the available concurrency control mechanisms for multithreaded environments, and together they convey all the topics required for writing a multithreaded program.

Chapter 15

Thread Execution

As we explained in the previous chapter, concurrency can be implemented using only one of the *multithreading* or *multi-processing* approaches within a POSIX-compliant system. Since these two approaches are such large topics to discuss, they've been split into four separate chapters in order to give each topic the coverage that it needs:

- **The multithreading approach** will be discussed in both this chapter and *Chapter 16, Thread Synchronization*
- **The multi-processing approach** will be covered in *Chapter 17, Process Execution*, and *Chapter 18, Process Synchronization*.

In this chapter, we're going to look at the anatomy of a thread and the APIs that can be used to create and manage threads. In the next chapter, *Chapter 16, Thread Synchronization*, we will go through the concurrency control mechanisms in a multithreaded environment to study how they are supposed to resolve concurrency-related issues.

Multi-processing is all about the idea of bringing concurrency into software by breaking its logic into concurrent processes, which eventually leads to multi-process software. Because of the existing differences between multithreading and multi-processing, we decided to move the discussion of multi-processing to two separate chapters.

In comparison, multithreading, the focus of the first two chapters, is limited to a single-process system. This is the most basic fact about threads and is the reason why we're focusing on it first.

In the previous chapter, we briefly explained the differences and similarities between multithreading and multi-processing. In this chapter, we are going to focus on multithreading, coupled with an exploration of the way they should be used in order to have several threads of execution running flawlessly in a single process.

The following topics are covered in this chapter:

- We begin by talking about threads. Both *user threads* and *kernel threads* are explained in this section, and some of the most important properties of threads are discussed. These properties help us to better understand a multithreaded environment.

- Then we move onto the next section, which is dedicated to basic programming using the **POSIX threading** library, or for short, the **pthread** library. This library is the main standard library that allows us to develop concurrent programs on POSIX systems, but it doesn't mean that non-POSIX-compliant operating systems don't support concurrency. For non-compliant operating systems like Microsoft Windows, they are still able to provide their own API for developing concurrent programs. The POSIX threading library provides support for both threads and processes. However, in this chapter, our focus is on the threading part, where we are looking at how the pthread library can both be used to create a thread and manage it further.

- In a further step, we also demonstrate a race condition together with a data race produced in some example C codes that are using the pthread library. This develops the basis for continuing our discussion in the next chapter regarding *thread synchronization*.

Note:
To be able to fully grasp the discussions that we are going to have in regard to the multithreading approach, it's highly recommended that you complete this chapter before moving onto *Chapter 16, Thread Synchronization*. This is because the themes introduced in this chapter are featured throughout the second part of our look into thread synchronization, which will come in the next chapter.

Before going any further, please bear in mind that we will only be covering the basic use of the POSIX threading library in this chapter. It's beyond the scope of this book to dive into the multiple and fascinating elements of the POSIX threading library and therefore, it is recommended that you take some time to explore the pthread library in more detail and gain sufficient practice through written examples to enable you to be comfortable with it. The more advanced usage of the POSIX threading library will be demonstrated across the remaining chapters of this book.

For now, though, let's delve deep into the concept of threads by beginning with an overview looking at everything we know about them. This is a key element in our understanding, as we are going to be introducing the other key concepts that we will be learning about in the remaining pages of this chapter.

Threads

In the previous chapter, we discussed threads as part of the multithreading approach that you can use when wanting to write concurrent programs in a POSIX-compliant operating system.

In this section, you will find a recap on everything you should know about threads. We will also bring in some new information that is relevant to topics we will discuss later. Remember that all of this information will act as a foundation for continuing to develop multithreaded programs.

Every thread is initiated by a process. It will then belong to that process forever. It is not possible to have a shared thread or transfer the ownership of a thread to another process. Every process has at least one thread that is its *main thread*. In a C program, the `main` function is executed as part of the main thread.

All the threads share the same **Process ID (PID)**. If you use utilities like `top` or `htop`, you can easily see the threads are sharing the same process ID, and are grouped under it. More than that, all the attributes of the owner process are inherited by all of its threads for example, group ID, user ID, current working directory, and signal handlers. As an example, the current working directory of a thread is the same as its owner process.

Every thread has a unique and dedicated **Thread ID (TID)**. This ID can be used to pass signals to that thread or track it while debugging. You will see that in POSIX threads, the thread ID is accessible via the `pthread_t` variable. In addition, every thread has also a dedicated signal mask that can be used to filter out the signals it may receive.

All of the threads within the same process have access to all of the *file descriptors* opened by other threads in that process. Therefore, all the threads can both read or modify the resources behind those file descriptors. This is also true regarding *socket descriptors* and opened *sockets*. In upcoming chapters, you'll learn more about file descriptors and sockets.

Threads can use all the techniques used by processes introduced in chapter 14 to share or transfer a state. Take note of the fact that having a shared state in a shared place (like a database) is different from transmitting it on a network for example, and this results in two different categories of IPC techniques. We will come back to this point in future chapters.

Here, you can find a list of methods that can be used by threads to share or transfer a state in a POSIX-compliant system:

- Owner process's memory (Data, Stack, and Heap segments). This method is *only* specific to threads and not processes.
- Filesystem.

- Memory-mapped files.
- Network (using internet sockets).
- Signal passing between threads.
- Shared memory.
- POSIX pipes.
- Unix domain sockets.
- POSIX message queues.
- Environment variables.

To proceed with the thread properties, all of the threads within the same process can use the same process's memory space to store and maintain a shared state. This is the most common way of sharing a state among a number of threads. The Heap segment of the process is usually used for this purpose.

The lifetime of a thread is dependent on the lifetime of its owner process. When a process gets *killed* or *terminated*, all the threads belonging to that process will also get terminated.

When the main thread ends, the process quits immediately. However, if there are other *detached* threads running, the process waits for all of them to be finished before getting terminated. Detached threads will be explained while explaining the thread creation in POSIX.

The process that creates a thread can be the kernel process. At the same time, it can also be a user process initiated in the user space. If the process is the kernel, the thread is called a *kernel-level thread* or simply a *kernel thread*, otherwise, the thread is called a *user-level thread*. Kernel threads typically execute important logic, and because of this they have higher priorities than that of user threads. As an example, a device driver may be using a kernel thread to wait for a hardware signal.

Similar to user threads that have access to the same memory region, kernel threads are also able to access the kernel's memory space and, subsequently, all the procedures and units within the kernel.

Throughout this book we will be mainly talking about user threads, not kernel threads. That's because the required API for working with user threads is provided by the POSIX standard. But there is no standard interface for creating and managing a kernel thread and they are only specific to each kernel.

Creating and managing kernel threads is beyond the scope of this book. Thus, from this point on, when we are using the term *thread*, we are referring to user threads and not kernel threads.

A user cannot create a thread directly. The user needs to spawn a process first, as only then can that process's main thread initiate another thread. Note that only threads can create threads.

Regarding the memory layout of threads, every thread has its own Stack memory region that can be considered as a private memory region dedicated to that thread. In practice, however, it can be accessed by other threads (within the same process) when having a pointer addressing it.

You should remember that all these Stack regions are part of the same process's memory space and can be accessed by any thread within the same process.

Regarding synchronization techniques, the same control mechanisms that are used to synchronize processes can be used to synchronize a number of threads. Semaphores, mutexes, and condition variables are part of the tools that can be used to synchronize threads, as well as processes.

When its threads are synchronized and no further data race or race condition can be observed, a program is usually referred to as a *thread-safe* program. Similarly, a library or a set of functions that can be easily used in a multithreaded program without introducing any new concurrency issue is called a *thread-safe library*. Our goal as programmers is to produce a thread safe piece of code.

Note:
In the following link, you can find more information about POSIX threads and the properties they share. The following link is about the NTPL implementation of the POSIX threading interface. This is dedicated to a Linux environment but most of it is applicable to other Unix-like operating systems.

```
http://man7.org/linux/man-pages/man7/
pthreads.7.html
```

In this section we looked at some foundational concepts and properties concerning threads in order to better understand the upcoming sections. You will see many of these properties in action later as we talk about various multithreaded examples.

The next section will introduce you to the first code examples on how to create a POSIX thread. The section is going to be simple because it only addresses the basics of threading in POSIX. These basics will lead us into more advanced topics afterwards.

POSIX threads

This section is dedicated to the POSIX threading API, better known as the *pthread library*. This API is very important because it's the main API used for creating and managing the threads in a POSIX-compliant operating system.

In non-POSIX-compliant operating systems such as Microsoft Windows, there should be another API designed for this purpose and it can be found in the documentation of that operating system. For example, in the case of Microsoft Windows, the threading API is provided as part of the Windows API, known as the Win32 API. This is the link to Microsoft's documentation regarding Windows' threading API: `https://docs.microsoft.com/en-us/windows/desktop/ procthread/process-and-thread-functions`.

However, as part of C11, we expect to have a unified API to work with threads. In other words, regardless of whether you're writing a program for a POSIX system or a non-POSIX system, you should be able to use the same API provided by C11. While this is highly desirable, not much support exists for such universal APIs among the various C standard implementations, like glibc, at this point in time.

To proceed with the topic, the pthread library is simply a set of *headers* and *functions* that can be used to write multithreaded programs in POSIX-compliant operating systems. Each operating system has its own implementation for pthread library. These implementations could be totally different from what another POSIX-compliant operating system have, but at the end of the day, they all expose the same interface (API).

One famous example is the **Native POSIX Threading Library**, or **NPTL** for short, which is the main implementation of pthread library for the Linux operating system.

As described by the pthread API, all threading functionality is available by including the header `pthread.h`. There are also some extensions to the pthread library that are only available if you include `semaphore.h`. As an example, one of the extensions involves operations that are semaphore-specific, for example, creating a semaphore, initializing it, destroying it, and so on.

The POSIX threading library exposes the following functionalities. They should be familiar to you since we have given detailed explanations to them in the previous chapters:

- Thread management, which includes thread creation, joining threads, and detaching threads
- Mutexes
- Semaphores
- Condition variables
- Various types of locks like spinlocks and recursive locks

To explain the preceding functionalities, we must start with the `pthread_` prefix. All pthread functions start with this prefix. This is true in all cases except for semaphores, which have not been part of the original POSIX threading library and have been added later as an extension. In this case, the functions will start with the `sem_` prefix.

In the following sections of this chapter, we will see how to use some of the preceding functionalities when writing a multithreaded program. To start with, we'll learn how to create a POSIX thread in order to run a code concurrent with the main thread. Here, we will learn about the `pthread_create` and `pthread_join` functions, which belong to the main API used for *creating* and *joining* threads, respectively.

Spawning POSIX threads

Having gone through all the fundamental concepts like interleaving, locks, mutexes, and condition variables, in the previous chapters, and introducing the concept of POSIX threads in this chapter, it is the time to write some code.

The first step is to create a POSIX thread. In this section, we are going to demonstrate how we can use the POSIX threading API to create new threads within a process. Following *example 15.1* describes how to create a thread that performs a simple task like printing a string to the output:

```c
#include <stdio.h>
#include <stdlib.h>

// The POSIX standard header for using pthread library
#include <pthread.h>

// This function contains the logic which should be run
// as the body of a separate thread
void* thread_body(void* arg) {
  printf("Hello from first thread!\n");
  return NULL;
}

int main(int argc, char** argv) {

  // The thread handler
  pthread_t thread;

  // Create a new thread
  int result = pthread_create(&thread, NULL, thread_body, NULL);
  // If the thread creation did not succeed
```

```
  if (result) {
    printf("Thread could not be created. Error number: %d\n",
           result);
    exit(1);
  }

  // Wait for the created thread to finish
  result = pthread_join(thread, NULL);
  // If joining the thread did not succeed
  if (result) {
    printf("The thread could not be joined. Error number: %d\n",
           result);
    exit(2);
  }
  return 0;
}
```

Code Box 15-1 [ExtremeC_examples_chapter15_1.c]: Spawning a new POSIX thread

The example code, seen in *Code Box 15-1*, creates a new POSIX thread. This is the first example in this book that has two threads. All previous examples were single-threaded, and the code was running within the main thread all the time.

Let's explain the code we've just looked at. At the top, we have included a new header file: pthread.h. This is the standard header file that exposes all the pthread functionalities. We need this header file so that we can bring in the declarations of both pthread_create and pthread_join functions.

Just before the main function, we have declared a new function: thread_body. This function follows a specific signature. It accepts a void* pointer and returns another void* pointer. As a reminder, void* is a generic pointer type that can represent any other pointer type, like int* or double*.

Therefore, this signature is the most general signature that a C function can have. This is imposed by the POSIX standard that all functions willing to be the *companion function* for a thread (being used as thread logic) should follow this generic signature. That's why we have defined the thread_body function like this.

Note:
The main function is a part of the main thread's logic. When the main thread is created, it executes the main function as part of its logic. This means that there might be other code that is executed before and after the main function.

Back to the code, as the first instruction in the `main` function, we have declared a variable of type `pthread_t`. This is a thread handle variable, and upon its declaration, it doesn't refer to any specific thread. In other words, this variable doesn't hold any valid thread ID yet. Only after creating a thread successfully does this variable contain a valid handle to the newly created thread.

After creating the thread, the thread handle actually refers to the thread ID of the recently created thread. While thread ID is the thread identifier in the operating system, the thread handle is the representative of the thread in the program. Most of the time, the value stored in the thread handle is the same as thread ID. Every thread is able to access its thread ID through obtaining a `pthread_t` variable that refers to itself. A thread can use the `pthread_self` function to obtain a self-referring handle. We are going to demonstrate the usage of these functions in future examples.

Thread creation happens when the `pthread_create` function is called. As you can see, we have passed the address of the `thread` handle variable to the `pthread_create` function in order to have it filled with a proper handle (or thread ID), referring to the newly created thread.

The second argument determines the thread's attributes. Every thread has some attributes like *stack size*, *stack address*, and *detach* state that can be configured before spawning the thread.

We show more examples of how to configure these attributes and how they affect the way the threads behave. If a `NULL` is passed as the second argument, it means that the new thread should use the default values for its attributes. Therefore, in the preceding code, we have created a thread that has attributes with default values.

The third argument passed to `pthread_create` is a function pointer. This is pointing to the thread's *companion function*, which contains the thread's logic. In the preceding code, the thread's logic is defined in the `thread_body` function. Therefore, its address should be passed in order to get bound to the handle variable `thread`.

The fourth and last argument is the input argument for the thread's logic, which in our case is `NULL`. This means that we don't want to pass anything to the function. Therefore, the parameter `arg` in the `thread_body` function would be `NULL` upon the thread's execution. In the examples provided in the next section, we'll look at how we can pass a value to this function instead of a `NULL`.

All pthread functions, including `pthread_create`, are supposed to return zero upon successful execution. Therefore, if any number other than zero is returned, then it means that the function has failed, and an *error number* has been returned.

Note that creating a thread using `pthread_create` doesn't mean that the thread's logic is being executed immediately. It is a matter of scheduling and cannot be predicted when the new thread gains one of the CPU cores and starts its execution.

After creating the thread, we join the newly created thread, but what exactly does that mean? As we explained before, each process starts with exactly one thread, which is the *main thread*. Except for the main thread, whose parent is the owning process, all other threads have a *parent thread*. In a default scenario, if the main thread is finished, the process will also be finished. When the process gets terminated, all other running or sleeping threads will also get terminated immediately.

So, if a new thread is created and it hasn't started yet (because it hasn't gained the use of the CPU) and in the meantime, the parent process is terminated (for whatever reason), the thread will die before even executing its first instruction. Therefore, the main thread needs to wait for the second thread to become executed and finished by joining it.

A thread becomes finished only when its companion function returns. In the preceding example, the spawned thread becomes finished when the `thread_body` companion function returns, and this happens when the function returns NULL. When the newly spawned thread is finished, the main thread, which was blocked behind calling `pthread_join`, is released and can continue, which eventually leads to successful termination of the program.

If the main thread didn't join the newly created thread, then it is unlikely that the newly spawned thread can be executed at all. As we've explained before, this happens due to the fact that the main thread exits even before the spawned thread has entered into its execution phase.

We should also remember that creating a thread is not enough to have it executed. It may take a while for the created thread to gain access to a CPU core, and through this eventually start running. If, in the meantime, the process gets terminated, then the newly created thread has no chance of running successfully.

Now that we've talked through the design of the code, *Shell Box 15-1* shows the output of running *example 15.1*:

```
$ gcc ExtremeC_examples_chapter15_1.c -o ex15_1.out -lpthread
$ ./ex15_1.out
Hello from first thread!
$
```

Shell Box 15-1: Building and running example 15.1

As you see in the preceding shell box, we need to add the `-lpthread` option to the compilation command. This is done because we need to link our program with the existing implementation of the pthread library. In some platforms, like macOS, your program might get linked without the `-lpthread` option as well; however, it is strongly recommended to use this option while you are linking programs that use pthread library. The importance of this advice is to make your *build scripts* working on any platform and prevent any cross-compatibility issues while building your C projects.

A thread that can be joined is known as *joinable*. The threads are joinable by default. Opposite to joinable threads, we have *detached* threads. Detached threads cannot be joined.

In *example 15.1*, the main thread could detach the newly spawned thread instead of joining it. This way, we would have let the process know that it must wait for the detached thread to become finished before it can get terminated. Note that in this case, the main thread can exit without the parent process being terminated.

In the final code of this section, we want to rewrite the preceding example using detached threads. Instead of joining the newly created thread, the main thread makes it detached and then exits. This way, the process remains running until the second thread finishes, despite the fact that the main thread has already exited:

```c
#include <stdio.h>
#include <stdlib.h>

// The POSIX standard header for using pthread library
#include <pthread.h>

// This function contains the logic which should be run
// as the body of a separate thread
void* thread_body(void* arg) {
  printf("Hello from first thread!\n");
  return NULL;
}

int main(int argc, char** argv) {

  // The thread handler
  pthread_t thread;

  // Create a new thread
  int result = pthread_create(&thread, NULL, thread_body, NULL);
  // If the thread creation did not succeed
  if (result) {
    printf("Thread could not be created. Error number: %d\n",
```

```
          result);
  exit(1);
}

// Detach the thread
result = pthread_detach(thread);
// If detaching the thread did not succeed
if (result) {
  printf("Thread could not be detached. Error number: %d\n",
          result);
  exit(2);
}

// Exit the main thread
pthread_exit(NULL);

  return 0;
}
```

Code Box 15-2 [ExtremeC_examples_chapter15_1_2.c]: Example 15.1 spawning a detached thread

The output of the preceding code is exactly the same as the previous code written using joinable threads. The only difference is the that way we managed the newly created thread.

Right after the creation of the new thread, the main thread has detached it. Then following that, the main thread exits. The instruction pthread_exit(NULL) was necessary in order to let the process know that it should wait for other detached threads to be finished. If the threads were not detached, the process would get terminated upon the exit of the main thread.

Note:
The *detach state* is one of the thread attributes that can be set before creating a new thread in order to have it detached. This is another method to create a new detached thread instead of calling pthread_detach on a joinable thread. The difference is that this way, the newly created thread is detached from the start.

In the next section, we're going to introduce our first example demonstrating a race condition. We will be using all the functions introduced in this section in order to write future examples. Therefore, you'll have a second chance to revisit them again in different scenarios.

Example of race condition

For our second example, we're going to look at a more problematic scenario. *Example 15.2*, shown in *Code Box 15-3*, shows just how interleavings happen and how we cannot reliably predict the final output of the example in practice, mainly because of the non-deterministic nature of concurrent systems. The example involves a program that creates three threads at almost the same time, and each of them prints a different string.

The final output of the following code contains the strings printed by three different threads but in an unpredictable order. If the invariant constraint (introduced in the previous chapter) for the following example was to see the strings in a specific order in the output, the following code would have failed at satisfying that constraint, mainly because of the unpredictable interleavings. Let's look at the following code box:

```c
#include <stdio.h>
#include <stdlib.h>

// The POSIX standard header for using pthread library
#include <pthread.h>

void* thread_body(void* arg) {
  char* str = (char*)arg;
  printf("%s\n", str);
  return NULL;
}

int main(int argc, char** argv) {

  // The thread handlers
  pthread_t thread1;
  pthread_t thread2;
  pthread_t thread3;

  // Create new threads
  int result1 = pthread_create(&thread1, NULL,
        thread_body, "Apple");
  int result2 = pthread_create(&thread2, NULL,
        thread_body, "Orange");
  int result3 = pthread_create(&thread3, NULL,
        thread_body, "Lemon");

  if (result1 || result2 || result3) {
    printf("The threads could not be created.\n");
    exit(1);
  }

  // Wait for the threads to finish
```

```
    result1 = pthread_join(thread1, NULL);
    result2 = pthread_join(thread2, NULL);
    result3 = pthread_join(thread3, NULL);

    if (result1 || result2 || result3) {
      printf("The threads could not be joined.\n");
      exit(2);
    }
    return 0;
}
```

Code Box 15-3 [ExtremeC_examples_chapter15_2.c]: Example 15.2 printing three different strings to the output

The code we've just looked at is very similar to the code written for *example 15.1*, but it creates three threads instead of the one. In this example, we use the same companion function for all three threads.

As you can see in the preceding code, we have passed a fourth argument to the pthread_create function, whereas in our previous example, *15.1*, it was NULL. These arguments will be accessible by the thread through the generic pointer parameter arg in the thread_body companion function.

Inside the thread_body function, the thread casts the generic pointer arg to a char* pointer and prints the string starting at that address using the printf function. This is how we are able to pass arguments to the threads. Likewise, it doesn't matter how big they are since we are only passing a pointer.

If you have multiple values that need to be sent to a thread upon their creation, you could use a structure to contain those values and pass a pointer to a structure variable filled by the desired values. We will demonstrate to how to do this in the next chapter, *Thread Synchronization*.

Note:
The fact that we can pass a pointer to a thread implies that the new threads should have access to the same memory region that the main thread has access to. However, access is not limited to a specific segment or region in the owning process's memory and all threads have full access to the Stack, Heap, Text, and Data segments in a process.

If you take *example 15.2* and run it several times, you'll see that the order of the printed strings can vary, as each run is expected to print the same strings but in a different order.

Shell Box 15-2 shows the compilation and the output of *example 15.2* after three consecutive runs:

```
$ gcc ExtremeC_examples_chapter15_2.c -o ex15_2.out -lpthread
$ ./ex15_2.out
Apple
Orange
Lemon
$ ./ex15_2.out
Orange
Apple
Lemon
$ ./ex15_2.out
Apple
Orange
Lemon
$
```

Shell Box 15-2: Running example 15.2 three times to observe the existing race condition and various interleavings

It is easy to produce the interleavings in which the first and second threads print their strings before the third thread, but it would be difficult to produce an interleaving in which the third thread prints its string, Lemon, as the first or second string in the output. However, this will certainly happen, albeit with a low probability. You might need to run the example many more times in order to produce that interleaving. This may require some patience.

The preceding code is also said to not be thread safe. This is an important definition; a multithreaded program is thread safe if, and only if, it has no race condition according to the defined invariant constraints. Therefore, since the preceding code has a race condition, it is not thread safe. Our job would be to make the preceding code thread safe through the use of proper control mechanisms that will be introduced in the next chapter.

As you see in the output of the preceding example, we don't have any interleaving between the characters of Apple or Orange. For example, we don't see the following output:

```
$ ./ex15_2.out
AppOrle
Ange
```

```
Lemon
$
```

Shell Box 15-3: An imaginary output that does not happen for the above example

This shows a fact that the printf function is *thread safe* and it simply means that it doesn't matter how interleavings happen, when one of the threads is in the middle of printing a string, printf instances in other threads don't print anything.

In addition, in the preceding code, the thread_body companion function was run three times in the context of three different threads. In the previous chapters and before giving multithreaded examples, all functions were being executed in the context of the main thread. From now on, every function call occurs in the context of a specific thread (not necessarily the main thread).

It's not possible for two threads to initiate a single function call. The reason is obvious because each function call needs to create a *stack frame* that should be put on top of the Stack of just one thread, and two different threads have two different Stack regions. Therefore, a function call can only be initiated by just one thread. In other words, two threads can call the same function separately and it results into two separate function calls, but they cannot share the same function call.

We should note that the pointer passed to a thread should not be a *dangling pointer*. It causes some serious memory issues that are hard to track. As a reminder, a dangling pointer points to an address in the memory where there is no allocated variable. More specifically, this is the case that at some moment in time; there might have been a variable or an array there originally, but as of the time when the pointer is about to be used, it's already been freed.

In the preceding code, we passed three literals to each thread. Since the memory required for these string literals are allocated from the Data segment and not from Heap or Stack segments, their addresses never become freed and the arg pointers won't become dangling.

It would be easy to write the preceding code in a way in which the pointers become dangling. The following is the same code but with dangling pointers, and you will see shortly that it leads to bad memory behaviors:

```c
#include <stdio.h>
#include <stdlib.h>
#include <string.h>

// The POSIX standard header for using pthread library
#include <pthread.h>
```

```
void* thread_body(void* arg) {
  char* str = (char*)arg;
  printf("%s\n", str);
  return NULL;
}

int main(int argc, char** argv) {

  // The thread handlers
  pthread_t thread1;
  pthread_t thread2;
  pthread_t thread3;

  char str1[8], str2[8], str3[8];
  strcpy(str1, "Apple");
  strcpy(str2, "Orange");
  strcpy(str3, "Lemon");

  // Create new threads
  int result1 = pthread_create(&thread1, NULL, thread_body, str1);
  int result2 = pthread_create(&thread2, NULL, thread_body, str2);
  int result3 = pthread_create(&thread3, NULL, thread_body, str3);

  if (result1 || result2 || result3) {
    printf("The threads could not be created.\n");
    exit(1);
  }

  // Detach the threads
  result1 = pthread_detach(thread1);
  result2 = pthread_detach(thread2);
  result3 = pthread_detach(thread3);

  if (result1 || result2 || result3) {
    printf("The threads could not be detached.\n");
    exit(2);
  }

  // Now, the strings become deallocated.
  pthread_exit(NULL);

  return 0;
}
```

Code Box 15-4 [ExtremeC_examples_chapter15_2_1.c]: Example 15.2 with literals allocated from the main thread's Stack region

The preceding code is almost the same as the code given in *example 15.2*, but with two differences.

Firstly, the pointers passed to the threads are not pointing to the string literals residing in Data segment, instead they point to character arrays allocated from the main thread's Stack region. As part of the `main` function, these arrays have been declared and in the following lines, they have been populated by some string literals.

We need to remember that the string literals still reside in the Data segment, but the declared arrays now have the same values as the string literals after being populated using the `strcpy` function.

The second difference is regarding how the main thread behaves. In the previous code it joined the threads, but in this code, it detaches the threads and exits immediately. This will deallocate the arrays declared on top of the main thread's Stack, and in some interleavings other threads may try to read those freed regions. Therefore, in some interleavings, the pointers passed to the threads can become dangling.

Note:
Some constraints, like having no crashes, having no dangling pointers, and generally having no memory-related issues, can always be thought of as being part of the invariant constraints for a program. Therefore, a concurrent system that yields a dangling pointer issue in some interleavings is definitely suffering from a serious race condition.

To be able to detect the dangling pointers, you need to use a *memory profiler*. As a simpler approach, you could run the program several times and wait for a crash to happen. However, you are not always fortunate enough to be able to see that and we are not lucky to see crashes in this example either.

To detect bad memory behavior in this example, we are going to use `valgrind`. You remember that we introduced this memory profiler in *Chapter 4*, *Process Memory Structure*, and *Chapter 5*, *Stack and Heap*, for finding the *memory leaks*. Back in this example, we want to use it to find the places where bad memory access has happened.

It's worth remembering that using a dangling pointer, and accessing its content, will not necessarily lead to a crash. This is especially true in the preceding code, in which the strings are placed on top of the main thread's Stack.

While the other threads are running, the Stack segment remains the same as it was when the main thread exited, therefore you can access the strings even though the `str1`, `str2`, and `str3` arrays are deallocated while leaving the `main` function. In other words, in C or C++, the runtime environment does not check if a pointer is dangling or not, it just follows the sequence of statements.

If a pointer is dangling and its underlying memory is changed, then bad things like crash or logical errors can happen but as long as the underlying memory is *untouched* then using the dangling pointers may not lead to a crash, and this is very dangerous and hard to track.

In short, just because you can access a memory region through a dangling pointer, that doesn't mean that you are allowed to access that region. This is the reason why we need to use a memory profiler like `valgrind` that will report on these invalid memory accesses.

In the following shell box, we compile the program and we run it with `valgrind` twice. In the first run, nothing bad happens but in the second run, `valgrind` reports a bad memory access.

Shell Box 15-4 shows the first run:

```
$ gcc -g ExtremeC_examples_chapter15_2_1.c -o ex15_2_1.out -lpthread
$ valgrind ./ex15_2_1.out
==1842== Memcheck, a memory error detector
==1842== Copyright (C) 2002-2017, and GNU GPL'd, by Julian Seward
et al.
==1842== Using Valgrind-3.13.0 and LibVEX; rerun with -h for
copyright info
==1842== Command: ./ex15_2_1.out
==1842==
Orange
Apple
Lemon
==1842==
==1842== HEAP SUMMARY:
==1842==     in use at exit: 0 bytes in 0 blocks
==1842==   total heap usage: 9 allocs, 9 frees, 3,534 bytes
allocated
==1842==
==1842== All heap blocks were freed -- no leaks are possible
==1842==
==1842== For counts of detected and suppressed errors, rerun with:
-v
==1842== ERROR SUMMARY: 0 errors from 0 contexts (suppressed: 0
from 0)
$
```

Shell Box 15-4: Running example 15.2 with valgrind for the first time

In the second run, valgrind reports some memory access issues (note that the full output will be viewable when you run it, but for purpose of length, we've refined it.):

```
$ valgrind ./ex15_2_1.out
==1854== Memcheck, a memory error detector
==1854== Copyright (C) 2002-2017, and GNU GPL'd, by Julian Seward
et al.
==1854== Using Valgrind-3.13.0 and LibVEX; rerun with -h for
copyright info
==1854== Command: ./ex15_2_1.out
==1854==
Apple
Lemon
==1854== Thread 4:
==1854== Conditional jump or move depends on uninitialised
value(s)
==1854==    at 0x50E6A65: _IO_file_xsputn@@GLIBC_2.2.5
(fileops.c:1241)
==1854==    by 0x50DBA8E: puts (ioputs.c:40)
==1854==    by 0x1087C9: thread_body (ExtremeC_examples_
chapter15_2_1.c:17)
==1854==    by 0x4E436DA: start_thread (pthread_create.c:463)
==1854==    by 0x517C88E: clone (clone.S:95)
==1854==
...
==1854==
==1854== Syscall param write(buf) points to uninitialised byte(s)
==1854==    at 0x516B187: write (write.c:27)
==1854==    by 0x50E61BC: _IO_file_write@@GLIBC_2.2.5
(fileops.c:1203)
==1854==    by 0x50E7F50: new_do_write (fileops.c:457)
==1854==    by 0x50E7F50: _IO_do_write@@GLIBC_2.2.5
(fileops.c:433)
==1854==    by 0x50E8402: _IO_file_overflow@@GLIBC_2.2.5
(fileops.c:798)
==1854==    by 0x50DBB61: puts (ioputs.c:41)
==1854==    by 0x1087C9: thread_body (ExtremeC_examples_
chapter15_2_1.c:17)
==1854==    by 0x4E436DA: start_thread (pthread_create.c:463)
==1854==    by 0x517C88E: clone (clone.S:95)
```

```
...
==1854==
Orange
==1854==
==1854== HEAP SUMMARY:
==1854==     in use at exit: 272 bytes in 1 blocks
==1854==   total heap usage: 9 allocs, 8 frees, 3,534 bytes
allocated
==1854==
==1854== LEAK SUMMARY:
==1854==    definitely lost: 0 bytes in 0 blocks
==1854==    indirectly lost: 0 bytes in 0 blocks
==1854==      possibly lost: 272 bytes in 1 blocks
==1854==    still reachable: 0 bytes in 0 blocks
==1854==         suppressed: 0 bytes in 0 blocks
==1854== Rerun with --leak-check=full to see details of leaked
memory
==1854==
==1854== For counts of detected and suppressed errors, rerun with:
-v
==1854== Use --track-origins=yes to see where uninitialised values
come from
==1854== ERROR SUMMARY: 13 errors from 3 contexts (suppressed: 0
from 0)
$
```

Shell Box 15-5: Running example 15.2 with valgrind for the second time

As you can see, the first run went well, with no memory access issues, even though the aforementioned race condition is still clear to us. In the second run, however, something goes wrong when one of the threads tries to access the string Orange pointed to by str2.

What this means is that the passed pointer to the second thread has become dangling. In the preceding output, you can clearly see that the stack trace points to line inside the thread_body function where there is the printf statement. Note that the stack trace actually refers to the puts function because our C compiler has replaced the printf statement with the equivalent puts statement. The preceding output also shows that the write system call is using a pointer named buf that points to a memory region that *is not initialized or allocated*.

Looking at the preceding example, valgrind doesn't conclude whether a pointer is dangling or not. It simply reports the invalid memory access.

Before the error messages regarding the bad memory access, you can see that the string `Orange` is printed even though the access for reading it is invalid. This just goes to show how easily things can get complicated when we have code running in a concurrent fashion.

In this section, we've taken a significant step forward in seeing how easy it is to write code that is not thread safe. Moving on, we're now going to demonstrate another interesting example that produces a data race. Here, we will see a more complex use of the pthread library and its various functions.

Example of data race

Example 15.3 demonstrates a data race. In previous examples, we didn't have a shared state, but in this example, we are going to have a variable shared between two threads.

The invariant constraint of this example is to protect the *data integrity* of the shared state, plus all other obvious constraints, like having no crashes, having no bad memory accesses, and so on. In other words, it doesn't matter how the output appears, but a thread must not write new values while the value of the shared variable has been changed by the other thread and the writer thread doesn't know the latest value. This is what we mean by "data integrity":

```
#include <stdio.h>
#include <stdlib.h>

// The POSIX standard header for using pthread library
#include <pthread.h>

void* thread_body_1(void* arg) {
  // Obtain a pointer to the shared variable
  int* shared_var_ptr = (int*)arg;
  // Increment the shared variable by 1 by writing
  // directly to its memory address
  (*shared_var_ptr)++;
  printf("%d\n", *shared_var_ptr);
  return NULL;
}

void* thread_body_2(void* arg) {
  // Obtain a pointer to the shared variable
  int* shared_var_ptr = (int*)arg;
  // Increment the shared variable by 2 by writing
  // directly to its memory address
  *shared_var_ptr += 2;
  printf("%d\n", *shared_var_ptr);
```

```
    return NULL;
}

int main(int argc, char** argv) {

    // The shared variable
    int shared_var = 0;

    // The thread handlers
    pthread_t thread1;
    pthread_t thread2;

    // Create new threads
    int result1 = pthread_create(&thread1, NULL,
            thread_body_1, &shared_var);
    int result2 = pthread_create(&thread2, NULL,
            thread_body_2, &shared_var);

    if (result1 || result2) {
      printf("The threads could not be created.\n");
      exit(1);
    }

    // Wait for the threads to finish
    result1 = pthread_join(thread1, NULL);
    result2 = pthread_join(thread2, NULL);

    if (result1 || result2) {
      printf("The threads could not be joined.\n");
      exit(2);
    }
    return 0;
}
```

Code Box 15-5 [ExtremeC_examples_chapter15_3.c]: Example 15.3 with two threads operating on a single shared variable

The shared state has been declared as the first line in the main function. In this example, we are dealing with a single integer variable allocated form the Stack region of the main thread, but in real applications it can be far more complex. The initial value of the integer variable is zero, and each thread contributes directly to an increase in its value by writing to its memory location.

In this example, there is no local variable that is keeping a copy of the shared variable's value in each thread. However, you should be careful about the increment operations in threads because they are not *atomic* operations, and therefore are subject to experiencing different interleavings. We have explained this thoroughly in the previous chapter.

Each thread is able to change the value of the shared variable by using the pointer that it receives inside its companion function through the argument `arg`. As you can see in both calls to `pthread_create`, we are passing the address of the variable `shared_var` as the fourth argument.

It's worth noting that the pointer never becomes dangling in threads because the main thread doesn't exit, and it waits for the threads to finish by joining them.

Shell Box 15-6 shows us the outputs of multiple runs of the preceding code in order to produce different interleavings. Remember that we want data integrity to be preserved for the shared variable `shared_var`.

So, based on the logic defined in `thread_body_1` and `thread_body_2`, we can only have `1  3` and `2  3` as the acceptable outputs:

```
$ gcc ExtremeC_examples_chapter15_3.c -o ex15_3.out -lpthread
$ ./ex15_3.out
1
3
$
. . .
. . .
. . .
$ ./ex15_3.out
3
1
$
. . .
. . .
. . .
$ ./ex15_3.out
1
2
$
```

Shell Box 15-6: Multiple runs of example 15.3, in which we eventually see that the data integrity of the shared variable is not preserved

As you can see, the last run reveals that the data integrity condition has not been met for the shared variable.

In the last run, the first thread, the thread that has `thread_body_1` as its companion function, has read the value of the shared variable and it is `0`.

The second thread, the thread that has `thread_body_2` as its companion function, has also read the shared value and it is `0`. After this point, both threads try to increment the value of the shared variable and print it immediately. This is a breach of data integrity because when one thread is manipulating a shared state, the other thread shouldn't be able to write to it.

As we explained before, we have a clear data race over `shared_var` in this example.

Note:
When executing *example 15.3* yourself, be patient and wait to see the `1 2` output. It might happen after running the executable 100 times! I could have observed the data race on both macOS and Linux.

In order to resolve the preceding data race, we need to use a control mechanism, such as a semaphore or a mutex, to synchronize the access to the shared variable. In the next chapter, we will introduce a mutex to the preceding code that will do that for us.

Summary

This chapter was our first step towards writing multithreaded programs in C using the POSIX threading library. As part of this chapter:

- We went through the basics of the POSIX threading library, which is the main tool for writing multithreaded applications in POSIX-compliant systems.
- We explored the various properties of threads and their memory structure.
- We gave some insight about the available mechanisms for threads to communicate and share a state.
- We explained that how the memory regions available to all threads within the same process are the best way to share data and communicate.
- We talked about the kernel threads and the user-level threads and how they differ.
- We explained the joinable and detached threads and how they differ from the execution point of view.
- We demonstrated how to use the `pthread_create` and `pthread_join` functions and what arguments they receive.

- Examples of a race condition and a data race were demonstrated using actual C code, and you saw how using dangling pointer can cause serious memory issues and eventually a crash or a logical error might occur.

In the following chapter, we will continue and develop our discussion into multithreading by looking at the concurrency-related issues and the available mechanisms to both prevent and resolve them.

Chapter 16

Thread Synchronization

In the previous chapter, we explained how to create and manage a POSIX thread. We also demonstrated two of the most common concurrency issues: race conditions and data races.

In this chapter, we are going to complete our discussion about multithreaded programming using the POSIX threading library and give you the required skills to control a number of threads.

If you remember from *Chapter 14, Synchronization*, we showed that concurrency-related problems are not actually issues; rather, they are consequences of the fundamental properties of a concurrent system. Therefore, you are likely to encounter them in any concurrent system.

We showed in the previous chapter that we could indeed produce such issues with the POSIX threading library as well. *Examples 15.2* and *15.3* from the previous chapter demonstrated the race condition and data race issues. Therefore, they will be our starting point to use the synchronization mechanisms provided by the pthread library in order to synchronize a number of threads.

In this chapter, we will cover the following topics:

- Using POSIX mutexes to protect critical sections accessing a shared resource.
- Using POSIX condition variables to wait for a specific condition.
- Using various types of locks together with mutexes and condition variables.
- Using POSIX barriers and the way they can help synchronize a number of threads.
- The concept of the semaphore and its counterpart object in the pthread library: the POSIX semaphore. You are going to find out that mutexes are just binary semaphores.
- The memory structure of a thread and how this structure can affect memory visibility in a multi-core system.

We start this chapter with a general talk about concurrency control. The following sections give you the necessary tools and constructs to write well-behaved multithreaded programs.

POSIX concurrency control

In this section, we are going to have a look at possible control mechanisms that are offered by the pthread library. Semaphores, mutexes, and condition variables alongside different types of locks are used in various combinations to bring determinism to multithreaded programs. First, we start with POSIX mutexes.

POSIX mutexes

The mutexes introduced in the pthread library can be used to synchronize both processes and threads. In this section, we are going to use them in a multithreaded C program in order to synchronize a number of threads.

As a reminder, a mutex is a semaphore that only allows one thread at a time to enter the critical section. Generally, a semaphore has the potential to let more than one thread enter its critical section.

Note:
Mutexes are also called *binary semaphores* because they are semaphores that accept only two states.

We start this section by resolving the data race issue observed as part of *example 15.3* in the previous chapter, using a POSIX mutex. The mutex only allows one thread at a time to enter the critical section and performs read and write operations on the shared variable. This way, it guarantees the data integrity of the shared variable. The following code box contains the solution to the data race issue:

```
#include <stdio.h>
#include <stdlib.h>

// The POSIX standard header for using pthread library
#include <pthread.h>

// The mutex object used to synchronize the access to
// the shared state.
pthread_mutex_t mtx;

void* thread_body_1(void* arg) {
  // Obtain a pointer to the shared variable
  int* shared_var_ptr = (int*)arg;
```

```
  // Critical section
  pthread_mutex_lock(&mtx);
  (*shared_var_ptr)++;
  printf("%d\n", *shared_var_ptr);
  pthread_mutex_unlock(&mtx);

  return NULL;
}

void* thread_body_2(void* arg) {
  int* shared_var_ptr = (int*)arg;

  // Critical section
  pthread_mutex_lock(&mtx);
  *shared_var_ptr += 2;
  printf("%d\n", *shared_var_ptr);
  pthread_mutex_unlock(&mtx);

  return NULL;
}

int main(int argc, char** argv) {

  // The shared variable
  int shared_var = 0;

  // The thread handlers
  pthread_t thread1;
  pthread_t thread2;

  // Initialize the mutex and its underlying resources
  pthread_mutex_init(&mtx, NULL);

  // Create new threads
  int result1 = pthread_create(&thread1, NULL,
          thread_body_1, &shared_var);
  int result2 = pthread_create(&thread2, NULL,
          thread_body_2, &shared_var);

  if (result1 || result2) {
    printf("The threads could not be created.\n");
    exit(1);
  }

  // Wait for the threads to finish
  result1 = pthread_join(thread1, NULL);
  result2 = pthread_join(thread2, NULL);
```

```
  if (result1 || result2) {
    printf("The threads could not be joined.\n");
    exit(2);
  }

  pthread_mutex_destroy(&mtx);

  return 0;
}
```

Code Box 16-1 [ExtremeC_examples_chapter15_3_mutex.c]: Using a POSIX mutex to resolve the data race issue found as part of example 15.3 in the previous chapter

If you compile the preceding code and run it as many times as you like, you will see only 1 3 or 2 3 in the output. That's because we are using a POSIX mutex object to synchronize the critical sections in the preceding code.

At the beginning of the file, we have declared a global POSIX mutex object as mtx. Then inside the main function, we have initialized the mutex with default attributes using the function pthread_mutex_init. The second argument, which is NULL, could be custom attributes specified by the programmer. We will go through an example of how to set these attributes in the upcoming sections.

The mutex is used in both threads to protect the critical sections embraced between the the pthread_mutex_lock(&mtx) and pthread_mutex_unlock(&mtx) statements.

Finally, before leaving the main function, we destroy the mutex object.

The first pair of pthread_mutex_lock(&mtx) and pthread_mutex_unlock(&mtx) statements, in the companion function thread_body_1, is making up the critical section for the first thread. Also, the second pair in the companion function thread_body_2 is making up the critical section for the second thread. Both critical sections are protected by the mutex, and at each time, only one of the threads can be in its critical section and the other thread should wait outside of its critical section until the busy thread leaves.

As soon as a thread enters the critical section, it locks the mutex, and the other thread should wait behind the pthread_mutex_lock(&mtx) statement to have the mutex unlocked again.

By default, a thread waiting for a mutex to become unlocked goes into sleeping mode and doesn't do a *busy-wait*. But what if we wanted to do *busy-waiting* instead of going to sleep? Then we could use a *spinlock*. It would be enough to use the following functions instead of all the preceding mutex-related functions. Thankfully, pthread uses a consistent convention in naming the functions.

The spinlock-related types and functions are as follows.

- `pthread_spin_t`: The type used for creating a spinlock object. It is similar to the `pthread_mutex_t` type.

- `pthread_spin_init`: Initializes a spinlock object. It is similar to `pthread_mutex_init`.

- `pthread_spin_destroy`: Similar to `pthread_mutex_destory`.

- `pthread_spin_lock`: Similar to `pthread_mutex_lock`.

- `pthread_spin_unlock`: Similar to `pthread_mutex_unlock`.

As you see, it's pretty easy to just replace the preceding mutex types and functions with spinlock types and functions to have a different behavior, busy-waiting in this case, while waiting for a mutex object to become released.

In this section, we introduced POSIX mutexes and how they can be used to resolve a data race issue. In the next section, we will demonstrate how to use a condition variable in order to wait for a certain event to occur. We will be addressing the race condition that occurred in *example 15.2*, but we will make some modifications to the original example.

POSIX condition variables

If you remember from *example 15.2* in the previous chapter, we faced a race condition. Now, we want to bring up a new example that is very similar to *example 15.2*, but one where it would be simpler to use a condition variable. *Example 16.1* has two threads instead of three (which was the case for *example 15.2*), and they are required to print the characters A and B to the output, but we want them to be always in a specific order; first A and then B.

Our invariant constraint for this example is to *see first A and then B in the output* (plus data integrity for all shared states, no bad memory access, no dangling pointer, no crashes, and other obvious constraints). The following code demonstrates how we use a condition variable to come up with a working solution written in C for this example:

```c
#include <stdio.h>
#include <stdlib.h>

// The POSIX standard header for using pthread library
#include <pthread.h>

#define TRUE  1
#define FALSE 0
```

```
typedef unsigned int bool_t;

// A structure for keeping all the variables related
// to a shared state
typedef struct {
  // The flag which indicates whether 'A' has been printed or not
  bool_t       done;
  // The mutex object protecting the critical sections
  pthread_mutex_t mtx;
  // The condition variable used to synchronize two threads
  pthread_cond_t  cv;
} shared_state_t;

// Initializes the members of a shared_state_t object
void shared_state_init(shared_state_t *shared_state) {
  shared_state->done = FALSE;
  pthread_mutex_init(&shared_state->mtx, NULL);
  pthread_cond_init(&shared_state->cv, NULL);
}

// Destroy the members of a shared_state_t object
void shared_state_destroy(shared_state_t *shared_state) {
  pthread_mutex_destroy(&shared_state->mtx);
  pthread_cond_destroy(&shared_state->cv);
}

void* thread_body_1(void* arg) {
  shared_state_t* ss = (shared_state_t*)arg;
  pthread_mutex_lock(&ss->mtx);
  printf("A\n");
  ss->done = TRUE;
  // Signal the threads waiting on the condition variable
  pthread_cond_signal(&ss->cv);
  pthread_mutex_unlock(&ss->mtx);
  return NULL;
}

void* thread_body_2(void* arg) {
  shared_state_t* ss = (shared_state_t*)arg;
  pthread_mutex_lock(&ss->mtx);
  // Wait until the flag becomes TRUE
  while (!ss->done) {
    // Wait on the condition variable
    pthread_cond_wait(&ss->cv, &ss->mtx);
  }
  printf("B\n");
  pthread_mutex_unlock(&ss->mtx);
  return NULL;
```

```
}

int main(int argc, char** argv) {

  // The shared state
  shared_state_t shared_state;

  // Initialize the shared state
  shared_state_init(&shared_state);

  // The thread handlers
  pthread_t thread1;
  pthread_t thread2;

  // Create new threads
  int result1 =
      pthread_create(&thread1, NULL, thread_body_1, &shared_state);
  int result2 =
      pthread_create(&thread2, NULL, thread_body_2, &shared_state);

  if (result1 || result2) {
    printf("The threads could not be created.\n");
    exit(1);
  }

  // Wait for the threads to finish
  result1 = pthread_join(thread1, NULL);
  result2 = pthread_join(thread2, NULL);

  if (result1 || result2) {
    printf("The threads could not be joined.\n");
    exit(2);
  }

  // Destroy the shared state and release the mutex
  // and condition variable objects
  shared_state_destroy(&shared_state);

  return 0;
}
```

Code Box 16-2 [ExtremeC_examples_chapter16_1_cv.c]: Using a POSIX condition variable to dictate a specific order between two threads

In the preceding code, it's good to use a structure in order to encapsulate the shared mutex, the shared condition variable, and the shared flag into a single entity. Note that we are only able to pass a single pointer to each thread. Therefore, we had to stack up the needed shared variables into a single structure variable.

As the second type definition (after `bool_t`) in the example, we have defined a new type, `shared_state_t`, as follows:

```
typedef struct {
  bool_t           done;
  pthread_mutex_t mtx;
  pthread_cond_t  cv;
} shared_state_t;
```

Code Box 16-3: Putting all shared variables required for example 16.1 into one structure

After the type definitions, we defined two functions in order to initialize and destroy the `shared_state_t` instances. They can be thought of as the *constructor* and *destructor* functions for the type `shared_state_t` respectively. To read more about constructor and destructor functions, please refer to *Chapter 6, OOP and Encapsulation*.

This is how we use a condition variable. A thread can *wait* (or *sleep*) on a condition variable, and then in the future, it becomes notified to wake up. More than that, a thread can *notify* (or *wake up*) all other threads waiting (or sleeping) on a condition variable. All these operations *must* be protected by a mutex, and that's why you should always use a condition variable together with a mutex.

We did the very same in the preceding code. In our shared state object, we have a condition variable, together with a companion mutex that is supposed to protect the condition variable. To emphasize again, a condition variable is supposed to be used only in critical sections protected by its companion mutex.

So, what happens in the preceding code? In the thread that is supposed to print A, it tries to lock the `mtx` mutex using a pointer to the shared state object. When the lock is acquired, the thread prints A, it sets the flag `done`, and it finally notifies the other thread, which could be waiting on the condition variable `cv`, by calling the `pthread_cond_signal` function.

On the other hand, if in the meantime the second thread becomes active and the first thread has not printed A yet, the second thread tries to acquire the lock over `mtx`. If it succeeds, it checks the flag `done`, and if it's false, it simply means that the first thread has not entered its critical section yet (otherwise the flag should have been true). Therefore, the second thread waits on the condition variable and immediately releases the CPU by calling the `pthread_cond_wait` function.

It is very important to note that upon waiting on a condition variable, the associated mutex becomes released and the other thread can continue. Also, upon becoming active and exiting the waiting state, the associated mutex should be acquired again. For some good practice in condition variables, you could go through other possible interleavings.

Note:
The function `pthread_cond_signal` can only be used to notify just one single thread. If you're going to notify all the threads waiting for a condition variable, you have to use the `pthread_cond_broadcast` function. We are going to give an example of this shortly.

But why did we use a `while` loop for checking the flag `done` when it could be a simple `if` statement? That's because the second thread can be notified by other sources rather than just the first thread. In those cases, if the thread could obtain the lock over its mutex upon exiting the wait and become active again, it could check the loop's condition, and if it is not met yet, it should wait again. It is an accepted technique to wait for a condition variable inside a loop, until its condition matches what we are waiting for.

The preceding solution satisfies the memory visibility constraint too. As we've explained in the previous chapters, all locking and unlocking operations are liable to trigger a memory coherence among various CPU cores; therefore, the values seen in different cached versions of the flag `done` are always recent and equal.

The race condition issue observed in examples 15.2 and 16.1 (in case of having no control mechanism in place), could also be resolved using POSIX barriers. In the next section, we are going to talk about them and rewrite *example 16.1* using a different approach.

POSIX barriers

POSIX barriers use a different approach for synchronizing a number of threads. Just like a group of people who are planning to do some tasks in parallel and at some points need to rendezvous, reorganize, and continue, the same thing can happen for threads (or even processes). Some threads do their tasks faster, and others are slower. But there can be a checkpoint (or rendezvous point) at which all threads must stop and wait for the others to join them. These checkpoints can be simulated by using *POSIX barriers*.

The following code uses barriers to propose a solution to the issues seen in *example 16.1*. As a reminder, in *example 16.1*, we had two threads. One of them was to `print` A, and the other thread was to `print` B, and we wanted to always see A first and B second in the output, regardless of various interleavings:

```
#include <stdio.h>
#include <stdlib.h>
```

```c
#include <pthread.h>

// The barrier object
pthread_barrier_t barrier;

void* thread_body_1(void* arg) {
  printf("A\n");
  // Wait for the other thread to join
  pthread_barrier_wait(&barrier);
  return NULL;
}

void* thread_body_2(void* arg) {
  // Wait for the other thread to join
  pthread_barrier_wait(&barrier);
  printf("B\n");
  return NULL;
}

int main(int argc, char** argv) {

  // Initialize the barrier object
  pthread_barrier_init(&barrier, NULL, 2);

  // The thread handlers
  pthread_t thread1;
  pthread_t thread2;

  // Create new threads
  int result1 = pthread_create(&thread1, NULL,
          thread_body_1, NULL);
  int result2 = pthread_create(&thread2, NULL,
          thread_body_2, NULL);

  if (result1 || result2) {
    printf("The threads could not be created.\n");
    exit(1);
  }

  // Wait for the threads to finish
  result1 = pthread_join(thread1, NULL);
  result2 = pthread_join(thread2, NULL);

  if (result1 || result2) {
    printf("The threads could not be joined.\n");
    exit(2);
  }

  // Destroy the barrier object
```

```
    pthread_barrier_destroy(&barrier);

    return 0;
}
```

Code Box 16-4 [ExtremeC_examples_chapter16_1_barrier.c]: A solution for example 16.1 using POSIX barriers

As you can see, the preceding code is much smaller than the code we wrote using condition variables. Using POSIX barriers, it would be very easy to synchronize some threads at some certain points during their execution.

First, we have declared a global barrier object of type `pthread_barrier_t`. Then, inside the `main` function, we have initialized the barrier object using the function `pthread_barrier_init`.

The first argument is a pointer to the barrier object. The second argument is the custom attributes of the barrier object. Since we are passing NULL, it means that the barrier object will be initialized using the default values for its attributes. The third argument is important; it is the number of threads that should become waiting on the same barrier object by calling the function `pthread_barrier_wait` and only after that are all of them released and allowed to continue.

For the preceding example, we set it to 2. Therefore, only when there are two threads waiting on the barrier object, both of them are unblocked and they can continue. The rest of the code is pretty similar to previous examples, and has been explained in the previous section.

A barrier object can be implemented using a mutex and a condition variable similar to what we did in the previous section. In fact, a POSIX-compliant operating system doesn't provide such a thing as a barrier in its system call interface, and most implementations are made using a mutex and a condition variable.

That's basically why some operating systems like macOS does not provide implementations for POSIX barriers. The preceding code cannot be compiled in a macOS machine since the POSIX barrier functions are not defined. The preceding code is tested both in Linux and FreeBSD and works on both of them. Therefore, be careful about using barriers, because using them makes your code less portable.

 The fact that macOS doesn't provide POSIX barrier functions simply means that it is partially POSIX-compliant and the programs using barriers (which is standard of course) cannot be compiled on macOS machines. This is against the C philosophy, which is *to write once, and compile anywhere.*

As the final note in this section, POSIX barriers guarantee memory visibility. Similarly to lock and unlock operations, waiting on barriers ensures that all the cached versions of the same variable are synchronized throughout various threads while they are going to leave the barrier point.

In the next section, we will be giving an example of semaphores. They are not used often in concurrent development, but they have their own special usages.

A specific type of semaphore, binary semaphores (interchangeably referred to as mutexes), is used often and you have seen a number of examples relating to that in the previous sections.

POSIX semaphores

In most cases, mutexes (or *binary semaphores*) are enough to synchronize a number of threads accessing a shared resource. That's because, in order to make read and write operations sequentially, only one thread should be able to enter the critical section at a time. It's known as *mutual exclusion*, hence, "mutex."

In some scenarios however, you might want to have more than one thread to enter the critical section and operate on the shared resource. This is the scenario in which you should use *general semaphores*.

Before we go into an example regarding general semaphores, let's bring up an example regarding a binary semaphore (or a mutex). We won't be using the `pthread_mutex_*` functions in this example; instead, we will be using `sem_*` functions which are supposed to expose semaphore-related functionalities.

Binary semaphores

The following code is the solution made using semaphores for *example 15.3*. As a reminder, it involved two threads; each of them incrementing a shared integer by a different value. We wanted to protect the data integrity of the shared variable. Note that we won't be using POSIX mutexes in the following code:

```
#include <stdio.h>
#include <stdlib.h>

// The POSIX standard header for using pthread library
#include <pthread.h>

// The semaphores are not exposed through pthread.h
#include <semaphore.h>
```

```c
// The main pointer addressing a semaphore object used
// to synchronize the access to the shared state.
sem_t *semaphore;

void* thread_body_1(void* arg) {
  // Obtain a pointer to the shared variable
  int* shared_var_ptr = (int*)arg;
  // Waiting for the semaphore
  sem_wait(semaphore);
  // Increment the shared variable by 1 by writing directly
  // to its memory address
  (*shared_var_ptr)++;
  printf("%d\n", *shared_var_ptr);
  // Release the semaphore
  sem_post(semaphore);
  return NULL;
}

void* thread_body_2(void* arg) {
  // Obtain a pointer to the shared variable
  int* shared_var_ptr = (int*)arg;
  // Waiting for the semaphore
  sem_wait(semaphore);
  // Increment the shared variable by 1 by writing directly
  // to its memory address
  (*shared_var_ptr) += 2;
  printf("%d\n", *shared_var_ptr);
  // Release the semaphore
  sem_post(semaphore);
  return NULL;
}

int main(int argc, char** argv) {

  // The shared variable
  int shared_var = 0;

  // The thread handlers
  pthread_t thread1;
  pthread_t thread2;

#ifdef __APPLE__
  // Unnamed semaphores are not supported in OS/X. Therefore
  // we need to initialize the semaphore like a named one using
  // sem_open function.
  semaphore = sem_open("sem0", O_CREAT | O_EXCL, 0644, 1);
#else
  sem_t local_semaphore;
  semaphore = &local_semaphore;
```

```
    // Initiliaze the semaphore as a mutex (binary semaphore)
    sem_init(semaphore, 0, 1);
#endif

    // Create new threads
    int result1 = pthread_create(&thread1, NULL,
            thread_body_1, &shared_var);
    int result2 = pthread_create(&thread2, NULL,
            thread_body_2, &shared_var);

    if (result1 || result2) {
      printf("The threads could not be created.\n");
      exit(1);
    }

    // Wait for the threads to finish
    result1 = pthread_join(thread1, NULL);
    result2 = pthread_join(thread2, NULL);

    if (result1 || result2) {
      printf("The threads could not be joined.\n");
      exit(2);
    }

#ifdef __APPLE__
    sem_close(semaphore);
#else
    sem_destroy(semaphore);
#endif

    return 0;
}
```

Code Box 16-5 [ExtremeC_examples_chapter15_3_sem.c]: A solution for example 15.3 using POSIX semaphores

The first thing you might notice in the preceding code is the different semaphore functions that we've used in Apple systems. In Apple operating systems (macOS, OS X, and iOS), *unnamed semaphores* are not supported. Therefore, we couldn't just use sem_init and sem_destroy functions. Unnamed semaphores don't have names (surprisingly enough) and they can only be used inside a process, by a number of threads. Named semaphores, on the other hand, are system-wide and can be seen and used by various processes in the system.

In Apple systems, the functions required for creating unnamed semaphores are marked as deprecated, and the semaphore object won't get initialized by sem_init. So, we had to use sem_open and sem_close functions in order to define named semaphores instead.

Named semaphores are used to synchronize processes, and we will explain them in *Chapter 18, Process Synchronization*. In other POSIX-compliant operating systems, Linux specifically, we still can use unnamed semaphores and have them initialized and destroyed by using the `sem_init` and `sem_destroy` functions respectively.

In the preceding code, we have included an extra header file, `semaphore.h`. As we've explained before, semaphores have been added as an extension to the POSIX threading library, and therefore, they are not exposed as part of the `pthread.h` header file.

After the header inclusion statements, we have declared a global pointer to a semaphore object. This pointer is going to point to a proper address addressing the actual semaphore object. We have to use a pointer here because, in Apple systems, we have to use the `sem_open` function, which returns a pointer.

Then, inside the `main` function, and in Apple systems, we create a named semaphore `sem0`. In other POSIX-compliant operating systems, we initialize the semaphore using `sem_init`. Note that in this case the pointer `semaphore` points to the variable `local_sempahore` allocated on top of the main thread's Stack. The pointer `semaphore` won't become a dangling pointer because the main thread doesn't exit and waits for the threads to get complete by joining them.

Note that we could distinguish between Apple and not - Apple systems by using the macro `__APPLE__`. This is a macro that is defined by default in C preprocessors being used in Apple systems. Therefore, we can rule out the code that is not supposed to be compiled on Apple systems by using this macro.

Let's look inside the threads. In companion functions, the critical sections are protected by `sem_wait` and `sem_post` functions which correspond to `pthread_mutex_lock` and `pthread_mutex_unlock` functions in the POSIX mutex API respectively. Note that `sem_wait` may allow more than one thread to enter the critical section.

The maximum number of threads that are allowed to be in the critical section is determined when initializing the semaphore object. We have passed the value 1 for the maximum number of threads as the last argument to the `sem_open` and `sem_init` functions; therefore, the semaphore is supposed to behave like a mutex.

To get a better understanding of semaphores, let's dive a bit more into the details. Each semaphore object has an integer value. Whenever a thread waits for a semaphore by calling the `sem_wait` function, if the semaphore's value is greater than zero, then the value is decreased by 1 and the thread is allowed to enter the critical section. If the semaphore's value is 0, the thread must wait until the semaphore's value becomes positive again. Whenever a thread exits the critical section by calling the `sem_post` function, the semaphore's value is incremented by 1. Therefore, by specifying the initial value 1, we will eventually get a binary semaphore.

We end the preceding code by calling `sem_destroy` (or `sem_close` in Apple systems) which effectively releases the semaphore object with all its underlying resources. Regarding the named semaphores, since they can be shared among a number of processes, more complex scenarios can occur when closing a semaphore. We will cover these scenarios in *Chapter 18, Process Synchronization*.

General semaphores

Now, it's time to give a classic example that uses general semaphores. The syntax is pretty similar to the preceding code, but the scenario in which multiple threads are allowed to enter the critical section could be interesting.

This classic example involves the creation of 50 water molecules. For 50 water molecules, you need to have 50 oxygen atoms and 100 hydrogen atoms. If we simulate each atom using a thread, we require two hydrogen threads, and one oxygen thread
to enter their critical sections, in order to generate one water molecule and have it counted.

In the following code, we firstly create 50 oxygen threads and 100 hydrogen threads. For protecting the oxygen thread's critical section, we use a mutex, but for the hydrogen threads' critical sections, we use a general semaphore that allows two threads to enter the critical section simultaneously.

For signaling purposes, we use POSIX barriers, but since barriers are not implemented in Apple systems, we need to implement them using mutexes and condition variables. The following code box contains the code:

```
#include <stdio.h>
#include <stdlib.h>
#include <string.h>
#include <limits.h>
#include <errno.h> // For errno and strerror function

// The POSIX standard header for using pthread library
#include <pthread.h>
// Semaphores are not exposed through pthread.h
#include <semaphore.h>


#ifdef __APPLE__
// In Apple systems, we have to simulate the barrier
functionality.
pthread_mutex_t barrier_mutex;
pthread_cond_t  barrier_cv;
unsigned int    barrier_thread_count;
```

```
unsigned int    barrier_round;
unsigned int    barrier_thread_limit;

void barrier_wait() {
  pthread_mutex_lock(&barrier_mutex);
  barrier_thread_count++;
  if (barrier_thread_count >= barrier_thread_limit) {
    barrier_thread_count = 0;
    barrier_round++;
    pthread_cond_broadcast(&barrier_cv);
  } else {
    unsigned int my_round = barrier_round;
    do {
      pthread_cond_wait(&barrier_cv, &barrier_mutex);
    } while (my_round == barrier_round);
  }
  pthread_mutex_unlock(&barrier_mutex);
}

#else
// A barrier to make hydrogen and oxygen threads synchronized
pthread_barrier_t water_barrier;
#endif

// A mutex in order to synchronize oxygen threads
pthread_mutex_t    oxygen_mutex;

// A general semaphore to make hydrogen threads synchronized
sem_t*             hydrogen_sem;

// A shared integer counting the number of made water molecules
unsigned int       num_of_water_molecules;

void* hydrogen_thread_body(void* arg) {
  // Two hydrogen threads can enter this critical section
  sem_wait(hydrogen_sem);
  // Wait for the other hydrogen thread to join
#ifdef __APPLE__
  barrier_wait();
#else
  pthread_barrier_wait(&water_barrier);
#endif
  sem_post(hydrogen_sem);
  return NULL;
}

void* oxygen_thread_body(void* arg) {
  pthread_mutex_lock(&oxygen_mutex);
```

```
  // Wait for the hydrogen threads to join
#ifdef __APPLE__
  barrier_wait();
#else
  pthread_barrier_wait(&water_barrier);
#endif
  num_of_water_molecules++;
  pthread_mutex_unlock(&oxygen_mutex);
  return NULL;
}

int main(int argc, char** argv) {

  num_of_water_molecules = 0;

  // Initialize oxygen mutex
  pthread_mutex_init(&oxygen_mutex, NULL);

  // Initialize hydrogen semaphore
#ifdef __APPLE__
  hydrogen_sem = sem_open("hydrogen_sem",
          O_CREAT | O_EXCL, 0644, 2);
#else
  sem_t local_sem;
  hydrogen_sem = &local_sem;
  sem_init(hydrogen_sem, 0, 2);
#endif

  // Initialize water barrier
#ifdef __APPLE__
  pthread_mutex_init(&barrier_mutex, NULL);
  pthread_cond_init(&barrier_cv, NULL);
  barrier_thread_count = 0;
  barrier_thread_limit = 0;
  barrier_round = 0;
#else
  pthread_barrier_init(&water_barrier, NULL, 3);
#endif

  // For creating 50 water molecules, we need 50 oxygen atoms and
  // 100 hydrogen atoms
  pthread_t thread[150];

  // Create oxygen threads
  for (int i = 0; i < 50; i++) {
    if (pthread_create(thread + i, NULL,
                oxygen_thread_body, NULL)) {
      printf("Couldn't create an oxygen thread.\n");
      exit(1);
```

```
    }
  }

  // Create hydrogen threads
  for (int i = 50; i < 150; i++) {
    if (pthread_create(thread + i, NULL,
              hydrogen_thread_body, NULL)) {
      printf("Couldn't create an hydrogen thread.\n");
      exit(2);
    }
  }

  printf("Waiting for hydrogen and oxygen atoms to react ...\n");
  // Wait for all threads to finish
  for (int i = 0; i < 150; i++) {
    if (pthread_join(thread[i], NULL)) {
      printf("The thread could not be joined.\n");
      exit(3);
    }
  }

  printf("Number of made water molecules: %d\n",
          num_of_water_molecules);

#ifdef __APPLE__
  sem_close(hydrogen_sem);
#else
  sem_destroy(hydrogen_sem);
#endif

  return 0;
}
```

Code Box 16-6 [ExtremeC_examples_chapter16_2.c]: Using a general semaphore to simulate the
process of creating 50 water molecules out of 50 oxygen atoms and 100 hydrogen atoms

In the beginning of the code, there are a number of lines that are surrounded by
#ifdef __APPLE__ and #endif. These lines are only compiled in Apple systems.
These lines are mainly the implementation and variables required for simulating
POSIX barrier behavior. In other POSIX-compliant systems other than Apple, we
use an ordinary POSIX barrier. We won't go through the details of the barrier
implementation on Apple systems here, but it is worthwhile to read the code
and understand it thoroughly.

As part of a number of global variables defined in the preceding code, we have
declared the mutex oxygen_mutex, which is supposed to protect the oxygen
threads' critical sections. At each time, only one oxygen thread (or oxygen atom)
can enter the critical section.

Then in its critical section, an oxygen thread waits for two other hydrogen threads to join and then it continues to increment the water molecule counter. The increment happens within the oxygen's critical section.

To elaborate more on the things that happen inside the critical sections, we need to explain the role of the general semaphore. In the preceding code, we have also declared the general semaphore `hydrogen_sem`, which is supposed to protect hydrogen threads' critical sections. At each time, only a maximum of two hydrogen threads can enter their critical sections, and they wait on the barrier object shared between the oxygen and hydrogen threads.

When the number of waiting threads on the shared barrier object reaches two, it means that we have got one oxygen and two hydrogens, and then voilà: a water molecule is made, and all waiting threads can continue. Hydrogen threads exit immediately, but the oxygen thread exists only after incrementing the water molecules counter.

We close this section with this last note. In *example 16.2*, we used the `pthread_cond_broadcast` function when implementing the barriers for Apple systems. It signals all threads waiting on the barrier's condition variable that are supposed to continue after having other threads joining them.

In the next section, we are going to talk about the memory model behind POSIX threads and how they interact with their owner process's memory. We will also look at examples about using the Stack and Heap segments and how they can lead to some serious memory-related issues.

POSIX threads and memory

This section is going to talk about the interactions between the threads and the process's memory. As you know, there are multiple segments in a process's memory layout. The Text segment, Stack segment, Data segment, and Heap segment are all part of this memory layout, and we covered them in *Chapter 4, Process Memory Structure*. Threads interact differently with each of these memory segments. As part of this section, we only discuss Stack and Heap memory regions because they are the most used and problematic areas when writing multithreaded programs.

In addition, we discuss how thread synchronization and a true understanding of the memory model behind a thread can help us develop better concurrent programs. These concepts are even more evident regarding the Heap memory because the memory management is manual there and in a concurrent system, threads are responsible for allocating and releasing Heap blocks. A trivial race condition can cause serious memory issues, therefore proper synchronization should be in place to avoid such disasters.

In the next subsection, we are going to explain how the Stack segment is accessed by different threads and what precautions should be taken.

Stack memory

Each thread has its own Stack region that is supposed to be private to that thread only. A thread's Stack region is part of the owner process's Stack segment and all threads, by default, should have their Stack regions allocated from the Stack segment. It is also possible that a thread has a Stack region that is allocated from the Heap segment. We will show in future examples how to do this, but for now, we assume that a thread's Stack is part of the process's Stack segment.

Since all threads within the same process can read and modify the process's Stack segment, they can effectively read and modify each other's Stack regions, but they *should not*. Note that working with other threads' Stack regions is considered dangerous behavior because the variables defined on top of the various Stack regions are subject to deallocation at any time, especially when a thread exits or a function returns.

That's why we try to assume that a Stack region is only accessible by its owner thread and not by the other threads. So, *local variables* (those variables declared on top the Stack) are considered to be private to the thread and should not be accessed by other threads.

In single-threaded applications, we have always one thread which is the main thread. Therefore, we use its Stack region like we use the process's Stack segment. That's because, in a single-threaded program, there is no boundary between the main thread and the process itself. But the situation is different for a multithreaded program. Each thread has its own Stack region which is different from another thread's Stack region.

When creating a new thread, a memory block is allocated for the Stack region. If not specified by the programmer upon creation, the Stack region will have a default Stack Size, and it will be allocated from the Stack segment of the process. The default Stack size is platform dependent and varies from one architecture to another. You can use the command `ulimit -s` to retrieve the default Stack size in a POSIX-compliant system.

On my current platform, which is macOS on an Intel 64-bit machine, the default Stack size is 8 MB:

```
$ ulimit -s
8192
$
```

Shell Box 16-1: Reading the default Stack size

The POSIX threading API allows you to set the Stack region for a new thread. In the following example, *example 16.3*, we have two threads. For one of them, we use the default Stack settings, and for the other one, we will allocate a buffer from the Heap segment and set it as the Stack region of that thread. Note that, when setting the Stack region, the allocated buffer should have a minimum size; otherwise it cannot be used as a Stack region:

```
#include <stdio.h>
#include <stdlib.h>
#include <limits.h>

#include <pthread.h>

void* thread_body_1(void* arg) {
  int local_var = 0;
  printf("Thread1 > Stack Address: %p\n", (void*)&local_var);
  return 0;
}

void* thread_body_2(void* arg) {
  int local_var = 0;
  printf("Thread2 > Stack Address: %p\n", (void*)&local_var);
  return 0;
}

int main(int argc, char** argv) {

  size_t buffer_len = PTHREAD_STACK_MIN + 100;
  // The buffer allocated from heap to be used as
  // the thread's stack region
  char *buffer = (char*)malloc(buffer_len * sizeof(char));

  // The thread handlers
  pthread_t thread1;
  pthread_t thread2;

  // Create a new thread with default attributes
  int result1 = pthread_create(&thread1, NULL,
          thread_body_1, NULL);

  // Create a new thread with a custom stack region
  pthread_attr_t attr;
  pthread_attr_init(&attr);
  // Set the stack address and size
  if (pthread_attr_setstack(&attr, buffer, buffer_len)) {
    printf("Failed while setting the stack attributes.\n");
    exit(1);
  }
```

```
    int result2 = pthread_create(&thread2, &attr,
            thread_body_2, NULL);

    if (result1 || result2) {
      printf("The threads could not be created.\n");
      exit(2);
    }

    printf("Main Thread > Heap Address: %p\n", (void*)buffer);
    printf("Main Thread > Stack Address: %p\n", (void*)&buffer_len);

    // Wait for the threads to finish
    result1 = pthread_join(thread1, NULL);
    result2 = pthread_join(thread2, NULL);

    if (result1 || result2) {
      printf("The threads could not be joined.\n");
      exit(3);
    }

    free(buffer);

    return 0;
}
```

Code Box 16-7 [ExtremeC_examples_chapter16_3.c]: Setting a Heap block as a thread's Stack region

To start the program, we create the first thread with the default Stack settings. Therefore, its Stack should be allocated from the Stack segment of the process. After that, we create the second thread by specifying the memory address of a buffer supposed to be the Stack region of the thread.

Note that the specified size is 100 bytes more than the already defined minimum Stack size indicated by the PTHREAD_STACK_MIN macro. This constant has different values on different platforms, and it is included as part of the header file limits.h.

If you build the preceding program and run it on a Linux device, you will see something like the following:

```
$ gcc ExtremeC_examples_chapter16_3.c -o ex16_3.out -lpthread
$ ./ex16_3.out
Main Thread > Heap Address: 0x55a86a251260
Main Thread > Stack Address: 0x7ffcb5794d50
Thread2 > Stack Address: 0x55a86a2541a4
```

```
Thread1 > Stack Address: 0x7fa3e9216ee4
$
```

Shell Box 16-2: Building and running example 16.3

As is clear from the output seen in *Shell Box 16-2*, the address of the local variable `local_var` that is allocated on top of the second thread's Stack belongs to a different address range (the range of the Heap space). This means that the Stack region of the second thread is within the Heap. This is not true for the first thread, however.

As the output shows, the address of the local variable in the first thread falls within the address range of the Stack segment of the process. As a result, we could successfully set a new Stack region allocated from the Heap segment, for a newly created thread.

The ability to set the Stack region of a thread can be crucial in some use cases. For example, in memory-constrained environments where the total amount of memory is low for having big Stacks, or in high-performance environments in which the cost of allocating the Stack for each thread cannot be tolerated, using some preallocated buffers can be useful and the preceding procedure can be employed to set a preallocated buffer as the Stack region of a newly created thread.

The following example demonstrates how sharing an address in one thread's Stack can lead to some memory issues. When an address from a thread is shared, the thread should remain alive otherwise all pointers keeping that address become dangling.

The following code is not thread-safe, therefore we expect to see crashes from time to time in successive runs. The threads also have the default Stack settings which means their Stack regions are allocated from the process's Stack segment:

```c
#include <stdio.h>
#include <stdlib.h>
#include <unistd.h>

#include <pthread.h>

int* shared_int;

void* t1_body(void* arg) {
  int local_var = 100;
  shared_int = &local_var;
```

```
    // Wait for the other thread to print the shared integer
    usleep(10);
    return NULL;
}

void* t2_body(void* arg) {
    printf("%d\n", *shared_int);
    return NULL;
}

int main(int argc, char** argv) {

    shared_int = NULL;

    pthread_t t1;
    pthread_t t2;

    pthread_create(&t1, NULL, t1_body, NULL);
    pthread_create(&t2, NULL, t2_body, NULL);

    pthread_join(t1, NULL);
    pthread_join(t2, NULL);

    return 0;
}
```

Code Box 16-8 [ExtremeC_examples_chapter16_4.c]: Trying to read a variable allocated from another thread's Stack region

At the beginning, we have declared a global shared pointer. Since it is a pointer, it can accept any address regardless of where the address points to in the process's memory layout. It could be from the Stack segment or the Heap segment or even the Data segment.

In the preceding code, inside the t1_body companion function, we store the address of a local variable in the shared pointer. This variable belongs to the first thread, and it is allocated on top of the first thread's Stack.

From now on, if the first thread exits, the shared pointer becomes dangling, and any dereferencing probably leads to a crash, a logical error, or a hidden memory issue in the best case. In some interleavings, this would happen, and you see crashes from time to time if you run the preceding program multiple times.

As an important note, proper synchronization techniques should be employed if one thread is willing to use a variable allocated from another thread's Stack region. Since the lifetime of a Stack variable is bound to its scope, the synchronization should aim at keeping the scope alive until the consumer thread is done with the variable.

Note that for simplicity we didn't check the results of the pthread functions. It is always advised to do so and check the return values. Not all pthread functions behave the same on different platforms; if something goes wrong, you will become aware by checking the return values.

In this section, generally speaking, we showed why the addresses belonging to Stack regions shouldn't be shared, and why shared states better not be allocated from Stack regions. The next section talks about Heap memory, which is the most common place for storing shared states. As you might have guessed, working with the Heap is also tricky, and you should be careful about memory leaks.

Heap memory

The Heap segment and the Data segment are accessible by all threads. Unlike the Data segment, which is generated at compile time, the Heap segment is dynamic, and it is shaped at runtime. Threads can both read and modify the contents of the Heap. In addition, the contents of the Heap can stay as long as the process lives, and stay independent of the lifetime of the individual threads. Also, big objects can be put inside the Heap. All these factors together have caused the Heap to be a great place for storing states that are going to be shared among some threads.

Memory management becomes a nightmare when it comes to Heap allocation, and that is because of the fact that allocated memory should be deallocated at some point by one of the running threads otherwise it could lead to memory leaks.

Regarding concurrent environments, interleavings can easily produce dangling pointers; hence crashes show up. The critical role of synchronization is to put things in a specific order where no dangling pointer can be produced, and this is the hard part.

Let's look at the following example, *example 16.5*. There are five threads in this example. The first thread allocates an array from the Heap. The second and third threads populate the array in this form. The second thread populates the even indices in the array with the capital alphabet letters starting from *Z* and moving backward to *A*, and the third thread populates the odd indices with small alphabet letters starting from *a* and moving forward to *z*. The fourth thread prints the array. And finally, the fifth thread deallocates the array and reclaims the Heap memory.

All the techniques described in the previous sections about POSIX concurrency control should be employed in order to keep these threads from misbehaving within the Heap. The following code has no control mechanism in place, and obviously, it is not thread-safe. Note that the code is not complete. The complete version with the concurrency control mechanisms in place will come in the next code box:

```
#include <stdio.h>
#include <stdlib.h>
```

```c
#include <unistd.h>

#include <pthread.h>

#define CHECK_RESULT(result) \
if (result) { \
  printf("A pthread error happened.\n"); \
  exit(1); \
}

int TRUE = 1;
int FALSE = 0;

// The pointer to the shared array
char* shared_array;
// The size of the shared array
unsigned int shared_array_len;

void* alloc_thread_body(void* arg) {
  shared_array_len = 20;
  shared_array = (char*)malloc(shared_array_len * sizeof(char*));
  return NULL;
}

void* filler_thread_body(void* arg) {
  int even = *((int*)arg);
  char c = 'a';
  size_t start_index = 1;
  if (even) {
    c = 'Z';
    start_index = 0;
  }
  for (size_t i = start_index; i < shared_array_len; i += 2) {
    shared_array[i] = even ? c-- : c++;
  }
  shared_array[shared_array_len - 1] = '\0';
  return NULL;
}

void* printer_thread_body(void* arg) {
  printf(">> %s\n", shared_array);
  return NULL;
}

void* dealloc_thread_body(void* arg) {
  free(shared_array);
  return NULL;
}
```

```
int main(int argc, char** argv) {
  ... Create threads ...
}
```

Code Box 16-9 [ExtremeC_examples_chapter16_5_raw.c]: Example 16.5 without any synchronization mechanism in place

It is easy to see that the preceding code is not thread-safe and it causes serious crashes because of the interference of the deallocator thread in deallocating the array.

Whenever the deallocator thread obtains the CPU, it frees the Heap-allocated buffer immediately, and after that the pointer shared_array becomes dangling, and other threads start to crash. Proper synchronization techniques should be used to ensure that the deallocation thread runs last and the proper order of logic in different threads are run.

In the following code block, we decorate the preceding code with POSIX concurrency control objects to make it thread-safe:

```
#include <stdio.h>
#include <stdlib.h>
#include <unistd.h>

#include <pthread.h>

#define CHECK_RESULT(result) \
if (result) { \
  printf("A pthread error happened.\n"); \
  exit(1); \
}

int TRUE = 1;
int FALSE = 0;

// The pointer to the shared array
char* shared_array;
// The size of the shared array
size_t shared_array_len;

pthread_barrier_t alloc_barrier;
pthread_barrier_t fill_barrier;
pthread_barrier_t done_barrier;

void* alloc_thread_body(void* arg) {
  shared_array_len = 20;
  shared_array = (char*)malloc(shared_array_len * sizeof(char*));
```

```
    pthread_barrier_wait(&alloc_barrier);
    return NULL;
}

void* filler_thread_body(void* arg) {
  pthread_barrier_wait(&alloc_barrier);
  int even = *((int*)arg);
  char c = 'a';
  size_t start_index = 1;
  if (even) {
    c = 'Z';
    start_index = 0;
  }
  for (size_t i = start_index; i < shared_array_len; i += 2) {
    shared_array[i] = even ? c-- : c++;
  }
  shared_array[shared_array_len - 1] = '\0';
  pthread_barrier_wait(&fill_barrier);
  return NULL;
}

void* printer_thread_body(void* arg) {
  pthread_barrier_wait(&fill_barrier);
  printf(">> %s\n", shared_array);
  pthread_barrier_wait(&done_barrier);
  return NULL;
}

void* dealloc_thread_body(void* arg) {
  pthread_barrier_wait(&done_barrier);
  free(shared_array);
  pthread_barrier_destroy(&alloc_barrier);
  pthread_barrier_destroy(&fill_barrier);
  pthread_barrier_destroy(&done_barrier);
  return NULL;
}

int main(int argc, char** argv) {

  shared_array = NULL;

  pthread_barrier_init(&alloc_barrier, NULL, 3);
  pthread_barrier_init(&fill_barrier, NULL, 3);
  pthread_barrier_init(&done_barrier, NULL, 2);

  pthread_t alloc_thread;
  pthread_t even_filler_thread;
  pthread_t odd_filler_thread;
```

```
pthread_t printer_thread;
pthread_t dealloc_thread;

pthread_attr_t attr;
pthread_attr_init(&attr);
int res = pthread_attr_setdetachstate(&attr,
        PTHREAD_CREATE_DETACHED);
CHECK_RESULT(res);

res = pthread_create(&alloc_thread, &attr,
        alloc_thread_body, NULL);
CHECK_RESULT(res);

res = pthread_create(&even_filler_thread,
        &attr, filler_thread_body, &TRUE);
CHECK_RESULT(res);

res = pthread_create(&odd_filler_thread,
        &attr, filler_thread_body, &FALSE);
CHECK_RESULT(res);

res = pthread_create(&printer_thread, &attr,
        printer_thread_body, NULL);
CHECK_RESULT(res);

res = pthread_create(&dealloc_thread, &attr,
        dealloc_thread_body, NULL);
CHECK_RESULT(res);

pthread_exit(NULL);

return 0;
}
```

Code Box 16-10 [ExtremeC_examples_chapter16_5.c]: Example 16.5 with synchronization mechanisms in place

To make the code found in *Code Box 16-9* thread-safe, we have only used the POSIX barriers in the new code. It is the easiest approach to form a sequential execution order between a number of threads.

If you compare *Code Boxes 16-9* and *16-10*, you see how POSIX barriers are used to impose an order between various threads. The only exception is between two filler threads. The filler threads can be running independently without blocking each other, and since they are changing odd and even indices separately, no concurrent issue can be raised. Note that the preceding code cannot be compiled on Apple systems. You need to simulate the barrier behavior using mutexes and condition variables in these systems (as we did for *example 16.2*).

The following is the output of the preceding code. No matter how many times you run the program, it never crashes. In other words, the preceding code is guarded against the various interleavings, and it is thread-safe:

```
$ gcc ExtremeC_examples_chapter16_5.c -o ex16_5 -lpthread
$ ./ex16_5
>> ZaYbXcWdVeUfTgShRiQ
$ ./ex16_5
>> ZaYbXcWdVeUfTgShRiQ
$
```

Shell Box 16-3: Building and running example 16.5

In this section, we gave an example of using the Heap space as a place holder for shared states. Unlike the Stack memory, where memory deallocation happens automatically, Heap space deallocation should be performed explicitly. Otherwise, memory leaks are an imminent side effect.

The easiest and sometimes the best available place to keep the shared states, in terms of least memory management effort for the programmer, is the Data segment in which both allocation and deallocation happen automatically. Variables residing in the Data segment are considered global, and have the longest possible lifetime, from the very beginning moments of the process's birth until its very last moments. But this long lifetime can be considered negative in certain use cases, especially when you're going to keep a big object in the Data segment.

In the next section, we will talk about memory visibility and how POSIX functions guarantee that.

Memory visibility

We explained *memory visibility* and *cache coherency* in the previous chapters, regarding the systems with more than one CPU core. In this section, we want to look at the pthread library and see how it guarantees memory visibility.

As you know, a cache coherency protocol among CPU cores ensures that all cached versions of a single memory address in all CPU cores remain synchronized and updated regarding the latest changes made in one of the CPU cores. But this protocol should be triggered somehow.

There are APIs in the system call interface to trigger the cache coherency protocol and make the memory visible to all CPU cores. In pthread also, there are a number of functions that guarantee the memory visibility before their execution.

You may have encountered some of these functions before. A list of them is presented below:

- `pthread_barrier_wait`
- `pthread_cond_broadcast`
- `pthread_cond_signal`
- `pthread_cond_timedwait`
- `pthread_cond_wait`
- `pthread_create`
- `pthread_join`
- `pthread_mutex_lock`
- `pthread_mutex_timedlock`
- `pthread_mutex_trylock`
- `pthread_mutex_unlock`
- `pthread_spin_lock`
- `pthread_spin_trylock`
- `pthread_spin_unlock`
- `pthread_rwlock_rdlock`
- `pthread_rwlock_timedrdlock`
- `pthread_rwlock_timedwrlock`
- `pthread_rwlock_tryrdlock`
- `pthread_rwlock_trywrlock`
- `pthread_rwlock_unlock`
- `pthread_rwlock_wrlock`
- `sem_post`
- `sem_timedwait`
- `sem_trywait`
- `sem_wait`
- `semctl`
- `semop`

Other than local caches in CPU cores, the compilers can also introduce caching mechanisms for the frequently used variables. For this to happen, the compiler needs to analyze the code and optimize it in a way that means frequently used variables are written to and read from the compiler caches. These are software caches that are put in the final binary by the compiler in order to optimize and boost the execution of the program.

While these caches can be beneficial, they potentially add another headache while writing multithreaded code and raise some memory visibility issues. Therefore, sometimes these caches must be disabled for specific variables.

The variables that are not supposed to be optimized by the compiler via caching can be declared as *volatile*. Note that a volatile variable still can be cached at the CPU level, but the compiler won't optimize it by keeping it in compiler caches. A variable can be declared as volatile using the keyword `volatile`. Following is a declaration of an integer that is volatile:

```
volatile int number;
```

Code Box 16-11: Declaring a volatile integer variable

The important thing about volatile variables is that they don't solve the memory visibility problems in multi-threaded systems. In order to solve this issue, you need to use the preceding POSIX functions in their proper places in order to ensure memory visibility.

Summary

In this chapter, we covered the concurrent control mechanisms provided by the POSIX threading API. We have discussed:

- POSIX mutexes and how they should be used
- POSIX condition variables and barriers and how they should be used
- POSIX semaphores, and how binary semaphores and general semaphores differ
- How threads interact with the Stack region
- How to define a new Heap-allocated Stack region for a thread
- How threads interact with the Heap space
- Memory visibility and POSIX functions that guarantee memory visibility
- Volatile variables and compiler caches

In the next chapter, we will continue our discussion and we will talk about another approach for having concurrency in a software system: multi-processing. We will discuss how a process can be executed and how it is different from a thread.

Chapter 17

Process Execution

We are now ready to talk about the software systems consisting of more than one process in their overall architecture. These systems are usually called multi-process or multiple-process systems. This chapter, together with the next chapter, is trying to cover the concepts of multi-processing and conduct a pros-and-cons analysis in order to compare it with multithreading, which we covered in *Chapter 15, Thread Execution*, and *Chapter 16, Thread Synchronization*.

In this chapter, our focus is the available APIs and techniques to start a new process and how process execution actually happens, and in the next chapter, we'll go through concurrent environments consisting of more than one process. We are going to explain how various states can be shared among a number of processes and what common ways of accessing shared state in a multi-processing environment are.

A proportion of this chapter is based on comparing multi-processing and multithreading environments. In addition, we briefly talk about single-host multi-processing systems and distributed multi-processing systems.

Process execution APIs

Every program is executed as a process. Before we have a process, we just have an executable binary file that contains some memory segments and probably lots of machine-level instructions. Conversely, every process is an individual instance of a program being executed. Therefore, a single compiled program (or an executable binary file) can be executed multiple times through different processes. In fact, that's why our focus is on the processes in this chapter, rather than upon the programs themselves.

In two previous chapters, we talked about threads in single-process software, but to follow our objective in this chapter, we are going to be talking about software with multiple processes. But first, we need to know how, and by using which API, a new process can be spawned.

Note that our main focus is on executing processes in Unix-like operating systems since all of them follow the Unix onion architecture and expose very well-known and similar APIs. Other operating systems can have their own ways for executing processes, but since most of them, more or less, follow the Unix onion architecture, we expect to see similar methods for process execution.

In a Unix-like operating system, there are not many ways to execute a process at the system call level. If you remember the *kernel ring* from *Chapter 11, System Calls and Kernel*, it is the most inner ring after the *hardware ring*, and it provides the *system call interface* to outer rings, *shell*, and *user*, in order to let them execute various kernel-specific functionalities. Two of these exposed system calls are dedicated to process creation and process execution; respectively, fork and exec (execve in Linux though). In *process creation*, we spawn a new process, but in *process execution* we use an existing process as the host, and we replace it with a new program; therefore, no new process is spawned in process execution.

As a result of using these systems calls, a program is always executed as a new process, but this process is not always spawned! The fork system call spawns a new process while the exec system call replaces the caller (the host) process with a new one. We talk about the differences between the fork and exec system calls later. Before that, let's see how these system calls are exposed to the outer rings.

As we explained in *Chapter 10, Unix – History and Architecture*, we have two standards for Unix-like operating systems, specifically about the interface they should expose from their shell ring. These standards are **Single Unix Specification** (**SUS**) and **POSIX**. For more information regarding these standards, along with their similarities and differences, please refer to *Chapter 10, Unix – History and Architecture*.

The interface that should be exposed from the shell ring is thoroughly specified in the POSIX interface, and indeed, there are parts in the standard that deal with process execution and process management.

Therefore, we would expect to find headers and functions for process creation and process execution within POSIX. Such functions do indeed exist, and we find them in different headers that provide the desired functionality. Following is a list of POSIX functions responsible for process creation and process execution:

- The function fork that can be found in the unistd.h header file is responsible for process creation.
- The posix_spawn and posix_spawnp functions that can be found in the spawn.h header file. These functions are responsible for process creation.
- The group of exec* functions, for example, execl and execlp, that can be found in the unistd.h header file. These functions are responsible for process execution.

Note that the preceding functions should not be mistaken for the `fork` and `exec` system calls. These functions are part of the POSIX interface exposed from the shell ring while the system calls are exposed from the kernel ring. While most Unix-like operating systems are POSIX-compliant, we can have a non-Unix-like system that is also POSIX-compliant. Then, the preceding functions exist in that system, but the underlying mechanism for spawning a process can be different at the system call level.

A tangible example is using Cygwin or MinGW to make Microsoft Windows POSIX-compliant. By installing these programs, you can write and compile standard C programs that are using the POSIX interface, and Microsoft Windows becomes partially POSIX-compliant, but there are no `fork` or `exec` system calls in Microsoft Windows! This is in fact very confusing and very important at the same time, and you should know that the shell ring does not necessarily expose the same interface that is exposed by the kernel ring.

Note:
You can find the implementation details of the `fork` function in Cygwin here: `https://github.com/openunix/cygwin/blob/master/winsup/cygwin/fork.cc`. Note that it doesn't call the `fork` system call that usually exists in Unix-like kernels; instead, it includes headers from the Win32 API and calls functions that are well-known functions regarding process creation and process management.

According to the POSIX standard, the C standard library is not the only thing that is exposed from the shell ring on a Unix-like system. When using a Terminal, there are prewritten shell utility programs that are used to provide a complex usage of the C standard API. About the process creation, whenever the user enters a command in the Terminal, a new process is created.

Even a simple `ls` or `sed` command spawns a new process that might only last less than a second. You should know that these utility programs are mostly written in C language and they are consuming the same exact POSIX interface which you would have been using when writing your own programs.

Shell scripts are also executed in a separate process but in a slightly different fashion. We will discuss them in future sections on how a process is executed within a Unix-like system.

Process creation happens in the kernel, especially in monolithic kernels. Whenever a user process spawns a new process or even a new thread, the request is received by the system call interface, and it gets passed down to the kernel ring. There, a new *task* is created for the incoming request, either a process or a thread.

Monolithic kernels like Linux or FreeBSD keep track of the tasks (process and threads) within their kernel, and this makes it reasonable to have processes being created in the kernel itself.

Note that whenever a new task is created within the kernel, it is placed in the queue of the *task scheduler unit* and it might take a bit of time for it to obtain the CPU and begin execution.

In order to create a new process, a parent process is needed. That's why every process has a parent. In fact, each process can have only one parent. The chain of parents and grandparents goes back to the first user process, which is usually called *init*, and the kernel process is its parent.

It is the ancestor to all other processes within a Unix-like system and exists until the system shuts down. Regularly, the init process becomes the parent of all *orphan processes* that have had their parent processes terminated, so that no process can be left without a parent process.

This parent-child relationship ends up in a big process tree. This tree can be examined by the command utility *pstree*. We are going to show how to use this utility in future examples.

Now, we know the API that can execute a new process, and we need to give some real C examples on how these methods actually work. We start with the fork API, which eventually calls the `fork` system call.

Process creation

As we mentioned in the previous section, the fork API can be used to spawn a new process. We also explained that a new process can only be created as a child of a running process. Here, we see a few examples of how a process can fork a new child using the fork API.

In order to spawn a new child process, a parent process needs to call the `fork` function. The declaration of the `fork` function can be included from the `unistd.h` header file which is part of the POSIX headers.

When the `fork` function is called, an exact copy of the caller process (which is called the parent process) is created, and both processes continue to run concurrently starting from the very next instruction after the `fork` invocation statement. Note that the child (or forked) process inherits many things from the parent process including all the memory segments together with their content. Therefore, it has access to the same variables in the Data, Stack, and Heap segments, and also the program instructions found in the Text segment. We talk about other inherited things in the upcoming paragraphs, after talking about the example.

Since we have two different processes now, the `fork` function returns twice; once in the parent process and another time in the child process. In addition, the `fork` function returns different values to each process. It returns 0 to the child process, and it returns the PID of the forked (or child) process to the parent process. *Example 17.1* shows how `fork` works in one of its simplest usages:

```
#include <stdio.h>
#include <unistd.h>

int main(int argc, char** argv) {
  printf("This is the parent process with process ID: %d\n",
         getpid());
  printf("Before calling fork() ...\n");
  pid_t ret = fork();
  if (ret) {
    printf("The child process is spawned with PID: %d\n", ret);
  } else {
    printf("This is the child process with PID: %d\n", getpid());
  }
  printf("Type CTRL+C to exit ...\n");
  while (1);
  return 0;
}
```

Code Box 17-1 [ExtremeC_examples_chapter17_1.c]: Create a child process using the fork API

In the preceding code box, we have used `printf` to print out some logs in order to track the activity of the processes. As you see, we have invoked the `fork` function in order to spawn a new process. As is apparent, it doesn't accept any argument, and therefore, its usage is very easy and straightforward.

Upon calling the `fork` function, a new process is forked (or cloned) from the caller process, which is now the parent process, and after that, they continue to work concurrently as two different processes.

Surely, the call to the `fork` function will cause further invocations on the system call level, and only then, the responsible logic in the kernel can create a new forked process.

Just before the `return` statement, we have used an infinite loop to keep both processes running and prevent them from exiting. Note that the processes should reach this infinite loop eventually because they have exactly the same instructions in their Text segments.

We want to keep the processes running intentionally in order to be able to see them in the list of processes shown by the `pstree` and `top` commands. Before that, we need to compile the preceding code and see how the new process is forked, as shown in *Shell Box 17-1*:

```
$ gcc ExtremeC_examples_chapter17_1.c -o ex17_1.out
$ ./ex17_1.out
This is the parent process with process ID: 10852
Before calling fork() …
The child process is spawned with PID: 10853
This is the child process with PID: 10853
Type CTRL+C to exit ...
$
```

Shell Box 17-1: Building and running example 17.1

As you can see, the parent process prints its PID, and that is 10852. Note that the PID is going to change in each run. After forking the child process, the parent process prints the PID returned by the fork function, and it is 10853.

On the next line, the child process prints its PID, which is again 10853 and it is in accordance with what the parent has received from the fork function. And finally, both processes enter the infinite loop, giving us some time to observe them in the probing utilities.

As you see in *Shell Box 17-1*, the forked process inherits the same stdout file descriptor and the same terminal from its parent. Therefore, it can print to the same output that its parent writes to. A forked process inherits all the open file descriptors at the time of the fork function call from its parent process.

In addition, there are also other inherited attributes, which can be found in fork's manual pages. The fork's manual page for Linux can be found here: http://man7.org/linux/man-pages/man2/fork.2.html.

If you open the link and look through the attributes, you are going to see that there are attributes that are shared between the parent and forked processes, and there are other attributes that are different and specific to each process, for example, PID, parent PID, threads, and so on.

The parent-child relationship between processes can be easily seen using a utility program like pstree. Every process has a parent process, and all of the processes contribute to building a big tree. Remember that each process has exactly one parent, and a single process cannot have two parents.

While the processes in the preceding example are stuck within their infinite loops, we can use the pstree utility command to see the list of all processes within the system displayed as a tree. The following is the output of the pstree usage in a Linux machine. Note that the pstree command is installed on Linux systems by default, but it might need to be installed in other Unix-like operating systems:

```
$ pstree -p
systemd(1)─┬─accounts-daemon(877)─┬─{accounts-daemon}(960)
           │                       └─{accounts-daemon}(997)
. . .
. . .
. . .
           ├─systemd-logind(819)
           ├─systemd-network(673)
           ├─systemd-resolve(701)
           ├─systemd-timesyn(500)───{systemd-timesyn}(550)
           ├─systemd-udevd(446)
           └─tmux: server(2083)─┬─bash(2084)───pstree(13559)
                                 └─bash(2337)───ex17_1.
out(10852)───ex17_1.out(10853)
$
```

Shell Box 17-2: Use pstree to find the processes spawned as part of example 17.1

As can be seen in the last line of *Shell Box 17-2*, we have two processes with PIDs 10852 and 10853 that are in the parent-child relationship. Note that process 10852 has a parent with PID 2337, which is a *bash* process.

It's interesting to note that on the line before the last line, we can see the pstree process itself as the child of the bash process with PID 2084. Both of the bash processes belong to the same *tmux* terminal emulator with PID 2083.

In Linux, the very first process is the *scheduler* process, which is part of the kernel image, and it has the PID 0. The next process, which is usually called *init*, has the PID 1, and it is the first user process which is created by the scheduler process. It exists from system startup until its shutdown. All other user processes are directly or indirectly the children of the init process. The processes which lose their parent processes become orphan processes, and they become abducted by the init process as its direct children.

However, in the newer versions of almost all famous distributions of Linux, the init process has been replaced by the *systemd daemon*, and that's why you see systemd(1) on the first line in *Shell Box 17-2*. The following link is a great source to read more about the differences between init and systemd and why Linux distro developers have made such a decision: https://www.tecmint.com/systemd-replaces-init-in-linux.

When using the fork API, the parent and forked processes are executed concurrently. This means that we should be able to detect some behaviors of concurrent systems.

The best-known behavior that can be observed is some interleavings. If you are not familiar with this term or you have not heard it before, it is strongly recommended to have a read of *Chapter 13, Concurrency*, and *Chapter 14, Synchronization*.

The following example, *example 17.2*, shows how the parent and forked processes can have non-deterministic interleavings. We are going to print some strings and observe how some various interleavings can happen in two successive runs:

```
#include <stdio.h>
#include <unistd.h>

int main(int argc, char** argv) {
  pid_t ret = fork();
  if (ret) {
    for (size_t i = 0; i < 5; i++) {
      printf("AAA\n");
      usleep(1);
    }
  } else {
    for (size_t i = 0; i < 5; i++) {
      printf("BBBBBB\n");
      usleep(1);
    }
  }
  return 0;
}
```

Code Box 17-2 [ExtremeC_examples_chapter17_2.c]: Two processes that print some lines to the standard output

The preceding code is very similar to the code we wrote for *example 17.1*. It creates a forked process, and after that, the parent and forked processes print some lines of text to the standard output. The parent process prints AAA 5 times, and the forked process prints BBBBBB five times. The following is the output of the two consecutive runs of the same compiled executable:

```
$ gcc ExtremeC_examples_chapter17_2.c -o ex17_2.out
$ ./ex17_2.out
AAA
AAA
AAA
AAA
AAA
BBBBBB
BBBBBB
```

```
BBBBBB
BBBBBB
BBBBBB
$ ./ex17_2.out
AAA
AAA
BBBBBB
AAA
AAA
BBBBBB
BBBBBB
BBBBBB
AAA
BBBBBB
$
```

Shell Box 17-3: Output of two successive runs of example 17.2

It is clear from the preceding output that we have different interleavings. This means we can be potentially suffering from a race condition here if we define our invariant constraint according to what we see in the standard output. This would eventually lead to all the issues we faced while writing multithreaded code, and we need to use similar methods to overcome these issues. In the next chapter, we will discuss such solutions in greater detail.

In the following section, we are going to talk about process execution and how it can be achieved using `exec*` functions.

Process execution

Another way to execute a new process is by using the family of `exec*` functions. This group of functions takes a different approach to execute a new process in comparison to the fork API. The philosophy behind `exec*` functions is to create a simple base process first and then, at some point, load the target executable and replace it as a new *process image* with the base process. A process image is the loaded version of a executable that has its memory segments allocated, and it is ready to be executed. In the future sections, we will discuss the different steps of loading an executable, and we will explain process images in greater depth.

Therefore, while using the `exec*` functions, no new process is created, and a process substitution happens. This is the most important difference between `fork` and `exec*` functions. Instead of forking a new process, the base process is totally substituted with a new set of memory segments and code instructions.

Code Box 17-3, containing *example 17.3*, shows how the execvp function, one of the functions in the family of exec* functions, is used to start an echo process. The execvp function is one of the functions in the group of exec* functions that inherits the environment variable PATH from the parent process and searches for the executables as the parent process did:

```
#include <stdio.h>
#include <unistd.h>
#include <string.h>
#include <errno.h>

int main(int argc, char** argv) {
  char *args[] = {"echo", "Hello", "World!", 0};
  execvp("echo", args);
  printf("execvp() failed. Error: %s\n", strerror(errno));
  return 0;
}
```

Code Box 17-3 [ExtremeC_examples_chapter17_3.c]: Demonstration of how execvp works

As you see in the preceding code box, we have invoked the function execvp. As we explained before, the execvp function inherits the environment variable PATH, together with the way it looks for the existing executables, from the base process. It accepts two arguments; the first is the name of the executable file or the script which should be loaded and executed, and the second is the list of arguments that should be passed to the executable.

Note that we are passing echo and not an absolute path. Therefore, execvp should locate the echo executable first. These executable files can be anywhere in a Unix-like operating system, from /usr/bin to /usr/local/bin or even other places. The absolute location of the echo can be found by going through all directory paths found in the PATH environment variable.

The exec* functions can execute a range of executable files. Following is a list of some file formats that can be executed by exec* functions:

- ELF executable files

- Script files with a *shebang* line indicating the *interpreter* of the script

- Traditional a.out format binary files

- ELF FDPIC executable files

After finding the `echo` executable file, the `execvp` does the rest. It calls the `exec` (`execve` in Linux) system call with a prepared set of arguments and subsequently, the kernel prepares a process image from the found executable file. When everything is ready, the kernel replaces the current process image with the prepared one, and the base process is gone forever. Now, the control returns to the new process, and it becomes executing from its `main` function, just like a normal execution.

As a result of this process, the `printf` statement after the `execvp` function call statement cannot be executed if the `execvp` has been successful, because now we have a whole new process with new memory segments and new instructions. If the `execvp` statement wasn't successful, then the `printf` should have been executed, which is a sign for the failure of `execvp` function call.

Like we said before, we have a group of `exec*` functions, and the `execvp` function is only one of them. While all of them behave similarly, they have slight differences. Next, you can find a comparison of these functions:

- `execl(const char* path, const char* arg0, ..., NULL)`: Accepts an absolute path to the executable file and a series of arguments that should be passed to the new process. They must end with a null string, `0` or `NULL`. If we wanted to rewrite *example 17.3* using `execl`, we would use `execl("/usr/bin/echo", "echo", "Hello", "World", NULL)`.

- `execlp(const char* file, const char* arg0, ..., NULL)`: Accepts a relative path as its first argument, but since it has access to the `PATH` environment variable, it can locate the executable file easily. Then, it accepts a series of arguments that should be passed to the new process. They must end with a null string, `0` or `NULL`. If we wanted to rewrite *example 17.3* using `execlp`, we would use `execlp("echo", "echo," "Hello," "World," NULL)`.

- `excele(const char* path, const char* arg0, ..., NULL, const char* env0, ..., NULL)`: Accepts an absolute path to the executable file as its first argument. Then, it accepts a series of arguments that should be passed to the new process followed by a null string. Following that, it accepts a series of strings representing the environment variables. They must also end with a null string. If we wanted to rewrite *example 17.3* using `execle`, we would use `execle("/usr/bin/echo", "echo", "Hello", "World", NULL, "A=1", "B=2", NULL)`. Note that in this call we have passed two new environment variables, `A` and `B`, to the new process.

- `execv(const char* path, const char* args[])`: Accepts an absolute path to the executable file and an array of the arguments that should be passed to the new process. The last element in the array must be a null string, `0` or `NULL`. If we wanted to rewrite *example 17.3* using `execl`, we would use `execl("/usr/bin/echo", args)` in which `args` is declared like this: `char* args[] = {"echo", "Hello", "World", NULL}`.

- `execvp(const char* file, const char* args[])`: It accepts a relative path as its first argument, but since it has access to the PATH environment variable, it can locate the executable file easily. Then, it accepts an array of the arguments that should be passed to the new process. The last element in the array must be a null string, `0` or `NULL`. This is the function that we used in *example 17.3*.

When `exec*` functions are successful, the previous process is gone, and a new process is created instead. Therefore, there isn't a second process at all. For this reason, we cannot demonstrate interleavings as we did for the `fork` API. In the next section, we compare the `fork` API and the `exec*` functions for executing a new program.

Comparing process creation and process execution

Based on our discussion and the given examples in previous sections, we can make the following comparison between the two methods used for executing a new program:

- A successful invocation of the `fork` function results in two separate processes; a parent process that has called the `fork` function and a forked (or child) process. But a successful invocation of any `exec*` function results in having the caller process substituted by a new process image and therefore no new process is created.

- Calling the `fork` function duplicates all memory contents of the parent process, and the forked process sees the same memory contents and variables. But calling the `exec*` functions destroys the memory layout of the base process and creates a new layout based on the loaded executable.

- A forked process has access to certain attributes of the parent process, for example, open file descriptors but using `exec*` functions. The new process doesn't know anything about it, and it doesn't inherit anything from the base process.

- In both APIs, we end up with a new process that has only one main thread. The threads in the parent process are not forked using the fork API.

- The `exec*` API can be used to run scripts and external executable files, but the `fork` API can be used only to create a new process that is actually the same C program.

In the next section, we'll talk about the steps that most kernels take to load and execute a new process. These steps and their details vary from one kernel to another, but we try to cover the general steps taken by most known kernels to execute a process.

Process execution steps

To have a process executed from an executable file, the user space and the kernel space take some general steps in most operating systems. As we noted in the previous section, executable files are mostly executable object files, for example, ELF, Mach, or script files that need an interpreter to execute them.

From the user ring's point of view, a system call like `exec` should be invoked. Note that we don't explain the `fork` system call here because it is not actually an execution. It is more of a cloning operation of the currently running process.

When the user space invokes the `exec` system call, a new request for the execution of the executable file is created within the kernel. The kernel tries to find a handler for the specified executable file based on its type and according to that handler, it uses a *loader program* to load the contents of the executable file.

Note that for the script files, the executable binary of the interpreter program that is usually specified in the *shebang line* on the first line of the script. The loader program has the following duties in order to execute a process:

- It checks the execution context and the permissions of the user that has requested the execution.
- It allocates the memory for the new process from the main memory.
- It copies the binary contents of the executable file into the allocated memory. This mostly involves the Data, and Text segments.
- It allocates a memory region for the Stack segment and prepares the initial memory mappings.
- The main thread and its Stack memory region are created.
- It copies the command-line arguments as a *stack frame* on top of the Stack region of the main thread.
- It initializes the vital registers that are needed for the execution.
- It executes the first instruction of the program entry point.

In the case of script files, the path to the script files is copied as the command-line argument of the interpreter process. The preceding general steps are taken by most kernels, but the implementation details can vary greatly from a kernel to another.

For more information on a specific operating system, you need to go to its documentation or simply search for it on Google. The following articles from LWN are a great start for those seeking more details about the process execution in Linux: `https://lwn.net/Articles/631631/` and `https://lwn.net/Articles/630727/`.

In the next section, we'll start to talk about concurrency-related topics. We prepare the ground for the next chapter, which is going to talk about multi-processing-specific synchronization techniques in great depth. We start here by discussing shared states, which can be used in multi-process software systems.

Shared states

As with threads, we can have some shared states between processes. The only difference is that the threads are able to access the same memory space owned by their owner process, but processes cannot have that luxury. Therefore, other mechanisms should be employed to share a state among a number of processes.

In this section, we are going to discuss these techniques and as part of this chapter, we focus on some of them that function as storage. In the first section, we will be discussing different techniques and trying to group them based on their nature.

Sharing techniques

If you look at the ways you can share a state (a variable or an array) between two processes, it turns out that it can be done in a limited number of ways. Theoretically, there are two main categories of sharing a state between a number of processes, but in a real computer system, each of these categories has some subcategories.

You either have to put a state in a "place" that can be accessed by a number of processes, or you must have your state *sent* or *transferred* as a message, signal, or event to other processes. Similarly, you either have to *pull* or *retrieve* an existing state from a "place," or *receive* it as a message, signal, or event. The first approach needs storage or a *medium* like a memory buffer or a filesystem, and the second approach requires you to have a messaging mechanism or a *channel* in place between the processes.

As an example for the first approach, we can have a shared memory region as a medium with an array inside that can be accessed by a number of processes to read and modify the array. As an example for the second approach, we can have a computer network as the channel to allow some messages to be transmitted between a number of processes located on different hosts in that network.

Our current discussion on how to share states between some processes is not in fact limited to just processes; it can be applied to threads as well. Threads can also have signaling between themselves to share a state or propagate an event.

In different terminology, the techniques found in the first group that requires a *medium* such as storage to share states are called *pull-based* techniques. That's because the processes that want to read states have to pull them from storage.

The techniques in the second group that require a *channel* to transmit states are called *push-based* techniques. That's because the states are pushed (or delivered) through the channel to the receiving process and it doesn't need to pull them from a medium. We will be using these terms from now on to refer to these techniques.

The variety in push-based techniques has led to various distributed architectures in the modern software industry. The pull-based techniques are considered to be legacy in comparison to push-based techniques, and you can see it in many enterprise applications where a single central database is used to share various states throughout the entire system.

However, the push-based approach is gaining momentum these days and has led to techniques such as *event sourcing* and a number of other similar distributed approaches used for keeping all parts of a big software system consistent with each other without having all data stored in a central place.

Between the two approaches discussed, we are particularly interested in the first approach throughout this chapter. We will focus more upon the second approach in *Chapter 19, Single-Host IPC and Sockets*, and *Chapter 20, Socket Programming*. In those chapters we are going to introduce the various channels available to transmit messages between processes as part of **Inter-Process Communication** (**IPC**) techniques. Only then will we be able to explore the various push-based techniques and give some real examples for the observed concurrency issues and the control mechanisms that can be employed.

The following is a list of pull-based techniques that are supported by the POSIX standard and can be used widely in all POSIX-compliant operating systems:

- **Shared memory**: This is simply a region in the main memory that is shared and accessible to a number of processes, and they can use it to store variables and arrays just like an ordinary memory block. A shared memory object is not a file on disk, but it is the actual memory. It can exist as a standalone object in the operating system even when there is no process using it. Shared memory objects can be removed whether by a process when not needed anymore or by rebooting the system. Therefore, in terms of surviving reboots, shared memory objects can be thought of as temporary objects.

- **Filesystem**: Processes can use files to share states. This technique is one of the oldest techniques to share some states throughout a software system among a number of processes. Eventually, difficulties with synchronizing access to the shared files, together with many other valid reasons, have led to the invention of **Database Management Systems** (**DBMSes**), but still, the shared files are being used in certain use cases.

- **Network services**: Once available to all processes, processes can use network storage or a network service to store and retrieve a shared state. In this scenario, the processes do not know exactly what is going on behind the scenes. They just use a network service through a well-defined API that allows them to perform certain operations on a shared state. As some examples, we can name **Network Filesystems** (**NFS**) or DBMSes. They offer network services that allow maintaining states through a well-defined model and a set of companion operations. To give a more specific example, we can mention *Relational DBMSes,* which allow you to store your states in a relational model through using SQL commands.

In the following subsections, we will be discussing each of the above methods found as part of the POSIX interface. We start with POSIX shared memory, and we show how it can lead to familiar data races known from *Chapter 16, Thread Synchronization.*

POSIX shared memory

Supported by POSIX standard, shared memory is one of the widely used techniques to share a piece of information among a number of processes. Unlike threads that can access the same memory space, processes do not have this power and access to the memory of other processes is prohibited by the operating system. Therefore, we need a mechanism in order to share a portion of memory between two processes, and shared memory is exactly that technique.

In the following examples, we go through the details of creating and using a shared memory object, and we start our discussion by creating a shared memory region. The following code shows how to create and populate a shared memory object within a POSIX-compliant system:

```
#include <stdio.h>
#include <unistd.h>
#include <fcntl.h>
#include <errno.h>
#include <string.h>
#include <sys/mman.h>

#define SH_SIZE 16

int main(int argc, char** argv) {
  int shm_fd = shm_open("/shm0", O_CREAT | O_RDWR, 0600);
  if (shm_fd < 0) {
    fprintf(stderr, "ERROR: Failed to create shared memory: %s\n",
```

```
            strerror(errno));
    return 1;
  }
  fprintf(stdout, "Shared memory is created with fd: %d\n",
          shm_fd);
  if (ftruncate(shm_fd, SH_SIZE * sizeof(char)) < 0) {
    fprintf(stderr, "ERROR: Truncation failed: %s\n",
            strerror(errno));
    return 1;
  }
  fprintf(stdout, "The memory region is truncated.\n");
  void* map = mmap(0, SH_SIZE, PROT_WRITE, MAP_SHARED, shm_fd, 0);
  if (map == MAP_FAILED) {
    fprintf(stderr, "ERROR: Mapping failed: %s\n",
            strerror(errno));
    return 1;
  }
  char* ptr = (char*)map;
  ptr[0] = 'A';
  ptr[1] = 'B';
  ptr[2] = 'C';
  ptr[3] = '\n';
  ptr[4] = '\0';
  while(1);
  fprintf(stdout, "Data is written to the shared memory.\n");
  if (munmap(ptr, SH_SIZE) < 0) {
    fprintf(stderr, "ERROR: Unmapping failed: %s\n",
            strerror(errno));
    return 1;
  }
  if (close(shm_fd) < 0) {
    fprintf(stderr, "ERROR: Closing shared memory failed: %s\n",
        strerror(errno));
    return 1;
  }
  return 0;
}
```

Code Box 17-4 [ExtremeC_examples_chapter17_4.c]: Creating and writing to a POSIX shared memory object

The preceding code creates a shared memory object named /shm0 with 16 bytes in it. Then it populates the shared memory with the literal ABC\n and finally, it quits by *unmapping* the shared memory region. Note that the shared memory object remains in place even when the process quits. Future processes can open and read the same shared memory object over and over again. A shared memory object is destructed either by rebooting the system or by getting *unlinked* (removed) by a process.

Note:
In FreeBSD, the names of the shared memory objects should start with /. This is not mandatory in Linux or macOS, but we did the same for both of them to remain compatible with FreeBSD.

In the preceding code, we firstly open a shared memory object using the shm_open function. It accepts a name and the modes that the shared memory object should be created with. O_CREAT and O_RDWR mean that the shared memory should be created, and it can be used for both reading and writing.

Note the creation won't fail if the shared memory object already exists. The last argument indicates the permissions of the shared memory object. 0600 means that it is available for reading and write operations performed by the processes that are initiated only by the owner of the shared memory object.

On the following lines, we define the size of the shared memory region by truncating it using ftruncate function. Note that this is a necessary step if you're about to create a new shared memory object. For the preceding shared memory object, we have defined 16 bytes to be allocated and then truncated.

As we proceed, we map the shared memory object to a region accessible by the process using the mmap function. As a result of this, we have a pointer to the mapped memory and that can be used to access the shared memory region behind. This is also a necessary step that makes the shared memory accessible to our C program.

The function mmap is usually used to map a file or a shared memory region (originally allocated from the kernel's memory space) to an address space that is accessible to the caller process. Then, the mapped address space can be accessed as a regular memory region using ordinary pointers.

As you can see, the region is mapped as a writable region indicated by PROT_WRITE and as a shared region among processes indicated by the MAP_SHARED argument. MAP_SHARED simply means any changes to the mapped area will be visible to other processes mapping the same region.

Instead of MAP_SHARED, we could have MAP_PRIVATE; this means that the changes to the mapped region are not propagated to other processes and are, rather, private to the mapper process. This usage is not common unless you want to use the shared memory inside a process only.

After mapping the shared memory region, the preceding code writes a null-terminated string ABC\n into the shared memory. Note the new line feed character at the end of the string. As the final steps, the process unmaps the shared memory region by calling the munmap function and then it closes the file descriptor assigned to the shared memory object.

Note:
Every operating system offers a different way to create an *unnamed* or *anonymous shared memory* object. In FreeBSD, it is enough to pass SHM_ANON as the path of the shared memory object to the shm_open function. In Linux, one can create an anonymous file using a memfd_create function instead of creating a shared memory object and use the returned file descriptor to create a mapped region. An anonymous shared memory is private to the owner process and cannot be used to share states among a number of processes.

The preceding code can be compiled on macOS, FreeBSD, and Linux systems. In Linux systems, shared memory objects can be seen inside the directory /dev/shm. Note that this directory doesn't have a regular filesystem and those you see are not files on a disk device. Instead, /dev/shm uses the shmfs filesystem. It is meant to expose the temporary objects created inside the memory through a mounted directory, and it is only available in Linux.

Let's compile and run *example 17.4* in Linux and examine the contents of the /dev/shm directory. In Linux, it is mandatory to link the final binary with the rt library in order to use shared memory facilities, and that's why you see the option -lrt in the following shell box:

```
$ ls /dev/shm
$ gcc ExtremeC_examples_chapter17_4.c -lrt -o ex17_4.out
$ ./ex17_4.out
Shared memory is created with fd: 3
The memory region is truncated.
Data is written to the shared memory.
$ ls /dev/shm
shm0
$
```

Shell Box 17-4: Building and running example 17.4 and checking if the shared memory object is created

As you can see on the first line, there are no shared memory objects in the /dev/shm directory. On the second line, we build *example 17.4*, and on the third line, we execute the produced executable file. Then we check /dev/shm, and we see that we've got a new shared memory object, shm0, there.

The output of the program also confirms the creation of the shared memory object. Another important thing about the preceding shell box is the file descriptor 3, which is assigned to the shared memory object.

For every file you open, a new file descriptor is opened in each process. This file is not necessarily on disk, and it can be a shared memory object, standard output, and so on. In each process, file descriptors start from 0 and go up to a maximum allowed number.

Note that in each process, the file descriptors 0, 1, and 2 are preassigned to the stdout, stdin, and stderr streams, respectively. These file descriptors are opened for every new process before having its main function run. That's basically why the shared memory object in the preceding example gets 3 as its file descriptor.

Note:
On macOS systems, you can use the pics utility to check active IPC objects in the system. It can show you the active message queues and shared memories. It shows you the active semaphores as well.

The /dev/shm directory has another interesting property. You can use the cat utility to see the contents of shared memory objects, but again this is only available in Linux. Let's use it on our created shm0 object. As you see in the following shell box, the contents of the shared memory object are displayed. It is the string ABC plus a new line feed character \n:

```
$ cat /dev/shm/shm0
ABC
$
```

Shell Box 17-5 Using the cat program to see the content of the shared memory object created
as part of example 17.4

As we explained before, a shared memory object exists as long as it is being used by at least one process. Even if one of the processes has already asked the operating system to delete (or *unlink*) the shared memory, it won't be actually deleted until the last process has used it. Even when there is no process unlinking a shared memory object, it would be deleted when a reboot happens. Shared memory objects cannot survive reboots, and the processes should create them again in order to use them for communication.

The following example shows how a process can open and read from an already existing shared memory object and how it can unlink it finally. *Example 17.5* reads from the shared memory object created in *example 17.4*. Therefore, it can be considered as complementary to what we did in *example 17.4*:

```c
#include <stdio.h>
#include <unistd.h>
#include <fcntl.h>
#include <errno.h>
#include <string.h>
#include <sys/mman.h>

#define SH_SIZE 16

int main(int argc, char** argv) {
  int shm_fd = shm_open("/shm0", O_RDONLY, 0600);
  if (shm_fd < 0) {
    fprintf(stderr, "ERROR: Failed to open shared memory: %s\n",
        strerror(errno));
    return 1;
  }
  fprintf(stdout, "Shared memory is opened with fd: %d\n", shm_fd);
  void* map = mmap(0, SH_SIZE, PROT_READ, MAP_SHARED, shm_fd, 0);
  if (map == MAP_FAILED) {
    fprintf(stderr, "ERROR: Mapping failed: %s\n",
            strerror(errno));
    return 1;
  }
  char* ptr = (char*)map;
  fprintf(stdout, "The contents of shared memory object: %s\n",
          ptr);
  if (munmap(ptr, SH_SIZE) < 0) {
    fprintf(stderr, "ERROR: Unmapping failed: %s\n",
            strerror(errno));
    return 1;
  }
  if (close(shm_fd) < 0) {
    fprintf(stderr, "ERROR: Closing shared memory fd filed: %s\n",
        strerror(errno));
    return 1;
  }
  if (shm_unlink("/shm0") < 0) {
    fprintf(stderr, "ERROR: Unlinking shared memory failed: %s\n",
        strerror(errno));
    return 1;
  }
  return 0;
}
```

Code Box 17-5 [ExtremeC_examples_chapter17_5.c]: Reading from the shared memory object created as part of example 17.4

As the first statement in the `main` function, we have opened an existing shared memory object named `/shm0`. If there is no such shared memory object, we will generate an error. As you can see, we have opened the shared memory object as read-only, meaning that we are not going to write anything to the shared memory.

On the following lines, we map the shared memory region. Again, we have indicated that the mapped region is read-only by passing the `PROT_READ` argument. After that, we finally get a pointer to the shared memory region, and we use it to print its contents. When we're done with the shared memory, we unmap the region. Following this, the assigned file descriptor is closed, and lastly the shared memory object is registered for removal by unlinking it through using the `shm_unlink` function.

After this point, when all other processes that are using the same shared memory are done with it, the shared memory object gets removed from the system. Note that the shared memory object exists as long as there is a process using it.

The following is the output of running the preceding code. Note the contents of `/dev/shm` before and after running *example 17.5*:

```
$ ls /dev/shm
shm0
$ gcc ExtremeC_examples_chapter17_5.c -lrt -o ex17_5.out
$ ./ex17_5.out
Shared memory is opened with fd: 3
The contents of the shared memory object: ABC


$ ls /dev/shm
$
```

Shell Box 17-6: Reading from the shared memory object created in example 17.4 and finally removing it

Data race example using shared memory

Now, it's time to demonstrate a data race using the combination of the fork API and shared memory. It would be analogous to the examples given in *Chapter 15, Thread Execution*, to demonstrate a data race among a number of threads.

In *example 17.6*, we have a counter variable that is placed inside a shared memory region. The example forks a child process out of the main running process, and both of them try to increment the shared counter. The final output shows a clear data race over the shared counter:

```c
#include <stdio.h>
#include <stdint.h>
#include <stdlib.h>
#include <unistd.h>
#include <fcntl.h>
#include <errno.h>
#include <string.h>
#include <sys/mman.h>
#include <sys/wait.h>

#define SH_SIZE 4

// Shared file descriptor used to refer to the
// shared memory object
int shared_fd = -1;

// The pointer to the shared counter
int32_t* counter = NULL;

void init_shared_resource() {
  // Open the shared memory object
  shared_fd = shm_open("/shm0", O_CREAT | O_RDWR, 0600);
  if (shared_fd < 0) {
    fprintf(stderr, "ERROR: Failed to create shared memory: %s\n",
        strerror(errno));
    exit(1);
  }
  fprintf(stdout, "Shared memory is created with fd: %d\n",
        shared_fd);
}

void shutdown_shared_resource() {
  if (shm_unlink("/shm0") < 0) {
    fprintf(stderr, "ERROR: Unlinking shared memory failed: %s\n",
        strerror(errno));
    exit(1);
  }
}

void inc_counter() {
  usleep(1);
  int32_t temp = *counter;
  usleep(1);
  temp++;
  usleep(1);
  *counter = temp;
  usleep(1);
}
```

```
int main(int argc, char** argv) {

  // Parent process needs to initialize the shared resource
  init_shared_resource();

  // Allocate and truncate the shared memory region
  if (ftruncate(shared_fd, SH_SIZE * sizeof(char)) < 0) {
    fprintf(stderr, "ERROR: Truncation failed: %s\n",
            strerror(errno));
    return 1;
  }
  fprintf(stdout, "The memory region is truncated.\n");

  // Map the shared memory and initialize the counter
  void* map = mmap(0, SH_SIZE, PROT_WRITE,
          MAP_SHARED, shared_fd, 0);
  if (map == MAP_FAILED) {
    fprintf(stderr, "ERROR: Mapping failed: %s\n",
            strerror(errno));
    return 1;
  }
  counter = (int32_t*)map;
  *counter = 0;

  // Fork a new process
  pid_t pid = fork();
  if (pid) { // The parent process
    // Increment the counter
    inc_counter();
    fprintf(stdout, "The parent process sees the counter as
%d.\n",
        *counter);

    // Wait for the child process to exit
    int status = -1;
    wait(&status);
    fprintf(stdout, "The child process finished with status
%d.\n",
        status);
  } else { // The child process
    // Incrmenet the counter
    inc_counter();
    fprintf(stdout, "The child process sees the counter as %d.\n",
        *counter);
  }

  // Both processes should unmap shared memory region and close
  // its file descriptor
```

```
    if (munmap(counter, SH_SIZE) < 0) {
      fprintf(stderr, "ERROR: Unmapping failed: %s\n",
            strerror(errno));
      return 1;
    }
    if (close(shared_fd) < 0) {
      fprintf(stderr, "ERROR: Closing shared memory fd filed: %s\n",
          strerror(errno));
      return 1;
    }

    // Only parent process needs to shutdown the shared resource
    if (pid) {
      shutdown_shared_resource();
    }

    return 0;
}
```

Code Box 17-6 [ExtremeC_examples_chapter17_6.c]: Demonstration of a data race using a POSIX
shared memory and the fork API

There are three functions in the preceding code other than the main function.
The function init_shared_resource creates the shared memory object. The
reason that I've named this function init_shared_resource instead of init_
shared_memory is the fact that we could use another pull-based technique in the
preceding example and having a general name for this function allows the main
function to remain unchanged in the future examples.

The function shutdown_shared_resource destructs the shared memory and unlinks
it. In addition, the function inc_counter increments the shared counter by 1.

The main function truncates and maps the shared memory region just like we
did in *example 17.4*. After having the shared memory region mapped, the forking
logic beings. By calling the fork function, a new process is spawned, and both
processes (the forked process and the forking process) try to increment the
counter by calling the inc_counter function.

When the parent process writes to the shared counter, it waits for the child process
to finish, and only after that, it tries to unmap, close, and unlink the shared memory
object. Note that the unmapping and the closure of the file descriptor happen in both
processes, but only the parent process unlinks the shared memory object.

As you can see as part of *Code Box 17-6*, we have used some unusual usleep calls
in the inc_counter function. The reason is to force the scheduler to take back the
CPU core from one process and give it to another process. Without these usleep
function calls, the CPU core is not usually transferred between the processes, and
you cannot see the effect of different interleavings very often.

One of the reasons for such an effect is having a small number of instructions in each process. If the number of instructions per process increases significantly, one can see the non-deterministic behavior of interleavings even without sleep calls. As an example, having a loop in each process that counts for 10,000 times and increments the shared counter in each iteration is very likely to reveal the data race. You can try this yourself.

As the final note about the preceding code, the parent process creates and opens the shared memory object and assigns a file descriptor to it before forking the child process. The forked process doesn't open the shared memory object, but it can use the same file descriptor. The fact that all open file descriptors are inherited from the parent process helped the child process to continue and use the file descriptor, referring to the same shared memory object.

The following in *Shell Box 17-7* is the output of running *example 17.6* for a number of times. As you can see, we have a clear data race over the shared counter. There are moments when the parent or the child process updates the counter without obtaining the latest modified value, and this results in printing 1 by both processes:

```
$ gcc ExtremeC_examples_chapter17_6 -o ex17_6.out
$ ./ex17_6.out
Shared memory is created with fd: 3
The memory region is truncated.
The parent process sees the counter as 1.
The child process sees the counter as 2.
The child process finished with status 0.
$ ./ex17_6
. . .
. . .
. . .
$ ./ex17_6.out
Shared memory is created with fd: 3
The memory region is truncated.
The parent process sees the counter as 1.
The child process sees the counter as 1.
The child process finished with status 0.
$
```

Shell Box 17-7: Running example 17.6 and demonstration of the data race happening over the shared counter

In this section, we showed how to create and use shared memory. We also demonstrated a data race example and the way concurrent processes behave while accessing a shared memory region. In the following section, we're going to talk about the filesystem as another widely used pull-based method to share a state among a number of processes.

File system

POSIX exposes a similar API for working with files in a filesystem. As long as the file descriptors are involved and they are used to refer to various system objects, the same API as that introduced for working with shared memory can be used.

We use file descriptors to refer to actual files in a filesystem like **ext4**, together with shared memory, pipes, and so on; therefore, the same semantic for opening, reading, writing, mapping them to a local memory region, and so on can be employed. Therefore, we'd expect to see similar discussion and perhaps similar C code regarding the filesystem as we had for the shared memory. We see this in *example 17.7*.

Note:
We usually map file descriptors. There are some exceptional cases, however, where *socket descriptors* can be mapped. Socket descriptors are similar to file descriptors but are used for network or Unix sockets. This link provides an interesting use case for mapping the kernel buffer behind a TCP socket which is referred to as a *zero-copy receive mechanism*: https://lwn.net/Articles/752188/.

Note that it's correct that the API employed for using the filesystem is very similar to the one we used for shared memory, but it doesn't mean that their implementation is similar as well. In fact, a file object in a filesystem backed by a hard disk is fundamentally different from a shared memory object. Let's briefly discuss some differences:

- A shared memory object is basically in the memory space of the kernel process while a file in a filesystem is located on a disk. At most, such a file has some allocated buffers for reading and writing operations.

- The states written to shared memory are wiped out by rebooting the system, but the states written to a shared file, if it is backed by a hard disk or permanent storage, can be retained after the reboot.

- Generally, accessing shared memory is far faster than accessing the filesystem.

The following code is the same data race example that we gave for the shared memory in the previous section. Since the API used for the filesystem is pretty similar to the API we used for the shared memory, we only need to change two functions from *example 17.6*; init_shared_resource and shutdown_ shared_resource. The rest will be the same. This is a great achievement that is accomplished by using the same POSIX API operating on the file descriptors. Let's get into the code:

```c
#include <stdio.h>
#include <stdint.h>
#include <stdlib.h>
#include <unistd.h>
#include <fcntl.h>
#include <errno.h>
#include <string.h>
#include <sys/mman.h>
#include <sys/wait.h>

#define SH_SIZE 4

// The shared file descriptor used to refer to the shared file
int shared_fd = -1;

// The pointer to the shared counter
int32_t* counter = NULL;

void init_shared_resource() {
  // Open the file
  shared_fd = open("data.bin", O_CREAT | O_RDWR, 0600);
  if (shared_fd < 0) {
    fprintf(stderr, "ERROR: Failed to create the file: %s\n",
        strerror(errno));
    exit(1);
  }
  fprintf(stdout, "File is created and opened with fd: %d\n",
        shared_fd);
}

void shutdown_shared_resource() {
  if (remove("data.bin") < 0) {
    fprintf(stderr, "ERROR: Removing the file failed: %s\n",
        strerror(errno));
    exit(1);
  }
}

void inc_counter() {
```

```
   ... As exmaple 17.6 ...
}

int main(int argc, char** argv) {
   ... As exmaple 17.6 ...
}
```

Code Box 17-7 [ExtremeC_examples_chapter17_7.c]: Demonstration of a data race using regular files and the fork API

As you see, the majority of the preceding code is obtained from *example 17.6*. The rest is a substitute for using the open and remove functions instead of the shm_open and shm_unlink functions.

Note that the file data.bin is created in the current directory since we've not given an absolute path to the open function. Running the preceding code also produces the same data race over the shared counter. It can be examined similarly to our approach for *example 17.6*.

So far, we have seen that we can use shared memory and shared files to store a state and access it from a number of processes concurrently. Now, it's time to talk about multithreading and multi-processing in a greater sense and compare them thoroughly.

Multithreading versus multi-processing

After discussing multithreading and multi-processing in *Chapter 14, Synchronization*, together with concepts we have covered throughout the recent chapters, we are in a good position to compare them and give a high-level description of situations in which each of the approaches should be employed. Suppose that we are going to design a piece of software that aims to process a number of input requests concurrently. We discuss this in the context of three different situations. Let's start with the first one.

Multithreading

The first situation is when you can write a piece of software that has only one process, and all the requests go into the same process. All the logic should be written as part of the same process, and as a result, you get a fat process that does everything in your system. Since this is single-process software, if you want to handle many requests concurrently, you need to do it in a multithreaded way by creating threads to handle multiple requests. Further, it can be a better design decision to go for a *thread pool* that has a limited number of threads.

There are the following considerations regarding concurrency and synchronization which should be taken care of. Note that we don't talk about using event loops or asynchronous I/O in this situation, while it can still be a valid alternative to multithreading.

If the number of requests increases significantly, the limited number of threads within the thread pool should be increased to overcome the demand. This literally means upgrading the hardware and resources on the machine on which the main process is running. This is called *scaling up* or *vertical scaling*. It means that you upgrade the hardware you have on a single machine to be able to respond to more requests. In addition to the possible downtime that clients experience while upgrading to the new hardware (though it can be prevented), the upgrade is costly, and you have to do another scale up when the number of requests grows again.

If processing the requests ends up in manipulating a shared state or a data store, synchronization techniques can be implemented easily, by knowing the fact that threads have access to the same memory space. Of course, this is needed whether they have a shared data structure that should be maintained or they have access to remote data storage that is not transactional.

All the threads are running on the same machine, and thus they can use all the techniques used for sharing a state that we explained so far, used by both threads and processes. This is a great feature and mitigates a lot of pain when it comes to thread synchronization.

Let's talk about the next situation, when we can have more than one process but all of them are on the same machine.

Single-host multi-processing

In this situation, we write a piece of software that has multiple processes, but all are deployed on a single machine. All of these processes can be either single-threaded, or they can have a thread pool inside that allows each of them to handle more than one request at a time.

When the number of requests increases, one can create new processes instead of creating more threads. This is usually called *scaling out* or *horizontal scaling*. When you have only one single machine, however, you must scale it up, or in other words, you must upgrade its hardware. This can cause the same issues we mentioned for the scaling up of a multithreaded program in the previous subsection.

When it comes to concurrency, the processes are being executed in a concurrent environment. They can only use the multi-processing ways of sharing a state or synchronizing the processes. Surely, it is not as convenient as writing multithreaded code. In addition, processes can use both pull-based or push-based techniques to share states.

Multi-processing on a single machine is not very effective, and it seems multithreading is more convenient when it comes to the effort of coding.

The next subsection talks about the distributed multi-processing environment, which is the best design to create modern software.

Distributed multi-processing

In the final situation, we have written a program that is run as multiple processes, running on multiple hosts, all connected to each other through a network, and on a single host we can have more than one process running. The following features can be seen in such a deployment.

When faced with significant growth in the number of requests, this system can be scaled out without limits. This is a great feature that enables you to use commodity hardware when you face such high peaks. Using the clusters of commodity hardware instead of powerful servers was one of the ideas that enabled Google to run its *Page Rank* and *Map Reduce* algorithms on a cluster of machines.

The techniques discussed in this chapter barely help because they have an important prerequisite: that all the processes are running within the same machine. Therefore, a completely different set of algorithms and techniques should be employed to make the processes synchronized and make shared states available to all processes within the system. *Latency, fault tolerance, availability, data consistency*, and many more factors should be studied and tuned regarding such a distributed system.

Processes on different hosts use network sockets to communicate in a push-based manner, but the processes on the same host may use local IPC techniques, for example, message queues, shared memory, pipes, and so on, to transfer messages and share state.

As a final word in this section, in the modern software industry, we prefer scaling out rather than scaling up. This will give rise to many new ideas and technologies for data storage, synchronization, message passing, and so on. It can even have an impact on the hardware design to make it suitable for horizontal scaling.

Summary

In this chapter, we explored multi-processing systems and the various techniques that can be used to share a state among a number of processes. The following topics were covered in this chapter:

- We introduced the POSIX APIs used for process execution. We explained how the `fork` API and `exec*` functions work.

- We explained the steps that a kernel takes to execute a process.

- We discussed the ways that a state can be shared among a number of processes.

- We introduced the pull-based and push-based techniques as the two top-level categories for all other available techniques.

- Shared memory and shared files on a filesystem are among common techniques to share a state in a pull-based manner.

- We explained the differences and similarities of multithreading and multi-processing deployments and the concepts of vertical and horizontal scaling in a distributed software system.

In the next chapter, we are going to talk about concurrency in single-host multi-processing environments. It will consist of discussions about concurrency issues and the ways to synchronize a number of processes in order to protect a shared resource. The topics are very similar to the ones you encountered in *Chapter 16, Thread Synchronization,* but their focus is on the processes rather than the threads.

Chapter 18

Process Synchronization

This chapter continues our discussion in the previous chapter, *Process Execution*, and our main focus will be on process synchronization. Control mechanisms in multi-process programs are different from the control techniques we met in multi-threaded programs. It is not just the memory which differs; there are other factors that you cannot find in a multi-threaded program, and they exist in a multi-process environment.

Despite threads that are bound to a process, processes can live freely on any machine, with any operating system, located anywhere within a network as big as the internet. As you might imagine, things become complicated. It will not be easy to synchronize a number of processes in such a distributed system.

This chapter is dedicated to process synchronization happening in just one machine. In other words, it mainly talks about single-host synchronization and the techniques around it. We discuss briefly the process synchronization in distributed systems, but we won't go into extensive detail.

This chapter covers the following topics:

- Firstly, we describe multi-process software where all processes are being run on the same machine. We introduce the techniques that are available in single-host environments. We use the knowledge from the previous chapter in order to give some examples that demonstrate these techniques.

- In our first attempt to synchronize a number of processes, we use named POSIX semaphores. We explain how they should be used and then we give an example that resolves a race condition issue we encountered in the previous chapters.

- After that, we talk about named POSIX mutexes and we show how we can use shared memory regions to have named mutexes up and working. As an example, we solve the same race condition resolved by semaphores, this time using named mutexes.

- As the last technique to synchronize a number of processes, we discuss named POSIX condition variables. Like named mutexes, they need to be put in a shared memory region to become accessible to a number of processes. We give a thorough example regarding this technique which shows how named POSIX condition variables can be used to synchronize a multi-process system.

- As our final discussion in this chapter, we briefly talk about the multi-process systems which have their own processes distributed around a network. We discuss their features and the problematic differences that they have in comparison to a single-host multi-process system.

Let us start the chapter with talking a bit more about single-host concurrency control and what techniques are available as part of it.

Single-host concurrency control

It is pretty common to be in situations where there are a number of processes running on a single machine that, at the same time, need to have simultaneous access to a shared resource. Since all of the processes are running within the same operating system, they have access to all the facilities which their operating system provides.

In this section, we show how to use some of these facilities to create a control mechanism that synchronizes the processes. Shared memory plays a key role in most of these control mechanisms; therefore, we heavily rely on what we explained about shared memory in the previous chapter.

The following is a list of POSIX-provided control mechanisms that can be employed while all processes are running on the same POSIX-compliant machine:

- **Named POSIX semaphores**: The same POSIX semaphores that we explained in *Chapter 16*, *Thread Synchronization*, but with one difference: they have a name now and can be used globally throughout the system. In other words, they are not *anonymous* or *private* semaphores anymore.

- **Named mutexes**: Again, the same POSIX mutexes with the same properties which were explained in *Chapter 16*, *Thread Synchronization*, but now named and can be used throughout the system. These mutexes should be placed inside a shared memory in order to be available to multiple processes.

- **Named condition variables**: The same POSIX condition variables which we explained in *Chapter 16*, *Thread Synchronization*, but like mutexes, they should be placed inside a shared memory object in order to be available to a number of processes.

In the upcoming sections, we discuss all the above techniques and give examples to demonstrate how they work. In the following section, we are going to discuss named POSIX semaphores.

Named POSIX semaphores

As you saw in *Chapter 16, Thread Synchronization*, semaphores are the main tool to synchronize a number of concurrent tasks. We saw them in multi-threaded programs and saw how they help to overcome the concurrency issues.

In this section, we are going to show how they can be used among some processes. *Example 18.1* shows how to use a POSIX semaphore to solve the data races we encountered in *examples 17.6* and *17.7* given in the previous chapter, *Process Execution*. The example is remarkably similar to *example 17.6*, and it again uses a shared memory region for storing the shared counter variable. But it uses named semaphores to synchronize the access to the shared counter.

The following code boxes show the way that we use a named semaphore to synchronize two processes while accessing a shared variable. The following code box shows the global declarations of *example 18.1*:

```c
#include <stdio.h>
...
#include <semaphore.h>  // For using semaphores

#define SHARED_MEM_SIZE 4

// Shared file descriptor used to refer to the
// shared memory object
int shared_fd = -1;

// The pointer to the shared counter
int32_t* counter = NULL;

// The pointer to the shared semaphore
sem_t* semaphore = NULL;
```

Code Box 18-1 [ExtremeC_examples_chapter18_1.c]: The global declarations of example 18.1

In *Code Box 18-1*, we have declared a global counter and a global pointer to a semaphore object which will be set later. This pointer will be used by both parent and child processes to have synchronized access to the shared counter, addressed by the counter pointer.

The following code shows the function definitions supposed to do the actual process synchronization. Some of the definitions are the same as we had in *example 17.6* and those lines are removed from the following code box:

```c
void init_control_mechanism() {
    semaphore = sem_open("/sem0", O_CREAT | O_EXCL, 0600, 1);
```

```
  if (semaphore == SEM_FAILED) {
    fprintf(stderr, "ERROR: Opening the semaphore failed: %s\n",
        strerror(errno));
    exit(1);
  }
}

void shutdown_control_mechanism() {
  if (sem_close(semaphore) < 0) {
    fprintf(stderr, "ERROR: Closing the semaphore failed: %s\n",
        strerror(errno));
    exit(1);
  }
  if (sem_unlink("/sem0") < 0) {
    fprintf(stderr, "ERROR: Unlinking failed: %s\n",
        strerror(errno));
    exit(1);
  }
}

void init_shared_resource() {
  ... as in the example 17.6 ...
}

void shutdown_shared_resource() {
  ... as in the example 17.6 ...
}
```

Code Box 18-2 [ExtremeC_examples_chapter18_1.c]: The definition of synchronization functions

We have added two new functions compared to *example 17.6*: init_control_mechanism and shutdown_control_mechanism. We also made some changes to the inc_counter function (shown in *Code Box 18-3*) to use the semaphore and form a critical section inside.

Inside the init_control_mechanism and shutdown_control_mechanism functions, we are using a similar API to the shared memory API to open, close, and unlink a named semaphore.

The functions sem_open, sem_close, and sem_unlink can be seen as similar to shm_open, shm_close, and shm_unlink. There is one difference and that is that the function sem_open returns a semaphore pointer instead of a file descriptor.

Note that the API used for working with the semaphore in this example is the same as we have seen before, so the rest of the code can remain unchanged as with *example 17.6*. In this example, the semaphore is initialized with value 1, which makes it a mutex. The following code box shows the critical section and how the semaphore is used to synchronize the read and write operations performed on the shared counter:

```
void inc_counter() {
  usleep(1);
  sem_wait(semaphore); // Return value should be checked.
  int32_t temp = *counter;
  usleep(1);
  temp++;
  usleep(1);
  *counter = temp;
  sem_post(semaphore); // Return value should be checked.
  usleep(1);
}
```

Code Box 18-3 [ExtremeC_examples_chapter18_1.c]: The critical section where the shared counter is being incremented

Comparing to *example 17.6*, in the function `inc_counter`, the functions `sem_wait` and `sem_post` are used to enter and exit the critical sections, respectively.

In the following code box, you can see the function `main`. It is almost the same as *example 17.6* and we only see some changes in the initial and final parts, and that is in accordance with the addition of two new functions seen in *Code Box 18-2*:

```
int main(int argc, char** argv) {

  // Parent process needs to initialize the shared resource
  init_shared_resource();

  // Parent process needs to initialize the control mechanism
  init_control_mechanism();

  ... as in the example 17.6 ...

  // Only parent process needs to shut down the shared resource
  // and the employed control mechanism
  if (pid) {
    shutdown_shared_resource();
    shutdown_control_mechanism();
  }

  return 0;
}
```

Code Box 18-4 [ExtremeC_examples_chapter18_1.c]: The main function of example 18.1

In the following shell box, you can see the output for two successive runs of *example 18.1*:

```
$ gcc ExtremeC_examples_chapter18_1.c -lrt -lpthread -o ex18_1.out
$ ./ex18_1.out
Shared memory is created with fd: 3
The memory region is truncated.
The child process sees the counter as 1.
The parent process sees the counter as 2.
The child process finished with status 0.
$ ./ex18_1.out
Shared memory is created with fd: 3
The memory region is truncated.
The parent process sees the counter as 1.
The child process sees the counter as 2.
The child process finished with status 0.
$
```

Shell Box 18-1: Building in Linux and two successive runs of example 18.1

Note that we need to link the above code with the `pthread` library because we are using POSIX semaphores. We need also to link it with the `rt` library in Linux in order to use the shared memories.

The preceding output is clear. Sometimes the child process gets the CPU first and increments the counter, and sometimes the parent process does so. There is no time when both enter the critical section, and therefore they satisfy the data integrity of the shared counter.

Note that it is not required to use the fork API in order to use named semaphores. Completely separated processes, which are not parent and child, can still open and use the same semaphores if they are run on the same machine and inside the same operating system. In *example 18.3*, we show how this is possible.

As the final note in this section, you should know that we have two types of named semaphores in Unix-like operating systems. One is *System V Semaphores*, and the other is *POSIX semaphores*. In this section, we explained the POSIX semaphores because they have a better reputation for their nice API and performance. The following link is a Stack Overflow question which nicely explains the differences between System V semaphores and POSIX semaphores: `https://stackoverflow.com/questions/368322/differences-between-system-v-and-posix-semaphores`.

Note:
Microsoft Windows is not POSIX-compliant in terms of using semaphores, and it has its own API to create and manage semaphores.

In the next section, we discuss named mutexes. In short, named mutexes are ordinary mutex objects that are put into a shared memory region.

Named mutexes

POSIX mutexes work simply in multi-threaded programs; we demonstrated this in *Chapter 16, Thread Synchronization*. This would not be the case with regard to multiple process environments, however. To have a mutex work among a number of processes, it would need to be defined within a place that is accessible to all of them.

The best choice for a shared place such as this is a shared memory region. Therefore, to have a mutex that works in a multi-process environment, it should be distributed in a shared memory region.

The first example

The following example, *example 18.2*, is a clone of *example 18.1*, but it solves the potential race condition using named mutexes instead of named semaphores. It also shows how to make a shared memory region and use it to store a shared mutex.

Since each shared memory object has a global name, a mutex stored in a shared memory region can be considered *named* and can be accessed by other processes throughout the system.

The following code box shows the declarations required for *example 18.2*. It shows what is needed for having a shared mutex:

```
#include <stdio.h>
...
#include <pthread.h> // For using pthread_mutex_* functions

#define SHARED_MEM_SIZE 4

// Shared file descriptor used to refer to shared memory object
int shared_fd = -1;

// Shared file descriptor used to refer to the mutex's shared
// memory object
int mutex_shm_fd = -1;

// The pointer to the shared counter
int32_t* counter = NULL;
```

```
// The pointer to shared mutex
pthread_mutex_t* mutex = NULL;
```

Code Box 18-5 [ExtremeC_examples_chapter18_2.c]: The global declarations of example 18.2

As you can see, we have declared:

- A global file descriptor for pointing to a shared memory region that is meant to store the shared counter variable
- A global file descriptor for the shared memory region storing the shared mutex
- A pointer to the shared counter
- A pointer to the shared mutex

These variables will be populated accordingly by the upcoming logic.

The following code boxes show all the functions we had in *example 18.1*, but as you see, the definitions are updated to work with a named mutex instead of a named semaphore:

```
void init_control_mechanism() {
  // Open the mutex shared memory
  mutex_shm_fd = shm_open("/mutex0", O_CREAT | O_RDWR, 0600);
  if (mutex_shm_fd < 0) {
    fprintf(stderr, "ERROR: Failed to create shared memory: %s\n"
      , strerror(errno));
    exit(1);
  }
  // Allocate and truncate the mutex's shared memory region
  if (ftruncate(mutex_shm_fd, sizeof(pthread_mutex_t)) < 0) {
    fprintf(stderr, "ERROR: Truncation of mutex failed: %s\n",
      strerror(errno));
    exit(1);
  }
  // Map the mutex's shared memory
  void* map = mmap(0, sizeof(pthread_mutex_t),
      PROT_READ | PROT_WRITE, MAP_SHARED, mutex_shm_fd, 0);
  if (map == MAP_FAILED) {
    fprintf(stderr, "ERROR: Mapping failed: %s\n",
        strerror(errno));
    exit(1);
  }
  mutex = (pthread_mutex_t*)map;
  // Initialize the mutex object
  int ret = -1;
  pthread_mutexattr_t attr;
```

```
    if ((ret = pthread_mutexattr_init(&attr))) {
      fprintf(stderr, "ERROR: Failed to init mutex attrs: %s\n",
          strerror(ret));
      exit(1);
    }
    if ((ret = pthread_mutexattr_setpshared(&attr,
                  PTHREAD_PROCESS_SHARED))) {
      fprintf(stderr, "ERROR: Failed to set the mutex attr: %s\n",
          strerror(ret));
      exit(1);
    }
    if ((ret = pthread_mutex_init(mutex, &attr))) {
      fprintf(stderr, "ERROR: Initializing the mutex failed: %s\n",
          strerror(ret));
      exit(1);
    }
    if ((ret = pthread_mutexattr_destroy(&attr))) {
      fprintf(stderr, "ERROR: Failed to destroy mutex attrs : %s\n"
          , strerror(ret));
      exit(1);
    }
  }
```

Code Box 18-6 [ExtremeC_examples_chapter18_2.c]: The function init_control_mechanism in example 18.2

As part of the function `init_control_mechanism`, we have created a new shared memory object named `/mutex0`. The size of the shared memory region is initialized to `sizeof(pthread_mutex_t)` which shows our intention to share a POSIX mutex object there.

Following that, we get a pointer to the shared memory region. Now we have a mutex which is allocated from the shared memory, but it still needs to be initialized. The next step is therefore to initialize the mutex object using the function `pthread_mutex_init`, with attributes that indicate that the mutex object should be shared and accessible by other processes. This is especially important; otherwise, the mutex does not work in a multi-process environment, even though it is placed inside a shared memory region. As you have seen in the preceding code box and as part of the function `init_control_mechanism`, we have set the attribute `PTHREAD_PROCESS_SHARED` to mark the mutex as shared. Let's look at the next function:

```
void shutdown_control_mechanism() {
  int ret = -1;
  if ((ret = pthread_mutex_destroy(mutex))) {
    fprintf(stderr, "ERROR: Failed to destroy mutex: %s\n",
        strerror(ret));
    exit(1);
```

```
  }
  if (munmap(mutex, sizeof(pthread_mutex_t)) < 0) {
    fprintf(stderr, "ERROR: Unmapping the mutex failed: %s\n",
        strerror(errno));
    exit(1);
  }
  if (close(mutex_shm_fd) < 0) {
    fprintf(stderr, "ERROR: Closing the mutex failed: %s\n",
        strerror(errno));
    exit(1);
  }
  if (shm_unlink("/mutex0") < 0) {
    fprintf(stderr, "ERROR: Unlinking the mutex failed: %s\n",
        strerror(errno));
    exit(1);
  }
}
```

Code Box 18-7 [ExtremeC_examples_chapter18_2.c]: The function destroy_control_mechanism in example 18.2

In the function `destroy_control_mechanism` we destroy the mutex object, and after that we close and unlink its underlying shared memory region. This is the same way that we destroy an ordinary shared memory object. Let's continue with other codes in the example:

```
void init_shared_resource() {
  ... as in the example 18.1 ...
}

void shutdown_shared_resource() {
  ... as in the example 18.1 ...
}
```

Code Box 18-8 [ExtremeC_examples_chapter18_2.c]: These functions are the same as we have seen in example 18.1

As you see, the preceding functions are not changed at all and they are the same as we had in *example 18.1*. Let's look at the critical section inside the function `inc_counter` which now uses a named mutex instead of a named semaphore.

```
void inc_counter() {
  usleep(1);
  pthread_mutex_lock(mutex); // Should check the return value.
  int32_t temp = *counter;
  usleep(1);
  temp++;
```

```
    usleep(1);
    *counter = temp;
    pthread_mutex_unlock(mutex); // Should check the return value.
    usleep(1);
}

int main(int argc, char** argv) {
    ... as in the example 18.1 ...
}
```

Code Box 18-9 [ExtremeC_examples_chapter18_2.c]: The critical section now uses a named mutex to protect the shared counter

Generally, as you see in the preceding code boxes, a few places are different from *example 18.1*, and we have had to change only three functions greatly. For instance, the function `main` has not changed at all, and it is the same as in *example 18.1*. This is simply because we have used a different control mechanism in comparison to *example 18.1*, and the remaining logic is the same.

As the final note about *Code Box 18-9*, in the function `inc_counter`, we have used the mutex object exactly as we did in a multi-threaded program. The API is the same, and it is designed in a way that mutexes can be used both in multi-threaded and multi-process environments using the same API. This is a great feature of POSIX mutexes because it enables us to use the same written code in both multi-threaded and multi-process environments when consuming these objects – while of course, the initialization and destruction can be different.

The output of the preceding code is very similar to what we observed for *example 18.1*. While the shared counter is protected by a mutex in this example, it was being protected by a semaphore in the previous example. The semaphore used in the previous example was actually a binary semaphore, and as we have explained in *Chapter 16, Thread Synchronization*, a binary semaphore can mimic a mutex. Therefore, not much is new in *example 18.2*, apart from replacing the binary semaphore with a mutex.

The second example

The named shared memories and mutexes can be used throughout the system by any process. It is not mandatory to have a forked process to be able to use these objects. The following example, *example 18.3*, tries to show how we can use a shared mutex and a shared memory to simultaneously terminate a number of processes that are all running at the same time. We expect to have all processes terminated after pressing the key combination *Ctrl + C* in only one of them.

Note that the code is going to be provided in multiple steps. The comments related to each step are provided right after it. Let's present the first step.

Step 1 – Global declarations

In this example, we write a single source file that can be compiled and executed multiple times to create multiple processes. The processes use some shared memory regions to synchronize their execution. One of the processes is elected to be the owner of the shared memory regions and manages their creation and destruction. Other processes just use the created shared memories.

The first step is going to declare some global objects that we need throughout the code. We will initialize them later on in the code. Note that the global variables defined in the following code box, such as mutex, are not actually shared between the processes. They have these variables in their own memory space but each of the processes maps their own global variable to the objects or variables located in the various shared memory regions:

```c
#include <stdio.h>
...
#include <pthread.h> // For using pthread_mutex_* functions

typedef uint16_t bool_t;

#define TRUE 1
#define FALSE 0

#define MUTEX_SHM_NAME "/mutex0"
#define SHM_NAME "/shm0"

// Shared file descriptor used to refer to the shared memory
// object containing the cancel flag
int cancel_flag_shm_fd = -1;

// A flag which indicates whether the current process owns the
// shared memory object
bool_t cancel_flag_shm_owner = FALSE;

// Shared file descriptor used to refer to the mutex's shared
// memory object
int mutex_shm_fd = -1;

// The shared mutex
pthread_mutex_t* mutex = NULL;

// A flag which indicates whether the current process owns the
// shared memory object
bool_t mutex_owner = FALSE;

// The pointer to the cancel flag stored in the shared memory
```

```
bool_t* cancel_flag = NULL;
```

Code Box 18-10 [ExtremeC_examples_chapter18_3.c]: The global declaration in example 18.3

In the preceding code, we can see the global declarations used in the code. We are going to use a shared flag to let the processes know about the cancellation signal. Note that, in this example, we are going to take the busy-wait approach to wait for the cancellation flag to become `true`.

We have a dedicated shared memory object for the cancellation flag and another shared memory object for the mutex protecting the flag as we did in *example 18.2*. Note that we could construct a single structure and define both the cancellation flag and the mutex object as its fields, and then use a single shared memory region to store them. But we have chosen to use separate shared memory regions to fulfill our purpose.

In this example, one important note about the shared memory objects is that the cleanup should be performed by the process which has created and initialized them in the first place. Since all processes are using the same code, somehow, we need to know which process has created a certain shared memory object and make that process the owner of that object. Then, while cleaning up the objects, only the owner process can proceed and do the actual cleanup. Therefore, we had to declare two Boolean variables for this purpose: `mutex_owner` and `cancel_flag_shm_owner`.

Step 2 – Cancellation flag's shared memory

The following code box shows the initialization of the shared memory region dedicated to the cancellation flag:

```
void init_shared_resource() {
  // Open the shared memory object
  cancel_flag_shm_fd = shm_open(SHM_NAME, O_RDWR, 0600);
  if (cancel_flag_shm_fd >= 0) {
    cancel_flag_shm_owner = FALSE;
    fprintf(stdout, "The shared memory object is opened.\n");
  } else if (errno == ENOENT) {
    fprintf(stderr,
            "WARN: The shared memory object doesn't exist.\n");
    fprintf(stdout, "Creating the shared memory object ...\n");
    cancel_flag_shm_fd = shm_open(SHM_NAME,
        O_CREAT | O_EXCL | O_RDWR, 0600);
    if (cancel_flag_shm_fd >= 0) {
      cancel_flag_shm_owner = TRUE;
      fprintf(stdout, "The shared memory object is created.\n");
    } else {
      fprintf(stderr,
```

```
            "ERROR: Failed to create shared memory: %s\n",
        strerror(errno));
    exit(1);
    }
} else {
    fprintf(stderr,
            "ERROR: Failed to create shared memory: %s\n",
        strerror(errno));
    exit(1);
}
if (cancel_flag_shm_owner) {
    // Allocate and truncate the shared memory region
    if (ftruncate(cancel_flag_shm_fd, sizeof(bool_t)) < 0) {
        fprintf(stderr, "ERROR: Truncation failed: %s\n",
            strerror(errno));
        exit(1);
    }
    fprintf(stdout, "The memory region is truncated.\n");
}
// Map the shared memory and initialize the cancel flag
void* map = mmap(0, sizeof(bool_t), PROT_WRITE, MAP_SHARED,
        cancel_flag_shm_fd, 0);
if (map == MAP_FAILED) {
    fprintf(stderr, "ERROR: Mapping failed: %s\n",
            strerror(errno));
    exit(1);
}
cancel_flag = (bool_t*)map;
if (cancel_flag_shm_owner) {
    *cancel_flag = FALSE;
}
}
```

Code Box 18-11 [ExtremeC_examples_chapter18_3.c]: Initialization of the cancellation flag's shared memory

The approach we took is different from what we did in *example 18.2*. That's because whenever a new process is run, it should check whether the shared memory object has already been created by another process. Note that we are not using the fork API to create new processes as part of this example and the user can use their shell and start a new process at will.

For this reason, a new process first tries to open the shared memory region by only providing the flag O_RDWR. If it succeeds, then it's a sign that the current process is not the owner of that region, and it proceeds with mapping the shared memory region. If it fails, it means that the shared memory region does not exist, and it is an indication that the current process should create the region and becomes its owner. So, it proceeds and tries to open the region with different flags; O_CREAT and O_EXCL. These flags create a shared memory object if it does not exist.

If the creation succeeds, the current process is the owner, and it continues by truncating and mapping the shared memory region.

There is a small chance that between the two successive calls of the shm_open function in the previous scenario, another process creates the same shared memory region, and therefore the second shm_open fails. The flag O_EXCL prevents the current process from creating an object which already exists, and then it quits by showing a proper error message. If this happens, which should be very rare, we can always try to run the process again and it won't face the same issue in the second run.

The following code is the reverse operation for destructing the cancellation flag and its shared memory region:

```c
void shutdown_shared_resource() {
  if (munmap(cancel_flag, sizeof(bool_t)) < 0) {
    fprintf(stderr, "ERROR: Unmapping failed: %s\n",
            strerror(errno));
    exit(1);
  }
  if (close(cancel_flag_shm_fd) < 0) {
    fprintf(stderr,
        "ERROR: Closing the shared memory fd filed: %s\n",
        strerror(errno));
    exit(1);
  }
  if (cancel_flag_shm_owner) {
    sleep(1);
    if (shm_unlink(SHM_NAME) < 0) {
      fprintf(stderr,
          "ERROR: Unlinking the shared memory failed: %s\n",
          strerror(errno));
      exit(1);
    }
  }
}
```

Code Box 18-12 [ExtremeC_examples_chapter18_3.c]: Closing the resources allocated for the cancellation flag's shared memory

As you can see in *Code Box 18-12*, the written logic is very similar to what we've seen so far, as part of previous examples, about releasing a shared memory object. But there is a difference here and it is the fact that only the owner process can unlink the shared memory object. Note that the owner process waits for 1 second before unlinking the shared memory object, in order to let other processes finalize their resources. This wait is not usually necessary due to the fact that, in most POSIX-compliant systems, the shared memory object remains in place until all depending processes quit.

Step 3 – Named mutex's shared memory

The following code box shows how to initialize the shared mutex and its associated shared memory object:

```c
void init_control_mechanism() {
  // Open the mutex shared memory
  mutex_shm_fd = shm_open(MUTEX_SHM_NAME, O_RDWR, 0600);
  if (mutex_shm_fd >= 0) {
    // The mutex's shared object exists and I'm now the owner.
    mutex_owner = FALSE;
    fprintf(stdout,
            "The mutex's shared memory object is opened.\n");
  } else if (errno == ENOENT) {
    fprintf(stderr,
            "WARN: Mutex's shared memory doesn't exist.\n");
    fprintf(stdout,
            "Creating the mutex's shared memory object ...\n");
    mutex_shm_fd = shm_open(MUTEX_SHM_NAME,
            O_CREAT | O_EXCL | O_RDWR, 0600);
    if (mutex_shm_fd >= 0) {
      mutex_owner = TRUE;
      fprintf(stdout,
              "The mutex's shared memory object is created.\n");
    } else {
      fprintf(stderr,
          "ERROR: Failed to create mutex's shared memory: %s\n",
          strerror(errno));
      exit(1);
    }
  } else {
    fprintf(stderr,
        "ERROR: Failed to create mutex's shared memory: %s\n",
        strerror(errno));
    exit(1);
  }
  if (mutex_owner) {
    // Allocate and truncate the mutex's shared memory region
  }
  if (mutex_owner) {
    // Allocate and truncate the mutex's shared memory region
    if (ftruncate(mutex_shm_fd, sizeof(pthread_mutex_t)) < 0) {
      fprintf(stderr,
          "ERROR: Truncation of the mutex failed: %s\n",
          strerror(errno));
      exit(1);
    }
  }
  // Map the mutex's shared memory
```

```
    void* map = mmap(0, sizeof(pthread_mutex_t),
            PROT_READ | PROT_WRITE, MAP_SHARED, mutex_shm_fd, 0);
    if (map == MAP_FAILED) {
      fprintf(stderr, "ERROR: Mapping failed: %s\n",
            strerror(errno));
      exit(1);
    }
    mutex = (pthread_mutex_t*)map;
    if (mutex_owner) {
      int ret = -1;
      pthread_mutexattr_t attr;
      if ((ret = pthread_mutexattr_init(&attr))) {
        fprintf(stderr,
            "ERROR: Initializing mutex attributes failed: %s\n",
            strerror(ret));
        exit(1);
      }
      if ((ret = pthread_mutexattr_setpshared(&attr,
                    PTHREAD_PROCESS_SHARED))) {
        fprintf(stderr,
            "ERROR: Setting the mutex attribute failed: %s\n",
            strerror(ret));
        exit(1);
      }
      if ((ret = pthread_mutex_init(mutex, &attr))) {
        fprintf(stderr,
            "ERROR: Initializing the mutex failed: %s\n",
            strerror(ret));
        exit(1);
      }
      if ((ret = pthread_mutexattr_destroy(&attr))) {
        fprintf(stderr,
            "ERROR: Destruction of mutex attributes failed: %s\n",
            strerror(ret));
        exit(1);
      }
    }
}
```

Code Box 18-13 [ExtremeC_examples_chapter18_3.c]: Initializing the shared mutex and its underlying shared memory region

Similarly to what we did while trying to create the shared memory region associated with the cancellation flag, we have done the same thing to create and initialize the shared memory region beneath the shared mutex. Note that, just like in *example 18.2*, the mutex has been marked as PTHREAD_PROCESS_SHARED, which allows it to be used by multiple processes.

The following code box shows how to finalize the shared mutex:

```
void shutdown_control_mechanism() {
  sleep(1);
  if (mutex_owner) {
    int ret = -1;
    if ((ret = pthread_mutex_destroy(mutex))) {
      fprintf(stderr,
          "WARN: Destruction of the mutex failed: %s\n",
          strerror(ret));
    }
  }
  if (munmap(mutex, sizeof(pthread_mutex_t)) < 0) {
    fprintf(stderr, "ERROR: Unmapping the mutex failed: %s\n",
        strerror(errno));
    exit(1);
  }
  if (close(mutex_shm_fd) < 0) {
    fprintf(stderr, "ERROR: Closing the mutex failed: %s\n",
        strerror(errno));
    exit(1);
  }
  if (mutex_owner) {
    if (shm_unlink(MUTEX_SHM_NAME) < 0) {
      fprintf(stderr, "ERROR: Unlinking the mutex failed: %s\n",
          strerror(errno));
      exit(1);
    }
  }
}
```

Code Box 18-14 [ExtremeC_examples_chapter18_3.c]: Closing the shared mutex and its associated shared memory region

Again, the owner process can only unlink the shared memory object of the shared mutex.

Step 4 – Setting the cancellation flag

The following code box shows the functions which allow the processes to read or set the cancellation flag:

```
bool_t is_canceled() {
  pthread_mutex_lock(mutex); // Should check the return value
  bool_t temp = *cancel_flag;
  pthread_mutex_unlock(mutex); // Should check the return value
  return temp;
}
```

```
void cancel() {
  pthread_mutex_lock(mutex); // Should check the return value
  *cancel_flag = TRUE;
  pthread_mutex_unlock(mutex); // Should check the return value
}
```

Code Box 18-15 [ExtremeC_examples_chapter18_3.c]: The synchronized functions that read and set the cancellation flag protected by the shared mutex

The preceding two functions allow us to have synchronized access to the shared cancellation flag. The function is_canceled is used to check the value of the flag, and the function cancel is used to set the flag. As you see, both are protected by the same shared mutex.

Step 5 – The main function

And finally, the following code box shows the main function and a *signal handler* which we explain shortly:

```
void sigint_handler(int signo) {
  fprintf(stdout, "\nHandling INT signal: %d ...\n", signo);
  cancel();
}

int main(int argc, char** argv) {

  signal(SIGINT, sigint_handler);

  // Parent process needs to initialize the shared resource
  init_shared_resource();

  // Parent process needs to initialize the control mechanism
  init_control_mechanism();

  while(!is_canceled()) {
    fprintf(stdout, "Working ...\n");
    sleep(1);
  }

  fprintf(stdout, "Cancel signal is received.\n");

  shutdown_shared_resource();
  shutdown_control_mechanism();

  return 0;
}
```

Code Box 18-16 [ExtremeC_examples_chapter18_3.c]: The function main and the signal handler function as part of example 18.3

As you see, the logic inside the `main` function is clear and straightforward. It initializes the shared flag and mutex and then goes into a busy-wait until the cancellation flag becomes `true`. Finally, it shuts down all shared resources and terminates.

One thing which is new here is the usage of the `signal` function which assigns a signal handler to a specific set of *signals*. Signals are one of the facilities provided by all POSIX-compliant operating systems and using it, the processes within the system can send signals to each other. The *terminal* is just one normal process that the user interacts with and it can be used to send signals to other processes. Pressing *Ctrl + C* is one convenient way to send `SIGINT` to the foreground process running in a terminal.

`SIGINT` is the *interrupt signal* which can be received by a process. In the preceding code, we assign the function `sigint_handler` to be the handler of the `SIGINT` signal. In other words, whenever the signal `SIGINT` is received by the process, the function `sigint_handler` will be called. If the signal `SIGINT` is not handled, the default routine is to terminate the process, but this can be overridden using signal handlers like above.

There are many ways to send a `SIGINT` signal to a process, but one of the easiest is to press the *Ctrl + C* keys on the keyboard. The process will immediately receive the `SIGINT` signal. As you see, within the signal handler, we set the shared cancellation flag to `true`, and after this point, all the processes start to exit their busy-wait loops.

Following is a demonstration of how the preceding code compiles and works. Let's build the preceding code and run the first process:

```
$ gcc ExtremeC_examples_chapter18_3.c -lpthread -lrt -o ex18_3.out
$ ./ex18_3.out
WARN: The shared memory object doesn't exist.
Creating a shared memory object ...
The shared memory object is created.
The memory region is truncated.
WARN: Mutex's shared memory object doesn't exist.
Creating the mutex's shared memory object ...
The mutex's shared memory object is created.
Working ...
Working ...
Working ...
```

Shell Box 18-2: Compilation of example 18.3 and running the first process

As you see, the preceding process is the first to be run, and therefore, it is the owner of the mutex and cancellation flag. The following is the run of the second process:

```
$ ./ex18_3.out
The shared memory object is opened.
The mutex's shared memory object is opened.
Working ...
Working ...
Working ...
```

Shell Box 18-3: Running the second process

As you see, the second process only opens the shared memory objects, and it is not the owner. The following output is showing when *Ctrl + C* has been pressed on the first process:

```
...
Working ...
Working ...
^C
Handling INT signal: 2 ...
Cancel signal is received.
$
```

Shell Box 18-4: The output of the first process when Ctrl + C has been pressed

As you see, the first process prints that it is handling a signal with the number 2 which is the standard signal number of the SIGINT. It sets the cancellation flag, and it exits immediately. And following it, the second process exits. The following is the output of the second process:

```
...
Working ...
Working ...
Working ...
Cancel signal is received.
$
```

Shell Box 18-5: The output of the second process when it sees that the cancellation flag is set

Also, you can send `SIGINT` to the second process and the result will be the same; both processes will get the signal and will quit. Also, you can create more than two processes and all of them will synchronously quit using the same shared memory and mutex.

In the next section, we demonstrate how to use condition variables. Like named mutexes, if you place a condition variable inside a shared memory region, it can be accessed and used by multiple processes using the shared memory's name.

Named condition variables

As we explained before, similar to named POSIX mutexes, we need to allocate a POSIX condition variable from a shared memory region in order to use it in a multi-processing system. The following example, *example 18.4*, shows how to do so in order to make a number of processes count in a specific order. As you know from *Chapter 16, Thread Synchronization*, every condition variable should be used together with a companion mutex object which protects it. Therefore, we will have three shared memory regions in *example 18.4*; one for the shared counter, one for the shared *named condition variable*, and one for the shared *named mutex* protecting the shared condition variable.

Note that instead of having three different shared memories, we could also use a single shared memory. This is possible by defining a structure that encompasses all the required objects. In this example, we are not going to take this approach and we will define a separate shared memory region for each object.

Example 18.4 is about a number of processes which should count in an ascending order. Each process is given a number, starting from 1 and up to the number of processes, and the given number indicates the process's rank within the other processes. The process must wait for the other processes with smaller numbers (ranks) to count first and then it can count its turn and exit. Of course, the process assigned the number 1 counts first, even if it is the latest spawned process.

Since we are going to have three different shared memory regions, each of which requiring its own steps to get initialized and finalized, we would have a lot of code duplication if we wanted to take the same approach as we have so far in the previous examples. For reducing the amount of code that we write, and factoring out the duplications into some functions, and having a better-organized code, we are going to make it object-oriented according to the topics and procedures discussed in *Chapter 6, OOP and Encapsulation, Chapter 7, Composition and Aggregation*, and *Chapter 8, Inheritance and Polymorphism*. We are going to write *example 18.4* in an object-oriented manner and use inheritance to reduce the amount of duplicated code.

We will define a parent class for all classes which need to be built upon a shared memory region. Therefore, while having the parent shared memory class, there will be one child class defined for the shared counter, one child class for the shared named mutex, and another child class for the shared named condition variable. Each class will have its own pair of header and source files, and all of them will be used finally in the main function of the example.

The following sections go through the mentioned classes one by one. First of all, let's being with the parent class: shared memory.

Step 1 – Class of shared memory

The following code box shows the declarations of the shared memory class:

```
struct shared_mem_t;

typedef int32_t bool_t;

struct shared_mem_t* shared_mem_new();
void shared_mem_delete(struct shared_mem_t* obj);

void shared_mem_ctor(struct shared_mem_t* obj,
                     const char* name,
                     size_t size);
void shared_mem_dtor(struct shared_mem_t* obj);

char* shared_mem_getptr(struct shared_mem_t* obj);
bool_t shared_mem_isowner(struct shared_mem_t* obj);
void shared_mem_setowner(struct shared_mem_t* obj, bool_t is_
owner);
```

Code Box 18-17 [ExtremeC_examples_chapter18_4_shared_mem.h]: The public interface
of the shared memory class

The preceding code contains the declarations (public API) needed to use a shared memory object. The functions `shared_mem_getptr`, `shared_mem_isowner`, and `shared_mem_setowner` are the behaviors of this class.

If this syntax is not familiar to you, please have a read of *Chapter 6, OOP and Encapsulation*, *Chapter 7, Composition and Aggregation*, and *Chapter 8, Inheritance and Polymorphism*.

The following code box shows the definitions of the functions declared as part of the public interface of the class, as seen in *Code Box 18-17*:

```
#include <stdio.h>
#include <stdlib.h>
```

```
#include <string.h>
#include <unistd.h>
#include <errno.h>
#include <fcntl.h>
#include <sys/mman.h>

#define TRUE 1
#define FALSE 0

typedef int32_t bool_t;

bool_t owner_process_set = FALSE;
bool_t owner_process = FALSE;

typedef struct {
  char* name;
  int shm_fd;
  void* map_ptr;
  char* ptr;
  size_t size;
} shared_mem_t;

shared_mem_t* shared_mem_new() {
  return (shared_mem_t*)malloc(sizeof(shared_mem_t));
}

void shared_mem_delete(shared_mem_t* obj) {
  free(obj->name);
  free(obj);
}

void shared_mem_ctor(shared_mem_t* obj, const char* name,
        size_t size) {
  obj->size = size;
  obj->name = (char*)malloc(strlen(name) + 1);
  strcpy(obj->name, name);
  obj->shm_fd = shm_open(obj->name, O_RDWR, 0600);
  if (obj->shm_fd >= 0) {
    if (!owner_process_set) {
      owner_process = FALSE;
      owner_process_set = TRUE;
    }
    printf("The shared memory %s is opened.\n", obj->name);
  } else if (errno == ENOENT) {
    printf("WARN: The shared memory %s does not exist.\n",
            obj->name);
    obj->shm_fd = shm_open(obj->name,
            O_CREAT | O_RDWR, 0600);
    if (obj->shm_fd >= 0) {
```

```c
        if (!owner_process_set) {
          owner_process = TRUE;
          owner_process_set = TRUE;
        }
        printf("The shared memory %s is created and opened.\n",
               obj->name);
        if (ftruncate(obj->shm_fd, obj->size) < 0) {
          fprintf(stderr, "ERROR(%s): Truncation failed: %s\n",
             obj->name, strerror(errno));
          exit(1);
        }
      } else {
        fprintf(stderr,
            "ERROR(%s): Failed to create shared memory: %s\n",
           obj->name, strerror(errno));
        exit(1);
      }
    } else {
       fprintf(stderr,
           "ERROR(%s): Failed to create shared memory: %s\n",
           obj->name, strerror(errno));
      exit(1);
    }
    obj->map_ptr = mmap(0, obj->size, PROT_READ | PROT_WRITE,
       MAP_SHARED, obj->shm_fd, 0);
    if (obj->map_ptr == MAP_FAILED) {
      fprintf(stderr, "ERROR(%s): Mapping failed: %s\n",
         name, strerror(errno));
      exit(1);
    }
    obj->ptr = (char*)obj->map_ptr;
}

void shared_mem_dtor(shared_mem_t* obj) {
  if (munmap(obj->map_ptr, obj->size) < 0) {
    fprintf(stderr, "ERROR(%s): Unmapping failed: %s\n",
       obj->name, strerror(errno));
    exit(1);
  }
  printf("The shared memory %s is unmapped.\n", obj->name);
  if (close(obj->shm_fd) < 0) {
    fprintf(stderr,
        "ERROR(%s): Closing the shared memory fd failed: %s\n",
       obj->name, strerror(errno));
    exit(1);
  }
  printf("The shared memory %s is closed.\n", obj->name);
  if (owner_process) {
    if (shm_unlink(obj->name) < 0) {
```

```
        fprintf(stderr,
            "ERROR(%s): Unlinking the shared memory failed: %s\n",
            obj->name, strerror(errno));
        exit(1);
    }
    printf("The shared memory %s is deleted.\n", obj->name);
  }
}

char* shared_mem_getptr(shared_mem_t* obj) {
  return obj->ptr;
}

bool_t shared_mem_isowner(shared_mem_t* obj) {
  return owner_process;
}

void shared_mem_setowner(shared_mem_t* obj, bool_t is_owner) {
    owner_process = is_owner;
}
```

Code Box 18-18 [ExtremeC_examples_chapter18_4_shared_mem.c]: The definitions of all functions found in the shared memory class

As you see, we have just copied the code we wrote for shared memories as part of the previous examples. The structure `shared_mem_t` encapsulates all we need to address a POSIX shared memory object. Note the global Boolean variable `process_owner`. It indicates whether the current process is the owner of all shared memory regions. It is set only once.

Step 2 – Class of shared 32-bit integer counter

The following code box contains the declaration of the shared counter class which is a 32-bit integer counter. This class inherits from the shared memory class. As you might have noticed, we are using the second approach we described as part of *Chapter 8, Inheritance and Polymorphism*, to implement the inheritance relationship:

```
struct shared_int32_t;

struct shared_int32_t* shared_int32_new();
void shared_int32_delete(struct shared_int32_t* obj);

void shared_int32_ctor(struct shared_int32_t* obj,
                       const char* name);
void shared_int32_dtor(struct shared_int32_t* obj);
```

```
void shared_int32_setvalue(struct shared_int32_t* obj,
                           int32_t value);
void shared_int32_setvalue_ifowner(struct shared_int32_t* obj,
                                   int32_t value);
int32_t shared_int32_getvalue(struct shared_int32_t* obj);
```

Code Box 18-19 [ExtremeC_examples_chapter18_4_shared_int32.h]: The public interface of
the shared counter class

And the following code box shows the implementations of the preceding
declared functions:

```
#include "ExtremeC_examples_chapter18_4_shared_mem.h"

typedef struct {
  struct shared_mem_t* shm;
  int32_t* ptr;
} shared_int32_t;

shared_int32_t* shared_int32_new(const char* name) {
  shared_int32_t* obj =
      (shared_int32_t*)malloc(sizeof(shared_int32_t));
  obj->shm = shared_mem_new();
  return obj;
}

void shared_int32_delete(shared_int32_t* obj) {
  shared_mem_delete(obj->shm);
  free(obj);
}

void shared_int32_ctor(shared_int32_t* obj, const char* name) {
  shared_mem_ctor(obj->shm, name, sizeof(int32_t));
  obj->ptr = (int32_t*)shared_mem_getptr(obj->shm);
}

void shared_int32_dtor(shared_int32_t* obj) {
  shared_mem_dtor(obj->shm);
}

void shared_int32_setvalue(shared_int32_t* obj, int32_t value) {
  *(obj->ptr) = value;
}

void shared_int32_setvalue_ifowner(shared_int32_t* obj,
                                   int32_t value) {
  if (shared_mem_isowner(obj->shm)) {
    *(obj->ptr) = value;
```

```
    }
  }
}

int32_t shared_int32_getvalue(shared_int32_t* obj) {
  return *(obj->ptr);
}
```

Code Box 18-20 [ExtremeC_examples_chapter18_4_shared_int32.c]: The definitions of all functions found in the shared counter class

As you can see, we have written a lot less code thanks to inheritance. All the necessary code for managing the associated shared memory object has been brought in by the field shm in the structure shared_int32_t.

Step 3 – Class of shared mutex

The following code box contains the declaration of the shared mutex class:

```
#include <pthread.h>

struct shared_mutex_t;

struct shared_mutex_t* shared_mutex_new();
void shared_mutex_delete(struct shared_mutex_t* obj);

void shared_mutex_ctor(struct shared_mutex_t* obj,
                       const char* name);
void shared_mutex_dtor(struct shared_mutex_t* obj);

pthread_mutex_t* shared_mutex_getptr(struct shared_mutex_t* obj);

void shared_mutex_lock(struct shared_mutex_t* obj);
void shared_mutex_unlock(struct shared_mutex_t* obj);

#if !defined(__APPLE__)
void shared_mutex_make_consistent(struct shared_mutex_t* obj);
#endif
```

Code Box 18-21 [ExtremeC_examples_chapter18_4_shared_mutex.h]: The public interface of the shared mutex class

As you see, the above class has three exposed behaviors as expected; shared_mutex_lock, shared_mutex_unlock, and shared_mutex_make_consistent. But there is one exception, which is that the behavior shared_mutex_make_consistent is only available in POSIX systems which are not macOS (Apple) based. That's because *robust mutexes* are not supported by Apple systems. We will discuss what a robust mutex is in the upcoming paragraphs. Note that we have used the macro __APPLE__ to detect whether we are compiling on an Apple system or not.

The following code box shows the implementation of the preceding class:

```
#include "ExtremeC_examples_chapter18_4_shared_mem.h"

typedef struct {
  struct shared_mem_t* shm;
  pthread_mutex_t* ptr;
} shared_mutex_t;

shared_mutex_t* shared_mutex_new() {
  shared_mutex_t* obj =
      (shared_mutex_t*)malloc(sizeof(shared_mutex_t));
  obj->shm = shared_mem_new();
  return obj;
}

void shared_mutex_delete(shared_mutex_t* obj) {
  shared_mem_delete(obj->shm);
  free(obj);
}

void shared_mutex_ctor(shared_mutex_t* obj, const char* name) {
  shared_mem_ctor(obj->shm, name, sizeof(pthread_mutex_t));
  obj->ptr = (pthread_mutex_t*)shared_mem_getptr(obj->shm);
  if (shared_mem_isowner(obj->shm)) {
    pthread_mutexattr_t mutex_attr;
    int ret = -1;
    if ((ret = pthread_mutexattr_init(&mutex_attr))) {
      fprintf(stderr,
          "ERROR(%s): Initializing mutex attrs failed: %s\n",
          name, strerror(ret));
      exit(1);
    }
#if !defined(__APPLE__)
    if ((ret = pthread_mutexattr_setrobust(&mutex_attr,
                    PTHREAD_MUTEX_ROBUST))) {
      fprintf(stderr,
          "ERROR(%s): Setting the mutex as robust failed: %s\n",
          name, strerror(ret));
      exit(1);
    }
#endif
    if ((ret = pthread_mutexattr_setpshared(&mutex_attr,
                    PTHREAD_PROCESS_SHARED))) {
      fprintf(stderr,
          "ERROR(%s): Failed to set as process-shared: %s\n",
          name, strerror(ret));
      exit(1);
    }
```

```
      if ((ret = pthread_mutex_init(obj->ptr, &mutex_attr))) {
        fprintf(stderr,
            "ERROR(%s): Initializing the mutex failed: %s\n",
            name, strerror(ret));
        exit(1);
      }
      if ((ret = pthread_mutexattr_destroy(&mutex_attr))) {
        fprintf(stderr,
            "ERROR(%s): Destruction of mutex attrs failed: %s\n",
            name, strerror(ret));
        exit(1);
      }
    }
}

void shared_mutex_dtor(shared_mutex_t* obj) {
  if (shared_mem_isowner(obj->shm)) {
    int ret = -1;
    if ((ret = pthread_mutex_destroy(obj->ptr))) {
      fprintf(stderr,
          "WARN: Destruction of the mutex failed: %s\n",
          strerror(ret));
    }
  }
  shared_mem_dtor(obj->shm);
}

pthread_mutex_t* shared_mutex_getptr(shared_mutex_t* obj) {
  return obj->ptr;
}

#if !defined(__APPLE__)
void shared_mutex_make_consistent(shared_mutex_t* obj) {
  int ret = -1;
  if ((ret = pthread_mutex_consistent(obj->ptr))) {
    fprintf(stderr,
        "ERROR: Making the mutex consistent failed: %s\n",
        strerror(ret));
    exit(1);
  }
}
#endif

void shared_mutex_lock(shared_mutex_t* obj) {
  int ret = -1;
  if ((ret = pthread_mutex_lock(obj->ptr))) {
#if !defined(__APPLE__)
    if (ret == EOWNERDEAD) {
        fprintf(stderr,
```

```
                    "WARN: The owner of the mutex is dead ...\n");
        shared_mutex_make_consistent(obj);
        fprintf(stdout, "INFO: I'm the new owner!\n");
        shared_mem_setowner(obj->shm, TRUE);
        return;
    }
#endif
    fprintf(stderr, "ERROR: Locking the mutex failed: %s\n",
        strerror(ret));
    exit(1);
  }
}

void shared_mutex_unlock(shared_mutex_t* obj) {
  int ret = -1;
  if ((ret = pthread_mutex_unlock(obj->ptr))) {
    fprintf(stderr, "ERROR: Unlocking the mutex failed: %s\n",
        strerror(ret));
    exit(1);
  }
}
```

Code Box 18-22 [ExtremeC_examples_chapter18_4_shared_mutex.c]: The definitions of all functions found in the shared named mutex class

In the preceding code, we do only the POSIX mutex initialization, finalization, and exposing some of the trivial behaviors such as locking and unlocking. Everything else regarding the shared memory object is being handled in the shared memory class. That's a benefit of using inheritance.

Note that in the constructor function `shared_mutex_ctor`, we set the mutex as a *shared process* mutex to be accessible to all processes. This is absolutely necessary to multi-process software. Note that in systems which are not Apple-based, we go further and configure the mutex as a *robust mutex*.

For an ordinary mutex that is locked by a process, if the process should suddenly die then the mutex goes into a non-consistent state. For a robust mutex, if this happens, the mutex can be put back in a consistent state. The next process, which is usually waiting for the mutex, can lock the mutex only by making it consistent. You can see how it can be done in the function `shared_mutex_lock`. Note that this functionality is not present in Apple systems.

Step 4 – Class of shared condition variable

The following code box shows the declaration of the shared condition variable class:

```
struct shared_cond_t;
struct shared_mutex_t;
```

```
struct shared_cond_t* shared_cond_new();
void shared_cond_delete(struct shared_cond_t* obj);

void shared_cond_ctor(struct shared_cond_t* obj,
                      const char* name);
void shared_cond_dtor(struct shared_cond_t* obj);

void shared_cond_wait(struct shared_cond_t* obj,
                      struct shared_mutex_t* mutex);
void shared_cond_timedwait(struct shared_cond_t* obj,
                           struct shared_mutex_t* mutex,
                           long int time_nanosec);
void shared_cond_broadcast(struct shared_cond_t* obj);
```

Code Box 18-23 [ExtremeC_examples_chapter18_4_shared_cond.h]: The public interface
of the shared condition variable class

Three behaviors are exposed; shared_cond_wait, shared_cond_timedwait, and shared_cond_broadcast. If you remember from *Chapter 16, Thread Synchronization,* the behavior shared_cond_wait waits for a signal on a condition variable.

Above, we have added a new version of waiting behavior; shared_cond_timedwait. It waits for the signal for a specified amount of time and then it gets timed out if the condition variable doesn't receive a signal. On the other hand, the shared_cond_wait never exists until it receives some sort of signal. We will use the timed version of waiting in *example 18.4*. Note that both waiting behavior functions receive a pointer to the companion shared mutex just like what we saw in multi-threaded environments.

The following code box contains the actual implementation of the shared condition variable class:

```
#include "ExtremeC_examples_chapter18_4_shared_mem.h"
#include "ExtremeC_examples_chapter18_4_shared_mutex.h"

typedef struct {
  struct shared_mem_t* shm;
  pthread_cond_t* ptr;
} shared_cond_t;

shared_cond_t* shared_cond_new() {
  shared_cond_t* obj =
      (shared_cond_t*)malloc(sizeof(shared_cond_t));
  obj->shm = shared_mem_new();
  return obj;
}
```

```
void shared_cond_delete(shared_cond_t* obj) {
  shared_mem_delete(obj->shm);
  free(obj);
}

void shared_cond_ctor(shared_cond_t* obj, const char* name) {
  shared_mem_ctor(obj->shm, name, sizeof(pthread_cond_t));
  obj->ptr = (pthread_cond_t*)shared_mem_getptr(obj->shm);
  if (shared_mem_isowner(obj->shm)) {
    pthread_condattr_t cond_attr;
    int ret = -1;
    if ((ret = pthread_condattr_init(&cond_attr))) {
      fprintf(stderr,
          "ERROR(%s): Initializing cv attrs failed: %s\n",
          name, strerror(ret));
      exit(1);
    }
    if ((ret = pthread_condattr_setpshared(&cond_attr,
                  PTHREAD_PROCESS_SHARED))) {
      fprintf(stderr,
          "ERROR(%s): Setting as process shared failed: %s\n",
          name, strerror(ret));
      exit(1);
    }
    if ((ret = pthread_cond_init(obj->ptr, &cond_attr))) {
      fprintf(stderr,
          "ERROR(%s): Initializing the cv failed: %s\n",
          name, strerror(ret));
      exit(1);
    }
    if ((ret = pthread_condattr_destroy(&cond_attr))) {
      fprintf(stderr,
          "ERROR(%s): Destruction of cond attrs failed: %s\n",
          name, strerror(ret));
      exit(1);
    }
  }
}

void shared_cond_dtor(shared_cond_t* obj) {
  if (shared_mem_isowner(obj->shm)) {
    int ret = -1;
    if ((ret = pthread_cond_destroy(obj->ptr))) {
      fprintf(stderr, "WARN: Destruction of the cv failed: %s\n",
          strerror(ret));
    }
  }
  shared_mem_dtor(obj->shm);
```

```
}

void shared_cond_wait(shared_cond_t* obj,
                      struct shared_mutex_t* mutex) {
  int ret = -1;
  if ((ret = pthread_cond_wait(obj->ptr,
                  shared_mutex_getptr(mutex)))) {
    fprintf(stderr, "ERROR: Waiting on the cv failed: %s\n",
            strerror(ret));
    exit(1);
  }
}

void shared_cond_timedwait(shared_cond_t* obj,
                           struct shared_mutex_t* mutex,
                           long int time_nanosec) {
  int ret = -1;

  struct timespec ts;
  ts.tv_sec = ts.tv_nsec = 0;
  if ((ret = clock_gettime(CLOCK_REALTIME, &ts))) {
    fprintf(stderr,
            "ERROR: Failed at reading current time: %s\n",
            strerror(errno));
    exit(1);
  }
  ts.tv_sec += (int)(time_nanosec / (1000L * 1000 * 1000));
  ts.tv_nsec += time_nanosec % (1000L * 1000 * 1000);

  if ((ret = pthread_cond_timedwait(obj->ptr,
                  shared_mutex_getptr(mutex), &ts))) {
#if !defined(__APPLE__)
    if (ret == EOWNERDEAD) {
      fprintf(stderr,
              "WARN: The owner of the cv's mutex is dead ...\n");
      shared_mutex_make_consistent(mutex);
      fprintf(stdout, "INFO: I'm the new owner!\n");
      shared_mem_setowner(obj->shm, TRUE);
      return;
    } else if (ret == ETIMEDOUT) {
#else
    if (ret == ETIMEDOUT) {
#endif
      return;
    }
    fprintf(stderr, "ERROR: Waiting on the cv failed: %s\n",
            strerror(ret));
    exit(1);
```

```
    }
  }

void shared_cond_broadcast(shared_cond_t* obj) {
    int ret = -1;
    if ((ret = pthread_cond_broadcast(obj->ptr))) {
      fprintf(stderr, "ERROR: Broadcasting on the cv failed: %s\n",
          strerror(ret));
      exit(1);
    }
}
```

Code Box 18-24 [ExtremeC_examples_chapter18_4_shared_cond.c]: The definitions of all functions found in the shared condition variable class

In our shared condition variable class, we have only exposed the *broadcasting* behavior. We could also expose the *signaling* behavior. As you might remember from *Chapter 16, Thread Synchronization*, signaling a condition variable wakes up only one of the many waiting processes, without the ability to specify or predict which one. Broadcasting in contrast will wake all the waiting processes. In *example 18.4* we'll only use broadcasting, and that's why we have only exposed that function.

Note that since every condition variable has a companion mutex, the shared mutex class should be able to use an instance of the shared mutex class, and that's why we have declared shared_mutex_t as a forward declaration.

Step 5 – The main logic

The following code box contains the main logic implemented for our example:

```
#include "ExtremeC_examples_chapter18_4_shared_int32.h"
#include "ExtremeC_examples_chapter18_4_shared_mutex.h"
#include "ExtremeC_examples_chapter18_4_shared_cond.h"

int int_received = 0;
struct shared_cond_t* cond = NULL;
struct shared_mutex_t* mutex = NULL;

void sigint_handler(int signo) {
  fprintf(stdout, "\nHandling INT signal: %d ...\n", signo);
  int_received = 1;
}

int main(int argc, char** argv) {
```

```
  signal(SIGINT, sigint_handler);

  if (argc < 2) {
    fprintf(stderr,
            "ERROR: You have to provide the process number.\n");
    exit(1);
  }

  int my_number = atol(argv[1]);
  printf("My number is %d!\n", my_number);

  struct shared_int32_t* counter = shared_int32_new();
  shared_int32_ctor(counter, "/counter0");
  shared_int32_setvalue_ifowner(counter, 1);

  mutex = shared_mutex_new();
  shared_mutex_ctor(mutex, "/mutex0");

  cond = shared_cond_new();
  shared_cond_ctor(cond, "/cond0");

  shared_mutex_lock(mutex);
  while (shared_int32_getvalue(counter) < my_number) {
    if (int_received) {
      break;
    }
    printf("Waiting for the signal, just for 5 seconds ...\n");
    shared_cond_timedwait(cond, mutex, 5L * 1000 * 1000 * 1000);
    if (int_received) {
      break;
    }
    printf("Checking condition ...\n");
  }
  if (int_received) {
    printf("Exiting ...\n");
    shared_mutex_unlock(mutex);
    goto destroy;
  }
  shared_int32_setvalue(counter, my_number + 1);
  printf("My turn! %d ...\n", my_number);
  shared_mutex_unlock(mutex);
  sleep(1);
  // NOTE: The broadcasting can come after unlocking the mutex.
  shared_cond_broadcast(cond);

destroy:
  shared_cond_dtor(cond);
  shared_cond_delete(cond);
```

```
    shared_mutex_dtor(mutex);
    shared_mutex_delete(mutex);

    shared_int32_dtor(counter);
    shared_int32_delete(counter);

    return 0;
}
```

Code Box 18-25 [ExtremeC_examples_chapter18_4_main.c]: The main function of example 18.4

As you can see, the program accepts an argument indicating its number. As soon as the process finds out about its number, it starts to initialize the shared counter, the shared mutex, and the shared condition variable. It then enters a critical section being protected by the shared mutex.

Inside a loop, it waits for the counter to become equal to its number. Since it waits for 5 seconds, there could be a timeout and we may leave the `shared_cond_timedwait` function after 5 seconds. This basically means that the condition variable has not been notified during that 5 seconds. The process then checks the condition again and it goes to sleep for another 5 seconds. This continues until the process gets the turn.

When this happens, the process prints its number, increments the shared counter, and by broadcasting a signal on the shared condition variable object, it notifies the rest of the waiting processes about the modification which it has made to the shared counter. Only then does it prepare to quit.

In the meantime, if the user presses *Ctrl + C*, the signal handler defined as part of the main logic sets the local flag `int_received` and as soon as the process leaves the function `shared_mutex_timedwait` when it is inside the main loop, it notices the interrupt signal and exits the loop.

The following shell box shows how to compile *example 18.4*. We are going to compile it in Linux:

```
$ gcc -c ExtremeC_examples_chapter18_4_shared_mem.c -o shared_
mem.o
$ gcc -c ExtremeC_examples_chapter18_4_shared_int32.c -o shared_
int32.o
$ gcc -c ExtremeC_examples_chapter18_4_shared_mutex.c -o shared_
mutex.o
$ gcc -c ExtremeC_examples_chapter18_4_shared_cond.c -o shared_
cond.o
```

```
$ gcc -c ExtremeC_examples_chapter18_4_main.c -o main.o
$ gcc shared_mem.o shared_int32.o shared_mutex.o shared_cond.o \
  main.o -lpthread -lrt -o ex18_4.out
$
```

Shell Box 18-6: Compiling the sources of example 18.4 and producing the final executable file

Now that we have got the final executable file `ex18_4.out`, we can run three processes and see how they count in sequence, no matter how you assign them the numbers and in what order they are run. Let's run the first process. We assign to this process the the number 3, by passing the number as an option to the executable file:

```
$ ./ex18_4.out 3
My number is 3!
WARN: The shared memory /counter0 does not exist.
The shared memory /counter0 is created and opened.
WARN: The shared memory /mutex0 does not exist.
The shared memory /mutex0 is created and opened.
WARN: The shared memory /cond0 does not exist.
The shared memory /cond0 is created and opened.
Waiting for the signal, just for 5 seconds ...
Checking condition ...
Waiting for the signal, just for 5 seconds ...
Checking condition ...
Waiting for the signal, just for 5 seconds ...
```

Shell Box 18-7: Running the first process which takes the number 3

As you see in the preceding output, the first process creates all the required shared objects and becomes the owner of the shared resources. Now, let's run the second process in a separate Terminal. It takes the number 2:

```
$ ./ex18_4.out 2
My number is 2!
The shared memory /counter0 is opened.
The shared memory /mutex0 is opened.
The shared memory /cond0 is opened.
Waiting for the signal, just for 5 seconds ...
```

```
Checking condition ...
Waiting for the signal, just for 5 seconds ...
```

Shell Box 18-8: Running the second process which takes the number 2

And finally, the last process takes the number 1. Since this process has been assigned the number 1, it prints its number immediately, increments the shared counter, and notifies the rest of the processes about it:

```
$ ./ex18_4.out 1
My number is 1!
The shared memory /counter0 is opened.
The shared memory /mutex0 is opened.
The shared memory /cond0 is opened.
My turn! 1 ...
The shared memory /cond0 is unmapped.
The shared memory /cond0 is closed.
The shared memory /mutex0 is unmapped.
The shared memory /mutex0 is closed.
The shared memory /counter0 is unmapped.
The shared memory /counter0 is closed.
$
```

Shell Box 18-9: Running the third process which takes the number 1. This process will exit immediately since it has the number 1.

Now, if you go back to the second process, it prints out its number, increments the shared counter, and notifies the third process about that:

```
...
Waiting for the signal, just for 5 seconds ...
Checking condition ...
My turn! 2 ...
The shared memory /cond0 is unmapped.
The shared memory /cond0 is closed.
The shared memory /mutex0 is unmapped.
The shared memory /mutex0 is closed.
The shared memory /counter0 is unmapped.
```

```
The shared memory /counter0 is closed.
$
```

Shell Box 18-10: The second process prints its number and exits

Finally, going back to the first process, it gets notified by the second process, then it prints out its number and exits.

```
...
Waiting for the signal, just for 5 seconds ...
Checking condition ...
My turn! 3 ...
The shared memory /cond0 is unmapped.
The shared memory /cond0 is closed.
The shared memory /cond0 is deleted.
The shared memory /mutex0 is unmapped.
The shared memory /mutex0 is closed.
The shared memory /mutex0 is deleted.
The shared memory /counter0 is unmapped.
The shared memory /counter0 is closed.
The shared memory /counter0 is deleted.
$
```

Shell Box 18-11: The first process prints its number and exits. It also deletes all shared memory entries.

Since the first process is the owner of all shared memories, it should delete them upon exiting. Releasing the allocated resources in a multi-processing environment can be quite tricky and complex because a simple mistake is enough to cause all the processes to crash. Further synchronization is required when a shared resource is going to be removed from the system.

Suppose that, in the preceding example, we'd run the first process with the number 2 and the second process with the number 3. Therefore, the first process should print its number before the second process. When the first process exits since it's the creator of all shared resources, it deletes the shared objects and the second process crashes as soon as it wants to access them.

This is just a simple example of how finalization can be tricky and problematic in multi-process systems. In order to mitigate the risk of such crashes, one needs to introduce further synchronization among processes.

During the previous sections, we covered the mechanisms which can be employed to synchronize a number of processes while all of them are running on the same host. In the following section, we are going to briefly talk about distributed concurrency control mechanisms and their features.

Distributed concurrency control

So far in this chapter we have assumed that all processes exist within the same operating system, and hence the same machine. In other words, we were constantly talking about a single-host software system.

But real software systems usually go beyond that. Conversely to the single-host software system, we have distributed software systems. These systems have processes distributed throughout a network, and they function through communicating over the network.

Regarding a distributed system of processes, we can see more challenges in some aspects that are not present in a centralized or single-host system in that degree. Next, we discuss some of them briefly:

- **In a distributed software system, you are probably experiencing parallelism instead of concurrency**. Since each process runs on a separate machine, and each process has its own specific processor, we will be observing parallelism instead of concurrency. Concurrency is usually limited to the borders of a single machine. Note that interleavings still exist and we might experience the same non-determinism as we saw in concurrent systems.

- **Not all processes within a distributed software system are written using a single programming language**. It is pretty common to see various programming languages being used in a distributed software system. It is also common to see the same diversity in the processes of a single-host software system. Despite our implicit assumption about the processes within a system, which is that all of them have been written using C, we can have processes written using any other language. Different languages provide different ways of having concurrency and control mechanisms. Therefore, for example, in some languages, you may not be able to use a named mutex very easily. Diverse technologies and programming languages used in a software system, single-host or distributed, force us to use concurrency control mechanisms that are abstract enough to be available in all of them. This might limit us to using a specific synchronization technique which is available in a certain technology or a programming language.

- **In a distributed system, you always have a network as the communication channel between two processes not residing on the same machine**. This is converse to our implicit assumption about the single-host system where all processes are running within the same operating system and using the available messaging infrastructures to communicate with each other.

- **Having a network in the middle means that you have latency**. There is a slight latency in single-host systems as well, but it is determined and manageable. It is also much lower than the latency you might experience in a network. Latency simply means that a process may not receive a message immediately because of many reasons having roots in the networking infrastructure. Nothing should be considered immediate in these systems.

- **Having a network in the middle also results in security issues**. When you have all the processes in one system, and all of them are communicating within the same boundary using mechanisms with extremely low latency, the security issues are greatly different. One has to firstly access the system itself in order to attack the system, but in a distributed system, all message passing is being done through the network. You might get an *eavesdropper* in the middle to sniff or, even worse, alter the messages. Regarding our discussion about synchronization in distributed systems, this is also applicable to messages meant to synchronize the processes within a distributed system.

- **Other than latency and security issues, you might have delivery issues that happen far less frequently in single-host multi-process systems**. Messages should be delivered to be processed. When a process sends a message to another process within the system, somehow the sender process should make sure that its message is received by the other end. *Delivery guarantee* mechanisms are possible, but they're costly and, in some scenarios, it is just not possible to use them at all. In those situations, a special kind of messaging problem is seen, which is usually modeled by the famous *Two Generals Problem*.

The preceding differences and possible issues are enough to force us to invent new ways of synchronization among processes and various components of giant distributed systems. Generally, there are two ways to make a distributed system transactional and synchronized:

- **Centralized process synchronization**: These techniques need a central process (or node) that manages the processes. All the other processes within the system should be in constant communication with this central node, and they need its approval in order to enter their critical sections.

- **Distributed (or peer-to-peer) process synchronization**: Having a process synchronization infrastructure that does not have a central node is not an easy task. This is actually an active field of research, and there are some ad hoc algorithms.

In this section, we tried to shine a little light over the complexity of concurrency control in a distributed multi-process system. Further discussions about distributed concurrency control would be out of the scope of this book.

Summary

In this chapter, we completed our discussion regarding multi-processing environments. As part of this chapter, we discussed the following:

- What a named semaphore is and how it can be created and used by multiple processes.

- What a named mutex is and how it should be used using a shared memory region.

- We gave an example which was about termination orchestration in which a number of processes were waiting for a sign to get terminated and the signal was received and handled by one of the processes and propagated to others. We implemented this example using shared mutexes.

- What a named condition variable is and how it can become shared and named using a shared memory region.

- We demonstrated another example of counting processes. As part of this example, we used inheritance to reduce the amount of code duplication for mutex and condition variable objects having an associated shared memory region.

- We briefly explored the differences and challenges found in a distributed system.

- We briefly discussed the methods which can be employed to bring concurrency control into distributed software.

In the upcoming chapter, we start our discussions regarding **Inter-Process Communication** (**IPC**) techniques. Our discussions will span two chapters and we will cover many topics such as computer networks, transport protocols, socket programming, and many more useful topics.

Chapter 19

Single-Host IPC and Sockets

In the previous chapter, we discussed the techniques by which two processes could operate on the same shared resource concurrently and in a synchronized fashion. In this chapter, we are going to expand these techniques and introduce a new category of methods that allow two processes to transmit data. These techniques, both those introduced in the previous chapter and the ones we are going to discuss in this chapter, are together referred to as **Inter-Process Communication (IPC)** techniques.

In this and the following chapter, we are going to talk about the IPC techniques that, despite the methods we discussed in the previous chapter, involve a kind of *message passing* or *signaling* between two processes. The transmitting messages are not stored in any shared place like a file or a shared memory, rather they are emitted and received by the processes.

In this chapter we cover two major topics. Firstly, we underpin the IPC techniques and we discuss single-host IPC and the POSIX API. Secondly, we begin to introduce socket programming and the surrounding topics. These topics include computer networks, the listener-connector model, and the sequences that exist for two processes to establish a connection.

As part of this chapter, we are going to discuss the following topics:

- Various IPC techniques. We introduce push-based and pull-based IPC techniques and as part of this section, we define the techniques discussed in the previous chapter to be pull-based IPC techniques.

- Communication protocols and the characteristics that a protocol usually has. We introduce what serialization and deserialization mean and how they contribute to a fully operational IPC.

- File descriptors and how they play a key role in establishing an IPC channel.

- The exposed API for POSIX signals, POSIX pipes, and POSIX message queues are discussed as part of this chapter. For each technique, an example is provided to demonstrate the basic usage.

- Computer networks and how two processes can communicate over an existing network.

- The listener-connector model and how two processes can establish a transport connection over a number of networks. This is the basis for our future discussions regarding socket programming.

- What socket programming is and what socket objects are.

- The sequences that exist for each of the processes participating in a listener-connector connection, and the API that they have to use from the POSIX socket library.

In the first section, we are going to revisit IPC techniques.

IPC techniques

An IPC technique generally refers to any means that is used by processes to communicate and transmit data. In the previous chapter, we discussed filesystems and shared memory as our beginning approach to share data between two processes. We didn't use the term 'IPC' for these techniques at that point, but this is in fact what they are! In this chapter, we will add a few more IPC techniques to the ones that we have encountered already, but we should remember that they are different in a number of ways. Before jumping to the differences and trying to categorize them, let's list some IPC techniques:

- Shared memory
- Filesystem (both on disk and in memory)
- POSIX signals
- POSIX pipes
- POSIX message queues
- Unix domain sockets
- Internet (or network) sockets

From the programming point of view, the shared memory and filesystem techniques are similar in certain ways and because of that they can be put into the same group, known as *pull-based* IPC techniques. The rest of the techniques stand out and they have their own category. We refer to them as *push-based* IPC techniques. This chapter together with the next chapter are dedicated to push-based IPC, and various techniques are discussed.

Note that the IPC techniques all are responsible for transmitting a number of messages between two processes. Since we are going to use the term *message* heavily in the upcoming paragraphs, it is worth defining it first.

Every message contains a series of bytes that are put together according to a well-defined interface, protocol, or standard. The structure of a message should be known by both processes dealing with that message, and it is usually covered as part of a communication protocol.

A list of differences between pull-based and push-based techniques can be seen as follows:

- In pull-based techniques, we have a shared resource or *medium* external to both processes and available in the user space. Files, shared memories, and even a network service like an **Network Filesystem (NFS)** server can be the shared resource. These mediums are the main place holders for the messages created and consumed by the processes. While in push-based techniques, there is no such a shared resource or medium and instead, there is a *channel*. Processes send and receive messages through this channel, and these messages are not stored in any intermediate medium.

- In pull-based techniques, each process must *pull* the available messages from the medium. In push-based techniques, the incoming messages are *pushed* (*delivered*) to the receiver end.

- In pull-based techniques, because of having a shared resource or medium, concurrent access to the medium must be synchronized. That's why we explored the various synchronization techniques for such IPC techniques in the previous chapter. Note that this is not the case regarding push-based techniques and there is no synchronization needed.

- In pull-based techniques, the processes can operate independently. That's because the messages can be stored in a shared resource and it can be fetched later. In other words, the processes can operate in an *async* fashion. Conversely, in a push-based IPC technique, both processes should be up and running at the same time, and because the messages are pushed instantly, the receiver process may lose some of the incoming messages if it's down. In other words, the processes operate in a *sync* fashion.

Note:
In push-based techniques, we have a temporary message buffer for each process that holds the incoming pushed messages. This message buffer resides in the kernel and lives as long as the process is running. This message buffer might be accessed concurrently, but the synchronization must be guaranteed by the kernel itself.

Messages being either transmitted in an IPC channel when using a push-based technique, or stored in an IPC medium when using a pull-based technique, should have a content that is understandable by the receiving process. This means that both processes – the sender end and the receiver end – must know how to create and parse the messages. Since messages are made up of bytes, this implies that both processes must know how to translate an object (a text or video) into a series of bytes, and how to resurrect the same object from the received bytes. We'll see shortly that the inter-operability of the processes is covered by a common *communication protocol* adapted by both of them.

In the following section, we'll discuss communication protocols in greater depth.

Communication protocols

Having just a communication channel or medium is not enough. Two parties willing to communicate over a shared channel need to understand one another, too! A very simple example is when two people want to talk to each other using the same language, such as English or Japanese. Here, the language can be considered as the protocol used by two parties in order to communicate.

In the context of IPC, processes are no exception; they need a common language so they can communicate. Technically, we use the term *protocol* to refer to this common language between any two parties. As part of this section, we are going to discuss communication protocols and their various characteristics such as the *message length* and the *message content*. Before being able to talk about these characteristics, we need to describe a communication protocol in a deeper sense. Note that our main focus in this chapter is IPC techniques; therefore, we only talk about communication protocols between two processes. Any kind of communication happening between parties other than processes cannot be covered as part of this chapter.

Processes can only transmit bytes. This effectively means that every piece of information must be translated into a series of bytes before being transmitted by one of the IPC techniques. This is called *serialization* or *marshalling*. A paragraph of text, a piece of audio, a music track, or any other kind of object must be serialized before being sent over an IPC channel, or being stored in an IPC medium. Hence, regarding the IPC communication protocols, this means that the messages transmitted between processes are a series of bytes in a very specific and well-defined order.

Conversely, when a process receives a series of bytes from an IPC channel, it should be able to reconstruct the original object out of the incoming bytes. This is called *deserialization* or *unmarshaling*.

To explain serialization and deserialization in the same flow, when a process wants to send an object to another process over any already established IPC channel, the sender process first serializes the object into a byte array. Then it transmits the byte array to the other party. On the receiver side, the process deserializes the incoming bytes and it resurrects the sent object. As you can see, these operations are the inverse of each other, and they are used by both ends in order to use a byte-oriented IPC channel to transmit information. This is something you can't escape from, and every IPC-based technology (RPC, RMI, and so on) relies heavily on the serialization and deserialization of various objects. From now on, we use the term serialization to refer to both serialization and deserialization operations.

Note that serialization is not limited to push-based IPC techniques that we have discussed so far. In pull-based IPC techniques such as filesystem or shared memory, we still need serialization. That's because the underlying mediums in these techniques can store a series of bytes and if a process wants to store an object in a shared file, for instance, it has to serialize it before being able to store it there. Therefore, serialization is universal to all IPC techniques; no matter which IPC method you are using, you have to deal with a great amount of serialization and deserialization while using the underlying channel or medium.

Choosing a communication protocol implicitly dictates the serialization because, as part of a protocol, we define the order of bytes very carefully. This is crucial because a serialized object must be deserialized back to the same object on the receiver side. Therefore, both the serializer and deserializer must obey the same rules dictated by the protocol. Having an incompatible serializer and deserializer at both ends effectively means no communication at all, simply because the receiver end cannot reconstruct the transmitted object.

 Note:
Sometimes, we use the term *parsing* as a synonym for *deserialization*, but they are in fact fundamentally different.

To make the discussion more tangible, let's talk about some real examples. A web server and a web client communicate using **Hyper Text Transfer Protocol (HTTP)**. Therefore, both sides are required to use compatible HTTP serializers and deserializers to speak to each other. As another example, let's talk about the **Domain Name Service (DNS)** protocol. Both the DNS client and server must use compatible serializers and deserializers so that they can communicate. Note that unlike HTTP, which has textual content, DNS is a binary protocol. We discuss this shortly in the upcoming sections.

Since serialization operations can be used in various components in a software project, they are usually provided as some libraries that can be added to any component wishing to use them. For famous protocol such as HTTP, DNS, and FTP, there are well-known third-party libraries that can be used without hassle. But for custom protocols specially designed for a project, the serialization libraries must be written by the team itself.

Note:
Well-known protocols such as HTTP, FTP, and DNS are standards and they are described in some official open documents called **request for comments** (**RFC**). For example, the HTTP/1.1 protocol is described in RFC-2616. A simple Google search will take you to the RFC page.

As a further note regarding *serialization libraries*, they can be provided in various programming languages. Note that a specific serialization itself is not dependent on any programming language because it only talks about the order of bytes and how they should be interpreted. Therefore, the serialization and deserialization algorithms can be developed using any programming language. That's a crucial requirement. In a big software project, we can have multiple components written in various programming languages, and there are situations in which these components must transmit information. Hence, we need the same serialization algorithms written in various languages. For instance, we have HTTP serializers written in C, C++, Java, Python, and so on.

To sum up the main point of this section, we need a well-defined protocol between two parties in order for them to talk to each other. An IPC protocol is a standard that dictates how the overall communication must take place and what details must be obeyed regarding the byte order and their meaning in various messages. We have to use some serialization algorithms in order to consume a byte-oriented IPC channel to transmit objects.

In the following section, we describe the characteristics of IPC protocols.

Protocol characteristics

IPC protocols have various characteristics. Briefly, every protocol can specify a different content type for the messages transmitted over an IPC channel. In another protocol, the messages can have a fixed length or a variable length. Some protocols dictate that the provided operations must be consumed in a synchronous fashion, while there are protocols that allow asynchronous usage. In the following sections, we will be covering these distinguishing factors. Note that the existing protocols can be categorized based on these characteristics.

Content type

Messages sent over IPC channels can have *textual* content or *binary* content or a combination of both of them. Binary content has bytes with values ranging over all possible numerical values between 0 to 255. But textual content has only characters that are used in text. In other words, only alphanumerical characters together with some symbols are allowed in textual content.

While textual content can be considered as a special case of binary content, we try to keep them separate and treat them differently. For instance, textual messages are good candidates to be compressed before sending, while binary messages suffer from a poor *compression ratio* (the actual size divided by the compressed size). It is good to know that some protocols are purely textual, such as JSON, and some others are fully binary, such as DNS. There are also protocols such as BSON and HTTP that allow message contents to be a combination of both textual and binary data. In these protocols, raw bytes can be mixed with text to form the final message.

Note that binary content can be sent as text. There are various encodings that allow you to represent binary content using textual characters. *Base64* is one of the most famous *binary-to-text encoding* algorithms that allows such a transformation. These encoding algorithms are widely used in purely textual protocols such as JSON to send binary data.

Length of messages

The messages produced according to an IPC protocol can be either *fixed-length* or *variable-length*. By fixed-length, we mean that all messages have the same length. Conversely, by variable-length, we mean that the produced messages can have different lengths. Receiving either fixed-length messages or variable-length messages have an immediate impact on the receiver side while deserializing the content of a message. Using a protocol that always produces fixed-length messages can reduce the burden of parsing receiving messages because the receiver already knows the number of bytes that it should read from the channel, and messages with the same size usually (not always) have the same structure. When reading fixed-length messages from an IPC channel, if all of them follow the same structure, we have a nice opportunity to use C structures to refer to those bytes through some already-defined fields, similar to what we did for objects placed in shared memories in the previous chapter.

With protocols that produce variable-length messages, finding where an individual message ends is not that easy, and the receiver side somehow (which we explain shortly) should decide whether it has read a complete message or more bytes must be read from the channel. Note that the receiver might read multiple chunks from the channel before reading a complete message, and a single chunk may contain data from two adjacent messages. We will see an example of this in the next chapter.

Since most protocols are variable-length and you usually don't have the luxury of dealing with fixed-length messages, it is worth discussing the methods that various protocols adopt to make their variable-length messages distinguishable or separable. In other words, these protocols use a mechanism to mark the end of a message and, this way, the receiver can use those marks to indicate that it has read a complete message. Next, you can see some of these methods:

- **Using a delimiter or a separator**: A delimiter or separator is a series of bytes (in binary messages) or characters (in textual messages) that indicates the end of a message. The delimiter should be chosen depending on the content of the messages, because it should be easily distinguishable from the actual content.

- **Length-prefix framing**: In these protocols, each message has a fixed-length prefix (usually 4 bytes or even more) that carries the number of bytes that should be read by the receiver in order to have a complete message. Various protocols such as all **Tag-Value-Length** (**TLV**) protocols, with **Abstract Syntax Notation** (**ASN**) as an example, use this technique.

- **Using a finite-state machine**: These protocols follow a *regular grammar* that can be modeled by a *finite-state machine*. The receiver side should be aware of the grammar of the protocol, and it should use a proper deserializer that works based on a finite-state machine to read a complete message from the IPC channel.

Sequentiality

In most protocols, we have a *conversation* happening between two processes that follows a *request-response* scheme. One of the parties sends a request and the other side replies. This scheme is usually used in client-server scenarios. The listener process, often the server process, waits for a message, and when the message is received, it replies accordingly.

If the protocol is synchronous or sequential, the sender (client) will wait until the listener (server) completes the request and sends back the reply. In other words, the sender stays in a *blocking* state until the listener replies. In an asynchronous protocol, the sender process isn't blocked, and it can continue with another task while the request is being processed by the listener. That is, the sender won't get blocked while the reply is being prepared.

In an asynchronous protocol, there should be a *pulling* or *pushing* mechanism in place, which allows the sender to check for the reply. In a pulling scenario, the sender will regularly ask the listener about the result. In a pushing scenario, the listener will push back the reply to the sender via the same or a different communication channel.

The sequentiality of a protocol is not limited to request-response scenarios. Messaging applications usually use this technique to have the maximum responsiveness both on the server-side and on the client-side.

Single-host communication

In this section, we are going to talk about single-host IPC. Multiple-host IPC will be the subject of our discussion in the next chapter. There are four main techniques that can be used by processes to communicate when they reside on the same machine:

- POSIX signals
- POSIX pipes
- POSIX message queues
- Unix domain sockets

POSIX signals, unlike the other preceding techniques, don't create a communication channel between the processes, but can be used as a way to notify a process about an event. In certain scenarios, such signals can be used by processes to notify each other about specific events in the system.

Before jumping to the first IPC technique, POSIX signals, let's discuss file descriptors. Other than POSIX signals, no matter which IPC technique you use, you will be dealing with file descriptors of some sort. Therefore, we'll now dedicate a separate section to them and discuss them further.

File descriptors

Two communicating processes can be running either on the same machine or on two different machines connected by a computer network. In this section and much of this chapter, our focus is on the first case, in which processes reside on the same machine. That's where file descriptors become immensely important. Note that in multiple-host IPC we will still be dealing with file descriptors, but they are called *sockets* there. We will discuss them thoroughly in the upcoming chapter.

A file descriptor is an abstract handle to an object within the system that can be used to read and write data. As you can see, despite the name, file descriptors can refer to a wide range of available mechanisms that deal with reading and modifying byte streams.

Regular files are certainly among the objects that can be referred to by file descriptors. Such files are located on filesystems, either on a hard disk or in memory.

Other things that can be referred to and accessed via file descriptors are devices. As we saw in *Chapter 10*, *Unix - History and Architecture*, each device can be accessed using a device file, which is usually found in the /dev directory.

Regarding push-based IPC techniques, a file descriptor can represent an IPC channel. In this case, the file descriptor can be used to read and write data from and to the represented channel. That's why the first step in setting up an IPC channel is to define a number of file descriptors.

Now that you know more about file descriptors and what they represent, we can move on and discuss the first IPC technique that can be used in single-host multi-process system; however, POSIX signals don't use file descriptors. You are going to hear more about file descriptors in the future sections dedicated to POSIX pipes and POSIX message queues. Let's begin with POSIX signals.

POSIX signals

In POSIX systems, processes and threads can send and receive a number of predefined signals. A signal can be sent either by a process, or a thread, or by the kernel itself. Signals are actually meant to notify a process or a thread about an event or error. For example, when the system is going to be rebooted, the system sends a SIGTERM signal to all processes to let them know that a rebooting is in progress and they must immediately quit. Once a process receives this signal, it should react accordingly. In some cases, nothing should be done, but in some cases, the current state of the process should be persisted.

The following table shows the available signals in a Linux system. The table is extracted from the Linux signals manual page that can be found at http://www.man7.org/linux/man-pages/man7/signal.7.html:

Signal	Standard	Action	Comment
SIGABRT	P1990	Core	Abort signal from abort(3)
SIGALRM	P1990	Term	Timer signal from alarm(2)
SIGBUS	P2001	Core	Bus error (bad memory access)
SIGCHLD	P1990	Ign	Child stopped or terminated
SIGCLD	-	Ign	A synonym for SIGCHLD
SIGCONT	P1990	Cont	Continue if stopped
SIGEMT	-	Term	Emulator trap
SIGFPE	P1990	Core	Floating-point exception
SIGHUP	P1990	Term	Hangup detected on controlling terminal
			or death of controlling process
SIGILL	P1990	Core	Illegal Instruction
SIGINFO	-		A synonym for SIGPWR
SIGINT	P1990	Term	Interrupt from keyboard

SIGIO	-	Term	I/O now possible (4.2BSD)
SIGIOT	-	Core	IOT trap. A synonym for SIGABRT
SIGKILL	P1990	Term	Kill signal
SIGLOST	-	Term	File lock lost (unused)
SIGPIPE	P1990	Term	Broken pipe: write to pipe with no readers; see pipe(7)
SIGPOLL	P2001	Term	Pollable event (Sys V). Synonym for SIGIO
SIGPROF	P2001	Term	Profiling timer expired
SIGPWR	-	Term	Power failure (System V)
SIGQUIT	P1990	Core	Quit from keyboard
SIGSEGV	P1990	Core	Invalid memory reference
SIGSTKFLT (unused)	-	Term	Stack fault on coprocessor
SIGSTOP	P1990	Stop	Stop process
SIGTSTP	P1990	Stop	Stop typed at terminal
SIGSYS	P2001	Core	Bad system call (SVr4); see also seccomp(2)
SIGTERM	P1990	Term	Termination signal
SIGTRAP	P2001	Core	Trace/breakpoint trap
SIGTTIN process	P1990	Stop	Terminal input for background
SIGTTOU process	P1990	Stop	Terminal output for background
SIGUNUSED	-	Core	Synonymous with SIGSYS
SIGURG (4.2BSD)	P2001	Ign	Urgent condition on socket
SIGUSR1	P1990	Term	User-defined signal 1
SIGUSR2	P1990	Term	User-defined signal 2
SIGVTALRM	P2001	Term	Virtual alarm clock (4.2BSD)
SIGXCPU	P2001	Core	CPU time limit exceeded (4.2BSD); see setrlimit(2)
SIGXFSZ	P2001	Core	File size limit exceeded (4.2BSD); see setrlimit(2)
SIGWINCH	-	Ign	Window resize signal (4.3BSD, Sun)

Table 19-1: List of all available signals in a Linux system

As you can see in the preceding table, not all of the signals are POSIX, and Linux has got its own signals. While most of the signals correspond to well-known events, there are two POSIX signals that can be defined by the user. This is mostly used in scenarios when you want to invoke a certain functionality in your program while the process is running. *Example 19.1* demonstrates how to use signals and how they can be handled in a C program. Next, you can find the code for *example 19.1*:

```
#include <stdio.h>
#include <stdlib.h>
```

```
#include <signal.h>

void handle_user_signals(int signal) {
  switch (signal) {
    case SIGUSR1:
      printf("SIGUSR1 received!\n");
      break;
    case SIGUSR2:
      printf("SIGUSR2 received!\n");
      break;
    default:
      printf("Unsupported signal is received!\n");
  }
}

void handle_sigint(int signal) {
  printf("Interrupt signal is received!\n");
}

void handle_sigkill(int signal) {
  printf("Kill signal is received! Bye.\n");
  exit(0);
}

int main(int argc, char** argv) {
  signal(SIGUSR1, handle_user_signals);
  signal(SIGUSR2, handle_user_signals);
  signal(SIGINT, handle_sigint);
  signal(SIGKILL, handle_sigkill);
  while (1);
  return 0;
}
```

Code Box 19-1 [ExtremeC_examples_chapter19_1.c]: Handling POSIX signals

In the preceding example, we have used the `signal` function to assign various signal handlers to some specific signals. As you can see, we have one signal handler for the user-defined signals, one handler for the SIGINT signal, and one for the SIGKILL signal.

The program is merely a never-ending loop, and all we want to do is to handle some signals. The following commands show how to compile and run the example in the background:

```
$ gcc ExtremeC_examples_chapter19_1.c -o ex19_1.out
$ ./ex19_1.out &
```

```
[1] 4598
$
```

Shell Box 19-1: Compiling and running example 19.1

Now that we know the PID of the program, we can send it some signals. The PID is 4598 and the program is running in the background. Note that the PID will be different for you. You can use the `kill` command to send a signal to a process. The following command is used to examine the preceding example:

```
$ kill -SIGUSR2 4598
SIGUSR2 received!
$ kill -SIGUSR1 4598
SIGUSR2 received!
$ kill -SIGINT 4598
Interrupt signal is received!
$ kill -SIGKILL 4598
$
[1]+  Stopped                 ./ex19_1.out
$
```

Shell Box 19-2: Sending different signals to the background process

As you can see, the program handles all signals except the `SIGKILL` signal. `SIGKILL` cannot be handled by any process and, usually, a parent process that has spawned the process can be notified about its child being killed.

Note that the `SIGINT` signal, or the interrupt signal, can be sent to a foreground program by pressing *Ctrl + C*. Therefore, whenever you press this combination of keys, you are actually sending an interrupt signal to the running program. The default handler just stops the program, but as you can see in the preceding example, we can handle the `SIGINT` signal and ignore it.

In addition to the ability to send a signal to a process using shell commands, a process also can send a signal to another process if it knows the target process's PID. You can use the `kill` function (declared in `signal.h`), which does exactly the same as its command-line version. It accepts two parameters: the first is the target PID and the second is the signal number. It is also possible for a process or a thread to use the `kill` or `raise` functions to send a signal to itself. Note that the `raise` function sends the signal to the current thread. These functions can be quite useful in scenarios in which you want to notify another part of your program about an event.

The last note about the preceding example is that, as you saw in *Shell Box 19-2*, it doesn't matter that the main thread is busy with the never-ending loop, the signals are delivered asynchronously. Therefore, you can be sure that you always receive the incoming signals.

Now it's time to talk about POSIX pipes as another single-host IPC technique that can be useful in certain circumstances.

POSIX pipes

POSIX Pipes in Unix are unidirectional channels that can be used between two processes that need to exchange messages. Upon creating a POSIX pipe, you will get two file descriptors. One file descriptor is used to write to the pipe, and the other one is used to read from the pipe. The following example shows the basic usage of a POSIX pipe:

```c
#include <stdio.h>
#include <stdlib.h>
#include <unistd.h>
#include <string.h>
#include <sys/types.h>

int main(int argc, char** argv) {
  int fds[2];
  pipe(fds);

  int childpid = fork();
  if (childpid == -1) {
    fprintf(stderr, "fork error!\n");
    exit(1);
  }
  if (childpid == 0) {
    // Child closes the read file descriptor
    close(fds[0]);
    char str[] = "Hello Daddy!";
    // Child writes to the write file descriptor
    fprintf(stdout, "CHILD: Waiting for 2 seconds ...\n");
    sleep(2);
    fprintf(stdout, "CHILD: Writing to daddy ...\n");
    write(fds[1], str, strlen(str) + 1);
  } else {
    // Parent closes the write file descriptor
    close(fds[1]);
    char buff[32];
    // Parent reads from the read file descriptor
    fprintf(stdout, "PARENT: Reading from child ...\n");
    int num_of_read_bytes = read(fds[0], buff, 32);
```

```
    fprintf(stdout, "PARENT: Received from child: %s\n", buff);
  }
  return 0;
}
```

Code Box 19-2 [ExtremeC_examples_chapter19_2.c]: Example 19.2 on using a POSIX pipe

As you can see, in the second line of the `main` function, we have used the `pipe` function. As we've already said, it accepts an array of two file descriptors and opens two file descriptors, one for reading from the pipe and the other one for writing to it. The first file descriptor, found at index 0, should be used for reading; and the second file descriptor, located at index 1, should be used for writing to the pipe.

In order to have two processes, we have used the fork API. As we've explained in *Chapter 17, Process Execution*, the fork API clones the parent process and creates a new child process. Therefore, the opened file descriptors are available to the child process after calling the `fork` function.

When the child process is spawned, the parent process enters the `else` block and the child process enters the `if` block. Firstly, each process should close the file descriptor that it is not going to use. In this example, the parent wants to read from the pipe and the child wants to write to the pipe. That's why the parent process closes the second file descriptor (the write file descriptor) and the child process closes the first file descriptor (the read file descriptor). Note that a pipe is unidirectional and reverse communication is not possible.

The following shell box shows the output of the preceding example:

```
$ gcc ExtremeC_examples_chapter19_2.c -o ex19_2.out
$ ./ex19_2.out
PARENT: Reading from child ...
CHILD: Waiting for 2 seconds ...
CHILD: Writing to daddy ...
PARENT: Received from child: Hello Daddy!
$
```

Shell Box 19-3: Output of running example 19.2

As you can see in *Code Box 19-2*, for reading and writing operations we use the `read` and `write` functions. As we mentioned before, in push-based IPC, a file descriptor refers to a byte channel, and when you have a file descriptor pointing to a channel, you can use the file descriptor's related functions. The `read` and `write` functions accept a file descriptor and no matter what kind of IPC channel is behind, they operate on the underlying channel the same way.

In the previous example, we used the fork API to spawn a new process. If a situation arises in which we have two different processes spawned separately, the question is, how can they communicate through a shared pipe? If a process demands access to a pipe object within the system, it should have the corresponding file descriptor. There are two options available:

- One of the processes should set up the pipe and transfer the corresponding file descriptors to the other process.

- The processes should use a named pipe.

In the first scenario, the processes must use a Unix domain socket channel in order to exchange file descriptors. The problem is that if such a channel exists between the two processes, they could use it for further communication and there would be no need to set up another channel (POSIX pipe) that has a less friendly API than Unix domain sockets.

The second scenario seems to be more promising. One of the processes could use the mkfifo function and create a queue file by providing a path. Then, the second process could use the path to the already created file and open it for further communication. Note that the channel is still unidirectional and, depending on the scenario, one of the processes should open the file in read-only mode and the other should open it in write-only mode.

One more point should be discussed about the previous example. As you can see, the child process waits for 2 seconds before writing to the pipe. In the meantime, the parent process is blocked on the read function. So, while there is no message written to the pipe, the process reading from the pipe becomes blocked.

As the final note in this section, we know that POSIX pipes are push-based. As we've explained this before, push-based IPC techniques have a corresponding temporary kernel buffer for holding the incoming pushed messages. POSIX pipes are no exception and the kernel holds the written messages until they are read. Note that if the owner process quits, the pipe object and its corresponding kernel buffer are destroyed.

In the following section, we will discuss POSIX message queues.

POSIX message queues

Kernel-hosted message queues are part of the POSIX standard. They differ significantly from POSIX pipes in a number of ways. Here, we examine the fundamental differences:

- The elements inside a pipe are bytes. Instead, message queues hold messages. Pipes are not aware of any existing structure in the written bytes, while message queues keep actual messages and each call to the `write` function results in a new message being added to the queue. Message queues preserve the boundaries between written messages. To elaborate more on this, suppose that we have three messages: the first one has 10 bytes, the second one has 20 bytes, and the third one has 30 bytes. We write these messages both to a POSIX pipe and to a POSIX message queue. The pipe only knows that it has 60 bytes inside, and it allows a program to read 15 bytes. But the message queue only knows that it has 3 messages and it doesn't allow a program to read 15 bytes because we don't have any messages with 15 bytes.

- Pipes have a maximum size, the unit of which is the number of bytes. Message queues instead have a maximum number of messages. In message queues, every message has a maximum size in terms of bytes.

- Every message queue, like a named shared memory or a named semaphore, opens a file. While these files are not regular files, they can be used by future processes to access the same message queue instance.

- Message queues can be prioritized, while pipes don't care about the priority of bytes.

And they have the following properties in common:

- Both are unidirectional. In order to have bidirectional communication, you need to create two instances of pipes or queues.

- Both have limited capacity; you cannot write any number of bytes or messages that you want.

- Both are represented using file descriptors in most POSIX systems; therefore, I/O functions such as `read` and `write` can be used.

- Both techniques are *connection-less*. In other words, if two different processes write two different messages, it is possible for one of them to read the other process's message. In other words, there is no ownership defined for the messages and any process can read them. This would be a problem, especially when there is more than one process operating on the same pipe or message queue concurrently.

 Note:
POSIX message queues explained in this chapter should not be confused with message queue brokers being used in the **Message Queue Middleware (MQM)** architecture.

There are various resources on the internet that explain POSIX message queues. The following link explains POSIX message queues specifically for the QNX operating system, but most of the content is still applicable to other POSIX systems: https://users.pja.edu.pl/~jms/qnx/help/watcom/clibref/mq_overview.html.

Now it is time to have an example. *Example 16.3* has the same scenario as we had in *example 16.2*, but it uses a POSIX message queue instead of a POSIX pipe. All the functions related to POSIX message queues are declared in the `mqueue.h` header file. We will explain some of them shortly.

Note that the following code doesn't compile on macOS because OS/X doesn't support POSIX message queues:

```
#include <stdio.h>
#include <stdlib.h>
#include <unistd.h>
#include <string.h>
#include <mqueue.h>

int main(int argc, char** argv) {
  // The message queue handler
  mqd_t mq;

  struct mq_attr attr;
  attr.mq_flags = 0;
  attr.mq_maxmsg = 10;
  attr.mq_msgsize = 32;
  attr.mq_curmsgs = 0;


  int childpid = fork();
  if (childpid == -1) {
    fprintf(stderr, "fork error!\n");
    exit(1);
  }
  if (childpid == 0) {
    // Child waits while the parent is creating the queue
    sleep(1);
    mqd_t mq = mq_open("/mq0", O_WRONLY);
    char str[] = "Hello Daddy!";
    // Child writes to the write file descriptor
    fprintf(stdout, "CHILD: Waiting for 2 seconds ...\n");
    sleep(2);
    fprintf(stdout, "CHILD: Writing to daddy ...\n");
    mq_send(mq, str, strlen(str) + 1, 0);
    mq_close(mq);
```

```
  } else {
    mqd_t mq = mq_open("/mq0", O_RDONLY | O_CREAT, 0644, &attr);
    char buff[32];
    fprintf(stdout, "PARENT: Reading from child ...\n");
    int num_of_read_bytes = mq_receive(mq, buff, 32, NULL);
    fprintf(stdout, "PARENT: Received from child: %s\n", buff);
    mq_close(mq);
    mq_unlink("/mq0");
  }
  return 0;
}
```

Code Box 19-3 [ExtremeC_examples_chapter19_3.c]: Example 19.3 on using a POSIX message queues

In order to compile the preceding code, run the following commands. Note that the preceding code should be linked with the `rt` library on Linux:

```
$ gcc ExtremeC_examples_chapter19_3.c -lrt -o ex19_3.out
$
```

Shell Box 19-4: Building example 19.3 on Linux

The following shell box demonstrates the output of *example 19.3*. As you can see, the output is exactly the same as we had for *example 19.2* but it uses POSIX message queues to perform the same logic that we wrote in *example 19.2*:

```
$ ./ex19_3.out
PARENT: Reading from child ...
CHILD: Waiting for 2 seconds ...
CHILD: Writing to daddy ...
PARENT: Received from child: Hello Daddy!
$
```

Shell Box 19-5: Running example 19.3 on Linux

Note that both POSIX pipes and message queues have a limited buffer in the kernel. Therefore, writing to pipes and message queues without having a consumer that reads their content can lead to all write operations being blocked. In other words, any `write` function call would remain blocked until a consumer reads a message from the message queue or some bytes from the pipe.

In the following section, we will briefly explain Unix domain sockets. They are usually the first choice when connecting two local processes in a single-host setup.

Unix domain sockets

Another technique that can be used by a number of processes to communicate in a single-host deployment is using Unix domain sockets. They are special kind of sockets that only operate within the same machine. Therefore, they are different from network sockets, which allow two processes from two different machines to talk to each other over an existing network. Unix domain sockets have various characteristics that make them important and sophisticated in comparison to POSIX pipes and POSIX message queues. The most important characteristic is the fact that Unix domain sockets are bidirectional. Therefore, a single socket object is enough to read from and write to the underlying channel. In other words, the channels operated by Unix domain sockets are full-duplex. In addition, Unix domain sockets can be both *session-aware* and *message-aware*. This makes them even more flexible. We will discuss session-awareness and message-awareness in the following sections.

Since Unix domain sockets cannot be discussed without knowing the basics of socket programming, we won't go any further than this in this chapter. Instead, in the following sections, we introduce socket programming and the concepts around it. A full discussion regarding Unix domain sockets will be given in the following chapter. Let's begin with socket programming.

Introduction to socket programming

As part of this chapter, we decided to discuss socket programming before going through the real C code examples as part of the next chapter. That's because there are some fundamental concepts that you need to know before jumping to the code.

Socket programming can be done both on single-host and multi-host deployments. As you might have guessed, the socket programming in a single-host system is done through Unix domain sockets. In a multi-host setup, socket programming is about creating and using network sockets. Both Unix sockets and network sockets more or less use the same API and share the same concepts, so it would make sense to cover them together in the next chapter.

One of the key concepts before using network sockets is how computer networks work. In the following section, we are going to talk about this and introduce you to computer networks. There are many terms and concepts that you should know before being able to write your first socket programming example.

Computer networks

The approach we take to explain the networking concepts in this section is different from the usual texts you might find about this topic. Our goal is to create a basic understanding of how things work in a computer network, especially between two processes. We want to look at this concept from a programmer's point of view. And the main actors in our discussion are processes, not computers. Therefore, you might find the order of sections a bit odd at first, but it will help you to get the idea of how IPC works over a computer network.

Note that this section shouldn't be considered a complete description of computer networks and, of course, it cannot be done in a few pages and in just one section.

Physical layer

First, let's forget about processes and just consider the computers, or simply the machines. Before moving forward, note that we use various terms to refer to a computer in a network. We can call it a computer, machine, host, node, or even a system. Of course, the context helps you to find out the true meaning behind a given term.

The first step toward having multi-host software is a number of computers that are connected together through a network or, more precisely, a computer network. For now, let's focus on two computers that we want to connect. In order to connect these two physical machines to one other, we certainly need some sort of physical medium such as a piece of wire or a wireless setup.

Of course, without such a physical medium (which doesn't need to be visible, like in a wireless network), the connection would not be possible. These physical connections are analogous to roads between cities. We will stick to this analogy because it can explain what is happening inside a computer network very closely.

All the hardware equipment required to connect two machines physically are considered to be part of the *physical layer*. This is the first and the most basic layer that we explore. Without having this layer, it is impossible to transmit data between two computers and assume them to be connected. Everything above this layer is not physical and all you find is a set of various standards regarding how the data should be transmitted.

Let's talk about the next layer, the link layer.

Link layer

While merely having roads is not sufficient for traffic to move along them, the same is true for the physical connections between computers. In order to use roads, we need laws and regulations about the vehicles, signs, materials, borders, speed, lanes, directions, and so on, and without them, traveling along the roads would be chaotic and problematic. Similar rules are needed for direct physical connections between two computers.

While the physical components and devices required to connect a number of computers all belong to the physical layer, the mandatory regulations and protocols that govern the way data is transmitted along the physical layer all belong to an upper layer called the *link layer*.

As part of the regulations enforced by the link protocols, messages should be broken into pieces called *frames*. This is analogous to the regulations in a road system that defines a maximum length of the vehicles traveling on a certain road. You cannot drive a 1 km-long trailer (presuming that it is physically possible) on a road. You have to break it down into smaller segments, or into smaller vehicles. Similarly, a long piece of data should be broken into multiple frames, and each frame must be traveling along the network freely, independent of the other frames.

It is worth mentioning that networks can exist between any two computational devices. They don't necessarily need to be computers. There are many devices and machines in industry that can be connected to each other to form a network. Industrial networks have their own standards for their physical wiring, connectors, terminators, and so on, and they have their own link protocols and standards.

Many standards describe such link connections, for instance, how a desktop computer can get connected to an industrial machine. One of the most prominent link protocols that is designed to connect a number of computers via a wire is *Ethernet*. Ethernet describes all the rules and regulations governing data transmission over computer networks. We have another widely used link protocol called IEEE 802.11, which governs wireless networks.

A network consisting of computers (or any other groups of homogenous computing machines or devices) connected by a physical connection via a specific link protocol is called a **Local Area Network** (**LAN**). Note that any device willing to join a LAN must use a physical component called a *network adapter* or a **Network Interface Controller** (**NIC**) attached to it. For instance, the computers wanting to join an Ethernet network must have an *Ethernet NIC*.

A computer can have multiple NICs attached. Each NIC can connect to a specific LAN, therefore a computer with three NICs is able to connect to three different LANs simultaneously.

It is also possible that it uses all its three NICs to connect to the same LAN. The way that you configure NICs and how you connect computers to various LANs should be designed beforehand and a precise plan should be in place.

Every NIC has a specific and unique address defined by the governing link protocol. This address will be used for data transmission between the nodes inside a LAN. The Ethernet and IEEE 802.11 protocols define a **media access control** (**MAC**) address for every compatible NIC. Therefore, any Ethernet NIC or IEEE 802.11 Wi-Fi adapter should have a unique MAC address in order to join a compatible LAN. Inside a LAN, the assigned MAC addresses should be unique. Note that ideally, any MAC address should be unique universally and unchangeable. However, this is not the case, and you can even set the MAC address of a NIC.

To summarize what we have explained so far, we have a stack of two layers, the physical layer beneath and the link layer above. This is enough to connect a number of computers on a single LAN. But it doesn't end here. We need another layer on top of these two layers to be able to connect computers from various LANs with or without any intermediate LANs in between.

Network layer

So far, we've seen that MAC addresses are used in Ethernet LANs in order to connect a number of nodes. But what happens if two computers from two different LANs need to connect to each other? Note that these LAN networks are not necessarily compatible.

For instance, one of the LANs could be a wired Ethernet network, while the other one could be a **fiber distributed data interface** (**FDDI**) network mainly using fiber optic as the physical layer. Another example is industrial machines connected to an **Industrial Ethernet** (**IE**) LAN that need to connect to operators' computers, which are on an ordinary Ethernet LAN. These examples and many more show that we need another layer on top of the aforementioned protocols in order to connect various nodes from different LANs. Note that we even need this third layer in order to connect compatible LANs. This would be even more crucial if we are going to transmit data from one LAN to another (compatible or heterogeneous) through a number of intermediate LANs. We explain this further in the upcoming paragraphs.

Just like the frames in the link layer, we have *packets* in the *network layer*. Long messages are broken into smaller pieces called packets. While frames and packets are referring to two different concepts in two different layers, for simplicity, we consider them the same and we stick to the term *packet* for the rest of this chapter.

As a key difference, you should know that frames encapsulate packets, in other words, a frame contains a packet. We won't go any deeper regarding frames and packets, but you can find numerous sources on the internet that describe various aspects of these concepts.

The *network protocol* fills the gap between various LANs in order to connect them to each other. While each LAN can have its own specific physical layer and its own specific link layer standards and protocols, the governing network protocol should be the same for all of them. Otherwise, heterogeneous (not compatible) LANs cannot connect to each other. The most famous network protocol at the moment is the **Internet Protocol** (**IP**). It is extensively used in large computer networks that usually consist of smaller Ethernet or Wi-Fi LANs. IP has two versions based on the length of its addresses: IPv4 and IPv6.

But how can two computers from two different LANs be connected? The answer lies in the *routing* mechanism. In order to receive data from an external LAN, there should be a *router* node. Suppose that we are going to connect two different LANs: LAN1 and LAN2. A router is simply another node that resides in both networks by having two NICs. One NIC is in LAN1 and the other one is in LAN2. Then, a special routing algorithm decides which packets to transfer and how they should be transferred between networks.

With the routing mechanism, multiple networks can have a bidirectional flow of data through the router nodes. For this to happen, within every LAN there should be a router node. Therefore, when you want to send data to a computer located in a different geographical zone, it could be that your data is being transmitted through tens of routers before hitting its target. I'm not going to go any further than this into the routing concept, but there are tons of great information about this mechanism on the web.

Note:
There is a utility program called *traceroute* that allows you to see the routers between your computer and the target computer.

At this point, two hosts from two different LANs can be connected to each other, with or without having intermediate LANs in between. Any further effort to make more specific connections should be done on top of this layer. Therefore, any communication happening between two programs, residing on two different nodes, must take place on top of a stack of three layers of protocols: the physical layer, the link layer, and finally the network layer. But what does it exactly mean when we say that two computers are connected to each other?

It is a bit vague to say that two nodes are connected, at least for programmers. To be more precise, the operating systems of these nodes are connected to each other, and they are the actors who transmit data. The ability to join a network and talk to other nodes in the same LAN or in a different LAN is intrinsically encoded in most current operating systems. Unix-based operating systems, which are our main focus in this book, are all operating systems that support networking, and they can be installed on the nodes participating in a network.

Linux, Microsoft Windows, and almost any modern operating system supports networking. Indeed, it is unlikely that an operating system could survive if it could not operate in a network. Note that it is the kernel, or to be precise a unit within the kernel, that manages network connections and, therefore, it is more exact to say that the actual networking functionality is provided by the kernel.

Since the networking functionality is provided by the kernel, any process in the user space can benefit from that, and it can get connected to another process residing on a different node within the network. As a programmer, you don't need to worry about the layers (physical, link, and network layers) operated by the kernel, and you can focus on the layers above them, those that relate to your code.

Every node in an IP network has an IP address. Like we said before, we have two versions of IP addresses: **IP version 4 (IPv4)** and **IP version 6 (IPv6)**. An IPv4 address consists of four segments, each of which can hold a numerical value between 0 and 255. Therefore, IPv4 addresses start from `0.0.0.0` and go up to `255.255.255.255`. As you can see, we only need 4 bytes (or 32 bits) in order to store an IPv4 address. For IPv6 addresses, this goes up to 16 bytes (or 128 bits). Also, we have private and public IP addresses, but the details are way beyond the subject of this chapter. It's sufficient for us to know that every node in an IP network has a unique IP address.

Building on the previous section, in a single LAN, every node has a link layer address together with an IP address, but we will use the IP address to make connections to that node and not the link layer address. As an example, in an Ethernet LAN, every node has two addresses; one is a MAC address and the other one is an IP address. The MAC address is used by the link layer protocols to transmit data within the LAN, and the IP address is used by the programs residing on various nodes to make network connections either within the same LAN or over a number of LANs.

The main functionality of the network layer is to connect two or more LANs. This will eventually lead to a big mesh of networks that are connected to each other, and they form a giant network with many individual LAN networks within it. In fact, such a network exists, and we know it as the internet.

Like any other network, every node that is accessible on the internet must have an IP address. But the main difference between a node that is accessible on the internet and a node that is not is that an internet node must have a public IP address, while a node that is not accessible through the internet usually has a private address.

To give an example, your home network might be connected to the internet, but an external node on the internet cannot get connected to your laptop because your laptop has a private IP address and not a public IP address. While your laptop is still accessible inside your home network, it is not available on the internet. Therefore, if your software is going to be available on the internet, it should be run on a machine that has a public IP address.

There is a tremendous amount of information about IP networking, and we are not going to cover all of it, but as a programmer it is important to know the difference between private and public addresses.

While in a network, ensuring the connectivity between the nodes is not the programmer's responsibility; it is considered part of your skillset to be able to detect network defects. This is very important because it can let you know whether a bug or misbehavior has roots in your code, or it is an infrastructure (or network) issue. That's why we have to touch on some more concepts and tools here.

The basic tool that guarantees that two hosts (nodes), either in the same LAN or located on different LANs, are capable of transmitting data, or that they can "see" each other, is the *ping* tool. You may already know of it. It sends a number of **Internet Control Message Protocol (ICMP)** packets that, if a reply is sent back, means that the other host is up, connected, and responding.

Note:
ICMP is another network layer protocol that is mainly used for monitoring and management of IP-based networks in case of connectivity or quality of service issues and failures.

Suppose you are going to check whether your computer can see the public IP address 8.8.8.8 (which it should if it is connected to the internet). The following commands will help you to check the connectivity:

```
$ ping 8.8.8.8
PING 8.8.8.8 (8.8.8.8): 56 data bytes
64 bytes from 8.8.8.8: icmp_seq=0 ttl=123 time=12.190 ms
```

```
64 bytes from 8.8.8.8: icmp_seq=1 ttl=123 time=25.254 ms
64 bytes from 8.8.8.8: icmp_seq=2 ttl=123 time=15.478 ms
64 bytes from 8.8.8.8: icmp_seq=3 ttl=123 time=22.287 ms
64 bytes from 8.8.8.8: icmp_seq=4 ttl=123 time=21.029 ms
64 bytes from 8.8.8.8: icmp_seq=5 ttl=123 time=28.806 ms
64 bytes from 8.8.8.8: icmp_seq=6 ttl=123 time=20.324 ms
^C
--- 8.8.8.8 ping statistics ---
7 packets transmitted, 7 packets received, 0.0% packet loss
round-trip min/avg/max/stddev = 12.190/20.767/28.806/5.194 ms
$
```

Shell Box 19-6: Using the ping utility to check the connectivity to the internet

As you can see in the output, it says that it has sent 7 ICMP ping packets and none of them have been lost during transmission. This means that the operating system behind the IP address 8.8.8.8 is up and responsive.

Note:
The public IP address 8.8.8.8 refers to the Google Public DNS service. More can be read here: https://en.wikipedia.org/wiki/Google_Public_DNS.

In this section, we explained how two computers can get connected via a network. Now, we are getting close to the point where two processes can actually get connected to each other and transmit data over a number of LANs. For this purpose, we need another layer on top of the network layer. That's where network programming begins.

Transport layer

So far, we have seen that two computers can get connected to each other via a stack of three layers: the physical layer, the link layer, and the network layer. For inter-process communication, we actually need two processes to be connected and talking to each other. But with two computers connected through these three layers, we can have many processes running on each of them, and any process running on the first machine might want to establish a connection with another process located on the second machine. Therefore, having a connection just based on the network layer is too general to support several distinct connections initiated by various processes.

That's why we need another layer on top of the network layer. The *transport layer* is there to address this need. While hosts are connected through the network layer, the processes running on those hosts can get connected through the transport layer established on top of the network layer. Like any other layer that has its own unique identifiers or unique addresses, this layer has a new concept as its unique identifier, usually known as a *port*. We will elaborate more on this in the upcoming sections, but before that, we have to explain the *listener-connector* model, which allows two parties to communicate over a channel. In the next section, we start to explain this model by giving an analogy between computer networks and telephone networks.

Analogy of telephone networks

The best example to start with is the **Public Switched Telephone Network** (or **PSTN**). While the similarity between computer networks and telephone networks might not seem very promising, there are strong similarities that allow us to explain the transport layer in a sensible fashion.

In our analogy, the people using the telephone network are like processes in a computer network. Therefore, a telephone call is equivalent to a *transport connection*. The people are able to make calls only if the necessary infrastructure has been installed. This is analogous to the networking infrastructure that should be in place in order to enable processes to communicate.

We suppose that the required underlying infrastructure is in place and it works perfectly and, based on that, we want to have two entities residing in these systems to make a channel and transmit data. This is analogous to two people in the PSTN and two processes residing on two different hosts in a computer network.

Anyone who wants to use PSTN needs to have a telephone device. This is analogous to the requirement of having a NIC for a computer node. On top of these devices, there are multiple layers consisting of various protocols. These layers building up the underlying infrastructure make the creation of a transport channel possible.

Now, in PSTN, one of the telephone devices that is connected to the PSTN waits until it receives a call. We call this the *listener* side. Note that a telephone device plugged into the PSTN always waits for a call signal from the network and, as soon as it receives the signal, it rings.

Now, let's talk about the other side, which makes the call. Note that making a call is equivalent to creating a transport channel. The other side also has a telephone device that is used to make a call. The listener is accessible through a telephone number, which can be thought of as the address of the listener. The *connector* side must know this telephone number in order to make the call. Therefore, the connector dials the listener's telephone number and the underlying infrastructure lets the listener know that there is an incoming call.

When the listener side answers the telephone, it accepts the incoming connection and a channel is established between the listener and the connector. From now on, it is up to the people sitting at each end to talk and continue the discussion over the created PSTN channel. Note that if one of the parties cannot understand the language of the other party, the communication cannot continue and one of the parties hangs up the phone, and the channel would be destroyed.

Connection-less versus connection-oriented transport communication

The preceding analogy tries to explain the transport communication in a computer network but, in fact, it describes *connection-oriented communication*. Here, we are going to introduce and describe another type of communication: *connection-less communication*. But before that, let's have a deeper look at connection-oriented communication.

In connection-oriented communication, a specific and dedicated channel is created for a connector. Therefore, if we have one listener communicating with three connectors, we have three dedicated channels. It doesn't matter how big the transmitting message is, the message will reach the other party in the correct form without any loss inside the channel. If multiple messages are sent to the same location, the order of the sent messages is preserved, and the receiving process won't notice any disturbances in the underlying infrastructure.

As we've explained in the previous sections, any message is always broken into smaller chunks called packets while being transmitted over a computer network. In a connection-oriented scheme however, none of the parties, neither the listener nor the connector, will notice anything about the underlying *packet switching*. Even if the sent packets are received in a different order, the receiver's operating system will rearrange the packets in order to reconstruct the message in its true form, and the receiver process won't notice anything.

More than that, if one of the packets gets lost while being transmitted, the receiver's operating system will request it again in order to revive the full message. As an example, **Transport Control Protocol (TCP)** is a transport layer protocol that behaves exactly as we have explained above. Therefore, TCP channels are connection-oriented.

Along with connection-oriented channels, we also have connection-less communication. In connection-oriented communication, we guarantee two factors: the *delivery* of the individual packets, and the *sequence* of the packets. A connection-oriented transport protocol such as TCP preserves these factors at the same time. Conversely, a connection-less transport protocol doesn't guarantee them.

In other words, you might have no guarantee for the delivery of the individual packets that the message is broken into, or you might not have a guarantee that all the packets will be in the correct order. Or you might not have both! For instance, the **User Datagram Protocol (UDP)** doesn't guarantee packet delivery or the order of the packets. Note that the guarantee of the correctness of contents of an individual packet is provided by the protocol in the network layer and the link layer.

Now it's time to explain two terms that are commonly used in network programming. The *stream* is the sequence of bytes that is transmitted over a connection-oriented channel. This means that connection-less transmission effectively doesn't offer a stream of data. We have a specific term for a unit of data being transmitted over a connection-less channel. We call it a *datagram*. A datagram is a piece of data that can be delivered as a whole in a connection-less channel. Any piece of data bigger than the maximum datagram size cannot be surely delivered or the final sequence might be wrong. Datagram is a concept defined in the transport layer, and it is the counterpart concept to packet in the network layer.

For instance, regarding UDP packets, it is guaranteed that every individual UDP datagram (packet) is transmitted correctly, but nothing more can be said about the correlation between two adjacent datagrams (packets). It is accepted that no integrity should exist beyond a UDP datagram, but this is not true of TCP. In TCP, because of the guarantee of delivery and preserving the sequence of the sent packets, we can put individual packets aside and look at it as a stream of bytes being transmitted between two processes.

Transport initialization sequences

In this subsection, we are going to talk about the steps that each process takes in order to establish a transport communication. We have different sequences for connection-oriented and connection-less schemes, so we are going to talk about them in two following subsections separately. Note that the difference appears only in the initialization of the channel, and after that, both sides will use more or less the same API in order to read from and write to the created channel.

The listener process always *binds* an endpoint (usually an IP address together with a port) and the connector process always *connects* to that endpoint. This is regardless of being a connection-oriented or a connection-less channel.

Note that in the following sequences, we have assumed that there is an IP network established between the computers hosting the listener and connector processes.

Connection-less initialization sequences

In order to establish a connection-less communication channel, the listener process will do the following:

1. The listener process binds a port on one of existing NICs, or even all of them. This means that the listener process asks its host operating system to redirect the incoming data to that port and, hence, to the listener process. The port is simply a number between 0 and 65535 (2 bytes) and must not be already bound by another listener process. Trying to bind a port that's already in use results in an error. Note that in the case of binding a port on a specific NIC, the operating system will redirect all incoming packets that are targeted at that bound port and received on that specific NIC to the listener process.

2. The process waits and reads the messages that become available on the created channel and responds to them by writing back to the channel.

And the connector process will do the following:

3. It must know the IP address and the port number of the listener process. Therefore, it tries to connect to the listener side by providing the IP address and the port number to its host operating system. If the target process is not listening on the specified port, or the IP address points to an invalid or the wrong host, the connection will fail.

4. When the connection is successfully established, the connector process can write to the channel and read from it in almost the same way, meaning the same API that the listener process uses.

Note that beside taking the preceding steps, the listener and connector processes should both be using the same transport protocol, otherwise the messages cannot be read and understood by their host operating systems.

Connection-oriented initialization sequences

In a connection-oriented scenario, the listener process will follow the following sequence in order to get initialized:

1. Bind a port, just like the connection-less scenario explained previously. The port is exactly the same as explained in the previous section and it follows the same constraints.

2. The listener process continues by configuring the size of its *backlog*. The backlog is a queue of pending connections that are not accepted yet by the listener process. In connection-oriented communication, the listener side should accept incoming connections before being able to transmit any data. After configuring the backlog, the listener process enters *listening mode*.

3. Now, the listener process begins to *accept* incoming connections. This is an essential step in establishing a transport channel. Only after accepting an incoming connection can they transmit data. Note that if the connector process sends a connection to the listener process, but the listener process cannot accept that connection, it will remain in the backlog until it gets either accepted or *timed out*. This can happen when the listener process is too busy with other connections and it cannot accept any further new connection. Then, the incoming connections will pile up in the backlog and when the backlog becomes full, new connections will be rejected immediately by the host operating system.

The sequence of the connector process is very similar to what we explained for the connection-less communication in the previous section. The connector connects to a certain endpoint by providing the IP address and the port, and after being accepted by the listener process, it can use the same API to read from and write to the connection-oriented channel.

Since the established channel is connection-oriented, the listener process has a dedicated channel to the connector side; therefore, they can exchange a stream of bytes that doesn't have an upper limit in terms of the number of bytes. Therefore, the two processes can transmit a huge amount of data, and its correctness is guaranteed by the governing transport and network protocols.

As the last note about the transport layer, we mentioned that the listener processes (regardless of the underlying channel being connection-oriented and connection-less) are required to bind an endpoint. Regarding UDP and TCP specifically, this endpoint is made up of an IP address and a port number.

Application layer

When a transport channel is established between two processes residing on two different ends, they should be able to talk to each other. By talking, we mean transmitting a series of bytes that can be understood by both ends. As we explained in the earlier sections in this chapter, a communication protocol is required here. Since this protocol resides in the *application layer* and it is used by the processes (or the applications running as processes), it is called an *application protocol*.

While there aren't many protocols used in link, network, and transport layers and they are mostly well-known, we have numerous application protocols that are used in the application layer. This is again analogous to telecommunication networks. While there aren't many standards for telephone networks, the number of languages that people use to communicate is large, and they differ greatly. In computer networks, every application run as a process needs to use an application protocol in order to communicate with another process.

Therefore, the programmers either use a well-known application protocol such as HTTP or FTP or they have to use a custom application protocol that is designed and built locally within a team.

So far, we have discussed five layers; physical, link, network, transport, and application. Now it's time to put all of them into a single body and use it as a reference to design and deploy computer networks. In the following section, we talk about the internet protocol suite.

Internet protocol suite

The network model that we see every day and that is widely applied is the **Internet Protocol Suite (IPS)**. IPS is mainly used on the internet, and since pretty much all computers want to have access to the internet, they have universally adapted to use IPS, which is not officially the standard approved by ISO. The standard model for computer networks is **Open System Interconnections (OSI)** model, which is more a theoretical model and is almost never publicly deployed and used. IPS has the following layers. Note that the prominent protocols in each layer are mentioned in the following list:

- Physical layer
- Link layer: Ethernet, IEEE 802.11 Wi-Fi
- Internet layer: IPv4, IPv6, and ICMP
- Transport layer: TCP, UDP
- Application layer: Numerous protocols such as HTTP, FTP, DNS, and DHCP, and so on.

As you can see, the layers have a nice correspondence to the layers that we discussed in this chapter, but with only one exception; the network layer is renamed the internet layer. This is because as part of IPS, the network protocols that are prominent in this layer are only IPv4 and IPv6. The rest of the explanations can be applied to IPS layers. IPS is the main model that we will be dealing with throughout this book and in the actual work environment.

Now that we know how computer networks work, we are in a good position to proceed and see what *socket programming* is. As part of the rest of this chapter and the upcoming chapter, you will see that there is a deep correspondence between the concepts discussed in the transport layer and the concepts we have in socket programming.

What is socket programming?

Now that we know about the IPS model and the various network layers, it is much easier to explain what socket programming is. Before delving into the technical discussions regarding the socket programming, we should define it as an IPC technique that allows us to connect two processes residing on either the same node or two different nodes having a network connectivity between them. If we put the single-host socket programming aside, the other form requires us to have an operational network between the two nodes. This very fact ties socket programming with computer networks and all we have explained so far.

To make it more technical, we should say that socket programming mainly happens in the transport layer. As we have already said, the transport layer is responsible for connecting two processes over an existing internet layer (network layer). Therefore, the transport layer is the key layer for establishing a socket programming context. Basically, that's why you as a programmer should know more about the transport layer and its various protocols. Some socket programming-related bugs have their origins in the underlying transport channel.

In socket programming, sockets are the main tools for establishing a transport channel. Note that despite what we have discussed so far, socket programming can go beyond transport layer or *process-to-process communications* and it can include internet layer (network layer) or *host-to-host communications* as well. This means that we can have internet-layer-specific sockets as well as transport layer sockets. With this in mind, most of the sockets that we see and work with are transport sockets and for the rest of this chapter and the next chapter, we will mainly be talking about transport sockets.

What is a socket?

As we have explained in the previous section, the transport layer is where the actual socket programming is taking place. Everything above it just makes the socket programming more specific; however, the actual underlying channel has been established in the transport layer.

We also discussed that the internet connection (network connection) on which the transport channel has been established is actually the connection between the operating systems, or more specifically the kernels of those operating systems. Therefore, there should be a concept in the kernel that resembles a connection. More than that, there could be many established connections initiated or accepted by the same kernel simply because there can be several processes running and hosted in that operating system and willing to have network connections.

The concept that we are looking for is the *socket*. For any established or soon-to-be-established connection in a system, there is a dedicated socket that identifies that connection. For a single connection made between two processes, there is exactly one socket on each side that addresses the same connection. As we explained before, one of these sockets belongs to the connector side and the other one belongs to the listener side. The API that allows us to define and manage a socket object is described by the *socket library* exposed by the operating system.

Since we are mainly talking about POSIX systems, we expect to have such a socket library as part of the POSIX API and, in fact, we do have such a library. In the rest of this chapter, we discuss the *POSIX socket library* and we explain how it can be used to establish a connection between two processes.

POSIX socket library

Every socket object has three attributes: *domain*, *type*, and *protocol*. While the manual pages of an operating system explain these attributes very well, we want to talk about some of the values that are commonly used for these attributes. We start with the domain attribute, which is also known as **address family (AF)** or **protocol family (PF)**. Some of the values that are widely used can be seen in the following list. Note that these address families support both connection-oriented and connection-less transport connections.

- `AF_LOCAL` or `AF_UNIX`: These are local sockets, which work only when both connector and listener processes are located on the same host.

- `AF_INET`: These sockets allow two processes to connect to each other over an IPv4 connection.

- `AF_INET6`: These sockets allow two processes to connect to each other over an IPv6 connection.

Note:
In some POSIX systems, in the constants used for the domain attribute, you might find the prefix `PF_` instead of `AF_`. It is often the case that `AF_` constants have the same values as `PF_` constants, so they can be used interchangeably.

In the next chapter, we will demonstrate the usage of the `AF_UNIX` and `AF_INET` domains, but it should be easy to find examples that use the `AF_INET6` domain. Also, there could be address families that are specific to a certain operating system and cannot be found on other systems.

The most well-known values for the type attribute of a socket object are as follows:

- SOCK_STREAM: This means that the socket will represent a connection-oriented transport communication that guarantees delivery, correctness, and the order of the sent content. As we've explained streams in the previous sections, the term STREAM also suggests this. Note that, at this point, you cannot predict that the actual underlying transport protocol is TCP because this is not true regarding local sockets that belong to the AF_UNIX address family.

- SOCK_DGRAM: This means that the socket will represent a connection-less transport communication. Note that the term datagram, abbreviated as DGRAM, like we explained in the previous sections, refers to a series of bytes that cannot be seen as a stream. Instead, they can be seen as some individual chunks of data that are called datagrams. In a more technical context, a datagram represents a packet of data transmitted over a network.

- SOCK_RAW: A raw socket can represent both connection-oriented and connection-less channels. The main difference between SOCK_RAW and SOCK_DGRAM or SOCK_STREAM is that the kernel actually knows about the underlying used transport protocol (UDP or TCP) and it can parse a packet and extract the header and the content. But with a raw socket, it doesn't do so, and it is up to the program that has opened the socket to read and extract various sections.

  In other words, when using SOCK_RAW, the packets are delivered directly to the program and it should extract and understand the packet structure itself. Note that if the underlying channel is a stream channel (connection-oriented), the recovery of lost packets and packet reordering are not done by the kernel, and the program should do them itself. This implies that recovery and packet reordering are actually done by the kernel when you select TCP as your transport protocol.

The third attribute, protocol, identifies the protocol that should be used for the socket object. Since most address families, together with the type, determine a certain protocol, this attribute can be chosen by the operating system upon the socket creation. In circumstances when we have multiple possible protocols, this attribute should be defined.

Socket programming offers solutions for both single-host and multiple-host IPC. In other words, while it is quite possible to connect two processes located on two different hosts and in two different LANs using internet (network) sockets, it is totally possible to connect two processes residing on the same host using Unix domain sockets.

As the last note in this section, we should add that socket connections are bidirectional and full-duplex. This means that both parties can read from and write to the underlying channel without interfering with the other end. This is a desired feature because it is usually a requirement in most IPC-related scenarios.

Now that you have been introduced to the concept of sockets, we have to revisit the sequences that we explained in the previous sections regarding listener and connector processes. But this time, we dive into more detail and describe how sockets can be used to perform these sequences.

Revisiting listener-connector sequences

As we mentioned before, as part of computer networks, in almost every connection one of the ends is always listening for incoming connections, and the other end tries to connect to the listener side. We also discussed an example regarding a telephone network, explaining how a telephone is used to listen to an incoming call, and how it can be used to make calls and connect to other listening devices. A similar situation exists in socket programming. Here, we want to explore the sequences that should be followed by the processes at two different ends in order to establish a successful transport connection.

In the following subsections, we will go deeper into the details of socket creation and the various operations that should be performed by both processes that want to engage in a connection. The sequences explained in the following subsections for the listener and connector processes are infrastructure agnostic and benefit from the generalization that socket programming provides over the various underlying transport connections.

As you should remember, we discussed the listener and connector sequences regarding connection-oriented and connection-less communications separately. We take the same approach here, and we firstly start with the stream (connection-oriented) listener sequence.

Stream listener sequence

The following steps should be followed by a process that wants to listen for new stream connections. You have been introduced to the binding, listening, and accepting phases in the previous sections, but here we will talk about them from a socket programming perspective. Note that most of the actual functionality is provided by the kernel and the process only needs to call the right functions from the socket library in order to put itself into listening mode:

1. The process should create a socket object using the `socket` function. This socket object is usually called a *listener socket*. The socket object represents the whole listener process, and it will be used to accept new connections. Depending on the underlying channel, the arguments sent to the `socket` function can vary. We could pass either `AF_UNIX` or `AF_INET` as the address family of the socket, but we have to use `SOCK_STREAM` as the type of the socket because we are going to have a stream channel. The protocol attribute of the socket object can be determined by the operating system. For example, if you choose `AF_INET` and `SOCK_STREAM` for a socket object, TCP will be selected by default for the protocol attribute.

2. Now, the socket must be bound to an *endpoint* that is reachable by the connector processes using the bind function. The details of the chosen endpoint heavily depend on the chosen address family. For example, for an internet channel, the endpoint should be a combination of an IP address and a port. For a Unix domain socket, the endpoint should be the path to a *socket file* located on the filesystem.

3. The socket must be configured for listening. Here, we use the listen function. As we have explained before, it simply creates a backlog for the listener socket. The backlog is a list of awaiting connections that have not yet been accepted by the listener process. While the listener process cannot accept new incoming connections, the kernel will keep the incoming connections in the corresponding backlog until the listener process becomes free and starts to accept them. Once the backlog is full, any further incoming connections will be rejected by the kernel. Choosing a low size for the backlog can lead to many connections being rejected when the listener process is congested and choosing a large size can lead to a pile of awaiting connections that will eventually get timed out and disconnected. The backlog size should be chosen according to the dynamics of the listener program.

4. After configuring the backlog, it is time to accept the incoming connections. For every incoming connection, the accept function should be called. Therefore, it is a widely used pattern to have the accept called in a never-ending loop. Whenever the listener process stops accepting new connections, the connector processes are put into the backlog and once the backlog is full, they get rejected. Note that every call to the accept function simply picks up the next connection waiting in the socket's backlog. If the backlog is empty and if the listener socket is configured to be blocking, then any call to the accept function will be blocked until a new connection comes in.

Note that the accept function returns a new socket object. This means that the kernel dedicates a new unique socket object to every accepted connection. In other words, a listener process that has accepted 100 clients is using at least 101 sockets: 1 for the listener socket and 100 sockets for its incoming connections. The returned socket from the accept function should be used for further communication with the client sitting at the other end of the channel.

Note that this sequence of function calls remains the same for all types of the stream (connection-oriented) socket-based IPC. In the next chapter, we show real examples of how these steps should be programmed using C. In the next subsection, we deal with the stream connector sequence.

Stream connector sequence

When the connector process wants to connect to a listener process that is already in listening mode, it should follow the following sequence. Note that the listener process should be in listening mode, otherwise the connection will get refused by the kernel of the target host:

1. The connector process should create a socket by calling the `socket` function. This socket will be used to connect to the target process. The characteristics of this socket should be similar or at least compatible with those we set for the listener socket, otherwise, we cannot establish a connection. Therefore, we need to set the same address family that we set for the listener socket. And the type should remain `SOCK_STREAM`.

2. Then it should use the `connect` function by passing the arguments that uniquely identify the listener endpoint. The listener endpoint should be reachable by the connector process and it should have been made available by the target process. If the `connect` function succeeds, it means that the connection has been accepted by the target process. Before this point, the connection might be waiting in the backlog of the target process. If the specified target endpoint is not available for any reason, the connection will fail, and the connector process will receive an error.

Just like `accept` function call in the listener process, the `connect` function returns a socket object. This socket identifies the connection and should be used for further communication with the listener process. In the upcoming chapter, we will give a demonstration of the preceding sequences in the calculator example.

Datagram listener sequence

A datagram listener process will do the following in order to get initialized:

1. Like the stream listener, the datagram listener process creates a socket object by calling the `socket` function. But this time, it must set the socket's type attribute as `SOCK_DGRAM`.

2. Now that the listener socket has been created, the listener process should bind it to an endpoint. The endpoint and its constraints are very similar to the stream listener end. Note that there won't be a listening mode or an accepting phase for a datagram listener socket because the underlying channel is connection-less, and we can't have a dedicated session for each incoming connection.

As explained, there is no listening mode or accepting phase with a datagram server socket. Also, the datagram listeners should use the `recvfrom` and `sendto` functions in order to read from and write back to a connector process. Reads can still be done using the `read` function, but writing the responses cannot be done just using a simple `write` function call. You will see why when we look at the datagram listener example as part of the upcoming chapter.

Datagram connector sequence

A datagram connector has almost the same sequence as a stream connector. The only difference is the socket type, which must be `SOCK_DGRAM` for the datagram connector. One special case for datagram Unix domain connector sockets is that they have to bind to a Unix domain socket file in order to receive the responses from the server. We will elaborate on this in the upcoming chapter as part of the datagram calculator example when using Unix domain sockets.

Now that we have gone through all the possible sequences, it's time to explain how sockets and *socket descriptors* are related. This is last section in this chapter, and by starting the next chapter, we will be giving real C examples that cover all the sequences.

Sockets have their own descriptors!

Unlike other push-based IPC techniques that work with file descriptors, socket-based techniques deal with socket objects. Every socket object is referred to by an integer value, which is a socket descriptor inside the kernel. This socket descriptor can be used to refer to the underlying channel.

Note that file descriptors and socket descriptors are different. File descriptors refer to a regular file or a device file while socket descriptors refer to socket objects created by `socket`, `accept`, and `connect` function calls.

While the file descriptors and socket descriptors are different, we still can use the same API or set of functions to read from and write to them. Therefore, it is possible to use `read` and `write` functions to work with sockets just like files.

These descriptors have another similarity; both of them can be configured to be non-blocking via the same API. Non-blocking descriptors can be used to work with the behind file or socket in a non-blocking fashion.

Summary

In this chapter, we started to talk about IPC techniques that allow two processes to communicate and transmit data. Our discussion in this chapter will be complete in the upcoming chapter where we talk specifically about socket programming, and we will give various real C examples.

As part of this chapter, we covered the following topics:

- Pull-based and push-based IPC techniques and how they are different and similar.

- We compared single-host IPC techniques versus multiple-host IPC techniques.

- You learned about communication protocols and their various characteristics.

- We went over the serialization and deserialization concepts and how they operate to fulfill a certain communication protocol.

- We explained how the content, length, and the sequentiality features of protocols can affect receiver processes.

- We explained POSIX pipes and demonstrated how to use them with an example.

- You saw what a POSIX message queue is and how it can be used to enable two processes to communicate.

- We briefly explained Unix domain sockets and their basic properties.

- We explained what computer networks are and how the stack of various network layers can lead to a transport connection.

- We explained what socket programming is.

- We explained the initialization sequences of listener and connector processes and the steps they take to become initialized.

- We compared file descriptors and socket descriptors.

In the next chapter, we continue our discussion about socket programming with a focus on providing real C examples. We will define an example of a calculator client and a calculator server. After that, we will use both Unix domain sockets and internet sockets to establish a fully functional client-server communication between the calculator client and its server.

Chapter 20

Socket Programming

In the previous chapter, we discussed single-host IPC and gave an introduction to socket programming. In this chapter, we want to complete our introduction and address socket programming in depth using a real client-server example: the calculator project.

The order of topics in this chapter might seem a bit unusual, but the purpose is to give you a better understanding about various types of sockets and how they behave in a real project. As part of this chapter, we discuss the following topics:

- Firstly, we give a review on what we explained in the previous chapter. Note that this review is just a short recap, and it is a must for you to read the second part of the previous chapter dedicated to socket programming.

- As part of the recap we discuss various types of sockets, stream and datagram sequences, and some other topics that are essential for our continuation of our calculator example.

- The client-server example, the calculator project, is described and fully analyzed. This prepares us to continue with various components in the example and to present C code.

- As a critical component of the example, a serializer/deserializer library is developed. This library is going to represent the main protocol used between a calculator client and its server.

- It is crucial to understand that a calculator client and a calculator server must be able to communicate over any type of socket. Therefore, we present various types of sockets integrated within the example and as the starting point, **Unix domain sockets (UDS)** are introduced.

- We show in our example how they are used to establish a client-server connection in a single-host setup.

- To continue with other types of sockets, we discuss network sockets. We present how TCP and UDP sockets can be integrated within the calculator project.

Let's begin the chapter with a summary of what we know about sockets and socket programming in general. It is highly recommended that you familiarize yourself with the second half of the previous chapter before delving into this chapter, as we assume some pre-existing knowledge here.

Socket programming review

In this section, we are going to discuss what sockets are, what their various types are, and generally what it means if we say that we are doing socket programming. This is going to be a short review, but it is essential to build this basis so that we can continue into deeper discussion in subsequent sections.

If you remember from the previous chapters, we have two categories of IPC techniques to be used by two or more processes to communicate and share data. The first category contains *pull-based* techniques that require an accessible *medium* (such as a shared memory or a regular file) to store data to and retrieve data from. The second category contains *push-based* techniques. These techniques require a *channel* to be established and the channel should be accessible by all processes. The main difference between these categories is regarding the way that data is retrieved from a medium in pull-based techniques, or a channel in push-based techniques.

To put it simply, in pull-based techniques, the data should be pulled or read from the medium, but in push-based techniques the data is pushed or delivered to the reader process automatically. In pull-based techniques, since the processes pull data from a shared medium, it is prone to race conditions if a number of them can write to that medium.

To be more exact about push-based techniques, the data is always delivered to a buffer in the kernel and that buffer is accessible to the receiver process through using a descriptor (file or socket).

Then the receiver process can either block until some new data is available on that descriptor or it can *poll* the descriptor to see if the kernel has received some new data on that descriptor and if not, continue to some other work. The former approach is *blocking I/O* and the latter is *non-blocking I/O* or *asynchronous I/O*. In this chapter, all push-based techniques use the blocking approach.

We know that socket programming is a special type of IPC that belongs to the second category. Therefore, all socket-based IPCs are push-based. But the main characteristic that distinguishes socket programming from other push-based IPC techniques is the fact that in socket programming we use *sockets*. Sockets are special objects in Unix-like operating systems, even in Microsoft Windows which is not Unix-like, that represent *two-way channels*.

In other words, a single socket object can be used to both read from and write to the same channel. This way, two processes located at two sides of the same channel can have *two-way communication*.

In the previous chapter, we saw that sockets are represented by socket descriptors, just like files that are represented by file descriptors. While socket descriptors and file descriptors are similar in certain ways such as I/O operation and being *poll-able*, they are in fact different. A single socket descriptor always represents a channel, but a file descriptor can represent a medium such as a regular file, or a channel like a POSIX pipe. Therefore, certain operations related to files such as seek are not supported for socket descriptors, and even for a file descriptor when it represents a channel.

Socket-based communication can be *connection-oriented* or *connection-less*. In connection-oriented communication, the channel represents a *stream* of bytes being transmitted between two specific processes, while in connection-less communication, *datagrams* can be transmitted along the channel and there is no specific connection between two processes. A number of processes can use the same channel for sharing states or transmitting data.

Therefore, we have two types of channels: *stream channels* and *datagram channels*. In a program, every stream channel is represented by a *stream socket* and every datagram channel is represented by a *datagram socket*. When setting up a channel, we have to decide if it should be either stream or datagram. We shortly see that our calculator example can support both channels.

Sockets have various types. Each type of socket exists for a certain usage and a certain situation. Generally, we have two types of socket: UDS and network sockets. As you may know and as we've explained in the previous chapter, UDS can be used whenever all the processes willing to participate in an IPC are located on the same machine. In other words, UDS can be used only in single-host deployments.

In contrast, network sockets can be used in almost any deployment no matter how processes are deployed and where they are located. They can be all on the same machine, or they can be distributed throughout a network. In case of having a single-host deployment, UDS are preferred because they are faster, and they have less overhead in comparison to network sockets. As part of our calculator example, we provide the support for both UDS and network sockets.

UDS and network sockets can represent both stream and datagram channels. Therefore, we have four varieties: UDS over a stream channel, UDS over a datagram channel, network socket over a stream channel, and finally network socket over a datagram channel. All these four variations are covered by our example.

A network socket offering a stream channel is usually a TCP socket. That's because, most of the time, we are using TCP as the transport protocol for such a socket. Likewise, a network socket offering a datagram channel is usually a UDP socket. That's because, most of the time, we are using UDP as the transport protocol for such a socket. Note that UDS socket offering either stream or datagram channels don't have any specific names because there is no underlying transport protocol.

In order to write actual C code for the different types of sockets and channels, it is better to do it when you are working on a real example. That's basically why we have taken this unusual approach. This way, you'll notice the common parts between various types of sockets and the channels, and we can extract them as units of code that can be reused again. In the next section, we are going to discuss the calculator project and its internal structure.

Calculator project

We are dedicating a separate section to explain the purpose of the calculator project. It is a lengthy example and thus it will be helpful to have a firm grounding before diving into it. The project should help you to achieve the following goals:

- Observe a fully functional example that has a number of simple and well-defined functionalities.

- Extract common parts among the various types of sockets and channels and have them as some reusable libraries. This reduces the amount of code we write significantly, and from a learning point of view, it shows you the boundaries that are common between various types of sockets and channels.

- Maintain communication using a well-defined application protocol. Ordinary socket programming examples lack this very important feature. They generally address very simple, and usually one-time, communication scenarios between a client and its server.

- Work on an example that has all the ingredients required for a fully functional client-server program such as an application protocol, supporting various types of channels, having serializer/deserializer, and so on, giving you a different perspective regarding socket programming.

With all that being said, we are going to present this project as our main example in this chapter. We do it step by step, and I will guide you through the various steps that culminate in a complete and working project.

The first step is to come up with a relatively simple and complete application protocol. This protocol is going to be used between the clients and the server. As we explained before, without a well-defined application protocol, the two parties cannot communicate. They can be connected and transmit data because that's the functionality that the socket programming offers, but they cannot understand each other.

That's why we have to dedicate a bit of time to understand the application protocol used in the calculator project. Before talking about the application protocol, let's present the source hierarchy that can be seen in the project code base. Then, we can find the application protocol and the associated serializer/deserializer library much easier in the project code base.

Source hierarchy

From a programmer's point of view, the POSIX socket programming API treats all the stream channels the same no matter whether the associated socket object is a UDS or a network socket. If you remember from the previous chapter, for stream channels, we had certain sequences for the listener-side and for the connector-side, and these sequences remain the same for different types of stream sockets.

Therefore, if you are going to support various types of sockets, together with various types of channels, it is better to extract the common part and write it once. That's exactly the approach that we take regarding the calculator project and that's what you see in the source code. Therefore, it is expected to see various libraries in the project and some of them contain the common code that is reused by other parts of the code.

Now, it's time to delve into the code base. First of all, the source code of the project can be found here: `https://github.com/PacktPublishing/Extreme-C/tree/master/ch20-socket-programming`. If you open the link and have a look at the code base, you see there are a number of directories that contain multiple source files. Obviously, we cannot demonstrate all of them because this would take too long, but we are going to explain important parts of the code. You are encouraged to look at the code and go through it, then try to build and run it; this will give you an idea of how the example has been developed.

Note that all the code relating to the examples of UDS, UDP sockets, and TCP sockets has been put in a single hierarchy. Next, we are going to explain the source hierarchy and the directories you find as part of the code base.

If you go to the root of the example and use the `tree` command to show the files and directories, you will find something similar to *Shell Box 20-1*.

The following shell box demonstrates how to clone the book's GitHub repository and how to navigate to the root of the example:

```
$ git clone https://github.com/PacktPublishing/Extreme-C
Cloning into 'Extreme-C'...
...
Resolving deltas: 100% (458/458), done.
$ cd Extreme-C/ch20-socket-programming
$ tree
.
├── CMakeLists.txt
├── calcser
...
├── calcsvc
...
├── client
│   ├── CMakeLists.txt
│   ├── clicore
...
│   ├── tcp
│   │   ├── CMakeLists.txt
│   │   └── main.c
│   ├── udp
│   │   ├── CMakeLists.txt
│   │   └── main.c
│   └── Unix
│       ├── CMakeLists.txt
│       ├── datagram
│       │   ├── CMakeLists.txt
│       │   └── main.c
│       └── stream
│           ├── CMakeLists.txt
│           └── main.c
├── server
│   ├── CMakeLists.txt
│   ├── srvcore
...
│   ├── tcp
│   │   ├── CMakeLists.txt
```

```
|   |       └── main.c
|   ├── udp
|   |   ├── CMakeLists.txt
|   |   └── main.c
|   └── Unix
|       ├── CMakeLists.txt
|       ├── datagram
|       |   ├── CMakeLists.txt
|       |   └── main.c
|       └── stream
|           ├── CMakeLists.txt
|           └── main.c
└── types.h

18 directories, 49 files
$
```

Shell Box 20-1: Cloning the calculator project's code base and listing the files and directories

As you can see in the listing of files and directories, the calculator project is made up of a number of parts, some of them being libraries, and each of them having its own dedicated directory. Next, we explain these directories:

- /calcser: This is the serializer/deserializer library. It contains the serialization/deserialization-related source files. This library dictates the application protocol that is defined between a calculator client and a calculator server. This library is eventually built into a static library file named libcalcser.a.

- /calcsvc: This library contains the sources for the calculation service. The *calculation service* is different from the server process. This service library contains the core functionality of the calculator and it is agnostic regarding being behind a server process and can be used individually as a separate standalone C library. This library eventually gets built into a static library file named libcalcsvc.a.

- /server/srvcore: This library contains the sources that are common between the stream and the datagram server processes, regardless of the socket type. Therefore, all calculator server processes, whether using UDS or network sockets, and whether operating on stream or datagram channels, can rely on this common part. The final output of this library is a static library file named libsrvcore.a.

- `/server/unix/stream`: This directory contains the sources for a server program using stream channels behind a UDS. The final build result of this directory is an executable file named `unix_stream_calc_server`. This is one of the possible output executables in this project that we can use to bring up a calculator server, this one listening on a UDS to receive stream connections.

- `/server/unix/datagram`: This directory contains the sources for a server program using datagram channels behind a UDS. The final build result of this directory is an executable file named `unix_datagram_calc_server`. This is one of the possible output executables in this project that we can use to bring up a calculator server, this one listening on a UDS to receive datagram messages.

- `/server/tcp`: This directory contains the sources for a server program using stream channels behind a TCP network socket. The final build result of this directory is an executable file named `tcp_calc_server`. This is one of the possible output executables in this project that we can use to bring up a calculator server, this one listening on a TCP socket to receive stream connections.

- `/server/udp`: This directory contains the sources for a server program using datagram channels behind a UDP network socket. The final build result of this directory is an executable file named `udp_calc_server`. This is one of the possible output executables in this project that we can use to bring up a calculator server, this one listening on a UDP socket to receive datagram messages.

- `/client/clicore`: This library contains the sources that are common between the stream and the datagram client processes, regardless of the socket type. Therefore, all calculator client processes, no matter whether they are using UDS or network sockets, and no matter operating on stream or datagram channels, can rely on this common part. It would be built into a static library file named `libclicore.a`.

- `/client/unix/stream`: This directory contains the sources for a client program using stream channels behind a UDS. The final build result of this directory is an executable file named `unix_stream_calc_client`. This is one of the possible output executables in this project that we can use to start a calculator client, this one connecting to a UDS endpoint and establishing a stream connection.

- `/client/unix/datagram`: This directory contains the sources for a client program using datagram channels behind a UDS. The final build result of this directory is an executable file named `unix_datagram_calc_client`. This is one of the possible output executables in this project that we can use to start a calculator client, this one connecting to a UDS endpoint and sending some datagram messages.

- `/client/tcp`: This directory contains the sources for a client program using stream channels behind a TCP socket. The final build result of this directory is an executable file named `tcp_calc_client`. This is one of the possible output executables in this project that we can use to start a calculator client, this one connecting to a TCP socket endpoint and establishing a stream connection.

- `/client/udp`: This directory contains the sources for a client program using datagram channels behind a UDP socket. The final build result of this directory is an executable file named `udp_calc_client`. This is one of the possible output executables in this project that we can use to start a calculator client, this one connecting to a UDP socket endpoint and sending some datagram messages.

Build the project

Now that we have gone through all the directories in the project, we need to show how to build it. The project uses CMake, and you should have it installed before moving on to build the project.

In order to build the project, run the following commands in the chapter's root directory:

```
$ mkdir -p build
$ cd build
$ cmake ..
. . .
$ make
. . .
$
```

Shell Box 20-2: The commands to build the calculator project

Run the project

There is nothing like running a project to see for yourself how it works. Therefore, before delving into technical details, I want you to bring up a calculator server, and then a calculator client, and finally see how they talk to each other.

Before running the processes, you need to have two separate Terminals (or shells) in order to enter two separate commands. In the first Terminal, in order to run a stream server listening on UDS, type the following command.

Note that you need to be in the `build` directory before entering the following command. The `build` directory was made as part of the previous section, *Build the Project*:

```
$ ./server/unix/stream/unix_stream_calc_server
```

Ensure the server is running. In the second Terminal, run the stream client built for using UDS:

```
$ ./client/unix/stream/unix_stream_calc_client
? (type quit to exit) 3++4
The req(0) is sent.
req(0) > status: OK, result: 7.000000
? (type quit to exit) mem
The req(1) is sent.
req(1) > status: OK, result: 7.000000
? (type quit to exit) 5++4
The req(2) is sent.
req(2) > status: OK, result: 16.000000
? (type quit to exit) quit
Bye.
$
```

Shell Box 20-4: Running the calculator client and sending some requests

As you see in the preceding shell box, the client process has its own command line. It receives some commands from the user, turns them into some requests according to the application protocol, and sends them to the server for further processing. Then, it waits for the response and, as soon as it receives it, prints the result. Note that this command line is part of the common code written for all clients and therefore, no matter the channel type or socket type the client is using, you always see the client command line.

Now, it's time to jump into the details of the application protocol and see how request and response messages look like.

Application protocol

Any two processes willing to communicate must obey an application protocol. This protocol can be custom, like the calculator project, or it can be one of the well-known protocols like HTTP. We call our protocol the *calculator protocol*.

The calculator protocol is a variable-length protocol. In other words, every message has its own length and every message should be separated from the next one using a delimiter. There is only one type of request message and one type of response message. The protocol is also textual. It means that we use only alphanumerical characters together with a few other characters as valid characters in request and response messages. In other words, the calculator messages are human-readable.

The request message has four fields: *request ID*, *method*, *first operand*, and *second operand*. Every request has a unique ID and the server uses this ID to relate a response to its corresponding request.

The method is an operation that can be performed by the calculator service. Next, you can see the `calcser/calc_proto_req.h` header file. This file describes the calculator protocol's request message:

```
#ifndef CALC_PROTO_REQ_H
#define CALC_PROTO_REQ_H

#include <stdint.h>

typedef enum {
  NONE,
  GETMEM, RESMEM,
  ADD, ADDM,
  SUB, SUBM,
  MUL, MULM,
  DIV
} method_t;

struct calc_proto_req_t {
  int32_t id;
  method_t method;
  double operand1;
  double operand2;
};

method_t str_to_method(const char*);
const char* method_to_str(method_t);

#endif
```

Code Box 20-1 [calcser/calc_proto_req.h]: Definition of the calculator request object

As you can see, we have nine methods defined as part of our protocol. As a good calculator, our calculator has an internal memory, and because of that we have memory operations associated with addition, subtraction, and multiplication.

For example, the ADD method simply adds two float numbers, but the ADDM method is a variation of the ADD method that adds those two numbers together with the value stored in the internal memory, and finally it updates the value in the memory for further use. It is just like when you use the memory button on your desktop calculator. You can find that button marked as +M.

We also have a special method for reading and resetting the calculator's internal memory. The division method cannot be performed on the internal memory, so we don't have any other variation.

Suppose that the client wants to create a request with ID 1000, using the ADD method, and with 1.5 and 5.6 as the operands. In C, it needs to create an object from the calc_proto_req_t type (the structure declared in the preceding header as part of *Code Box 20-1*) and fill it with the desired values. Next, you can see how to do it:

```
struct calc_proto_req_t req;
req.id = 1000;
req.method = ADD;
req.operand1 = 1.5;
req.operand2 = 5.6;
```

Code Box 20-2: Creating a calculator request object in C

As we explained in the previous chapter, the req object in the preceding code box needs to be serialized to a request message before being sent to the server. In other words, we need to serialize the preceding *request object* to the equivalent *request message*. The serializer in the calculator project, according to our application protocol, serializes the req object as follows:

```
1000#ADD#1.5#5.6$
```

Code Box 20-3: The serialized message equivalent to the req object defined in Code Box 20-2

As you can see, the # character is used as the *field delimiter*, and the $ character is used as the *message separator*. In addition, each request message has exactly four fields. A *deserializer* object on the other side of the channel uses these facts to parse the incoming bytes and revive the request object again.

Conversely, the server process needs to serialize the response object while replying to a request. A calculator response object has three fields: *request ID*, *status*, and *result*. The request ID determines the corresponding request. Every request has a unique ID and this way, the server specifies the request that it wants to respond to.

The `calcser/calc_proto_resp.h` header file describes what a calculator response should look like, and you can see it in the following code box:

```
#ifndef CALC_PROTO_RESP_H
#define CALC_PROTO_RESP_H

#include <stdint.h>

#define STATUS_OK               0
#define STATUS_INVALID_REQUEST  1
#define STATUS_INVALID_METHOD   2
#define STATUS_INVALID_OPERAND  3
#define STATUS_DIV_BY_ZERO      4
#define STATUS_INTERNAL_ERROR   20

typedef int status_t;

struct calc_proto_resp_t {
  int32_t req_id;
  status_t status;
  double result;
};

#endif
```

Code Box 20-4 [calcser/calc_proto_resp.h]: Definition of the calculator response object

Similarly, in order to create a *response object* for the preceding request object, `req`, mentioned in *Code Box 20-2*, the server process should do this:

```
struct calc_proto_resp_t resp;
resp.req_id = 1000;
resp.status = STATUS_OK;
resp.result = 7.1;
```

Code Box 20-5: Creating a response object for the request object req defined as part of Code Box 20-2

The preceding response object is serialized as follows:

```
1000#0#7.1$
```

Code Box 20-6: The serialized response message equivalent to the resp object created in the Code Box 20-5

Again, we use # as the field delimiter and $ as the message separator. Note that the status is numerical, and it indicates the success or failure of the request. In the case of failure, it is a non-zero number, and its meaning is described in the response header file, or to be exact, in the calculator protocol.

Now, it is time to talk a bit more about the serialization/deserialization library and what its internals look like.

Serialization/deserialization library

In the previous section, we described how the request and response messages look like. In this section, we are going to talk a bit more about the serializer and deserializer algorithms used in the calculator project. We are going to use the `serializer` class, with `calc_proto_ser_t` as its attribute structure, for providing the serialization and deserialization functionalities.

As said before, these functionalities are provided to other parts of the project as a static library named `libcalcser.a`. Here, you can see the public API of the `serializer` class found in `calcser/calc_proto_ser.h`:

```c
#ifndef CALC_PROTO_SER_H
#define CALC_PROTO_SER_H

#include <types.h>

#include "calc_proto_req.h"
#include "calc_proto_resp.h"

#define ERROR_INVALID_REQUEST            101
#define ERROR_INVALID_REQUEST_ID         102
#define ERROR_INVALID_REQUEST_METHOD     103
#define ERROR_INVALID_REQUEST_OPERAND1   104
#define ERROR_INVALID_REQUEST_OPERAND2   105


#define ERROR_INVALID_RESPONSE           201
#define ERROR_INVALID_RESPONSE_REQ_ID    202
#define ERROR_INVALID_RESPONSE_STATUS    203
#define ERROR_INVALID_RESPONSE_RESULT    204


#define ERROR_UNKNOWN   220

struct buffer_t {
  char* data;
  int len;
};

struct calc_proto_ser_t;

typedef void (*req_cb_t)(
        void* owner_obj,
        struct calc_proto_req_t);
```

```
typedef void (*resp_cb_t)(
        void* owner_obj,
        struct calc_proto_resp_t);

typedef void (*error_cb_t)(
        void* owner_obj,
        const int req_id,
        const int error_code);

struct calc_proto_ser_t* calc_proto_ser_new();
void calc_proto_ser_delete(
        struct calc_proto_ser_t* ser);

void calc_proto_ser_ctor(
        struct calc_proto_ser_t* ser,
        void* owner_obj,
        int ring_buffer_size);

void calc_proto_ser_dtor(
        struct calc_proto_ser_t* ser);

void* calc_proto_ser_get_context(
        struct calc_proto_ser_t* ser);

void calc_proto_ser_set_req_callback(
        struct calc_proto_ser_t* ser,
        req_cb_t cb);

void calc_proto_ser_set_resp_callback(
        struct calc_proto_ser_t* ser,
        resp_cb_t cb);
void calc_proto_ser_set_error_callback(
        struct calc_proto_ser_t* ser,
        error_cb_t cb);

void calc_proto_ser_server_deserialize(
        struct calc_proto_ser_t* ser,
        struct buffer_t buffer,
        bool_t* req_found);

struct buffer_t calc_proto_ser_server_serialize(
        struct calc_proto_ser_t* ser,
        const struct calc_proto_resp_t* resp);

void calc_proto_ser_client_deserialize(
        struct calc_proto_ser_t* ser,
        struct buffer_t buffer,
        bool_t* resp_found);
```

```
struct buffer_t calc_proto_ser_client_serialize(
        struct calc_proto_ser_t* ser,
        const struct calc_proto_req_t* req);

#endif
```

Code Box 20-7 [calcser/calc_proto_ser.h]: The public interface of the Serializer class

Apart from the constructor and destructor functions required for creating and destroying a serializer object, we have a pair of functions that should be used by the server process, and another pair of functions that should be used by the client process.

On the client side, we serialize the request object and we deserialize the response message. Meanwhile on the server side, we deserialize the request message and we serialize the response object.

In addition to serialization and deserialization functions, we have three *callback functions*:

- A callback for receiving a request object that has been deserialized from the underlying channel
- A callback for receiving a response object that has been deserialized from the underlying channel
- A callback for receiving the error when a serialization or a deserialization has failed

These callbacks are used by client and server processes to receive incoming requests and responses and also the errors that are found during serialization and deserialization of a message.

Now, let's have a deeper look at serialization/deserialization functions for the server side.

Server-side serializer/deserializer functions

We have two functions for the server process to serialize a response object and deserialize a request message. We begin with the response serialization function.

The following code box contains the code for the response serialization function calc_proto_ser_server_serialize:

```
struct buffer_t calc_proto_ser_server_serialize(
```

```
    struct calc_proto_ser_t* ser,
    const struct calc_proto_resp_t* resp) {
  struct buffer_t buff;
  char resp_result_str[64];
  _serialize_double(resp_result_str, resp->result);
  buff.data = (char*)malloc(64 * sizeof(char));
  sprintf(buff.data, "%d%c%d%c%s%c", resp->req_id,
          FIELD_DELIMITER, (int)resp->status, FIELD_DELIMITER,
      resp_result_str, MESSAGE_DELIMITER);
  buff.len = strlen(buff.data);
  return buff;
}
```

Code Box 20-8 [calcser/calc_proto_ser.c]: The server-side response serializer function

As you can see, `resp` is a pointer to a response object that needs to be serialized. This function returns a `buffer_t object`, which is declared as follows as part of the `calc_proto_ser.h` header file:

```
struct buffer_t {
  char* data;
  int len;
};
```

Code Box 20-9 [calcser/calc_proto_ser.h]: The definition of buffer_t

The serializer code is simple and it consists mainly of a `sprintf` statement that creates the response string message. Now, let's look at the request deserializer function. Deserialization is usually more difficult to implement, and if you go to the code base and follow the function calls, you see how complicated it can be.

Code Box 20-9 contains the request deserialization function:

```
void calc_proto_ser_server_deserialize(
    struct calc_proto_ser_t* ser,
    struct buffer_t buff,
    bool_t* req_found) {
  if (req_found) {
    *req_found = FALSE;
  }
  _deserialize(ser, buff, _parse_req_and_notify,
          ERROR_INVALID_REQUEST, req_found);
}
```

Code Box 20-9 [calcser/calc_proto_ser.c]: The server-side request deserialization function

The preceding function seems to be simple, but in fact it uses the _deserialize and _parse_req_and_notify private functions. These functions are defined in the calc_proto_ser.c file, which contains the actual implementation of the Serializer class.

It would be intense and beyond the scope of this book to bring in and discuss the code we have for the mentioned private functions, but to give you an idea, especially for when you want to read the source code, the deserializer uses a *ring buffer* with a fixed length and tries to find $ as the message separator.

Whenever it finds $, it calls the function pointer, which in this case points to the _parse_req_and_notify function (the third argument passed in the _deserialize function). The _parse_req_and_notify function tries to extract the fields and resurrect the request object. Then, it notifies the registered *observer*, in this case the server object that is waiting for a request through the callback functions, to proceed with the request object.

Now, let's look at the functions used by the client side.

Client-side serializer/deserializer functions

Just as for the server side, we have two functions on the client side. One for serializing the request object, and the other one meant to deserialize the incoming response.

We begin with the request serializer. You can see the definition in *Code Box 20-10*:

```
struct buffer_t calc_proto_ser_client_serialize(
    struct calc_proto_ser_t* ser,
    const struct calc_proto_req_t* req) {
  struct buffer_t buff;
  char req_op1_str[64];
  char req_op2_str[64];
  _serialize_double(req_op1_str, req->operand1);
  _serialize_double(req_op2_str, req->operand2);
  buff.data = (char*)malloc(64 * sizeof(char));
  sprintf(buff.data, "%d%c%s%c%s%c%s%c", req->id, FIELD_DELIMITER,
          method_to_str(req->method), FIELD_DELIMITER,
          req_op1_str, FIELD_DELIMITER, req_op2_str,
          MESSAGE_DELIMITER);
  buff.len = strlen(buff.data);
  return buff;
}
```

Code Box 20-10 [calcser/calc_proto_ser.c]: The client-side request serialization function

As you can see, it accepts a request object and returns a `buffer` object, totally similar to the response serializer on the server side. It even uses the same technique; a `sprintf` statement for creating the request message.

Code Box 20-11 contains the response deserializer function:

```
void calc_proto_ser_client_deserialize(
    struct calc_proto_ser_t* ser,
    struct buffer_t buff, bool_t* resp_found) {
  if (resp_found) {
    *resp_found = FALSE;
  }
  _deserialize(ser, buff, _parse_resp_and_notify,
        ERROR_INVALID_RESPONSE, resp_found);
}
```

Code Box 20-11 [calcser/calc_proto_ser.c]: The client-side response deserialization function

As you can see, the same mechanism is employed, and some similar private functions have been used. It is highly recommended to read these sources carefully, in order to get a better understanding of how the various parts of the code have been put together to have the maximum reuse of the existing parts.

We won't go any deeper than this into the `Serializer` class; it's up to you to dig into the code and finds out how it works.

Now that we have the serializer library, we can proceed and write our client and server programs. Having a library that serializes objects and deserializes messages based on an agreed application protocol is a vital step in writing multi-process software. Note that it doesn't matter if the deployment is single-host or contains multiple hosts; the processes should be able to understand each other, and proper application protocols should have been defined.

Before jumping to code regarding socket programming, we have to explain one more thing: the calculator service. It is at the heart of the server process and it does the actual calculation.

Calculator service

The calculator service is the core logic of our example. Note that this logic should work independently of the underlying IPC mechanism. The upcoming code shows the declaration of the calculator service class.

As you can see, it is designed in such a way that it can be used even in a very simple program, with just a `main` function, such that it doesn't even do any IPC at all:

```
#ifndef CALC_SERVICE_H
#define CALC_SERVICE_H

#include <types.h>

static const int CALC_SVC_OK = 0;
static const int CALC_SVC_ERROR_DIV_BY_ZERO = -1;

struct calc_service_t;

struct calc_service_t* calc_service_new();
void calc_service_delete(struct calc_service_t*);

void calc_service_ctor(struct calc_service_t*);
void calc_service_dtor(struct calc_service_t*);

void calc_service_reset_mem(struct calc_service_t*);
double calc_service_get_mem(struct calc_service_t*);
double calc_service_add(struct calc_service_t*, double, double b,
    bool_t mem);
double calc_service_sub(struct calc_service_t*, double, double b,
    bool_t mem);
double calc_service_mul(struct calc_service_t*, double, double b,
    bool_t mem);
int calc_service_div(struct calc_service_t*, double,
        double, double*);

#endif
```

Code Box 20-12 [calcsvc/calc_service.h]: The public interface of the calculator service class

As you can see, the preceding class even has its own error types. The input arguments are pure C types, and it is in no way dependent on IPC-related or serialization-related classes or types. Since it is isolated as a standalone logic, we compile it into an independent static library named `libcalcsvc.a`.

Every server process must use the calculator service objects in order to do the actual calculations. These objects are usually called the *service objects*. Because of this, the final server program must get linked against this library.

An important note before we go further: if, for a specific client, the calculations don't need a specific context, then having just one service object is enough. In other words, if a service for a client doesn't require us to remember any state from the previous requests of that client, then we can use a *singleton* service object. We call this a *stateless service object*.

Conversely, if handling the current request demands knowing something from the previous requests, then for every client, we need to have a specific service object. This is the case regarding our calculator project. As you know, the calculator has an internal memory that is unique for each client. Therefore, we cannot use the same object for two clients. These objects are known as *stateful service objects*.

To summarize what we said above, for every client, we have to create a new service object. This way, every client has its own calculator with its own dedicated internal memory. Calculator service objects are stateful and they need to load some state (the value of the internal memory).

Now, we are in a good position to move forward and talk about various types of sockets, with examples given in the context of the calculator project.

Unix domain sockets

From the previous chapter, we know that if we are going to establish a connection between two processes on the same machine, UDS are one of the best options. In this chapter, we expanded our discussion and talked a bit more about push-based IPC techniques, as well as stream and datagram channels. Now it's time to gather our knowledge from previous and current chapters and see UDS in action.

In this section, we have four subsections dedicated to processes being on the listener side or the connector side and operating on a stream or a datagram channel. All of these processes are using UDS. We go through the steps they should take to establish the channel, based on the sequences we discussed in the previous chapter. As the first process, we start with the listener process operating on a stream channel. This would be the *stream server*.

UDS stream server

If you remember from the previous chapter, we had a number of sequences for listener and connector sides in a transport communication. A server stands in the position of a listener. Therefore, it should follow the listener sequence. More specifically, since we are talking about stream channels in this section, it should follow a stream listener sequence.

As part of that sequence, the server needs to create a socket object first. In our calculator project, the stream server process willing to receive connections over a UDS must follow the same sequence.

The following piece of code is located in the main function of the calculator server program, and as can be seen in *Code Box 20-13*, the process firstly creates a `socket` object:

```
int server_sd = socket(AF_UNIX, SOCK_STREAM, 0);
if (server_sd == -1) {
  fprintf(stderr, "Could not create socket: %s\n",
strerror(errno));
  exit(1);
}
```

Code Box 20-13 [server/unix/stream/main.c]: Creating a stream UDS object

As you can see, the `socket` function is used to create a socket object. This function is included from `<sys/socket.h>`, which is a POSIX header. Note that this is just a socket object, and yet it is not determined whether this is going to be a client socket or a server socket. Only the subsequent function calls determine this.

As we explained in the previous chapter, every socket object has three attributes. These attributes are determined by the three arguments passed to the `socket` function. These arguments specify the address family, the type, and the protocol used on that socket object respectively.

According to the stream listener sequence and especially regarding the UDS after creating the socket object, the server program must bind it to a *socket file*. Therefore, the next step is to bind the socket to a socket file. *Code Box 20-14* has been used in the calculator project to bind the socket object to a file located at a predetermined path specified by the `sock_file` character array:

```
struct sockaddr_un addr;
memset(&addr, 0, sizeof(addr));
addr.sun_family = AF_UNIX;
strncpy(addr.sun_path, sock_file, sizeof(addr.sun_path) - 1);

int result = bind(server_sd, (struct sockaddr*)&addr,
sizeof(addr));
if (result == -1) {
  close(server_sd);
  fprintf(stderr, "Could not bind the address: %s\n",
strerror(errno));
  exit(1);
}
```

Code Box 20-14 [server/unix/stream/main.c]: Binding a stream UDS object to a socket file specified by the sock_file char array

The preceding code has two steps. The first step is to create an instance, named `addr`, of the type `struct sockaddr_un` and then initialize it by pointing it to a socket file. In the second step, the `addr` object is passed to the `bind` function in order to let it know which socket file should be *bound* to the socket object. The `bind` function call succeeds only if there is no other socket object bound to the same socket file. Therefore, with UDS, two socket objects, probably being in different processes, cannot be bound to the same socket file.

Note:

In Linux, UDS can be bound to *abstract socket addresses*. They are useful mainly when there is no filesystem mounted to be used for having a socket file. A string starting with a null character, `\0`, can be used to initialize the address structure, `addr` in the preceding code box, and then the provided name is bound to the socket object inside the kernel. The provided name should be unique in the system and no other socket object should be bound to it.

On a further note about the socket file path, the length of the path cannot exceed 104 bytes on most Unix systems. However, in Linux systems, this length is 108 bytes. Note that the string variable keeping the socket file path always include an extra null character at the end as a `char` array in C. Therefore, effectively, 103 and 107 bytes can be used as part of the socket file path depending on the operating system.

If the `bind` function returns `0`, it means that the binding has been successful, and you can proceed with configuring the size of the *backlog*; the next step in the stream listener sequence after binding the endpoint.

The following code shows how the backlog is configured for the stream calculator server listening on a UDS:

```
result = listen(server_sd, 10);
if (result == -1) {
  close(server_sd);
  fprintf(stderr, "Could not set the backlog: %s\n",
strerror(errno));
  exit(1);
}
```

Code Box 20-15 [server/unix/stream/main.c]: Configuring the size of the backlog for a bound stream socket

The `listen` function configures the size of the backlog for an already bound socket. As we have explained in the previous chapter, when a busy server process cannot accept any more incoming clients, a certain number of these clients can wait in the backlog until the server program can process them. This is an essential step in preparing a stream socket before accepting the clients.

According to what we have in the stream listener sequence, after having the stream socket bound and having its backlog size configured, we can start accepting new clients. *Code Box 20-16* shows how new clients can be accepted:

```
while (1) {
  int client_sd = accept(server_sd, NULL, NULL);
  if (client_sd == -1) {
    close(server_sd);
    fprintf(stderr, "Could not accept the client: %s\n",
        strerror(errno));
    exit(1);
  }
  ...
}
```

Code Box 20-16 [server/unix/stream/main.c]: Accepting new clients on a stream listener socket

The magic is the `accept` function, which returns a new socket object whenever a new client is received. The returned socket object refers to the underlying stream channel between the server and the accepted client. Note that every client has its own stream channel, and hence its own socket descriptor.

Note that if the stream listener socket is blocking (which it is by default), the `accept` function would block the execution until a new client is received. In other words, if there is no incoming client, the thread calling the `accept` function is blocked behind it.

Now, it's time to see the above steps together in just one place. The following code box shows the stream server from the calculator project, which listens on a UDS:

```
#include <stdio.h>
#include <string.h>
#include <errno.h>
#include <unistd.h>
#include <stdlib.h>
#include <pthread.h>

#include <sys/socket.h>
#include <sys/un.h>

#include <stream_server_core.h>

int main(int argc, char** argv) {
  char sock_file[] = "/tmp/calc_svc.sock";

  // ---------- 1. Create socket object ------------------
```

```
int server_sd = socket(AF_UNIX, SOCK_STREAM, 0);
if (server_sd == -1) {
  fprintf(stderr, "Could not create socket: %s\n",
          strerror(errno));
  exit(1);
}

// ---------- 2. Bind the socket file ------------------

// Delete the previously created socket file if it exists.
unlink(sock_file);

// Prepare the address
struct sockaddr_un addr;
memset(&addr, 0, sizeof(addr));
addr.sun_family = AF_UNIX;
strncpy(addr.sun_path, sock_file, sizeof(addr.sun_path) - 1);

int result = bind(server_sd,
        (struct sockaddr*)&addr, sizeof(addr));
if (result == -1) {
  close(server_sd);
  fprintf(stderr, "Could not bind the address: %s\n",
          strerror(errno));
  exit(1);
}

// ---------- 3. Prepare backlog ------------------
result = listen(server_sd, 10);
if (result == -1) {
  close(server_sd);
  fprintf(stderr, "Could not set the backlog: %s\n",
          strerror(errno));
  exit(1);
}

// ---------- 4. Start accepting clients ---------
accept_forever(server_sd);

return 0;
}
```

Code Box 20-17 [server/unix/stream/main.c]: The main function of the stream calculator service listening on a UDS endpoint

It should be easy to find the code blocks that perform the aforementioned steps in initializing a server socket. The only thing that is missing is the client-accepting code. The actual code for accepting new clients is put in a separate function that is called `accept_forever`. Note that this function is blocking and blocks the main thread until the server stops.

In the following code box, you can see the definition of the `accept_forever` function. The function is part of the server common library located in the `srvcore` directory. This function should be there because its definition remains the same for other stream sockets such as TCP sockets. Therefore, we can reuse the existing logic instead of writing it again:

```
void accept_forever(int server_sd) {
  while (1) {
    int client_sd = accept(server_sd, NULL, NULL);
    if (client_sd == -1) {
      close(server_sd);
      fprintf(stderr, "Could not accept the client: %s\n",
              strerror(errno));
      exit(1);
    }
    pthread_t client_handler_thread;
    int* arg = (int *)malloc(sizeof(int));
    *arg = client_sd;
    int result = pthread_create(&client_handler_thread, NULL,
            &client_handler, arg);
    if (result) {
      close(client_sd);
      close(server_sd);
      free(arg);
      fprintf(stderr, "Could not start the client handler
thread.\n");
      exit(1);
    }
  }
}
```

Code Box 20-18 [server/srvcore/stream_server_core.c]: The function accepting new clients on a stream socket listening on a UDS endpoint

As you can see in the preceding code box, upon accepting a new client, we spawn a new thread that is in charge of handling the client. This effectively entails reading bytes from the client's channel, passing the read bytes into the deserializer, and producing proper responses if a request has been detected.

Creating a new thread for every client is usually the pattern for every server process that operates on a blocking stream channel, no matter what the type of socket is. Therefore, in such use cases, multithreading and all the surrounding topics become enormously important.

 Note:
Regarding non-blocking stream channels, a different approach known as *event loop* is usually used.

When you have the socket object of a client, you can use it for reading from the client, as well writing to the client. If we follow the path that we've taken so far in the `srvcore` library, the next step is to look into the companion function of a client's thread; `client_handler`. The function can be found next to the `accept_forever` in the code base. Next, you can see the code box containing the function's definition:

```c
void* client_handler(void *arg) {
  struct client_context_t context;

  context.addr = (struct client_addr_t*)
      malloc(sizeof(struct client_addr_t));
  context.addr->sd = *((int*)arg);
  free((int*)arg);

  context.ser = calc_proto_ser_new();
  calc_proto_ser_ctor(context.ser, &context, 256);
  calc_proto_ser_set_req_callback(context.ser, request_callback);
  calc_proto_ser_set_error_callback(context.ser, error_callback);

  context.svc = calc_service_new();
  calc_service_ctor(context.svc);

  context.write_resp = &stream_write_resp;

  int ret;
  char buffer[128];
  while (1) {
    int ret = read(context.addr->sd, buffer, 128);
    if (ret == 0 || ret == -1) {
      break;
    }
    struct buffer_t buf;
    buf.data = buffer; buf.len = ret;
    calc_proto_ser_server_deserialize(context.ser, buf, NULL);
  }

  calc_service_dtor(context.svc);
  calc_service_delete(context.svc);

  calc_proto_ser_dtor(context.ser);
  calc_proto_ser_delete(context.ser);

  free(context.addr);

  return NULL;
}
```

Code Box 20-19 [server/srvcore/stream_server_core.c]: The companion function of the client-handling thread

There are many details regarding the preceding code, but there are a few important ones that I want to mention. As you see, we are using the `read` function to read chunks from the client. If you remember, the `read` function accepts a file descriptor but here we are passing a socket descriptor. This shows, despite the differences between file descriptors and socket descriptors, regarding I/O functions, we can use the same API.

In the preceding code, we read chunks of bytes from the input and we pass them to the deserializer by calling the `calc_proto_ser_server_deserialize` function. It is possible to call this function three or four times before having a request fully deserialized. This is highly dependent on the chunk size that you read from the input and the length of the messages transmitting on the channel.

On a further note, every client has its own serializer object. This is also true for the calculator service object. These objects are created and destroyed as part of the same thread.

And as the last note about the preceding code box, we are using a function to write responses back to the client. The function is `stream_write_response` and it is meant to be used on a stream socket. This function can be found in the same file as the preceding code boxes. Next, you can see the definition of this function:

```c
void stream_write_resp(
        struct client_context_t* context,
        struct calc_proto_resp_t* resp) {
  struct buffer_t buf =
      calc_proto_ser_server_serialize(context->ser, resp);
  if (buf.len == 0) {
    close(context->addr->sd);
    fprintf(stderr, "Internal error while serializing
response\n");
    exit(1);
  }
  int ret = write(context->addr->sd, buf.data, buf.len);
  free(buf.data);
  if (ret == -1) {
    fprintf(stderr, "Could not write to client: %s\n",
            strerror(errno));
    close(context->addr->sd);
    exit(1);
  } else if (ret < buf.len) {
    fprintf(stderr, "WARN: Less bytes were written!\n");
    exit(1);
  }
}
```

Code Box 20-20 [server/srvcore/stream_server_core.c]: The function used for writing the responses back to the client

As you see in the preceding code, we are using the `write` function to write a message back to the client. As we know, the `write` function can accept file descriptors, but it seems socket descriptors can also be used. So, it clearly shows that the POSIX I/O API works for both file descriptors and socket descriptors.

The above statement is also true about the `close` function. As you can see, we have used it to terminate a connection. It is enough to pass the socket descriptor while we know that it works for file descriptors as well.

Now that we have gone through some of the most important parts of the UDS stream server and we have an idea of how it operates, it is time to move on and discuss the UDS stream client. For sure, there are plenty places in the code that we haven't discussed but you should dedicate time and go through them.

UDS stream client

Like the server program described in the previous section, the client also needs to create a socket object first. Remember that we need to follow the stream connector sequence now. It uses the same piece of code as server does, with exactly the same arguments, to indicate that it needs a UDS. After that, it needs to connect to the server process by specifying a UDS endpoint, similarly to how the server did. When the stream channel is established, the client process can use the opened socket descriptor to read from and write to the channel.

Next, you can see the `main` function of the stream client connecting to a UDS endpoint:

```
int main(int argc, char** argv) {
  char sock_file[] = "/tmp/calc_svc.sock";

  // ---------- 1. Create socket object ------------------

  int conn_sd = socket(AF_UNIX, SOCK_STREAM, 0);
  if (conn_sd == -1) {
    fprintf(stderr, "Could not create socket: %s\n",
            strerror(errno));
    exit(1);
  }

  // ---------- 2. Connect to server ---------------------

  // Prepare the address
  struct sockaddr_un addr;
  memset(&addr, 0, sizeof(addr));
  addr.sun_family = AF_UNIX;
```

```
  strncpy(addr.sun_path, sock_file, sizeof(addr.sun_path) - 1);

  int result = connect(conn_sd,
          (struct sockaddr*)&addr, sizeof(addr));
  if (result == -1) {
    close(conn_sd);
    fprintf(stderr, "Could no connect: %s\n", strerror(errno));
    exit(1);
  }

  stream_client_loop(conn_sd);

  return 0;
}
```

Code Box 20-21 [client/unix/stream/main.c]: The main function of the stream client connecting to a UDS endpoint

As you can see, the first part of the code is very similar to the server code but afterward, the client calls `connect` instead of `bind`. Note that the address preparation code is exactly the same as that of the server.

When `connect` returns successfully, it has already associated the `conn_sd` socket descriptor to the opened channel. Therefore, from now on, `conn_sd` can be used to communicate with the server. We pass it to the `stream_client_loop` function, which brings up the client's command line and does the rest of the actions performed by the client. It is a blocking function that runs the client until it quits.

Note that the client also uses `read` and `write` functions to transmit messages back and forth from and to the server. *Code Box 20-22* contains the definition of the `stream_client_loop` function, which is part of the client common library that is used by all stream clients, regardless of the socket type and is shared between UDS and TCP sockets. As you see, it uses the `write` function to send a serialized request message to the server:

```
void stream_client_loop(int conn_sd) {
  struct context_t context;

  context.sd = conn_sd;
  context.ser = calc_proto_ser_new();
  calc_proto_ser_ctor(context.ser, &context, 128);
  calc_proto_ser_set_resp_callback(context.ser, on_response);
  calc_proto_ser_set_error_callback(context.ser, on_error);

  pthread_t reader_thread;
  pthread_create(&reader_thread, NULL,
```

```
              stream_response_reader, &context);

  char buf[128];
  printf("? (type quit to exit) ");
  while (1) {
    scanf("%s", buf);
    int brk = 0, cnt = 0;
    struct calc_proto_req_t req;
    parse_client_input(buf, &req, &brk, &cnt);
    if (brk) {
      break;
    }
    if (cnt) {
      continue;
    }
    struct buffer_t ser_req =
        calc_proto_ser_client_serialize(context.ser, &req);
    int ret = write(context.sd, ser_req.data, ser_req.len);
    if (ret == -1) {
      fprintf(stderr, "Error while writing! %s\n",
              strerror(errno));
      break;
    }
    if (ret < ser_req.len) {
      fprintf(stderr, "Wrote less than anticipated!\n");
      break;
    }
    printf("The req(%d) is sent.\n", req.id);
  }
  shutdown(conn_sd, SHUT_RD);
  calc_proto_ser_dtor(context.ser);
  calc_proto_ser_delete(context.ser);
  pthread_join(reader_thread, NULL);
  printf("Bye.\n");
}
```

Code Box 20-22 [client/clicore/stream_client_core.c]: The function executing a stream client

As you can see in the preceding code, every client process has only one serializer object and it makes sense. This is opposite to the server process, where every client had a separate serializer object.

More than that, the client process spawns a separate thread for reading the responses from the server side. That's because reading from the server process is a blocking task and it should be done in a separate flow of execution.

As part of the main thread, we have the client's command line, which receives inputs from a user through the Terminal. As you see, the main thread joins the reader thread upon exiting and it waits for its completion.

On a further note regarding the preceding code, the client process uses the same I/O API for reading from and writing to the stream channel. Like we said before, the `read` and `write` functions are used and the usage of the `write` function can be seen in *Code Box 20-22*.

In the following section, we talk about datagram channels but still using the UDS for that purpose. We start with the datagram server first.

UDS datagram server

If you remember from the previous chapter, datagram processes had their own listener and connector sequences regarding transport transmission. Now it's time to demonstrate how a datagram server can be developed based on UDS.

According to the datagram listener sequence, the process needs to create a socket object first. The following code box demonstrates that:

```
int server_sd = socket(AF_UNIX, SOCK_DGRAM, 0);
if (server_sd == -1) {
  fprintf(stderr, "Could not create socket: %s\n",
          strerror(errno));
  exit(1);
}
```

Code Box 20-23 [server/unix/datagram/main.c]: Creating a UDS object meant to operate on a datagram channel

You see that we have used `SOCK_DGRAM` instead of `SOCK_STREAM`. This means that the socket object is going to operate on a datagram channel. The other two arguments remain the same.

As the second step in the datagram listener sequence, we need to bind the socket to a UDS endpoint. As we said before, this is a socket file. This step is exactly the same as for the stream server, and therefore we don't bother to demonstrate it below and you can see it in *Code Box 20-14*.

For a datagram listener process, these steps were the only ones to be performed, and there is no backlog associated to a datagram socket to be configured. More than that, there is no client-accepting phase because we can't have stream connections on some dedicated 1-to-1 channels.

Next, you can see the `main` function of the datagram server listening on a UDS endpoint, as part of the calculator project:

```
int main(int argc, char** argv) {
  char sock_file[] = "/tmp/calc_svc.sock";

  // ---------- 1. Create socket object ------------------
  int server_sd = socket(AF_UNIX, SOCK_DGRAM, 0);
  if (server_sd == -1) {
    fprintf(stderr, "Could not create socket: %s\n",
            strerror(errno));
    exit(1);
  }

  // ---------- 2. Bind the socket file ------------------

  // Delete the previously created socket file if it exists.
  unlink(sock_file);

  // Prepare the address
  struct sockaddr_un addr;
  memset(&addr, 0, sizeof(addr));
  addr.sun_family = AF_UNIX;
  strncpy(addr.sun_path, sock_file, sizeof(addr.sun_path) - 1);

  int result = bind(server_sd,
          (struct sockaddr*)&addr, sizeof(addr));
  if (result == -1) {
    close(server_sd);
    fprintf(stderr, "Could not bind the address: %s\n",
            strerror(errno));
    exit(1);
  }

  // ---------- 3. Start serving requests ---------
  serve_forever(server_sd);

  return 0;
}
```

Code Box 20-24 [server/unix/datagram/main.c]: The main function of the datagram server listening on a UDS endpoint

As you know, datagram channels are connection-less, and they don't operate like stream channels. In other words, there cannot be a dedicated 1-to-1 connection between two processes. Therefore, the processes can only transmit datagrams along the channel. A client process can only send some individual and independent datagrams and likewise, the server process can only receive datagrams and send back some other datagrams as responses.

So, the crucial thing about a datagram channel is that the request and response messages should be fit into a single datagram. Otherwise, they cannot be split between two datagrams and the server or client cannot handle the message. Fortunately, our messages in the calculator project are mostly short enough to be fit into a single datagram.

The size of a datagram is highly dependent on the underlying channel. For example, regarding datagram UDS this is quite flexible because it happens through the kernel, but regarding UDP sockets, you are bound to the configuration of the network. Regarding the UDS the following link can give you a better idea of how to set the correct size: `https://stackoverflow.com/questions/21856517/whats-the-practical-limit-on-the-size-of-single-packet-transmitted-over-domain`.

Another difference that we can mention regarding datagram and stream sockets is the I/O API that is used to transmit data along them. While the `read` and `write` functions can still be used for datagram sockets just like the stream sockets, we use other functions for reading from and sending to a datagram channel. The `recvfrom` and `sendto` functions are usually used.

That's because in stream sockets the channel is dedicated, and when you write to a channel both ends are determined. Regarding datagram sockets, we have only one channel that is being used by many parties. Therefore, we can lose track of the process owning a specific datagram. These functions can keep track of and send the datagram back to the desired process.

Next, you can find the definition for the `serve_forever` function used in *Code Box 20-24* at the end of the `main` function. This function belongs to the server common library and is specific to datagram servers, regardless of the socket type. You can clearly see how the `recvfrom` function has been used:

```
void serve_forever(int server_sd) {
  char buffer[64];
  while (1) {
    struct sockaddr* sockaddr = sockaddr_new();
    socklen_t socklen = sockaddr_sizeof();
    int read_nr_bytes = recvfrom(server_sd, buffer,
            sizeof(buffer), 0, sockaddr, &socklen);
    if (read_nr_bytes == -1) {
      close(server_sd);
      fprintf(stderr, "Could not read from datagram socket: %s\n",
            strerror(errno));
      exit(1);
    }
    struct client_context_t context;
```

```
    context.addr = (struct client_addr_t*)
        malloc(sizeof(struct client_addr_t));
    context.addr->server_sd = server_sd;
    context.addr->sockaddr = sockaddr;
    context.addr->socklen = socklen;

    context.ser = calc_proto_ser_new();
    calc_proto_ser_ctor(context.ser, &context, 256);
    calc_proto_ser_set_req_callback(context.ser, request_
callback);
    calc_proto_ser_set_error_callback(context.ser, error_
callback);

    context.svc = calc_service_new();
    calc_service_ctor(context.svc);

    context.write_resp = &datagram_write_resp;

    bool_t req_found = FALSE;
    struct buffer_t buf;
    buf.data = buffer;
    buf.len = read_nr_bytes;
    calc_proto_ser_server_deserialize(context.ser, buf, &req_
found);

    if (!req_found) {
      struct calc_proto_resp_t resp;
      resp.req_id = -1;
      resp.status = ERROR_INVALID_RESPONSE;
      resp.result = 0.0;
      context.write_resp(&context, &resp);
    }

    calc_service_dtor(context.svc);
    calc_service_delete(context.svc);

    calc_proto_ser_dtor(context.ser);
    calc_proto_ser_delete(context.ser);

    free(context.addr->sockaddr);
    free(context.addr);
  }
}
```

Code Box 20-25 [server/srvcore/datagram_server_core.c]: The function handling the datagrams found in the server common library, and dedicated to the datagram servers

As you see in the preceding code box, the datagram server is a single-threaded program and there is no multithreading around it. More than that, it operates on every datagram individually and independently. It receives a datagram, deserializes its content and creates the request object, handles the request through the service object, serializes the response object and puts it in a new datagram, and sends it back to the process owning the original datagram. It does the same cycle over and over again for every incoming datagram.

Note that every datagram has its own serializer object and its own service object. We could design this in a way that we had only one serializer and one service object for all the datagrams. This might be something interesting for you to think about with regard to how it is possible and why that might not be possible for the calculator project. This is a debatable discussion and you might receive different opinions from various people.

Note that in *Code Box 20-25*, we store the client address of a datagram upon receiving it. Later, we can use this address to write directly back to that client. It is worth having a look at how we write back the datagram to the sender client. Just like the stream server, we are using a function for this purpose. *Code Box 20-26* shows the definition of the datagram_write_resp function. The function is in the datagram servers' common library next to the serve_forever function:

```
void datagram_write_resp(struct client_context_t* context,
        struct calc_proto_resp_t* resp) {
  struct buffer_t buf =
      calc_proto_ser_server_serialize(context->ser, resp);
  if (buf.len == 0) {
    close(context->addr->server_sd);
    fprintf(stderr, "Internal error while serializing object.\n");
    exit(1);
  }
  int ret = sendto(context->addr->server_sd, buf.data, buf.len,
      0, context->addr->sockaddr, context->addr->socklen);
  free(buf.data);
  if (ret == -1) {
    fprintf(stderr, "Could not write to client: %s\n",
            strerror(errno));
    close(context->addr->server_sd);
    exit(1);
  } else if (ret < buf.len) {
    fprintf(stderr, "WARN: Less bytes were written!\n");
    close(context->addr->server_sd);
    exit(1);
  }
}
```

Code Box 20-26 [server/srvcore/datagram_server_core.c]: The function writing datagrams back to the clients

You can see that we use the sorted client address and we pass it to the `sendto` function together with the serialized response message. The rest is taken care of by the operating system and the datagram is sent back directly to the sender client.

Now that we know enough about the datagram server and how the socket should be used, let's look at the datagram client, which is using the same type of socket.

UDS datagram client

From a technical point of view, stream clients and datagram clients are very similar. It means that you should see almost the same overall structure but with some differences regarding transmitting datagrams instead of operating on a stream channel.

But there is a big difference between them, and this is quite unique and specific to datagram clients connecting to UDS endpoints.

The difference is that the datagram client is required to bind a socket file, just like the server program, in order to receive the datagrams directed at it. This is not true for datagram clients using network sockets, as you will see shortly. Note that the client should bind a different socket file, and not the server's socket file.

The main reason behind this difference is the fact that the server program needs an address to send the response back to, and if the datagram client doesn't bind a socket file, there is no endpoint bound to the client socket file. But regarding network sockets, a client always has a corresponding socket descriptor that is bound to an IP address and a port, so this problem cannot occur.

If we put aside this difference, we can see how similar the code is. In *Code Box 20-26* you can see the `main` function of the datagram calculator client:

```
int main(int argc, char** argv) {
  char server_sock_file[] = "/tmp/calc_svc.sock";
  char client_sock_file[] = "/tmp/calc_cli.sock";

  // ----------- 1. Create socket object ------------------

  int conn_sd = socket(AF_UNIX, SOCK_DGRAM, 0);
  if (conn_sd == -1) {
    fprintf(stderr, "Could not create socket: %s\n",
            strerror(errno));
    exit(1);
  }

  // ----------- 2. Bind the client socket file ------------
```

```
// Delete the previously created socket file if it exists.
unlink(client_sock_file);

// Prepare the client address
struct sockaddr_un addr;
memset(&addr, 0, sizeof(addr));
addr.sun_family = AF_UNIX;
strncpy(addr.sun_path, client_sock_file,
        sizeof(addr.sun_path) - 1);

int result = bind(conn_sd,
        (struct sockaddr*)&addr, sizeof(addr));
if (result == -1) {
  close(conn_sd);
  fprintf(stderr, "Could not bind the client address: %s\n",
          strerror(errno));
  exit(1);
}

// ----------- 3. Connect to server --------------------

// Prepare the server address
memset(&addr, 0, sizeof(addr));
addr.sun_family = AF_UNIX;
strncpy(addr.sun_path, server_sock_file,
        sizeof(addr.sun_path) - 1);

result = connect(conn_sd,
        (struct sockaddr*)&addr, sizeof(addr));
if (result == -1) {
  close(conn_sd);
  fprintf(stderr, "Could no connect: %s\n", strerror(errno));
  exit(1);
}

datagram_client_loop(conn_sd);

return 0;
}
```

Code Box 20-26 [server/srvcore/datagram_server_core.c]: The function writing datagrams back to the clients

As we explained earlier, and as can be seen in the code, the client is required to bind a socket file. And of course, we have to call a different function to start the client loop, at the end of the `main` function. The datagram client calls the `datagram_client_loop` function.

If you look at the function datagram_client_loop, you still see many similarities between the stream client and the datagram client. Despite the small differences, a big difference is using the recvfrom and sendto functions instead of the read and write functions. The same explanation given for these functions as part of the previous section, still holds true for the datagram client.

Now it's time to talk about network sockets. As you will see, the main function in the client and server programs is the only code that changes when moving from UDS to network sockets.

Network sockets

The other socket address family that is widely used is AF_INET. It simply refers to any channel established on top of a network connection. Unlike the UDS stream and datagram sockets, which have no protocol name assigned to them, there are two well-known protocols on top of network sockets. TCP sockets establish a stream channel between every two processes, and UDP sockets establish a datagram channel that can be used by a number of processes.

In the following sections, we are going to explain how to develop programs using TCP and UDP sockets and see real some examples as part of the calculator project.

TCP server

A program using a TCP socket to listen and accept a number of clients, in other words a TCP server, is different from a stream server listening on a UDS endpoint in two ways: firstly, it specifies a different address family, AF_INET instead of AF_UNIX, when calling the socket function. And secondly, it uses a different structure for the socket address required for binding.

Despite these two differences, everything else would be the same for a TCP socket in terms of I/O operation. We should note that a TCP socket is a stream socket, therefore the code written for a stream socket using UDS should work for a TCP socket as well.

If we go back to the calculator project, we expect to see the differences just in the main functions where we create the socket object and bind it to an endpoint. Other than that, the rest of the code should remain unchanged. In fact, this is what we actually see. The following code box contains the main function of the TCP calculator server:

```
int main(int argc, char** argv) {
```

```
// ---------- 1. Create socket object ------------------
int server_sd = socket(AF_INET, SOCK_STREAM, 0);
if (server_sd == -1) {
  fprintf(stderr, "Could not create socket: %s\n",
          strerror(errno));
  exit(1);
}

// ---------- 2. Bind the socket file ------------------

// Prepare the address
struct sockaddr_in addr;
memset(&addr, 0, sizeof(addr));
addr.sin_family = AF_INET;
addr.sin_addr.s_addr = INADDR_ANY;
addr.sin_port = htons(6666);

...

// ---------- 3. Prepare backlog ------------------
...

// ---------- 4. Start accepting clients ---------
accept_forever(server_sd);

return 0;
}
```

Code Box 20-27 [server/tcp/main.c]: The main function of the TCP calculator client

If you compare the preceding code with the main function seen in *Code Box 20-17*, you will notice the differences we explained earlier. Instead of using the sockaddr_un structure, we are using the sockaddr_in structure for the bound endpoint address. The listen function is used the same, and even the same accept_forever function has been called to handle the incoming connections.

As a final note, regarding I/O operations on a TCP socket, since a TCP socket is a stream socket, it inherits all the properties from a stream socket; therefore, it can be used just like any other stream socket. In other words, the same read, write, and close functions can be used.

Let's now talk about the TCP client.

TCP client

Again, everything should be very similar to the stream client operating on a UDS. The differences mentioned in the previous section are still true for a TCP socket on a connector side. The changes are again limited to the main function.

Next, you can see the `main` function of the TCP calculator client:

```
int main(int argc, char** argv) {

  // ----------- 1. Create socket object ------------------

  int conn_sd = socket(AF_INET, SOCK_STREAM, 0);
  if (conn_sd == -1) {
    fprintf(stderr, "Could not create socket: %s\n",
          strerror(errno));
    exit(1);
  }

  // ------------ 2. Connect to server-- ------------------

  // Find the IP address behind the hostname
  ...

  // Prepare the address
  struct sockaddr_in addr;
  memset(&addr, 0, sizeof(addr));
  addr.sin_family = AF_INET;
  addr.sin_addr = *((struct in_addr*)host_entry->h_addr);
  addr.sin_port = htons(6666);

  ...

  stream_client_loop(conn_sd);

  return 0;
}
```

Code Box 20-27 [server/tcp/main.c]: The main function of the TCP calculator server

The changes are very similar to the ones we saw for the TCP server program. A different address family and a different socket address structure have been used. Apart from that, the rest of the code is the same, and we therefore do not need to discuss the TCP client in detail.

Since TCP sockets are stream sockets, we can use the same common code for handling the new clients. You can see this by calling the `stream_client_loop` function, which is part of the client common library in the calculator project. Now, you should get the idea of why we extracted two common libraries, one for the client programs and one for the server programs, in order to write less code. When we can use the same code for two different scenarios, it is always best to extract it as a library and reuse it in the scenarios.

Let's look at UDP server and client programs; we will see that they are more or less similar to what we saw regarding TCP programs.

UDP server

UDP sockets are network sockets. Other than that, they are datagram sockets. Therefore, we expect to observe a high degree of similarity between the code we wrote for the TCP server together with the code we wrote for the datagram server operating on a UDS.

In addition, the main difference between a UDP socket and a TCP socket, regardless of being used in a client or server program, is the fact that the socket type is SOCK_DGRAM for the UDP socket. The address family remains the same, because both of them are network sockets. The following code box contains the main function of the calculator UDP server:

```
int main(int argc, char** argv) {

  // ----------- 1. Create socket object -----------------
  int server_sd = socket(AF_INET, SOCK_DGRAM, 0);
  if (server_sd == -1) {
    fprintf(stderr, "Could not create socket: %s\n",
            strerror(errno));
    exit(1);
  }

  // ----------- 2. Bind the socket file -----------------

  // Prepare the address
  struct sockaddr_in addr;
  memset(&addr, 0, sizeof(addr));
  addr.sin_family = AF_INET;
  addr.sin_addr.s_addr = INADDR_ANY;
  addr.sin_port = htons(9999);

  ...

  // ----------- 3. Start serving requests ---------
  serve_forever(server_sd);

  return 0;
}
```

Code Box 20-28 [server/udp/main.c]: The main function of the UDP calculator server

Note that UDP sockets are datagram sockets. Therefore, all the code written for datagram sockets operating on UDS is still valid for them. For instance, we have to use the `recvfrom` and `sendto` functions to work with UDP sockets. So, as you can see, we have used the same `serve_forever` function to serve incoming datagrams. This function is part of the server common library meant to contain the datagram-related code.

We've said enough regarding the UDP server's code. Let's see what the UDP client's code looks like.

The UDP client

UDP client code is very similar to the TCP client code, but it uses a different socket type and it calls a different function for handling the incoming messages, which is the same function that the datagram client based on UDS used. You can see the following `main` function:

```c
int main(int argc, char** argv) {

    // ----------- 1. Create socket object ------------------

    int conn_sd = socket(AF_INET, SOCK_DGRAM, 0);
    if (conn_sd == -1) {
        fprintf(stderr, "Could not create socket: %s\n",
                strerror(errno));
        exit(1);
    }

    // ----------- 2. Connect to server-- ------------------
    ...

    // Prepare the address
    ...

    datagram_client_loop(conn_sd);

    return 0;
}
```

Code Box 20-28 [client/udp/main.c]: The main function of the UDP calculator client

That was the final concept for this chapter. In this chapter, we went through the various well-known socket types and together with that, we showed how the listener and connector sequences for both stream and datagram channels can be implemented in C.

There are many things in the calculator project that we didn't even talk about. Therefore, it is highly recommended to go through the code, find those places, and try to read and understand it. Having a fully working example can help you to examine the concepts in real applications.

Summary

In this chapter, we went through the following topics:

- We introduced various types of communications, channels, mediums, and sockets as part of our review of IPC techniques.

- We explored a calculator project by describing its application protocol and the serialization algorithm that it uses.

- We demonstrated how UDS can be used to establish a client-server connection, and we showed how they are used in the calculator project.

- We discussed the stream and datagram channels established using Unix domain sockets, separately.

- We demonstrated how TCP and UDP sockets can be used to make a client-server IPC channel, and we used them in the calculator example.

The next chapter is about integrating of C with other programming languages. By doing so, we can have a C library loaded and used in another programming language like Java. As part of the next chapter, we cover integration with C++, Java, Python, and Golang.

Chapter 21

Integration with Other Languages

Knowing how to write a C program or library can be more valuable than you might expect. Due to the important role of C in developing operating systems, C is not limited to its own world. C libraries have the potential to be loaded and used in other programming languages as well. While you are reaping the benefits of writing code in a higher-level programming language, you can have the rocket power of C as a loaded library inside your language environment.

In this chapter we are going to talk more about this, and demonstrate how C shared libraries can be integrated with some well-known programming languages.

In this chapter, we will cover the following key topics:

- We discuss why integration is possible in the first place. The discussion is important because it gives you the basic idea of how integration works.
- We design a C stack library. We build it as a shared object file. This shared object file is going to be used by a number of other programming languages.
- We go through C++, Java, Python, and Golang and see how the stack library can be loaded first and then used.

As a general note in this chapter, since we are going to work on five different subprojects, each having different programming languages, we only present the builds for Linux in order to prevent any issues regarding the builds and executions. Of course, we give enough information about the macOS system, but our focus is to build and run sources on Linux. Further scripts are available in the book's GitHub repository that help you to build the sources for macOS.

The first section talks about the integration itself. We see why the integration with other programming languages is possible and it makes a basis for expanding our discussion within other environments rather than C.

Why integration is possible?

As we have explained in *Chapter 10, Unix – History and Architecture*, C revolutionized the way we were developing operating systems. That's not the only magic of C; it also gave us the power to build other general-purpose programming languages on top of it. Nowadays, we call them higher-level programming languages. The compilers of these languages are mostly written in C and if not, they've been developed by other tools and compilers written in C.

A general-purpose programming language that is not able to use or provide the functionalities of a system is not doing anything at all. You can write things with it, but you cannot execute it on any system. While there could be usages for such a programming language from a theoretical point of view, certainly it is not plausible from an industrial point of view. Therefore, the programming language, especially through its compiler, should be able to produce programs that work. As you know, the functionalities of a system are exposed through the operating system. Regardless of the operating system itself, a programming language should be able to provide those functionalities, and the programs written in that language, and being run on that system, should be able to use them.

This is where C comes in. In Unix-like operating systems, the C standard library provides the API to use the available functionalities of the system. If a compiler wants to create a working program, it should be able to allow the compiled program to use the C standard library in an indirect fashion. No matter what the programming language is and whether it offers some specific and native standard library, like Java, which offers **Java Standard Edition (Java SE)**, any request for a specific functionality made by the written program (such as opening a file) should be passed down to the C standard library and from there, it can reach the kernel and get performed.

As an example, let's talk a bit more about Java. Java programs are compiled to an intermediate language called *bytecode*. In order to execute a Java bytecode, one needs to have **Java Runtime Environment (JRE)** installed. JRE has a virtual machine at its heart that loads the Java bytecode and runs it within itself. This virtual machine must be able to simulate the functionalities and services exposed by the C standard library and provide them to the program running within. Since every platform can be different in terms of the C standard library and its compliance with POSIX and SUS standards, we need to have some virtual machines built specifically for each platform.

As a final note about the libraries that can be loaded in other languages, we can only load shared object files and it is not possible to load and use static libraries. Static libraries can only be linked to an executable or a shared object file. Shared object files have the `.so` extension in most Unix-like systems but they have the `.dylib` extension in macOS.

In this section, despite its short length, I tried to give you a basic idea of why we are able to load C libraries, shared libraries specifically, and how most programming languages are already using C libraries, since the ability to load a shared object library and use it exists in most of them.

The next step would be writing a C library and then loading it in various programming languages in order to use it. That's exactly what we want to do soon but before that you need to know how to get the chapter material and how to run the commands seen in the shell boxes.

Obtaining the necessary materials

Since this chapter is full of sources from five different programming languages, and my hope is to have you all able to build and run the examples, I dedicated this section to going through some basic notes that you should be aware of regarding building the source code.

First of all, you need to obtain the chapter material. As you should know by now, the book has a repository in which this chapter has a specific directory named `ch21-integration-with-other-languages`. The following commands show you how to clone the repository and change to the chapter's root directory:

```
$ git clone https://github.com/PacktPublishing/Extreme-C.git
...
$ cd Extreme-C/ch21-integration-with-other-languages
$
```

Shell Code 21-1: Cloning the book's GitHub repository and changing to the chapter's root directory

Regarding the shell boxes in this chapter, we assume that before executing the commands in a shell box, we are located in the root of the chapter, in the `ch21-integration-with-other-languages` folder. If we needed to change to other directories, we provide the required commands for that, but everything is happening inside the chapter's directory.

In addition, in order to be able to build source code, you need to have **Java Development Kit (JDK)**, Python, and Golang installed on your machine. Depending on whether you're using Linux or macOS, and on your Linux distribution, the installation commands can be different.

As the final note, the source code written in other languages than C should be able to use the C stack library that we discuss in the upcoming section. Building those sources requires that you've already built the C library. Therefore, make sure that you read the following section first and have its shared object library built before moving on to the next sections. Now that you know how to obtain the chapter's material, we can proceed to discuss our target C library.

Stack library

In this section, we are going to write a small library that is going to be loaded and used by programs written in other programming languages. The library is about a Stack class that offers some basic operations like *push* or *pop* on stack objects. Stack objects are created and destroyed by the library itself and there is a constructor function, as well as a destructor function, to fulfill this purpose.

Next, you can find the library's public interface, which exists as part of the `cstack.h` header file:

```c
#ifndef _CSTACK_H_
#define _CSTACK_H_

#include <unistd.h>

#ifdef __cplusplus
extern "C" {
#endif

#define TRUE 1
#define FALSE 0

typedef int bool_t;

typedef struct {
  char* data;
  size_t len;
} value_t;

typedef struct cstack_type cstack_t;

typedef void (*deleter_t)(value_t* value);

value_t make_value(char* data, size_t len);
value_t copy_value(char* data, size_t len);
void free_value(value_t* value);

cstack_t* cstack_new();
void cstack_delete(cstack_t*);

// Behavior functions
void cstack_ctor(cstack_t*, size_t);
void cstack_dtor(cstack_t*, deleter_t);

size_t cstack_size(const cstack_t*);

bool_t cstack_push(cstack_t*, value_t value);
```

```
bool_t cstack_pop(cstack_t*, value_t* value);

void cstack_clear(cstack_t*, deleter_t);

#ifdef __cplusplus
}
#endif

#endif
```

Code Box 21-1 [cstack.h]: The public interface of the Stack library

As we have explained in *Chapter 6, OOP and Encapsulation,* the preceding declarations introduce the public interface of the Stack class. As you see, the companion attribute structure of the class is cstack_t. We have used cstack_t instead of stack_t because the latter is used in the C standard library and I prefer to avoid any ambiguity in this code. By the preceding declarations, the attribute structure is forward declared and has no fields in it. Instead, the details will come in the source file that does the actual implementation. The class also has a constructor, a destructor, and some other behaviors such as push and pop. As you can see, all of them accept a pointer of type cstack_t as their first argument that indicates the object they should act on. The way we wrote the Stack class is explained as part of *implicit encapsulation* in *Chapter 6, OOP and Encapsulation.*

Code Box 21-2 contains the implementation of the stack class. It also contains the actual definition for the cstack_t attribute structure:

```
#include <stdlib.h>
#include <assert.h>

#include "cstack.h"

struct cstack_type {
  size_t top;
  size_t max_size;
  value_t* values;
};

value_t copy_value(char* data, size_t len) {
  char* buf = (char*)malloc(len * sizeof(char));
  for (size_t i = 0; i < len; i++) {
    buf[i] = data[i];
  }
  return make_value(buf, len);
}
```

```
value_t make_value(char* data, size_t len) {
  value_t value;
  value.data = data;
  value.len = len;
  return value;
}

void free_value(value_t* value) {
  if (value) {
    if (value->data) {
      free(value->data);
      value->data = NULL;
    }
  }
}

cstack_t* cstack_new() {
  return (cstack_t*)malloc(sizeof(cstack_t));
}

void cstack_delete(cstack_t* stack) {
  free(stack);
}

void cstack_ctor(cstack_t* cstack, size_t max_size) {
  cstack->top = 0;
  cstack->max_size = max_size;
  cstack->values = (value_t*)malloc(max_size * sizeof(value_t));
}

void cstack_dtor(cstack_t* cstack, deleter_t deleter) {
  cstack_clear(cstack, deleter);
  free(cstack->values);
}

size_t cstack_size(const cstack_t* cstack) {
  return cstack->top;
}

bool_t cstack_push(cstack_t* cstack, value_t value) {
  if (cstack->top < cstack->max_size) {
    cstack->values[cstack->top++] = value;
    return TRUE;
  }
  return FALSE;
}

bool_t cstack_pop(cstack_t* cstack, value_t* value) {
  if (cstack->top > 0) {
```

```
      *value = cstack->values[--cstack->top];
      return TRUE;
    }
    return FALSE;
  }


  void cstack_clear(cstack_t* cstack, deleter_t deleter) {
    value_t value;
    while (cstack_size(cstack) > 0) {
      bool_t popped = cstack_pop(cstack, &value);
      assert(popped);
      if (deleter) {
        deleter(&value);
      }
    }
  }
```

Code Box 21-2 [cstack.c]: The definition of the stack class

As you see, the definition implies that every stack object is backed with an array, and more than that, we can store any value in the stack. Let's build the library and produce a shared object library out of it. This would be the library file that is going to be loaded by other programming languages in the upcoming sections.

The following shell box shows how to create a shared object library using the existing source files. The commands found in the text box work in Linux and they should be slightly changed in order to work in macOS. Note that before running the build commands, you should be in this chapter's root directory as explained before:

```
$ gcc -c -g -fPIC cstack.c -o cstack.o
$ gcc -shared cstack.o -o libcstack.so
$
```

Shell Box 21-2: Building the stack library and producing the shared object library file in Linux

As a side note, in macOS, we can run the preceding exact commands if the gcc is a known command and it is pointing to the clang compiler. Otherwise, we can use the following commands to build the library on macOS. Note that the extension of shared object files is .dylib in macOS:

```
$ clang -c -g -fPIC cstack.c -o cstack.o
$ clang -dynamiclib cstack.o -o libcstack.dylib
$
```

Shell Box 21-3: Building the stack library and producing the shared object library file in macOS

We now have the shared object library file, and we can write programs in other languages that can load it. Before giving our demonstration on how the preceding library can be loaded and used in other environments, we need to write some tests in order to verify its functionality. The following code creates a stack and performs some of the available operations and checks the results against the expectations:

```
#include <stdio.h>
#include <stdlib.h>
#include <assert.h>

#include "cstack.h"

value_t make_int(int int_value) {
  value_t value;
  int* int_ptr = (int*)malloc(sizeof(int));
  *int_ptr = int_value;
  value.data = (char*)int_ptr;
  value.len = sizeof(int);
  return value;
}

int extract_int(value_t* value) {
  return *((int*)value->data);
}

void deleter(value_t* value) {
  if (value->data) {
    free(value->data);
  }
  value->data = NULL;
}

int main(int argc, char** argv) {
  cstack_t* cstack = cstack_new();
  cstack_ctor(cstack, 100);
  assert(cstack_size(cstack) == 0);

  int int_values[] = {5, 10, 20, 30};

  for (size_t i = 0; i < 4; i++) {
    cstack_push(cstack, make_int(int_values[i]));
  }
  assert(cstack_size(cstack) == 4);

  int counter = 3;
  value_t value;
  while (cstack_size(cstack) > 0) {
    bool_t popped = cstack_pop(cstack, &value);
```

```
        assert(popped);
        assert(extract_int(&value) == int_values[counter--]);
        deleter(&value);
    }
    assert(counter == -1);
    assert(cstack_size(cstack) == 0);

    cstack_push(cstack, make_int(10));
    cstack_push(cstack, make_int(20));
    assert(cstack_size(cstack) == 2);

    cstack_clear(cstack, deleter);
    assert(cstack_size(cstack) == 0);

    // In order to have something in the stack while
    // calling destructor.
    cstack_push(cstack, make_int(20));

    cstack_dtor(cstack, deleter);
    cstack_delete(cstack);
    printf("All tests were OK.\n");
    return 0;
}
```

Code Box 21-3 [cstack_tests.c]: The code testing the functionality of the Stack class

As you can see, we have used assertions to check the returned values. The following is the output of the preceding code after being built and executed in Linux. Again, note that we are in the chapter's root directory:

```
$ gcc -c -g cstack_tests.c -o tests.o
$ gcc tests.o -L$PWD -lcstack -o cstack_tests.out
$ LD_LIBRARY_PATH=$PWD ./cstack_tests.out
All tests were OK.
$
```

Shell Box 21-4: Building and running the library tests

Note that in the preceding shell box, when running the final executable file cstack_tests.out, we have to set the environment variable LD_LIBRARY_PATH to point to the directory that contains the libcstack.so, because the executed program needs to find the shared object libraries and load them.

As you see in *Shell Box 21-4*, all tests have passed successfully. This means that from the functional point of view, our library is performing correctly. It would be nice to check the library against a non-functional requirement like memory usage or having no memory leaks.

The following command shows how to use valgrind to check the execution of the tests for any possible memory leaks:

```
$ LD_LIBRARY_PATH=$PWD valgrind --leak-check=full ./cstack_tests.
out
==31291== Memcheck, a memory error detector
==31291== Copyright (C) 2002-2017, and GNU GPL'd, by Julian Seward
et al.
==31291== Using Valgrind-3.13.0 and LibVEX; rerun with -h for
copyright info
==31291== Command: ./cstack_tests.out
==31291==
All tests were OK.
==31291==
==31291== HEAP SUMMARY:
==31291==     in use at exit: 0 bytes in 0 blocks
==31291==   total heap usage: 10 allocs, 10 frees, 2,676 bytes
allocated
==31291==
==31291== All heap blocks were freed -- no leaks are possible
==31291==
==31291== For counts of detected and suppressed errors, rerun
with: -v
==31291== ERROR SUMMARY: 0 errors from 0 contexts (suppressed: 0
from 0)
$
```

Shell Box 21-5: Running the tests using valgrind

As you can see, we don't have any memory leaks, and this gives us more trust in the library that we have written. Therefore, if we see any memory issue in another environment, the root cause should be investigated there first.

In the following chapter, we will cover unit testing in C. As a proper replacement for the assert statements seen in *Code Box 21-3*, we could write unit tests and use a unit testing framework like CMocka to execute them.

In the following sections, we are going to integrate the stack library in programs written by four programming languages. We'll start with C++.

Integration with C++

Integration with C++ can be assumed as the easiest. C++ can be thought of as an object-oriented extension to C. A C++ compiler produces similar object files to those that a C compiler produces. Therefore, a C++ program can load and use a C shared object library easier than any other programming language. In other words, it doesn't matter whether a shared object file is the output of a C or C++ project; both can be consumed by a C++ program. The only thing that can be problematic in some cases is the C++ *name mangling* feature that is described in *Chapter 2, Compilation and Linking*. As a reminder, we'll briefly review it in the following section.

Name mangling in C++

To elaborate more on this, we should say that symbol names corresponding to functions (both global and member functions in classes) are mangled in C++. Name mangling is mainly there to support *namespaces* and *function overloading*, which are missing in C. Name mangling is enabled by default, therefore if C code gets compiled using a C++ compiler, we expect to see mangled symbol names. Look at the following example in *Code Box 21-4*:

```
int add(int a, int b) {
  return a + b;
}
```

Code Box 21-4 [test.c]: A simple function in C

If we compile the preceding file using a C compiler, in this case `clang`, we see the following symbols in the generated object file, shown in *Shell Box 21-6*. Note that the file `test.c` doesn't exist in the book's GitHub repository:

```
$ clang -c test.c -o test.o
$ nm test.o
0000000000000000 T _add
$
```

Shell Box 21-6: Compiling test.c with a C compiler

As you see, we have a symbol named _add that refers to the function `add` defined above. Now, let's compile the file with a C++ compiler, in this case `clang++`:

```
$ clang++ -c test.c -o test.o
clang: warning: treating 'c' input as 'c++' when in C++ mode, this
behavior is deprecated [-Wdeprecated]
$ nm test.o
0000000000000000 T __Z3addii
$
```

Shell Box 21-7: Compiling test.c with a C++ compiler

As you can see, `clang++` has generated a warning that says that in the near future, the support for compiling C code as C++ code will be dropped. But since this behavior is not removed yet (and it is just deprecated), we see that the symbol name generated for the preceding function is mangled and is different from the one generated by `clang`. This can definitely lead to problems in the linking phase when looking for a specific symbol.

To eliminate this issue, one needs to wrap the C code inside a special scope that prevents a C++ compiler from mangling the symbol names. Then, compiling it with `clang` and `clang++` produces the same symbol names. Look at the following code in *Code Box 21-5*, which is a changed version of the code introduced in *Code Box 21-4*:

```
#ifdef __cplusplus
extern "C" {
#endif

int add(int a, int b) {
  return a + b;
}

#ifdef __cplusplus
}
#endif
```

Code Box 21-5 [test.c]: Putting the function declaration into the special C scope

The preceding function is put in the scope `extern "C" { ... }` only if the macro __cplusplus is already defined. Having the macro __cplusplus is a sign that the code is being compiled by a C++ compiler. Let's compile the preceding code with `clang++` again:

```
$ clang++ -c test.c -o test.o
clang: warning: treating 'c' input as 'c++' when in C++ mode, this
behavior is deprecated [-Wdeprecated]
$ nm test.o
0000000000000000 T _add
$
```

Shell Box 21-8: Compiling the new version of test.c with clang++

As you see, the generated symbol is not mangled anymore. Regarding our stack library, based on what we explained so far, we need to put all declarations in the scope `extern "C" { ... }` and this is exactly the reason behind having that scope in *Code Box 21-1*. Therefore, when linking a C++ program with the stack library, the symbols can be found inside `libcstack.so` (or `libcstack.dylib`).

Note:

`extern "C"` is a *linkage specification*. More information can be found via the following links:

`https://isocpp.org/wiki/faq/mixing-c-and-cpp`

`https://stackoverflow.com/questions/1041866/
what-is-the-effect-of-extern-c-in-c`

Now, it's time to write the C++ code that uses our stack library. As you'll see shortly, it's an easy integration.

C++ code

Now that we know how to disable name mangling when bringing C code into a C++ project, we can proceed by writing a C++ program that uses the stack library. We start by wrapping the stack library in a C++ class, which is the main building block of an object-oriented C++ program. It is more appropriate to expose the stack functionality in an object-oriented fashion instead of having the stack library's C functions be called directly.

Code Box 21-6 contains the class that wraps the stack functionality derived from the stack library:

```
#include <string.h>

#include <iostream>
#include <string>
```

```
#include "cstack.h"

template<typename T>
value_t CreateValue(const T& pValue);

template<typename T>
T ExtractValue(const value_t& value);

template<typename T>
class Stack {
public:
  // Constructor
  Stack(int pMaxSize) {
    mStack = cstack_new();
    cstack_ctor(mStack, pMaxSize);
  }

  // Destructor
  ~Stack() {
    cstack_dtor(mStack, free_value);
    cstack_delete(mStack);
  }

  size_t Size() {
    return cstack_size(mStack);
  }

  void Push(const T& pItem) {
    value_t value = CreateValue(pItem);
    if (!cstack_push(mStack, value)) {
      throw "Stack is full!";
    }
  }

  const T Pop() {
    value_t value;
    if (!cstack_pop(mStack, &value)) {
      throw "Stack is empty!";
    }
    return ExtractValue<T>(value);
  }

  void Clear() {
    cstack_clear(mStack, free_value);
  }

private:
```

```
    cstack_t* mStack;
};
```

Code Box 21-6 [c++/Stack.cpp]: A C++ class that wraps the functionalities exposed by the stack library

Regarding the preceding class, we can point out the following important notes:

- The preceding class keeps a private pointer to a `cstack_t` variable. This pointer addresses the object created by the static library's `cstack_new` function. This pointer can be thought of as a *handle* to an object that exists at the C level, created and managed by a separate C library. The pointer `mStack` is analogous to a file descriptor (or file handle) that refers to a file.

- The class wraps all behavior functions exposed by the stack library. This is not essentially true for any object-oriented wrapper around a C library, and usually a limited set of functionalities is exposed.

- The preceding class is a template class. This means that it can operate on a variety of data types. As you can see, we have declared two template functions for serializing and deserializing objects with various types: `CreateValue` and `ExtractValue`. The preceding class uses these functions to create a byte array from a C++ object (serialization) and to create a C++ object from a byte array (deserialization) respectively.

- We define a specialized template function for the type `std::string`. Therefore, we can use the preceding class to store values with the `std::string` type. Note that `std::string` is the standard type in C++ for having a string variable.

- As part of the stack library, you can have multiple values from different types pushed into a single stack instance. The value can be converted to/from a character array. Look at the `value_t` structure in *Code Box 21-1*. It only needs a `char` pointer and that's all. Unlike the stack library, the preceding C++ class is *type-safe* and every instance of it can operate only on a specific data type.

- In C++, every class has at least one constructor and one destructor. Therefore, it would be easy to initialize the underlying stack object as part of the constructor and finalize it in the destructor. That's exactly what you see in the preceding code.

We want our C++ class to be able to operate on string values. Therefore, we need to write proper serializer and deserializer functions that can be used within the class. The following code contains the function definitions that convert a C char array to an `std::string` object and vice versa:

```
template<>
value_t CreateValue(const std::string& pValue) {
  value_t value;
  value.len = pValue.size() + 1;
  value.data = new char[value.len];
  strcpy(value.data, pValue.c_str());
  return value;
}

template<>
std::string ExtractValue(const value_t& value) {
  return std::string(value.data, value.len);
}
```

Code Box 21-7 [c++/Stack.cpp]: Specialized template functions meant for serialization/deserialization of the std::string type. These functions are used as part of the C++ class.

The preceding functions are std::string *specialization* for the declared template function used in the class. As you can see, it defines how a std::string object should be converted to a C char array, and conversely how a C char array can be turned into an std::string object.

Code Box 21-8 contains the main method that uses the C++ class:

```
int main(int argc, char** argv) {
  Stack<std::string> stringStack(100);
  stringStack.Push("Hello");
  stringStack.Push("World");
  stringStack.Push("!");
  std::cout << "Stack size: " << stringStack.Size() << std::endl;
  while (stringStack.Size() > 0) {
    std::cout << "Popped > " << stringStack.Pop() << std::endl;
  }
  std::cout << "Stack size after pops: " <<
      stringStack.Size() << std::endl;
  stringStack.Push("Bye");
  stringStack.Push("Bye");
  std::cout << "Stack size before clear: " <<
      stringStack.Size() << std::endl;
  stringStack.Clear();
  std::cout << "Stack size after clear: " <<
      stringStack.Size() << std::endl;
  return 0;
}
```

Code Box 21-8 [c++/Stack.cpp]: The main function using the C++ stack class

The preceding scenario covers all the functions exposed by the stack library. We execute a number of operations and we check their results. Note that the preceding code uses a `Stack<std::string>` object for testing functionality. Therefore, one can only push/pop `std::string` values into/from the stack.

The following shell box shows how to build and run the preceding code. Note that all the C++ code that you've seen in this section is written using C++11, hence it should be compiled using a compliant compiler. Like we said before, we are running the following commands when we are in the chapter's root directory:

```
$ cd c++
$ g++ -c -g -std=c++11 -I$PWD/.. Stack.cpp -o Stack.o
$ g++ -L$PWD/.. Stack.o -lcstack -o cstack_cpp.out
$ LD_LIBRARY_PATH=$PWD/.. ./cstack_cpp.out
Stack size: 3
Popped > !
Popped > World
Popped > Hello
Stack size after pops: 0
Stack size before clear: 2
Stack size after clear: 0
$
```

Shell Box 21-9: Building and running the C++ code

As you can see, we have indicated that we are going to use a C++11 compiler by passing the `-std=c++11` option. Note the `-I` and `-L` options, which are used for specifying custom include and library directories respectively. The option `-lcstack` asks the linker to link the C++ code with the library file `libcstack.so`. Note that on macOS systems, the shared object libraries have the `.dylib` extension, and therefore you might find `libcstack.dylib` instead of `libcstack.so`.

For running the `cstack_cpp.out` executable file, the loader needs to find `libcstack.so`. Note that this is different from building the executable. Here we want to run it, and the library file must be located before having the executable run. Therefore, by changing the environment variable `LD_LIBRARY_PATH`, we let the loader know where it should look for the shared objects. We have discussed more regarding this in *Chapter 2, Compilation and Linking*.

The C++ code should also be tested against memory leaks. `valgrind` helps us to see the memory leaks and we use it to analyze the resulting executable. The following shell box shows the output of `valgrind` running the `cstack_cpp.out` executable file:

```
$ cd c++
$ LD_LIBRARY_PATH=$PWD/.. valgrind --leak-check=full ./cstack_cpp.
out
==15061== Memcheck, a memory error detector
==15061== Copyright (C) 2002-2017, and GNU GPL'd, by Julian Seward
et al.
==15061== Using Valgrind-3.13.0 and LibVEX; rerun with -h for
copyright info
==15061== Command: ./cstack_cpp.out
==15061==
Stack size: 3
Popped > !
Popped > World
Popped > Hello
Stack size after pops: 0
Stack size before clear: 2
Stack size after clear: 0
==15061==
==15061== HEAP SUMMARY:
==15061==     in use at exit: 0 bytes in 0 blocks
==15061==   total heap usage: 9 allocs, 9 frees, 75,374 bytes
allocated
==15061==
==15061== All heap blocks were freed -- no leaks are possible
==15061==
==15061== For counts of detected and suppressed errors, rerun
with: -v
==15061== ERROR SUMMARY: 0 errors from 0 contexts (suppressed: 0
from 0)
$
```

Shell Box 21-10: Building and running the C++ code using valgrind

As is clear from the preceding output, we don't have any leaks in the code. Note that having 1081 bytes in the `still reachable` section doesn't mean that you have had a leak in your code. You can find more about this in `valgrind`'s manual.

In this section, we explained how to write a C++ wrapper around our C stack library. While mixing C and C++ code seems to be easy, some extra care about name mangling rules in C++ should be taken. In the next section, we are going to briefly talk about the Java programming language and the way that we are going to load our C library in a program written in Java.

Integration with Java

Java programs are compiled by a Java compiler into Java bytecode. Java bytecode is analogous to the object file format specified in the **Application Binary Interface (ABI)**. Files containing Java bytecode cannot be executed like ordinary executable files, and they need a special environment to be run.

Java bytecode can only be run within a **Java Virtual Machine (JVM)**. The JVM is itself a process that simulates a working environment for the Java bytecode. It is usually written in C or C++ and has the power to load and use the C standard library and the functionalities exposed in that layer.

The Java programming language is not the only language that can be compiled into Java bytecode. Scala, Kotlin, and Groovy are among programming languages that can be compiled to Java bytecode hence they can be run within a JVM. They are usually called *JVM languages*.

In this section, we are going to load our already built stack library into a Java program. For those who have no prior knowledge of Java, the steps we take may seem complicated and hard to grasp. Therefore, it is strongly recommended that readers come into this section with some basic knowledge about Java programming.

Writing the Java part

Suppose that we have a C project that it is built into a shared object library. We want to bring it into Java and use its functions. Fortunately, we can write and compile the Java part without having any C (or native) code. They are well separated by the *native methods* in Java. Obviously, you cannot run the Java program with just the Java part, and have the C functions called, without the shared object library file being loaded. We give the necessary steps and source code to make this happen and run a Java program that loads a shared object library and invokes its functions successfully.

The JVM uses **Java Native Interface (JNI)** to load shared object libraries. Note that JNI is not part of the Java programming language; rather, it is part of the JVM specification, therefore an imported shared object library can be used in all JVM languages such as Scala.

In the following paragraphs, we show how to use JNI to load our target shared object library file.

As we said before, JNI uses native methods. Native methods don't have any definition in Java; their actual definitions are written using C or C++ and they reside in external shared libraries. In other words, native methods are ports for the Java programs to communicate to the world outside of the JVM. The following code shows a class that contains a number of static native methods and it is supposed to expose the functionalities provided by our stack library:

```java
package com.packt.extreme_c.ch21.ex1;

class NativeStack {

  static {
    System.loadLibrary("NativeStack");
  }

  public static native long newStack();
  public static native void deleteStack(long stackHandler);

  public static native void ctor(long stackHandler, int maxSize);
  public static native void dtor(long stackHandler);

  public static native int size(long stackHandler);

  public static native void push(long stackHandler, byte[] item);
  public static native byte[] pop(long stackHandler);

  public static native void clear(long stackHandler);
}
```

Code Box 21-9 [java/src/com/packt/extreme_c/ch21/ex1/Main.java]: The NativeStack class

As the method signatures imply, they correspond to the functions we have in the C stack library. Note that the first operand is a `long` variable. It contains a native address read from the native library and acts as a pointer that should be passed to other methods to denote the stack instance. Note that, for writing the preceding class, we don't need to have a fully working shared object file beforehand. The only thing we need is the list of required declarations to define the stack API.

The preceding class has also a *static constructor*. The constructor loads a shared object library file located on the filesystem and tries to match the native methods with the symbols found in that shared object library. Note that the preceding shared object library is not `libcstack.so`. In other words, this is not the shared object file that we produced for our stack library. JNI has a very precise recipe for finding symbols that correspond to native methods. Therefore, we cannot use our symbols defined in `libcstack.so`; instead we need to create the symbols that JNI is looking for and then use our stack library from there.

This might be a bit unclear at the moment, but in the following section, we clarify this and you'll see how this can be done. Let's continue with the Java part. We still need to add some more Java code.

The following is a generic Java class named `Stack<T>` that wraps the native methods exposed by JNI. Generic Java classes can be regarded as twin concepts for the template classes that we had in C++. They are used to specify some generic types that can operate on other types.

As you see in the `Stack<T>` class, there is a *marshaller* object, from the type `Marshaller<T>`, that is used to serialize and deserialize the methods' input arguments (from type `T`) in order to put them into, or retrieve them from, the underlying C stack:

```
interface Marshaller<T> {

  byte[] marshal(T obj);

  T unmarshal(byte[] data);
}

class Stack<T> implements AutoCloseable {
  private Marshaller<T> marshaller;
  private long stackHandler;

  public Stack(Marshaller<T> marshaller) {
    this.marshaller = marshaller;
    this.stackHandler = NativeStack.newStack();
    NativeStack.ctor(stackHandler, 100);
  }

  @Override
  public void close() {
    NativeStack.dtor(stackHandler);
    NativeStack.deleteStack(stackHandler);
  }

  public int size() {
    return NativeStack.size(stackHandler);
  }

  public void push(T item) {
    NativeStack.push(stackHandler, marshaller.marshal(item));
  }

  public T pop() {
    return marshaller.unmarshal(NativeStack.pop(stackHandler));
```

```
  }
  public void clear() {
    NativeStack.clear(stackHandler);
  }
}
```

Code Box 21-10 [java/src/com/packt/extreme_c/ch21/ex1/Main.java]: The Stack<T> class and the
Marshaller<T> interface

The following points seem to be noticeable regarding the preceding code:

- The class Stack<T> is a generic class. It means that its different instances can operate on various classes like String, Integer, Point, and so on, but every instance can operate only on the type specified upon instantiation.

- The ability to store any data type in the underlying stack requires the stack to use an external marshaller to perform serialization and deserialization of the objects. The C stack library is able to store byte arrays in a stack data structure and higher-level languages willing to use its functionalities should be able to provide that byte array through serialization of the input objects. You will see shortly the implementation of the Marshaller interface for the String class.

- We inject the Marshaller instance using the constructor. This means that we should have an already created marshaller instance that is compatible with the *generic* type of the class T.

- The Stack<T> class implements the AutoCloseable interface. This simply means that it has some native resources that should be freed upon destruction. Note that the actual stack is created in the native code and not in the Java code. Therefore, the JVM's *garbage collector* cannot free the stack when it is not needed anymore. AutoCloseable objects can be used as resources which have a specific scope and when they are not needed anymore, their close method is called automatically. Shortly, you will see how we use the preceding class in a test scenario.

- As you see, we have the constructor method and we have initialized the underlying stack using the native methods. We keep a handler to the stack as a long field in the class. Note that unlike in C++, we don't have any destructors in the class. Therefore, it is possible not to have the underlying stack freed and for it eventually to become a memory leak. That's why we have marked the class as an AutoCloseable. When an AutoCloseable object is not needed anymore, its close method is called and as you see in the preceding code, we call the destructor function from the C stack library to release the resources allocated by the C stack.

Generally, you cannot trust the garbage collector mechanism to call *finalizer methods* on Java objects and using the `AutoCloseable` resources is the correct way to manage native resources.

The following is the implementation of `StringMarshaller`. The implementation is very straightforward thanks to the great support of the `String` class in working with byte arrays:

```
class StringMarshaller implements Marshaller<String> {

  @Override
  public byte[] marshal(String obj) {
    return obj.getBytes();
  }

  @Override
  public String unmarshal(byte[] data) {
    return new String(data);
  }
}
```

Code Box 21-11 [java/src/com/packt/extreme_c/ch21/ex1/Main.java]: The StringMarshaller class

The following code is our `Main` class that contains the test scenario for demonstration of C stack functionalities through Java code:

```
public class Main {
  public static void main(String[] args) {
    try (Stack<String> stack = new Stack<>(new
StringMarshaller())) {
      stack.push("Hello");
      stack.push("World");
      stack.push("!");
      System.out.println("Size after pushes: " + stack.size());
      while (stack.size() > 0) {
        System.out.println(stack.pop());
      }
      System.out.println("Size after pops: " + stack.size());
      stack.push("Ba");
      stack.push("Bye!");
      System.out.println("Size after before clear: " + stack.
size());
      stack.clear();
```

```
        System.out.println("Size after clear: " + stack.size());
      }
    }
  }
```

Code Box 21-12 [java/src/com/packt/extreme_c/ch21/ex1/Main.java]: The Main class that contains the test
scenario to check the functionalities of the C stack library

As you see, the reference variable stack is being created and used inside a try block. This syntax is usually called *try-with-resources* and it has been introduced as part of Java 7. When the try block is finished, the method close is called on the resource object and the underlying stack becomes freed. The test scenario is the same as the scenario we wrote for C++ in the previous section, but this time in Java.

In this section, we covered the Java part and all the Java code that we need to import the native part. All the sources above can be compiled but you cannot run them because you need the native part as well. Only together can they lead to an executable program. In the next section, we talk about the steps we should take to write the native part.

Writing the native part

The most important thing we introduced in the previous section was the idea of native methods. Native methods are declared within Java, but their definitions reside outside of the JVM in a shared object library. But how does the JVM find the definition of a native method in the loaded shared object files? The answer is simple: by looking up certain symbol names in the shared object files. The JVM extracts a symbol name for every native method based on its various properties like the package, the containing class, and its name. Then, it looks for that symbol in the loaded shared object libraries and if it cannot find it, it gives you an error.

Based on what we established in the previous section, the JVM forces us to use specific symbol names for the functions we write as part of the loaded shared object file. But we didn't use any specific convention while creating the stack library. So, the JVM won't be able to find our exposed functions from the stack library and we must come up with another way. Generally, C libraries are written without any assumption about being used in a JVM environment.

Figure 21-1 shows how we can use an intermediate C or C++ library to act as a glue between the Java part and the native part. We give the JVM the symbols it wants, and we delegate the function calls made to the functions representing those symbols to the correct function inside the C library. This is basically how JNI works.

We'll explain this with an imaginary example. Suppose that we want to make a call to a C function, `func`, from Java, and the definition of the function can be found in the `libfunc.so` shared object file. We also have a class `Clazz` in the Java part with a native function called `doFunc`. We know that the JVM would be looking for the symbol `Java_Clazz_doFunc` while trying to find the definition of the native function `doFunc`. We create an intermediate shared object library `libNativeLibrary.so` that contains a function with exactly the same symbol that the JVM is looking for. Then, inside that function, we make a call to the `func` function. We can say that the function `Java_Clazz_doFunc` acts as a relay and delegates the call to the underlying C library and eventually the `func` function.

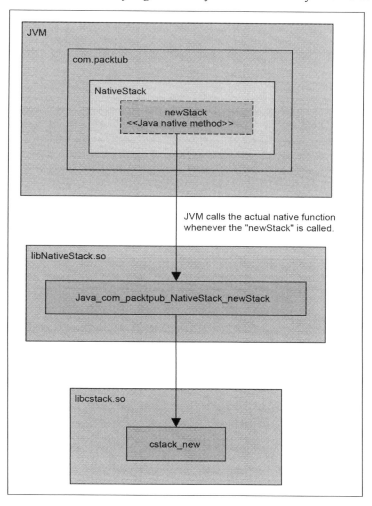

Figure 21-1: The intermediate shared object libNativeStack.so which is used to delegate function calls from Java to the actual underlying C stack library, libcstack.so.

In order to stay aligned with JVM symbol names, the Java compiler usually generates a C header file out of the native methods found in a Java code. This way, you only need to write the definitions of those functions found in the header file. This prevents us from making any mistakes in the symbol names that the JVM eventually would be looking for.

The following commands demonstrate how to compile a Java source file and how to ask the compiler to generate a header file for the found native methods in it. Here, we are going to compile our only Java file, `Main.java`, which contains all the Java code introduced in the previous code boxes. Note that we should be in the chapter's root directory when running the following commands:

```
$ cd java
$ mkdir -p build/headers
$ mkdir -p build/classes
$ javac -cp src -h build/headers -d build/classes \
src/com/packt/extreme_c/ch21/ex1/Main.java
$ tree build
build
├── classes
│   └── com
│       └── packt
│           └── extreme_c
│               └── ch21
│                   └── ex1
│                       ├── Main.class
│                       ├── Marshaller.class
│                       ├── NativeStack.class
│                       ├── Stack.class
│                       └── StringMarshaller.class
└── headers
    └── com_packt_extreme_c_ch21_ex1_NativeStack.h

7 directories, 6 files
$
```

Shell Box 21-11: Compiling the Main.java while generating a header for native methods found in the file

As shown in the preceding shell box, we have passed the option `-h` to `javac`, which is the Java compiler. We have also specified a directory that all headers should go to. The `tree` utility shows the content of the `build` directory in a tree-like format. Note the `.class` files. They contain the Java bytecode which will be used when loading these classes into a JVM instance.

In addition to class files we see a header file, `com_packt_extreme_c_ch21_ex1_NativeStack.h`, that contains the corresponding C function declarations for the native methods found in the `NativeStack` class.

If you open the header file, you will see something like *Code Box 21-13*. It has a number of function declarations with long and strange names each of which being made up of the package name, the class name, and the name of the corresponding native method:

```
/* DO NOT EDIT THIS FILE - it is machine generated */
#include <jni.h>
/* Header for class com_packt_extreme_c_ch21_ex1_NativeStack */

#ifndef _Included_com_packt_extreme_c_ch21_ex1_NativeStack
#define _Included_com_packt_extreme_c_ch21_ex1_NativeStack
#ifdef __cplusplus
extern "C" {
#endif
/*
 * Class:     com_packt_extreme_c_ch21_ex1_NativeStack
 * Method:    newStack
 * Signature: ()J
 */
JNIEXPORT jlong JNICALL Java_com_packt_extreme_1c_ch21_ex1_
NativeStack_newStack
  (JNIEnv *, jclass);

/*
 * Class:     com_packt_extreme_c_ch21_ex1_NativeStack
 * Method:    deleteStack
 * Signature: (J)V
 */
JNIEXPORT void JNICALL Java_com_packt_extreme_1c_ch21_ex1_
NativeStack_deleteStack
  (JNIEnv *, jclass, jlong);

 . . .
 . . .
 . . .


#ifdef __cplusplus
}
#endif
#endif
```

Code Box 21-13: The (incomplete) content of the generated JNI header file

The functions declared in the preceding header file carry the symbol names that the JVM would be looking for when loading the corresponding C function for a native method. We have modified the preceding header file and used macros to make it compact in order to have all the function declarations in a smaller area. You can see it in *Code Box 21-14*:

```
// Filename: NativeStack.h
// Description: Modified JNI generated header file

#include <jni.h>

#ifndef _Included_com_packt_extreme_c_ch21_ex1_NativeStack
#define _Included_com_packt_extreme_c_ch21_ex1_NativeStack

#define JNI_FUNC(n) Java_com_packt_extreme_1c_ch21_ex1_
NativeStack_##

#ifdef __cplusplus
extern "C" {
#endif

JNIEXPORT jlong JNICALL JNI_FUNC(newStack)(JNIEnv* , jclass);
JNIEXPORT void JNICALL JNI_FUNC(deleteStack)(JNIEnv* , jclass,
jlong);

JNIEXPORT void JNICALL JNI_FUNC(ctor)(JNIEnv* , jclass, jlong,
jint);
JNIEXPORT void JNICALL JNI_FUNC(dtor)(JNIEnv* , jclass, jlong);

JNIEXPORT jint JNICALL JNI_FUNC(size)(JNIEnv* , jclass, jlong);

JNIEXPORT void JNICALL JNI_FUNC(push)(JNIEnv* , jclass, jlong,
jbyteArray);
JNIEXPORT jbyteArray JNICALL JNI_FUNC(pop)(JNIEnv* , jclass,
jlong);

JNIEXPORT void JNICALL JNI_FUNC(clear)(JNIEnv* , jclass, jlong);

#ifdef __cplusplus
}
#endif
#endif
```

Code Box 21-14 [java/native/NativeStack.h]: The modified version of the generated JNI header file

As you see, we have created a new macro `JNI_FUNC` that factors out a big portion of the function name that is common for all of the declarations. We have also removed the comments in order to make the header file even more compact.

We will be using the macro `JNI_FUNC` in both the header file and the following source file, which are shown as part of *Code Box 21-15*.

Note:

It is not an accepted behavior to modify the generated header file. We did it because of educational purposes. In real build environments, it is desired to use the generated files directly without any modification.

In *Code Box 21-15*, you will find the definitions of the preceding functions. As you see, the definitions only relay the calls to the underlying C functions included from the C stack library:

```c
#include <stdlib.h>

#include "NativeStack.h"
#include "cstack.h"

void defaultDeleter(value_t* value) {
  free_value(value);
}

void extractFromJByteArray(JNIEnv* env,
                           jbyteArray byteArray,
                           value_t* value) {
  jboolean isCopy = false;
  jbyte* buffer = env->GetByteArrayElements(byteArray, &isCopy);
  value->len = env->GetArrayLength(byteArray);
  value->data = (char*)malloc(value->len * sizeof(char));
  for (size_t i = 0; i < value->len; i++) {
    value->data[i] = buffer[i];
  }
  env->ReleaseByteArrayElements(byteArray, buffer, 0);
}

JNIEXPORT jlong JNICALL JNI_FUNC(newStack)(JNIEnv* env,
                                           jclass clazz) {
  return (long)cstack_new();
}

JNIEXPORT void JNICALL JNI_FUNC(deleteStack)(JNIEnv* env,
                                             jclass clazz,
                                             jlong stackPtr) {
  cstack_t* cstack = (cstack_t*)stackPtr;
  cstack_delete(cstack);
}
```

```
JNIEXPORT void JNICALL JNI_FUNC(ctor)(JNIEnv *env,
                                      jclass clazz,
                                      jlong stackPtr,
                                      jint maxSize) {
  cstack_t* cstack = (cstack_t*)stackPtr;
  cstack_ctor(cstack, maxSize);
}

JNIEXPORT void JNICALL JNI_FUNC(dtor)(JNIEnv* env,
                                      jclass clazz,
                                      jlong stackPtr) {
  cstack_t* cstack = (cstack_t*)stackPtr;
  cstack_dtor(cstack, defaultDeleter);
}

JNIEXPORT jint JNICALL JNI_FUNC(size)(JNIEnv* env,
                                      jclass clazz,
                                      jlong stackPtr) {
  cstack_t* cstack = (cstack_t*)stackPtr;
  return cstack_size(cstack);
}

JNIEXPORT void JNICALL JNI_FUNC(push)(JNIEnv* env,
                                      jclass clazz,
                                      jlong stackPtr,
                                      jbyteArray item) {
  value_t value;
  extractFromJByteArray(env, item, &value);

  cstack_t* cstack = (cstack_t*)stackPtr;
  bool_t pushed = cstack_push(cstack, value);
  if (!pushed) {
    jclass Exception = env->FindClass("java/lang/Exception");
    env->ThrowNew(Exception, "Stack is full!");
  }
}

JNIEXPORT jbyteArray JNICALL JNI_FUNC(pop)(JNIEnv* env,
                                           jclass clazz,
                                           jlong stackPtr) {
  value_t value;
  cstack_t* cstack = (cstack_t*)stackPtr;
  bool_t popped = cstack_pop(cstack, &value);
  if (!popped) {
    jclass Exception = env->FindClass("java/lang/Exception");
    env->ThrowNew(Exception, "Stack is empty!");
  }
```

```
    jbyteArray result = env->NewByteArray(value.len);
    env->SetByteArrayRegion(result, 0,
            value.len, (jbyte*)value.data);
    defaultDeleter(&value);
    return result;
}


JNIEXPORT void JNICALL JNI_FUNC(clear)(JNIEnv* env,
                                       jclass clazz,
                                       jlong stackPtr) {
    cstack_t* cstack = (cstack_t*)stackPtr;
    cstack_clear(cstack, defaultDeleter);
}
```

Code Box 21-15 [java/native/NativeStack.cpp]: The definitions of the functions declared in the JNI header file

The preceding code is written in C++. It is possible to write the definitions in
C as well. The only thing demanding attention is the conversion from C byte
arrays into Java byte arrays happening in push and pop functions. The function
extractFromJByteArray has been added to create a C byte array based on a Java
byte array received from the Java part.

The following commands create the intermediate shared object libNativeStack.
so in Linux, which is going to be loaded and used by the JVM. Note that you
need to set the environment variable JAVA_HOME before running the following
commands:

```
$ cd java/native
$ g++ -c -fPIC -I$PWD/../.. -I$JAVA_HOME/include \
  -I$JAVA_HOME/include/linux NativeStack.cpp -o NativeStack.o
$ g++ -shared -L$PWD/../.. NativeStack.o -lcstack -o
libNativeStack.so
$
```

Shell Box 21-12: Building the intermediate shared object library libNativeStack.so

As you see, the final shared object file is linked against the C stack library's
shared object file libcstack.so which simply means the libNativeStack.
so has to load libcstack.so in order to work. Therefore, the JVM loads the
libNativeStack.so library and then it loads libcstack.so library, and
eventually the Java part and the native part can cooperate and let the Java
program be executed.

The following commands run the test scenario shown in *Code Box 21-12*:

```
$ cd java
$ LD_LIBRARY_PATH=$PWD/.. java -Djava.library.path=$PWD/native \
  -cp build/classes com.packt.extreme_c.ch21.ex1.Main
Size after pushes: 3
!
World
Hello
Size after pops: 0
Size after before clear: 2
Size after clear: 0
$
```

Shell Box 21-13: Running the Java test scenario

As you see, we have passed the option `-Djava.library.path=...` to the JVM. It specifies the place where shared object libraries can be found. As you see, we have specified the directory which should contain the `libNativeStack.so` shared object library.

In this section, we showed how to load a native C library into the JVM and use it together with other Java source code. The same mechanism can be applied for loading bigger and multi-part native libraries.

Now, it's time to go through the Python integration and see how the C stack library can be used from Python code.

Integration with Python

Python is an *interpreted* programming language. This means that the Python code is read and run by an intermediate program that is called an *interpreter*. If we are going to use an external native shared library, it is the interpreter that loads the shared library and makes it available to the Python code. Python has a special framework for loading external shared libraries. It is called *ctypes* and we are going to use it in this section.

Loading the shared libraries using `ctypes` is very straightforward. It only requires loading the library and defining the inputs and output of the functions that are going to be used. The following class wraps the ctypes-related logic and makes it available to our main `Stack` class, shown in the upcoming code boxes:

```python
from ctypes import *

class value_t(Structure):
    _fields_ = [("data", c_char_p), ("len", c_int)]

class _NativeStack:
    def __init__(self):
        self.stackLib = cdll.LoadLibrary(
                "libcstack.dylib" if platform.system() == 'Darwin'
                else "libcstack.so")

        # value_t make_value(char*, size_t)
        self._makevalue_ = self.stackLib.make_value
        self._makevalue_.argtypes = [c_char_p, c_int]
        self._makevalue_.restype = value_t

        # value_t copy_value(char*, size_t)
        self._copyvalue_ = self.stackLib.copy_value
        self._copyvalue_.argtypes = [c_char_p, c_int]
        self._copyvalue_.restype = value_t

        # void free_value(value_t*)
        self._freevalue_ = self.stackLib.free_value
        self._freevalue_.argtypes = [POINTER(value_t)]

        # cstack_t* cstack_new()
        self._new_ = self.stackLib.cstack_new
        self._new_.argtypes = []
        self._new_.restype = c_void_p

        # void cstack_delete(cstack_t*)
        self._delete_ = self.stackLib.cstack_delete
        self._delete_.argtypes = [c_void_p]

        # void cstack_ctor(cstack_t*, int)
        self._ctor_ = self.stackLib.cstack_ctor
        self._ctor_.argtypes = [c_void_p, c_int]

        # void cstack_dtor(cstack_t*, deleter_t)
        self._dtor_ = self.stackLib.cstack_dtor
        self._dtor_.argtypes = [c_void_p, c_void_p]

        # size_t cstack_size(cstack_t*)
        self._size_ = self.stackLib.cstack_size
        self._size_.argtypes = [c_void_p]
        self._size_.restype = c_int

        # bool_t cstack_push(cstack_t*, value_t)
```

```
self._push_ = self.stackLib.cstack_push
self._push_.argtypes = [c_void_p, value_t]
self._push_.restype = c_int

# bool_t cstack_pop(cstack_t*, value_t*)
self._pop_ = self.stackLib.cstack_pop
self._pop_.argtypes = [c_void_p, POINTER(value_t)]
self._pop_.restype = c_int

# void cstack_clear(cstack_t*, deleter_t)
self._clear_ = self.stackLib.cstack_clear
self._clear_.argtypes = [c_void_p, c_void_p]
```

Code Box 21-17 [python/stack.py]: The ctypes-related code that makes the stack library's C functions available to the rest of Python

As you can see, all the functions required to be used in our Python code are put in the class definition. The handles to the C functions are stored as private fields in the class instance (private fields have _ on both sides) and they can be used to call the underlying C function. Note that in the above code, we have loaded the libcstack.dylib, as we are in a macOS system. And for Linux systems, we need to load libcstack.so.

The following class is the main Python component that uses the above wrapper class. All other Python code uses this class to have the stack functionality:

```
class Stack:
  def __enter__(self):
    self._nativeApi_ = _NativeStack()
    self._handler_ = self._nativeApi_._new_()
    self._nativeApi_._ctor_(self._handler_, 100)
    return self

  def __exit__(self, type, value, traceback):
    self._nativeApi_._dtor_(self._handler_, self._nativeApi_._
freevalue_)
    self._nativeApi_._delete_(self._handler_)

  def size(self):
    return self._nativeApi_._size_(self._handler_)

  def push(self, item):
    result = self._nativeApi_._push_(self._handler_,
            self._nativeApi_._copyvalue_(item.encode('utf-8'),
len(item)));
    if result != 1:
```

```
    raise Exception("Stack is full!")

  def pop(self):
    value = value_t()
    result = self._nativeApi_._pop_(self._handler_, byref(value))
    if result != 1:
      raise Exception("Stack is empty!")
    item = string_at(value.data, value.len)
    self._nativeApi_._freevalue_(value)
    return item

  def clear(self):
    self._nativeApi_._clear_(self._handler_, self._nativeApi_._
freevalue_)
```

Code Box 21-16 [python/stack.py]: The Stack class in Python that uses the loaded C functions from the stack library

As you see, the Stack class keeps a reference to the `_NativeStack` class in order to be able to call the underlying C functions. Note that the preceding class overrides `__enter__` and `__exit__` functions. This allows the class to be used as a resource class and be consumed in the `with` syntax in Python. You will see shortly what the syntax looks like. Please note that the preceding Stack class only operates on string items.

The following is the test scenario, which is very similar to the Java and C++ test scenarios:

```
if __name__ == "__main__":
  with Stack() as stack:
    stack.push("Hello")
    stack.push("World")
    stack.push("!")
    print("Size after pushes:" + str(stack.size()))
    while stack.size() > 0:
      print(stack.pop())
    print("Size after pops:" + str(stack.size()))
    stack.push("Ba");
    stack.push("Bye!");
    print("Size before clear:" + str(stack.size()))
    stack.clear()
    print("Size after clear:" + str(stack.size()))
```

Code Box 21-18 [python/stack.py]: The test scenario written in Python and using the Stack class

In the preceding code, you can see Python's `with` statement.

Upon entering the with block, the __enter__ function is called and an instance of the Stack class is referenced by the stack variable. When leaving the with block, the __exit__ function is called. This gives us the opportunity to free the underlying native resources, the C stack object in this case, when they are not needed anymore.

Next, you can see how to run the preceding code. Note that all the Python code boxes exist within the same file named stack.py. Before running the following commands, you need to be in the chapter's root directory:

```
$ cd python
$ LD_LIBRARY_PATH=$PWD/.. python stack.py
Size after pushes:3
!
World
Hello
Size after pops:0
Size before clear:2
Size after clear:0
$
```

Shell Box 21-14: Running the Python test scenario

Note that the interpreter should be able to find and load the C stack shared library; therefore, we set the LD_LIBRARY_PATH environment variable to point to the directory that contains the actual shared library file.

In the following section, we show how to load and use the C stack library in the Go language.

Integration with Go

The Go programming language (or simply Golang) has an easy integration with native shared libraries. It can be considered as the next generation of the C and C++ programming languages and it calls itself a system programming language. Therefore, we expect to load and use the native libraries easily when using Golang.

In Golang, we use a built-in package called *cgo* to call C code and load the shared object files. In the following Go code, you see how to use the cgo package and use it to call the C functions loaded from the C stack library file. It also defines a new class, Stack, which is used by other Go code to use the C stack functionalities:

```
package main
```

```
/*
#cgo CFLAGS: -I..
#cgo LDFLAGS: -L.. -lcstack
#include "cstack.h"
*/
import "C"
import (
  "fmt"
)

type Stack struct {
  handler *C.cstack_t
}

func NewStack() *Stack {
  s := new(Stack)
  s.handler = C.cstack_new()
  C.cstack_ctor(s.handler, 100)
  return s
}

func (s *Stack) Destroy() {
  C.cstack_dtor(s.handler, C.deleter_t(C.free_value))
  C.cstack_delete(s.handler)
}

func (s *Stack) Size() int {
  return int(C.cstack_size(s.handler))
}

func (s *Stack) Push(item string) bool {
  value := C.make_value(C.CString(item), C.ulong(len(item) + 1))
  pushed := C.cstack_push(s.handler, value)
  return pushed == 1
}

func (s *Stack) Pop() (bool, string) {
  value := C.make_value(nil, 0)
  popped := C.cstack_pop(s.handler, &value)
  str := C.GoString(value.data)
  defer C.free_value(&value)
  return popped == 1, str
}

func (s *Stack) Clear() {
  C.cstack_clear(s.handler, C.deleter_t(C.free_value))
}
```

Code Box 21-19 [go/stack.go]: The Stack class using the loaded libcstack.so shared object file

In order to use the cgo package, one needs to import the C package. It loads the shared object libraries specified in the pseudo #cgo directives. As you see, we have specified the libcstack.so library to be loaded as part of the directive #cgo LDFLAGS: -L.. -lcstack. Note that the CFLAGS and LDFLAGS contain the flags that are directly passed to the C compiler and to the linker respectively.

We have also indicated the path that should be searched for the shared object file. After that, we can use the C struct to call the loaded native functions. For example, we have used C.cstack_new() to call the corresponding function from the stack library. It is pretty easy with cgo. Note that the preceding Stack class only works on string items.

The following code shows the test scenario written in Golang. Note that we have to call the Destroy function on the stack object when quitting the main function:

```go
func main() {
  var stack = NewStack()
  stack.Push("Hello")
  stack.Push("World")
  stack.Push("!")
  fmt.Println("Stack size:", stack.Size())
  for stack.Size() > 0 {
    _, str := stack.Pop()
    fmt.Println("Popped >", str)
  }
  fmt.Println("Stack size after pops:", stack.Size())
  stack.Push("Bye")
  stack.Push("Bye")
  fmt.Println("Stack size before clear:", stack.Size())
  stack.Clear()
  fmt.Println("Stack size after clear:", stack.Size())
  stack.Destroy()
}
```

Code Box 21-20 [go/stack.go]: The test scenario written in Go and using the Stack class

The following shell box demonstrates how to build and run the test scenario:

```
$ cd go
$ go build -o stack.out stack.go
$ LD_LIBRARY_PATH=$PWD/.. ./stack.out
Stack size: 3
Popped > !
Popped > World
Popped > Hello
```

```
Stack size after pops: 0
Stack size before clear: 2
Stack size after clear: 0
$
```

Shell Box 21-15: Running the Go test scenario

As you see in Golang, unlike Python, you need to compile your program first, and then run it. In addition, we still need to set the LD_LIBRARY_PATH environment variable in order to allow the executable to locate the libcstack.so library and load it.

In this section, we showed how to use the cgo package in Golang to load and use shared object libraries. Since Golang behaves like a thin wrapper around C code, it has been easier than using Python and Java to load an external shared object library and use it.

Summary

In this chapter, we went through the integration of C within other programming languages. As part of this chapter:

- We designed a C library that was exposing some stack functionality such as push, pop, and so on. We built the library and as the final output we generated a shared object library to be used by other languages.

- We discussed the name mangling feature in C++, and how we should avoid it in C when using a C++ compiler.

- We wrote a C++ wrapper around the stack library that could load the library's shared object file and execute the loaded functionalities within C++.

- We continued by writing a JNI wrapper around the C library. We used native methods to achieve that.

- We showed how to write native code in JNI and connect the native part and Java part together, and finally run a Java program that uses the C stack library.

- We managed to write Python code that was using the ctypes package to load and use the library's shared object file.

- As the final section, we wrote a program in Golang that could load the library's shared object file with help from the cgo package.

The next chapter is about unit testing and debugging in C. We will introduce some C libraries meant for writing unit tests. More than that, we talk about debugging in C, and some of the existing tools that could be used to debug or monitor a program.

Chapter 22
Unit Testing and Debugging

It doesn't really matter which programming language you are using or what type of application you are developing, it is always important to thoroughly test it before delivering it to the customer.

Writing tests is not a new thing and as of today, you can find hundreds or even thousands of tests in almost every software project. Nowadays writing tests for software is a must and delivering a piece of code or feature without having it tested properly is strongly discouraged. That's why we have a dedicated chapter to talk about testing software written in C, and various libraries that exist today for this purpose.

Testing is not the only topic in this chapter, however. We will also be discussing the debugging tools and techniques that can be used to troubleshoot a C program. Testing and debugging have complimented one another from the start, and whenever a test fails, a series of investigations are followed and debugging the target code is a common follow-up action.

In this chapter, we won't go through the philosophy of testing and we assume that testing is good. Instead, we will give you a short introduction about the basic terminology and the guidelines that a developer should follow in order to write testable code.

This chapter has two sections. In the first section, we talk about testing and the existing libraries that can be used in modern C development. The second section of this chapter is going to talk about debugging, starting with a discussion about various categories of bugs. Memory issues, concurrency issues, and performance issues are the most common cases in which further debugging seems to be necessary in order to establish a successful investigation.

We will also cover the most used debugging tools available for C (and C++). The final goal of this chapter is to let you know about the testing and debugging utilities available for C and give you some basic background knowledge about them.

The first section introduces you to the basic terminology of software testing in general. It is not specific to C, and the ideas and concepts can be applied to other programming languages and technologies as well.

Software testing

Software testing is a big and important subject in computer programming, and it has its own specific terminology and many concepts. In this section, we are going to give you a very basic introduction to software testing. Our purpose is to define some terms that we are going to use in the first half of this chapter. Therefore, you should be aware that this is not a thorough chapter about testing and further study is strongly encouraged.

When it comes to testing software, the first question that comes to mind is, what are we testing, and what is this testing about? In general, we test an aspect of a software system. This aspect can be *functional* or *non-functional*. In other words, the aspect may be related to a certain functionality of the system, or it can be related to a certain variable of a system when performing a functionality. Next, we give some examples.

Functional testing is about testing a defined functionality requested as part of the *functional requirements*. These tests provide a certain input to a *software element* such as a *function*, a *module*, a *component*, or a *software system*, and expect a certain output from them. Only if the expected output is seen as part of a test is that test considered as *passed*.

Non-functional testing is about the *quality level* to which a software element, such as a function, a module, a component, or a software system as a whole, completes a specific functionality. These tests are usually supposed to *measure* various *variables* like *memory usage*, *time to completion*, *lock contention*, and *level of security*, and assess how well that element has done its job. A test is passed only when the measured variables are within the expected ranges. The *expectations* for these variables are derived from the *non-functional requirements* defined for the system.

Apart from functional and non-functional testing, we can have different *levels* of testing. These levels are designed in a way to cover some orthogonal aspects. Some of these aspects are size of the tested element, the actor of the test, and the extent of the functionalities that should be tested.

For instance, regarding the size of the element, these levels are defined from the smallest possible piece of functionality, which we know as a function (or a method), up to the biggest possible piece of functionality that it is exposed from a software system as a whole.

In the following section, we are going to introduce these levels in a deeper sense

Testing levels

For every software system, the following levels of testing can be considered and planned. These are not the only existing testing levels and you can find more of them in other references:

- Unit testing
- Integration testing
- System testing
- Acceptance testing
- Regression testing

In *unit testing*, we test a *unit* of functionality. This unit can be a function that performs a certain job, or a group of functions together to satisfy a need, or a class that has a final goal to perform a certain functionality, or even a component that has a specific task to do. A *component* is a part of a software system that has a well-defined set of functionalities and, together with other components, joins and becomes the whole software system.

In the case of having components as units, we call the testing process *component testing*. Both functional and non-functional testing can be done at the level of units. When testing a unit, that unit should become isolated from its surrounding units, and for this to happen, the surrounding environment should be simulated in some way. This level would be the only level that we cover as part of this chapter and we provide real code to demonstrate how unit testing and component testing can be done in C.

When the units join together, they form a component. In component testing, a component is tested alone in isolation. But when we group some of these components, we need a different level of testing that checks the functionality or the variables for that specific group of components. This level is *integration testing*. As the name implies, the tests in this level check if the integration of some of the components works well and they together still satisfy the defined requirements for the system.

At a different level, we test the functionality of the whole system. This will contain a complete set of all components fully integrated. This way, we test if the exposed system functionalities and system variables are in accordance with the requirements defined for the software system.

On a different level, we evaluate a software system to check if it is in accordance with the business requirements defined for that system from the *stakeholder* or *end user* point of view. This level is called *acceptance testing*. While both system testing and acceptance testing is about the whole software system, they are actually quite different. To name a few differences:

- System testing is done by developers and testers, but acceptance testing is usually done by the end user or the stakeholder.

- System testing is about checking both functional and non-functional requirements, but acceptance testing is only about functional requirements.

- In system testing, we usually use a prepared small set of data as the input, but in acceptance testing, the actual real-time data is fed to the system.

A great link that explains all the differences can be found at https://www.javatpoint.com/acceptance-testing.

When a change is introduced to a software system, it is required to check if the current functional and non-functional tests are still in a good shape. This is done at a different level known as *regression testing*. The purpose of regression testing is to confirm that there is no *regression* after introducing a change. As part of regression testing, all the functional and non-functional tests found as unit tests, integration tests, and end-to-end (system) tests are run again to see if any of them fail following a change.

In this section, we introduced various levels of testing. For the rest of this chapter, we are going to discuss unit testing. In the upcoming section, we start talking about it by giving a C example and trying to write test cases for it.

Unit testing

As we explained in the previous section, as part of unit testing, we test isolated units and a unit can be as small as a function or as big as a component. In C, it can be a function or a whole component written in C. The same discussion can be applied to C++ as well, but there we can have other units like classes.

The most important thing about unit testing is that units should be tested in isolation. For example, if the target function depends on the output of another function, we need to find a way to test the target function in isolation. We are going to explain this using a real example.

Example 22.1 prints the factorials of even numbers less than 10, but not in the usual way. The code is well-organized in one header and two source files. The example is about two functions; one of them generates the even numbers less than 10 and the other function receives a function pointer and uses it as a source for reading an integer number, and finally calculates its factorial.

The following code box contains the header file containing the function declarations:

```
#ifndef _EXTREME_C_EXAMPLE_22_1_
#define _EXTREME_C_EXAMPLE_22_1_

#include <stdint.h>
#include <unistd.h>
```

```
typedef int64_t (*int64_feed_t)();

int64_t next_even_number();

int64_t calc_factorial(int64_feed_t feed);

#endif
```

Code Box 22-1 [ExtremeC_examples_chapter22_1.h]: The header file of example 22.1

As you can see, the function `calc_factorial` accepts a function pointer that returns an integer. It will use the function pointer in order to read an integer and calculate its factorial. The following code is the definition of the preceding functions:

```
#include "ExtremeC_examples_chapter22_1.h"

int64_t next_even_number() {
  static int feed = -2;
  feed += 2;
  if (feed >= 10) {
    feed = 0;
  }
  return feed;
}

int64_t calc_factorial(int64_feed_t feed) {
  int64_t fact = 1;
  int64_t number = feed();
  for (int64_t i = 1; i <= number; i++) {
    fact *= i;
  }
  return fact;
}
```

Code Box 22-2 [ExtremeC_examples_chapter22_1.c]: The definitions of the functions used in example 22.1

The `next_even_number` function has an internal static variable that acts as a feed for the caller function. Note that it never exceeds 8 and after that, it goes back to 0. Therefore, you can simply call this function as many times as you like, and you never get a number greater than 8 and lower than zero. The following code box contains the content of the source file that contains the `main` function:

```
#include <stdio.h>

#include "ExtremeC_examples_chapter22_1.h"
```

```
int main(int argc, char** argv) {
  for (size_t i = 1; i <= 12; i++) {
    printf("%lu\n", calc_factorial(next_even_number));
  }
  return 0;
}
```

Code Box 22-3 [ExtremeC_examples_chapter22_1_main.c]: The main function of example 22.1

As you see, the `main` function calls the `calc_function` 12 times and prints the returned factorials. In order to run the preceding example, you need to compile both source files first and then link their corresponding relocatable object files together. The following shell box contains the required commands to build and run the example:

```
$ gcc -c ExtremeC_examples_chapter22_1.c -o impl.o
$ gcc -c ExtremeC_examples_chapter22_1_main.c -o main.o
$ gcc impl.o main.o -o ex22_1.out
$ ./ex22_1.out
1
2
24
720
40320
1
2
24
720
40320
1
2
$
```

Shell Box 22-1: Building and running example 22.1

In order to write tests for the preceding functions, we need to give a bit of introduction first. As you can see, we have two functions (not including the `main` function) in the example. Therefore, there are two different units, in this case functions, that should be tested separately and in isolation from each other; one is the `next_even_number` function and the other one is the `calc_factorial` function. But as it is clear in the main function, the `calc_factorial` function depends on the `next_even_number` function and one might think that this dependency is going to make the isolation of the `calc_factorial` function much harder than we anticipated. But this is not true.

In fact, the `calc_factorial` function does not depend on the `next_even_number` function at all. It only depends on the *signature* of `next_even_number` and not its definition. Therefore, it is possible to replace `next_even_number` with a function that follows the same signature, but always returns a fixed integer. In other words, we can provide a simplified version of `next_even_number` that is intended to be used only in the *test cases*.

So, what is a test case? As you know, there are various scenarios to test a specific unit. The simplest example is to provide various inputs to a certain unit and *expect* a predetermined output. In the preceding example, we can provide 0 as the input for the `calc_factorial` function and wait for 1 as its output. We can also provide -1 and wait for 1.

Every one of these scenarios can be a test case. Therefore, regarding a single unit, we can have multiple test cases addressing all different corner cases of that unit. A collection of test cases is called a *test suite*. All the test cases found in a test suite are not necessarily related to the same unit.

We start by creating a test suite for the `next_even_number` function. Since `next_even_number` can be easily tested in isolation, there is no need for extra work. Following are the test cases written for the `next_even_number` function:

```c
#include <assert.h>

#include "ExtremeC_examples_chapter22_1.h"

void TESTCASE_next_even_number__even_numbers_should_be_returned()
{
    assert(next_even_number() == 0);
    assert(next_even_number() == 2);
    assert(next_even_number() == 4);
    assert(next_even_number() == 6);
    assert(next_even_number() == 8);
}

void TESTCASE_next_even_number__numbers_should_rotate() {
    int64_t number = next_even_number();
    next_even_number();
    next_even_number();
    next_even_number();
    next_even_number();
    int64_t number2 = next_even_number();
    assert(number == number2);
}
```

Code Box 22-4 [ExtremeC_examples_chapter22_1__next_even_number__tests.c]: The test cases written for the next_even_number function

As you see, we have defined two test cases in the preceding test suite. Note that I have used my own convention to give names to the above test cases; however, there is no standard regarding this. The whole purpose of naming test cases is to realize what a test case does from its name and more important than that, to find it easily in the code when the test case fails or needs to be modified.

I used the capital TESTCASE as a prefix to function names to make them distinguished from other ordinary functions. The names of the functions also try to describe the test case and the concern it is addressing.

Both test cases have assert at the end. This is the thing that all test case functions do when evaluating the expectations. If the condition inside the parentheses of assert is not true, the *test runner*, a program that is running the tests, quits and an error message is printed. More than that, the test runner returns a non-zero *exit code* that indicates one or more of the test cases have failed. The test runner program must return 0 when all tests have been successful.

It would be nice to go through the test cases on your own and try to understand how they evaluate our expectations by calling the next_even_number function in the preceding two scenarios.

Now, it's time to write test cases for the calc_factorial function. Writing test cases for the calc_factorial function needs a *stub function* as its feed that returns the test input. We explain what stubs are shortly.

Following are three test cases that are only testing the calc_factorial unit:

```
#include <assert.h>

#include "ExtremeC_examples_chapter22_1.h"

int64_t input_value = -1;

int64_t feed_stub() {
  return input_value;
}

void TESTCASE_calc_factorial__fact_of_zero_is_one() {
  input_value = 0;
  int64_t fact = calc_factorial(feed_stub);
  assert(fact == 1);
}

void TESTCASE_calc_factorial__fact_of_negative_is_one() {
  input_value = -10;
  int64_t fact = calc_factorial(feed_stub);
```

```
    assert(fact == 1);
}

void TESTCASE_calc_factorial__fact_of_5_is_120() {
  input_value = 5;
  int64_t fact = calc_factorial(feed_stub);
  assert(fact == 120);
}
```

Code Box 22-5 [ExtremeC_examples_chapter22_1 __calc_factorial__tests.c]: The test cases written for the calc_
factorial function

As you can see, we have defined three test cases for the `calc_factorial` function. Note the `feed_stub` function. It follows the same contract that `next_even_number` is following, as can be seen in *Code Box 22-2*, but it has a very simple definition. It just returns a value stored in the static variable `input_value`. This variable can be set by the test cases before calling the `calc_facorial` function.

Using the preceding stub function, we could isolate `calc_factorial` and test it individually. The same approach is valid for object-oriented programming languages like C++ or Java, but there we define *stub classes* and *stub objects*.

In C, a *stub* is a function definition that conforms to a function declaration that the target unit would use as part of its logic, and more importantly, the stub doesn't have a complex logic and it just returns a value that is going to be used just by the test case.

In C++, a stub can still be a function definition that conforms to a function declaration, or a class that implements an interface. In other object-oriented languages where you cannot have standalone functions, for instance Java, a stub can only be a class that implements an interface. Then, a stub object is an object from such stub classes. Note that in all cases, a stub should have a simple definition that is only usable in tests, and not in production.

Finally, we need to be able to run the test cases. As we said previously, we need a test runner to run tests. Therefore, we need a specific source file with a `main` function that only runs the test cases one after another. The following code box contains the code of the test runner:

```
#include <stdio.h>

void TESTCASE_next_even_number__even_numbers_should_be_returned();
void TESTCASE_next_even_number__numbers_should_rotate();

void TESTCASE_calc_factorial__fact_of_zero_is_one();
void TESTCASE_calc_factorial__fact_of_negative_is_one();
void TESTCASE_calc_factorial__fact_of_5_is_120();
```

```
int main(int argc, char** argv) {
  TESTCASE_next_even_number__even_numbers_should_be_returned();
  TESTCASE_next_even_number__numbers_should_rotate();
  TESTCASE_calc_factorial__fact_of_zero_is_one();
  TESTCASE_calc_factorial__fact_of_negative_is_one();
  TESTCASE_calc_factorial__fact_of_5_is_120();
  printf("All tests are run successfully.\n");
  return 0;
}
```

Code Box 22-6 [ExtremeC_examples_chapter22_1 _tests.c]: The test runner used in example 22.1

The above code returns 0 only if all the test cases within the main functions are executed successfully. For building the test runner, we need to run the following commands. Note the -g option that adds debugging symbols to the final test runner executable. Performing a *debug build* is the most common way to build tests since if a test case fails, we immediately need the precise *stack trace* and further debugging information to proceed with investigation. More than that, the assert statements are usually removed from *release builds*, but we need to have them in the test runner executable:

```
$ gcc -g -c ExtremeC_examples_chapter22_1.c -o impl.o
$ gcc -g -c ExtremeC_examples_chapter22_1__next_even_number__
tests.c -o tests1.o
$ gcc -g -c ExtremeC_examples_chapter22_1__calc_factorial__tests.c
-o tests2.o
$ gcc -g -c ExtremeC_examples_chapter22_1_tests.c -o main.o
$ gcc impl.o tests1.o tests2.o main.o -o ex22_1_tests.out
$ ./ex22_1_tests.out
All tests are run successfully.
$ echo $?
0
$
```

Shell Box 22-2: Building and running the test runner of example 22.1

The preceding shell box shows that all the tests have been passed. You can also check the exit code of the test runner process by using the echo $? command and see that it has returned zero.

Now, by applying a simple change in one of the functions, we can fail the tests. Let's see what happens when we change calc_factorial as follows:

```
int64_t calc_factorial(int64_feed_t feed) {
  int64_t fact = 1;
  int64_t number = feed();
  for (int64_t i = 1; i <= (number + 1); i++) {
    fact *= i;
  }
  return fact;
}
```

Code Box 22-7: Changing the calc_factorial function to fail the tests

With the preceding change, shown in bold font, the test cases about the 0 and negative inputs still pass, but the last test case, which is about the calculation of the factorial of 5, fails. We are going to build the test runner again and the following is the output of the execution on a macOS machine:

```
$ gcc -g -c ExtremeC_examples_chapter22_1.c -o impl.o
$ gcc -g -c ExtremeC_examples_chapter22_1_tests.c -o main.o
$ ./ex22_1_tests.out
Assertion failed: (fact == 120), function TESTCASE_calc_
factorial__fact_of_5_is_120,
file .../22.1/ExtremeC_examples_chapter22_1__calc_factorial__
tests.c, line 29.
Abort trap: 6
$ echo $?
134
$
```

Shell Box 22-3: Building and running the test runner after changing the calc_factorial function

As you can see, `Assertion failed` appears in the output and the exit code is `134`. This exit code is usually used and reported by the systems running the tests periodically, such as *Jenkins*, to check if the tests have been run successfully.

As a rule of thumb, whenever you have a unit that should be tested in isolation, you need to find a way to provide its dependencies as some kind of input. Therefore, the unit itself should be written in a way that makes it *testable*. Not all code is testable, and testability is not limited to unit testing, and this is very important to be aware of. This link provides good information on how to write testable code: `https://blog.gurock.com/highly-testable-code/`.

To clarify the above discussion, suppose that we have written the `calc_factorial` function like below to use the `next_even_number` function directly instead of using a function pointer. Note that in the following code box, the function doesn't receive a function pointer argument and it calls the `next_even_number` function directly:

```
int64_t calc_factorial() {
  int64_t fact = 1;
  int64_t number = next_even_number();
  for (int64_t i = 1; i <= number; i++) {
    fact *= i;
  }
  return fact;
}
```

Code Box 22-8: Changing the calc_factorial function's signature to not accept a function pointer

The preceding code is less testable. There is no way to test `calc_factorial` without having the `next_even_number` called – that is, without employing some hacks to change the definition behind the symbol `next_even_number` as part of the final executable, as we do in *example 22.2*.

In fact, both versions of `calc_factorial` do the same thing, but the definition in *Code Box 22-2* is more testable because we could test it in isolation. Writing testable code is not easy, and you should always think carefully in order to implement code and have it be testable.

Writing testable code usually demands more work. There are various opinions about the overhead percentage of writing testable code but it is certain that writing tests brings some extra cost in terms of time and effort. But this extra cost surely has great benefits. Without having tests for a unit, you will lose track of it as time goes by and more changes are introduced to the unit.

Test doubles

In the preceding example, while writing test cases, we introduced stub functions. There are a few other terms about the objects that try to mimic a unit's dependencies. These objects are called *test doubles*. Next, we are going to introduce two other test doubles: *mock* and *fake* functions. First, let's briefly explain again what stub functions are.

Note two things in this short section. Firstly, there are never-ending debates on the definition of these test doubles, and we try to give a proper definition that matches our usage in this chapter. Secondly, we keep our discussion only relevant to C, so there is no object and everything we have is a function.

When a unit is dependent on another function, it simply depends on the signature of that function, therefore that function can be replaced by a new one. This new function, based on some properties that it might have, can be called a stub, a mock, or a fake function. These functions are just written to satisfy the test requirements and they cannot be used in production.

We explained a stub to be a function that is very simple, usually just returning a constant value. As you saw in *example 22.1*, it was indirectly returning a value just set by the running test case. In the following link, you can read more about the test doubles that we are talking about and a few more of them: `https://en.wikipedia.org/wiki/Test_double`. If you open the link, a stub is defined as something that provides an *indirect input* to the testing code. If you accept this definition, the `feed_stub` function seen in *Code Box 22-5* is a stub function.

Mock functions, or generally mock objects as part of object-oriented languages, can be manipulated by specifying the output for a certain input. This way, you set whatever should be returned from a mock function for a certain input before running the test logic and during the logic it will act as you have set beforehand. Mock objects in general can have expectations as well and they perform the required assertions accordingly. As stated in the preceding link, for mock objects, we set expectations before running the test. We are going to give a C example of mock functions as part of the component testing section.

Finally, a fake function can be used to give a very simplified functionality for a real and maybe complex functionality as part of the running test. For example, instead of using a real filesystem, one may use some simplified in-memory storage. In component testing, for instance, other components that have complex functionalities can be replaced by fake implementations in the tests.

Before ending this section, I want to talk about *code coverage*. In theory, all units should have corresponding test suites and each test suite should contain all test cases that go through all possible branches of code. As we said, this is in theory, but in practice you usually have test units only for a percentage of units. Often, you don't have test cases that cover all possible branches of code.

The proportion of units that have proper test cases is called code coverage or *test coverage*. The higher the proportion, the better placed you are for getting notified about unwanted modifications. These unwanted modifications are not usually introduced by bad developers. In fact, these breaking changes are usually introduced while someone is working on a piece of code for fixing a bug or implementing a new feature.

Having covered test doubles, we talk about component testing in the next section.

Component testing

As we explained in the previous section, units can be defined as a single function, a group of functions, or a whole component. Therefore, component testing is a special type of unit testing. In this section, we want to define a hypothetical component as part of *example 22.1* and put the two functions found in the example into this component. Note that a component usually results in an executable or a library. We can suppose that our hypothetical component would result in a library that contains the two functions.

As we said before, we have to be able to test the functionality of a component. In this section, we still want to write test cases but the difference between the tests written in this section and the previous section is to do with the units that should be isolated. In the previous section, we had functions that should have been isolated, but in this section, we have a component, compromising of two functions working hand in hand, that needs to be isolated. So, the functions must be tested when they are working together.

Next, you can find the test cases we have written for the component defined as part of *example 22.1*:

```
#include <assert.h>

#include "ExtremeC_examples_chapter22_1.h"

void TESTCASE_component_test__factorials_from_0_to_8() {
  assert(calc_factorial(next_even_number) == 1);
  assert(calc_factorial(next_even_number) == 2);
  assert(calc_factorial(next_even_number) == 24);
  assert(calc_factorial(next_even_number) == 720);
  assert(calc_factorial(next_even_number) == 40320);
}

void TESTCASE_component_test__factorials_should_rotate() {
  int64_t number = calc_factorial(next_even_number);
  for (size_t i = 1; i <= 4; i++) {
    calc_factorial(next_even_number);
  }
  int64_t number2 = calc_factorial(next_even_number);
  assert(number == number2);
}

int main(int argc, char** argv) {
  TESTCASE_component_test__factorials_from_0_to_8();
  TESTCASE_component_test__factorials_should_rotate();
  return 0;
}
```

Code Box 22-9 [ExtremeC_examples_chapter22_1_component_tests.c]: Some component tests written for our hypothetical component as part of example 22.1

As you see, we have written two test cases. Like we said before, in our hypothetical component, the functions calc_factorial and next_even_number must work together, and as you see, we have passed next_even_number as the feed to calc_factorial. The preceding test cases, and other similar test cases, should guarantee that the component is working properly.

It requires a lot of effort to prepare a basis for writing test cases. Therefore, it is very common to use a testing library for this purpose. These libraries prepare the playground for the test cases; they initialize every test case, run the test case, and finally tear down the test case. In the upcoming section, we are going to talk about two of the testing libraries available for C.

Testing libraries for C

In this section, we are going to demonstrate two of the well-known libraries used to write tests for C programs. For unit testing in C, we use libraries that are written in C or C++. That's because we can integrate them easily and use the units directly from a C or C++ testing environment. In this section, our focus is on unit testing and component testing in C.

For integration testing, we are free to choose other programming languages. Generally, the integration and system testing are much more complex, and we therefore need to use some testing automation frameworks in order to write tests easier and run them without too much hassle. Using a **domain-specific language (DSL)** is part of this automation, in order to write test scenarios more easily and make test execution much simpler. Many languages can be used for this purpose, but scripting languages like Unix shell, Python, JavaScript, and Ruby are among the most favorite ones. Some other programming languages like Java are also used heavily in test automation.

The following is a list of some well-known unit testing frameworks which can be used to write unit tests for C programs. This list below can be found at the following link: `http://check.sourceforge.net/doc/check_html/check_2.html#SEC3`:

- Check (from the author of the preceding link)
- AceUnit
- GNU Autounit
- cUnit
- CUnit
- CppUnit
- CuTest
- embUnit
- MinUnit
- Google Test
- CMocka

In the following sections, we will introduce two popular testing frameworks: *CMocka*, which is written in C, and *Google Test*, which is written in C++. We won't explore all features of these frameworks, but this is just to give you an initial feeling about a unit testing framework. Further study is highly encouraged in this domain.

In the next section, we are going to write unit tests for *example 22.1* using CMocka.

CMocka

The first great thing about CMocka is that it is written purely in C, and it only depends on the C standard library – not on any other libraries. So, you can use a C compiler to compile the tests, and this gives you the confidence that the test environment is very close to the actual production environment. CMocka is available on many platforms like macOS, Linux, and even Microsoft Windows.

CMocka is the *de facto* framework for unit testing in C. It supports *test fixtures*. Test fixtures may allow you to initialize and clear the testing environment before and after each test case. CMocka also supports *function mocking*, which is very useful when trying to mock any C function. As a reminder, a mock function can be configured to return a certain value when a certain input is provided. We will give an example of mocking the `rand` standard function used in *example 22.2*.

The following code box contains the same test cases that we saw for *example 22.1* but written in CMocka this time. We have put all test cases in just one file, which has its own `main` function:

```
// Required by CMocka
#include <stdarg.h>
#include <stddef.h>
#include <setjmp.h>
#include <cmocka.h>

#include "ExtremeC_examples_chapter22_1.h"

int64_t input_value = -1;

int64_t feed_stub() {
  return input_value;
}

void calc_factorial__fact_of_zero_is_one(void** state) {
  input_value = 0;
```

```
    int64_t fact = calc_factorial(feed_stub);
    assert_int_equal(fact, 1);
}

void calc_factorial__fact_of_negative_is_one(void** state) {
    input_value = -10;
    int64_t fact = calc_factorial(feed_stub);
    assert_int_equal(fact, 1);
}

void calc_factorial__fact_of_5_is_120(void** state) {
    input_value = 5;
    int64_t fact = calc_factorial(feed_stub);
    assert_int_equal(fact, 120);
}
void next_even_number__even_numbers_should_be_returned(void**
state) {
    assert_int_equal(next_even_number(), 0);
    assert_int_equal(next_even_number(), 2);
    assert_int_equal(next_even_number(), 4);
    assert_int_equal(next_even_number(), 6);
    assert_int_equal(next_even_number(), 8);
}

void next_even_number__numbers_should_rotate(void** state) {
    int64_t number = next_even_number();
    for (size_t i = 1; i <= 4; i++) {
        next_even_number();
    }
    int64_t number2 = next_even_number();
    assert_int_equal(number, number2);
}

int setup(void** state) {
    return 0;
}

int tear_down(void** state) {
    return 0;
}

int main(int argc, char** argv) {
    const struct CMUnitTest tests[] = {
        cmocka_unit_test(calc_factorial__fact_of_zero_is_one),
        cmocka_unit_test(calc_factorial__fact_of_negative_is_one),
        cmocka_unit_test(calc_factorial__fact_of_5_is_120),
        cmocka_unit_test(next_even_number__even_numbers_should_be_
returned),
        cmocka_unit_test(next_even_number__numbers_should_rotate),
```

```
    };
    return cmocka_run_group_tests(tests, setup, tear_down);
}
```

Code Box 22-10 [ExtremeC_examples_chapter22_1_cmocka_tests.c]: CMocka test cases for example 22.1

In CMocka, every test case should return void and receive a void** argument. The pointer argument will be used to receive a piece of information, called a state, which is specific to a test case. In the main function, we create a list of test cases, and then finally we call the cmocka_run_group_tests function to run all the unit tests.

In addition to test case functions, you see two new functions: setup and tear_down. As we said before, these functions are called test fixtures. Test fixtures are called before and after every test case and their responsibility is to set up and tear down the test case. The fixture setup is called before every test case and the fixture tear_down is called after every test case. Note that the names are optional, and they could be named anything, but we use setup and tear_down for clarity.

Another important difference between the test cases we wrote before and the test cases written using CMocka is the use of different assertion functions. This is one of the advantages of using a unit testing framework. There are a wide range of assertion functions as part of a testing library that can give you more information about their failure, rather than the standard assert function, which terminates the program immediately and without giving much information. As you can see, we have used assert_int_equal in the preceding code, which checks the equality of two integers.

In order to compile the preceding program, you need to have CMocka installed first. On a Debian-based Linux system, it is enough to run sudo apt-get install libcmocka-dev, and on macOS systems, it is enough to install it by using the command brew install cmocka. There will be a lot of help available online that can help you get through the installation process.

After having CMocka installed, you can use the following commands to build the preceding code:

```
$ gcc -g -c ExtremeC_examples_chapter22_1.c -o impl.o
$ gcc -g -c ExtremeC_examples_chapter22_1_cmocka_tests.c -o
cmocka_tests.o
$ gcc impl.o cmocka_tests.o -lcmocka -o ex22_1_cmocka_tests.out
$ ./ex22_1_cmocka_tests.out
[==========] Running 5 test(s).
[ RUN      ] calc_factorial__fact_of_zero_is_one
```

```
[      OK  ]  calc_factorial__fact_of_zero_is_one
[ RUN       ]  calc_factorial__fact_of_negative_is_one
[      OK  ]  calc_factorial__fact_of_negative_is_one
[ RUN       ]  calc_factorial__fact_of_5_is_120
[      OK  ]  calc_factorial__fact_of_5_is_120
[ RUN       ]  next_even_number__even_numbers_should_be_returned
[      OK  ]  next_even_number__even_numbers_should_be_returned
[ RUN       ]  next_even_number__numbers_should_rotate
[      OK  ]  next_even_number__numbers_should_rotate
[==========]  5 test(s) run.
[  PASSED  ]  5 test(s).
$
```

Shell Box 22-4: Building and running CMocka unit tests written for example 22.1

As you can see, we had to use `-lcmocka` in order to link the preceding program with the installed CMocka library. The output shows the test case names and the number of passed tests. Next, we change one of the test cases to make it fail. We just modify the first assertion in the `next_even_number__even_numbers_should_be_returned` test case:

```
void next_even_number__even_numbers_should_be_returned(void**
state) {
  assert_int_equal(next_even_number(), 1);
  ...
}
```

Code Box 22-11: Changing one of the CMocka test cases in example 22.1

Now, build the tests and run them again:

```
$ gcc -g -c ExtremeC_examples_chapter22_1_cmocka_tests.c -o
cmocka_tests.o
$ gcc impl.o cmocka_tests.o -lcmocka -o ex22_1_cmocka_tests.out
$ ./ex22_1_cmocka_tests.out
[==========]  Running 5 test(s).
[ RUN       ]  calc_factorial__fact_of_zero_is_one
[      OK  ]  calc_factorial__fact_of_zero_is_one
[ RUN       ]  calc_factorial__fact_of_negative_is_one
[      OK  ]  calc_factorial__fact_of_negative_is_one
```

```
[ RUN       ] calc_factorial__fact_of_5_is_120
[       OK ] calc_factorial__fact_of_5_is_120
[ RUN       ] next_even_number__even_numbers_should_be_returned
[   ERROR  ] --- 0 != 0x1
[    LINE  ] --- .../ExtremeC_examples_chapter22_1_cmocka_
tests.c:37: error: Failure!
[  FAILED  ] next_even_number__even_numbers_should_be_returned
[ RUN       ] next_even_number__numbers_should_rotate
[       OK ] next_even_number__numbers_should_rotate
[==========] 5 test(s) run.
[  PASSED  ] 4 test(s).
[  FAILED  ] 1 test(s), listed below:
[  FAILED  ] next_even_number__even_numbers_should_be_returned

 1 FAILED TEST(S)
$
```

Shell Box 22-5: Building and running CMocka unit tests after modifying one of them

In the preceding output, you see that one of the test cases has been failed and the reason is shown as an error in the middle of the logs. It shows an integer equality assertion failure. As we have explained before, using `assert_int_equal` instead of using an ordinary `assert` call allows CMocka to print a helpful message in the execution log instead of just terminating the program.

Our next example is about using CMocka's function mocking feature. CMocka allows you to mock a function and this way, you can instrument the function to return a specific result when a certain input is provided.

In the next example, *example 22.2*, we want to demonstrate how to use the mocking feature. In this example, the standard function `rand` is used to generate random numbers. There is also a function, named `random_boolean`, that returns a Boolean based on the oddity of the number returned from the `rand` function. Before showing CMocka's mocking feature, we want to show how to create a stub for the `rand` function. You see that this example is different from *example 22.1*. Next, you can see the declaration of the `random_boolean` function:

```
#ifndef _EXTREME_C_EXAMPLE_22_2_
#define _EXTREME_C_EXAMPLE_22_2_

#define TRUE 1
```

```
#define FALSE 0

typedef int bool_t;

bool_t random_boolean();

#endif
```

Code Box 22-12 [ExtremeC_examples_chapter22_2.h]: The header file of example 22.2

And the following code box contains the definition:

```
#include <stdlib.h>
#include <stdio.h>

#include "ExtremeC_examples_chapter22_2.h"

bool_t random_boolean() {
  int number = rand();
  return (number % 2);
}
```

Code Box 22-13 [ExtremeC_examples_chapter22_2.c]: The definition of the random_boolean function in example 22.2

First of all, we cannot let `random_boolean` use the actual `rand` definition in the tests because, as its name implies, it generates random numbers and we cannot have a random element in our tests. Tests are about checking expectations and the expectations, and the provided inputs, must be predictable. More than that, the definition of the `rand` function is part of the C standard library, for instance *glibc* in Linux, and using a stub function for it won't be easy like what we did in *example 22.1*.

In the previous example, we could send a function pointer to the stub definition very easily. But in this example, we are using the `rand` function directly. We cannot change the definition of `random_boolean`, and we have to come up with another trick to use the stub function for `rand`.

In order to use a different definition for the `rand` function, one of the easiest ways in C is to play with *symbols* in the final object file. In the *symbol table* of the resulting object file, there is an entry for `rand` which refers to its actual definition in the C standard library. If we change this entry to refer to a different definition of the `rand` function in our testing binaries, we can easily substitute the definition of `rand` with our stub one.

In the following code box, you can see how we have defined the stub function and the tests together. This would be very similar to what we did for *example 22.1*:

```c
#include <stdlib.h>

// Required by CMocka
#include <stdarg.h>
#include <stddef.h>
#include <setjmp.h>
#include <cmocka.h>

#include "ExtremeC_examples_chapter22_2.h"

int next_random_num = 0;

int __wrap_rand() {
  return next_random_num;
}

void test_even_random_number(void** state) {
  next_random_num = 10;
  assert_false(random_boolean());
}

void test_odd_random_number(void** state) {
  next_random_num = 13;
  assert_true(random_boolean());
}
int main(int argc, char** argv) {
  const struct CMUnitTest tests[] = {
    cmocka_unit_test(test_even_random_number),
    cmocka_unit_test(test_odd_random_number)
  };
  return cmocka_run_group_tests(tests, NULL, NULL);
}
```

Code Box 22-14 [ExtremeC_examples_chapter22_2_cmocka_tests_with_stub.c]: Writing CMocka test cases using a stub function

As you can see, the preceding code is mostly following the same pattern that we saw as part of the CMocka tests written for *example 22.1* in *Code Box 22-10*. Let's build the preceding file and run the tests. What we expect is to have all tests failed because, no matter how you define the stub function, the `random_boolean` is picking the `rand` from the C standard library:

```
$ gcc -g -c ExtremeC_examples_chapter22_2.c -o impl.o
$ gcc -g -c ExtremeC_examples_chapter22_2_cmocka_tests_with_stub.c
-o tests.o
```

```
$ gcc impl.o tests.o -lcmocka -o ex22_2_cmocka_tests_with_stub.out
$ ./ex22_2_cmocka_tests_with_stub.out
[==========] Running 2 test(s).
[ RUN      ] test_even_random_number
[   ERROR  ] --- random_boolean()
[   LINE   ] --- ExtremeC_examples_chapter22_2_cmocka_tests_with_
stub.c:23: error: Failure!
[  FAILED  ] test_even_random_number
[ RUN      ] test_odd_random_number
[   ERROR  ] --- random_boolean()
[   LINE   ] --- ExtremeC_examples_chapter22_2_cmocka_tests_with_
stub.c:28: error: Failure!
[  FAILED  ] test_odd_random_number
[==========] 2 test(s) run.
[  PASSED  ] 0 test(s).
[  FAILED  ] 2 test(s), listed below:
[  FAILED  ] test_even_random_number
[  FAILED  ] test_odd_random_number

 2 FAILED TEST(S)
$
```

Shell Box 22-6: Building and running CMocka unit tests for example 22.2

Now it's time do the trick and change the definition behind the `rand` symbol defined as part of the `ex22_2_cmocka_tests_with_stub.out` executable file. Note that the following commands are only applicable to Linux systems. We do it as follows:

```
$ gcc impl.o tests.o -lcmocka -Wl,--wrap=rand -o ex22_2_cmocka_
tests_with_stub.out
$ ./ex22_2_cmocka_tests_with_stub.out
[==========] Running 2 test(s).
[ RUN      ] test_even_random_number
[       OK ] test_even_random_number
[ RUN      ] test_odd_random_number
[       OK ] test_odd_random_number
[==========] 2 test(s) run.
[  PASSED  ] 2 test(s).
```

```
$
```

Shell Box 22-7: Building and running CMocka unit tests for example 22.2 after wrapping the rand symbol

As you see in the output, the standard `rand` function is not being called anymore and instead, the stub function returns what we have told it to return. The main trick that makes the function `__wrap_rand` be called instead of standard `rand` function lies in using the option `-Wl,--wrap=rand` in the `gcc` link command.

Note that this option is only available for the `ld` program in Linux and you have to use other tricks like *inter-positioning* to call a different function in macOS or other systems using a linker other than the GNU linker.

The option `--wrap=rand` tells the linker to update the entry for the symbol `rand` in the final executable's symbol table, which is going to refer to the definition of the `__wrap_rand` function. Note that this is not a custom name and you have to name the stub function like that. The function `__wrap_rand` is said to be a *wrapper function*. After updating the symbol table, any call to the `rand` function results in calling the `__wrap_func` function. This can be verified by looking at the symbol table of the final test binary.

Apart from updating the `rand` symbol in the symbol table, the linker also creates another entry. The new entry has the symbol `__real_rand`, which refers to the actual definition of the standard `rand` function. Therefore, if we needed to run the standard `rand`, we still can use the function name `__real_rand`. This is a great usage of the symbol table and the symbols in it, in order to call a wrapper function, despite the fact that some people don't like it and they prefer to preload a shared object that wraps the actual `rand` function. Whichever method you use, you need to finally redirect the calls to the `rand` symbol to another stub function.

The preceding mechanism would be the basis to demonstrate how function mocking works in CMocka. Instead of having a global variable `next_random_num`, as seen in *Code Box 22-14*, we can use a mocked function to return the specified value. Next, you can see the same CMocka tests but using a mocked function to read the test inputs:

```c
#include <stdlib.h>

// Required by CMocka
#include <stdarg.h>
#include <stddef.h>
#include <setjmp.h>
#include <cmocka.h>
```

```
#include "ExtremeC_examples_chapter22_2.h"

int __wrap_rand() {
  return mock_type(int);
}

void test_even_random_number(void** state) {
  will_return(__wrap_rand, 10);
  assert_false(random_boolean());
}

void test_odd_random_number(void** state) {
  will_return(__wrap_rand, 13);
  assert_true(random_boolean());
}
int main(int argc, char** argv) {
  const struct CMUnitTest tests[] = {
    cmocka_unit_test(test_even_random_number),
    cmocka_unit_test(test_odd_random_number)
  };
  return cmocka_run_group_tests(tests, NULL, NULL);
}
```

Code Box 22-15 [ExtremeC_examples_chapter22_2_cmocka_tests_with_mock.c]: Writing CMocka test cases using a mock function

Now that we know how the wrapper function __wrap_rand is called, we can explain the mocking part. Mocking functionality is provided by the pair of functions will_return and mock_type. First, will_return should be called, which specifies the value that the mock function should return. Then, when the mock function, in this case __wrap_rand, is called, the function mock_type returns the specified value.

As an example, we define 10 to be returned from __wrap_rand by using will_return(__wrap_rand, 10), and then the value 10 is returned when the function mock_type is called inside __wrap_rand. Note that every will_return must pair with a mock_type call; otherwise, the test fails. Therefore, if __wrap_rand is not called because of any reason, the test fails.

As the last note in this section, the output of the preceding code would be the same as we saw in Shell Boxes 22-6 and 22-7. In addition, the same commands, of course for the source file ExtremeC_examples_chapter22_2_cmocka_tests_with_mock.c, must be used to build the code and run the tests.

In this section, we showed how we can use the CMocka library to write test cases, perform assertions, and write mock functions. In the next section, we talk about Google Test, another testing framework that can be used to unit test C programs.

Google Test

Google Test is a C++ testing framework that can be used for unit testing both C and C++ programs. Despite being developed in C++, it can be used for testing C code. Some consider this as a bad practice, because the test environment is not set up using the same compiler and linker that you are going to use for setting up the production environment.

Before being able to use Google Test for writing test cases for *example 22.1*, we need to modify the header file in *example 22.1* a bit. The following is the new header file:

```
#ifndef _EXTREME_C_EXAMPLE_22_1_
#define _EXTREME_C_EXAMPLE_22_1_

#include <stdint.h>
#include <unistd.h>

#if __cplusplus
extern "C" {
#endif

typedef int64_t (*int64_feed_t)();

int64_t next_even_number();

int64_t calc_factorial(int64_feed_t feed);

#if __cplusplus
}
#endif

#endif
```

Code Box 22-16 [ExtremeC_examples_chapter22_1.h]: The modified header file as part of example 22.1

As you can see, we have put the declarations in the extern C { ... } block. We do that only if the macro _cplusplus is defined. The preceding change simply means that when the compiler is C++, we want to have the symbols *unmangled* in the resulting object files, otherwise we will get link errors when the linker tries to find definitions for *mangled symbols*. If you don't know about C++ *name mangling*, please refer to the last section in *Chapter 2, Compilation and Linking*.

Now, let's continue and write the test cases using Google Test:

```
// Required by Google Test
#include <gtest/gtest.h>
```

```
#include "ExtremeC_examples_chapter22_1.h"

int64_t input_value = -1;

int64_t feed_stub() {
  return input_value;
}

TEST(calc_factorial, fact_of_zero_is_one) {
  input_value = 0;
  int64_t fact = calc_factorial(feed_stub);
  ASSERT_EQ(fact, 1);
}

TEST(calc_factorial, fact_of_negative_is_one) {
  input_value = -10;
  int64_t fact = calc_factorial(feed_stub);
  ASSERT_EQ(fact, 1);
}

TEST(calc_factorial, fact_of_5_is_120) {
  input_value = 5;
  int64_t fact = calc_factorial(feed_stub);
  ASSERT_EQ(fact, 120);
}

TEST(next_even_number, even_numbers_should_be_returned) {
  ASSERT_EQ(next_even_number(), 0);
  ASSERT_EQ(next_even_number(), 2);
  ASSERT_EQ(next_even_number(), 4);
  ASSERT_EQ(next_even_number(), 6);
  ASSERT_EQ(next_even_number(), 8);
}

TEST(next_even_number, numbers_should_rotate) {
  int64_t number = next_even_number();
  for (size_t i = 1; i <= 4; i++) {
    next_even_number();
  }
  int64_t number2 = next_even_number();
   ASSERT_EQ(number, number2);
}

int main(int argc, char** argv) {
  ::testing::InitGoogleTest(&argc, argv);
  return RUN_ALL_TESTS();
}
```

Code Box 22-17 [ExtremeC_examples_chapter22_1_gtests.cpp]: The test cases written using Google Test for example 22.1

The test cases are defined using the TEST(...) macro. This is an example of how well macros can be used to form a DSL. There are also other macros like TEST_F(...) and TEST_P(...), which are C++ specific. The first argument passed to the macro is the test's class name (Google Test is written for object-oriented C++), which can be thought of as the test suite that contains a number of test cases. The second argument is the name of the test case.

Note the ASSERT_EQ macro, which is used to assert the equality of objects, not just integers. There are a great number of expectation checker macros in Google Test, which makes it a complete unit testing framework. The final part is the main function, which runs all the defined tests. Note that the above code should be compiled using a C++11-compliant compiler like g++ and clang++.

The following commands build the preceding code. Note using the g++ compiler and the option -std=c++11 which is passed to it. It indicates that C++11 should be used:

```
$ gcc -g -c ExtremeC_examples_chapter22_1.c -o impl.o
$ g++ -std=c++11 -g -c ExtremeC_examples_chapter22_1_gtests.cpp -o
gtests.o
$ g++ impl.o gtests.o -lgtest -lpthread -o ex19_1_gtests.out
$ ./ex19_1_gtests.out
[==========] Running 5 tests from 2 test suites.
[----------] Global test environment set-up.
[----------] 3 tests from calc_factorial
[ RUN      ] calc_factorial.fact_of_zero_is_one
[       OK ] calc_factorial.fact_of_zero_is_one (0 ms)
[ RUN      ] calc_factorial.fact_of_negative_is_one
[       OK ] calc_factorial.fact_of_negative_is_one (0 ms)
[ RUN      ] calc_factorial.fact_of_5_is_120
[       OK ] calc_factorial.fact_of_5_is_120 (0 ms)
[----------] 3 tests from calc_factorial (0 ms total)

[----------] 2 tests from next_even_number
[ RUN      ] next_even_number.even_numbers_should_be_returned
[       OK ] next_even_number.even_numbers_should_be_returned (0
ms)
[ RUN      ] next_even_number.numbers_should_rotate
[       OK ] next_even_number.numbers_should_rotate (0 ms)
[----------] 2 tests from next_even_number (0 ms total)

[----------] Global test environment tear-down
```

```
[==========] 5 tests from 2 test suites ran. (1 ms total)
[  PASSED  ] 5 tests.
$
```

Shell Box 22-8: Building and running Google Test unit tests for example 22.1

The above output shows a similar output to the CMocka output. It indicates that five test cases have been passed. Let's change the same test case as we did for CMocka to break the test suite:

```
TEST(next_even_number, even_numbers_should_be_returned) {
  ASSERT_EQ(next_even_number(), 1);
  ...
}
```

Code Box 22-18: Changing one of the test cases written in Google Test

Let's build the tests again and run them:

```
$ g++ -std=c++11 -g -c ExtremeC_examples_chapter22_1_gtests.cpp -o
gtests.o
$ g++ impl.o gtests.o -lgtest -lpthread -o ex22_1_gtests.out
$ ./ex22_1_gtests.out
[==========] Running 5 tests from 2 test suites.
[----------] Global test environment set-up.
[----------] 3 tests from calc_factorial
[ RUN      ] calc_factorial.fact_of_zero_is_one
[       OK ] calc_factorial.fact_of_zero_is_one (0 ms)
[ RUN      ] calc_factorial.fact_of_negative_is_one
[       OK ] calc_factorial.fact_of_negative_is_one (0 ms)
[ RUN      ] calc_factorial.fact_of_5_is_120
[       OK ] calc_factorial.fact_of_5_is_120 (0 ms)
[----------] 3 tests from calc_factorial (0 ms total)

[----------] 2 tests from next_even_number
[ RUN      ] next_even_number.even_numbers_should_be_returned
.../ExtremeC_examples_chapter22_1_gtests.cpp:34: Failure
Expected equality of these values:
  next_even_number()
```

```
      Which is: 0
    1
  [  FAILED  ] next_even_number.even_numbers_should_be_returned (0
  ms)
  [ RUN      ] next_even_number.numbers_should_rotate
  [       OK ] next_even_number.numbers_should_rotate (0 ms)
  [----------] 2 tests from next_even_number (0 ms total)

  [----------] Global test environment tear-down
  [==========] 5 tests from 2 test suites ran. (0 ms total)
  [  PASSED  ] 4 tests.
  [  FAILED  ] 1 test, listed below:
  [  FAILED  ] next_even_number.even_numbers_should_be_returned

  1 FAILED TEST
  $
```

Shell Box 22-9: Building and running Google Test unit tests for example 22.1 after modifying one of the test cases

As you can see and exactly like CMocka, Google Test also prints out where the tests are broken and shows a helpful report. As a final note on Google Test, it supports test fixtures but not in the same way that CMocka supports. Test fixtures should be defined in a *test class*.

Note:
For having mock objects and the mocking functionality, the *Google Mock* (or *gmock*) library can be used, but we don't cover it in this book.

In this section, we went through two of the most well-known unit testing libraries for C. In the next part of the chapter, we dive into the topic of debugging, which is of course a necessary skill for every programmer.

Debugging

There are situations in which one test or a group of tests fail. Also, there are times when you find a bug. In both of these situations, there is a bug, and you need to find the root cause and fix it. This involves many sessions of debugging and going through the source code to search for the cause of the bug and planning the required fixes. But what does it mean to *debug* a piece of software?

Note:
It is a popularly held belief that the term "debug" originates from the days when computers were so large that real bugs (such as moths) could get caught in the system's machinery and lead to malfunctions. Therefore, some people, officially called *debuggers*, were sent into the hardware room to remove the bugs from the equipment. See this link for more information: https://en.wikipedia.org/wiki/Debugging.

Debugging is an investigative task to find the root cause of an observed bug by looking inside and/or outside of a program. When running a program, you usually look at it as a black box. When something is wrong with the results or something interrupts the execution, however, you need to have a deeper look inside and see how the issue is produced. This means that you have to observe the program as a white box in which everything can be seen.

That's basically why we can have two different builds for a program: *release* and *build*. In release builds, the focus is on the execution and the functionality, and the program is mostly seen as a black box, but in debug builds, we can trace all the events happening and see the inside of the program as a white box. Debug builds are generally useful for development and test environments, but release builds are targeted at deployment and production environments.

In order to have a debug build, all of the products of a software project, or a limited set of them, need to contain *debugging* symbols, which enable a developer to track and see the *stack trace* and the execution flow of the program. Usually, a release product (executable or libraries) is not suitable for debugging purposes because it is not transparent enough to let an observer examine the internals of a program. In *Chapter 4*, *Process Memory Structure*, and *Chapter 5*, *Stack and Heap*, we discussed how we can build C sources for debugging purposes.

For debugging a program, we mainly use debuggers. Debuggers are standalone programs that attach to the target process in order to control or monitor it. While debuggers are our main tools for our investigation when working on an issue, other debugging tools can also be used to study the memory, concurrent execution flows, or the performance of a program. We will talk about these tools in the following sections.

A great portion of bugs are *reproducible*, but there are bugs that cannot be reproduced or observed in debugging sessions; this is mostly because of the *observer effect*. It says, when you want to look at the internals of a program, you alter the way it works, and it might prevent some bugs from happening. These sorts of issues are disastrous, and they are usually very hard to fix because you cannot use your debugging tools to investigate the root cause of the problem!

Some threading bugs in high-performance environments can be categorized in this group.

In the following sections, we are going to talk about different categories of bugs. Then, we introduce the tools that we use in modern C/C++ development in order to investigate bugs.

Bug categories

There can be thousands of bugs reported in a piece of software throughout the years that it is in use by a customer. But if you look at the types of these bugs, they are not many. Next, you can see a list of bug categories that we think are important and require special skills to deal with. For sure, this list is not complete and there can be other types of bugs that we are missing:

- **Logical bugs**: In order to investigate these bugs, you need to know the code and the execution flow of the code. To see the actual execution flow of a program, a debugger should be attached to a running process. Only then, the execution flow can be *traced* and analyzed. *Execution logs* can also be used when debugging a program, especially when debugging symbols are not available in the final binaries or a debugger cannot be used to attach to an actual running instance of the program.

- **Memory bugs**: These bugs are memory related. They occur usually because of dangling pointers, buffer overflows, double frees, and so on. These bugs should be investigated using a *memory profiler*, which acts as a debugging tool for observing and monitoring memory.

- **Concurrency bugs**: Multi-processing and multithreading programs have always been the birthplace of some of the hardest-to-solve bugs found in the software industry. You need special tools like *thread sanitizers* in order to detect particularly difficult issues such as race conditions and data races.

- **Performance bugs**: New developments may result in *performance degradation* or performance bugs. These bugs should be investigated using further and more focused testing and even debugging. Execution logs, which contain annotated historical data for the previous executions, can be useful in order to find the exact change or changes that have initiated the degradation.

In the following sections, we are going to talk about various tools introduced in the preceding list.

Debuggers

We have talked about debuggers, especially gdb, in *Chapter 4*, *Process Memory Structure*, and we used it to see inside a process's memory. In this section, we are going to give debuggers a second look and describe their role in daily software development. The following is a list of common features provided by most modern debuggers:

- A debugger is a program, and like all other programs, it runs as a process. The debugger process can attach to another process given the target process ID.

- A debugger can control the execution of the instructions in the target process after a successful attachment; therefore, the user is able to pause and continue the flow of the execution in the target process, using an interactive debugging session.

- Debuggers can see inside the protected memory of a process. They can also modify the contents, therefore a developer can run the same group of instructions while the memory content is being changed deliberately.

- Almost all of the known debuggers, if the debugging symbols are provided while compiling the sources to relocatable object files, can trace back the instructions to the source code. In other words, when you pause on an instruction, you can go to its corresponding line of code in the source file.

- If the debugging symbols are not provided in the target object file, the debugger can show the disassembly code of a target instruction, which can still be useful.

- Some debuggers are language-specific, but most of them are not. **Java Virtual Machine (JVM)** languages such as Java, Scala, and Groovy have to use JVM debuggers in order to see and control the internals of a JVM instance.

- Interpreted languages like Python have also their own debuggers, which can be used to pause and control a script. While the low-level debuggers like gdb are still usable for JVM or scripting languages, they try to debug the JVM or interpreter processes instead of the executing Java bytecode or Python script.

A list of the debuggers can be found on Wikipedia as part of the following link: https://en.wikipedia.org/wiki/List_of_debuggers. From this list, the following debuggers are eye-catching:

1. **Advanced Debugger (adb)**: The default Unix debugger. It has different implementations based on the actual Unix implementation. It has been the default debugger on Solaris Unix.

2. **GNU Debugger (gdb)**: The GNU version of the Unix debugger, which is the default debugger on many Unix-like operating systems including Linux.

3. **LLDB**: A debugger mainly designed for debugging object files produced by LLVM compilers.

4. **Python Debugger**: Used in Python to debug Python script.

5. **Java Platform Debugger Architecture (JPDA)**: This one is not a debugger, but it is an API designed for debugging programs running inside a JVM instance.

6. **OllyDbg**: A debugger and disassembler used in Microsoft Windows for debugging GUI applications.

7. **Microsoft Visual Studio Debugger**: The main debugger used by Microsoft Visual Studio.

In addition to gdb, one can use cgdb. The cgdb program shows a terminal code editor next to the gdb interactive shell that allows you to move between the code lines easier.

In this section, we discussed debuggers as the main tools for investigating an issue. In the next section, we will be talking about memory profilers, which are vital for investigating memory-related bugs.

Memory checkers

Sometimes when you encounter a memory-related bug or a crash, a debugger alone cannot help much. You need another tool that can detect the memory corruptions and invalid read or writes to the memory cells. The tool you need is a *memory checker* or a *memory profiler*. It could be part of a debugger, but it is usually provided as a separate program and the way it detects memory misbehaviors is different from a debugger.

We usually can expect the following features from a memory checker:

* Reporting the total amount of allocated memory, freed memory, used static memory, Heap allocations, Stack allocations, and so on.

* Memory-leak detection, which can be considered as the most important feature that a memory checker provides.

- Detection of invalid memory read/write operations like out-of-bound access regarding buffers and arrays, writes to an already freed memory region, and so on.

- Detection of a *double free* issue. It happens when a program tries to free an already freed memory region.

So far, we have seen memory checkers like *Memcheck* (one of the Valgrind's tools) in some of the chapters, particularly *Chapter 5*, *Stack and Heap*. We have also discussed the different types of memory checkers and memory profilers in chapter 5. Here, we want to explain them again, and give more details about each of them.

Memory checkers all do the same thing, but the underlying technique they use to monitor memory operations can be different. Therefore, we group them based on the technique they use:

1. **Compile-time overriding**: For using a memory checker employing this technique, you need to make some, usually slight, changes to your source code like including a header file from the memory checker library. Then, you need to compile your binaries again. Sometimes, it is necessary to link the binaries against the libraries provided by the memory checker. The advantage is that the performance drop of the executing binary is less than the other techniques, but the disadvantage is that you need to recompile your binaries. **LLVM AddressSanitizer (ASan)**, Memwatch, Dmalloc, and Mtrace are memory profilers using this technique.

2. **Link-time overriding**: This group of memory checkers is like the previous group of memory checkers, but the difference is that you don't need to change your source code. Instead, you only have to link the resulting binaries with the provided libraries from the memory checker and no change is made to the source code. The *heap checker* utility in *gperftools* can be used as a link-time memory checker.

3. **Runtime interception**: A memory checker using this technique sits between the program and the OS and tries to intercept and track all memory-related operations and report whenever a misbehavior or invalid access is seen. It also can give leak reports based on the total allocations and freed memory blocks. The main advantage of using this technique is that you don't need to recompile or relink your program in order to use the memory checker. The big disadvantage is the significant overhead it introduces to the execution of the program. Also, the memory footprint would be much higher than when running the program without the memory checker. This is definitely not an ideal environment to debug high-performance and embedded programs. The Memcheck tool in Valgrind can be used as a runtime interceptor memory checker. These memory profilers should be used with a debug build of the code base.

4. **Preloading libraries**: Some memory checkers use *inter-positioning* in order to wrap standard memory functions. Therefore, by preloading the memory checker's shared libraries using the LD_PRELOAD environment variable, the program can use the wrapper functions and the memory checker can intercept the calls to underlying standard memory functions. The *heap checker* utility in *gperftools* can be used like this.

Usually, it is not enough to use a specific tool for all memory issues because each of them has its own advantages and disadvantages, which make that tool specific to a certain context.

In this section, we went through the available memory profilers and categorized them based on the technique they use to record memory allocations and deallocations. In the next section, we are going to talk about thread sanitizers.

Thread debuggers

Thread sanitizers or *thread debuggers* are programs that are used to debug multithreading programs to find concurrency-related issues while the program is running. Some of the issues they can find are as follows:

- Data races, and the exact places in different threads where the read/write operations have caused the data race
- Misusing the threading API, especially POSIX threading API in POSIX-compliant systems
- Possible deadlocks
- Lock ordering issues

Both thread debuggers and memory checkers can detect issues as *false positives*. In other words, they may find and report some issues but after being investigated, it becomes clear that they are not issues. This really depends on the technique these libraries use for tracking the events, and making a final decision about that event.

In the following list, you can find a number of well-known available thread debuggers:

- **Helgrind (from Valgrind)**: It is another tool inside Valgrind mainly used for thread debugging. DRD is also another thread debugger as part of the Valgrind toolkit. The list of features and differences can be seen in these links: http://valgrind.org/docs/manual/hg-manual.html and http://valgrind.org/docs/manual/drd-manual.html. Like all other tools from Valgrind, using Helgrind doesn't need you to modify your source. For running Helgrind, you need to run the command valgrind --tool=helgrind [path-to-executable].

- **Intel Inspector**: This successor to *Intel Thread Checker* performs an analysis of threading errors and memory issues. Therefore, it is a thread debugger as well as a memory checker. It is not free like Valgrind, and proper licenses must be purchased in order to use the tool.

- **LLVM ThreadSanitizer (TSan)**: This is part of the LLVM toolkit, and it comes with LLVM AddressSanitizer, described in the previous section. Some slight compile-time modifications are needed in order to use the debugger and the code base should be recompiled.

In this section, we discussed thread debuggers and we introduced some of the available thread debuggers in order to debug threading issues. In the next section, we provide the programs and toolkits that are used to tune the performance of a program.

Performance profilers

Sometimes the results of a group of non-functional tests indicate a degradation in performance. There are specialized tools for investigating the cause of the degradation. In this section, we are going to have a quick look at the tools which can be used to analyze performance and find performance bottlenecks.

These performance debuggers usually offer a subset of the following features:

- Gather statistics about every single function call
- Provide a *function call graph* used to trace function calls
- Gather memory-related statistics for each function call
- Gather lock contention statistics
- Gather memory allocation/deallocation statistics
- Cache analysis, giving cache usage statistics and showing parts of the code that are not cache-friendly
- Gather statistics about threading and synchronization events

The following is a list of the most well-known programs and toolkits that can be used for performance profiling:

- **Google Performance Tools (gperftools)**: This is actually a performant `malloc` implementation, but as it says on its home page, it provides some performance analytics tools like *heap checker*, which was introduced in the previous sections as a memory profiler. It should be linked with the final binary in order to be usable.

- **Callgrind (as part of Valgrind)**: Mainly gathers statistics about the function calls and the caller/callee relationship between two functions. There is no need to change the source code or link the final binaries and it can be used on the fly, with a debug build, of course.

- **Intel VTune**: This is a performance profiling suite from Intel that is a complete set of all the features given in the preceding list. Proper licenses must be purchased in order to use it.

Summary

This chapter was about unit testing and debugging C programs. As a summary, in this chapter:

- We talked about testing, and why it is important to us as software engineers and development teams.

- We also discussed the different levels of testing like unit testing, integration testing, and system testing.

- Functional and non-functional testing were also covered.

- Regression testing was explained.

- CMocka and Google Test, as two well-known testing libraries for C, were explored and some examples were given.

- We talked about debugging and various types of bugs.

- We discussed debuggers, memory profilers, thread debuggers, and performance debuggers which can help us to have a more successful investigation while working on a bug.

The next chapter is about the *build systems* available for C projects. We will discuss what a build system is and what features it can bring in, which will eventually help us to automate the process of building a huge C project.

Chapter 23

Build Systems

For us programmers, building a project and running its various components is the first step in developing a new feature or fixing a reported bug in a project. In fact, this is not limited to C or C++; almost any project with a component written in a compiled programming language, such as C, C++, Java, or Go, needs to be built first.

Therefore, being able to build a software project quickly and easily is a fundamental demand required by almost any party working in the software production pipeline, whether they be developers, testers, integrators, DevOps engineers, or even customer support.

More than that, when you join a team as a newbie, the first thing you do is to build the code base that you are going to work on. Considering all this, then, it's clear that addressing the ability to build a software project is justified, given its importance within the software development process.

Programmers need to build code bases frequently in order to see the results of their changes. Building a project with only a few source files seems to be easy and fast, but when the number of source files grows (and believe me, it happens), building a code base frequently becomes a real obstacle to development tasks. Therefore, a proper mechanism for building a software project is crucial.

People used to write shell scripts to build a huge number of source files. Even though it worked, it took a lot of effort and maintenance to keep the scripts general enough to be used in various software projects. Following that, around 1976 at Bell Labs, the first (or, at least, one of the earliest ones) *build system*, named *Make*, was developed and it was used in internal projects.

After that, Make was used on a massive scale in all C and C++ projects, and even in other projects in which C/C++ were n-ot the main languages.

In this chapter, we are going to talk about widely used *build systems* and *build script generators* for C and C++ projects. As part of this chapter, we will talk about the following topics:

- First, we will look at what build systems are and what they are good for.

- Then, we will cover what Make is and how Makefiles should be used.

- CMake is the next topic. You will read about build script generators and you will learn how to write simple `CMakeLists.txt` files.

- We'll see what Ninja is and how it is different from Make.

- The chapter will also explore how CMake should be used to generate Ninja build scripts.

- We'll delve into what Bazel is and how it should be used. You will learn about `WORKSPACE` and `BUILD` files and how they should be written in a simple use case.

- Finally, you will be given links to some already-published comparisons of various build systems.

Note that the build tools used in this chapter all need to be installed on your system beforehand. Proper resources and documentation should be available on the internet, since these build tools are being used on a massive scale.

In the first section, we are going to explore what a build system actually is.

What is a build system?

Put simply, a build system is a set of programs and companion text files that collectively build a software code base. Nowadays, every programming language has its own set of build systems. For instance, in Java, you have *Ant, Maven, Gradle*, and so on. But what does "building a code base" mean?

Building a code base means producing final products from source files. For example, for a C code base, the final products can be executable files, shared object files, or static libraries, and the goal of a C build system is to produce these products out of the C source files found in the code base. The details of the operations needed for this purpose depend heavily on the programming language or the languages involved in the code base.

Many modern build systems, especially in projects written in a *JVM language* such as Java or Scala, provide an extra service.

They do *dependency management* as well. This means that the build system detects the dependencies of the target code base, and it downloads all of them and uses the downloaded artifacts during the *build process*. This is very handy, especially if there are a great many dependencies in a project, which is usually the case in big code bases.

For instance, *Maven* is one of the most famous building systems for Java projects; it uses XML files and supports dependency management. Unfortunately, we don't have great tools for dependency management in C/C++ projects. Why we haven't got Maven-like build systems for C/C++ projects yet is a matter for debate, but the fact that they have not been developed yet could be a sign that we don't need them.

Another aspect of a build system is the ability to build a huge project with multiple modules inside. Of course, this is possible using shell scripts and writing recursive *Makefiles* that go through any level of modules, but we are talking about the intrinsic support of such a demand. Unfortunately, Make does not offer this intrinsically. Another famous build tool, CMake, does offer that, however. We will talk more about this in the section dedicated to CMake.

As of today, many projects still use Make as their default build system, however, through using CMake. Indeed, this is one of the points that makes CMake very important, and you need to learn it before joining a C/C++ project. Note that CMake is not limited to C and C++ and can be used in projects using various programming languages.

In the following section, we are going to discuss the Make build system and how it builds a project. We will give an example of a multi-module C project and use it throughout this chapter to demonstrate how various build systems can be used to build this project.

Make

The Make build system uses Makefiles. A Makefile is a text file with the name "Makefile" (exactly this and without any extension) in a source directory, and it contains *build targets* and commands that tell Make how to build the current code base.

Let's start with a simple multi-module C project and equip it with Make. The following shell box shows the files and directories found in the project. As you can see, it has one module named `calc`, and another module named `exec` is using it.

The output of the `calc` module would be a static object library, and the output of the `exec` module is an executable file:

```
$ tree ex23_1
ex23_1/
├── calc
│   ├── add.c
│   ├── calc.h
│   ├── multiply.c
│   └── subtract.c
└── exec
    └── main.c

2 directories, 5 files
$
```

Shell Box 23-1: The files and directories found in the target project

If we want to build the above project without using a build system, we must run the following commands in order to build its products. Note that we have used Linux as the target platform for this project:

```
$ mkdir -p out
$ gcc -c calc/add.c -o out/add.o
$ gcc -c calc/multiply.c -o out/multiply.o
$ gcc -c calc/subtract.c -o out/subtract.o
$ ar rcs out/libcalc.a out/add.o out/multiply.o out/subtract.o
$ gcc -c -Icalc exec/main.c -o out/main.o
$ gcc -Lout out/main.o -lcalc -o out/ex23_1.out
$
```

Shell Box 23-2: Building the target project

As you can see, the project has two artifacts: a static library, `libcalc.a`, and an executable file, `ex23_1.out`. If you don't know how to compile a C project, or the preceding commands are strange to you, please read *Chapter 2, Compilation and Linking*, and *Chapter 3, Object Files*.

The first command in *Shell Box 23-2* creates a directory named `out`. This directory is supposed to contain all the relocatable object files and the final products.

Following that, the next three commands use gcc to compile the source files in the calc directory and produce their corresponding relocatable object files. Then, these object files are used in the fifth command to produce the static library libcalc.a.

Finally, the last two commands compile the file main.c from the **exec** directory and finally link it together with libcalc.a to produce the final executable file, ex23_1.out. Note that all these files are put inside the **out** directory.

The preceding commands can grow as the number of source files grows. We could maintain the preceding commands in a shell script file called a *build script*, but there are some aspects that we should think about beforehand:

- Are we going to run the same commands on all platforms? There are some details that differ in various compilers and environments; therefore, the commands might vary from one system to another. In the simplest scenario, we should maintain different shell scripts for different platforms. Then, it effectively means that our script is not *portable*.
- What happens when a new directory or a new module is added to the project? Do we need to change the build script?
- What happens to the build script if we add new source files?
- What happens if we need a new product, like a new library or a new executable file?

A good build system should handle all or most of the situations covered above. Let's present our first Makefile. This file is going to build the above project and generate its products. All the files written for build systems, in this section and the following sections, can be used to build this particular project and nothing more than that.

The following code box shows the content of the simplest Makefile that we can write for the above project:

```
build:
    mkdir -p out
    gcc -c calc/add.c -o out/add.o
    gcc -c calc/multiply.c -o out/multiply.o
    gcc -c calc/subtract.c -o out/subtract.o
    ar rcs out/libcalc.a out/add.o out/multiply.o out/subtract.o
    gcc -c -Icalc exec/main.c -o out/main.o
    gcc -Lout -lcalc out/main.o -o out/ex23_1.out
clean:
    rm -rfv out
```

Code Box 23-1 [Makefile-very-simple]: A very simple Makefile written for the target project

The preceding Makefile contains two targets: `build` and `clean`. Targets have a set of commands, which should be executed when the target is summoned. This set of commands is called the *recipe* of the target.

In order to run the commands in a Makefile, we need to use the `make` command. You need to tell the `make` command which target to run, but if you leave it empty, `make` always executes the first target.

To build the preceding project using the Makefile, it is enough to copy the lines from *Code Box 23-1* to a file named `Makefile` and put it in the root of the project. The content of the project's directory should be similar to what we see in the following shell box:

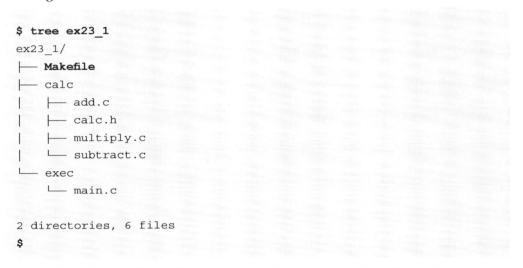

```
$ tree ex23_1
ex23_1/
├── Makefile
├── calc
│   ├── add.c
│   ├── calc.h
│   ├── multiply.c
│   └── subtract.c
└── exec
    └── main.c

2 directories, 6 files
$
```

Shell Box 23-3: The files and directories found in the target project after adding the Makefile

Following that, you can just run the `make` command. The `make` program automatically looks for the `Makefile` file in the current directory and executes its first target. If we wanted to run the `clean` target, we would have to use the `make clean` command. The `clean` target can be used to remove the files produced as part of the build process, and this way, we can start a fresh build from scratch.

The following shell box shows the result of running the `make` command:

```
$ cd ex23_1
$ make
mkdir -p out
gcc -c -Icalc exec/main.c -o out/main.o
```

```
gcc -c calc/add.c -o out/add.o
gcc -c calc/multiply.c -o out/multiply.o
gcc -c calc/subtract.c -o out/subtract.o
ar rcs out/libcalc.a out/add.o out/multiply.o out/subtract.o
gcc -Lout -lcalc out/main.o -o out/ex23_1.out
$
```

Shell Box 23-4: Building the target project using the very simple Makefile

You might ask, "What is the difference between a build script (written in a shell script), and the above Makefile?" You'd be right to ask this! The preceding Makefile does not represent the way we usually use Make to build our projects.

In fact, the preceding Makefile is a naive usage of the Make build system, and it doesn't benefit from the features we know that Make has to offer.

In other words, so far, a Makefile has been remarkably similar to a shell script, and we could still just use shell scripting (though, of course, that would involve more effort). Now we get to the point where Makefiles become interesting and really different.

The following Makefile is still simple, but it introduces more of the aspects of the Make build system that we are interested in:

```
CC = gcc

build: prereq out/main.o out/libcalc.a
    ${CC} -Lout -lcalc out/main.o -o out/ex23_1.out

prereq:
    mkdir -p out

out/libcalc.a: out/add.o out/multiply.o out/subtract.o
    ar rcs out/libcalc.a out/add.o out/multiply.o out/subtract.o

out/main.o: exec/main.c calc/calc.h
    ${CC} -c -Icalc exec/main.c -o out/main.o

out/add.o: calc/add.c calc/calc.h
    ${CC} -c calc/add.c -o out/add.o

out/subtract.o: calc/subtract.c calc/calc.h
    ${CC} -c calc/subtract.c -o out/subtract.o

out/multiply.o: calc/multiply.c calc/calc.h
```

```
    ${CC} -c calc/multiply.c -o out/multiply.o

clean: out
    rm -rf out
```

Code Box 23-2 [Makefile-simple]: A new, but still simple, Makefile written for the target project

As you can see, we can declare a variable in a Makefile and use it in various places, just as we have declared CC in the preceding code box. Variables, together with conditions in a Makefile, allow us to write flexible build instructions with less effort than it takes to write a shell script that would achieve the same flexibility.

Another cool feature of Makefiles is the ability to include other Makefiles. This way, you can benefit from existing Makefiles that you have written in your previous projects.

As you can see in the preceding Makefile, each Makefile can have several targets. Targets start at the beginning of a line and end with a colon, ":". One tab character *must* be used to indent all the instructions within a target (the recipe) in order to make them recognizable by the make program. Here is the cool thing about targets: they can be dependent on the other targets.

For example, in the preceding Makefile, the build target depends on the prereq, out /main.o, and out/libcalc.a targets. Then, whenever the build target is invoked, first, its depending targets will be checked, and if they are not yet produced, then those targets will be invoked first. Now, if you pay more attention to the targets in the preceding Makefile, you should be able to see the flow of execution between targets.

This is definitely something that we miss in a shell script; a lot of control flow mechanisms (loops, conditions, and so on) would be needed to make a shell script work like this. Makefiles are less verbose and more declarative, and that is why we use them. We want to only declare what needs to be built, and we do not need to know about the path it takes to get built. While this is not totally achieved by using Make, it is a start to having a fully featured build system.

Another feature of the targets in a Makefile is that if they are referring to a file or a directory on the disk, such as out/multiply.o, the make program checks for recent modifications to that file or directory, and if there is no modification since the last build, it skips that target. This is also true for the dependency of out/ multiply.o, which is calc/multiply.c. If the source file, calc/multiply.c, has not been changed recently and it has been compiled before, it doesn't make sense to compile it again. This is again a feature that you cannot simply obtain by writing shell scripts.

By having this feature, you only compile the source files that have been modified from the last build, and this reduces a huge amount of compilation for sources that have not been changed since the last build. Of course, this feature will work after having the whole project compiled at least once. After that, only modified sources will trigger a compilation or linkage.

Another crucial point in the preceding Makefile is the `calc/calc.h` target. As you can see, there are multiple targets, mostly source files, that are dependent on the header file, `calc/calc.h`. Therefore, based on the functionality we explained before, a simple modification to the header file can trigger multiple compilations for the source files depending on that header file.

This is exactly why we try to include only the required header files in a source file, and use forward declarations wherever possible instead of inclusion. Forward declarations are not usually made in source files because there, we often demand access to the actual definition of a structure or a function, but it can be easily done in header files.

Having a lot of dependencies between header files usually leads to build disasters. Even a small modification to a header file included by many other header files, and eventually included by many source files, can trigger building the whole project or something on that scale. This will effectively reduce the quality of development as well as lead to a developer having to wait for minutes between builds.

The preceding Makefile is still too verbose. We have to change the targets whenever we add a new source file. We expect to change the Makefile upon adding a new source file, but not by adding a new target and changing the overall structure of a Makefile. This effectively prevents us from reusing the same Makefile in another project similar to the current one.

More than that, many targets follow the same pattern, and we can benefit from the *pattern matching* feature available in Make to reduce the number of targets and write less code in a Makefile. This is another super feature of Make whose effect you cannot easily achieve by writing shell scripts.

The following Makefile will be our last one for this project, but still is not the best Makefile that a Make professional can write:

```
BUILD_DIR = out
OBJ = ${BUILD_DIR}/calc/add.o \
            ${BUILD_DIR}/calc/subtract.o \
            ${BUILD_DIR}/calc/multiply.o \
            ${BUILD_DIR}/exec/main.o
CC = gcc
```

```
HEADER_DIRS = -Icalc
LIBCALCNAME = calc
LIBCALC = ${BUILD_DIR}/lib${LIBCALCNAME}.a
EXEC = ${BUILD_DIR}/ex23_1.out

build: prereq ${BUILD_DIR}/exec/main.o ${LIBCALC}
    ${CC} -L${BUILD_DIR} -l${LIBCALCNAME} ${BUILD_DIR}/exec/main.o
-o ${EXEC}

prereq:
    mkdir -p ${BUILD_DIR}
    mkdir -p ${BUILD_DIR}/calc
    mkdir -p ${BUILD_DIR}/exec

${LIBCALC}: ${OBJ}
    ar rcs ${LIBCALC} ${OBJ}

${BUILD_DIR}/calc/%.o: calc/%.c
    ${CC} -c ${HEADER_DIRS} $< -o $@

${BUILD_DIR}/exec/%.o: exec/%.c
    ${CC} -c ${HEADER_DIRS} $< -o $@

clean: ${BUILD_DIR}
    rm -rf ${BUILD_DIR}
```

Code Box 23-3 [Makefile-by-pattern]: A new Makefile written for the target project that uses pattern matching

The preceding Makefile uses pattern matching in its targets. The variable OBJ keeps a list of the expected relocatable object files, and it is used in all other places when a list of object files is needed.

This is not a book on how Make's pattern matching works, but you can see that there are a bunch of wildcard characters, such as %, $<, and $@, that are used in the patterns.

Running the preceding Makefile will produce the same results as the other Makefiles, but we can benefit from the various nice features that Make offers, and eventually have a reusable and maintainable Make script.

The following shell box shows how to run the preceding Makefile and what the output is:

```
$ make
```

```
mkdir -p out
mkdir -p out/calc
mkdir -p out/exec
gcc -c -Icalc exec/main.c -o out/exec/main.o
gcc -c -Icalc calc/add.c -o out/calc/add.o
gcc -c -Icalc calc/subtract.c -o out/calc/subtract.o
gcc -c -Icalc calc/multiply.c -o out/calc/multiply.o
ar rcs out/libcalc.a out/calc/add.o out/calc/subtract.o out/calc/
multiply.o out/exec/main.o
gcc -Lout -lcalc out/exec/main.o -o out/ex23_1.out
$
```

Shell Box 23-5: Building the target project using the final Makefile

In the following sections, we will be talking about CMake, a great tool for generating true Makefiles. In fact, a while after Make became popular, a new generation of build tools emerged, *build script generators*, which could generate Makefiles or scripts from other build systems based on a given description. CMake is one of them, and it is probably the most popular one.

Note:
Here is the main link to read more about GNU Make, which is the implementation of Make made for the GNU project: https://www.gnu.org/software/make/manual/html_node/index.html.

CMake – not a build system!

CMake is a build script generator and acts as a generator for other build systems such as Make and Ninja. It is a tedious and complex job to write effective and cross-platform Makefiles. CMake or similar tools, like *Autotools*, are developed to deliver finely tuned cross-platform build scripts such as Makefiles or Ninja build files. Note that Ninja is another build system and will be introduced in the next section.

Note:
You can read more about Autotools here: https://www.gnu.org/software/automake/manual/html_node/Autotools-Introduction.html.

Dependency management is also important, which is not delivered through Makefiles. These generator tools can also check for installed dependencies and won't generate the build scripts if a required dependency is missing from the system. Checking the compilers and their versions, and finding their locations, their supported features, and so on is all part of what these tools do before generating a build script.

Like Make, which looks for a file named Makefile, CMake looks for a file named CMakeLists.txt. Wherever you find this file in a project, it means that CMake can be used to generate proper Makefiles. Fortunately, and unlike Make, CMake supports nested modules. In other words, you can have multiple CMakeLists.txt in other directories as part of your project and all of them can be found and proper Makefiles would be generated for all of them, just by running CMake in the root of your project.

Let's continue this section by adding CMake support to our example project. For this purpose, we add three CMakeLists.txt files. Next, you can see the hierarchy of the project after adding these files:

```
$ tree ex23_1
ex23_1/
├── CMakeLists.txt
├── calc
│   ├── CMakeLists.txt
│   ├── add.c
│   ├── calc.h
│   ├── multiply.c
│   └── subtract.c
└── exec
    ├── CMakeLists.txt
    └── main.c

2 directories, 8 files
$
```

Shell Box 23-6: The project hierarchy after introducing three CMakeLists.txt files

As you can see, we have three CMakeLists.txt files: one in the root directory, one in the calc directory, and the other one in the exec directory. The following code box shows the content of the CMakeLists.txt file found in the root directory. As you can see, it adds subdirectories of calc and exec.

These subdirectories must have a CMakeLists.txt file inside and, in fact, they do, according to our setup:

```
cmake_minimum_required(VERSION 3.8)

include_directories(calc)

add_subdirectory(calc)
add_subdirectory(exec)
```

Code Box 23-4 [CMakeLists.txt]: The CMakeLists.txt file found in the root directory of the project

The preceding CMake file adds the calc directory to the include directories that will be used by the C compiler when compiling the source files. Like we said before, it also adds two subdirectories: calc and exec. These directories have their own CMakeLists.txt files that explain how to compile their content. The following is the CMakeLists.txt file found in the calc directory:

```
add_library(calc STATIC
    add.c
    subtract.c
    multiply.c
)
```

Code Box 23-5 [calc/CMakeLists.txt]: The CMakeLists.txt file found in the calc directory

As you can see, it is just a simple *target declaration* for the calc target, meaning that we need to have a static library named calc (actually libcalc.a after build) that should contain the corresponding relocatable object files for the source files, add.c, subtract.c, and multiply.c. Note that CMake targets usually represent the final products of a code base. Therefore, specifically for the calc module, we have only one product, which is a static library.

As you can see, nothing else is specified for the calc target. For instance, we didn't specify the extension of the static library or the filename of the library (even though we could). All other configurations required to build this module are either inherited from the parent CMakeLists.txt file or have been obtained from the default configuration of CMake itself.

For example, we know that the extension for shared object files is different on Linux and macOS. Therefore, if the target is a shared library, there is no need to specify the extension as part of the target declaration. CMake is able to handle this very platform-specific difference, and the final shared object file will have the correct extension based on the platform that it is being built on.

The following `CMakeLists.txt` file is the one found in the `exec` directory:

```
add_executable(ex23_1.out
  main.c
)

target_link_libraries(ex23_1.out
  calc
)
```

Code Box 23-6 [exec/CMakeLists.txt]: The CMakeLists.txt file found in the exec directory

As you can see, the target declared in the preceding `CMakeLists.txt` is an executable, and it should be linked to the `calc` target that is already declared in another `CMakeLists.txt` file.

This really gives you the power to create libraries in one corner of your project and use them in another corner just by writing some directives.

Now it's time to show you how to generate a Makefile based on the `CMakeLists.txt` file found in the root directory. Note that we do this in a separate directory named `build` in order to have the resulting relocatable and final object files kept separated from the actual sources.

If you're using a **source control management (SCM)** system like *git*, you can ignore the `build` directory because it should be generated on each platform separately. The only files that matter are the `CMakeLists.txt` files, which are always kept in a source control repository.

The following shell box demonstrates how to generate build scripts (in this case, a Makefile) for the `CMakeLists.txt` file found in the root directory:

```
$ cd ex23_1
$ mkdir -p build
$ cd build
$ rm -rfv *
...
$ cmake ..
-- The C compiler identification is GNU 7.4.0
-- The CXX compiler identification is GNU 7.4.0
-- Check for working C compiler: /usr/bin/cc
-- Check for working C compiler: /usr/bin/cc -- works
-- Detecting C compiler ABI info
```

```
-- Detecting C compiler ABI info - done
-- Detecting C compile features
-- Detecting C compile features - done
-- Check for working CXX compiler: /usr/bin/c++
-- Check for working CXX compiler: /usr/bin/c++ -- works
-- Detecting CXX compiler ABI info
-- Detecting CXX compiler ABI info - done
-- Detecting CXX compile features
-- Detecting CXX compile features - done
-- Configuring done
-- Generating done
-- Build files have been written to: .../extreme_c/ch23/ex23_1/
build
$
```

Shell Box 23-7: Generating a Makefile based on the CMakeLists.txt file found in the root directory

As you can see from the output, the CMake command has been able to detect the working compilers, their ABI info (for more on ABI, refer to *Chapter 3, Object Files*), their features, and so on, and finally it has generated a Makefile in the `build` directory.

 Note:
In *Shell Box 23-7*, we assumed that we could have had the `build` directory in place; therefore, we removed all of its content first.

You can see the content of the `build` directory and the generated Makefile:

```
$ ls
CMakeCache.txt  CMakeFiles  Makefile  calc  cmake_install.cmake
exec
$
```

Shell Box 23-8: Generated Makefile in the build directory

Now that you've got a Makefile in your `build` directory, you're free to run the make command. It will take care of the compilation and display its progress nicely for you.

Note that you should be in the `build` directory before running the `make` command:

```
$ make
Scanning dependencies of target calc
[ 16%] Building C object calc/CMakeFiles/calc.dir/add.c.o
[ 33%] Building C object calc/CMakeFiles/calc.dir/subtract.c.o
[ 50%] Building C object calc/CMakeFiles/calc.dir/multiply.c.o
[ 66%] Linking C static library libcalc.a
[ 66%] Built target calc
Scanning dependencies of target ex23_1.out
[ 83%] Building C object exec/CMakeFiles/ex23_1.out.dir/main.c.o
[100%] Linking C executable ex23_1.out
[100%] Built target ex23_1.out
$
```

Shell Box 23-9: Executing the generated Makefile

Currently, many big projects use CMake, and you can build their sources by using more or less the same commands that we've shown in the previous shell boxes. *Vim* is one such project. Even CMake itself is built using CMake after having a minimum CMake system built by Autotools! CMake now has lots of versions and features and it would take a whole book to discuss them in extensive detail.

Note:
The following link is the official documentation of the latest version of CMake and it can help you to get an idea of how it works and what features it has: https://cmake.org/cmake/help/latest/index.html.

As a final note in this section, CMake can create build script files for Microsoft Visual Studio, Apple's Xcode, and other development environments.

In the following section, we will be discussing the Ninja build system, a fast alternative to Make that has been gaining momentum recently. We also explain how CMake can be used to generate Ninja build script files instead of Makefiles.

Ninja

Ninja is an alternative to Make. I hesitate to call it a replacement, but it is a faster alternative. It achieves its high performance by removing some of the features that Make offers, such as string manipulation, loops, and pattern matching.

Ninja has less overhead by removing these features, and because of that, it is not wise to write Ninja build scripts from scratch.

Writing Ninja scripts can be compared to writing shell scripts, the downsides of which we explained in the previous section. That's why it is recommended to use it together with a build script generator tool like CMake.

In this section, we show how Ninja can be used when Ninja build scripts are generated by CMake. Therefore, in this section, we won't go through the syntax of Ninja, as we did for Makefiles. That's because we are not going to write them ourselves; instead, we are going to ask CMake to generate them for us.

Note:
For more information on Ninja syntax, please follow this link:
`https://ninja-build.org/manual.html#_writing_your_own_ninja_files`.

As we explained before, it is best to use a build script generator to produce Ninja build script files. In the following shell box, you can see how to use CMake to generate a Ninja build script, `build.ninja`, instead of a Makefile for our target project:

```
$ cd ex23_1
$ mkdir -p build
$ cd build
$ rm -rfv *
...
$ cmake -GNinja ..
-- The C compiler identification is GNU 7.4.0
-- The CXX compiler identification is GNU 7.4.0
-- Check for working C compiler: /usr/bin/cc
-- Check for working C compiler: /usr/bin/cc -- works
-- Detecting C compiler ABI info
-- Detecting C compiler ABI info - done
-- Detecting C compile features
```

```
-- Detecting C compile features - done
-- Check for working CXX compiler: /usr/bin/c++
-- Check for working CXX compiler: /usr/bin/c++ -- works
-- Detecting CXX compiler ABI info
-- Detecting CXX compiler ABI info - done
-- Detecting CXX compile features
-- Detecting CXX compile features - done
-- Configuring done
-- Generating done
-- Build files have been written to: .../extreme_c/ch23/ex23_1/
build
$
```

Shell Box 23-10: Generating build.ninja based on CMakeLists.txt found in the root directory

As you can see, we have passed the option -GNinja to let CMake know that we are demanding Ninja build script files instead of Makefiles. CMake generates the build.ninja file and you can find it in the build directory as follows:

```
$ ls
CMakeCache.txt   CMakeFiles   build.ninja   calc   cmake_install.cmake
exec   rules.ninja
$
```

Shell Box 23-11: Generated build.ninja in the build directory

To compile the project, it is enough to run the ninja command as follows. Note that just as the make program looks for the Makefile in the current directory, the ninja program looks for build.ninja in the current directory:

```
$ ninja
[6/6] Linking C executable exec/ex23_1.out
$
```

Shell Box 23-12: Executing generated build.ninja

In the following section, we are going to talk about *Bazel*, another build system that can be used for building C and C++ projects.

Bazel

Bazel is a build system developed at Google to address the internal need to have a fast and scalable build system that can build any project no matter what the programming language is. Bazel supports building C, C++, Java, Go, and Objective-C projects. More than that, it can be used to build Android and iOS projects.

Bazel became open source around 2015. It is a build system, so it can be compared with Make and Ninja, but not CMake. Almost all of Google's open source projects use Bazel for their builds. For example, we can name *Bazel* itself, *gRPC*, *Angular*, *Kubernetes*, and *TensorFlow*.

Bazel is written in Java. It is famous for parallel and scalable builds, and it really makes a difference in big projects. Parallel builds are also available in Make and Ninja, both by passing the -j option (Ninja is parallel by default, however).

Note:
The official documentation of Bazel can be found here:
https://docs.bazel.build/versions/master/bazel-
overview.html.

The way to use Bazel is similar to what we did for Make and Ninja. Bazel requires two kinds of files to be present in a project: WORKSPACE and BUILD files. The WORKSPACE file should be in the root directory, and the BUILD files should be put into the modules that should be built as part of the same workspace (or project). This is more or less similar to the case with CMake, where we had three CMakeLists.txt files distributed in the project, but note that, here, Bazel itself is the build system and we are not going to generate any build script for another build system.

If we want to add the Bazel support to our project, we should obtain the following hierarchy in the project:

```
$ tree ex23_1
ex23_1/
├── WORKSPACE
├── calc
│   ├── BUILD
│   ├── add.c
│   ├── calc.h
│   ├── multiply.c
│   └── subtract.c
```

```
    └── exec
        ├── BUILD
        └── main.c


2 directories, 8 files
$
```

Shell Box 23-13: The project hierarchy after introducing Bazel files

The content of the WORKSPACE file would be empty in our example. It is usually used to indicate the root of the code base. Note that you need to refer to the documentation to see how these files, WORKSPACE and BUILD, should be propagated throughout the code base if you have even more nested and deeper modules.

The content of the BUILD file indicates the targets that should be built in that directory (or module). The following code box shows the BUILD file for the calc module:

```
c_library(
    name = "calc",
    srcs = ["add.c", "subtract.c", "multiply.c"],
    hdrs = ["calc.h"],
    linkstatic = True,
    visibility = ["//exec:__pkg__"]
)
```

Code Box 23-7 [calc/BUILD]: The BUILD file found in the calc directory

As you see, a new target, calc, is declared. It is a static library and contains the three source files found in the directory. The library is also visible to the targets residing in the exec directory.

Let's look at the BUILD file in the exec directory:

```
cc_binary(
    name = "ex23_1.out",
    srcs = ["main.c"],
    deps = [
        "//calc:calc"
    ],
    copts = ["-Icalc"]
)
```

Code Box 23-8 [exec/BUILD]: The BUILD file found in the exec directory

With the preceding files in their places, we can now run Bazel and build the project. You need to go to the project's root directory. Note that there is no need to have a build directory as we did for CMake:

```
$ cd ex23_1
$ bazel build //...
INFO: Analyzed 2 targets (14 packages loaded, 71 targets
configured).
INFO: Found 2 targets...
INFO: Elapsed time: 1.067s, Critical Path: 0.15s
INFO: 6 processes: 6 linux-sandbox.
INFO: Build completed successfully, 11 total actions
$
```

Shell Box 23-14: Building the example project using Bazel

Now, if you look at the `bazel-bin` directory found in the root directory, you should be able to find the products:

```
$ tree bazel-bin
bazel-bin
├── calc
│   ├── _objs
│   │   └── calc
│   │       ├── add.pic.d
│   │       ├── add.pic.o
│   │       ├── multiply.pic.d
│   │       ├── multiply.pic.o
│   │       ├── subtract.pic.d
│   │       └── subtract.pic.o
│   ├── libcalc.a
│   └── libcalc.a-2.params
└── exec
    ├── _objs
    │   └── ex23_1.out
    │       ├── main.pic.d
    │       └── main.pic.o
    ├── ex23_1.out
    ├── ex23_1.out-2.params
```

```
    ├── ex23_1.out.runfiles
    │   ├── MANIFEST
    │   └── __main__
    │       └── exec
    │           └── ex23_1.out -> .../bin/exec/ex23_1.out
    └── ex23_1.out.runfiles_manifest

9 directories, 15 files
$
```

Shell Box 23-15: The content of bazel-bin after running the build

As you can see in the preceding list, the project is built successfully, and the products have been located.

In the next section, we are going to close our discussion in this chapter and compare various build systems that exist for C and C++ projects.

Comparing build systems

In this chapter, we tried to introduce three of the most well-known and widely used build systems. We also introduced CMake as a build script generator. You should know that there are other build systems that can be used to build C and C++ projects.

Note that your choice of build system should be considered as a long-term commitment; if you start a project with a specific build system, it would take significant effort to change it to another one.

Build systems can be compared based on various properties. Dependency management, being able to handle a complex hierarchy of nested projects, build speed, scalability, integration with existing services, flexibility to add a new logic, and so on can all be used to make a fair comparison. I'm not going to finish this book with a comparison of build systems because it is a tedious job to do, and, more than that, there are already some great online articles covering the topic.

A nice Wiki page on Bitbucket that does a pros/cons comparison on available build systems, together with build script generator systems can be found here: https://bitbucket.org/scons/scons/wiki/SconsVsOtherBuildTools.

Note that the result of a comparison can be different for anyone. You should choose a build system based on your project's requirements and the resources available to you. The following links lead to supplementary resources that can be used for further study and comparison:

```
https://www.reddit.com/r/cpp/comments/8zm66h/an_overview_of_build_
systems_mostly_for_c_projects/
```

```
https://github.com/LoopPerfect/buckaroo/wiki/Build-Systems-
Comparison
```

```
https://medium.com/@julienjorge/an-overview-of-build-systems-
mostly-for-c-projects-ac9931494444
```

Summary

In this chapter, we discussed the common build tools available for building a C or C++ project. As part of this chapter:

- We discussed the need for a build system.
- We introduced Make, one of the oldest build systems available for C and C++ projects.
- We introduced Autotools and CMake, two famous build script generators.
- We showed how CMake can be used to generate the required Makefiles.
- We discussed Ninja and we showed how CMake can be used to generate Ninja build scripts.
- We demonstrated how Bazel can be used to build a C project.
- Finally, we provided some links to a number of online discussions regarding the comparison of various build systems.

Epilogue

And the final words ...

If you are reading this, it means that our journey has come to an end! We went through several topics and concepts as part of this book, and I hope that the journey has made you a better C programmer. Of course, it cannot give you the experience; you must obtain that by working on various projects. The methods and tips we discussed in this book will ramp up your level of expertise, and this will enable you to work on more serious projects. Now you know more about software systems, from a broader point of view, and possess a top-notch knowledge about the internal workings.

Though this book was heavier and lengthier than your usual read, it still could not cover all the topics found within C, C++, and system programming. Therefore, a weight remains on my shoulders; the journey is not yet done! I would like to continue to work on more Extreme topics, maybe more specific areas, such as Asynchronous I/O, Advanced Data Structures, Socket Programming, Distributed Systems, Kernel Development, and Functional Programming, in time.

Hope to see you again on the next journey!

Kamran

Other Books You May Enjoy

If you enjoyed this book, you may be interested in these other books by Packt:

C# 8.0 and .NET Core 3.0 – Modern Cross-Platform Development - Fourth Edition

Mark J. Price

ISBN: 978-1-78847-812-0

- Build cross-platform applications for Windows, macOS, Linux, iOS, and Android
- Explore application development with C# 8.0 and .NET Core 3.0
- Explore ASP.NET Core 3.0 and create professional web applications
- Learn object-oriented programming and C# multitasking
- Query and manipulate data using LINQ
- Use Entity Framework Core and work with relational databases
- Discover Windows app development using the Universal Windows Platform and XAML
- Build mobile applications for iOS and Android using Xamarin.Forms

DevOps Paradox

Viktor Farcic

ISBN: 978-1-78913-363-9

Expert opinions on:

- Introducing DevOps into real-world, chaotic business environments
- Deciding between adopting cutting edge tools or sticking with tried-and-tested methods
- Initiating necessary business change without positional power
- Managing and overcoming fear of change in DevOps implementations
- Anticipating future trends in DevOps and how to prepare for them
- Getting the most from Kubernetes, Docker, Puppet, Chef, and Ansible
- Creating the right incentives for DevOps success across an organization
- The impact of new techniques, such as Lambda, serverless, and schedulers, on DevOps practice

Leave a review - let other readers know what you think

Please share your thoughts on this book with others by leaving a review on the site that you bought it from. If you purchased the book from Amazon, please leave us an honest review on this book's Amazon page. This is vital so that other potential readers can see and use your unbiased opinion to make purchasing decisions, we can understand what our customers think about our products, and our authors can see your feedback on the title that they have worked with Packt to create. It will only take a few minutes of your time, but is valuable to other potential customers, our authors, and Packt. Thank you!

Index

Printed in Great Britain
by Amazon